When Adaline Glasheen's *Census of Finnegans Wake* was published in 1956, it was acclaimed as one of the most important guides to a rewarding but difficult novel. Mingled with critical applause, however, was the fervent wish that someday Mrs. Glasheen might expand her intriguing but brief index. Now this *Second Census* more than fulfills that hope by one-third over the original. The most valuable change is in the fully revised synopsis of the *Wake* narrative running to almost forty pages and providing the reader with a detailed and authoritative outline of the novel. Mrs. Glasheen has also devised an ingenious chart: *Who Is Who When Everybody is Someone Else* which identifies at a glance the many transformations of the major characters in *Finnegans Wake*. For scholar or novice, *A Second Census of Finnegans Wake* is an indispensable guide and companion to one of the richest novels of the twentieth century.

A Sec

A SECOND CENSUS of

FINNEGANS WAKE

An Index of the Characters and Their Roles

Revised and Expanded from the First *Census*
By ADALINE GLASHEEN

NORTHWESTERN UNIVERSITY PRESS 1963

Foreword to the First *Census* (1956)

By Richard Ellmann

James Joyce's picture of the mind at work and at play in *Finnegans Wake* was an attempt at literal representation and not a trick played tediously on his friends for sixteen years. If he hides the name of Abraham in "abramanation" or "Allbrewham", or the name of Anna Livia in "Hanah Levy" or "allalluvial", it is not to pull our legs but to stretch our daytime imaginations. That the mind works this way in certain states of tension or repose was recognized long before Joyce, as before Freud. Among the forerunners, Count Rostov in *War and Peace*, as he rides towards the front at Austerlitz, passes a black knoll with a white patch, and his mind responds queerly to it. "Was it a clearing in the wood, lighted up by the moon," he asks himself, "or the remains of snow, or white houses?" In his nervousness about the impending battle, his mind answers: "It must be snow—that spot: a spot—*une tache*. But that's not a *tache* . . . Na . . . tasha, my sister, her black eyes. Na . . . tasha . . . tasha . . . sabre-tache. . . ." A hussar warns him he is riding into the bushes, but hardly interrupts his revery: "But, I say, what was I thinking? I mustn't forget. Now I am going to speak to the Emperor? No, not that—that's tomorrow. Yes, yes! Natasha, attacks, tacks us—whom? The hussars. Ah, the hussars with their moustaches." These plays on words are like those in *Finnegans Wake*, and if that book seems eccentric it seems so only because of the audacity with which the method is sustained. Shapes merge into shapes, persons into persons, names into other names with the ambiguities of a pun, or a dream.

Yet, even when we accept Joyce's methods, the difficulties of reading his book are not cleared away. It has been evident since *Finnegans Wake* was published in 1939 that it requires, much more urgently than *Ulysses*, a critical apparatus with which to board it. If Joyce had lived, he would have commissioned someone to perform for his last book the service which Stuart Gilbert performed for *Ulysses*. As it is, we have only *Our exagmination round his factification for incamination of Work in Progress*, a series of essays by friends published ten years before the book was finished. The work of subsequent

v

scholars has been slowed by Joyce's absence. Harry Levin and Edmund Wilson have thrown light on the book, and so have other critics; but only one full-length explanation has been attempted, *A Skeleton Key to Finnegans Wake* by Joseph Campbell and Henry Morton Robinson, published in 1944. Since it appeared, many passages have been illuminated by the discovery of Joyce's sources, many clues to the interconnections of parts have been found, so that this work, indispensable as it is, is already a little out of date.

Part of our difficulty in reading *Finnegans Wake* is suspending the whole intricate pattern in our heads. Some kind of index to its 628 large pages has obviously been needed. There is the precedent of Miles L. Hanley's *Word Index to James Joyce's Ulysses*, but the complications of a word index to the *Wake* are so great that the mind boggles before them. It is Adaline Glasheen's distinction that she perceived the possibility of making a more specialized list which would require only half a decade to complete 'and would have uses that a mere index would lack.

Her *Census* names all, or almost all, the characters in *Finnegans Wake*, tables their appearances in various distorted forms, and then proceeds to identify most of them. This job will seem easy or mechanical only to someone who has not tried it. Standard reference works are rarely of much use. Hunting down Joyce's people in the novels of LeFanu, the plays of Boucicault, Irish songbooks, ecclesiastical history, and a hundred other out-of-the-way places requires an inspired power of detection.

Once the name has been identified, the critical task of determining the relevance to *Finnegans Wake* and its themes needs to be performed. Here Mrs Glasheen's discoveries and conjectures extend greatly the usefulness of her book. She presents the information with a mixture of wit and conscience, ingredients appropriate to her author. The lighthearted subtleties of the Glasheen *Census* will not surprise those who read her article, "*Finnegans Wake* and the Girls from Boston, Mass.", in the *Hudson Review*, Spring, 1954, where she solved one of the *Wake's* more teasing problems, the provenance of the famous nightletter in Boston. Her *Census* displays a series of solutions of puzzles comparable in their mysteriousness.

In other ways, too, the *Census* will help both dabblers and probers into *Finnegans Wake*. A reader who remembers a reference to Jack Sharkey, Vercingetorix, or Lady Precious Stream, but cannot bring himself to re-read the whole book to hunt it down, need no longer feel thwarted. A reader who wishes to trace themes will find the *Census* of characters makes his work much easier. And besides the *Census* proper there are in Mrs Glasheen's book three other aids which seem to me of much importance. The first is her preface, which goes far to show Joyce's point of view in all his works and especially in this one. The second is her "Synopsis" of the chapters of *Finnegans Wake*; a comparison with the similar synopsis in the *Skeleton Key* will show her advance in fathoming the book's structure and plot. The third is the table of "Who Is Who When Everybody Is Somebody Else", which demonstrates more clearly than any less graphic presentation how the characters change names and epochs in the book according to system rather than caprice.

As Adaline Glasheen emphasizes, this *Census* will not end research on *Finnegans Wake*. Every reader will want to add to it a few buried names that only he has exhumed, or to identify some that she has not succeeded in characterizing. Yet the book is of great consequence in Joyce studies. It makes available for Joyce the same kind of detailed information that is becoming available for those other inscrutable masters, Eliot and Pound. Joyce is quoted as having asked of his readers only that they devote their lives to reading his works. The Glasheen *Census* may enable them to spend some years less than a lifetime in comprehending *Finnegans Wake*. We may now understand a little better what so far we have perhaps only admired.

Preface to the First *Census*

J OYCE did not forsake received religion and then enslave himself, as most rationalists do, to received history. He carried uncertainty to its logical end and questioned all systems that man has shored against his chaos. Especially history ("a nightmare from which I am trying to awake") because the presumption of the historian is so overweening and has been so little challenged. The historian claims that the past can be divided into fact and fancy, Waterloo called a real and the Resurrection a mythical event.

For the purpose of *Finnegans Wake*, Joyce assumes that, as far as anyone knows, Waterloo and the Resurrection are events of the same order, equally credible, equally incredible. Man may have created them to satisfy a psychological need; just as likely, they are acts in a divine drama. Is either real? "Search me," Joyce says, being very much his definition of the Artist: ". . . like the God of the creation . . . within or behind or beyond or above his handiwork, invisible, refined out of existence, indifferent, paring his fingernails."

Finnegans Wake is a simulacrum of the world as the consciousness of man perceives it, presented with good-tempered nihilism, without explanation or apology. It has no First Cause, only a First Riddler, who may or may not know why a raven is like a writing-desk. Only the riddle is real, the riddle and man's passionate itch to solve it.

In *Moby Dick* Melville isolated the quest for ultimate truth by putting men on a ship in a timeless ocean and causing them to speak out of Shakespeare and the Bible. Joyce achieves a like isolation from time, space and the language of men, by using the dream; and his crew has no idea whether they are out after a white whale or a school of red herring.

The reader of *Finnegans Wake*, along with the characters in *Finnegans Wake*, finds himself on the well-trodden darkling plain, swept with confused alarms of struggle and flight. He and Joyce set out to explore the plain, to find out who is fighting and why. All night they walk in Viconian circles round the plain and come back with nothing to report save that the game goes on. If the reader had walked with Kafka, say, or Arnold, morning would see him near dead with discouragement; but Joyce is an athletic and exhilarating guide. He tells jokes all night; he is brave without calling attention to his bravery; he finds struggles, however ignorant, a sign of vitality; he has no grievance, no notion that it is all a dirty trick. "It was," Joyce says, "allso agreenable . . . touring the no placelike no timelike absolent. . . ."

Finnegans Wake is a highly agreeable book. It is also a misunderstood, confusing, obscure, and pretty well unread book. One trouble is that everybody has heard that *Finnegans Wake* is a dream, and dreams, as Huxley's young man observed, merely connote Freud, and Freud has, of course, become hopelessly middle-brow. Joyce uses Freud in *Finnegans Wake*, just as he uses *The Golden Bough* and Ossian and Rowntree's *Poverty* and *The Sorrows of Satan*; but *Finnegans Wake* is not an exploration of the individual subconsciousness of Humphrey Chimpden Earwicker or of James Joyce. In *Finnegans Wake*, as in *The Pilgrim's Progress* or *Piers Plowman*, the dream is a device for the suspension of disbelief. The book's obscurities are not to be dismissed by chatter about dreams having a logic of their own. Likely they do have, but the logic of *Finnegans Wake* is the logic of sharp, waking, verbal wit. It is one of the least subjective books ever written and one of the least irrelevant. It is hard to read because its relevance is all too rich.

Thousands of people are mentioned in *Finnegans Wake*, but only a few are characters in the novelist's sense of the word. These characters are the archetypal Earwickers, who have opposite but identical modes of being. Humphrey Chimpden Earwicker, an innkeeper of Chapelizod (a Dublin environ), is microcosmic; simultaneously, he is macrocosmic as Here Comes Everybody. The initials HCE designate both micro-and-macrocosm.

There are five Earwickers—father, mother, twin sons, daughter. They are distinct from one another, instantly recognizable by the rhythm of their speech, and they have varying degrees of fictional reality. The father, HCE, has a towering vitality, an expansive presence, which makes all the others look pale. His seedy magniloquence, his preposterous aplomb are reminiscent of Mr Micawber, O'Casey's Paycock and the late W. C. Fields. "An imposing everybody he always indeed looked, constantly the same as and equal to himself and magnificently well worthy of any and all such universalisation. . . ." He has no interior reality, his voice rises only in public boast or defense, and this does much to make him a credible Everyman.

HCE's wife, Anna Livia, is Everywife, mother, woman, but she plays these parts superficially. Anna Livia is Nature, at once sweetly pretty and deadly; specifically, she is Dublin's river Liffey, eternally "the same anew". A kind of Undine, prisoned in an alien and man-made world, her reality is poetic, not prosaic. The other Earwickers belong whole-hog to the world of men, but in her swan-song Anna Livia mourns, "My people were not their sort . . .".

The Earwicker children are vivid and memorable, and, like HCE, are what Mr Forster calls "flat characters". Issy, the girl, is tempta-tion made flesh and has but to murmur erotic nothings—an eternal enough humor, but not a living girl. The twin sons, Shem and Shaun, personify opposites, in whose endless war of black against white, the chiaroscuro that is man is often forgotten. Shem is Evil, Satan; Shaun is Good, St Michael; Shem is Mercy, Shaun Justice; Shem is the Heretic, Shaun the Infallible; Shem is energy (in Blake's sense), Shaun a loud-mouthed passivity, and so on. The brothers battle to no discernible victory. They lack their father's vitality and exist in his sense of guilt. To their mother, they are just little boys.

Characters of second rank (or they may turn out to be forms of the Earwickers) are: Kate, the slavey (sister to Butler's Mrs Jupp), who is Joyce's version of Kathleen ni Houlihan; a man servant, so mys-terious that I don't know his name; twelve drinkers at the bar; twenty-nine leap-year girls; seven rainbow "girls". Then there are the four old men—Matt Gregory, Mark Lyons, Luke Tarpey and Johnny MacDougal, who stand for many a four this and that, but over-all are the irrational, law-giving conscience: "And whatever it was one did they said, the fourlings, that on no accounts you were not to."

Man and father, HCE looms over the other characters, sole hero of the piece. Between micro-and-macrocosm, between Humphrey Chimpden Earwicker and Here Comes Everybody, between these poles human diversity flashes, dies away, and is renewed. Microcosm and macrocosm are identical, though opposite, states of union that exist, static and containing, for the instant of their realization. Then they split like the atom into a burst of energy that is the human race. Split and diverse, humanity then makes a counter movement to union.

Joyce is careful not to say whether reality lies in union or diversity. On the one hand, he shows Everyman made up of millions of men; on the other hand, he shows we are all of us members of one another. The archetype speaks through the historical individual; the individual becomes archetypal.

Finnegans Wake is not a dramatic book, but its easiest analogy is theatrical. The Earwickers play human history in a series of dramatic roles. They are like the old Dublin stock companies which Shaw describes as:

> . . . a readymade cast that had to fit all plays, from *Hamlet* down to the latest burlesque; and as it never fitted any of them completely, and seldom fitted at all, the casts were more or less grotesque misfits . . . each claimed . . . the part which came nearest to his or her specialty; and each played his parts in exactly the same way.

Much of the fun of *Finnegans Wake* hangs on the Earwickers being such very bad actors. They will not sink their own clamorous voices in their parts, they continually break off their lines to address the audience or rail at one another. People from one drama wander into a second: Swift's Struldbrugs leer at the mating of Tristan and Isolde and then, as the Elders, proposition Susanna; Brutus and Cassius quarrel over Cleopatra; the Flying Dutchman marries an Irish girl and settles down in Dublin. A single actor often plays several parts at once: HCE first falls as Noah, Tim Finnegan, Finn MacCool, Old Parr, and Halvard Solness; Issy is both Isoldes, both Swift's Esthers and plays parts as diverse as Alice and Ophelia. Sometimes an actor hands a favorite role to another: Shem and Shaun do this all the time, to exemplify, I guess, the absurd and illusory nature of Principles. Shem, for example, starts by playing a debased Miltonic Satan, but in Book III, section i,ii, Shaun takes over the part and interprets it as Blake's "Antichrist, Creeping Jesus".

It is all very confusing (". . . that sword of certainty which would identifide the body never falls . . ."), especially since the reader cannot know, till he has finished reading *Finnegans Wake*, whether a given name belongs to a character, a character's role, or is a mere allusion, existing on the level of language. Joyce, of course, means to confuse. He is out to get history by patiently demonstrating the chaos of the past and the pathos (Camus would call it the absurdity) of our attempts to know anything at all about the past. Three whole sections of *Finnegans Wake* (Book I, ii,iii,iv) go to prove Carlyle right when he called "Foolish History" the synopsis of rumor; then Joyce goes on to show that rumor is as valid a source of history as contemporary documents, scholarship, literature, art, mathematics, psychoanalysis, or table-turning. Misunderstanding, malice, sympathy, space, time, wit, learning, art, language, shifts in sensibility— all combine to distort the past out of recognition.

In *Finnegans Wake* nothing but Anna Livia's swan song comes to us direct. "They say", "We are told", "The fall . . . is retaled".

Uncertainty beats through the book. No person stands directly before us: Shaun describes Shem; the gray ass describes Shaun; washerwomen describe Anna Livia; HCE speaks through a medium —" . . . the unfacts, did we possess them, are too imprecisely few to warrant our certitude. . . ."

Another way in which Joyce mocks at history is by refusing to admit distinction of kind or degree between the mythical, the fictitious, and the so-called "historical" person, or between lowly and great, vulgar and aristocratic. Hamlet and the Colleen Bawn are assumed to be creations of equal statute and to be real as Osiris, Bernard Shaw, Leopold Bloom, James Joyce and Humphrey Earwicker are real. Great or small, Joyce agrees with Whitman, they furnish their parts toward the soul. Joyce's characters play role after role, casually egalitarian; but Joyce's own egalitarianism is, I think, grimly determined. Joyce had to sing the common man.

He had already sung Leopold Bloom who is precisely the sort of man Yeats told the Irish not to sing—"Base-born products of base beds." Bloom, commonest of men, saves Stephen Dedalus, and the moral of *Ulysses* (*Ulysses* sometimes seems to me *all* moral) is that art is not born till the artist climbs down from his ivory tower and joins forces with the man-in-the-street. Bloom saves Stephen from despair and the drunken soldiery, Stephen saves Bloom for art. Did he save him only to burlesque Homer's heroics? Surely not. "I mean my Ulysses to be a good man", Joyce said.

Having drunk cocoa with the common man and found him lovable, Joyce went on in *Finnegans Wake* to put history's darlings level with the common Dubliner. But it is not for love of man alone, or just to tease history that Joyce is determinedly democratic. Symbolically speaking, his salvation depended on democracy.

In *A Portrait of the Artist* Stephen made a symbolically disastrous choice when he identified himself with Satan and Icarus and poised for flight under the protection of a greater than himself: "Old father, old artificer, stand me now and ever in good stead." The flight failed: Stephen fell into despair, hell, the sea, and the Arian heresy. He readily divined that he failed because he assumed the role of disobedient son who cannot safely soar, instead of the role of potent, creative father. *Ulysses* traces Stephen's climb from the Arian to the Athanasian posture and leaves him at a triumphant height, consubstantial with the father. (The peaks of exaltation on which Joyce liked to leave his heroes, stand for "the affirmation of the spirit of man in literature".)

For every height, of course, a fall. The height Stephen attained at the end of *Ulysses* was dizzier far than anything Satan or Icarus dreamed of. As Stephen asserted in his Shakespearean discourse, the Artist-Father is a creator, even as God. When Shakespeare wrote *Hamlet*:

> . . . he was not the father of his own son merely, but being no more a son, he was and felt himself the father of all his race, the father of his own grandfather, the father of his unborn grandson.

The disobedience of the non-creative son is a flea-bite to the monstrous effrontery that makes the Artist-Father into God's rival in the matter of creation. In *Finnegans Wake* Joyce deals with the fate of the father.

Ibsen's Masterbuilder Solness was, for Joyce, the symbol of the Artist-Father who does not come down from his tower until he is thrown down by the conjunction of youth and a jealous rival—God. Halvard Solness is a horrid warning against futile, lonely death upon lonely life which overtakes the Artist who isolates himself in pride of his powers. Become a father and an artist himself, Joyce was, I think, concerned to provide symbolically against isolation and destruction by allying himself with the human race. He could not make himself into a common man, but he could declare every man an artist.

In *Finnegans Wake* all falls are one fall, all creations one. All men are equal, all men are artists and creators in the sign of the erect phallus, and in this sign they eternally affirm. In this sign they also fall into sin and death. HCE carries his sin on his humped back like Christian, his stutter betrays his knowledge that he has sinned, but he is not alone. "We all, for whole men is lepers. . . ."

In *Finnegans Wake* Joyce does more than state man's equality in sin and creation, he carries his leveling as far as possible and makes his popular epic out of material mainly vulgar. From all periods, all peoples, he sweeps up the rag-tag, the trashy tittle-tattle of speech and fills his book with it, saves for art the verbal garbage of the race. The individual mind, the race mind collects this stuff like a squirrel: Hastings was fought in 1066; Mrs Patrick Campbell became Mrs Cornwallis-West; Bosquet said, "*C'est magnifique, mais ce n'est pas la guerre*"; *avond* is Dutch for "evening"; Claribel wrote "Come Back to Erin"; the helicopter is here to stay; e equals mc squared; Campanella catches for the Dodgers. Our minds teem with this kind of thing; out of it we make art, philosophy, morals, science, but raw facts in themselves have a good deal of charm and importance. Joyce exploited the trashy irrelevance of Bloom's mind and did it brilliantly, but Bloom is one man, anchored in time and space, restricted in trash as in abstract thought. In *Finnegans Wake* HCE has the local information of Humphrey Chimpden Earwicker of Chapelizod and the world knowledge of Here Comes Everybody. Joyce, the old artificer, creates the illusion that the wide world is dreaming.

The illusion of the universal depends mainly on the strange, beautiful, funny speech of *Finnegans Wake*, a cunning web of multilingual puns, allusions, quotations, metaphors. This language is clear, exuberant, gay as a fine morning or an Elizabethan play, but it has not yet been greatly liked. Pound, for example, defined great literature as ". . . simply language charged with meaning to the utmost degree". But he was flummoxed by *Finnegans Wake*. No, it is not fashionable to take liberties with the language. A surprising number of people absolutely dislike verbal fun and games. Some can't cope, more have a nagging suspicion that verbal wit is frivolity and frivolity not highly serious. They prefer translations from English to French and back to English so that language may be sanitized.

No question, *Finnegans Wake* is a very hard book to get used to, and for the first year or two the hardest thing about it is the language. The language is the first thing that stops the reader in his tracks, and it was the last thing Joyce added to *Finnegans Wake*—though "added" is not the exact word.

The early drafts of *Finnegans Wake* are written in approximately standard English. They are amazingly dull, discontinuous, and read as distressingly as any dozen pages of *A Skeleton Key*. Instead of being what Lamb calls "beautiful bare narratives", these drafts are meager and embryonic. They are little more than a framework (Joyce hardly ever blotted a framework), and, strangely enough, they are more obscure than the published version of *Finnegans Wake*.*

First, apparently, Joyce made his strong, unbeautiful framework; then gradually he gave it beauty, color, and variety by turning it into his peculiar language, not as you ice a cake, but as a sculptor first roughs in the semblance of a human head and then works the clay into individual meaning and beauty.

The language of *Finnegans Wake* serves to explain and describe its substance—a common enough use of language. Subject and language in *Finnegans Wake* are, however, more mutually dependent than is usual in literature, and little can be removed from the text without

* I have seen early drafts of perhaps a third of *Finnegans Wake*, or rather, copies of the drafts, made by Mr J. S. Atherton and Mr M. J. C. Hodgart from papers Miss Harriet Weaver deposited in the British Museum. I have only seen one draft with any pretension to charm—the Tristan and Isolde episode which became part of II,iv.

outraging text and quotation. A few phrases—like "yung and easily freudened"—can be taken for themselves alone, but they sound slick and smarty, lose savor out of context. *Finnegans Wake* is never irrelevant, and this is probably its great fault, for a little something at random is good for literature, and relevance too steady wearies the reading mind.

I am not here concerned with the language of *Finnegans Wake*, but with the thousands of proper names that occur on the language level of the book and do not refer to the actors or their roles in the dream drama. I call these thousands of people "tropes", though I should like to be given a better word. Most of these tropes were added (some quite mechanically) after the frameworks were made, and like the language, they serve to describe, explain, color.

A distinction must first be made between proper tropes (e.g. "yung and easily freudened") and the names of the characters and their roles which serve as *leitmotivs* and recur again and again, punned on, alluded to. Because of the circular construction of *Finnegans Wake*, characters and roles often show up before their particular drama has been acted: the first persons mentioned in *Finnegans Wake* are Adam and Eve, but the temptation does not take place until "Anna Livia Plurabelle", some two hundred pages later; the second person mentioned is Tristram whose drama takes place almost four hundred pages later. These running allusions, which are often used as tropes, are vastly confusing to the beginning reader of *Finnegans Wake* because he has no way of telling the running allusion from proper tropes, which are local and passing, until he has finished the book.

The proper or local trope is an allusion that illuminates thought, mood, act in the way that "I am not Prince Hamlet" illuminates the thought, mood, act of Prufrock. When a trope does not, in some way, illuminate, the reader may be sure he has made a false identification or does not know enough about the person named, or has not the wit to take Joyce's point.

For example, there is a list of kings and military leaders on p. 88 of *Finnegans Wake*, and it contains the name Bentley. I could think of no famous Bentley but the 18th century classicist, who did not seem to fit. Then one day a friend pointed out to me that Bentley was a leader of the Moderns in *The Battle of the Books*. Or look at the first page of *Finnegans Wake*: "The fall . . . of a once wallstrait oldparr is retaled early in bed and later on life down through all christian minstrelsy." To many readers this may correctly suggest that Joyce compares HCE's fall to the crash of '29. The trope that brings in

Thomas or Old Parr (1483-1635) is irrelevant and obstructive so long as one thinks of Old Parr as a man who lived a long time; but, according to William Harvey, Old Parr "did public penance under a conviction for incontinence after he had passed his hundredth year". This information clarifies the trope, shows Old Parr as representing a sexual fall, a theme on which many changes are rung in *Finnegans Wake*. Further, Old Parr means "old young salmon"; it will be used later to express the union of opposites—like Tristram Shandy—and to express the renewal of the old, and the fertility of fish.

In the following *Census*, I am sure I omit many of Joyce's tropes, failing to see them as they lurk in the language. I fail to identify many that I list. I have likely listed people who are not people but rivers or dirty words in seventeen languages. I have made false identifications in my ignorance, and incomplete identifications in my lack of wit and learning. But people who work on *Finnegans Wake* must be willing to expose the partial mind and hope others can complete it.

To go back to the trope, it obscures where it is not understood or is partially understood, it blunts the narrative, breaks up the reading process. Understood, it is explanatory and descriptive. There is, however, no reason to think Joyce believed that common or uncommon readers could identify his tropes out of hand, or that he wanted readers to so identify them.

A great many well-known names occur in *Finnegans Wake*; but they are often in distorted, riddling form, and many of the tropes are people of truly stygian obscurity. Who knows the identity of: Brassolis, Julia Bride, Concessa, Gipsy Devereux, Kate Strong, Strongbow? (For the answers see *Census*.) I choose them because they appear in undistorted form and normal context, but surely they are an obscure lot. Identified, they clarify a phrase, a sentence, at most, a paragraph. Ignored (and everyone has to ignore some tropes), they are so many stumbling stones.

Why did Joyce pepper his book with tropes? Part of the answer has been given: he uses them to create an illusion of diversity, democracy, universality. But if diversity, democracy, and universality were all Joyce was after, he could have stuck to well-known names and would not have turned well-known names into puzzles like: Bill C. Babby, R. E. Meehan, Mavis Toffeelips, Bill Shasser, Andrew Clays, Population Peg, Beatified Biddy, Talop, Nama Knatut. (For answers, see *Census*.)

No question, Joyce is out to trick the reader, play jokes, pose puzzlers, lead up garden paths; but only that queer little band that has always hated Joyce could suppose he had no reason for his tricks. The reason is obvious: *Finnegans Wake* is a model of our universe as we perceive it. It is mysterious as a whole and in its parts; Joyce imitates God and is mysterious in his turn. It is not true to say that *Finnegans Wake* is mysterious because of Joyce's great learning, and could we but duplicate that learning, did we know Vico and seventeen languages—why then the book would be plain as a pike-staff. No. *Finnegans Wake* is wilfully obscure. It was conceived as obscurity, it was executed as obscurity, it is about obscurity, ". . . the fog of the cloud in which we toil and the cloud of the fog under which we labour". The language of *Finnegans Wake* is the first layer of fog and the reader must penetrate it, just as a child must his native speech. Readers of *Finnegans Wake* are, of course, accomplished readers of conventional prose, and they don't much like having to be as little child readers, "babes awondering in a wold made fresh where with the hen in the storyaboot we start from scratch".

Acknowledgement

This *Census* of *Finnegans Wake* owes so much to other people that the mere statement of my being grateful to Mr So and So would be shabby indeed. A short account of its making will better pay my debt.

In 1950 I started, hit or miss, to draw up an alphabetical list of such proper names as I could discern in *Finnegans Wake*. I did it for the diversion of the thing and because I never could find passages or people. I also had a vague idea that listing people would solve the riddle of the book. Now, five years later, I know the riddle is not solved and that I have not listed nearly all the people in the book. I stop in simple exhaustion, but I do know that the *Census*, as it now stands, is a very fair index to *Finnegans Wake*, that its identifications clear up many a murky passage, and that it brings together most of the running themes of the book. Others, I trust, will work on from the *Census*, and in twenty years I hope it will be outmoded.

When my list was inchoate and contained no identifications, I had it mimeographed and sent it to a few Joyceans. One of these was Mr Thornton Wilder who treated it with heavenly kindness and generosity. He gave me many valuable identifications and wrote me at length about *Finnegans Wake*. He has a writer's creative understanding of the book that no harmless drudge can hope to duplicate. I am specially indebted to him for interesting me in the four fascinating old men. Most of all, he encouraged me to expand the *Census* and add as many identifications as I could.

A later manuscript, with such identifications as I could muster, was sent to Mr J. S. Atherton of Wigan, Lancashire. He worked over it very thoroughly, correcting many errors, subduing many eccentric suppositions, and giving me perhaps 150 identifications, and these some of the best in the *Census*. He did more work on the *Census* than anyone except myself.

The manuscript was later read by Mr Matthew Hodgart of Pembroke College, Cambridge, who also gave very generously of his time and contributed about 50 identifications. Later still, it was read by Mr Hugh Kenner of Santa Barbara, California, who added some identifications and very valuable general comment.

Finally, Mr Richard Ellmann of Northwestern University read the manuscript and gave me more splendid identifications, especially of people from Joyce's Dublin. He interested Northwestern Studies in English in my manuscript and made its publication possible.

None of these five people was known to me. They had nothing in common but an interest in Joyce and a desire that *Finnegans Wake* should become more available to the common reader. Their generosity to the *Census* was disinterested and speaks very well for the intellectual climate of our time.

I also want to thank personal friends who gave me encouragement and identifications. I thank the late Mr Charles Bennett, who gave me my first copy of *Finnegans Wake*, Mr Ignatius Mattingley, Mr David Patton, Mr Warren Smith. Most of all, I thank my husband—"And ook, ook, ook, fanky! All the charictures in the drame!"

Note to the Second *Census*

HERE are the old and lots of new "charictures in the drame", and the end is not by a long-shot yet. In doing better by the old lot and rounding up the new, I have had most patient, open-handed and intelligent help from other players at *Finnegans Wake*, and I am grateful. Before I become specifically grateful, I must take responsibility for all the gaps and silly mistakes in the *Census* and for the eccentric conviction that *Finnegans Wake* is about William Shakespeare.

The people who helped most with this second edition are: Mr Wilder of Connecticut, Mr Atherton of Lancashire, Mr Clive Hart of New South Wales, Mr John Kelleher of Harvard, and Mr Fritz Senn of Zurich who also edited the manuscript and saw it through the press.

I was given many fine identifications by Mr Bernard Benstock, Mr Helmut Bonheim, Mr Philip Lamar Graham, Mr Fred Higginson, Mr J. Mitchell Morse, Father William Noon, S.J., Mr Peter Spielberg, and Mrs Ruth von Phul.

Fewer but no less telling additions and corrections were received from Mr Alan Cohn, Mr T. E. Connolly, Mr Jack Dalton, Mr Richard Ellmann, Mr Christopher Fyfe, Mr Martin Gardner, Mr Philip Graham Jr, Mr Matthew Hodgart, Mrs Helen Joyce, Mr Hugh Kenner, Mr Walton Litz, Mr Jon Morse, Mr Gerard O'Flaherty, Mr George Painter, Mr Joseph Prescott, Mr Warren Smith, Mr Bjorn Tysdahl, Miss Mabel Worthington.

Only those who are married to a reader of *Finnegans Wake* can know how much I owe to my husband Frank and my daughter Alison.

Contents

A Revised Synopsis of
*Finnegans Wake**

BOOK I, section i (3-29) The Wake

As *Ulysses* freely retells the *Odyssey*, this section—somewhat less
freely—retells the ballad "Finnegan's Wake", found under Finnegan
in this *Census*. I will assume that the reader knows the ballad, Vico,
and the Bible.

3.27-7.19

Joyce describes Masterbuilder (q.v.) Finnegan, how he gets drunk
while building a wall, falls from a ladder, dies. At his wake his wife
spreads his body as food for the guests, but he vanishes and they are
not fed.

7.20-10.24

Today we can perhaps approximate the missing meal by visiting
the Willingdone (q.v.) Museyroom, where wax-works, devoted to
the battle of Waterloo, are exhibited (fed) to the public. Our guide is
ignorant Kate (q.v.), and what she calls Waterloo is the human family's
sexual battle. The father, Willingdone, sits on his "big white harse",
peeping through a telescope at his two (q.v.) daughters, the jinnies
(q.v.), while they study how to make war (or water) on him. The

* This synopsis gives a flat, meager impression of FW because it
leaves out Joyce's fine nonsense, his infinite variety; but I think
people need to be reminded that FW is not a lot of fragments,
some of them suitable for public recitation or scholarly explanation or proving what Joyce thought of given men and institutions.
FW is a narrative, tight and tailored as *Ulysses*. My understanding
of the narrative is weak, uneven, full of holes, crawling with
mistakes and ignorance, and what I want this synopsis to do is
stimulate better readers to attend to narrative connection and
narrative progress in FW.

   The titles prefixed to the seventeen units of this synopsis are
the titles under which Joyce published parts of his *Work in
Progress*, or they are the informal titles which he used in his
letters and early manuscripts.

passive mother hides three (q.v.) soldier sons, the lipoleums (q.v.), who spy on their father, want to bring him down, but murder each other instead. The jinnies send a forged letter, signed "Nap", to Willingdone, which provokes him into firing (thundering, defecating) at his children. (For Joyce, dung is the stuff of creation, noisome and fertile.) The girls flee, the lipoleums stay. One lipoleum is an Irish-Hindu-Corsican rebel—for this is also political rebellion—and he throws a bomb which puts an end to Willingdone's "big white harse". Willingdone has, however, put half the lipoleum's hat on his horse's tail and lent the lipoleum a match to light his bomb. In *Finnegans Wake* exchange of belongings means exchange of roles, though not of personality: it is like the exchange of Rafe Rackstraw and the Captain at the end of *Pinafore*. The son-become-tyrant (Vico says they always do) blows up or castrates the father-overthrown-and-oppressed. Napoleon loses the Battle of Waterloo, lies buried on the field (10.35).

10.25-13.3

Outside the Museyroom is a peace-loving hen (q.v.), gathering spoils, relics, on the deserted battlefield. As we shall learn, she gathers bits of a letter which clears her husband's name, confounds his enemies. She is faithful, provident, keeps home-fires burning, babies coming. By her information, Man is a victim; his tomb is in Phoenix (q.v.) Park, and there his sons, in the guise of oppressors of Ireland—Williamite English, Danes—dance on his bones.

Shrewish Kate shows Man as provoked by females, committing a crime, meeting retribution. The saintly hen shows him victim. Roughly, then, Kate's is the First Adam, the hen's is the Second Adam. These opposing opinions are Joyce's equivalent of the war of women at the wake; Waterloo is the war of the men.

13.4-14.27

Four (q.v.) old men—historians, elders, evangelists—now come to Dublin. They were at the earlier wake scene (6.29-7.8) and find the scene in Phoenix Park familiar. Four aspects of it, they take to be unfailing and present them as Irish Annal entries: 1) father as dead fish to be eaten; 2) mother gathering turf, giving birth; 3) daughter mourning the dead; 4) twin sons, Primas and Caddy (q.v.)—one goes for a soldier and "drills", i.e., "shoots" his father (as at Waterloo), the other writes a farce about, presumably, his father. To the Four these things are unchanging as stars in the sky and the entries are signs of the zodiac: Pisces, Aries, Virgo, Libra. They have only four bits of him, not the whole man.

14.28-18.16

A transitional passage brings us to the dramatic dialogue of Mutt and Jute, which is Caddy's farce, acted by himself and his brother. It takes place on the battlefield (now become Clontarf—see Brian Boru) and is about a traveller who thinks he is buying, as it were, Manhattan from an Indian for a wooden nickel. He gets the lesser breed to swop hats (exchange roles), asks him a string of questions and, when he can't understand the answers, he prepares to go. The lesser breed coaxes him to stay, and, with true realtor's enthusiasm, shows him the qualities of the isle, leads him to a hoard of "litters from aloft" which are buried in a mound. The mound is a reeking dung-heap (the one committed at Waterloo) and the traveller recoils. The native, however, shows him it is a treasure-hoard, a viking's barrow, and the grave of the ancestors all seek. The traveller bought it with a wooden coin and in his own word, he is "thonthorstrok". In Vico and *Finnegans Wake*, to be thunderstruck is to have lost innocence. The traveller thought he was despoiling the lesser breed, playing Jacob (q.v.) to his Esau, and it was really Adam to the native's Satan. What he bought was knowledge.

18.17-20.18

According to Vico, man learned speech from the thunder*. Joyce goes along with this and adds the notion that written language was in the thunder's dung. The hoard contains the alphabet, "litters from aloft", indeed, for Vico says all peoples think letters are of divine origin. "Please stop," the Four beg. "Please stoop," the Devil begs. Jute stoops to the mound and finds in it letters, evolving from runes to Gutenberg. At all its stages the alphabet confusedly suggests Man's fall, and the printing press adds more confusion.

20.19-23.15

Movable type moves and writes, at the buried father's dictation, an account of how the woman tempted him. The sources of the story of the Prankquean and Jarl van Hoother can be found in this *Census* under Grace O'Malley, Dermot and Grania, the Masterbuilder (q.q.v.).

* Thunder speaks ten times: pp. 3, 23, 44, 90, 113, 257, 314, 332, 414, 424. Nine times it says one hundred letters. The tenth time it says one hundred and one.

I don't always know what happens in this story, but "what the mis-chievmiss made a man do" is what the jinnies made him do at Waterloo—come out fighting, make war-thunder-dung. Jarl van Hoother is passive, dead; then the prankquean comes knocking at the door, bringing fertile substances—woman, fire and water (fire-water). Twice rejected, she finally provokes, tempts him to act.

23.16-24.15

The act is evil, man does not understand it or understand the woman, but we would not be here today if he hadn't acted. For he had dug his grave and ours till he thought of a better story, i.e., the story of resurrection he has just told. He will wake again if she whis-pers, if the phoenix is reborn, if the elders (Four) tell truth about him to the young. . . . Suddenly the father's voice breaks in, singing of brides and waking from the dead. He ends with a cry—*Usquead-baugham!* Whisky or Usque*ad*baugh*am*, the water of life breaks over Adam. This is the climax of the ballad and of "The Wake", the moment when whisky breaks over Finnegan and he rises, crying, "Souls to the devil! Do you think I'm dead?"

24.16-29.36

The question is not rhetorical, and the rest of "The Wake" is given to the Four historians who say, yes, you are dead or ought to be. In a keen, the first coaxes him to be aisy because times have changed for the worse and his memory is greatly honored (24.16-26.24). He is content to lie down when the second tells him his sons are grow-ing up, eating of the tree of knowledge; but when the second de-scribes his daughters —the one relighting the phoenix flame, the other doing a sexy dance (26.25-27.21)—then Finnegan starts up again and the Four hold him down by main force (27.22-30). The third reconciles him to death by describing his middle-aged wife, a dear creature who still desires him (27.31-28.34). The fourth tells him he has a successor, a double who has taken his place, is even blamed for all the trouble in "Edenborough". I take the double to be Every-man-in-the-living-present, and he on the bier, Everyman-in-the-dead-past—see 619.11-14 (28.35-29.36).

I do not describe the first two paragraphs of "The Wake" (3.13-26) because they are too complex for synopsis. With the help of Joyce's "Key" (letter to Miss Weaver, 15 November 1926) the reader can work out the paragraphs for himself. Two things should be said about the Wake: first, "The Wake" moves in a geographical circle from the church of Adam and Eve on Merchant's Quay in Dublin to "Edenborough" or Eden and Burgh Quays which are opposite on the Liffey in Dublin; second, everything in *Finnegans Wake* has happened before. This is necessarily so since the scheme of *Finnegans Wake* is Viconian, and, according to Vico, man in his primal innocence could not speak, had no family, did not create. The typical fall in *Finnegans Wake* is the fall of man when he is building something. If he is building, he has fallen before.

BOOK I, section ii (30-47)   Ballad

This section is easy to read, not so easy to interpret. Knowing Vico on the class-struggle helps.

There are two stories of how Humphrey Chimpden Earwicker (q.v.) got his name, i.e., his reputation: he got it from the king; he got it from the rabble.

30.13-32.2

William the Conk (q.v.), out fox-hunting, stops to drink water in the inn-yard of his vassal, Harold, who also keeps a turnpike or toll-gate there. William and his two gallowglasses are the three soldiers, sons, become usurpers, tyrants; Harold is the father overthrown and become a Viconian plebe. Harold has potholed the king's highway—a crime. The king asks, did he do it to trap lobsters (redcoats)? Harold answers, he was just catching earwigs. The king gets off a witticism about Harold being both a trusty turnpiker and an ear-wigger. Harold and William exchange water for a name, hence exchange roles.

32.2-33.13

Ever after, our hero signs himself HCE and becomes an Irish viceroy, tyrant. The admiring populace interprets HCE as Here Comes Everybody (q.v.), and at the same time call him good Duke Humphrey (q.v.) for English tyranny meant hunger to Ireland. His humble inn is now a splendid theatre (inns and theatres are synonymous in *Finnegans Wake*) and there he sits in style, enjoying a play about Napoleon and/or Henry VIII (q.q.v.), *A Royal Divorce*, the theme of which emphasizes his Protestantism.

33.14-34.29

Slander finds baser meaning in the initials, and it is put about that HCE is a homosexual (see Wilde) who annoyed three soldiers in

Phoenix Park; the soldiers say, no, HCE exposed himself to two servant girls in the park.

34.30-36.34

The second story is that long after the alleged homosexual crime, HCE happens to meet in Phoenix Park a cad (q.v.) with a pipe. The cad greets him in Irish and asks the time. HCE mistakes the Irish for a' homosexual proposal, and stoutly denies he is homosexual; the request for time he receives in its Masonic sense, gives the correct Masonic response—twelve noon—declares himself Protestant and British to his backbone.

36.35-42.16

The cad now believes the scandal true, and his imperfect recollection of the encounter passes from ear to Dublin ear. It finally reaches three down-and-out perverts—Cloran, O'Mara and Hosty (q.q.v.), a poet. They are the three soldiers become plebs in the water-name exchange. They go to a tavern and write a scurrilous "Ballad of Persse O'Reilly", *perce-oreille* being French for "earwig".

42.17-47.33

The ballad is first sung to an overflow crowd of representative Dubliners near the tollgate where William and Harold met, and in the shadow of Parnell's monument. Irish bards had power to rhyme their enemies to death, and HCE is dead and buried by the ballad's end.

The performance of the ballad, its wild acceptance by the mob, the catholicity of its accusation, all these mark the expulsion of a scapegoat, in Cromwell's words "To Connaught or hell". The refrain: ". . . the rann, the rann, the rann, the king of all ranns . . ." echoes the catch sung on December 26, when Irish boys parade about with a dead bird on a pole:

> The wren, the wren, the king of all birds,
> St Stephen's Day was caught in the furze.

This "hunting of the wren" was known all over Europe, and Frazer calls it the prime example of sacred animal or fertility god, slain and paraded so all can share in his virtue. HCE as wren, British Viceroy, and St Stephen is stoned by the rabble; they do cast their sins on him, but the hoped-for virtue is lost when the stones break the chalice (44.19-21). The broken chalice had already been used by Joyce in

"The Sisters" to signify the curse that turns Ireland into the Waste Land—see Weston.

The ballad itself is a good imitation of the ferocious Irish street ballad—compare Swift's "The Yahoo's Overthrow", John Murphy's poem on David Gleeson, and "The Hackler from Grouse Hall". It accuses HCE of being a foreigner, of heterosexual and homosexual crimes, Protestantism, tyranny, murder, sharp business practices and attempts to civilize the Irish. It threatens him with jail, his wife, death and no resurrection.

BOOK I, section iii (48-74)   Goat

In section ii rumor raced straight through Dublin, space. Now it moves crooked through mists of time—syntax foggy, weather precipitating—till nothing is so easily lost as identity. The section rehabilitates and sentimentalizes HCE and ends on a note exactly opposite the end of section ii: Everyman sleeps, is not dead, will rise one day to answer God's call. Another scapegoat is sought, the enemy who made HCE fall or threw stones. Is the enemy man or woman?

48.13-57.29

Those involved with Hosty's ballad were a theatrical troupe, later to act "The Mime". All disappear but one who recreates the encounter of HCE and the cad for three truant schoolboys. Although "the unfacts, did we possess them, are too imprecisely few to warrant our certitude", there are many readings of HCE's part, he is exhibited in wax and in the "notional gullery". Public opinion continues to judge him.

57.30-69.29

Individual judgments are taken from representative Dubliners. (They are those who flung stones at HCE in "The Ballad"—see 62.20-25; they are those on whom HCE's wife has revenge later—see 210-212.) Their notions of the case are wildly dissimilar, but they turn in a general verdict of "human, erring and condonable", meaning he was more sinned against than sinning, but all the same—Guilty.

The first judgment is that of the three soldiers who say HCE was souped by the two girls (58.23-29); the last is that of two girls who say three soldiers were behind it all (61.25-27). The male and female views are hereafter offered, turn and turn about, till the female view prevails (69.5-74.19).

The male story is that HCE was an old geezer who involved himself with two young girls. One killed herself, the other turned whore and led him to a sexual fall. This story is at 64.22-65.33 and 67.28-69.4.

The female story is that one foggy night a tall man who might be HCE was threatened with a pistol by a masked man who was jealous over two girls. HCE defied him and who—if anybody—was shot is unclear, for, when arrested, the gunman insisted he was only kicking and hammering with a bottle on HCE's gateway; and at his trial, the gunman denied even this much and told the policeman he was "deepknee in error", a phrase not clarified till section iv. Nor was HCE out that night because his servants had locked him inside his gate so he couldn't go out and be clodded with eggs by the populace, i.e., they were keeping him in his grave. This story is found at 62.26-64.21, 67.7-27, and perhaps at 66.10-67.6.

69.30-74.19

Under the title "Der Fall Adams", a German newspaper man writes up the story from the female point of view: HCE was inside his gate and a drunken enemy (Satan, Man's accuser) shouted threats and bad names through the keyhole and threw stones at the gate. HCE could have called for help, but he hoped for his enemy's redemption and so did nothing but compile a list of the bad names. Sure enough, the enemy put down the stones and left, still threatening. Those stones will be gathered on Doomsday when God's horn rolls over Ireland and lost heroes return. Then God will call Everyman-Abraham and he will answer, like Colonel Newcome, "Add some", or like Abraham promise to be fertile at an advanced age. "Souls to the Devil, do you think I'm dead?"

He is not dead but in perfect health, sleeping in the rain. Wait till the rain and the sleep are over.

BOOK I, section iv (75-103)   Lion

75.13-76.9

Like a caged lion, the besieged (of 70.10-73.22) dreams of Liliths who undid him, of wheat fields and his daughter, Issy (q.v.), of founding a race of outcasts, sons of Ham (q.v.) on whom all crime can be fixed.

76.10-79.13

The public gave him a grave, but HCE blew it up and built his own. Here he lives in style, supported by public offerings and earth's riches. It is the dump, the treasure-howe of Mutt and Jute, and is so valuable that when North and South are done fighting in the American Civil War, they combine and come against his "heights of Abraham". They would plunder the howe because they are all unemancipated, starving, and Kate, the cook, says HCE is a great fish to feed on. HCE makes himself scarce. (Repeats 7.8-19.)

79.14-80.36

Once Kate was a temptress with a bare bodkin and she married HCE. Now a widow, she gives an ugly description of "old dumplan"—The rubbish tip—where she carried her own soil. There in Phoenix Park, with the help of the Four (as gravediggers) she buried the reconciling letter, which may have come from the thunder (God) or may have been a love-letter. Here at the dump God spoke . . . Kate breaks off to curse and scatter a flock of girls, little Issies who would roll away the stone from HCE's grave. (This passage cannot be understood without reference to *Ulysses*, 192-193 249-250.)

81.1-85.19

The offensive of the starving and unemancipated takes place at the howe and is reduced to combat between a negro attacker and one who may or may not be HCE. I think we are not meant to know whether this is the same old father-son battle or the brother-battle which is increasingly important from now on. The men fight, make peace, exchange kisses; the attacked gives the attacker money for drink, then reports him to the police. Their talk has to do with a duty imposed on Irish spirits—see Victoria.

85.20-93.21

Little headway is made in solving this last crime till Festy King (or Pegger Festy) is tried at Old Bailey for—if I follow the plot—stealing coal and taking off his clothes in public. An unfriendly witness accuses Festy of attacking two men. It is the nature of Irish trials to be comic, confusing and perjured—see Lover's *Rory O'More*, MacDonald's account of the Parnell (q.v.) Commission, see also Pigott in this *Census*. I make no coherence out of evidence about a hyacinth (q.v.) which turns into somebody named Hyacinth O'Donnell, B.A.—a pig, Cliopatrick (q.v.) who eats a doorway—a witness who sees a fight by moonlight when no moon shines—cipher ogham—twins as indistinguishable as the Dromios (q.v.), etc., etc. The Four judges find no one guilty, but twenty-nine female lawyers make a hero of the unfriendly witness, who is HCE's son, Shaun the

Post; and they shun Pegger Festy King, who is Shaun's twin, Shem the Penman (q.v.).

93.22-96.24

The Four cry for Kate to produce the letter, but (I suspect) she can't read and fancies it runs from Alpha to Omega, and is made up of snatches of Irish song. A very affecting letter, Kate thinks, but no one can really read it but "old hunks", a blind Elizabethan bear. The Four sit, therefore, in their judges' chambers, and gossip about the past when HCE was undone by a young girl. A couple of them claim to have had her, too, but the others call them liars (see Elders) and quarrel; Lally (q.v.) makes peace between them.

96.25-100.36

They conclude that by escaping all firm identification, by playing possum, our ancestor HCE may have saved himself. Dogs ran him over half Ireland as a fox, newspapers, radio, police, the populace chased him the wide world over, thought they'd found him in a hundred forms, were sure he was finally dead. But next morning smoke issued from one of the towers he had built over his grave, showing he was there—the lion with his little lady. This proves he was a fact, no fable.

101.1-103.12

Who is his little lady? It is A.L.P. (see Anna Livia), his faithful stay-at-home wife, mother of his children. She shelters him after his fall, crushes slander's head, pleads for him, lets no one rob his grave. He left her and spent his strength on seven (q.v.) whores, causing her sorrow, but he returns.

BOOK I, section v (104-125)   Hen

Sections ii,iii,iv are a unit, describing the fluctuations of the father's public reputation. Now he falls into the background a while, stays a caged lion, potent but passive, while his wife and children steal the scene. "Hen" is written by Shem and deals with the letter that the hen gathered on p. 11 and Kate buried on p. 80.

104.13-107.7

Anna Livia, faithful Mrs Earwicker, wants to write her husband's story, clear his name, confound his slanderers, but when she has listed possible titles, inspiration fails and she hands over her evidence—part of a letter from Boston, Mass. to her son, Shem the Penman, who often hereafter is said to have written the letter at his mother's dictation. (Alternatively, he stole the letter—see 125.21-22.) Shem writes no defense of his father, but makes good fun of the letter and achieves a charming burlesque of textual exegesis.

107.8-111.4

Insisting that all will come clear, Shem shows that nobody knows who wrote the thing, but it is probably a feminine fiction, a feminine clothing of bare facts. The letter was dug up from the dung-hill or scratched on it one spring day by a cold little hen, Biddy Doran (q.v.), while cold little Kevin (q.v.) or Shaun the Post looks on. Shaun will eventually deliver the letter, in the form of a pious sermon. Writing or delivering, the sons distort the mother's meaning and she finally writes her own letter or letters, 615.12-628.16.

111.5-113.22

As given here, the letter seems much ado about nothing. It sounds like the letter of a barely literate Irish female to a friend or relation, also female; it comes from Boston, Mass. (see Sally, Delia Bacon, Artemis), is addressed to Dear Maggy (q.v.); the signature is blotted out with a tea-stain; we have only fragments of the original and odd things happened to it underground. If you feel at a loss about the letter, trust the hen. She has a lovely character, ladylike principles, no pretensions to learning. All she wants is to tell the truth about him.

113.23-125.23

Shem now examines the letter—handwriting, writing materials; he subjects it to Freudian, Marxian comment, discusses the relation of language and love, insists we believe it genuine and authoritative; for at some time somebody wrote it and it is not nonsense, "it only looks like it as damn it"; and we are lucky to have any document from the past. Shem then drops into parody of Sir Edward Sullivan's introduction to the *Book of Kells* and discusses the significance of the letters large and small. Last of all, we study the punctuation marks and, discarding the theory that a professor (Shaun) made them, decide they were made by "Dame Partlet on her dungheap".

The final paragraph establishes that Shem, not Shaun, wrote the "Hen" section.

Book I, section vi (126-168) Questions and Answers

Joyce called this section "a picture history from the family album". Twelve questions, set by Shem, are answered by Shaun in a public lecture. (Book III, section i repeats the questioning of brother by brother.) Shaun wants to carry out his mother's wishes, exalt his father, debase the enemy, who, for Shaun, is always Shem.

126.13-139.14

1 A picture of the father by way of a long list of achievements and epithets which make him an imposing Everybody indeed. "Finn MacCool" (q.v.) is the right answer because Finn is HCE's mythical and heroic aspect.

139.15-28

2 A short sexy picture of the mother. Her full-length portrait is painted by Shem in "Anna Livia Plurabelle".

139.29-140.7

3 A picture of HCE's inn, a riddling question about the inn's name. I don't get it.

140.8-141.7

4 A picture of the Four, courting Issy as on pp. 398-399. The answer to all four parts of the question is "Dublin". Shaun answers it wrongly: Belfast, Cork, Dublin Georgia, Galway, capitals (except for Dublin, Ga.) of the four Irish provinces. Shaun always tries to please the Four.

141.8-27

5 A picture of the Earwickers' Man Servant (q.v.) in the form of a Help Wanted.

141.28-142.7

6 A picture of Kate, the Earwickers' slavey.

142.8-29

7 A picture of the Twelve (q.v.) as Dublin environs and apostles.

142.30-143.2

8 A picture of the Maggies (q.v.).

143.3-28

9 A picture of the Seven (q.v.).

143.29-148.32

10 A picture of Issy in the form of a dramatic monologue, with interruptions by her mirror self—see Sally, Rachel and Leah. I can't tell which Isolde (q.v.) she is, but she is certainly busy seducing Tristram (q.v.) or Shem.

148.33-168.12

11 A picture of Shaun, lecturing. In *Finnegans Wake* Shaun always describes Shem with plainly biased hatred; clever Shem lets Shaun open his mouth and make himself intolerable.

Shem's question is: if a man—exile, rebel, homosexual, starving —asks for food and begs you to save his soul, will you? No, Shaun answers and justifies himself at length for refusing to spare a dime. He tells the story of The Mookse and the Gripes (q.v.) to show he cannot save the soul of a brother who refuses to call him infallible. Then in another story, Burrus and Caseous (Butter and Cheese, Brutus and Cassius, q.v.), Shaun makes it plain that, though he and his brother are both regicides, he (Burrus) is a *noble* regicide and Caseous low.

The Mookse and the Gripes, Burrus and Caseous are two kinds of brother-battle, which will recur. The first is a male or homosexual battle in which the combatants are indifferent to the wiles of their sister, Nuvoletta (q.v.), and drive her to an Ophelia-like suicide; the second is a quarrel over the sister, Margareen-Cleopatra, who leaves them flat for Antony (q.v.), a wop.

168.13-14

12 *Sacer esto?* (Let him be cursed-sacred?)
Semus sumus! (?We are Shem!)
This is all there is to No. 12. The next section enlarges Shem's picture.

BOOK I, section vii (169-195)   Shem

An enlargement of No. 12 in "Questions and Answers", "Shem" is a portrait of the artist painted by Shaun, his mortal enemy. Shaun sees Shem as dispossessed, criminal, black Ham-Satan, not a grand Miltonic Satan, but "low", a squalid Satan, given to small vanities, social failures, personal nastiness, loss of nerve. All this Shaun reveals in a torrent of vituperation which has the happy verve of "The Flyting of Dunbar and Kennedie" or of a Church father denouncing a heretic.

Superficially at least, the section is easy reading and filled with echoes of attacks made on Joyce and his books. Shaun uses most of the section (169.13-193.30) to savage Shem and establish himself as a chum of the angels; Shem has a briefer turn (193.31-194.6). Near the end of the section, the brothers emerge as Justice and Mercy (q.v.) and plead their cases to their mother, Anna Livia (187.24 ff.). Shaun asks for justice in view of his upright life and is given a death or pointing bone which can still the quick, send them to sleep. (He sends the washerwomen to sleep in "Anna Livia Plurabelle", 214-216.) Shem admits himself Cain and a sinner who forswore his mother's womb because it also bore his righteous brother. Anna Livia's voice flows into Shem's (194.12-195.4), and for the first time she is clearly revealed as the river Liffey (or *Lifé*). She scolds Shem for laughing at her (in "The Hen"), for forgetting her; but she sees Satan in Miltonic-Blakeian terms, "windblasted tree of the knowledge of beautiful andevil, ay, clothed upon with the metuor and shimmering", and she picks him over his brother, Shaun, to tell her story in "Anna Livia Plurabelle". She gives Shem "the lifewand", he raises it and the dumb speak (195.5-6). They are the washerwomen of the next section and they speak at Shem's command.

BOOK I, section viii (196-216)   Anna Livia Plurabelle

. . . a chattering dialogue across the river by two washerwomen who as night falls become a tree and a stone. The river is named Anna Liffey. . . . Dublin is a city founded by Vikings. The Irish name is . . . Ballyclee = Town of Ford of Hurdles. Her Pandora's box contains the ills flesh is heir to. The stream is quite brown, rich in salmon, very devious, shallow.
                              Joyce to Miss Weaver, 7 March 1924

"Anna Livia" is written in river language, i.e., contains hundreds of river-names and water-words, and its prose moves like devious, shallow water. Everywoman is a river and a river goddess (see Artemis); her life moves with the river: we see her first in Dublin's Phoenix Park (middle-age), move upstream to the Liffey's (q.v.) source in the Wicklow hills (childhood, youth), move downstream to Dublin (middle-age again), move to Dublin harbor and the sea (old-age, death). The rural hills are Eden; to come down to man-made Dublin is to lose Eden. "Anna Livia" is a faithful (faithful for Joyce) retelling of *Paradise Lost*, and it begins with Adam and Eve cast out.

196.13-200.32

The washerwomen themselves move up and down the Liffey (and tributaries?), are sometimes in a boat, sometimes on opposite banks, scrubbing what dirty linen they find. They start on HCE who is here Dublin and the builder of Dublin where he gets their water so black. They rehash the scandal of three soldiers, two girls and HCE in Phoenix Park, talk of his arrest and trial. They remember how grand he was before his fall. They wonder if he and Anna Livia are legally married or not.

Anna Livia is as bad as HCE because she calls young girls (seven of them) in to enliven her erring husband, for since his fall, Old Humber sits sunk in gloom and impotence, asking "queasy quizzers of his ruful continence," dreading Doomsday, reading his children's obituaries in the papers. Anna Livia tried to cheer him up with food and song, but he hates her—throws plates at her or makes no more response than the mangle weight. She hopes the girls succeed where she has failed.

200.33-201.20

The Grail Quest theme (see Weston) runs strong in "Anna Livia". HCE is not just Adam ybounden and grousing, he is also a slain-wounded fertility god—Adonis, Fisher King. Anna Livia sings a song about her life in the Waste Land—bankside worn out, husband impotent, no food—and hopes some lord or knight will feed them. The song marks a turn towards the Liffey's source where she was-is-will be fed. We are off, then, on a successful fertility quest, which is, at the same time, the slaying of Adam.

201.21-204.20

We move backwards through Anna Livia's childbearing (proof of fertility found) to the fathering of the children. Who was the first man to know her? One washer thinks Anna Livia, the young moon, was raped by the sun when she was bridged for the first time. The other insists that the first time, the occasion of the "happy fault" or Adam's fall, was in Wicklow, "garden of Erin", long before Anna Livia went to Dublin and had to work for a living.

In the dale of Luggelaw (Loch Tay in Wicklow) there lived a chaste priest and eremite, Michael Arklow (q.v.). One summer day when he was hot and thirsty, Anna Livia came by, looking sweet and cool. He could not help himself, he plunged his hands into her lovely hair, he drank her cool water (thus accomplishing the Grail Quest), he kissed her, telling her all the while (like Milton's Adam) never to do it. This theogamy parallels those nature myths (see *From Ritual to Romance*) in which a land is barren till a girl temps a particularly

chaste man to sex. But pagan fertility is the death of Adam; Father
Michael is slain, becomes cross, impotent Old Humber.

As for the little murderess, it is a happy occasion, for she is healed
of barrenness, rises in her own estimation. Before Father Michael,
when a mere child, she knew slight sexual incidents, but the first,
worst, real encounter is now when she falls out of Eden and down to
the evil, the fallen state of Dublin (black pools). Escaping the Devil's
snare, which is the sense of guilt, she laughs "innocefree".

204.21-212.19

Back in Dublin (as at 198-200) Adam's fall gets to be known and
his children, the rabble, mock. Anna Livia swears revenge. She makes
herself beautiful, like Hera dressing up to wheedle Zeus, and gets her
husband's permission to go out for a little. To lull suspicion that she
is Pandora (q.v.)—a Greek bearing gifts—she dresses up as a dowdy,
mad figure of fun, and steps out into Dublin harbor with a bag of
presents for her children—the ills the flesh is heir to. Death, disease,
cold, misery—the children accept these gifts from their delusive
mother.

212.20-216.5

When they finally run from "her pison plague", it is too late. The
washerwomen are representative of those scandalmongering children
and they are shown having to bring forth in pain (213.17-19) and
labor in the cold (214.24-28). Pandora's last gift, hope, comes in the
form of the Annunciation (214.11-215.4), promise of a new day. Hope
causes the washerwomen to forgive their parents, but the gift is delusive. The washers are pagans who die before the coming of Christ.
Night falls, they turn to a tree and a stone.

"Anna Livia Plurabelle" is about how a woman—hugely enjoying
herself—brought sin into the world, death to her husband and children.

BOOK II, section i (219-259)   The Mime of Mick, Nick and the Maggies

The scheme of the piece . . . is the game we used to call Angels and
Devils or colours. The Angels, girls, are grouped behind the Angel, Shawn,
and the Devil has to come over three times and ask for a colour. If the
colour he asks for has been chosen by any girl she has to run and he tries
to catch her. As far as I have written he has come twice and been twice
baffled. The piece is full of rhythms taken from English singing games.
When first baffled vindictively he thinks of publishing blackmail stuff
about his father, mother, etc etc etc. The second time he maunders off
into sentimental poetry. . . . This is interrupted by a violent pang of

toothache after which he throws a fit.* When he is baffled a second time
the girl angels sing a hymn of liberation around Shawn . . . the wild
flowers are the lilts of children. Note specially the treatment of the double
rainbow in which the iritic colours are first normal and then reversed.
                              Joyce to Miss Weaver, 22 November 1930

Finnegans Wake is a dream, but no more a night book than *Ulysses*.
In Book I most important events happen by day and night falls at
the end of "Anna Livia"; Book II takes place between about 8-12 p.m.;
it is midnight at the start of Book III; it dawns in Book III, iv and
is 6 a.m.; the sun rises in Book IV. All parts of *Finnegans Wake* are
shaped by their hour.

"The Mime" catches the twilit texture of childhood and of children
at their sportive and sinister game, Angels and Devils. Irrational, they
communicate mostly by gesture (the language of Vico's First Age) at
an hour when gestures cannot well be seen; they guess at colors and
flowers when colors fade, flowers close. The Devil (Glugg, q.v., or
Shem) tries to guess "heliotrope", which is a flower, gem, color and
his sister Issy, who is seven (q.v.) Rainbow Girls. For all Issy's hints,
Shem cannot guess right, maybe because there is no real sun in the
sky for her to turn to, only the Angel (Chuff, q.v., or Shaun) playing
the part of the sun. I do not understand Joyce on optics, but see
611-613 where Shem is more successful with color.

In "The Mime" Joyce used *The Golden Bough* and Norman
Douglas's *London Street Games* (those on 176 are mostly from Douglas);
both Frazer and Douglas hold that games like Angels and Devils are
survivals of fertility rites. Issy (and girls) is avid for sex and does all
she can to rouse the boys; but Shaun is too pure (or ignorant, as the
next section shows); and Shem, though he wills sex, cannot. The girls
laud Shaun for purity, deride Shem for incapacity.

"The Mime" is not, however, a failed fertility rite; for the father
has watched it from the start (219.25), like the Willingdone at Waterloo. Now—as in "The Wake", 27—he starts up (253.32-36), roused by
the dancing girl (girls). She-they are the seven girls Anna Livia taught
to dance and called in to her passive husband (compare 200.18-27
with 256.2-11, 257.3-5); now she calls, the girl-girls come running and
the father—fairy-tale giant or god from the machine—picks her up
and carries her off into the house, while the sons sing of this as the
fertile meeting of Old Father Barley and Ruth Wheatacre. The

---

* See *Finnegans Wake*, 231: poetry, toothache, fit, come, like the blackmail stuff,
after the first baffling on 225, and before the second, 233. After the second baffle
Shem goes to hell, reforms, pretends to be his father.
"The Mime" was first called "Twilight Games".

door-thunder bangs (257.27-28), marking a fall-creation for the
father and an end to the daughter's barrenness. This repeats the end
of the Prankquean story.

The sons have quarrelled over their sister and lost her to an older
man, as in the Burrus and Caseous story. For them the thunder is
their father's anger. They flee but return and abase themselves,
proclaim their father's greatness, ask him to hear their pleas for mercy
(259.26-259.10).

The game-rite is also "The Mime of Mick, Nick and the Maggies",
presented by a troop of child actors, who rival their elders like the
"little eyases" of *Hamlet*. Like the old guild players they move about,
acting their mystery play, from street to street in Phoenix Park.
They fetch up near their father's inn, which is on the Liffey in
Chapelizod. (q.v.). In the inn, as we shall see, there are more plays
to be acted. Indeed, the four sections of Book II are a cycle of
plays, taking Man from the impotence of childhood in "The Mime"
to the impotence of senility in "Mamalujo".

"The Mime of Mick, Nick and the Maggies" is about the dubious
battle on the plains of heaven. Nick-Shem is the rebel who would
presume to seize his father's prerogative of sex-creation. Mick-Shaun
is the pure, sexless angel who opposes Satan, but, as in *Paradise Lost*,
it is necessary for the father to intervene. Both sons run in fear of the
thunder, but Michael is sure he will have heaven, while his brother
will be "havonfalled".

In so far as the father is Adam, he—not St Michael or Satan—gets
the girl. In so far as the father is God, he takes that which he has
created in order to create further, for, as the next section has it,
"maker mates with made".

BOOK II, section ii (260-308)   Night Lessons*

> . . . the technique here is a reproduction of a schoolboy's (and school-
> girl's) old classbook complete with marginalia by the twins, who change
> sides at half time, footnotes by the girl (who doesn't), a Euclid diagram,
> funny drawings, etc. It was like that in Ur of the Chaldees too, I daresay.
>
> Joyce to Frank Budgen, End July 1939

260.13-266.19

Youth and ignorance defeated the sons in "The Mime". At the
start of "Night Lessons" they are lost and wonder how to get back

* According to Mr Litz, Joyce published 260-275, 304-308 under the title,
Storiella As She Is Syung; 282-304 was informally called, first "The Triangle",
then "The Muddest Thick That Was Ever Heard Dump". Under this last title,
it was published, along with "The Mookse and the Gripes" and "The Ondt and
the Gracehoper" in *Tales Told of Shem and Shaun*.

to their father's "pint of porter place", his bar, and bring him down. The way there is a circle of learning, by which, in the Viconian nature of things, they will come to the time of overthrowing the father—the time arrives in the next section; the circle of learning begins and ends with their mother—knowing her will make men of them. Till they get knowledge, they must go in fear, "natural, simple, slavish, filial". Thus when they get back to Chapelizod, they don't mind their father, calling them into his place; instead, they linger along the Liffey (their mother), throw a brick at the bar and go upstairs to the "studiorum" where their sister sits and knits.

266.20-272.8

The boys are obsessed with the past because it contains the mating of their father and seven-colored sister. In their awe-struck eyes the maker mates with the seven wonders of the ancient world (260.28-261.22), and he mates, as the Kabbalist Ainsoph (q.v.) with his emanations (261.23-262.19). The act was religious, magic, mythical, all-fertile. But after sojourning by the Liffey, their interest turns to the feminine. Before settling down to study they consider their sister and the education her mother gave her so she would be Leda (q.v.) and a dish for the god.

272.9-281.29

The mother now recalls the boys and the girl from the haunted past, so they can fight for themselves—as at Waterloo—and then mourn and praise their fallen father at his wake. The first thing they must know is their letters (272.9-278.24).

"The Wake" established letters-of-the-alphabet as the knowledge of good and evil, the knowledge or power for which Adam lost his innocence. Here, Issy is Eve who has eaten the apple; she knows letters and two parts of her split personality promptly write (279, note 1; 280.1-281.3): first, a mash note, thanking the male teacher who taught her to err; second, a Dear Maggy, using the Boston letter (111) as a model. The mother has told the boys that they need to know the young female heart, and from Issy's letters they could learn that her heart is a pearl, a flower, a cloud; but the boys are like Brutus and Cassius, Othello and Iago (q.q.v.), more concerned with war (against their father, against each other) than with a girl's heart (281.4-29).

282.1-287.17

Issy-Eve and Shem-Satan have eaten of the apple, know their letters. Shaun does not and "The Mime" showed he was not tempted by young female charm. If the war against the father is to succeed,

Shaun-Adam must be made "vicewise", as in Mutt and Jute. Shem takes on the job with tears, but pep.

Shaun is bad at algebra and geometry, finding all problems equal to "aosch" or "chaos". He asks his brother to do his geometry problem for him: "Concoct an equoangular trillitter", or "Construct an equilateral triangle". Shem agrees and tells Shaun to start by drawing two circles on mud taken from the mother-river.

An equilateral triangle is a geometric figure. It is also the female counterpart of the phallus and the Greek letter Delta (q.v.), which is Anna Livia's sign, stands at the beginning of "Anna Livia Plurabelle". A delta is an alluvial deposit at the mouth of a river; and in this section the delta is the mother's dung-heap on which Shaun constructs the triangle, for "Love has pitched his mansion in the place of excrement". The letter Shaun must learn to make is Delta or D, which is the first letter in Dear, the first word in most letters. (The Hebrew letter Daleth or door is also important here).

287.18-292.32

The lesson is interrupted by a Latin message from the Liffey, to the effect that everything flows safely like a river, that the contents of the (dung?) heap will remain in the river, that everything is recognized by its opposite, that rivers are embraced by rival banks. The Latin is part of a long sentence of seven clauses, dealing (I guess) with some of the important roles, played by those opposites, those rivals, the twins. After it, they exchange sides of the margin, which must mark an important change or mixing of roles, as when the Prankquean mixes them, perhaps. I don't make the sentence out and have little confidence in my reading of the section from now on.

293.1-304.4

The geometry lesson resumes. Shem teaches Shaun to construct a triangle and then to look behind it at his mother's organs of generation. Apparently Shaun is uncomprehending, has no sense of sin, for he is easily flattered into going on to show that he can write a letter, beginning with a big D(ear), and write it as well as his father. The letter is written in Shaun's blood (300.31-301.2) and is a Faustian pact with the Devil. Shaun is also Esau, selling his birthright, and later—when, in some fashion, he realizes what he has done—he knocks his brother down.

304.5-306.7

Shem thanks him for favors received. The blow makes him see rainbows and recall his little sister who has watched the fight, while dreaming of her father, and now throws a tea-cup at Shem. (As in Ibsen's *Love's Comedy* tea stands for sex.) Moreover Shaun has lost his innocence, which is what Shem wanted him to do. Shaun now begins his career as a hypocrite and insists he did no such thing: his brother forged the letter in blood, his brother is Cain. Their quarrel ends temporarily when they remember they still have to meet with their father who will offer them sweetmeats, but give them his "Noblett's surprise"—blow them up with TNT. For the fight against their father they are united, "singulfied".

306.8-308.30

The father comes in to ask what they have been learning. "Natural, simple, slavish, filial", they answer with utmost duplicity that they have studied: "Art, literature, politics, economy, chemistry, humanity", subjects which make an acrostic of their parents' initials. They have still a composition to write—expressing of course Nobel's (q.v.) sense of idealism. They ignore a long list of suggested topics because time is short, tea's waiting. When they fall to their tea, they and their sister have concocted a "trillitter"—or at any rate, a letter containing three "ds" and signed by the three of them. It seems to wish their parents a merry Christmas, but in fact wishes them dead. The young people are now, all of them, accomplices.

BOOK II, section iii (309-382)   Scene in the Pub

. . . McCann's story, told to John Joyce, of a hunchbacked Norwegian captain who ordered a suit from a Dublin tailor, J. H. Kerse of 34 Upper Sackville Street. The finished suit did not fit him, and the captain berated the tailor for being unable to sew, whereupon the irate tailor denounced him for being impossible to fit.

Ellmann, *James Joyce*, 22

. . . his father's story of Buckley and the Russian General. . . . Buckley . . . was an Irish soldier in the Crimean War who drew a bead on a Russian general, but when he observed his splendid epaulettes and decorations, he could not bring himself to shoot . . . he raised his rifle again, but just then the general let down his pants to defecate. The sight of his enemy in so helpless and human a plight was too much for Buckley, who again lowered his gun. But when the general prepared to finish the operation with a piece of grassy turf, Buckley lost all respect for him and fired.

Ellmann, *James Joyce*, 411

He then narrated the story of Buckley; when he came to the piece of turf, Beckett remarked, "Another insult to Ireland".

Ellmann, *James Joyce*, 411, note

HCE's pub goes by nearly as many names as he does, but it is, at any rate, the "pint of porter place". Here the innkeeper and customers spend the hour before closing-time watching two plays (written by Shem?) and a musical program on a TV set, given by certain Irish invaders—the sons (309.13-311.4).

The plays—*The Norwegian Captain* and *How Buckley Shot the Russian General* (311.5-332.9, 337.32-355.7)—and the music (359.31-361.31) are about the overthrow of the father by, respectively, Shem, Shaun, Issy. Shem takes his father's daughter from him; Shaun shoots him dead; Issy as moon priestess castrates him.

Thereafter—apparently in fact, not TV—HCE's sons come knocking at the door, singing another version of "The Ballad of Persse O'Reilly", and his daughter comes to say she's off with a younger man (370.23-373.12). The sons capture HCE, threaten, mock, taunt, try him and beat him up for his sins (373.13-380.5).

Alone in the pub, HCE plays Roderick O'Connor, last native king of Ireland, who was overthrown by the Anglo-Normans. He drinks up the guests' leavings, falls dead drunk. As always, Anna Livia shelters him after fall; as the stout ship *Nansy Hans*, she bears him by starlight over the sea from Ireland to "Nattenlander" (380.6-382.30).

The Norwegian Captain (q.v.) is a comedy of love intrigue, and I cannot follow the ins and outs of the intrigue, much less explain what the ill-fitting suit means to the plot. (Suit as clothes—suit as courtship?) The story seems to be about a wild, pagan sea-rover (all Ireland's Viking invaders) who steals away the daughter of an Irish innkeeper (also known as the Ship's Husband) from her father and from a rival suitor, Kersse the tailor. Later, by some female stratagem, the captain is converted to landlubber, Christian, Irish and becomes a respectable husband and father; the Ship's Husband reconciles him and Kersse (q.v.). The captain is hunchbacked, called Humphrey, and the girl is Anne; therefore, they recall the courtship and marriage of HCE and ALP (compare 197, 624.27-30), and the play warns the father (the watching innkeeper, not the TV innkeeper) that, as he took a daughter, so his daughter will be taken. The marriage of the captain and the daughter ends in an outburst of joy, peace and fertility for Ireland.

How Buckley Shot the Russian General (a rerun of the events at Waterloo) is a tragedy with a *Hamlet* feeling about it and a Freudian feeling, too; for Buckley—anguished in indecision and pity—kills not only a father, but the totem ancestor, the uncanny deer or bear or bull or white whale that haunts a man's dreams and is a more precious part of himself than his trigger-finger. As Butt and Taff (q.v.), both sons will the general's death and at different times both assume the role of Buckley. One (who I take to be Shem or Mercy) is merciful when the general defecates and is so human; the other (who I take to be Shaun or Justice) kills for the honor of Ireland, thus being Brutus, the high-minded trigger-man.

When the play is over the customers at the bar say Buckley was right to shoot, and the innkeeper agrees (355.8,21), thus finding against himself—Guilty but fellow culprits . . . (363.20). It is why, after all have attacked him, he drinks symbolic hemlock and falls. "All men," Anna Livia says later, "has done something. Be the time they've come to the weight of old fletch."

BOOK II, section iv (383-399)   Mamalujo

> Many thanks for your letter and kind appreciation of the foursome episode. It is strange that on the day I sent off to you a picture of an epicene professor of history in an Irish university college seated in the hospice for the dying etc after "eating a bad crab in the red sea" . . .
>   Joyce to Miss Weaver, 23 October 1923

"Mamalujo" is short and collective for Matthew, Mark, Luke and John (see Four Evangelists) or Matt Gregory, Mark Lyons, Luke Tarpey, Johnny MacDougall (q.q.v.). As Joyce says, the section is mostly a picture of these dreadful old creatures. Always old in *Finnegans Wake*, they are never so old as here where they are a monumental Senility and, by their peevish, lunatic flux of memory, they shrink history to something monstrous and small.

We have seen them as Repression, holding down the old Adam when he would rise to life, judging, censoring, law-giving; and we have seen Repression's other face (94.23-96.24, 140.15-141.7), lewd, envious, hypocritic. Over and over Joyce calls them "the Elders" (q.v.), those judges, lechers, liars in *Susanna* (q.v.). One way or another —as sycamores, elders, bed-posts, etc.—they leer at all mating in *Finnegans Wake* and are emblematic of the voyeurist, the poisoned imagination.

In "Mamalujo" they are the muttering waves across which the ship moves from Ireland. His sons are HCE when young, and the Four are HCE in impotence and dissolution; they make up the unhappy viewpoint of Mark of Cornwall (q.v.), watching young Tristan (Shem) take Isolde of Ireland. For this is the ship of the first act of *Tristan und Isolde*, and the Four are treated to a luscious scene of the young people's mating (395.26-396.33), described as a football match. The sight revitalizes the old men (in fact or fancy) and in turn they serenade Issy, first propositioning her, then claiming, like the Elders, to have known her.

Book II begins with childhood. It ends with second childhood.

It is easy to forget that Tristram is also Sir Amory Tristram (q.v.), the stranger who takes Ireland for his bride.

BOOK III, section i (403-428)   First Watch of Shaun

. . . Shawn . . . is a description of a postman travelling backwards in the night through the events already narrated. It is written in the form of a *via crucis* of 14 stations but in reality is only a barrel rolling down the river Liffey.

Joyce to Miss Weaver, 24 May 1924*

The "First Watch" begins with a flurry of allusions to *A Midsummer-Night's Dream*, for it is midnight, the hour when fairies, witches and evil spirits wake. The narrator or dreamer is Bottom (q.v.), translated to an ass (q.v.), the ass which is the property of the Four. He is narrator of sections i,ii, and perhaps of all Book III. The ass is a lot of other people, too: in so far as the Four are Irish provinces, he is Meath, the dispossessed or missing Fifth province; in so far as he is their servant, he is St Patrick (q.v.) when a slave in Ireland; in so far as the Four are the evangelists, the ass is Christ, unknown as at Emmaus. He is also Jerry (q.v.) or Shem.

403.13-407.9

Unlike Shakespeare's Bottom, nothing so agreeable as the fairy queen happens to the ass. He sees Oberon and Titania (the parents) asleep and then meets up with his brother, Shaun the Post, acting— among other things—Moonshine. Anna Livia is, of course, moon and moon goddess, but Shaun and his lantern playact Moonshine, i.e., Nonsense and a leaking barrel of stout (471.36). In the "Second Watch" he will be Dionysus (q.v.), surrounded by maenads. That Moonshine's real name is Starveling partly accounts for Shaun's eating constantly, eating steak (because they drive stakes through witches' hearts?), bacon (to prove he's not a Jew), drinking his brother's blood.

John McCormack (q.v.), the Irish tenor, was one of the principal models for Shaun in III, i and ii. A man composed of wondrous

---

* Book III, sections i and ii were once one section, and I think the *via crucis* extends across both. It may, however, extend across all Book III. Because i,ii make up a mock-passion, Joyce's "backwards" may also mean "Bachwards".

quantities of flesh and sentiment, McCormack was made a papal count and, in the first two Watches, Joyce uses him to mount a slashing satire, very medieval, on the gross materiality, the indelicate chastity, the degradation of sensibility which mark popular Catholicism. Shaun is not, of course, Christ or a member of the Roman Catholic Church. He is a heretic, a wizard, and Antichrist (q.v.). He walks the *via crucis* backwards, and, like Antichrist in the old morality play, claims to do everything Christ did. At the end of III,ii, Shaun tries to fly to heaven and cannot.

409.8-419.11

As in I,vi, Shem puts to Shaun calculated, ironic questions that wheedle Shaun into showing himself conceited, mercenary and merciless. The fable of "The Ondt and the Gracehoper" (q.v.) is a companion piece to "The Mookse and the Gripes": Shaun the Ondt (Ant or Don't) will not feed his starving brother; he forgoes girls in this world so he can have houris in heaven.

Shem's ironic questions also aim to get Shaun to admit his knowledge of the letter (Delta-epistle), knowledge gained and then denied in "Night Lessons". Shaun does not seem to recognize his brother-as-ass, but he is quick to anger and on the defensive about the letter. He insists he was condemned to carry it, is tired of the job, but can get no other, and so does his duty like a good pious boy who has always believed. There follow questions I don't understand, but Shaun takes them as an accusation that he has spent money-virtue as he shouldn't; he denies the charge and says someday he will defend himself, write a "savings book" and dedicate it to that killed-with-sexual-cold female, Swift's Stella (q.q.v.). Next he tells "The Ondt and the Gracehoper" to show himself the prudent Ant who spends nothing, just hoards money and virtue.

419.12-424.22

The ass still tries to get Shaun to admit he carries a fertility symbol and that he knows about that symbol. Won't Shaun read and explain the letter? Shaun cannot, for it is all Greek (Delta) to him. Though he cannot read it, he knows the letter is trash, dirt, written by his mother and brother. It is addressed to HCE, but the address is always wrong or HCE not at home. Has not Shaun written just as sinful letters as his brother? Shaun denies it, says he will be revenged on his brother who put his mother up to the letter-writing and then tried to say the letter is partly Shaun's. How will he be revenged? Shaun will excommunicate Shem. Why? For his "root language" (the rude language of the creative thunder-peal) that he put into his invention of letters.

424.23-426.4

Couldn't Shaun "come near" (cf. 297.14-15) that rude language himself? No one in his senses could, Shaun answers, for the language is "incendiary" and Shem (like Prometheus?) stole it from Heaven. For a reason unclear to me, Shaun takes a swig of John Jameson (q.v.) from his "treestem sucker cane" (424.28), which turns out to mean he drinks the blood of his brother, Tristram-Cain (425.9); and this drink apparently affects his next and last and reckless reply. The ass flatters—Shaun is so brainy (cf. 300.1-2), he can surely use worse language than his brother. Shaun has recognized the ass as Shem (425.30-31), and says, yes he could, much worse, but he never would—here we have the prudent Ondt—because he is "too fly and hairyman", i.e. smart and Ahriman (q.v.) or Devil-like; he adds that he will send to the flames any incendiarist who set his mother on fire, —on fire sexually, I suppose.

426.5-428.27

Shaun has now admitted, though only to his brother, that he knows the wicked letter, and is now creating his own version of the Devil-Antichrist. After the admission Shaun falls from his own weight and, as a barrel, rolls backward and down the Liffey, bound for the life of the remittance man in America.

I am pretty sure that this is the Ninth Station of the Cross (Jesus Falls for the Third Time) because most of the next section is the Eighth Station. The fall and disappearance doubtless have further meaning. Does Shaun go to hell? Is he born in a breech delivery? However that may be, Shaun leaves Ireland and is prayed to return.

BOOK III, section ii (429-473)   Second Watch of Shaun*

The "Second Watch" is mostly the Eighth Station of the Cross: Jesus speaks to the Daughters of Jerusalem: it is also John McCormack's long-drawn farewell to the operatic stage, singing a medley of *Don Giovanni* and the *St John Passion*.

Shaun—now called Jaun—is still a barrel of Moonshine, talks nonsense and affects young women like a dose of Dionysus. He is compounded of Don Juan, Henry VIII, Swift and Othello

---

* A helpful note on *Finnegans Wake*, 469 ff.—too long to print here—is found in Joyce's letter to Miss Weaver, 8 August 1928.

(q.q.v.) because he is "the killingest ladykiller all by kindness"; because he kills with kindness, does not give himself, preaches chastity to a sister, he is St Benedict, Pascal, Laertes (q.q.v.); he is the dying god of infertility, winter, a carnival figure of Lent; and he is still Boucicault's Sean the Post and Antichrist. Beautiful, chaste, sexy, he preaches while leaning against a blond policeman (see Man Servant) who is dead-drunk and buried upright in the soil like a log or phallic symbol. The ass is again narrator, but has nothing to do or say.

It is Lent (till 453.36) and Jaun's audience is composed of twenty-nine hysterically devoted maenads, members of a coven, hens, February girls; or, to be precise, there are twenty-eight daughters of infertile February (see St Bridget), twenty-eight phases of the chaste moon. The twenty-ninth is Jaun's sister, Issy, and to her he addresses his plea for chastity and spiritual love of himself alone. Issy is, however, a leap-year girl and makes her own choice.

431.21-457.24

Jaun's sermon or letter on female chastity is the "savingsbook", dedicated to Swift's chaste, dead Stella, which he promised in the First Watch (412.30-413.26). It is based, Jaun says, on the advice of Father Michael (203.36)—"niver to, niver to, nevar"—which was uttered at the moment Father Michael succumbed to female wiles; and Jaun uses words "taken in triumph" from Shem (433.7-9). Jaun's letter entirely justifies his boast (425.9-31) that he can write worse letters than his brother, worse than Shem's exposition of Delta or Triangle in "Night Lessons".

It has been established that Jaun knows the Triangle, the sexual nature of woman, as well as Shem. To his young girl audience, he exhibits and corrupts that knowledge in order to make the Triangle or Cross not fertile. Joyce is a great writer and makes it possible to feel sorry for Jaun, by showing the devastating strength, envy, greed and sadism of the virile personality, caught in the net of chastity; but Joyce, along with Blake and Lawrence and, for that matter, Milton (*Paradise Lost*, x, 979-1046), perceives that infertility is the plea of the Devil. It is bad enough to dirty sex, as Jaun does, but far worse to urge chastity as a matter of prudent calculation—Give up boys in this world, sisters, and enjoy ME, the prize of all eternity, hereafter.

457.25-461.32

When Jaun stops talking, Issy agrees with every word he says. As Veronica (Sixth Station of the Cross) she gives him a handkerchief as a pledge of faithful love (the Cressida touch), which turns out to be a letter to Shem, asking him, while Jaun is away, to "Coach me how to tumble, Jaime . . .". In other words, Issy wants love here and hereafter.

461.33-468.22

Jaun makes the best of this by pretending he always meant to leave the Holy Ghost or Shem (here also Simon of Cyrene and David to Shaun's Jonathan) behind to console the girls. Jaun then acts the part of Pandarus, and with the most vulgar hectoring urges Shem and Issy into each other's arms, assuring them he will always be at their bedside. He has failed to strike down sex in a vital girl, but men are sensitive plants and shame, the Irish "national umbloom", comes "greeping ghastly" out of Shem. I am not sure, but I think he and Shaun become, as on other occasions, one.

468.23-473.25

If Jaun has queered Shem's sexual pitch, Shem now queers Jaun's pretensions to be Christ by suggesting he fly to heaven or America. Twice Jaun tries to fly away and falls. The girls weep and praise him as a dying god, apparently for the purpose of getting him to leave them, for, according to Joyce's note on the passage, they regard him as a yesterday. When Jaun is about to try for the third time and tumble in the river, "the gentlest weaner" (Issy being Veronica again? Anna Livia?), gives him a stamp, which may be her way of trying to get rid of him, mail him to America. He takes it for a mark of her faith in him and sticks it on his brow. Exactly what happens next I am not sure. I guess that after waving goodbye to the girls (who respond with the word "Peace" in twenty-nine languages) he soars up among the stars who are angry (see Stella), falls a third time and then goes off like a postman on foot. The girls praise him and pray he will come again.

Book III, section iii (474-554) Third Watch of Shaun*

It was predicted that Shaun-Jaun would grow till he filled space (429.23-24). Now called Yawn and sleeping in a poppy-field like the Cowardly Lion, he covers the whole of Ireland, an angelic, gargantuan baby, sweetly wailing. As Magi, the Four come with their ass to his crib (cf. 6.29-35), come to the hill of Uisnech, traditionally the center of Ireland, the place where the four provinces meet. Here they hold inquiry—half seance, half inquest.

* 532-554 was published as *Haveth Childers Everywhere*.

The Four are old, silly, quarrelsome, but not near so senile as in "Mamalujo". Each has pet phrases, each speaks in the accents of his quarter of Ireland. I once pretty well determined which old man asks what question, but I couldn't see what difference it made, except that Mark Lyons dominates the questioning and Johnny MacDougal doesn't ask his share. The ass is the missing fifth province and sometimes interprets between the Four and the sleeper, or rather, between the Four and the voices that speak through "Pure Yawn's" baby lips, using him like a radio station, a telephone exchange, or as spirit controls use the lips of a medium.

This is a coroner's inquest which anciently had jurisdiction, not only over unexplained deaths (like HCE's) but also over treasure-troves and royal fish, caught near the coast or washed ashore. The Four are concerned with fish because they are evangelists, but on 477.18-30, 524-525 their coroners' duty reinforces this concern. As for treasure-troves, the Four are entirely taken up with one from 477.35-501.5. Thereafter, until displaced by a youthful braintrust (529.5), they inquire into the circumstances surrounding the death of H. C. Earwicker.

The treasure-trove is, of course, the contents of the barrow or dung-heap, where, as Mutt told Jute, are buried countless "livestories", "litters from aloft", and most important, Anna Livia and HCE (17.27- 18.11), the object of all treasure hunts.

The coroners' first care is to establish that this is indeed the letter-hoard (477.35-478.6); they examine letters and livestories, comment on them till they come on Anna Livia, at once exhibiting and defending her husband (492.5-495.33), and then on HCE in the mound, lying as at his wake (497-499).

477.31-486.31

The way to the parents lies through difficult passages about the sons. The first letter or voice is Shem's, speaking as St Patrick (q.v.), not the saint of legends, but of the wonderful *Confession*. A Tantric T on temple, lips and breast causes Patrick to have (as he actually did) three visions. The visions are other roles of Shem's—Tristram, Swift, and a third I don't understand.

487.7-491.36

Shaun as postman speaks next. He has figured in the preceding passage as Patrick's Judas and "counterfeit Kevin". Now Shaun has his turn and savages Shem. Then—what I don't at all follow—he talks of himself and his brother as Browne and Nolan (q.v.), opposite and identical.

499.16-501.5

To return to HCE or Finnegan at his wake (497-499), he is the object of their inquest, the ultimate treasure of the trove, the epiphany they have come for. He stirs—Do you think I'm dead?—and the Four, as always, will not let him speak. Instead, they set up "zounds of sounds upon him", jam radio communications as in a magnetic storm, let loose a whirlwind of ancestral voices, prophesying war— Cromwell, Patrick, Parnell, Swift—and after, there is radio silence.

501.9-528.26

The curtain drops and the inquest on the treasure-trove is over. The spirit radio is now tuned to HCE's fall. Back we go through variations on persons and events that were presented in I,ii-iv, till the Four, who have become increasingly silly and quarrelsome, are replaced by "bright young chaps of the brandnew braintrust", the sons, who we have seen a little earlier (525.10-526.15) making really serious efforts to catch the father-as-fish. They come "with maternal sanction" (529.6), for as muck-raker or white-washer, Anna Livia is always determined that her husband shall be known.

528.26-532.5

After hearing from the family servants, the young brains close down the program, say, "Arise, sir ghostus!", and switch on their father's voice. They are doing what the Four would not do, calling the most important witness to the stand, but note they do not call him back in the flesh, only as a ghost, a radio voice. It is not a true epiphany.

532.6-534.2

As Amsterdam (q.v.) or Protestant (he really does protest too much), HCE first addresses Rome and in his divinely unconvincing way, denies he was ever anything but a faithful husband. He did not chase girls.

534.7-535.21

Then as Big Calm he denies the charges against him and blames them on that criminal, that strangler of green parrots, the cad. As for the girls, they were whores.

535.26-539.16

Next he announces himself as Old Whitehowth or Sebastion and is not to be distinguished from Oscar Wilde (q.v.). He assumes the pathetic whine of *De Profundis*, admits he is guilty and deserving of punishment; but it should be a light prison term, for all men are guilty, he will "discontinue entyrely all practices", all the charges made against him are not true, and he repents.

539.16-554.10

Scarcely has he uttered the word "repent" when the frail dam of virtue breaks. He launches into a high-spirited, boyish boast, the boast of the builder, a Whitman-like catalogue of What Man Hath Wrought; and he makes no distinction between, feels no greater pride in the Parthenon than in the slums of York in 1906—see Rowntree.

The first part of the boast (to 546.24) is a masculine thing—Adam before Eve, I suppose. Thereafter, HCE created of, on, for Anna Livia, reforming and altcring Nature whether she liked it or not—"I was firm with her."

HCE's boast damns him, not because he does not have a desirable social attitude to slums and criminals, not because he raped Nature, but because as masterbuilder of civilization—a wall, a city, a family—he successfully rivals God's prerogative of creation. He fell because he built.

BOOK III, section iv (555-590) Fourth Watch of Shaun

> I know that [Shaun] d ought to be about roads, all about dawn and roads. . . .
>
> Joyce to Miss Weaver, 29 August 1925

555.13-558.31

Another go through the picture album brings us to the father and mother in bed, as at the opening of Book III. Then it was midnight and they were Oberon and Titania; now it is almost six in the morning and they are not that fairy pair, but Albert and Victoria (q.v.) Liffey quays and a notably mundane royal couple.

558.35-560.21

The "Fourth Watch" leads down from the imaginative reach of Everybuilder's boast and reminds us that HCE is also a single member of the human race. To this end Joyce shows us the humble inn in Chapelizod, the bedchamber, homely as the Blooms'. It is natural to

think the homely and unbeautiful must be the real, and suppose that
from this place the big innkeeper and his little wife rise to playact
the kings and queens who so abound in this section. But note, humble
life is particularly shown as a scene upon a stage. We cannot be sure
if the Earwickers (here called Porters) act royalty or royalty acts low
life like Marie Antoinette at the Petit Trianon.

At the corners of the bed stand the Four Evangelists and each in
turn describes (influences?) the action as seen from his particular
vantage point. I suppose the Fourth Watch is a sort of Play of
Marriage in four acts, with a different critic for each act. Matthew
begins 559.22, Mark 564.2, Luke 582.28, John 590.23.

558.32-563.36

The parents are waked by a cry from little Shem-Jerry. (It is the
ass's cry at the end of the "Third Watch".) The mother rises like
Dawn from her bed and, bearing a lamp, rushes upstairs, her husband
after her. (Like Dawn, Anna Livia is saffron robed, rises with a light
from a cold bed and goes after a younger male.) They go into the
first room where infant Issy lies in lovely slumber. Her father looks
at her with wonder and desire and the passage is full of references to
sleeping Imogen. Then they go to the twins' room. The father looks
at angelic Kevin on the left and devilish Jerry on the right. It is not
easy to tell them apart, the good from the bad, both seem worth
something—so HCE leaves his blessing between them, "kerryjevin".
This ends Act I.

564.1-565.32

HCE's blessing is his fortune, his man's estate. It is the dream vision
of that estate—symbolized as Phoenix Park seen as the father's
bottom—that frightened Jerry-Shem in the first place. Now his
brother joins in the bawling and when their father can't convince
them he's their friend, he tells them, shame on you—shut up!—thus
dividing his curse between them. The mother comforts Shem—it was
all a dream, a "magic nation", there are no panthers, no bad fathers
in the room, tomorrow Father will go away to Dublin on business,
slap bad Father.

565.33-570.25

While the mother kneels and comforts the boy, the really high life
above stairs begins in the father's "magic nation". His household
forms itself into a gratifying scene of a royal court where the sons

are princes in the tower (to be murdered), the mother kneels passive, the daughter bows to his drawn sword. It is followed by a royal progress, a time of peace, celebration, lovely weather. Now a mayor, HCE receives the king, is knighted, makes an address; bells peal; food, music, plays, fancy ladies are provided. Yes, Lord Pournter-familias is a good married man with two boys and a girl.

570.26-572.17

The thought of the daughter rouses the father sexually and he imagines himself Tristram, knowing Isolde. His wife's voice interrupts him (like Mrs Mitty's), speaking of Shem—quieter now. Resentfully, the father thinks he is legally entitled to his wife and is not a wild beast (panther). As they leave the boys' room he thinks how soon the younger generation will come knocking at the door. He opens his daughter's door and looks at her again.

572.18-576.9

HCE's household forms into another kind of court—domestic relations. He was in gratifying command of the royal court and particularly virile; now his wife brings a charge of impotence against him. The situation of Honuphrius and Anita is modelled on Father Matharan's (q.v.) collection of marital problems, solved by the Catholic Church. I do not understand the problem or the trial that follows, where the matter is argued in terms of a dud check and brought before the Dail.

576.17-582.27

The parents resume their progress downstairs to bed, while Joyce lists titles and achievements which make them our ancestors, Everyman and Everywoman. Once below stairs they become little people again, and their descendants accept them with resignation and no enthusiasm. This ends Act II.

(582.28-590.22)

In bed again, the parents' copulation is told as a cricket-match and news of it flashes over the world and the planets. It ends when the cock crows for dawn. What is not at first publicly known is that HCE has used a birth preventative. In his ensuing sadness, he thinks of this failure to procreate becoming known and merging into all that scandal about the three soldiers and two girls. No devastation, no indignity will be spared him—they'll put him on the stage; his children will boo; he'll be tried in court; his daughter will leave him; he'll lose an election; he'll never triumph with a woman again, etc. etc. This ends Act III.

(590.23-30)

Act IV: while the male torments himself, the queenbee enjoyed it all so much and "blesses her bliss".

BOOK IV (593-628)

> In Part IV there is in fact a triptych—though the central window is scarcely illuminated. Namely the supposed windows of the village church gradually lit up by the dawn, the windows, i.e., representing on one side the meeting of St Patrick (Japanese) and the (Chinese) Archdruid Bulkely (this by the way is all about colour) and the legend of the progressive isolation of St Kevin, the third being St Lawrence O'Toole, patron saint of Dublin, buried in Eu in Normandy.
>
> Joyce to Frank Budgen (dictated)

> . . . the hagiographic triptych in Part IV (S. L. O'Toole is only adumbrated). Much more is intended in the colloquy between Berkeley the arch druid and his pidgin speech and Patrick the [?] and his Nippon English. It is also the defense and indictment of the book itself, B's theory of colours and Patrick's practical solution of the problem. Hence the phrase in the preceding Mutt and Jeff banter 'Dies is Dorminus master' = Deus est Dominus noster plus the day is Lord over sleep, i.e. when it days.
>
> Joyce to Frank Budgen, 20 August 1939

As Joyce indicates, Book IV is shaped like a triptych whose parts are:

1) 600.5-606.12 or 607.16—on the left, St Kevin (q.v.) remains pure when tempted by an amorous girl. The scene is Glendalough in County Wicklow.

2) 609.1-613.14—on the right, St Patrick kindles the flame of Christianity on Holy Saturday in defiance of King Laoghaire's (q.v.) orders; then in a contest of truth and skill, Patrick defeats the Archdruid and uses the shamrock to teach the doctrine of the Trinity. The scene is Slane and Tara in County Meath.

3) 613.15-628.16—in the center, St Lawrence O'Toole (q.v.)—of whom I know no memorable legend—is "adumbrated" (613.15-16). I fancy he is to be thought of as dead, not on Irish soil, and his picture replaced by one of HCE and Anna Livia, older patrons of Dublin —hill and river. The scene is Howth and Dublin City in County Dublin.

For all I know, the "hagiographic triptych" is a real window in the

village church of Chapelizod or in Adam and Eve's on Merchant's
Quay. I do know that if you trace the outlines of counties Wicklow,
Dublin, Meath, you find they are contiguous and make a very fair
triptych. The triptych is, then—geographical as well as architectural
—three eastern counties lit by dawn.

At the start of Book IV (593.13-600.4) there is a deal of talk about
the sun (lots of Sanscrit words and English anagrams—why?). I
don't think it is the actual rising of the sun, rather, an invocation,
desiring the sun to rise. HCE himself must be the sun when he rises
and goes to the top of Howth (619.25-624.11) and then down to the
Liffey valley (626.7). In III,iv we saw Anna Livia as Aurora, but in
Book IV she carries no lamp (621.5) for dawn's light goes out with
the sun. She is also the old moon, going down into the sea (627.34)
as the new moon rises over the Wicklow hills (627.3-6—compare
202.26-29).

600.5-606.12

The parts of the triptych have more correspondence than is found
in family portraits, saints' legends, architecture and geography. For
one thing, the pictures retell earlier parts of *Finnegans Wake*.

The "isolation of St Kevin" retells that part of "Anna Livia
(202.35-204.20) where the water-woman successfully tempts the chaste
eremite to drink the pagan grail, causing his spiritual death, her
physical fertility. That was paradise lost, the fall of the First Adam.
In Book IV the Second Adam attains the isolation of perfect chastity
when he does not drink from the pagan chalice. Into his own chalice
or tub he puts exorcized, sanctified water and then gets into it—
regaining paradise and the womb of Mother Church. This time the
female is physically murdered, i.e., condemned to perpetual chastity;
the male uses her for the practical purpose of making himself clean,
fostering his spiritual fertility.

609.1-613.14

The contest between St Patrick and Archdruid Berkeley (q.v.)
I do not well understand; but it retells and reverses Patrick's
failure to guess the color "heliotrope" in "The Mime" (see Joyce to
Frank Budgen, End July 1939). Whatever Patrick's "practical
solution" may be, he wins the prize this time—Ireland—and ends
HCE's division of his kingdom between his two sons (compare
563.29-30 and 610.10-12). Note that both Kevin and Patrick find
practical solutions to the problem of woman-seven, expressed as

water, then as color. Note, too, that both legends were formerly told
in reverse, but now they are told straight—St Kevin did master
female temptation, St Patrick did overcome the Archdruid.

The side windows of the triptych show Christianity conquering
paganism—first Shaun conquers, then Shem. The center window
shows the opposite: Christian St Lawrence O'Toole dead and buried
abroad and his place taken by HCE and Anna Livia who rise up from
bed and make a progress, not (as in III,iv) downstairs, upstairs,
downstairs in the inn, but up from Phoenix Park to the top of Howth
and down again to the Liffey (621.1, 624.11, 626.7). Joyce was a
dreadfully consistent mind, so I guess this progress must reverse the
earlier one.

614.27-619.19

Before the godlike progress comes a letter which ostensibly defends
"that direst of housebounds" and in fact rakes up all the sour old
scandals about him (compare the letters, 492-495). The shrew side of
Mrs Earwicker-Finnegan writes it and limns the mean proportions of
what is historical man to the Four historians. His "fooneral will sneak
place", she assures us, and there is no word of his rising. This is not
the letter from Boston, that is yet to come (623.29-36); this letter
comes from Dublin, is written to a man, has a signature, etc. But this
belittling letter is an important reminder that HCE Inglorious is just
as real as the Glorious HCE that follows, "another he what stays
under the himp of holth" (619.11-12—compare 28.35-29.36). Only he
does not stay—the sleeping giant rises from the landscape, and as
rising sun, rousing force, fairly blots out memory of the "direst of
housebounds".

619.20-628.16

The voice of the shrew makes no man rise, but now the Liffey says,
"Rise up, man of the hooths, you have slept so long!" He rises in this
dream, dreamed by a dying woman, a waning moon, a river going out
to sea. When he boasted, in III,iii, of his building he was a voice,
speaking through the lips of his son. Now he does not speak, is a
physical presence, a colossus felt. Nor does his wife boast of his
accomplishments. She notes casually he is a great poet and the only
man who can "eat crushts of lobsters", but the magnificence she
feels is in him, not in his works. No woman in *Finnegans Wake* ever
admires a man for anything he made or gave her.

Anna Livia's dramatic monologue, her swan-song, is beautiful, romantic, poetic, imaginative, moving, frail. I don't care to turn it into indifferent paraphrase. Enough to say she causes her husband to rise and shine; she takes leave of this world—children, house, land; she blesses her husband when, grown young, he turns to a daughterwife. When she lets go her last human illusion—his magnificence—she is bitter, inhumanly separate, and gives herself to her cold mad father, the sea. But as she surrenders to the inconceivable, she catches hold of human love again, cries, "Finn again!". The dream breaks off to begin again in Dublin and with a quotation from another broken dream poem.

The comparison with "Kubla Khan" is well enough, for we cannot be too often reminded that *Finnegans Wake* is supremely a work of imagination which treats, from first to last, the supernatural. It is not, however, a lyric work, but an epic whose argument is History, surely the most ambitious argument since Milton explained God's ways. For an epic, 628 pages long, the person from Porlock is not enough. An epic cannot dangle, must come to a massive conclusion—like Molly Bloom.

In Book IV Joyce manages to have it both ways. He gets the "Kubla Khan" effect—the dream dangle—by breaking off in the middle of a poetic sentence; and he gets the strength of no dangle by finishing up the broken sentence at the start of *Finnegans Wake*. He also gets mass—literal mass—by bringing on the stage the colossus whose head is Howth, whose feet stick up in Phoenix Park, whose body lies under Dublin City. In so doing he achieves something like a definite conclusion. Finnegan does wake and is magnificent, stronger and more magnificent than cold old mad father Lear who is death or the sea.

But affirmation of life over death is not precisely what we have been seeking. From the start of *Finnegans Wake* we have not chased after a presence or an affirmation, but after a missing meal, after rational, truthful explanation of what can be called Historical Truth or Man. In the chase we came on all sorts of serendipities—engaging, horrid, consoling, silly, profound—but on a firm answer—never! Over and over, gently, persuasively, Joyce has sent our expectation up and then down, so that in the rise and fall of expectation we experienced nervously, kinetically almost, the historical constant of hope raised and hope dashed, and we moved—though palely—in the rhythm of *Finnegans Wake*.

WHO IS WHO WHEN EVERYBODY IS SOMEBODY ELSE

HCE	⋀ SHAUN	⊏ SHEM	I ISSY	△ ALP	OTHER
Tim Finnegan	Male guests who fight at the wake		1) Female mourners at wake; 2) Whisky	Mrs Finnegan	4 are guests at wake who hold down rising Finnegan—not in ballad
Divine and human builder	What, among other things, he builds		Nature ← →		4 are 4 elements, winds, NSEW
Masterbuilder Solness	Younger generation		Hilda	Aline	
Sun, all that fertilizes, now vital, now dormant			Stars, esp. Venus	Moon	
Howth, Dublin, Phoenix Park are the body of the sleeping giant	Left bank of the Liffey, Co. Wicklow	Right bank of the Liffey, Co. Meath	?Chapelizod	River Liffey	ALP's father is Lir, the sea. 4 are Irish provinces. Ass is missing 5th province, Meath
Invaders of Ireland: Norse, English	Native Irish who emigrates	Alien who becomes Irish	Ireland — Dark Rosaleen	Poor Old Woman	Kate is Cathleen Ni Houlihan
Earwig	Ondt (Ant)	Gracehoper	Insect girls		
Fish		Ass		Hen	Man Servant is bear. 4 are angel (or man), lion, calf (or ox), eagle
Sometimes fox, lion, bull, swan, deer, etc.	Mookse (Pope Adrian IV)	Gripes	Nuvoletta (cloud)	Moon	

God the Father	God the Son	Holy Ghost			
God the Father	God the Son	Holy Ghost			HCE is the three members of the Trinity but at times the sons play at being the second and third persons, just as they play at Adam
God as Creator Adam as Creator, sinner	St Michael (Mick, Chuff) ?Father Michael	Satan (Nick, Glugg)	Eve—temptress Rainbow girl (Maggies)	Mother Eve	Impossible to distinguish God and Adam as creators
Adam exiled	Abel (Butcher)	←→Cain (Baker) Seth		Mother Eve	?Kate is Lilith
	Antichrist	Christ as ass, unknown	Virgin, Church	Mother Mary	4 are Evangelists, 12 are Apostles
St Lawrence O'Toole	St Kevin	St Patrick	St Bridget, Kevin's girl, Cathleen		
	Kevin	Jerry (Jeremiah)			II, ii, Jerry is called Dolph
Abraham	Isaac	Ishmael	Sally—Sarah young	Sarah old	Sarah or Island Bridge is where the Liffey meets the tide Kate is Hagar
Isaac	Esau	←→Jacob	Rachel and Leah	Rebecca	
Lot			Daughters	Mrs Lot	
			Susanna		4 are Elders

WHO IS WHO WHEN EVERYBODY IS SOMEBODY ELSE

EE EE HCE	∧ SHAUN	⊏ SHEM	I ISSY	△ ALP	OTHER
Noah	Ham, Shem, Japhet Shem, Ham or Sham		Rainbow Strong Drink	Mrs Noah Ark (moon)	
Deucalion				Pyrrha	
Zeus and all sky and thunder gods			Zeus's women, esp. Leda	Hera	
Thor					
Adonis, Fisher King and all fertility gods				Grail ←→Venus, etc.	
				Artemis Aurora Pandora	
Bacchus					Shaun is Bacchus in III, ii
Osiris and all divided gods	Horus	Set		Isis	
Hindu Triad					
Buddha					
Mohammed					
Finn MacCool	Goll	Dermot	Grania		

lxii

		Tristram	Ireland	
			2 Isoldes	
Mark of Cornwall				
Amory Tristram		Tristram		
Jarl van Hoother (Earl of Howth)		Jiminies	Grace O'Malley	Who dummy?
Brian Boru	Sitric Brodhar			
Roderick O'Connor	Anglo-Normans		Ireland	
Laoghaire (see Lear, Lir)	Archdruid Berkeley	St Patrick	?Rainbow Ireland	
Harold the Saxon	← William the Conk			William is all King Williams of England HCE is all English kings. Irish viceroys, Dublin mayors
Cromwell				
?Peter Sawyer	Dean Swift	Draper Swift	2 Esthers	
Daniel O'Connell				
Wellington	← Hindu	Napoleon Three Soldiers	Jinnies Two girls Josephine and Marie Louise	
?Isaac Butt ?Captain O'Shea	Pigott	Parnell	Mrs O'Shea	I think I have this somehow wrong for Parnell is also a father-figure

WHO IS WHO WHEN EVERYBODY IS SOMEBODY ELSE

ΞΞ HCE	∨ SHAUN	⊏ SHEM	I ISSY	△ ALP	OTHER
Gladstone			Fallen girls		
Lewis Carroll			Alice		
Oscar Wilde	Alfred Douglas				
Persse O'Reilly		Hosty ?Cad			
		Festy King Pegger Festy			
Ship's Husband	Kersse	Norwegian Captain	Daughter		The captain is also HCE when young
Russian General	Buckley Butt (Budd)	Taff			
	Jute	Mutt			
	Primas	Caddy			
	Browne ←→Nolan				
Benjamin Guinness	John Jameson				
	Sean the Post	Shem the Penman	Arrah-na-Pogue		

lxiv

Honuphrius	Jaun / John McCormack / Don Giovanni / Yawn	Jeremias	Felicia	Anita	
John Joyce, Sr	Eugenius / John Stanislaus Joyce	James Joyce		Mary Murray Joyce	
James Joyce	Giorgio Joyce		Lucia Joyce / Nora young	Nora Joyce	
Simon Dedalus / Leopold Bloom	Buck Mulligan	Stephen Dedalus	Milly Bloom	May Dedalus / ?Molly Bloom	
Gabriel Conroy	Michael Furey			Gretta Conroy	
William Shakespeare	Mr W. H. (Willy Hughes)	?Hamnet Shakespeare	Susanna Shakespeare, identical with Lizzy Hall who doubles with Elizabeth I	Ann Hathaway / Dark Lady	Young Ann is Issy / Dark Lady is also partly Issy / ?Judith
King Hamlet (ghost) / Claudius	Shakespeare / Laertes	↔ F. Bacon / Prince Hamlet	Ophelia	Delia Bacon / Gertrude	
King Lear				Cordelia	See Sea, Laoghaire above
	?MacDuff	Macbeth			
	Othello	Iago	Desdemona		
	Romeo		Juliet		

WHO IS WHO WHEN EVERYBODY IS SOMEBODY ELSE

E E E HCE	∧ SHAUN	⊏ SHEM	I ISSY	△ ALP	OTHER
	Justius	Mercius		Portia	
Oberon	Moonshine	Bottom Puck		Titania	
Julius Caesar Antony	Brutus (Burrus or Butter)	Cassius (Caseous or Cheese)	Cleopatra (Margarine)	Fulvia	
Richard III					
Falstaff					
Henry VIII			Baby Elizabeth	Anne Boleyn and other wives	ALP is all Queen Annes of England
	Angelo		Isabella		
	Dromios		Rosalind Viola Cressida Perdita Miranda Mariana Imogen, etc.		Young Anna Livia is Venus Kate is Kate-the-Shrew
Michael Gunn					
Mr Porter					And Family

lxvi

Census II

167.18 means page 167, line 18 of *Finnegans Wake*. On some pages of FW, poetic or dramatic passages, much of the textbook section (II,ii), I give up page and line and use whatever seems reasonable. On the opening page of each section, where print is dropped, I give lines the number they would have on a full page of print.

An asterisk means I don't know who somebody is. A dagger means a composite drawn from the names of two or more people.

For *Ulysses* the pagination of both the American and the English edition are given, thus *Ulysses* 372/494 refers to page 372 of the American edition, Random House, New York, and page 494 of the English reset edition, published by The Bodley Head, London, 1960.

A

Aaron–first high-priest of the Jews, brother of Moses. Also a black villain in Shakespeare's *Titus Andronicus* (q.q.v.). 204.31.

Abbey or Abby–see Yeats.

Abdul the Bulbul Amir–title character in a ballad by Percy French (q.v.). Abdul and Ivan Slavinsky Slavar (q.v.) fight each other into hamburger. 355.10-11.

Abel–see Cain.

Abel, Robert–19th century cricketer. †584.2—with Cain and Abel (q.v.).

Abelard and Heloise–Peter Abelard (1079-1142), scholastic philosopher; Heloise, his pupil, love, correspondent. †237.34-35—with Abel (q.v.); †453.26—with Issy (q.v.).

Abijah–nine different people in the Old Testament. 389.3.

Abraham (born Abram) and Sarah–

Biblical patriarch and his sister-wife who, at an advanced age, produced Isaac (q.v.)—see also Hagar and Ishmael. In FW they are often types of old age and sorrow. Joyce identifies Sarah with Sarah Bridge (Island Bridge) where the Liffey (q.v.) meets the ocean tide, and he puns on the fact that *sara* is Sanscrit "salt"; but Sarah and her laugh also stand for regeneration, the birth of a new female personality, and on this account she is identified with Sally (q.v.). See also Saar. To the 18th century "Abram" meant naked.

11.34	sair
14.3	sawl
†26.16,19-20	babe . . .abramanation—with Abraham Lincoln (q.v.)
74.6-7	Allprohome
†76.27,29	sally . . . sillying—with Sally (q.v.)

1

†78.15   Abraham—with Abraham Lincoln (q.v.) and the heights near Quebec
97.16   Allbrewham
104.32-33   Aldborougham . . . Sahara
105.3   a-be
106.28   Abe . . . Sare
127.26   Sahara
†210.30   Saara—with Saar and Sarah Curran (q.q.v.)
254.12   Sara's
307.left margin   Abraham
333.20,33   sari . . . bramborry
336.15   awebrume . . . Sahara
346.5   Alibey Ibrahim . . . Bella Suora
†364.30-31   sally . . . abery ham— with Sally and Ham (q.q.v.)
403.23-24   Zeehere . . . eggbrooms
418.18   marhaba
446.1   sands . . . Amberhann
481.18,24   apabhramsa, sierrah . . . Abrahamsk
531.10   Abarm's
546.17   abram
570.19,29   aproham . . . sairey's
†571.24   saarsplace—with Saar (q.v.)
600.5   Saras
624.14   sarra . . . a brambling ram

Acacius–4th century bishop of Caesarea who taught that the Father and Son were alike in will alone. The acacia is sacred to Freemasons. 160.12.

*Achburn, Soulpetre and Ashreborn, Messrs. 59.17-18.

Achilles–Greek hero, character of Homer's and Shakespeare's (q.q.v.). 154.18; 248.11.

*Achin–see Deacon and Bacon. 257.21.

Adah (dawn) and Zillah (shadow)– the two wives of Lamech (Genesis 4). 102.3.

Adam and Eve. The story of our first parents in "Milton's (q.v.) Park" underlies all falls in FW. It does not, however, dominate FW as the *Odyssey* dominates *Ulysses*, making events assume a predetermined form and sequence; rather, it is a foundation on which Joyce raises a fantastic, allegorical structure, much as Bunyan does in *The Pilgrim's Progress*. HCE's (q.v.) crime in Phoenix (q.v.) Park is Adam's, and with St Augustine (q.v.), if not for his reasons, Joyce says, "*O felix culpa!*" To Joyce, as to Vico (q.v.), all civilization, all art are born of the fall.

Eve is Hebrew for "life" ("*Lifé*" is the earliest form of "Liffey"—see Anna Livia); Adam is Hebrew for "man", a word derived from other words, meaning "ground" and "to make". When Eve was born, Adam called her "Isshah" (see Issy) because she was taken from the side of *ish* or man. Since Eve was born from Adam's body she is both daughter and wife. The Hebrew form of her name is Havvah, Latin Heva. FW is full of puns on all these words. Eve was, by the by, Adam's 13th and crooked rib. Adam and Eve's is a Roman Catholic church on Merchant's Quay, Dublin. In reading FW, remember that Adam and Eve, God, Satan, Cain, Abel, Seth (q.q.v.) are characters in the old mystery plays. See also Amsterdam, Lilith, Atom.

3.13   Eve and Adam's
†5.11,29-30   eve . . . abe . . . ivvy's —with Ivy (q.v.)
7.5   a tum
19.25,30   eve . . . Damadam
21.6   Adam . . . madameen
24.14   Usque*ad*baugh*am*! (my italics)
†28.32   Adams and Sons—with James Adam (q.v.)
30.26   Eve
31.12   adamale
34.22   eventide
†38.30   Havvah - ban - Annah— with Anna Livia (q.v.)
39.24   Mr Adams
61.6   evew

65.5	sweatyfunnyadams (see F . . . A . . .)
69.10-11	eddams . . . aves
70.5	Adams
76.2-3	predamanant
77.26	adamelegy
83.22	Adam and Eve's
86.4	Alum . . . Even
89.1	evesdripping
96.28	a dim's
104.14	eve
106.29	Eve
113.4	adamologists
117.19	eve
124.34	Père Adam
130.3	Even
133.22	Mister Mudson
173.30-31	eaveswater
176.4	Adam . . . Ell
197.12	Adam and Eve's
205.31	Ahdahm
210.30	Eva Mobbely (q.v.)
215.4	eve . . . eve
222.32	evelings
226.13	Eve's
228.31	heave a hevy
235.3-4	evings . . . Even
†242.28	Avenlith (q.v.)
†246.28	Adam Leftus—with Adam Loftus (q.v.)
251.28	Headmaster Adam . . . Eva Harte's (see Hart?)
266.27	eves
†267.18	Adamman see (Adamnan)
271.25	Heva
278.note 7	Eddems
291.3	Adam-he-used-to
†24	Dammad—with Dermot (q.v.)
293.31	Eve
296.6	Hoddum and Heave
298.23	Aha
303.13,18	Upanishadem . . . pup padums
306.left margin	Adam, Eve
313.12	Adams
314.25	eve
321.16	eve
324.7	Ede (q.v.)
338.14	dada, mwilshuni . . . even
341.34	damas
346.17	daddam
354.25	ivies (see Holly)

377.16	Eve . . . Alum
379.15	Evas
†381.19	Adams — with Aram (q.v.)
†387.35	mand—with my man Godfrey (q.v.)
389.20	eve
393.24	alum and oves
395.1	adim
396.4,9,21	add them . . . madapolam . . . Edem . . . noavy
410.35	eve
436.7	madam's
445.13	Aveh
455.3,17	eve . . . atoms and ifs
488.24	Eve
494.15,26	Eva's . . . heva heva
496.20-21	Ma's da. Da's ma. Madas. Sadam.
505.13	Evovae
514.23-24	Earl Adam Fitzadam
517.3-4	a dumm
530.28-29	preadamite
532.6	Amtsadam (see Amsterdam)
538.25	Haddam
541.5	a dome
†549.33	Adam—with Adam Loftus (q.v.)
551.22	adams
552.25	adimdim adoom adimadim
†558.10	Adam Findlater (q.v.)
†559.2	Adam's—with Robert Adam (q.v.)
565.9	Amsterdam (q.v.)
568.3-4	a damson . . . evabusies
595.6	evar . . . a damse
596.24	atman . . . evars
601.23	S. Eddaminiva's
615.6	adomic
617.23-24	preadaminant
†619.3	Adam . . . Finnlatter—see Findlater
626.3	adamant evar

Adam, James, and Sons–Dublin Auctioneers. †28.32—with Adam (q.v.).

Adam, Robert (1782-92)–English architect and designer. †559.2—with Adam (q.v.).

*****Adamantaya** Liubokovskva, 498.15.

Adamnan, St (624-708)–Irish saint, biographer of St Columba (q.v.). †267.18—with Adam (q.v.).

Adams, Henry (1838-1918)–American historian, author of *The Education of Henry Adams* in which he steadily refers to himself as "the ex-private secretary". The FW reference includes Swift (q.v.) who was an ex-private secretary to Sir William Temple (q.v.). 40.16.

Adelaide–words by John Oxenford, music by Beethoven (q.v.). 450.17.

*Adgigasta, 81.5.

Adolphos, Phil–a play on "Off to Philadelphia", a song which indicates that Shaun (q.v.), one of the Earwicker brothers (Gr. *adelphos*), is leaving Ireland for America. 93.33.

Adonis–youth beloved of Venus (q.v.), who was slain by a boar, restored to life, worshipped as a fertility god. He is also a Shakespearean (q.v.) character. †434.27 —with Jonah (q.v.).

Adrian IV, Pope 1154-59–born Nicholas Breakspear, he was the only English pope. He did much to uphold the power of the Papacy, especially against Barbarossa (q.v.). To Henry II (q.v.), Adrian granted (or did not grant) a Bull, *Laudabiliter,* which Henry later used to regularize the conquest of Ireland. In FW Adrian is the Mookse (q.v.) and is not distinct from Shakespeare (q.v.). 152.31.33; 153.20; 155.31?

AE–see Russell.

Aegisthus–murdered by Orestes (q.v.). 343.34.

Aegyptus–in classic myth, an Egyptian king, twin of Danaus. His fifty sons married the fifty Danaides (q.v.), and forty-nine sons were slain by their wives. 263.6.

Aemilia–mother of the high-born twins in Shakespeare's (q.v.) *The Comedy of Errors.* There are Emilias in *Othello* (q.v.) and *The Winter's Tale.* 410.23.

Aeneas–hero of Virgil's (q.v.) *Aeneid.* 185.27; 240.33 (alios).

Aengus–pagan Irish god, son of Dagda (q.v.). 90.34 (Oincuish); 248.4; 377.1 (ter).

Aesculapius–Greek god of medicine. 540.33.

Aesop (fl. 570 B.C.)–fable writer of whom Vico (q.v.) makes much use. I think Joyce spells his name "Esop" so as not to mix in AE (q.v.). 29.13; †289.5—with Cain and Esau (q.q.v.); 307.left margin; †414.17—with Esau (q.v.); 422.22.

Aetius–Roman general who, with Theodoric, defeated Attila (q.v.) near Chalons in 451. 266.25.

Agatha, St–patron of Catania, Sicily. She and the following saints have their feasts in February—see Sts Bridget, Scolastica. 430.35.

*Aghatharept, 250.27.

Agnès–Paris milliner, patronized by Nora Joyce (q.v.). 548.22.

Agni–Hindu god of fire, miraculously reborn each day. 80.24; 594.2.

*Agonistes–maybe Samson (q.v.). 333.20 (agony stays).

*Agrah, Jane–*a ghrádh* (love), an Irish endearment. 358.32.

Agricola–German painter or scientist or protestant reformer, a raft of German musicians, a Dutch scholar, a Roman general. 173.16-17.

Agrippa, Henricus Cornelius of Nettesheim (1486-1535)–writer on occult sciences. 84.16; 94.13; †154.6—with Gripes (q.v.).

Aguilar, Padre–see Johnny MacDougal whose symbol is the eagle. 184.35.

Ahab–a Biblical king, a captain in Melville's (q.v.) *Moby Dick.* I am not sure Ahab is intended in these references. 283.26 (aabs); †492.22 —with Patrick Joyce (q.v.) (*A*famado *H*airductor *A*chmed *B*orumborad).

*A'Hara (Okaroff)–perhaps a reference to Vishnu and Siva (q.q.v.) who are sometimes called Hari and Hara; *a chara* is Irish for "friend", used like "Dear Sir". See Joseph O'Mara. 49.3.

Ahriman–see Ormazd.

Aïda–negress, title heroine of Verdi's (q.v.) opera. Dark Lady (q.v.)? 59.4; †204.10—with Leda; 418.18.

Ailbey or Ailbe, St–with Ciaran, Declan (q.v.) and Ibar, one of the four (q.v.) Christian bishops who were in Ireland before St Patrick (q.v.). At first they opposed Patrick, but were finally reconciled. 484.23.

Aimee–see MacPherson, Amy.

Ainsoph or En Soph–in Kabbalistic doctrine, the god who is boundless, beyond thought or being. To make himself comprehensible, he created the universe by means of the ten Sephiroth or intelligences. 261.23.

Ajax–Homeric and Shakespearean (q.q.v.) character, a Greek, noted for strength without brains. 53.16; 306.left margin; 338.27; †547.23—with Jacob (q.v.).

Akenhead, Mary–founded the Irish Sisters of Charity in Dublin in 1815. 262.note 6.

Alacoque, St Marguerite Marie (1647-90)–French nun who established the cult of the Sacred Heart. †214.23—with Martha and Mary (q.v.).

Aladdin–hero of a story in the *Arabian Nights*, title character in an English pantomime—see Michael Gunn. 108.27; 407.27; 560.19.

Alaric (c. 370-410)–Gothic conqueror, first Teutonic leader to conquer Rome. †336.12—with Attila (q.v.).

*Alastor or Alastair–*alastor* is Hebrew "avenger", also the title hero of a poem of Shelley's (q.v.). 32.26; 354.3.

?Albany–character in Shakespeare's *King Lear* (q.q.v.). 137.7; 489.32.

Albern–see Nyanza.

Albert I, "The Bear" (1100-70)– Margrave of Brandenburg. 539.30-31.

Albert, Prince Consort–see Nyanza.

Albert Victor, Prince, Duke of Clarence and Avondale, "Collars and Cuffs"–heir apparent to Edward VII, he was for a time a Hussar and stationed in Dublin. He was betrothed to Princess May of Teck (208.34), and when he died she married the Duke of York (209.4), later George V, and became Queen Mary. 209.6-7; 214.29; 322.36; 614.10.

*Albiony, Swed–maybe Albion, maybe Albany (q.v.). Goldsmith (q.v.) quotation. 137.7.

Alcibiades (450-404 B.C.)–Athenian general, politician, friend of Socrates (q.v.). Also a character in Shakespeare's *Timon of Athens* (q.q.v.). 306.left margin.

Alcott, Louisa May (1832-88)– American author of *Little Women*, whose heroines had trouble with gloves at a ball. 434.5-6.

Alday, Paul (1764-1835)–founded a Dublin music-school. †155.36— with Hildebrand (q.v.).

*Aldrich, 548.35.

*Alexander–whether an eminent Russian or Alexander the Great, I don't know. 310.15; 339.25; 439.34.

*Alexi, 180.36.

*Alexis, Nestor, 73.25.

Alfred the Great (871-901)–king of the West Saxons. The second reference deals with his having tended cakes for a poor woman.

While he worked out plans for defeating the Danes, he let the cakes burn and was scolded. The third reference is to the White Horse of Wanstead, cut in a chalk hill to celebrate Alfred's victory over the Danes. 19.9; 392.32; 600.28.

Algy, Autest–see Swinburne. 434.35.

Ali Baba and the Forty Thieves–oriental story, English pantomime. *Punch*, 2 July 1887, calls the Parliamentary Parnellites (q.v.) "The Forty Thieves". I do not know if the name was common. 176.2 (Joyce cancelled this); †176.12-13 – with Tim Healy (q.v.); 243.24; 481.20; 622.23-24.

Alice in Wonderland and Through the Looking-Glass (Alice Liddell) –Lewis Carroll's (q.v.) child heroine. Joyce identifies her with the child Issy (q.v.) and Lewis Carroll with the elderly man who tampers with her. There is further identification with Lizzy, Shakespeare's (q.q.v.) little "lump of love" (*Ulysses*, 193/250, 210/273). See also Sally, Isa Bowman, Alice Barnham.

7.33	alliance
?†21.20-21	grace o'malice—with Grace O'Malley (q.v.)
32.3	alicence
?40.27	ifidalicence
48.16	liddled
57.28	Alys
115.22	'alices
144.12	alliance
†200.31	a lizzy a · lossie—with Lizzy (q.v.)
†203.8	Alesse — with Lizzy (q.v.)
207.26	liddel
†226.29	a lessle, a lissle—with Lizzy (q.v.)
237.9	alisten
†270.20-21	Alis, alas . . . Liddell— with Lizzy (q.v.)
†276.note 7	A liss in hunterland— with Lizzy (q.v.)
293.32	alass
294.8	Ellis (q.v.)
321.31	alice

333.10	allied
351.31	alliance
†359.32-33	Alys Alysaloe—with Lizzy (q.v.)
35	allies
407.27	alas
421.4	Dalicious
†440.18	Mary Liddlelambe's— with Mary Lamb (q.v.)
448.25	liddle
491.24	allies
†526.32	salices—with Sally (q.v.)
35	Secilas
528.17-18	Alicious . . . alas
618.23	alce

Alice–elephant in a song who said "I love you" to her mate, Jumbo. 105.17; †528.18—with Alice in Wonderland (q.v.)

*****Alice Jane,** 214.24-25.

Alina–by spoonerism becomes *gallina*, Latin "hen" (q.v.). A possible reference to Aline, the Masterbuilder's (q.v.) wife, or to Aliena—see Celia. 320.24; 608.18.

Allat–female counterpart of Allah in the pre-Islamic pantheon. 309.20.

Alldaybrandy–see Alday, Hildebrand.

*****Allen,** Hillary–probably not the American biographer, but the Hill of Allen in the Fenian cycle. ?532.10; 618.23.

Alley Croker–air to which Moore's (q.v.) "Through Erin's Isle" is sung. 391.15-16.

Allgood, Sara–acted in the early days of the Abbey (q.v.) Theatre. 21.30.

*****Allolosha**–Alyosha Karamazov? 106.23.

Ally Sloper–grotesque, disreputable figure in the late 19th century comic paper. Also a brand of pickles and a sauce. 248.10; 288.note 4; 291.26; 319.18.

Almayer–I suppose the title character of Conrad's novel, *Almayer's Folly* (1895). 371.26; 625.6?

Aloyse, Mère–see Marie Louise, Ravel.

Alph the sacred river–Mr Senn points out that FW opens with a quotation from Coleridge's "Kubla Khan". Anna Livia (q.v.) is often Alpha.

Alphos–see Three Musketeers.

Alsop–brand of British ale. Joyce's spelling "Allsap" may be an anagram of Pallas—see Athena. 264.3 ; 377.33-34.

Altoid's – English confection—"Those curiously strong peppermints". 210.9.

*Altrues, 191.14.

Alwayswelly, olderman K.K.–always Willy (q.v.)? See W. W. Kelly. 365.30.

*Alzette, 578.36.

Amalthea–foster-mother of Zeus (q.v.), perhaps a goat. 338.20.

*A'Mara, Mrs, 460.17.

Amaryllis–often a mistress in pastoral poems, also a lily. 180.10 ; 184.20 ; †268.left margin —with Anna Livia (q.v.) ; 609.12.

Amazia–see Amazon.

Amazon–as a river-nymph, Anna Livia (q.v.) has two attendants, the Nile and the Amazon. These rivers are also two of Shakespeare's (q.v.) queens, Cleopatra and Hippolita (q.q.v.), the Amazon of *A Midsummer Night's Dream.* The word "Amazon" is usually derived from "without breast" or from the Circassian word for "moon" (q.v.), *maza.*
I have an unproved suspicion that the Amazon and the Nile, come down in the world, are the washwomen of "Anna Livia Plurabelle". At 198.1, one woman calls the other "ijypt", but I can't find any similar use of the Amazon. †104.13—with Anna Livia ; 364.13 ; 494.35 ; 548.2 ; 627.28.

Ambree, Mary–ballad heroine, who, disguised as a man, fought the

Prince of Parma in 1584. 127.35-36 (myrioscope . . . ambries).

Ambrose, St (340-407)–Church father, bishop of Milan. 605.30-31.

Amen or Ammon or Ammun–Egyptian god, sometimes associated with Ra (q.v.). 411.11.

Amenhotep or Akhenaton–the reference is probably to Amenhotep IV who fostered monotheism, the worship of the visible sun-disk, Aton (q.v.). See Solsking. 237.26-27 (Amanti . . . Notep).

*Amenius–probably combines Arminius and Comenius (q.q.v.). 155.34.

Amenti–not a person, the Egyptian region of the dead. 62.26 ; 237.26 ; 613.18.

Aminah–mother of Mohammed (q.v.). 309.26 (Himana).

*Amni the fay–Anna Livia (q.v.). 18.11.

Amoret–in Spenser's *Faerie Queene* (q.v.), III, she is twin sister of Belphoebe and her adventures are said to reflect Elizabeth's (q.v.) displeasure at the relations of Raleigh (q.v.) and Elizabeth Throgmorton. Spenser's sonnets, "Amoretti", reflect his wooing of Elizabeth Boyle. 350.5.

Amoricas Champius–see Tristram. 395.35.

Amory–see Tristram, see Blaine.

Amos–prophet and book of the Old Testament. 550.34.

Ampère, André Marie (1775-1836) –French physicist, name of an electrical unit. 549.16.

Amphion–son of Zeus (q.v.). He and his twin, Zethus, destroyed Thebes. Amphion rebuilt its walls by playing wonderfully on the lyre. 222.7.

Amsterdam–HCE (q.v.) calls himself Amsterdam because he is William of Orange (q.v.), because he is a protestant, because its citizens write Amsterdam—A'dam (q.v.). 138.24; 319.16-17; 352.24; 532.6.

Amundsen, Roald–Norwegian who discovered the South Pole in 1911. 325.22.

***Amy**–see MacPherson?—106.32; 227.14.

Ana or Anu–earth goddess of the Tuatha Dé Danaan, perhaps identical with Dana or Danu (q.v.). Cormack's glossary calls her *mater deorum hibernensium*. She is listed under Anna Livia (q.v.), from whom she is inseparable. *Ana* means "riches" in Irish.

Anacletus II (d. 1133)–anti-pope, opposed to Innocent II (q.v.) 13.30.

Anacletus the Jew–probably the 3rd bishop of Rome, 77-88. 155.34.

Anacreon–6th century B.C., Greek poet. "Anacreon in Heaven" is an old drinking song from which Joyce quotes; its tune is "The Star Spangled Banner". 279.note 1; 559.10 (seapan nacre . . . on).

Anaks–race of giants in Canaan, destroyed by the Israelites (Josh. 10). Perhaps also a play on Gr. *anax*, "lord". 240.27.

Ananias–Biblical liar, (Acts, 5). 170.31.

Anastasia–see Anna Livia. *Anastasie* is the French Mrs Grundy (q.v.).

Anatoli, Jacob (1199-1256)–Hebrew translator who made Arabic learning accessible to the West. His great work was a translation of Averroes (q.v.). 504.30.

Anaxagoras (b. 500 B.C.)–Greek philosopher. 155.32-33.

Ancient–sometimes refers to Iago (q.v.). To Pistol (q.v.)?

Ancient Mariner–title and subject of a poem by Coleridge. 123.23-24; 324.8; 607.1?

Ancus Martius (640-616 B.C.)–4th legendary king of Rome, a bridge

builder. †467.33—with Martin Cunningham (q.v.).

***Anders**, Miss–not, I think, a proper name but a reference to the sender of the letter from Boston, Mass. See Sanders. 414.2.

Andersen, Hans Christian (1805-75) –Danish poet and fabulist. 138.16.

***Andersen**, Mevrouw von–see Anders. 413.15.

Anderson, Elizabeth Garrett (1836-1917)–founded the first London medical school for women. †389.10-11—with Margaret Anderson (q.v.).

Anderson, John–elderly subject of a poem by Burns (q.v.). 318.28.

Anderson, Margaret and Jane Heap–editors of *The Little Review* in which *Ulysses* was first published. Margaret Anderson wrote *My Thirty Years War, an Autobiography.*   †389.10-11—with Elizabeth Anderson (q.v.); †406.7 —with Maggies (q.v.).

Andreini, Francesco–Italian actor. His son Giambattista wrote a play, *L'Adamo*. 414.13.

***Andrew**–Apostle? Handy Andy? †227.14—with Rue (q.v.); 501. 34,36; †504.20—with Corcoran (q.v.); 510.9.

Androcles–hero of a story by Aulus Gellius (q.v.) and of a play by Shaw (q.v.). He took a thorn from a lion's paw and on a subsequent occasion was not eaten by the lion. 468.32-33; 471.34.

Andycox–Antioch and Luke Tarpey (q.v.) as a city. 124.36.

Angelina–heroine of *Trial by Jury*, by Gilbert and Sullivan (q.v.). 233.5.

Angelo–whited sepulchre in Shakespeare's (q.v.) *Measure for Measure*. See Isabella. †230.3— with Michelangelo (q.v.); 257.1?; 296.16.

***Anglys**, 512.23.

Angot–in the French opera, *La*

Fille de Madame Angot, Madame is a washwoman. 214.19.

Anguish, King–father of Isold of Ireland (q.v.). Aengus (q.v.) may be included. 189.19; 265.20; 603.21.

Ani–Egyptian scribe for whom most of the recensions in *The Book of the Dead* were written. In every case he doubles with Anna Livia (q.v.). 243.4; 493.32; 498.19.

Anit–Egyptian goddess, equated with Hathor (q.v.). 332.16.

Anita–see Anna Livia.

*Ankers, 30.19; 329.9.

*Anklegazer, Mr–Shem (q.v.) is intended. 193.12.

Anna, Donna–see Anne Whitefield, Don Giovanni.

Anna Livia Plurabelle–heroine of FW, Mother Eve (q.v.), Mrs H. C. Earwicker, Everywoman, Every woman, Every goddess, Every river. Specifically, she is Dublin's little brown river, Anna Liffey, which rises in the Wicklow hills and meets salt Dublin Bay at Island Bridge—see Sarah.

Mr Kelleher tells me that Joyce sent Mr Frank O'Connor a postcard from Paris, asking, "What was the old name of the Liffey?" Mr O'Connor answered, *Ruirtech*, which means "swift running". In time the river assumed the name of the land through which it ran, *Magh* (pronounced "moy") *Life* or Plain of Life. The meaning of *Life* is unknown.

Irish *abha* is pronounced "avain" and means "river". It was Anglicized, by way of the genitives *abhna* and *abhann*, into avon, aven, anna. The root of *abha* is in Sanscrit *ap* (water) and is related to Latin *aqua, amnis*. The root appears, more or less disguised, in water names all over Europe—Avon, Aune, Anne, Ive, Inney, Aff, Avenza, Avono—and is also present in the Asian Punjab. (See the 11th *Britannica*, "Avon".) Anna is, then, a comprehensive name for a "Lady of Rivers"—see Artemis.

In *The White Goddess* Mr Graves declares that if one needs "a single, simple, inclusive name for the Great Goddess, Anna is the best choice . . .". He cites the Italian Anna Perenna (goddess of the circle or "ring" of the year, by some called a moon (q.v.) goddess); and the Irish goddess Ana (q.v.), a title of Dana (q.v.). Ana (Irish for "riches") was in one aspect Plenty and in Cormac's glossary is called Buan-ann or "Good Mother"; in another aspect she led a malign trinity of Fates, together known as Marrigan (12.6) or Great Queen (q.v.). Mr Graves adds that *An* is Sumerian for "heaven". One way and another, these meanings are used in FW. Joyce also makes much of Anna meaning "grace" (q.v.) in Hebrew, and of *ana* representing the Greek for "back, again, anew". Anastasia means "resurrection", and, if it matters, *Anastasie* is French argot for D.O.R.A. or Mrs Grundy (q.q.v.). See also Ani, St Anne, Queen Anne, etc.

Plurabelle refers, I guess, to Anna Livia's great beauty and to the plurality of belles (see Issy) or daughters of Eve to whom she gives birth. Joyce often associates the name with Vico's (q.v.) *pura et pia bella*. Perhaps he means that woman is man's joy and all his bliss because she combines his two great pleasures—love and war. Oddly enough, Anna Livia's full name occurs only once in FW in undistorted form—215.24. Usually she is called Anna, Ann, Nan, Nancy, Nan, or Livia, Livy, Liv, Liffey, Life, ALP, Delta (q.v.), or by some name which matches the role her husband is playing. German *Alp* means "nightmare" or "incubus".

Anna Livia is, of cousre, all female creatures in FW. As Kate (q.v.) the Cleaner, she is the shrew on the hearth who rakes muck about her husband, as Biddy Doran (q.v.) she promotes the letter which will clear his name. Her daughter, Issy, is her past and future, a girl with "myriads of drifting minds" which must be brought together before her "muddied name" can be "Missisliffi". Issy is the temptress Eve who preceded Mother Eve, she is the "daughterwife" from the hills who supplants the aging mother. Joyce makes fun of Issy, cruel fun sometimes, but he is polite, almost awed with Anna Livia who is, he perceives, most deadly when most sweetly pretty—see Pandora.

I hold that FW is about Shakespeare (q.v.) and that Anna Livia is identical with Ann Hathaway (q.v.), who lived upon the Avon.

I Anna Livia Plurabelle

41.23	appy, leppy and playable
104.13-14	Annah the Allmaziful (see Amazon), the Everliving, the Bringer of Plurabilities
153.2	Amnis Limina Permanent
†207.8-9	Annushka Lutetiavitch Pufflovah — with Pavlova (q.v.)
215.24	Anna . . . Livia . . . Plurabelle
268.28-29	analectual pygmyhop
297.25	appia lippia pluvaville
299.26-27	analytical plausible
†325.4-5	Anna Lyncha Pourable—with Anne Lynch (q.v.)
327.6	anny livving plusquebelle
512.10	Annabella Lovabella Pullabella
16	antelithual paganellas
548.6	Appia Lippia Pluviabilla
568.4-5	annamation . . . livlianess . . . plurity of bells
569.12	Alla tingling pealabelles
619.16	Alma Luvia, Pollabella
627.27-28	allaniuvia pulchrabelled

II Anna Livia

13.30,31	leaves of the living . . . annals
63.13-14	ann . . . liv
81.17	livland
86.9	any luvial
128.14	Anna Livia
139.19	Ann alive
154.4,5	aulne and lithial . . . awn and liseias
182.27	anna loavely
195.4	Anna Livia
196.15,16,17	Anna Livia
198.10	Anna Livia (bis)
199.11	Anna Livia
†34	Annona . . . Nivia—with Annona (q.v.)
200.16,36	Anna Liv . . . Anna Livia
207.19	Anna Livia
213.32	Allalivial, allalluvial
215.12,35	Anna Livia . . . All Livia's
236.17-18	Anneliuia
†242.28	Avenlith (q.v.)
265.14	an litlee plads of liefest
273.11	Hanah Levy
287.7	Anny liffle
†293.25	ann linch—with Anne Lynch (q.v.)
28-29,30	A . . . Anna . . . L . . . liv . . . aunty annalive
309.35	an eliminium
333.4-5	anni slavey
337.8	annapal livibel
340.22	annal livves
348.36	ohosililesvienne
355.32	An-Lyph
373.34	allalility
†392.32	Anne Lynch (q.v.)
†406.27	Anne Lynch (q.v.)
451.15	liffey . . . annyblack
452.18-19	annals . . . livy
463.10,16	anny living . . . nanna
496.27	Abha na Lifé
†506.34	Anna Lynsha's—with Anne Lynch (q.v.)
549.16	Livania's
562.7	Allaliefest

580.25	ambling limfy	200.32	haven
583.22	nivia . . . nan	†203.21	Nance the Nixie . . .
†586.35-36	ham and livery . . . ham		Nanon L'Escaut—
	in livery—with Ham		with Manon Lescaut
	(q.v.)		(q.v.)
600.5	Innalavia	†36	Anna - na - Poghue —
608.14	And a live		with Arrah-na-Pogue
			(q.v.)

III **Anne, Annie, Anna** and
variations

		207.28	Amnisty Ann
4.28	Annie	†209.6	Avondale—with Albert
†7.25,26,27	Anny Ruiny . . . Anna		Victor (q.v.)
	Rayiny—with Annie	34-35	Annchen . . . Anna
	Rooney (q.v.) . . .	220.19	Ann
	nannygoes nancing	242.29	Avenlith (q.v.)
9.14	ann	36	manna
10.26	annaone	†243.2,4	annams . . . Ani (q.v.)
†12.6	marriedann—with St	244.20,29	Nancy Hands . . . deer-
	Anne (q.v.)		haven
14.17	annadominant	?†248.26,27	Deanns . . . threaspan-
18.11	Amni the fay		ning—with Dean
19.26,30	anntisquattor . . . Nan		(q.v.)
20.35	ann	254.15,26	Nan . . . cycloannalism
?24.1	Novo Nilbud (Dublin)	258.14	havonfalled . . . haven
28.31	Anna Stacey's		hevens
†38.30	Havvah-ban-Annah —	†268.left margin	annaryllies—with
	with Eve (q.v.)		Amaryllis (q.v.)
49.11	haven	†275.14	Airyanna—with Ari-
53.26	Havana		ana (q.v.)
54.4-5	Ann van Vogt	277.12,18	Anna . . . annews
†55.5	Fennyana—with Finn	280.3,9	annalykeses . . . A.N.
	MacCool (q.v.)	284.15	anan
67.8	analectralyse	286.19	ann
71.36	Nancy's	293.22	Antiann
72.1	Annie's	†294.29	Gaudyanna — with
80.20	propagana		Anne Whitefield
94.16	ana (q.v.)		(q.v.)
101.36	anngreen	301.7	anny
104.20	Anna Stessa's (see	302.1	Ann
	Anastasia)	308.1-2	Gobble Anne
105.9	Anny	†311.12	Ana (q.v.)
†106.31	Airy Ann—with Ariana	312.1	Eireann
	(q.v.)	†9	Tanneiry—with Anne
†113.18	Add dapple inn—with		Whitefield and Tan-
	Ann Hathaway		ner (q.q.v.)
	(q.v.)	318.11,24-25	Annexandreian . . .
†117.16	Nanette—with Anne		Annapolis
	Boleyn (q.v.)	†327.12	Anny Roners—with
139.8	haven		Annie Rooney (q.v.)
22	Ann's	328.14,19	Nanny Ni Sheeres . . .
143.10	hopeinhaven		annas
179.14	Annamite	?330.25	Nova
†182.27	anne —with Anne	†331.25	nana karlikeevna—
	Whitesides (q.v.)		with Nana and Anna
			Karenina (q.q.v.)

340.25,29	psychophannies . . . fannacies
342.28	annuysed
†350.8	Hanar—with hen (see Biddy Doran)
†23	juliannes—with Julia and Juliet (q.q.v.)
361.15	anny
364.22	Analbe (Eblana or Dublin)
374.32	Avenance
378.2	Annie Delap
382.27	Nansy Hans
403.23	Anastashie
†406.27,28	Anne Lynch (q.v.) . . . Houseanna
419.20	anaglyptics
422.26	Ann
423.2	Ananymus
426.3	annyma
439.8-9	nancyfree
†444.31	Annybettyelsas—with Elizabeth and Elsa (q.q.v.)
452.34	Annanmeses
†454.6-7	Ann Posht the Shorn— with Shaun (q.v.)
†463.16	nanna — with Nana (q.v.)
475.21	annywom
478.16	hopenhaven
492.8	Annie Delittle
493.5	annaversary
†32	Ani Latch—see Ani
?494.10	Nova Ardonis
495.33	Amn. Anm. Amn. Ann
496.4	haven
†498.19	pani's annagolorum— with Ani (q.v.)
501.11	Gobble Ann's (goblins?)
504.33	annettes
†512.18	puttagonnianne—with Maud Gonne (q.v.)
514.6	Annie's
516.32	annusual
521.24	Annybody's
532.21,24	Any . . . anniece (see Niece)
?535.8	Nova Tara
†537.6-7	Christina Anya—with Christine Beauchamp (q.v.)
†548.10	annie . . . lauralad— with Annie Laurie

	and Laura (q.q.v.)
11	havenliness
†551.6	Duanna—with Diana (q.v.)
†553.2	ana (q.v.)
559.34	nanny's
†567.15	Nan Nan Nanetta— with Anne of Denmark and Ann Boleyn (q.q.v.)
568.17-18	Nancy's . . . Nanny's
571.26	Annshee
572-573	Anita (occurs 9 times)
575.6-7	Ann Doyle . . . Doyle (Ann)—see Doyle
576.8	Nancy
578.21	ninya-nanya
584.32	anne
585.22,30	Anunska . . . Anny
586.31	eitheranny
600.10	Nin
603.5	tanny
†606.30	Panniquanne—with Prankquean (q.v.)
607.11-12	anniverse . . . a nam . . . a nam
610.17	Haven
620.34	haven
†623.34	an . . . an . . . hath an an—with Ann Hathaway (q.v.)
626.1-2	Annamores

IV Livia, Liffey and variations

3.36	livvy
7.1-2,35	livvylong . . . lyffing-in-waiting
11.5,32,35	liv . . . livving . . . laffing
14.29-30	Liber Lividus
†23.20-21	Livia Noanswa—with Nyanza (q.v.)
26.8	Liffey
†16	Laffayette (q.v.)
42.18,25	Riau Liviau . . . liffey-side
50.14	Levey
54.24	moyliffey
64.17	liffopotamus
88.34	laving
126.25	liffeyette
146.23	leapy
159.12-13	Missisliffi
172.19	Liffey
179.26	Tumblin-on-the-Leafy

203.6	lifey		518.33	bella . . . pura
204.5	Liffy		610.21	Piabelle . . . purabelle
†208.5	Liviam Liddle—with Alice in Wonderland (q.v.)		**VI Alp, Lap, Pal, etc.**	
			7.2	dalppling
215.33-34,35	liffeying . . . Livia's		†8.28	Delian alps—with Delia (q.v.)—are these the Mountains of the Moon?
†224.29	Madama Lifay—with Morgana le Fay (q.v.)			
230.25	liffe			
245.11,23-24	Liffeyetta's . . . Livmouth		30	alps
			17.34	alp
260.21,25	Livius (*bis*)		57.11	alplapping
268.note 6	Mrs Lappy		66.18,26	lappish . . . halpbrother
†275.12	lavy—with Lavinia (q.v.)		85.11	alpenstuck
			102.23	A.L.P.
289.28	Liv's		105.21	Lapps
310.5	liffing		106.24	Aples
317.32	obliffious		119.20	alp
318.4	live		126.29	lapapple
328.17	Lif . . . lif		148.22	alpin
332.17	lifflebed		†183.13	alphybettyformed— with Elizabeth (q.v.)
342.25	Leavybrink			
361.18,26	o'liefing . . . leavely of leaftimes		209.9	Alp
			243.29	Alpoleary (*Bearlagair Na Saer* for "Dublin")
380.3	Liffey			
382.13,27	Litvian . . . Liff			
420.11,34	livetree . . . Laffey		256.34	alps
445.34	Liffalidebankum		264.3	pal
447.23	liffe		287.9	alp
451.15	liffey		293.fig.	ALP
452.19	livy		294.3	AL
474.32	lif		296.5	P
493.14	Lithia		297.11	A.L.P.
495.21	lifing		298.1	apl lpa
503.4	realithy		299.17	lap
512.6	liffey		300.20	halp
526.1	liffeybank		314.33	lappel
547.17,34	liffsloup . . . lieflang		318.12,13,32	lap . . . pal . . . Alpyssinia
548.1	Livland			
553.4	Livvy		332.3	alpy
568.4-5	livlianess		340.6	Alps
578.6	livite		362.14	lap
583.21	Liv		393.20	lapper
595.8	liv		420.18	Alp
617.1	Levia		441.31	lapwholp
619.20,29	leafy . . . leafy		478.10	alpman
624.22	Leafiest		†483.19	alpybecca—with Rebecca (q.v.)
V Plurabelle				
			528.18	pal
11.25	pleures of bells		553.25-26	alpine plurabelle
27.16	Pia de Purebelle		577.24	alptrack
201.35	Pluhurabelle		†595.19	alpsulumply—with Lamp (q.v.)
224.10,25	deplurabel... plurielled			
264.2	plurable		624.25	Alpine
290.24	plurible		625.27	lapped

*Annanmeses, 452.34.

Anne, St–patron of riches. See Ana, Mother of Mary (q.v.). †12.6— with Anna Livia (q.v.).

Anne of Denmark (1574-1619)– queen of James I (q.v.). The fury of the gales forced her to lie abroad. Later, she and James had an elaborate progress from Edinburgh to London, a progress for which Ben Jonson (q.v.) devised Entertainments and Masques. †567.13,15—with Anna Livia and Ann Boleyn (q.q.v.).

*Annesley–an Irish river. 130.21.

Annona, St–a Dublin church. In Roman myth Annona was the female personification of the produce of the year. 44.6; †199.34 —with Anna Livia (q.v.).

*Ansighosa, 246.10.

Ant–see Ondt.

Ant–mythological fish in *The Book of the Dead.* See Ondt. 418.5-6.

Anthea or Antheia–epithet of Aphrodite (q.v.) as goddess of flowers —Gr. *anthos.* 354.22.

Antheil, George–son of a New Jersey shoemaker, composer, lived in Paris, set some of Joyce to music. †133.27—with Schubert (q.v.); 360.34.

Anthony, St, of Padua–invoked by devout Catholics to secure the safe conduct of letters through the mail. They sometimes write S.A.G. on their letters—St Anthony Guide. 66.17; †409.7—with Anthony Trollope (q.v.); †621.7-8 —with Arcturus and Sir Arthur Guinness (q.v.).

Anthony, St–the first Christian monk, resisted temptation. He had a pet pig and became patron of swineherds. The smallest pig in a litter was formerly devoted to St Anthony and called an "Anthony pig". An "Anthony pig" is also a hanger-on or sponger. †86.13—with Anthony Bacon (q.v.).

Antichrist–a great antagonist, a pseudo-Messianic wonder-worker, who will subdue the weak and be destroyed at Christ's second coming. Epiphanes, Nero (q.q.v.) and the Pope have been advanced as likely candidates. In FW III,i,ii Jaun (q.v.) plays—among other things—Antichrist from the old Chester miracle play. 308.note 1; 346.4.

Antinous–1) leader of Penelope's (q.v.) suitors in the *Odyssey*; 2) beautiful Bithynian, beloved and deified by Hadrian. In *Ulysses* Buck Mulligan and Blazes Boylan (q.q.v.) are Antinous. 190.33.

Antonines–Roman emperors. 167.3.

Antonio–Shakespeare's (q.v.) *Merchant of Venice*; the usurping brother of Prospero (q.v.) in *The Tempest.* †483.17—with Mark Antony and Mark Lyons (q.q.v.).

Antony, Marcus–triumvir, hero of Shakespeare's *Antony and Cleopatra* (q.v.). See Brutus, Julius Caesar. †152.21—with Rowley, Romeo; 167.3,4; 271.6; †483.17 —with Mark Lyons, Antonio (q.q.v.); 568.9.

Apep–Egyptian snake-god of darkness, eternal enemy of Ra (q.v.). 494.15.

Aphrodite–Greek goddess of love and beauty. See Venus. 203.27-28; 299.left margin; 354.22 (Anthea).

Apnorval–see Norval.

Apollo–Greek god of the sun and poetry, twin of Delia (q.v.). 167.12; †431.36—with Pollux (q.v.).

Apollyon–"foul fiend" who assaulted Christian in the Valley of Humiliation. During the Napoleonic wars his name was often given Napoleon's. †273.27—with Napoleon.

Apopi–Egyptian god. 67.22 (I appop pie).

Apostles–see Twelve.

*Appelredt's, 406.9.

Appleton–a geological layer. Maybe Appleton Morgan (q.v.). 323.30.

Apsaras–in Hindu myth, female spirits of the clouds, handmaids of Indra (q.v.). They dance before his throne and rule over gambling. 60.20.

Aquinas, St Thomas (1227-74)–scholastic philosopher who greatly influenced Joyce's thinking. †93.9 —with Ass (q.v.); 145.10; 240.8; 245.12; 296.20; 299.8; 417.8; 510.18; 514.17.

Aram–in the Bible, son of Shem (q.v.). Probably also Eugene Aram (1704-59), who discovered the Celtic languages were Indo-European and murdered his wife's lover. 228.15; 256.6 (bis); 262.note 4; 381.19; 396.15; 490.3-4.

*Arans, Kings of, Duke of–the Arans are three islands in Galway Bay. The second reference plays with the Iron Duke, Wellington (q.v.). 87.25; 595.22.

*Arber, Sir–the reference here may be to Shakespeare (q.v.). In FW many Tree (q.v.) references and "woodman spare" references include him. See the use of "woodman" in Measure for Measure, IV iii, 170. 1) Tradition says that when young he slept off a drunk under a particular crabtree. 2) Tradition also says that when he retired to Stratford, he planted a mulberry tree at New Place, which Francis Gastrell cut down in 1758 because he was mad at Stratford. See Wood, see Gladstone. 504.15-16.

*Archer, 254.11; 283.19.

Archer, Charles–villain of LeFanu's (q.v.) The House by the Churchyard. Through most of the novel, Archer is known as Dangerfield (q.v.); he stuns, with deadly intent, Sturk (q.v.), who later undergoes a kind of resurrection. The crime is committed in Phoenix Park. 80.9.

Archer, Colores–the rainbow—see Seven. 63.13.

Archer, William (1856-1924)–dramatic critic, translator of Ibsen (q.v.). There was also an Irish William Archer, naturalist and librarian, renowned for his admirable dictionary catalogue of the National Library in Dublin. 440.3-4.

Archdruid–see Berkeley.

*Archibald–see Rowan? MacLeish? 65.3.

Archimedes (287-212 B.C.)–Greek mathematician who worked out the theory of the lever. 230.34.

Arcobaleine–see Balenoarch. 175.16.

Arcoforty–see Strongbow.

Arcoiris–the rainbow—see Seven.

Arditi, Luigi (1822-1903)–Italian composer and conductor. 44.22.

Ardrey–the "ardri" or high king in ancient Ireland. 261.left margin.

Areopagus–the Hill of Area (q.v.) in Athens. Spenser so named the literary group that gathered round Sidney (q.v.) at Leinster House. Perhaps also a Miltonic (q.v.) work. 5.33.

Ares–Greek god of war. 5.33; 88.17; 122.7; 269.17; 421.23.

Argan–Molière's imaginary invalid. 234.33.

Argyle, Duke–subject of a jocular remark, "God bless the Duke of Argyle"—made when one rubs oneself against a post. The English are so odd. 71.18-19.

*Ar home, Edith–Wharton (q.v.)? 34.10-11.

*Arhone, Helen, 210.32.

Ariane and Barbe Bleu–French for Bluebeard (q.v.) and his wife.

Ariel–a sprite in Shakespeare's (q.v.) The Tempest. 228.8; 449.30; 471.24.

Arion of Lesbos (fl. 625 B.C.)–semi-legendary poet and musician. 75.14.

Aristobulus–see Hyrcan. 219.26.

Aristophanes (448-380 B.C.)–Greek comic poet, author of *The Wasps*—see 414.29. 414.28 (airy processes).

Aristotle (378-322 B.C.)–Greek philosopher. †110.17—with Harry (q.v.); 306.left margin; 417.16.

Arius (d. 346)–heretic. 75.14; 440.7; 530.18.

*****Arklow**, Michael–Father Michael? Arklow is a town in Wicklow. 203.18.

*****Arkwright**–possibly Sir Richard (1732-92), inventor of the spinning jenny. 560.9.

Arminius, Jacobus (1560-1609)–Dutch theologian. †155.34—with Comenius (q.v.); 296.8.

*****Armitage**–a bookseller of this name was last King of Dalkey (q.v.). 379.34.

Armory–see Tristram.

*****Armstrong**, 275.18.

Armsworth–see Harmsworth.

*****Arnolff's**, 443.22.

*****Arnott**, 580.1.

Arp, Hans–contemporary painter. 66.28; 508.33.

Arrah-na-Pogue or Nora of the Kiss–lower-class heroine and title character of Boucicault's (q.v.) play. She is foster-sister to the high-born hero, and gets him out of jail by means of a message, hidden in her mouth, which she gives him with a kiss. She marries Sean the Post (q.v.). I think Joyce identifies Arrah with Nora Barnacle (q.v.). I think he spells "pogue" as "poghue" in order to include Mr W.H. (q.v.). 7.25; 68.12; †203.36—with Anna Livia (q.v.); 297.4; 376.19,21; 385.22,32; 388.25-26; 391.3; 404.4; 460.2; 492.12; 588.29; 600,32-33; 626.6.

Artalone the Weeps–seems from context to personify the artist in isolation, and also includes Art the Lone or the Solitary, a hero of Irish mythology, son of Conn (q.v.). Artho (q.v.) is Macpherson's (q.v.) rendering of the name. 418.1.

*****Artahut**, Poulchinello–see Punch, Casudas. 43.23.

Artaxerxes–three ancient Persian kings, all warlike. See Flavin and see Taff. 337.35-36.

Artemis–the goddess illustrates the fact that you cannot unravel all, or perhaps even the most important part, of FW by means of names. I cannot find the name "Artemis" in FW, except in a handful of Delias (q.v.), and yet Artemis is all over the place, is, as Moon, one of the most important aspects of Anna Livia (q.v.).

Joyce indicates Artemis by her attributes, the forms in which she was worshipped, etc. He could have found these in any classical dictionary. I found them in Graves, Frazer, "Artemis" in the 11th *Britannica*.

Artemis was originally a fertility goddess, worshipped in orgiastic totem cults, but she was chastened into a queen and huntress, chaste and fair—see Elizabeth I. This parallels the turning of Brigid (q.v.) into St Bridget (q.v.). Artemis was called Delia because she was born on Delos, Apollo's (q.v.) twin. In various times and places, she healed and she destroyed, she was peaceful, she was orgiastic. She was "The Lady of Rivers" (see Anna Livia, 110.1) and of the Moon (q.v.); she took her share of first fruits (12.19); she collected "spoils" of vegetables and animals (11.18-19, 209.28, 273.12); she was goddess of the chase and of all wild animals (112.16, 113.3); she was a virgin (q.v.) (110.25), she was a mother, patron of generation, the rearing of all young animals and humans, and of the field (112.13-18, 244.8-11); she was a bear goddess (110.2-3), a lion goddess (112.22); she was worshipped as a fir tree (113.6, 235.17), a nut tree (113.3, 273.note 3, 360.15-16, 623.32-33—these also include references to Nut (q.v.) and to the Irish hazel-nuts of wisdom), a date-palm (20.3-4, 112.26, ?117.16, 136.2, 235.17, ?275.left margin, 318.16-17, 347.7); and finally, Artemis or Delia was worshipped on the Acropolis as a guinea-hen (q.v.) (236.9-10—*parelhoen* is Dutch for guinea-hen, 479.5, 482.19). See Biddy Doran who is Delia the goddess and Delia Bacon (q.v.), manifest as a guinea-hen.

Anyone who will study these references with care will find that Anna Livia is the Moon, as the two temptresses are the Stars (q.v.). See also Diana, Hecate, Selene, Elizabeth I, Lamp.

Artho–father of Cormac (q.v.), king of Ireland in Macpherson's Ossian (q.q.v.), see the poem "Temora". See also Arthur and Artalone. †254.36—with Gautama Buddha and Arthur Capel (q.q.v.).

Arthur–in FW the name refers by times to King Arthur, Prince Arthur, Gautama, Wellington, Sir Arthur Guinness, Arthur Capel, Earl of Essex (q.q.v.), and sometimes to no one I can clearly identify. †9.5—Wellington—with Thor (q.q.v.); 44.12; 52.17; 59.7 —Gautama (q.v.); 71.23; 73-74 —King Arthur; †91.13—King Arthur, with Mark of Cornwall and Melkarth (q.q.v.); 93.7; 112.29; 151.20— King Arthur (q.v.); 175.11—Wellington (q.v.); 229.7; 246.7; 252.20—Wellington (q.v.); 254.36—see Artho; †285.left margin—King Arthur with Sir Arthur Guinness (q.q.v.); 335.30—Wellington (q.v.); †347.9 —Wellington with Gautama (q.q.v.); 358.29—Wellington

(q.v.); 359.15-16—King Arthur (q.v.); †361.3—King Arthur— with Sir Arthur Guinness (q.q.v.); 375.8 — King Arthur (q.v.); ?380.22 — Art Macmurrough (q.v.); 387.32 — King Arthur (q.v.); †420.36—Wellington with Prince Arthur (q.q.v.); 488.3— Essex (q.v.); 498.23—King Arthur (q.v.); †510.30—Wellington with Essex (q.q.v.); 514.6; 578.34; 593.23; 594.2 — King Arthur (q.v.); 608.7—Essex (q.v.); 621.8—Sir Arthur Guinness (q.v.), 621.20 — King Arthur (q.v.).

Arthur, King–legendary king of Britain, who, like Finn MacCool (q.v.) will come again. The triangle of Arthur-Guinevere-Lancelot (q.q.v.) parallels that of Finn-Grainia-Dermot, Mark-Isolde-Tristram, Shakespeare-Dark Lady-Fair Man (q.q.v.). See also Arthur. 73-74; †91.13— with Mark of Cornwall and Melkarth (q.q.v.); 93.7,22; 151.20; †285.left margin—with Sir Arthur Guinness (q.v.); 359.15-16; †361.3 —with Sir Arthur Guinness (q.v.); 375.8; 387.32; †420.36—with Wellington; 498.23; †594.2—with Arcturus; 621.20.

Arthur, Prince–Shakespeare's (q.v.) boy-prince who dies in *King John* (q.v.). I am confident that some one of the Arthurs refers to him, but I am not sure of this reference. †420.36.

Artsa–read backwards is astra or star (q.v.). 29.13.

*Arvanda, 37.22.

Asa see Odin.

Aschenbrödel–German for Cinderella (q.v.). 445.6.

*Ashburner, G. B. W., Mr–partly G. B. Shaw (q.v.). 369.7-8.

*Ashe and Whitehead, 97.26; 311.24; 321.34; 328.4.

Ashtoreth–see Astarte. 601.8.

*Asitas, sanit–a saint? 60.16.

Aske–in Norse legend, the first man —see Adam. Perhaps also Robert Aske (d. 1537), leader of the English rebellion called The Pilgrimage of Grace. 4.15; †320.8— with Ass (q.v.).

Askold–semi-legendary Scandinavian or Varangian (see 310.15) who, with Dir, seized Kiev. They were followers of Ruric (q.v.) and were succeeded by Oleg (q.v.). 310.16.

Ass–companion of the Four (q.v.), special property of Johnny Mac-Dougal (q.v.), narrator of FW III,i,ii. In so far as the Four are provinces—Ulster, Munster, Leinster, Connaught—the ass is Midhi or Meath (see 87.24, 352.12), which is the "lost province", "the missing fifth" of Ireland. Meath was bisected by a great ancient road, *Slighe Assail*; in the center of Meath—by tradition the center of Ireland as well —was the hill of Uisnech where Yawn (q.v.) lies (474.6). Because Uisnech is the hill of the ass, the ass acts as interpreter or dragoman (see Dragonman) in the Yawn episode. Later, the dragoman is questioned for his own sake and melts into St Patrick (q.v.), who was also a servant for Four Masters (q.v.). Since a good deal is made of the ass being man's servant—e.g. 364.19—I assume there is a strong link, perhaps absolute identification, between the-ass-as-Ham and the Man Servant (q.q.v.).

The roles of dispossessed and/or servant belong, by and large, to Shem (q.v.) who often goes by a donkey's name, Jerry (q.v.). In some fashion I can't explain, it seems that Johnny MacDougal and his ass are Shaun and Shem. Certainly they are Shaun and Shem in III,i,ii where they play the roles of Shakespeare's Moonshine and Bottom (q.q.v.). According to Paracelsian (q.v.) geography the west or Johnny MacDougal is the human bottom. The ass may be all aspects of the bottom which are dispossessed in polite society.

I have no notion when, how, why Shem is metamorphosed into an ass. It may happen in "The Mime" where Shem-Glugg throws a fit and Midhe is mentioned, 231.17, but I am not sure. A clue to why may lie in the fact that, by certain Sanscrit laws, the man who censures his teachers, however richly they deserve it, is reborn ass. Shem spites his teachers, the Four—see 184.35, 223-224.

I think the foregoing information does a lot to clear up the ass in FW, but not nearly enough. There is a strong possibility that the ass is Christ. See Set, Dwyer Gray, Jerry, Moke, Cuddy, Ned.

14.35; 20.25,26; †24.22—with St Patrick (q.v.); 50.25; 57.10; 69.22; 84.3; †93.9—with Aquinas (q.v.); 96.1; †101.9—with St Thomas (Doubting); 111.29,30, 32; 127.18,19; 153-154; 159.30; 164.13; 184.35 (see Baldwin); ?200.12—with hen (q.v.); 202.4; 214.32; †231.18—with Silla (q.v.); †234.4—with Don Quixote (q.v.); †242.1—with Neelson (q.v.); 252.13; †260.30—with Hugh (q.v.); 285.14 and note 5; †320.8 —with Aske (q.v.); 323.6; 326.10; 334.25; 340.10,24; 342.10; 343.22; †347.10—with Tom, St Thomas?; 364.19; †372.4—with Mark of Cornwall and Swan (q.q.v.); 373.4; 377.33; †380.25—with Palisse (q.v.); 383.35; 398.2 —see Dwyer Gray; ?399.st. 2; 405.6-7; †408.26—see Egari; 423.18; 427.8—see Esellus; 479.9; 480.6; †482.9,14—with Don Quixote (q.v.); †495.15—with Pallas?; ?512.35; 518.33; 520.5,20; 522.19,30; 523.22; 528.32; †529.23 —with Jonah (q.v.); 538.32; 566.31; 567.27; 595.2; 602.14-15,23; 604.2; 607.25 (*bis*); 609.9 (*bis*); 625.27.

*Assoluta, 527.13.

Astarte–Semitic goddess, Ashtoreth (q.v.) in the Bible. Her male counterpart was Baal (q.v.). †91.14—with Baal (q.v.); 232.12.

Aster–see Stella.

Asthoreth–see Ashtoreth.

Astley's Amphitheatre–18th and 19th century place of entertainment. 214.14.

Aston's–a Dublin quay. All the quays along the Liffey (q.v.) are in FW, mostly in "Anna Livia Plurabelle". 447.35.

*Astrid–various women, prominent in Norse history. The reference may also be to an asteroid in Killiney which is between a druid's (q.v.) chair and a druid's altar. 279.note 1.

Atahualpa – Macaulay, "Lord Clive": "Every schoolboy knows who imprisoned Montezuma and who strangled Atahualpa." †339. 32—with Attila (q.v.).

Atalanta–the ancient Greeks' Wilma Rudolph. 336.27.

Ate–Greek goddess of mischief. In FW Joyce scarcely ever uses any other form of the verb "to eat". 86.28; 258.6; 318.15; 368.20; 376.36; 378.3; 385.16; 397.20; 421.21; 479.32; 480.22; 490.33; 538.20.

Atem–see Tem.

Athena–Greek goddess of wisdom. The owl was her bird and in FW is probably the goddess herself. 602.30 (touthena).

Athlone, earl of–the original earl was William III's (q.v.) general, Godart van Ginkel who captured Athlone 30 June 1691. 450.28.

*Athma, 33.18.

Atkins, Fred–a perjured witness at Oscar Wilde's (q.v.) trial. He may always be included in the Tommy Atkins (q.v.) references. See Watkins for reference.

Atkins, Tommy–an enlisted man in the British army. See Tom, Three, Fred Atkins. 8.6; 125.11; 210.8 (in the transition version of "Anna Livia Plurabelle", "Chummy the Guardsman" is called "Tommy the Soldier"); 241.25; 281.left margin; 350.27; 436.11; 534.33; 588.18.

Atkinson–see Elliot and Fry.

Atlas–in Greek myth supported on his shoulders the pillars that supported the heavens. 132.3; 324.3; 368.30.

Atom–some Toms, Atems, etc. (q.v.), may be partly accounted for by the atom, of which, it once seemed, matter was ultimately composed. Joyce puns on Atom-Adam (q.v.). Pp. 13-14 the initial letters of the Annal entries are M-O Silence A-T and represent, I think, a split and scattered atom.

Atreox–see Atreus.

Atreus–father of Agamemnon, founder of a doomed house. See Orestes. 55.3.

*Atterbom, Ebba–see Gorman's (q.v.) biography, p. 310. 103.2.3.4.

Attila (d. 453)–king of the Huns, harried Rome, battled his brother. 70.31; 251.1 (bis); 266.25; †336.12 —with Alaric (q.v.); †339.32— with Atahualpa (q.v.); 378.9.

Attis–Phrygian god, connected with the cult of the Great Mother, Son of Nana (q.v.). See Tammuz. 297.15; 461.30; 625.27 (sitta).

*Attraente, 105.25.

Aubrey, John (1626-97)–author of Brief Lives, which contains material about Shakespeare and Bacon (q.q.v.) which Joyce used. 604.19-20.

Auden–see Odin. 297.note 1.

Augustine, St (354-430)–Bishop of Hippo, father of the Latin church. Joyce quotes him in FW. 38.29-30.

Augustus, Caius Julius Caesar Octavianus (63 B.C.—A.D. 14)—

first Roman emperor, a triumvir with Mark Antony and Lepidus (q.q.v.). His Greek name was Sebastos. His wife was Livia (q.v.). He is also a character in Shakespeare's (q.v.) *Antony and Cleopatra* (q.v.). 104.18; 271.5-6 (Oxthievious — maybe with Hermes or Ulysses's, q.q.v., men who, on separate occasions, stole Apollo's cattle); 281.24; 353.3; †467.8—with Don Ottavio (q.v.); 521.33; 532.11.

Auliffe–first letter of the Hebrew alphabet, *aleph*, plus Anna Livia (q.v.). 582.9.

Aunt–in FW does not commonly refer to a female relative. To the Elizabethans (q.v.) an aunt was a light woman.

Aurelian (212-274)–Roman emperor. 478.14.

*****Aurell**, Piers–see Persse O'Reilly. 496.15.

Aurora–Roman goddess of dawn. 244.33; 587.1.

Ausonius, Decimus Magnus (310-95)–Roman poet, etc. 267.6.

Avebury, John Lubbock, 1st baron –author of *The Pleasures of Life*. He introduced bank holidays into England and one of these—the first Monday in August—was known once as "St Lubbock's Day". 113.34-35; 189.7; 222.28; 292.5.

*****Aveling**, 613.30.

Aven, Avon–see Anna Livia.

Avenlith–Anna Livia. Perhaps also Lilith, Eve (q.q.v.), Avan, who, with Azura, is given in the Apocryphal books as the female offspring of Adam and Eve, and Avon Lily (q.v.). †242.28.

Averroes or Abul Walid Mohammed Ben Ahmed Ibn Roshd (1126-98)–Moslem philosopher. 488.7,15.

Avicenna or Ibn Sen (980-1037)–Arabian philosopher. Ibsen (q.v.) may be included. 488.6,7,15.

*****Avis**–Willobie's Avisa fits into context. 250.1.

Avril, Jenny–dancer painted by Toulouse-Lautrec (q.v.). 415.11.

Awlining, Brian–see Brian O'Linn (q.v.).

Ayessha or Ayesha (pronounced Assha)–heroine of Rider Haggard's *She*. She was 2,000 years old and lived in rocky circumstances. 105.20; †284.24-25—with Aysha (q.v.).

Aysha–child-wife of Mohammed (q.v.). †284.24-25—with Ayessha, Lily, Anna Livia (q.q.v.).

*****Azava**–probably Ahura Mazda— see Ormazd. 73.36.

?Aziz, Dr–hero of Forster's *A Passage to India*. 4.14.

Azrael–angel of death in Jewish and Mohammedan religions. 258.7.

B

Ba's–not a person. The Ebers Papyrus (1550 B.C.) gives an augury as to whether a child will live or die, according to whether its first cry is ni (415.29) or ba. See also 224.28; 225.6; 415.31; 607.18.

Baal–Semitic god of fertility, the male principle as Astarte (q.v.) is the female. †13.36—with Balfour (q.v.); 52.19; †91.14—with As-tarte (q.v.); †455.6—with Abel (q.v.); 593.27.

Babau–bogie with which nurses in Languedoc terrify unruly children. 466.1.

Babby, Bill C.–see Beelzebub, Bill. 230.4.

Babes in the Wood–brother and sister abandoned to die in a wood and covered by the robins with

leaves. Also an English pantomime. 386.16-17; 504.22; 561.3;
619.23-24.

*Babwith, Bichop, 241.36.

Bacbuc–Pantagruel's (q.v.) divine
oracle bottle. 118.16.

Bacchus or Dionysus–Greek and
Roman god of wine, patron of
tragedy. He is almost buried at
3.14, but Joyce's original draft
read "brings us back" (see J. to
Miss Weaver, 15 November 1926).
Bacchus must, of course, preside
over Finnegan's (q.v.) tipsy wake.
At the opening of III,ii, Shaun
appears to be, among other things,
Bacchus. I don't know why.
3.14; 56.27; †83.3—with Bach
(q.v.); 118.16; 243.21; 262.26;
276.13; †365.6—with Buckley
(q.v.); 378.3.

Bach, Johann Sebastian (1685-
1750)–German composer. I have
the feeling of not getting the
point of a lot of Bach jokes in
FW. On 597.26 Joyce plays with
his cantata, "Sleepers Awake".
In III,i,ii I suspect Jaun (q.v.)
moves not merely backward, but
also Bach-ward in a mock passion.
Since bache is MHG for "bacon",
Bach may connect with Francis
Bacon (q.v.) or the elaborate Pig
(q.v.) theme. 73.21; †83.3—with
Bacchus; 176.34; 213.17; 287.6;
328.10; 346.23; 360.9; 426.34;
508.34; 526.30-31; †533.21—with
Johnny MacDougal (q.v.); 597.27;
603.6.

Bacon, Anthony–Francis Bacon's
(q.v.) brother. †86.13—with St
Anthony (q.v.).

Bacon, Delia (1811-59)–American,
author of The Philosophy of
Shakespeare's (q.v.) Plays Un-
folded, 1857. In popular opinion,
Delia is the original Baconian
(q.v.). She went to Stratford to
rape the lock of Shakespeare's
tomb (see Belinda) in order to
find documentary proof of her
theory; she lost her nerve, but
not her faith, and went mad. See

Hawthorne's (q.v.) "Recollections
of a Gifted Woman". See also
Pandora, Biddy Doran.
  In FW Delia is the hen (q.v.)
who met with Francis Bacon in
mutual refrigeration on Highgate
Hill. She is also Delia or Artemis
(q.v.) as guinea-hen (q.v.). Over-
all, I guess her role is that of the
Muse as a Victorian virgin. See
Delia for references to her.

Bacon, Francis, first Baron Verul-
am and Viscount St Albans
(1561-1626); brother of Anthony
Bacon (q.v.); married Alice Barnham (q.v.); Solicitor General,
Attorney General, Lord Keeper
(see Keeper), Lord Chancellor.
Charged with corruption and
bribery in 1621, Bacon was de-
prived of the Great Seal, fined,
dismissed from office and the
favor of James I (q.v.). He died
in the spring of 1626 from a chill
he caught from a hen (q.v.) he
stuffed with snow in order to see
if he could preserve her from
decay. Joyce's source on Bacon
and his hen seems to be Macaulay's
(q.v.) essay, "Francis Bacon".
See also St Kevin, Essex, Delia,
Delia Bacon, Biddy Doran.
  Bacon wrote a lot of books
whose titles may be found in the
encyclopaedia. For FW his most
important work is "The Colours
of Good and Evil", which (in a
way I do not understand) probably underlies "The Mime" and
the episode of St Patrick and the
Archdruid (q.q.v.). See also Idol.
  Bacon's importance to FW is
his role as a leading Shakespeare
(q.v.) pretender. This I can see,
but only understand and explain
confusedly because, as yet, the
whole Bacon-Ham-Hamlet-Pig-
Swine-Sow-Pork, etc. (see Pig)
theme is not clear to me. I merely
note its vast importance. I think
it is safe to say that, like Swift
(q.v.), Francis Bacon is divided
by name, between Shem and
Shaun (q.v.). "Bacon" is Shem

(and the Man Servant?)—Shaun eats him: Francis is Frank (q.v.) or Shaun. Of this I am also sure: there are two Francis Bacons or two ideas of Francis Bacon in FW: 1) the intelligent, corrupt, traitorous homosexual who founded modern science; 2) the saint of the Baconian cult. Joyce makes much of this. I list below references to the name Bacon. For Francis—see Frank. For extended coverage, see what you can do with Pig.

7.10 (see Butcher); †39.17—with Packenham, Ham; 41.13; ?56.27; 57.25 (flashback in); 59.20; 71.12,24 (see York); 85.18; †100. 19—with Disraeli (q.v.); 141.8,21 (*flesk* is Norwegian for Bacon); 160.17; 179.14; 199.17; 205.19 (see Beggar); 222.36; 257. 15,22; 267.12; 311.31; †318.21 —with Ham and Buckingham in a quotation from Shakespeare (q.q.v.); 320.29; 325.21; ?342.23 (see William, Bailey); 345.30; 358.25 (see William, Bailey); 363.17; †382.11 — with Delia Bacon (q.v.); ?403.25; 405.33; 406.3,15; ?412.29; 428.22; 456.22 (naboc); 508.4; 546.31; 553.10; 603.1-2; 615.31; 618.7.

Badbols–Finn's (q.v.) nurses were Bodhmall, a female druid, and Liathluachra ("the Grey of Luachair"). See Skerry, Grey One. 376.26.

Baddelaries–see Baudelaire.

?Badman, Mr–protagonist of Bunyan's *Life and Death of Mr Badman*. 113.20.

*Bagot–there is a Baggot Street in Dublin. The reference may include the feast of Adonis (q.v.) which is sometimes called *El Bûgat*, Arabic for "The feast of weeping women". 71.12; 345.15,25; 346.34; 352.27; 490.20; 491.6.

Bailey–"Burnham and Bailey" refers to: 1) Barnum (q.v.) and Bailey Circus; 2) and the Burnham light at Bristol and the Bailey light on Howth (q.v.). 71.21.

Bailey, Bill–subject of a song by Hughie Cannon, 1902. Bill is a brakeman on the B&O, whose wife wants him to come home, as, say, Penelope and Ann Hathaway (q.q.v.) wanted their husbands home. In FW he doubles with the Bailey light on Howth (q.v.) and perhaps with the recruiting sergeant, William Bailey who stood at Dunphy's Corner, tooraloo. See Bill. 127.6; 317.30; 448.19; 480.18.

Baird–British inventor of what the English call "telly". 349.9.

Bairnsfather, Bruce–English cartoonist of trench life in World War I. His most famous drawing was captioned: "If you know a better 'ole, go to it." 99.12.

Balaam–Biblical prophet (Num. 22 ff.). His ass (q.v.) spoke and warned him of the wrath of Yahweh. 178.13; †441.25—with John Braham (q.v.); 566.9.

Balbus (Latin "Stammerer")–civil servant under Julius Caesar (q.v.), sent to Gaul on an engineering job, where he had troubles over a wall. I have an idea that Balbus and his wall are a sort of cat-sat-on-the-mat in schoolboy Latin. 4.30; 37.16; 173.27-28; 192.36— with Elizabeth (q.v.); 287.19; 467.16; 518.34; 552.19.

Balder–Odin's (q.v.) son in Norse myth, god of the summer sun. He was killed when Loki (q.v.) got blind Hodur to throw mistletoe at him. Balder means "the white god". †263.5-6—with Theobald (q.v.); 331.14; 364.1 (rebald).

Balenoarch–mixed-up Italian rainbow—see Seven. 175.16; 612.27,28.

Balfe, Michael (1808-70) – Irish composer, best known for *The Bohemian Girl* and *The Rose of*

Castille. His songs are all over FW. 199.29.

Balfour, Arthur James, Earl of Balfour (1848-1930)–British statesman, efficient, coercing Irish secretary. †13.36—with Baal (q.v.); 52.19.

Bali–Indian Pluto (q.v.). 19.19.

Balkis–Queen of Sheba who visited Solomon (q.v.), 1 Kings, 10. 29.26; 68.21; 198.3; 543.14; 577.9.

Ball, Francis Elrington (1863-1928) –Irish historian who edited Swift (q.v.), and wrote *Howth and its Environs.* †55-56—with Thomas Elrington (q.v.).

Ball, John–in a nursery rhyme, "shot them all". 130.10.

***Ballantine**–Since R. L. Stevenson (q.v.) is indicated here, this may combine *The Master of Ballantrae* (a story of opposed brothers which owes almost everything to Hogg's (q.v.) *Justified Sinner*) and Scott's publishers, the Ballantines. 106.9.

Bally, Belly–see Billy.

Bally, Charles–Swiss philologist. 523.11.

Banba–queen of the Tuatha De Danaan, whose name is poetically given to Ireland. 132.26; 294.note 4; 325.24; 330.21; 469.6-7; 596.8.

***Bancorot**–see Corot? 266.23.

Baptiste, Nicholas (1761-1835)– French actor who specialized in Noble Fathers. 204.36.

Barat, St Madeleine Sophie–foundress of the Congregation of the Sacred Heart, which educates girls. The allusion on 155 seems to be to a Dublin school. 155.26; ?171.14.

Barbara, St–patron of armorers, gunsmiths, gunners and thunderstorms. Since Shaw's (q.v.) *Major Barbara* is based on the saint's legend, Barbara Undershaft is included in these references.

105.15; 335.27; 348.36; 410.26; 561.32.

Barbarossa or Frederick I of Germany (1152-90)–German emperor who sleeps in a cave and will return at his country's need. In life, he was a determined opponent of Adrian IV (q.v.). The Barbarossa is a kind of grape. 154.23; 280.left margin.

Bard–see Shakespeare. Note that Joyce mostly puns on "bard" and "bird". Shakespeare is a bird by way of swan and crow (q.q.v.). 10.34; 37.17; 48.19; 60.10; 172. 28; 251.35 (ter); 363.5; 373.33; 465.28; 504.16.

Bare, mere–see Meyerbeer. 360.7.

Barebones or Barbon, Praise-God (1596-1679)–English leather-seller and Fifth Monarchy man. †85.8, 14,17—with Billy Bones (q.v.).

Barham, Richard (1788-1854)– English author of *The Ingoldsby* (q.v.) *Legends.* †518.28—with Ham (q.v.).

Barkers–London department store. 127.11.

Barkis–"willin" (see Will) in *David Copperfield* (q.v.). 62.31.

***Barindens,** 600.28.

***Barley,** Father–connected with Lear's (q.v.) "ancient uncle Arley". See also Burghley. 257. 10,17,29.

***Barlow,** 553.20.

***Barmabrac's,** Saint, 274.12.

Barmecides–noble Persians in *The Arabian Nights.* A "Barmecide Feast" is an imaginary banquet. 79.6-7; 387.21.

***Barnabas** (son of exhortation)– the solicitor who Lily Kinsella (q.v.) carries on with. 572.34.

***Barnaby** (son of prophecy)–Barnaby Bright or Long Barnaby or St Barnabas's day was June 11, which, old style, was the longest day of the year. 237.15.

Barnacle, Nora–maiden name of

Mrs James Joyce. See Arrah-na-Pogue, Gretta Greene, Doll. 3.21 (nor avoice); 399; 423.22; 452.36.

Barnardo, Thomas John (1845-1905)–founder of orphans' homes in England. He was born in Dublin, and the particular reference here is to a shop which relatives of his opened in Grafton Street, Dublin. 253.31.

*Barnet, 20.28.

Barnett, Samuel Augustus–English cleric and reformer. For the poor of his parish, he provided music, reasonable entertainment, and a book called *Practical Socialism.* 480.2.

Barney - the - Bark – G. B. Shaw (q.v.). I list other Barneys here, but I am not sure they refer to Shaw. 200.6; 211.2; 330.34.

Barnham, Alice–the very young girl who Francis Bacon (q.v.) married and did not get on with. I think she is included in the Alice in Wonderland (q.v.) references.

Barnhelm, Minna von–title heroine of Lessing's greatest comedy. †331.35-36—with Wild Man from Borneo (q.v.).

Barnum, Phineas T. (1810-91)–American circus man. 29.5; 71.21 —see also Bailey.

Barraclough–tenor mentioned in *Ulysses,* 273/357, 647/773. 48.17 (cloud barrage).

*Barren–see Warren. 575.2.

*Barrentone, Zerobubble–maybe Jonah Barrington (q.v.). Here he seems to be one of the Four (q.v.). For Zerubbabel, see Ezra 3:2. 536.32.

Barrett–see Barat.

Barrington, Sir Jonah (1760-1834) –Irish lawyer and historian. †536.32—with Jonah and with Whelley.

Barry, Coogan–Kevin Barry (q.v.) and the poem "Gougaune Barra" by J. J. Callanan. 93.28.

Barry, Kevin (1902-20)–another martyr for Old Ireland, another murder for the Crown. 93.28; †555.28—with Kevin (q.v.).

Barry, Spranger (1719-77)–Dublin-born actor who rivalled Garrick (q.v.) in London. He built the Crow Street Theatre in Dublin. 134.11; ?184.21; 569.30.

Bartolo–old man in love with young Rosina (q.v.) in Rossini's (q.v.) *Barber of Seville.* †21.35—with Van Hoother (q.v.); 247.10; 527.25.

*Baruch, Braham–maybe Brian Boru (q.v.). 284.note 4.

*Basil–maybe just Greek *basileus* or king. 105.9-10; 374.31.

*Basilico's ointment. *Basilico* is Italian for sweet basil. The word could have to do with Gr. *basileus* and the King's evil. Basilico is a braggart knight in *Solyman and Perseda,* by Kyd (q.v.) perhaps, referred to in Shakespeare's (q.v.) *King John,* I, i, 244. 25.9.

Bastien and Bastienne–title characters of Mozart's (q.v.) comic opera. 254.14.

*Bates, Master–maybe the captain in Gulliver (q.v.). No one fits into the context so well as Harry Bates (1850-99), English sculptor, whose *Pandora* (q.v.) is in the Tate Gallery. 209.8.

Bathsheba–wife of Uriah the Hittite (q.v.), taken in adultery by David (q.v.), (2 Sam. 11). See Peele. 188.26; 468.36.

Batiste–type-name for a French-Canadian. 54.15.

Batta–stuttering king of Cyrene. 44.20; 98.29; 177.29.

Battersby Sisters–Battersby Bros., Dublin auctioneers. 386.24; 515.30-31.

Baudelaire, Charles Pierre (1821-67)–French poet who wrote of: "Those who like me are contemned—I would even say contemptible if I cared to flatter nice people." (Fusées, 26) In French *baudelaire* is a 14th century scimitar or a spear. 4.3; 207.11.

Baudwin, Layteacher – the ass (q.v.). Baldwin is the name of the ass in the Reynard (q.v.) cycle. 184.35.

Baughkley–see Buckley. 447.24.

*Baws, 262.25.

Bax, Arnold (b. 1883)–English composer. See Joyce to Miss Weaver, 22 Nov. 1929. 542.29.

Baxter–see Butcher and Baker.

*Baywindaws Bros, 141.18-19.

Beach, Sylvia–owner of the Paris bookshop, Shakespeare and Company, first publisher of *Ulysses*, 1922. Doubtless some one of the Sylvias (q.v.) refers to her.

*Beacher, 305.30.

Bear–see Man Servant.

*Beardall, Mister, 587.32.

Beardsley, Aubrey (1874-94)–English artist in black and white, who wrote some prose and poetry, but is best known for his illustrations of other men's works, including Wilde's (q.v.) *Salome*. †357.2-3—with Oberon (q.v.); 357.6,8.

Beardwood–friend of Joyce's father—see Woodenbeard, Blogg. 169.17; 467.15.

*Beatrice–maybe Miss Portinari —see *Purgatorio*, xxxii 97. Maybe Shakespeare's (q.v.) girl in *Much Ado About Nothing* or Joyce's in *Exiles*. Some of the "Trix" and "Trixies" may be Beatrice. See Hero. ?8.8; 227.14.

*Beatsoon, 286.24.

*Beatties–Betties (q.v.) ?19.9.

Beauchamp–one of the towers of the Tower of London, named for Earl Thomas Beauchamp who was imprisoned by Richard II. 77.19.

Beauchamp, Christine (pronounced Beecham)–pseudonym of the young New England girl, studied by Dr Morton Prince (q.v.) of Boston in *The Dissociation of a Personality*. See the Maggies, see Sally. 11.27; †111.14—with Jesus 207.12; 281.21-22 (cinder . . . Christinette . . . chumming . . . be) —with Cinderella (q.v.); †537.6-7 —with Anna Livia (q.v.).

Beaufort–a noble family and an English hunt. 393.22; 396.36; 511.10; 567.25.

Beauty and the Beast–fairy-tale and English pantomime. †487.16-17—with Bewley (q.v.); †541.30-31—with Sleeping Beauty (q.v.); 560.21.

Beaverbrook, William, 1st Baron (b. 1879)–English newspaper publisher. 72.10.

Bebel, Ferdinand August–German socialist. 118.18.

Beck, Jakob Sigismund (1761-1803) –German expounder of Kant (q.v.). 415.10.

Becket, Thomas or Thomas à Becket (1118-70)–English saint and martyr, killed in Canterbury cathedral for the convenience of Henry II (q.v.). In FW he is usually paired with St Lawrence O'Toole (q.v.), his contemporary. As far as I know the two men had no contact with each other, and I am sometimes tempted to suppose that Becket and O'Toole are T. S. Eliot and D. H. Lawrence (q.q.v.). Some of these Beckets may include Samuel Beckett (q.v.). 5.3; 59.6-7,24; 70.27; 77.2; 388.15; ?397.6; †510.19—with Beggar (q.v.); 543.11; 601.27; †617.12-13—with St Lawrence O'Toole (q.v.).

Beckett, Samuel–Irish writer, one of the Twelve (q.v.), friend of Joyce's, called by Joyce "the boy". †112.3,5—with Brushwood Boy (q.v.).

Bective–Irish football team. 451.10.

Bede, the Venerable (673-735)–English historian and theologian. ?3.29; 185.31-32; 548.30.

Bedevere–knight of the Round Table. 266.10.

Beelzebub–called "prince of devils", Matt., 12. Milton (q.v.) made him next to Satan in power of evil. 64.11; 230.4; 239.33; 580.14.

Beery, Noah–American movie star. Also Noah, Guinness (q.q.v.). 64.33.

Beethoven, Ludwig van (1770-1827)–German composer. 360.8.

Beeton–town eaten up by Los Angeles, as Mr Morse has shown. 154.24.

Beeton, Mrs (1836-65)–author of a groan English cookbook. 333.34; †437.24—with Elizabeth I (q.v.).

*****Beggar**–a mysterious figure, almost certainly the Cad (q.v.)—but who's the Cad? perhaps Hamlet (q.v.), "the absentminded beggar" of *Ulysses*, 185/239. The note on p. 37 of Scribbledehobble could mean that Oscar Wilde (q.v.) is "rented" by the Beggar (Pegger Festy (q.v.)?); on the other hand, Wilde was, after his prison term, an abject beggar. "Oscar is too dreadful," Lord Alfred Douglas (q.v.) wrote, "he begs and begs and of course I have given him money. . . ." The whole thing is made more mysterious by the fact that the "six victolios fifteen" (82.12-13) refer, so Mr Graham tells me, to Statutes 6 Victoria 15: An act to impose an additional duty on spirits and to repeal the allowance on spirits made from malt only in Ireland. 29 April 1842. 7.24; †15.30—with Biggar (q.v.); †70.34-35; 79.31; 82.5,29 (see Billy); 130.6; 135.13; 145.22; 149.7,15; 163.13; 168.5; 205.16; 239.6; 257.19; 332.25-26; 388.15 — with Becket; 494.36; †510.19 — with Becket (q.v.); 542.35; 584.6,35; 588.2.

*****Begge**–there is a Dublin wine merchant of this name. 58.16,17; 262.note 7.

*****Behan**–Joyce would have liked the coincidence of Brendan Behan writing a book called *The Quare Fellow*. See Man Servant. 27.31.

Behemoth–intensive plural of Hebrew *b'hima*, meaning a beast, mentioned in Job (q.v.) 40:15, probably the hippopotamus. †244.36—with Boehme (q.v.).

Bel–Babylonian earth-god. 405.13.

*****Belchum**–Belgium, but what else? I think he is the Man Servant (q.v.). 9.1,4,10,13,15, 30-31.

Belial–one of Milton's (q.v.) fallen angels. 301.10.

Belinda–heroine of Pope's (q.v.) "Rape of the Lock". Joyce joins her to Biddy Doran (q.v.) because Biddy is Delia Bacon (q.v.) who wished to rape the lock on Shakespeare's (q.v.) tomb. †111.5—with Biddy Doran.

Belisha, Leslie Hore–British homesecretary who introduced the pedestrian-crossing sign, popularly called "Belisha Beacon". 267.12.

Bell, Alexander Graham (1847-1922)–American inventor of the telephone. 122.7.

Bell, Alexander Melville (1819-1905)–American author of *Fundamentals of Elocution*. 72.16; 381.18.

Bell, Currer, Ellis, Acton–pen names of the Brontës (q.v.), who dominate this paragraph. 7.33.

Belle–see Anna Livia, Issy.

Bellezza, Betty–see Elizabeth. *Bellezza* is Italian for "beauty". 211.13-14; 328.36.

*****Bellina,** Una–maybe Una out of *The Faerie Queene* (q.v.). 576.6.

Bellingham, Sir Edward (d. 1549) –Lord Deputy of Ireland. 6.22.

Bellini, Vincenzo (1801-35)–Italian operatic composer. Bellini and

Tosti were also pioneers in radio-telegraphy. †309.31—with Tosti (q.v.); 360.7 (Bill Heeny).

Bellona–Roman goddess of war. 78.31; 494.6.

Belly the First–see William I. 26.28.

Belshazzar–last king of Babylon, whose doom was foretold by the writing on the wall, which was interpreted by Daniel (q.v.), Dan. 5. 146.13; 494.20.

Ben–see Franklin, Jonson.

Benedict or Benedick–the following references probably take in: 1) the founder of the Benedictines —see St Scolastica; 2) Sir Julius Benedict (1804-85) who composed *The Lily* (q.v.) *of Killarney*; 3) the bachelor of Shakespeare's (q.v.), *Much Ado About Nothing* —see Beatrice, Hero. 248.30; 431.18; 469.23; 596.17; 613.15.

Benedict X–Pope from 1058-1059, called Mincius, meaning lout or dolt. Hildebrand (q.v.) degraded him to the rank of simple priest. 432.4.

Benjamin–youngest, favorite son of Jacob (q.v.)—Gen. 36 etc. I cannot see that he or Franklin or Jonson (q.q.v.) fit in very well. 38.2; 457.29.

*Benkletter, the Daughters, 60.10.

Bentley, Richard (1662-1742)–English classical scholar, one of the leaders on the Modern side and slain in Swift's (q.v.) *The Battle of the Books.* 88.23.

Benvolio–character in Shakespeare's *Romeo and Juliet* (q.q.v.). See Phoenix. 450.11.

*Beppy–short for Joseph in Italian. The people of Basle are called the Beppi. 415.36.

Béranger, Pierre Jean de (1780-1857)–French song-writer, revolutionist, author of *Le Sénateur.* 372.12.

*Berbeck, 64.31.

Berchert, St–at Tullyease of St

Berchert there is a limestone boulder round which pilgrims make "rounds" in a sun-wise direction. †430.2—with St Bridget (q.v.).

Berenice, Mayde–wife of Ptolemy III who dedicated her hair as a votive offering for her husband's safety in war. The hair was stolen and became the constellation Coma Berenices. 243.26.

*Bergins–possibly Dan Bergin's Public House, *Ulysses,* 218/283, 597/704. 12.26,27,28; 206.9.

Bergerac, Cyrano de (1619-55)–gallant French soldier and playwright, himself the subject of a play by Rostand. 338.24?

Bergson, Henri (1859-1941)–French philosopher whose *Durée et simultanéité,* 1922, discussed Einstein's (q.v.) theories. 149.20 (Bitchson).

Bering, Vitius Jonassen (1681-1741)–Danish navigator who discovered America from the east. The Bering Strait is named for him. 628.9.

Berkeley, George (1685-1752)–Anglican bishop of Cloyne, philosopher. I can see that Joyce associates him with Buckley (q.v.), but beyond this I do not understand his use in FW. I do not know why he is the Archdruid. 260.23; 287.19; 312.29; 330.17; †391.31—with Buckley (q.v.); †423.32—with Buckley (q.v.); †435.11—with Bishop Bulkeley (q.v.); †610.1—with Buckley (q.v.), 12; 611.2,5,27; 612.32.

Bern, Berchtold von–founder of Berne, Switzerland. See Bear. 525.36.

Bernadette, St (1844-79)–French religious. 430.35.

*Berrboel, 437.8.

*Bertha–must surely include the heroine of *Exiles.* I have found no famous Bertha of Tartar nationality. Maybe Joyce is thinking of

Bertha, "the White Lady" of German legend who founded the Orange (q.v.) family. Maybe he means Bertha was hard to live with. 330.28; 514.24.

Besant, Annie (1847-1933)–Fabian, feminist, theosophist, disciple of Madame Blavatsky (q.v.). 234.5; 432.32.

Bessemer, Sir Henry (1813-98)–English inventor of a steel process. 359.4.

Best, Mr–assistant librarian, present in the "Scylla and Charybdis" section of *Ulysses*, where Stephen (q.v.) puns on his name very much as he does in FW. 76.33; 121.32; 256.16; 414.35-36.

Bethel, Jakob van der–see Jacob. 607.8.

Bethgelert–see Gelert. According to Saxo Grammaticus, Hamlet (q.q.v.) was brought up under a dog's name to save him from his uncle, Feng (q.v.). 177.22.

*Betreffender, Herr–probably not a person. The word is German for "before-mentioned". 69.32.

*Betterlies, 293.note 1.

Betty, Bet–see Elizabeth.

Beurla–Irish word for the English language. 132.27.

*Bevradge, 289.23.

*Bewey, 277.note 4.

Bewley–Dublin baker. 487.16—with Beauty and the Beast (q.v.).

Bezouts, Étienne–18th century French mathematician. 301.28.

Bianconi, Charles–in the 19th century he provided Ireland with a transportation system and was known to Dubliners as Brian Connolly. 240.18; 321.9.

Bias of Priene–one of Greece's seven sages. 365.10.

Bickerstaff, Isaac–invented by Swift (q.v.). A cobbler, John Partridge (q.v.), published certain astrological predictions. In 1708 Swift parodied Partridge in "Predictions for the ensuing year, by Isaac Bickerstaff", and predicted Partridge's death. 178.23; †366.19 —with Butt and Taff (q.v.); 413.29.

*Biddles–not, I think, the noble American family. It seems to be an imaginary playmate of the child Issy, perhaps another part of her personality, perhaps a doll (q.v.). Biddy? 561.36; 562.2,3.

Biddy–see Biddy Doran, St Bridget.

Biene–Ger. "bee". 414.25; 417.18, 30; 418.15; 458.33.

Biggar, Joseph–one of Parnell's most trusted parliamentary aides, a "character" of whom many stories were told. He was hunchbacked and misshapen. See Beggar. 15.50; 70.34-35; 141.22; 444.14.

Bigods–earls of Norfolk, lords of Carlow. 366.12.

Bile–in Celtic myth, ruler of the underworld. 447.5.

Bill, Billy–the ancient and contemporary name for Dublin is Baile Atha Cliath, which means "town of the ford of hurdles" and is pronounced approximately "Bally clay". Of this name Joyce makes much. Most of the Bails, Baileys, Bellys, Bullys, Ballys, Bollys, Billys, Bills, Bulls, Balls, etc. refer to, or at any rate, memoralize the city. Many of them of course also refer to specific persons named William (q.v.), as indicated below. Since I believe that FW is about William Shakespeare (q.v.) I take the "Bill-Billy" theme to refer to or memoralize him as well. Dublin is Bill Shakespeare's clay. See also Billy Budd.
    6.22,33,35; ?8-13,15; 9.24; 10.21; ?13.12; 14.18; 15.18; †17.9 —with Abel (q.v.); 18.33,34; 19.19; 21.7,9; ?22.25; 23.3,17;

?24.6; †26.28—with William I (q.v.); ?30.36; 31.27,32,36; 32.3; 35.7,30; †37.35—with Little Billee (q.v.); 39.34; ?40.28; 42.13; 43.22; 45.st. 4 (ter); 46.10; 47.st. 1; ?52.16,19; ?53.12; †53.36—with William III (q.v.); 54.22; 56.6; 70.15,21-22; 72.11,26; 73.8,23; †75.27—with William III (q.v.) 33; 79.4,31; 80.13; 82.5,29—see Beggar; 83.27,28; 84.2-3,9,15; 85.8 (bellybone is Elizabethan for sweetheart), 13,26; 86.24-25; 87.15,21; 88.10,19,28; ?91.14—with Baal (q.v.); ?95.2-3,26; ?98.31; ?100.7,8; †?102.19,20—with Balkis (q.v.); 104.18; ?105.9—see Ballantine; ?106.15; 107.15; †111.21—with Masterbuilder (q.v.); 113.36; 114.27; 115.28; †116.6—with Buckley (q.v.); 116.6,13; 117.21-22; 118.7,29; ?119.16; 120.7,14; ?121.36; ?122.7,26; 125.13; †127.6—with Bill Bailey (q.v.); ?128.1,22; 130.10,21; ?134.1,18; 136.33; †137.12—with Huck Finn (q.v.), 13; ?141.4,5; 142.2-3; †146.13—with Belshazzar (q.v.); 147.4; ?152.23; ?153.29; 154.1,7,22, 34; 157.7; 159.30; †160.19—with Wilde (q.v.), †27—with Faust; 162.9; 170.33; ?175.27; 177.23,24, 25,27; ?179.4,14,35; 180.24, ?27; ?187.2; 188.7; 190.5,28; ?192.36; 197.7; ?198.4; 205.27; 206.4; 209.13; 210.7, ?†16—with Bully Hayes (q.v.), 19; 211.19,34; 215.18; 219.16, ?31; ?221.18; 225.10; †229.15—with Polyphemus (q.v.); ?231.19,21; 232.15; †233.25—with Nancy (q.v.); 234.32; 235.23; 236.14,21; 237.14; †238.4—see Isabel, Eve, 32, †33—with Beelzebub; 242.21; †248.21—with Swan, Swine (q.q.v.); 353.21; †255.13—with John Bull (q.v.); ?262.25-26.left margin; 263.4; 264.left margin; ?267.20; 270. note 2; 272.29,30; 273.1,2; ?275.10, †14—with Bill Hart (q.v.); 277. note 1; 279.8; 285.25-26, ?left margin; ?287.19,29; ?289.14—see Billy Hayes; †292.25—with Cymbeline, note 1; 295.note 1; 304.13;

305.2,14; 309.13, †31—with Bellini (q.v.), 34; 310.12,29,36; ?†311.18—with O'Connell (q.v.); 313.21, 29; 314.13,21; 315.28; 316.21,23; 317.12,14,19, †30—with Bill Bailey (q.v.); 318.6; 320.33,34; 321.15,17; 323.7,16,17; 324.2,25; 326.1,25,34; 328.26; 331.26; 333.18; 334.4; 335.13; 337.16, †18-19—with Masterbuilder (q.v.) 30,35; ?339.8,10,11,19,20; †342.25—with Bailey and Bacon (q.q.v.); 344.27,28; ?346.21,25; 350.13,22; 352.23; 353.13; 356.30; †358.25—with Bailey, Bacon (q.v.), 31; 359.1-2; †360.7—with Bellini (q.v.); 365.6; 366.3,6,11; 368.10, 15; 373.23, ?33; 375.17; 378.1, 15; 381.23; ?384.29; ?386.1; 387. 9; 393.12, †18—with Gladstone (q.v.); 403.21-22; 404.13; †405.13—with Bel (q.v.), 27; 406.7,34; 410.10; 414.28; 416.8; ?420.25; 424.2,27,33; 425.16,17; ?429.28; ?†432.21—with Delia (q.v.); 435.1-2,9; †436.27—with Billy Sunday (q.v.); 438.5,8,20,23; 440.25; †445.20,24—with Anne Boleyn (q.v.); 447.17,20; †448.19—with Bill Bailey (q.v.), 20; †448.19—with Bill Bailey (q.v.), 33; †450.29—with Lily (q.v.); 453.3; 454.11; 455.6; 456.3; 460. 12; 463.32; 464.18,21,27,28; ?465.26; 466.30; 467.1; 472.2; 475.13; 480.13, †18—with Bill Bailey (q.v.); ?483.6; 485.32; ?486.32; 488.35; 490.35; 491.1,10; ?492.24,36; ?494.19, †20—with Belshazzar (q.v.); 495.3; ?498.18, 23,36; ?488.1; 506.8,24; 508.32; 509.33; 510.14; 511.9,34; 512.10; †513.25—with Lily and Issy (q.q.v.); 516.10; ?517.9; 518.1, 19-20; 520.24; 522.1,2,15; 523.10, 11,12; 525.28; 529.11,18,22; 533. 36; 536.10; 537.3,18,20; 540.20; 542.35; 543.1,8,11; 550.4; 557.10, 11,12; 559.30,36; 566.4; 567.5,36; 568.14,15,18,23; 579.18; †580.14—with Beelzebub (q.v.); 583.4; 584.28; 587.7; 589.8; †593.27—with Feghin, Baal (q.q.v.); 608.8-9; †611.6—with Berkeley (q.v.); 612.15,32; 618.7,34; 624.19.

*Bill–the Bustonly, Bowlbeggar—
see Bill, Beggar. 82.29; 135.13.

Billee, Little–Thackeray's (q.v.)
hero who just missed being eaten
by his shipmates. 37.35.

*Billups, Mr–see Phillips. 537.20.

*Bindmerollingeyes, 11.6-7.

*Biorwik's–Earwickers? 550.18.

Bird–"Bird" Milligan was a Dublin
cut-up who played a joke involv-
ing the Ballast Office, two alarm
clocks and the hour of noon.
(Gogarty, q.v., *A Week-end in the
Middle of the Week*, pp. 175-181.)
See also Swan. 37.13.

Birkett, T. A.—see Becket. 77.2.

Biron, hero of Shakespeare's (q.v.)
Love's Labour's Lost. Like Lord
Byron (q.v.) he became a poet.
See Rosaline, Costard, Longaville.
†41.16—with H. J. Byron (q.v.);
†91.3—with Byron; 296.23; †435.
10—with Byron and Boylan;
†541.17—with Brian Boru (q.v.);
563.12.

Bismarck, Prince (1815-98)–German statesman. 9.32; 601.36.

Bissavolo–Italian *bisavolo* or
great-grandfather. 68.19.

*Bisse, Bina de, 279.note 1.

Bitchson—see Bergson. 149.20.

Bjornson, Bjornstjerne (1832-1910)
–Norwegian writer, *Bjorn* is Norwegian "bear" (q.v.). 471.30;
529.16.

Blackham,   McCarthy–English
cricketer.   †584.2—with Ham
(q.v.).

Black Prince, Edward (1330-76)–
son of Edward III, father of
Richard II. Stephen Dedalus
(q.v.) calls Hamlet (q.v.) the
Black Prince. 387.20.

Blackstone, Sir William (1723-80)
–English jurist. See Whitestone.
5.17.

Blaine, Amory–hero of Scott Fitzgerald's *This Side of Paradise*,
1920. He has a girl named Isabelle (q.v.), but it is Rosalind
(q.v.) with whom he has this
conversation: "I love you, Amory,
with all my heart."/"Always, will
you?"/"All my life—Oh Amory
—" See Tristram. ?43.10; 148.31.

Blair, Robert (1699-1746)–Scottish
poet, author of "The Grave".
256.11.

*Blaire, Loftonant-Cornel, 607.29.

Blaise, St—patron of actors. 12.12;
?21.17; 52.19.

Blake, William (1757-1827)–English poet and painter. 219.36;
220.13; 409.23; 563.13,15.

*Blanchards, 609.16.

*Blanche de Blanche–in FW
Blanche is probably always a
reference to Isolde of the White
Hands (q.v.). Other "whites"
refer, however to Finn MacCool
(q.v.). See also White Patch.
248.33.

*Blanchisse–just a laundress?
210.24.

Blavatsky, Madame Helena Pe-
trovna, née Hahn-Hahn (1831-91)
–Russian theosophist, author of
Isis Unveiled, etc. For listing, see
Hahn.

*Blayncy's, D.–Dublin? 99.34.

*Blennercassel of the brogue—
maybe Harman Blennerhasset, a
rich, idealistic Irishman who got
mixed up in Aaron Burr's con-
spiracy. He did not have a castle,
but built a most palatial house on
an island in the Ohio. 376.32.

*Blogg, Mr Bbyrdwood de Trop–
"Blogg" is English slang for a
vulgarian. See Beardwood. 169.17.

*Blong's, 406.2.

Bloom, Leopold and Molly–hero
and heroine, Ulysses and Penelope (q.q.v.) in Joyce's *Ulysses.*
See also Virag, Mary, Fox. 55.28;
78.27; 93.35; 113.16; 223.31;
241.4; 245.7; 260.29; 346.26;
360.28; 385.25; 389.27; †456.16
—with Finn MacCool (q.v.);

?466.33; 467.11,13 (Caius Cocoa Codinhand); 495.28; †560.20— with Bluebeard (q.v.); 564.23; 587.27; †600.33—with Dolly Varden (q.v.); 620.2.

Bloom, Milly–daughter of the above. 249.36; 600.23.

?Bloom, Rudy–son of the Blooms (q.v.). 386.2.

***Blount,** Captain Chaplain, 39.8.

***Blownose,** Mistral–wind? 453.17.

Blowyhart–see Bill Hart. 275.14.

Blucher, Gebhard Leberecht, von (1742-1819)–Prussian marshal who came to Wellington's (q.v.) support at Waterloo. 9.22; 133. 21-22; 338.9; ?351.34; 587.16.

Bluebeard–villain of a story of Perrault's, of an opera by Dukas and Maeterlinck (q.v.), of an English pantomime. His wife, or his wife's sister was named Anne and doubles with Anna Livia (q.v.). 106.31; ?169.16; 275.14; 332.22; 501.29; †560.20—with L. Bloom (q.v.).

***Blusterboss,** 273.23.

Boanerges or Sons of Thunder–the name Christ gave to the apostles, James and John (q.v.), Mark 3:17. 22.32.

Boar–see Pig, Richard III, Francis Bacon.

***Boaro,** 136.14.

***Boas**–Boaz? There were an archaeologist and a Shakespeare (q.v.) critic of this name. 353.25.

***Boawwll**–partly A. M. Bell (q.v.). 72.16.

Boaz–found Ruth (q.v.) amid the alien corn and married her. 257.21.

***Bob,** Bigamy – thingamabob? 48.15.

Bobrikoff, General–Russian governor of Finland, shot 16 June, 1904 by a young Finn, Eugene Schauman. See Eugenius. 338.32 (bobbycop).

Boccaccio, Giovanni (1313-75)– Italian author of the *Decameron.* 561.24.

Bode, Wilhelm–director of the Kaiser Friedrich Museum in Berlin who, in 1910 was involved in a controversy over a wax figure —see 11th *Britannica,* "Wax Figures". *Bode* is also OE for "messenger", hence the reference may be to Shaun the Post (q.v.) or some angel. 9.10.

Bodkin, Michael ("Sonny")–a beau of Nora Joyce's (q.v.) from Galway who became Michael Furey in *The Dead.* Joyce steadily plays on Furey-Furies and Hamlet's (q.v.) bare bodkin. I believe that Michael is Father Michael (q.v.), but the subject is a very murky one. 25.27; 79.20; 188.34; 249.18; 268.15; 353.3 (Gragious One); 377.27; 424.15 (gracious one); 446.5; 500.2; 578.16.

Boehme or Behmon, Jakob (1575-1624)–German mystical writer. †244.36—with Behemoth (q.v.).

Boerne, Karl Ludwig–German political satirist. 263.19.

Bogaleen, Miles na–see Miles na Copaleen. 343.11-12.

***Boghas,** 75.14.

***Bogy** Bobow, 576.27.

Bohemond (1058-1111)–leader of the first crusade. 170.10.

Boileau, Nicolas (1636-1711)– French writer. 527.13.

Boissy d'Anglas (1756-1828)– French Revolutionary statesman, exiled for reacting against the terror. George Chapman wrote plays, *Bussy D'Ambois* and *The Revenge of Bussy D'Ambois.* 485,6, 12,13,29.

***Bolche,** 330.23.

Boldmans, Isas–see Isa Bowman, Issy. 361.22.

Boleyn or Bullen, Anne (1507-36)– Queen of Henry VIII (q.v.), mother of Elizabeth I (q.v.), character in Shakespeare's *Henry VIII* (q.q.v.). †117.16—with Anna Livia; 445.24; †567.13,15 —with Anna Livia and Anne of Denmark (q.v.).

Bolivar, Simon (1783-1830)–hero of South American independence. †453.13—with Gulliver (q.v.).

Bonapart–see Napoleon.

Bonaventura, St (1221-74)–Franciscan theologian. 207.26.

Bond, Oliver–United Irishman of 1798, condemned to death, but died first of apoplexy. 211.3.

Bones, Billy–pirate who stole the map in Stevenson's (q.v.) *Treasure Island.* See Billy, John Silver. To the Elizabethans, a "bellybone" was a bonny lass. †84.33—with Napoleon (q.v.); †85.8—with Praise-God Barebones (q.v.).

*****Bonhamme,** Paddy–pig (q.v.)? Jacques Bonhomme is a French peasant. 351.16; 459.24-25.

Boniface–generic name for innkeepers. Some of the references below allude to the Irish licensing laws which permit "bona fide" travellers to have alcohol when it is forbidden local citizens. HCE (q.v.) is, of course, the innkeeper of FW. †46.20—with Oscar Wilde (q.v.); 315.9; 321.5; 337.6; †371. 22—with Wilde (q.v.); 380.3; 577.11.

Boore–see Moore and Burgess. 62.30.

*****Boorman's**–just poor man's? 257.9.

Boosey and Hawkes–English music publishers. 448.36.

Booslaeugh, Wassaily–see Buslaevitch. 5.5-6.

*****Boote's**–maybe Bootes, a constellation, maybe a chain of English drugstores. 262.21.

*****Bootenfly,** Mester, †291.note 4— with Esther (q.v.).

Bootersbay, Sisters–see Battersby.

*****Booth,** 332.35; 480.30.

?Booth, John Wilkes (1839-65)– actor who killed Lincoln (q.v.). 26.10; 35.10; 188.7; 257.19; ?351. 28.

Booth, William (1829-1912)–founder of the Salvation Army. 188.7; 552.15.

*****Bootherbrowth,** 121.33.

Bopeep–nursery rhyme and pantomime subject. 227.12; 248.17,18, 19; 435.25; 508.27; 624.9.

Boreas–north wind. See Matthew Gregory (q.v.). 269.18.

Borgia–Italian family. The second reference is to either of two Borgia popes—Callixtus III or Alexander VI. 130.12; 152.27; 538.11 (scatab orgias).

Borkman, John Gabriel–title hero of Ibsen's (q.v.) play. 85.13.

Borneo, Wild Man from–see Wild.

*****Borrough,** 538.8.

Borrow, George (1803-81)–English writer, authority on gipsies who called him "Romany Rye". 210.7; 472.22; 600.30.

Borry–see Spranger Barry. 569.30.

Borsalino–a brand of Italian hat. 32.36; 288.18; 337.33; 471.12-13; 483.11; 520.9

Borumborad–see Patrick Joyce, Ahab.

*****Borumoter,** Big Bil Brine–see Brian Boru, Bill? 331.26-27.

Bosquet (1810-61)–French marshal who said the Charge of the Light Brigade was pretty but was it art? 523.25.

*****Bossford,** 583.12.

Boswell, James (1740-95)–Scottish biographer. See Johnson. 40.7.

Botha, Louis "Oom" (1863-1919)– Transvaal leader, Boer general. 200.14; 479.31.

*****Bott,** 268.26.

Botticelli, Sandro (1444-1510)– Florentine painter. 435.7.

Bottom, Nick "Bully"–weaver

(q.v.) who plays Pyramus (q.v.) in Shakespeare's (q.v.) *A Midsummer Night's Dream*. In FW III,i,ii, Shem (q.v.) assumes the role of Bottom-as-Ass, while Shaun is Moonshine (q.v.). Elsewhere Bottom is indistinguishable from the ass (q.v.) which accompanies the Four (q.v.). See also Woeful Dane's Bottom. 69.3; 78.32; 93.18; ?98.7; 110.26; †163.19—with Butt (q.v.), 21; 164.29; 173.28; 191.28 (but him); 248.12; 278.note 2; 281.note 2; 296.6; 312.7; †313.26—with Bottomley (q.v.); 315.4; 319.6; 342.31-32; 343.25; 350.15; 375.3; 381.33-34; 445.13 (mottob); 565.23.

Bottomley, Horatio–English journalist who blackmailed various English politicians and went to jail. See Bottom? 313.26; 534.10,18.

Boucicault, Dion (1822-90)–Irish actor and playwright. FW makes great use of his plays, *The Colleen Bawn* or Fair Girl (see Eily O'Connor and *The Lily of Killarney*), and *Arrah-na-Pogue* (q.v.), and mentions others, such as *Daddy O'Dowd* and *The Octoroon, The Corsican Brothers* (q.q.v.). 95.8; 385.3; †391.23—with Dion Cassius (q.v.); 555.24-25; 569.35.

Boudeville–Frenchman hired by the Free State to put the Dublin street-cleaning department in order—see 138.12. 294.18.

Boulanger, George Ernest Jean Marie (1837-91)–French general with whom Irish revolutionists, including Maud Gonne (q.v.), conspired. The reference may be to the song of Boulangisme, *"En Revenant de la Revue"*. 190.29.

Bound, Oliver–see Bond.

*Bourne, 31.33; 190.21; 268.16; 321.8; 365.5; 366.14; 379.35; 513.9.

Bouvard and Pécuchet–title characters of a novel by Flaubert to which *Ulysses* was compared by Wyndham Lewis (q.v.). Bouvard and Pécuchet live together and study everything under the sun. 302.9-10.

Bowdler, Thomas (1754-1825)–expurgated Shakespeare, Gibbon (q.q.v.) and the Old Testament. 179.28; 517.8-9.

*Bowen, 371.23.

*Bowers, 379.35.

Bowie, James–invented a knife and died at the Alamo. 345.7.

Bowman, Isa–child actress who first played Alice (q.v.) in *Alice in Wonderland*, child-friend of Lewis Carroll (q.v.). In FW she is identified with Issy. 226.4,7; 238.3; 361.22.

Box and Cox–title character of a farce by J. M. Morton. *Cox and Box* is an operetta by Sir F. Burnand and Sir Arthur Sullivan (q.v.). 105.5; 308.left margin; 347.29; 409.35; 517.17-18.

Boyce, William (1710-79)–English composer of ecclesiastical music who began his career as a chorister at St Paul's. ?†4.5—with Whoyteboyce (q.v.); †536.22—with Lord Alfred Douglas (q.v.).

Boycott, Captain Charles Cunningham (1832-97)–agent for the estates of the Earl of Erne in Mayo. A "boycott" of the estates gave a word to the language. †9.8—with Cotton and Creasy (q.q.v.); 60.30; 95.33-34; 185.4; 496.3.

*Boyd, 180.7; 609.4.

Boyg, The–vague, sinister, troll-like monster in Norwegian folklore and in *Peer Gynt* (q.v.). 313.13.

Boylan, Blazes – character in *Ulysses*. See Antinous. †435.10—with Byron (q.v.).

*Boyle, 34.11; 44.8; 343.3.

Boyles, Conan–see Doyle.

Bracegirdle, Mrs Anne (1674-1748) –English actress. 59.1; 134.9-10; 245.20.

Brache, Tycho–see Brahe.

*Braddon–Irish *brádan* or salmon? 59.35.

Bradlaugh, Charles (1833-91)– English free-thinker, always being elected to Parliament and being thrown out for refusing to swear on the Bible. 252.34.

*Bradogue, Melissa–the Bradoge is one of Dublin's rivers. 212.9.

Brady, Joe–leader of the Invincibles who murdered in Phoenix Park. Joyce is also punning on the Greek word for "slow". 35.20.

*Brady, Mike, 381.12.

Brae, Dolly–see Gray.

Bragshaw–see B. G. Shaw.

Bragspear–see Adrian IV and Shakespeare.

Braham, John (1774-1856)–English tenor who had the longest career of singing supremacy on record. He composed "The Death of Nelson" (q.v.). 200.4; 422.26; †441.25–with Balaam (q.v.).

Brahe, Tycho (1546-1601)–Danish astronomer. Tycho is one of the Hyades. 59.15; 260.22-23.

Brahma–supreme god of Hinduism, the creator. †81.7–with Brahms (q.v.); 106.29.

Brahms, Johannes (1833-97)–German composer. †81.7—with Brahma (q.v.).

*Brakeforth, Mr–see Brer Fox (q.v.), 575.11.

Bramble, Matthew–character in Smollett's *Humphrey Clinker* (q.q.v.). 507.13.

Bran–dog and niece of Finn McCool (q.v.). 232.28; 376.29.

Bran–Irish and Welsh god. The *Mabinogion* contains "The Voyage of Bran". 486.31.

Brand–title character of Ibsen's (q.v.) play. *Brand* means "fire" in Norwegian. Some Brand references may include Brandes (q.v.).

311.31; 374.32; 484.13,34; ?583. 29; 617.16.

Brandes, Georg–Danish critic, friend of Ibsen (q.v.). It is for his book on Shakespeare (q.v.), 1897-98, that he is important to Joyce. Mr Schutte has shown it to be the prime source of "Scylla and Charybdis" in *Ulysses*, and it is also one of the main sources of F.W. On p. 80 Joyce is quoting a passage from *Ulysses*, 193/250, in which Brandes' name occurs. See Brand. 80.14.

*Brassenaarse, Dr–maybe an Oxford don. 301.2.

Brassey, Hugh de–see Hudibras.

*Brasslattin, Mr–a name for Johnny MacDougal (q.v.) as the Brazen Age. 519.16.

Brassolis–girl whose brother kills her lover in Macpherson's "Fingal" (q.q.v.). She kills herself after that. 228.12.

*Braten's, Kitzy–probably Swiss-German *Gitzibraten* or "roast goat's meat". 406.9.

*Bratislavoff, Brothers, 219.26.

Brauchbar, Edmund–friend of Joyce's, richest silk-merchant in Switzerland. 481.18.24.

*Breakfast, Will–probably Leopold Bloom (q.v.) who, at the end of *Ulysses*, tells his wife he will breakfast in bed. See Will, Brer Fox. 575.29-30.

*Breedabrooda, 78.17.

*Breen–there are Breens in *Ulysses*. 463.35.

Brendan, Brandon or Brandan, St (484-578)–Irish hero of a legendary voyage into the Atlantic. St Brendan's island was long believed a real place and an earthly paradise. 213.35; 327.2; 442.14; 488.25.

*Brennan's–includes the Brenner Pass. 81.14.

Brennan-on-the-Moor–outlaw hero

of an Irish ballad, hung. 211.27-28; 276.21.

*Brereton–maybe one of Anne Boleyn's (q.v.) lovers, maybe Priscilla or Mrs Kemble. 437.6.

Brewer–as in *The Dictionary of Phrase and Fable* which Joyce uses extensively in FW. 95.26.

*Brewster, 29.4-5.

*Brewster, Blanchette, 537.24.

*Brewster, Brigid–see Biddy Doran? 39.36.

Brian Boru (Brian of the Tribute)–Irish hero-king who defeated the Danes at Clontarf in 1041. He was known as the "Terror of the Danes", but was slain by a Dane, Brodhar (q.v.), after the battle. See Man Servant, Bruin. 16.26; 22.32; 24.34; 73.7; ?110.2; 133.28; 211.6-7; ?284.note 4—see Baruch; 316.9; 331.26-27; 337.15; 338.28; †339.14—with Oriana, Oberon (q.q.v.); 340.20; 351.5; 376.8-9; 385.15; 485.18-19; 498.25; †541.17—with Biron (q.v.); 625. 18-19.

Brian O'Linn–see O'Linn.

Briand, Aristide (1862-1932)– French statesman. †17.12—with Brian O'Linn (q.v.).

*Brices, Saint, 390.1.

*Brichashert, 352.5.

Bride, St–see St Bridget. I cannot make up my mind whether all "brides" in FW refer to or memoralize St Bridget or whether they don't. See also Brinabride.

Bride, Julia–title heroine of a story by Henry James (whose name must surely be included among the James (q.v.) of FW). Julia has been too often engaged. A former fiancé, in cruel, hypocritic condescension sets out to wreck her present engagement to a young man of whom she is "proud", Basil French (q.v.). See also Shakespeare's Julia (q.q.v.), a jilted girl. †465.2—with St Bridget (q.v.).

Bridget, Bride, Breed St (452-523)– female patron saint of Ireland as Patrick (q.v.) is the male. She is known as the Mary (q.v.) of the Gael and is thought to be a Christian remaking of the pagan goddess, two-faced Brigid (q.v.) —see also Artemis. St Bridget made her cell (the first in Ireland) at *Kil-dara*, "church of the oaks". I am sure that FW is full of legends about her. By extending Brigid-Bridget to Biddy Doran (q.v.), Joyce makes a use of her too elaborate to consider here. See Bride.

12.22	scentbreeched
53.30	Bri Head
66.36	bride or brides
172.3	bridewell (the prison was named for her)
207.16	bridely
210.25,29	breechettes . . . beatified Biddy
213.36	Biddy's
214.2	marygold
237.6	bridawl
256.5-6	blessed brigid
305.19	Biddy's . . . Biddy's
309.16	bride's
324.34	brider
328.28-29	bride . . . breed
362.9	bride
367.28	breide
388.27	Bride Street
389.31	brythe
?390.1	St Brices
404.35	Huggisbrigid
†430.2	St Berched (q.v.)
433.11	brideworship
462.9	bridle's
†465.2	Julia Bride (q.v.)
526.34	bridelittle
547.27,29	bride . . . bryllupswibe (Nor. "marriage", literally "bride race")
561.16,21	auntybride . . . marygold
562.13	brigidschool
563.11,17	bride . . . bridest
566.16	maidbrides
569.11	Bride-and-Audeons-be-hind-Wardborg
589.11	bridling

Bright, Honor–Dublin prostitute,

found murdered in the Wicklow hills. 211.33.

Bright, John (1811-89)–radical English politician who opposed Home Rule and told the Irish they "exhibited a boundless sympathy for criminals and murderers". 542.19.

Brigid–goddess of poetry and fertility of the Tuatha Dé Danaan, beautiful on one side of her face, ugly on the other. She was chastened and Christianized into St Bridget (q.v.) and with her makes, in FW, a two-faced female concept. Brigid means "bright" or "burning". See also Artemis, Biddy Doran.

Brillat-Savarin, Anthelme (1755-1826)–French gastronomist. 59.30.

Brimstoker–see Bram Stoker.

*****Brinabride** – certainly Venus (q.v.), perhaps a little St Bridget (q.v.). 13.26-27; 148.19; 399. stanza 2; 469.19; 500.21-22,27,30; 501.3; 502.9; 595.5.

*****Bristol** and Balrothery, queen of, 405.27.

*****Bro** Cahlls, 423.36.

Brock–the badger in the Reynard (q.v.) cycle. 272.25.

Brodhar or Brodar–Danish sorcerer who killed Brian Boru (q.v.) after the battle of Clontarf. 22.2; 70.26-27; 481.33.

Brody, Dr Daniel–published Joyce's works in German. 243.6.

Brohan, Augustine Susanna (1807-87)–French actress. She and her daughters, Joséphine and Emilie, won prizes for comedy. †251.33-34—with Browne and Nolan (q.v.).

Brontë–the whole family is all over the paragraph that runs from 7.20 to 8.8. Brontë (thunder) is found at 7.22,28. Anne is at 7.25,26–with Anna Livia (q.v.). Heathcliff (with Howth, q.v., or Ben Edar) is at 7.28. Isabella Linton is at 7.29 perhaps. 7.30-31

suggests the end of *Wuthering Heights.* 7.32 "sisterin", Bell (q.v.) at 7.33. *Villette* (which takes place in Belgium) is at 8.3. Patrick is at 8.6. Cathy Earnshaw may be included with Kate (q.v.) at 8.8. The Duke of Wellington (q.v.) was Charlotte's favorite hero, and the little Brontë children played at war-and-Wellington with their tin soldiers.

*****Brookbear,** 481.24. See Brauchbar.

Brooke, G. V.–Dublin-born actor who died a hero when the *S.S. London* foundered in the Bay of Biscay in 1866. Wearing red velvet pants, he manned the pumps and sank with an excellent line. 210.23.

*****Brophy,** Rev. B. B. of Swords, 266.note 2.

*****Brosna,** Briery–in some manner the Irish river, Brosna. 212.7.

Broughton, Rhoda (1840-1920)–English novelist, author of *Red as a Rose is She.* 569.33.

*****Brown,** 286.1; 424.36.

Brown bomber–probably not Joe Louis but a horse in a comic column by J. B. Morton (Beachcomber). 341.28.

*****Browne** and Nolan–usually Shaun and Shem respectively, but the change about and getting to be Nolan seems to have to do with one's eyes changing from brown to blue—FW, 344.12, 418.32. It has been suggested that the names are derived from Bruno of Nola (q.v.) who believed in the identity of opposites, and from Browne and Nolan, Dublin publishers. See Man Servant.

37.23   blowne . . . noran
38.26,28 Mr Browne . . . Nolan
42.8   Browne's
50.18,19,23 Father San Browne
      . . . Padre Don Bruno . . . Fratomistor Nawlanmore and Brawne

93.1 Nolans Brumans
97.5-6 noelan . . . bruin
113.28 browned or nolensed
128.25,26 O'Bruins . . . Noolahn
152.11 Bruno Nowlan
159.22 Nolan Browne
163.24 Nolanus
†177.20 Davy Browne Nowlan
—with David (q.v.)
†187.24,28 Brawn . . . Nayman of Noland—with Philip Nolan (q.v.)
211.32 Browne . . . Nolan
†251.33-34 B. Rohan . . . N. Ohlan with Brohan (q.v.)
268.8-9 Browne and Nolan's
271.20-21 nolens . . . brune
300.29 noland's browne
303.note 3 The Brownes de Browne-Browne of Castlehacknolan
†321.8 Glasthule Bourne . . . Roehernapark Nolagh —with Bourne, Gladstone, Napoleon (q.q.v.)
†334.6-7 Mr "Gladstone Browne" —with Gladstone (q.v.)
9-10 Mr "Bonaparte Nolan" —with Napoleon (q.v.)
13-14 glance dowon his browen . . . born appalled noodlum—with Gladstone, Napoleon (q.q.v.)
†336.33,35 The Nolan of the Calabashes . . . Saint Bruno (q.v.)
341.25-26,28 Mr Twomass Noholan . . . browne
†351.1 nowells and brownings —with Knowell and Browning (q.q.v.)
352.16 bron a nuhlan
†372.15,29 Brownhazelwood . . . Brownaboy Fuinnninuinn's—with St Finian (q.v.)
†373.16 Bruni Lanno . . . Brani Lonni—with Bruni (q.v.)
380.31-32 widow Nolan's . . . Brownes girls

391.14-15,21 brownesberrow in nolandsland . . . bronnanoleum
412.36 Nolaner and Browno
418.32 Nolans . . . Bruneyes
442.5 Attaboy Knowling
461.12 Bruin and Noselong
488.4,7,8,9,11 Bruno and Nola . . . Nola Bruno . . . egobruno . . . alionola . . . brunoipso . . . Nola
†14 Bruin . . . Noble (q.q.v.)
15 Nolans
489.13 E. Obiit Nolan
490.7-8,26-27 Nolan . . . Mr Nolan . . . Mr Nobru . . . Mr Anol
†503.34-35 Browne's . . . Nolan's— with W. J. Browne (q.v.)
520.17-18 Brown . . . Anlone
522.32,34 psychoanolised . . . broons
567.22-23 brigadier-general Nolan . . . buccaneer-admiral Browne
569.32 Senior Nowno and Senior Brolano
†587.36 Jocko Nowlong—with Jibbo Nolan (q.v.)
588.13 brown
599.23 Browne . . . Noland

*Browne, Mother–probably refers to the song "Knees Up, Mother Brown". 144.31.

Browne, Peter (1665-1735)–Bishop of Cork and Ross. He engaged in a theological dispute with Berkeley (q.v.). Archbishop George Browne was the first protestant to occupy the see of Dublin. 76.29; 537.6.

Browne, W. J.–author of *Botany for Schools*, 1881, published by Browne and Nolan. †503.34— with Browne and Nolan (q.v.).

Browning, Elizabeth Barrett– English poetess.?132.9-10; 171.14.

Browning, Robert (1812-89)–English poet. †351.1–with Browne and Nolan (q.v.); 467.9.

Bruce, Edward and Robert–Scottish national heroes, conducted an expedition to Ireland in 1327. 108.14; 596.15.

Bruin–bear in the Reynard (q.v.) cycle. See also Man Servant, Brian Boru.   †488.14—with Browne and Nolan (q.v.).

*Bruisanose, 125.20.

Brummell, Beau (1778-1840)–English man of fashion. 322-323; ?491.21.

Bruni, Leonardo (1369-1444) Italian scholar, wrote a history of Florence.   †373.16—with Browne and Nolan (q.v.).

Bruno, Giordano (1548-1600)– Italian philosopher, born near Nola, burned as a heretic. I have not read his philosophy, but his doctrine of the identity of opposites is said to be important to FW. He is, of course, comprehended in every Browne and Nolan (q.v.) reference. 117.12; 246.32; 287.24; †336.35—with St Bruno (q.v.); †369.8—with St Bruno; 424.36.

Bruno, St (1030-1101)–founder of the Carthusians. †336.35—with Bruno, Browne and Nolan (q.q.v.); †369.8—with Bruno.

Brushwood Boy or George Cottar, hero of Kipling's story. He loves a girl named Annieandlouise; they dream true and meet at Lily Lock, "lost in the world's fourth dimension". †112.3-4— with Beckett (q.v.).

*Bruton–Bruno? 595.18.

Brutus or Brute–legendary founder of Britain, great-grandson of Aeneas (q.v.), subject of *The Brut* by Layamon (q.v.). 60.26 (*bis*); 254.5; 292.note 2; 359.17; 451.24.

Brutus and Cassius–Romans who conspired against Julius Caesar (q.v.), characters in Shakespeare's (q.v.) *Julius Caesar*. In FW they are Shaun and Shem (q.v.), and not so much conspirators as rivals (Burrus-Butter and Caseous-Cheese) for the affections of Mar-

garine, a cleopatrician (q.q.v.). The Burrus-Caseous episode is a burlesque Shavian (q.v.) preface. 161-168, *passim*; 278.left margin; †281.15-16—with Cassio (q.v.); 366.25-26; 568.8; 620.28.

Bryant and May make most British matches. 80.2.

Bryllars, Llewellys ap–see Lévy-Bruhl.

*Bryne, 595.5.

Bubble, Madam–wicked temptress in *The Pilgrim's Progress*. See Stand-fast. 273.7.

Buccas–see Bacchus. 378.3.

Buccleuch, Dukes of–Scottish ducal family. Maybe the duke in *The Lay of the Last Minstrel* is indicated.†346.20—with Buckley.

Buchan, Alexander (1829-1907)– British meteorologist who stated that certain dates were "cold spots". 81.13.

?Buck, Sir George–Elizabethan censor. 412.35.

Buckingham, Duke of–since the name is played on in a quotation from Shakespeare's *Richard III* (q.q.v.), it is natural to assume this is the Buckingham of that play; but the pun also takes in Francis Bacon (q.v.) who toadied to James I's (q.v.) favorite, George Villiers, Duke of Buckingham. Identification is further complicated by the fact that the vintner in the quotation may be that sad fellow, Mr Davenant (q.v.). †318.21—with Bacon and Ham (q.q.v.).

Buckle–mostly Buckley (q.v.), but may include H. T. Buckle (1821-62), English historian. At the time of the Parnell (q.v.) Commission, a Buckle edited *The Times.* 346.24.

Buckley and the Russian General–according to Mr Ellmann, p. 411, this was a story John Joyce (q.v.) told: "Buckley . . . was an Irish soldier in the Crimean War who drew a bead on a Russian general, but when he observed his splendid epaulettes and decorations, he could not bring himself to shoot. After a moment, alive to his duty, he raised his rifle again, but just then the general let down his pants to defecate. The sight of his enemy in so helpless and human a plight was too much for Buckley, who again lowered his gun. But when the general prepared to finish the operation with a piece of grassy turf, Buckley lost all respect for him and fired." Joyce went on to make the turf Irish and the general insulting Ireland.

To know a source of Joyce's is not to understand what he does with it. Since Buckley melts into Berkeley (q.v.), it is fair to assume that he slays the material universe. But who exactly is Buckley? He starts out being one of the twins and is merciful; then he changes into the other twin (344.8-12) and is not merciful. I think this means he is first Shem (q.v.), then Shaun—see Justius and Mercius—but I am not sure. Who is the Russian General? The Russian General is a tyrant and father figure, object of all parricide.

The following—scattered and disjointed—have occasionally to do with Buckley. In German *der Buckel* means "the hunchback"— the adjective is *bucklig*. "Buckley's Chance" is an Australian expression meaning "a very remote chance". To the Irish "buckshot" suggested "Buckshot" Foster, an Irish secretary who told his soldiers, "Don't hesitate to shoot" (see *Ulysses*, 185/239-240). I think that all the many "bucks" in FW probably tie on to Buckley, and I think "buck" likely to suggest Buck Mulligan (q.v.) to Joyce. In German *einen Bock schiessen* (literally "to shoot a buck") means to make a blunder. The answer to the vexing question of who struck

Buckley has been discovered by Mr Atherton: Buckley struck himself without knowing it. "Who struck Buckley?" became a cant phrase, used to annoy 19th century Irishmen. See O'Dunnochoo, Butt and Taff, Billy Budd.

11.26 bucklied
42.11 bouckaleens shout their roscan generally
49.8 Blanco Fusilovna Bucklovitch
50.31 the General
81.35 general Boukeleff
101.15,19,20-21 Buckley . . . Buckleyself . . . Russian generals . . . Buckley
105.21-22 Buckling Shut at Rush in January
116.6-7 Gemral . . . Bulsklivism
137.13-14 buckshotbackshattered
138.14 buckeley
192.2-3 bulkily . . . Ructions gunorrhal
220.15 rudskin gunerally
221.36 Buckley
258.5 buncskleydoodle
272.8 buckets
†290.note 7 bookley . . . rusin's
†292.note 1 Buickley . . . Rudge engineral—with Buick and Barnaby Rudge (q.q.v.)
†312.29 Burklley—with Berkeley, Burke and Hare (q.q.v.)
?314.32 bouchal
†335.13-14,20 Bullyclubber burgherly . . . rush in general . . . rawshorn generand — with Burghley (q.v.)
337.34 rucks on Gereland
†338.2-3 Burghley . . . rackushant Germanon — with Burghley (q.v.)
†340.26-27 bulchrichudes . . . roshashanaral—with Rose (q.v.)
341.5,6-7,29-30 Buckily buckily . . . Rumjar Journaral . . . Backlegs . . . racing kenneldar
†346.11-12,20-21,24 Burkeley's . . . ructiongetherall . . .

Buccleuch — rosing girnirilles . . . Buckle —with Burke, Berkeley, Buccleuch, Rose, Buckle (q.q.v.)

†349.20-21 Popey O'Donoshough . . . jesuneral of the russuates—with Jesus

350.6 ruttengenerously . . . blucky

352.1,30,33 urssian gemenal . . . buckbeshottered . . . fourstar Russkakruscam

†354.34-35 budly . . . rising germinal . . . bodley . . . badley—with Budd (q.v.)

†361.25 budkley—with Budd (q.v.)

†365.6-7 Bacchulus . . . rousing gutteral—with Bacchus (q.v.)

368.8 bungley . . . rising gianerant

†372.6-7 butly . . . rouged engenerand—with Butt (q.v.)

†375.23-24 Don Gouverneur Buckley's . . . Rhutian Jhanaral—with Donal Buckley (q.v.)

376.24 bunkledoodle

388.33-34 Bockleyshuts the rahjahn gerachknell

390.2,4 burglar he shoved the wretch in churneroil . . . Lagener (anagram of General)

†391.31 general of the Berkeleyites—with Berkeley (q.v.)

†423.32-33 Berkeley . . . reason generously — with Berkeley (q.v.)

444.18 backly
445.20 bulkier
447.24 Baughkley
471.19-20,22 region's general . . . bouchal
518.25 Bucclis
530.2 buckleybackers
536.15 buckely
†610.1,12-13 Bulkily . . . burkeley

. . . Eurasian Generalissimo—with Berkeley (q.v.)

†611.2,4,5,27 bookley . . . bullocky . . . Balkelly . . . Bilkilly-Belkelly — see Bill

612.32 Bilkilly - Belkelly - Balkally

†620.4 buckly . . . Rosensharonals—with Rose (q.v.)

622.25 Bugley

Buckley, Donal–last governor-general of Ireland. Thus, like HCE (q.v.) in I,ii, Buckley is both tyrant and rebel. †375.23—with Buckley (q.v.).

Budd, Billy–hero of Herman Melville's (q.v.) novel. Billy or "Beauty" or "Baby" Budd is foretopman in a British man-of-war in 1797; he is radiantly good, beautiful, and tenderly loved by his shipmates—in short, an almost perfect natural man in Rousseau's sense. (Joyce echoes and parodies Melville's description of Billy in the long paragraph on 234, where Billy is Shaun, q.v.) Billy has, however, a mark of the fallen, "an organic hesitancy—in fact more or less of a stutter or even worse", which comes on him in moments of crisis. He has also an enemy in one of the ship's officers, John "Jimmy Legs" Claggart who is the naturally depraved man of Calvinism. Claggart falsely accuses Billy of mutiny and, rendered dumb by his stutter, Billy strikes Claggart dead with a single, unmeant blow. Captain Vere (q.v.) as divine justice, acquits Billy: as human justice, he hangs him. See Buckley, Butt, Buddha. Rose? 21.8-9; †25.25—with Buddha (q.v.); 95.36; †100. 7-8—with Buddha and Abel (q.q.v.); †234.14—with Buddha; 236.14—see Billy; 309.32; †329.3, 14; 337.16.21,24,26,32,36—see Billy, Will, Ulick Dean; †338.13-14—with Buddha (q.v.); 340.11;

†346.26—with Huck Finn (q.v.); 346.31-34; ?350.22; †354.34-35 —with Buckley (q.v.); 355.8,13; †361.25—with Buckley; 445.7; †485.16—with Paddy Riley (q.v.); †544.24—with Buddha; †620.3— with Buddha (q.v.).

Buddha–see Gautama.

Budgen, Frank–painter, friend of Joyce's, author of *James Joyce and the Making of "Ulysses".* ?376.4.

Buffalo Bill or William Cody (1846-1917)–Indian fighter, wild-west showman. 118.7.

*****Buggaloffs,** journeyall–possibly Vasily Buslaevitch (q.v.) who did go "Jerusalemfaring in Arssia Manor". 26.3-4.

*****Bugle** and Bitch, 379.4.

Buick–American automobile. †292. note 1—with Buckley (q.v.).

Bulkeley, Miss–probably Anna Livia (q.v.) because she conquers the Norwegian Captain (q.v.) as Buckley (q.v.) conquers the Russian General. This is the more likely since Mrs Bulkley played Kate Hardcastle (q.v.) in Goldsmith's (q.v.) *She Stoops to Conquer.* 327.26.

Bulkeley, Bishop Lancelot–17th century Archbishop of Dublin. †435.11—with Berkeley.

Bull, Bully–see Bill? The Bulls are two great wastes of sand on the north and south of Dublin Bay. They roar with the surf. "Bull" in Irish is "tarb", pronounced "tarf" as in Clontarf or "Bull's Meadow".

Bull, John–England's Uncle Sam. †99.32-33—with O'Roarke; †138.17—with Ivan the Terrible (q.v.); 366.20.

Buller, C. F.–19th century cricketer. 584.8.

*****Bullingdon**–see Wellington. 333. 18.

*****Bulljon** Brossbrute–maybe John Bull (q.v.). 255.13.

*****Bunnicombe,** prince of, 254.35.

*****Bunting,** Captive–a Bunting wrote *Ancient Music of Ireland,* Dublin, 1890. 607.28.

Burbage, Richard (1567-1619)–the man who first acted Shakespeare's (q.v.) tragic heroes, including Hamlet and Richard III (q.q.v.) —see *Ulysses,* 199/258. †134.11— with Richard III; ?539.21.

Burbank, Mr–not, I think, Luther, but Eliot's (q.v.) "Burbank with a Baedeker: Bleistein with a Cigar". 64.31.

*****Burgaans,** Le King of the–Plato's leaking barrel? 72.3.

Burgess, Charles (Cathal Brugha) –IRA leader, Irish statesman. See also Moore and Burgess, which double with all these references. †62.30; 130.12—with Borgia (q.v.); 516.32.

*****Burgess,** Peter, 277.10.

Burghley, 1st Baron, William Cecil (1520-98)–Elizabethan statesman, Bacon's (q.v.) uncle. ?257.10,17; †335.13—with Buckley (q.v.); †338.2-3—with Buckley; ?362.3; 511.24.

*****Burgley,** Davy or Titus–see David, Titus Andronicus. 70.14.

*****Burke**–see Three. 343.3.

Burke, Edmund (1729-97)–British statesman, political writer, born in Dublin. Some of the following references may be to other Burkes. ?5.35; †64.23—see Three Musketeers; ?106.6; 256.11-12; 303.6; 503.36; 542.19; 588.30.

Burke and Hare–Edinburgh resurrectionists, natives of Ireland. See Knox. 443.16; 580.31-32.

Burke, John (1787-1848)–as in *Burke's Peerage,* Dublin born. 71.30; 235.13.

*****Burke,** Philip's, 420.29.

Burke, Thomas Henry–permanent undersecretary for Ireland who, with Lord Frederick Cavendish, was murdered by the Invincibles in Phoenix (q.v.) Park in 1882. *Tom Burke of Ours* is a novel of Lever's (q.v.). 106.6; 132.33.

Burk-Lee–see Berkeley. 330.17.

*****Burleigh,** Farmer–see Barley. Burghley? 257.17.

Burns, Robert (1759-96)–Scottish poet. 204.6; 248.35; 520.26.

*****Burroman,** Dr–probably Burrus (q.v.). 163.35.

Burrus and Caseous–Butter and Cheese—see Brutus and Cassius.

Burtt, Sir Edwin Arthur–author of *The Metaphysical Foundations of Modern Physical Science.* 293. note 2.

Bury, J. B.–19th century historian, author of *The Life of St Patrick* (q.v.), which Joyce used in FW. 291.11.

*****Burymeleg,** 11.6.

Buschmann, J. C. E.–collected world-wide forms of "father" and "mother". 207.34.

Bushe, Charles Kendal–legal light of 19th century Dublin, author of *Cease Your Funning.* 256.12; 586.11.

*****Bushe,** Peganeen, 331.10.

Bushmills–Irish whisky and town. 357.4; 521.15; 577.21.

Buslaevitch, Vasily–hero of Russian ballad cycle of Novgorod. See Buggaloffs. 5.5.

Butcher and Baker–most often and most simply, Abel and Cain (q.v.), the meatman and the vegetarian; but HCE (q.v.) occasionally seems to be both. Some references include Shakespeare (q.v.), the butcher-boy (see *Ulysses*, 185/239) and Bacon-baken (q.v.). See also Fleischmann, Baxter. 7.10; 41.13; 50.1; 63.16; 64.18; 67.15; 70.11; 80.8; 90.2; 136.4; 144.30; 172.5,7; 190.5; 212.20; 213.26; 257.19,22; 265.note 5; 290.27; 315.1; 320. 29; 338.9; 351.19; 406.2; 422.3; 491.28; 498.20; 518.12,13; 600.29; 603.6; 607.12.

Butler–family famous in Irish history. In 1328 they became Irish earls with the title of Ormond (q.v.). I think one or more "Butlers" refers to the two Samuel Butlers. †12.4—with Butt (q.v.); 118.5; 372.7; 385.15; 519. 5-6.

?**Butler,** Samuel (1835-1902) English writer, author of *The Way of All Flesh.* 189.8.

*****Butt** and Hocksett's, 529.17.

*****Butt** and Taff—names adopted by Shaun and Shem (q.v.) in the TV skit "Buckley and the Russian General" (q.v.). They make up one of the major themes of FW and I wish I knew why. Butt has something to do with Isaac Butt and Billy Budd (q.q.v.), Taff is, of course, David (q.v.), and Taffy was a Welshman. See Butter. See Bottom? †3.22,23—with Isaac Butt (q.v.); 6.7—Isaac Butt and Herbert (q.q.v.); 7.12-13; †8.7,23 —with David (q.v.); 10.1; 11.19, 25; 12.4,11,23; 13.14; 16.16,20, 22; 23.32; 34.17; 35.27,34; 42.7; 45.4; 48.29-30; 65.31; 70.14; 71.13; †85.15—with Isaac Butt (q.v.); †87.24—with Mutt and Jute (q.v.); 88.35,36; 96.11; 100. 15,17; 106.33; 124.1 (*bis*); 130.13; 135.34; 145.7,14; 148.1; 169.14- 18; †172.26—see David; †177.20, 29—with Browne and Nolan (q.v.); 186.29; 188.29; 191.28,36; 192.9,11-12; 196.18,21,34; 211. 15,32; 221.6,11; 225.17,21; 249. 29; 268.26,left margin; 271.19; 272.6,7,8; 277.11; 288.20; 291.24; 302.10,11; 306.note 1; 309.13; 310.34; 311.8; 312.7; 313.31; 315.1,12,32; 316.18,19; 320.23,29; 334.6,15; †337.3,32-36—with Budd, Flavin, Dunne (q.q.v.); †338.9,12-13,16—with Budd, Adam (q.q.v.); 339.20; 340.31-32; 341.16; †342.3,27,30-32—with Bottom (q.v.); 343.25; 346.36; 349.8,9; 354.9,33-36; †358.22— with Mookse and Mockturtle (q.q.v.); 359.11; †366.19—with Bickerstaff (q.v.); 369.1; 372.6,7;

374.19; 378.26,27; 419.27,33; 428.27; ?429.31; ?431.7; †433.25 —with Buttercup (q.v.); 434.24, 25; 440.30; †441.11-12—see Toffeelips; 444.17; 446.18; 451.19 —see David; 457.22; 458.24; ?459.3; †462.5,17,30— see David; 463.36—see David; †464.3,20— see David, Crozier; †464.36—see David, Davitt, David French; 478.8; 469.7; 471.17; ?483.24; †489.30—see Davitt, David; 492. 3,4; 494.24; 497.20; 509.28; 510. 19; ?517.2; 524.22,30; †525.35— with Herbert (q.v.); ?529.17; 530.2; 532.5; 533.35,36; 534.1; 536.4,14; 538.31,34; 539.19; 557. 10; 559.10,28; ?561.12—see Buttercup; ?562.7; ?567.10; 577.12; 580.32; ?581.33,34; 582.8; 593.18, 36; †594.12—with Bottom; †595. 7-8,9—with Elizabeth (q.v.); 598. 21,22; 603.7,13; ?604.4; 605.2; 616.29,36; †607.36—with Gladstone (q.v.); 610.35,36; 615.31; †624.2,17-18; 625.17,18.

Butt, Isaac (1813-79)–Irish nationalist leader. Because of his caution, Parnell (q.v.) ousted him as head of the Irish party. One of the bridges across the Liffey (q.v.) is Butt Bridge. It is extremely hard to disentangle him from Butt (q.v.). †3.23—with Isaac (q.v.); †6.7—with Herbert (q.v.); 85.15; 254.13; 421.4.

Butter and Cheese are Brutus and Cassius. Butter presumably melts to Butt (q.v.).

Butter, Nathaniel, registered and published *King Lear* (q.v.) in 1608. 356.22.

Buttercup, Little–of *Pinafore*. She mixed those children up—see FW 21.33. 145.14; 321.16; 428.27; 561.12.

?Button Moulder–"character" in *Peer Gynt* (q.v.). 18.8.

Buvard–see Bouvard.

Buylan–see Byron, Boylan.

Bygmester and variations–see Masterbuilder.

Byng, General–with Wellington (q.v.) at Waterloo. 8.12.

Byrne, Alfy–mayor of Dublin, friend of John Joyce (q.v.). 568.32.

*Byrnes–maybe Davy Byrne's pub in *Ulysses*, maybe J. F. Byrne, the original of Cranly in *Portrait of the Artist*. 51.29; 289.13.

*Byrns, 455.2, 586.11.

Byron, George Gordon, Lord (1788-1824)–English poet. All references to him may double with Biron (q.v.). 91.3; †435.10—with Boylan (q.v.); 465.17; 563.12.

Byron, Henry James (1834-84)–author of plays, including *Our Boys*, a domestic drama which ran for 1,362 performances in London. †41.16—with Biron (q.v.).

Bywaters and Thompson–defendants in a British murder trial of the 1920s. If Mr Atherton is right and Joyce does name all his sources, these people are in FW (103.12?), for a letter of Mrs Thompson's to Bywaters, a sailor, is echoed 226.8-9, 232.25: "This time really will be the last you will go away—like things are, won't it? We said it before, darlint . . . I'm telling you—if things are the same again then I'm going with you—wherever it is if it's to sea I am coming too —and if it's to nowhere—I'm also coming, darlint. . . ." Frazer says the forsaken sweetheart or bride is common in May Day festivities.

C

*Cabbanger, Archdukon–see Coppinger. 71.35.

*Cabler, Negoist–seems to be Shem (q.v.) and to tie onto Capel (q.v.). 488.21.

Cabot, John (1450-98)–Italian navigator who discovered Newfoundland for England. His son Sebastian (1476-1557) was also a voyager. †312.8—with Thor and Mendoza (q.q.v.); 315.22; 512.18.

*Cad with a pipe–a man who accosted John Joyce (q.v.) in Phoenix Park. James Joyce says somewhere that the meeting between his father and the Cad is the basis of FW. (Joycean remarks of this sort are likely to be, in the popular sense of the term, jesuitical.) The Cad seems, at various times to be Beggar, Caddy, Gilly, Magrath (q.q.v.). 3.23; 14.12; 35.11; 38.9; 54.20; 88.13; 101.21; 127.7; 145.10; 167.8; 178.2; 220.26; 270.7; 303.29; 332.25; 341.1; 358.2,9; 420.6; 511.32; 518.12; 520.10,21; 534.26; †587.7—with Cadbury; 588.10; 618.3; 624.1; 625.6.

Cadbury–English chocolate and cocoa. 193.15; †587.7—with Cad (q.v.).

Cadderpollard, Mr Lhugewhite–see Oscar Wilde, Mr W. H. 350.11.

*Caddy and Primas–may be Shem and Shaun (q.v.) as Cadet and First Born—see Cad, Jacob and Esau (q.q.v.). Caddy may owe something to caddi, "I fell" as in Inferno, III, 136. I read the entry 14.11-15 this way: Primas shot ("drilled") all decent people, meaning his father, HCE (q.v.), while Caddy attacked his father with words, made mock of him. In other words, Caddy goes on to be Hosty (q.v.), Primas to be Buckley (q.v.). See Santry. 14.12-13; 69.17-18; 101.35; ?405.14;

623.32; 624.1. (In this last entry the twins' roles are reversed.)

Cadenus–anagram of Decanus or Deacon, used by Swift (q.v.) in "Cadenus and Vanessa", a poem which describes his relations with Vanessa (q.v.). ?55.30; 413.27; 624.26.

Cadman–see Caedmon. 113.20.

Cadmus–King of Phoenicia, brother of Europa (q.v.), inventor of agriculture, the alphabet, etc. 307.left margin.

Cadwan, Cadwallon and Cadwalloner–kings of ancient Wales. 152.6.

?Caedmon (fl. 670)–Anglo-Saxon poet. 113.20.

Caesar–see Julius.

*Cahills–Dublin printers? 44.8.

Cain and Abel–sons of Adam and Eve (q.v.), first murderer and his victim, vegetarian and meateater, characters in the old mystery plays. Shem (q.v.) is Cain, Shaun is Abel. See also Seth, Jacob and Esau, Butcher and Baker, Kane.

5.30	abbles
16.24,31	wiseable . . . coyne
†28.19	kanekannan and abbely —with Concannen (q.v.)
29.28	cane
41.3	able
47.last line	able . . . Cain
59.10	uncained
61.28,29	fablings . . . Can
†62.15-16	franchisables—with Frank (q.v.)
†63.7,9,16,29	Kane . . . able . . . Abelbody . . . peaceablest—with Kane (q.v.)
†64.9,10	Mullingcan Inn . . . babel—with Mulligan, Canaan (q.q.v.)
71.13	Cainandabler
83.15,21	coctable . . . keenest
99.14	kaind

101.15 cainozoic
102.2-3 keen . . . able
106.33 Caines
121.11 cainapple
154.31,36 connow . . . abler
159.14 fables . . . "keen"
193.32 Cain
201.33 cane . . . abbles
211.29-30 Karmalite Kane (see Kane)
†237.34 Abel—with Abelard (q.v.)
?273.left margin Kine
275.20 crime and fable
283.13-14 tables . . . chains
287.11-12 cain . . . able
†289.4,5 veritably . . . esoupcans —with Esau, Aesop (q.q.v.)
9 beam . . . cable
303.21,32 able . . . misocain
†305.11,18,19 culpable . . . Old Keane . . . jubalee Keane—with Kean and Jubal Cain (q.v.)
307.left margin Cain
336.13 keen and able
362.5 Camnabel
374.33 Cainfully
?391.33 Cailcainnin
410.30,33 able . . . able
416.3 abelboobied
419.34 crime and libel
421.5 Kainly
424.28 cane
427.19 able
436.35 cancan
446.29 Abelite (the Abelites were a 4th century Christian sect that lived continent and adopted children)
448.3 Kane (q.v.)
†455.6 a bail—with Baal (q.v.)
18,21 Kain . . . abel
490.34-35 a bull
491.1,16 a bull . . . Ebell Teresa Kane (q.v.)
516.23 kanes (q.v.)
536.27 Kanes (q.v.)
560.36 hable
583.28-29 Cainmaker's
†584.2 abbels—with Robert Abel (q.v.)

Cairnes, John Elliot (1823-75)– Irish political economist. 594.24; 604.6.

Cairpre, King–several legendary Irish kings, one an enemy of St Patrick (q.v.). 390.35.

Caius–see Gracchi. 128.15.

Caius, Pope (283-96). 282.29.

*****Calaman,** Aratar, 59.24.

*****Calavera**–may just mean "hot-head". 255.14.

Caliban–servant monster, dispos-sessed heir in Shakespeare's (q.v.) *The Tempest.* His name is usually explained as an anagram of "cannibal", or as having to do with gipsy *cauliban* or "black"— see Ham. FW 193 echoes the opening of *Ulysses,* p. 8/6, where Mulligan (q.v.) shows Stephen (q.v.) his face in a mirror and quotes *Dorian Gray*: "The rage of Caliban at not seeing his face in a mirror." The "Mutt and Jute" (q.v.) episode (FW 16-18) is partly based on Caliban's inter-views with Stephano and Trin-culo (q.v.). It must be remem-bered that Sir Sidney Lee (q.v.) makes much of Caliban being an American Indian; Joyce makes him a Utah (16.10). Caliban is identified with the Man Servant (q.v.). 193.32; 600.1.

Caligula–Roman emperor. 4.23; 60.26; 237.12.

Calomnequiller–see St Columkill. 50.9-10.

Calvin, John (1509-64)–Genevan re-former and divine. 519.26.

Calypso nymph in the *Odyssey,* episode in *Ulysses.* 229.13; 613.17.

*****Camac,** Zusan–the Camac is one of Dublin's rivers. See Susanna? 212.8.

Cambrensis, Giraldus (1146-1220) –Welsh churchman who accom-panied Prince John to Ireland in 1184, wrote *Topographia Hiber-nica.* 151.31-32; 573.21.

Cambronne, General (1770-1842)–
one of Napoleon's (q.v.) generals
who said *merde* in public. 9.27;
134.8; 352.21-22; 421.13-14.

*****Camellus,** 90.18.

*****Camhelsson,** Fjorgn, 124.29.

*****Camilla,** Dromilla, Ludmilla,
Mamilla–Camilla and Mamilla are
heroines of Robert Greene's (q.v.).
211.8.

Camille–Marguerite Gautier, heroine of *La Dame aux Camélias* by
Dumas *fils.* 334.17; 432.21.

*****Campbell,** 343.3.

*****Campbell,** Cacao, 73.10.

*****Campdens,** 517.22.

Canaan the Hateful–After Ham
(q.v.) had seen Noah (q.v.) naked,
Noah said, "Cursed be Canaan; a
servant of servants shall he be
unto his brethren" (Gen. 9).
Canaan means "low region"
which accounts in part for all the
"lows" in "Shem the Penman"
(q.v.). †64.8-9 (pig . . . Mullingcan Inn)—with Mulligan, Cain
(q.q.v.); 264.9-10.

*****Canavan** of Canmakenoise (Clon-
macnoise) – 31.21-22. Irish *o*
ceanndhubhain is black head,
ceannbhan is white head (see
Finn): both are anglicized as
"Canavan".

*****Canby**–American critic? 48.21.

*****Canicula** (the dog star), said to
be the wife of Mauritius (q.v.).
573.30.

Cannily–see James Connolly.

*****Cannmatha,** 329.14-15.

*****Cannon,** Sir–I guess that Joyce
plays on military, legal and
musical canons. He illustrates the
latter 222.5-6, and in all FW.
104.21.

Cantelman–as in Wyndham
Lewis's (q.v.) *Cantelman's Spring
Mate.* 165.24; 172.6; 236.7.

Canter, Manoel–see Kant. 440.17. .

Cantrell and Cochrane–Dublin sup-
pliers of mineral water, made
from the water of St Patrick's
(q.v.) well. 137.7-8.

Canute or Cnut, King (995-1035)–
king of Denmark and England.
He could not persuade the sea to
retire. ?84.23; 139.5; 512.16-17;
†520.23—Connaught, see Four.

Canwyll y Cymry–see Pritchard.
464.6.

*****Cape**–perhaps Jonathan Cape,
publishers. 573.33.

Capel–a Dublin street. *Capal* is
Irish for "horse". See Arthur
Capel, Earl of Essex.

*****Capellisato**–see Essex? 255.1.

Capet, Hugh–king of the Franks,
elected 987. †197.8–with HCE
(q.v.); 369.31-32 (who goes . . .
cupital).

*****Capilla,** Rubretta and Melcamo-
milla, 492.13.

Capponi, Gino, Marquis (1792-
1876)–Italian statesman and historian who made a vast collection
of documents for a history of the
Church. 155.35.

Caractacus–British chieftain who
resisted the Roman invaders,
48-51, but was finally captured
and sent to Rome. 54.4; 518.22;
617.14.

*****Caramis**–see Three Musketeers.
64.23.

*****Carberry**–possibly Cairpre (q.v.).
Possibly Carbery—3rd century
Irish king who defeated the
Fianna at Gabhra, sending, as it
were, Ossian (q.v.) into banish-
ment in fairyland. 228.18.

Carbo–noted Roman family that
supported the plebeians. 232.3.

*****Carchingarri,** Cardinal–see Mark
Lyons. 180.14.

Cardigan, Earl of (1707-1868)–
English lieutenant-general in
charge of the Light Brigade at
Balaclava. 339.12.

Carême – French gastronome. 184.32.

Carey, Mother–in sailor's use, an anglicization of Mater Cara, an epithet of the Virgin (q.v.). Her chickens are the stormy petrels. 370.6.

Carlisle, A. Briggs–not a person but Carlisle Bridge across the Liffey (q.v.). 514.26.

Carlyle, Jane Welsh (1801-66)–wife of Thomas, subject of Landor's poem, "Jenny Kissed Me" which is faintly echoed here. †59.26— with Ginger Jane (q.v.).

Carlyle, Thomas (1795-1881)–English author. 517.22.

*Carme, Conte, 418.3.

Carmen–title and gipsy heroine of Bizet's opera. 448.12.

Carmen Sylva–pen-name of Queen Elizabeth of Rumania (1843-1916). See Carmen, Sylvia, Elizabeth. 360.13.

*Carminia–Carmen? 239.24.

Carolan–last of the Irish bards. Several people were. 369.9.

*Carprimustimus, 108.12-13.

*Carpulenta, Gygasta–fat woman with a big stomach? 99.9.

*Carr–private in *Ulysses?* 264.16.

Carr, Winnie–vinegar. See Carte. 279.note 1.

Carrison–see Carson. 532.1-2.

*Carroll, Barney, 285.note 2.

Carroll, Lewis (Charles Lutwidge Dodgson) (1832-98)–English mathematician, author of *Alice* (q.v.) *in Wonderland* and *Through the Looking-Glass.* In FW, Lewis Carroll usually represents an old man with lecherous feelings for a little girl. 57.26; 234.15, †20— with Kevin (q.v.); 294.7; 361.21 —with Lodewijk (q.v.); 374.2; 482.1; 501.36; †538.3—with Muggleton, Ludwig (q.q.v.); 601.16, 17.

Carson, Sir Edward (1854-1935)– Ulster politician, a schoolmate of Wilde's, who led for the other side at one of his trials. ?241.33; 532.1-2.

Carte, Richard D'Oyly (1844-1901) –producer of the most famous players of Gilbert and Sullivan's (q.v.) operas. 279.note 1; †574.1 —with Doyle and Owens (q.q.v.).

Carus, Marcus Aurelius–Roman emperor from 282-283, murdered like Vitellus (q.v.). †406.15—with Caruso (q.v.).

Caruso, Enrico (1873-1921)–Italian operatic tenor. †406.15—with Carus (q.v.).

Carver, George Washington (1864-1943)–American negro botanist. 78.35.

Casabianca, Louis (1755-98)– father of the boy on the burning deck, immortalized by Mrs Hemans (q.v.). 342.9.

Casanova (1725-98)–Italian lover and adventurer. See Casanuova. 230.15.

Casanuova, Mondamoiseau of–refers to Ann Hathaway (q.v.) and/ or her daughter(s). Ann was Mrs Bird (swan) of New Place, and a female Casanova, according to Stephen Dedalus (q.v.) in "Scylla and Charybdis". According to other commentators she was a Mademoiselle from Armentiers (q.v.) who hadn't been kissed in however many years. †230.14-15 —with Casanova (q.v.).

*Casemate, Lady Jales–maybe Roger Casement (q.v.). 387.22-23.

Casement, Sir Roger (1864-1916)— Irish rebel. I feel that Casement must be in FW rather than find him certainly there. Joyce must have been interested in his "Black Book", his Christansen (q.v.), etc. ?80.13; ?478.17; ?559.4.

Casey–"Comic Cuts" had a large panel called "Casey's Court", showing all kinds of capering, Mr

Atherton says. †286.9—with John Casey (q.v.).

Casey, John–mathematics professor at the Catholic University, Dublin, author of *Sequel to Euclid*. He was noted for his demonstrations of the circle. Mr Senn suggests that the "frost book" rings in Robert Frost who was published in England by J. Cape. 206.12; †286.9—see Casey above.

*Caspi, 256.35.

?Cassandra–Priam's (q.v.) prophetic daughter in the *Iliad*. 124.36 (Olecasandrum).

Cassels, Richard–German architect, brought to Dublin in 1727. He designed, among other buildings, Tyrone House, the Rotunda Hospital, the dining-hall and printing house of Trinity College and Leinster House. 552.11.

*Cassidy, 45.stanza 4; 87.15; 98.31.

Cassio–character in Shakespeare's *Othello* (q.q.v.). †281.16—with Cassius (q.v.).

Cassiodorus (490-585)–historian, statesman, monk. 255.21.

Cassius–see Brutus.

Cassivelaunus or Cassibellaum (Cassibelan in *Cymbeline*, q.v.)– ruler of the country north of the Thames, defeated by Julius Caesar (q.v.). 77.3.

Castlemallard, Lord–minor character in LeFanu's (q.v.) *The House by the Churchyard*. His agent, Nutter (q.v.) engages in a duel with Fireworker O'Flaherty (q.v.). 80.9.

Castlevillainous – see Cassivelaunus.

Castor and Pollux–twin sons of Leda (q.v.), brothers of Helen (q.v.) and Clytemnestra. 28.5-6; †229.31–with Caxton (q.v.); 307. left margin; 340.28; 418.23,24; †431-432—with Apollo (q.v.); 489.16.

Castorp, Hans–hero of Mann's (q.v.) *The Magic Mountain*. 310.20.

Castrucci–18th century violinist, brought to Dublin by Dr Bartholomew Mosse (q.v.) to play for the benefit of the Lying-in Hospital. 533.16.

Catherine II or the Great (1729-96) –Empress of Russia. *Great Catherine* is a playlet of Bernard Shaw's (q.v.). The reference may include Catherine of Aragon, Henry VIII's (q.v.) queen and a Shakespearean (q.v.) character. 498.12-13; 538.22.

Cathleen, Countess–title heroine of Yeats's (q.v.) play. She sells her soul to the devil to relieve the starving Irish. The Irish found this insulting and rioted at the Abbey Theatre. She is, of course, Cathleen ni Houlihan. 39.30; 189.11; ?239.21; 441.11; †448. 10—with Kate (q.v.).

Cathlin–girl who dies beautifully in "Cathlin of Clutha", one of the Ossian (q.v.) poems. 329.15.

*Cathmon-Carbery, 194.2.

Catilina, L. Sergius (108-62 B.C.)– Roman conspirator, unmasked by Cicero (q.v.). 307.left margin.

Cato, Marcus Porcius (234-149 B.C.) –Roman statesman and Orator. Young Cato is a character in Shakespeare's *Julius Caesar* (q.q.v.). 306.left margin.

Catullus, Gaius Valerius (84-54 B.C.)–Roman poet. ?111.20; 527.1.

Caudle, Mrs–her curtain lectures, by Douglas Jerrold appeared in *Punch*, 1845. To Joyce she is a synonym for a shrew—see Kate— *Ulysses*, 188/244. 271.11; 333.35; 415.14; 485.3.

*Caulofat's–maybe just "caliphate". 533.28.

Cavel, Edith (1865-1915)–English nurse, executed by the Germans. She said patriotism was not enough. 529.24.

*Caxons the Coswarn, 397.13.

Caxton, William (1422-91)–first English printer. †229.31 —with Castor (q.v.).

*Cecil, 33.3.

Cecilia, St–patron of music. There is a Cecilia Street, Dublin. 41.33; 230.9; 279.note 1; 354.14; 424.7.

Cedric Silkyshag–see Sitric. 16.34.

*Celeste, 232.16.

Celestine or Celestian–five popes. 154.20; 191.15.

Celia–girl in Shakespeare's (q.v.) *As You Like It.* In Arden she calls herself Aliena. See Rosaline, Jacques, Touchstone, Oliver, Lang, Greenwood. 147.11; †526.32,35—with Alice (q.v.).

Cerf, Bennett–as editor of Random House published the first legal American edition of *Ulysses*, subsequently a professional humorist. 113.11.

*Cerisia Cerosia, 128.14.

*Cernilius, 228.34.

?Cervantes, Miguel de (1547-1616) –Spanish novelist, thought to have written *Don Quixote* (q.v.), though many Baconians (q.v.) claim it for Shakespeare (q.v.). 174.11.

Chamberlain, Joseph (1836-1914) –British politician, wrecked Home Rule, may have been behind Captain O'Shea (q.v.). 129.25.

Chambers, Sir E. K.–author of *The Elizabethan Stage* (1923) and *William Shakespeare* (1930), author, in this last work, of a sentence which should not slip into oblivion: "We cannot, I think, ascribe to Shakespeare that rigid propriety of sexual conduct, the absence of which in more modern poets it has too often been the duty of their family biographers to conceal." 105.4.

Chambers, Ephraim (d. 1740)– English encyclopaedist. 334.2.

Chance, Charley–Dubliner, original of McCoy in *Ulysses*. Mr Ellmann suggests that Joyce combined him with "Mr Hunter" (q.v.) to make up the character of Bloom (q.v.). 65.16.

*Chandler–maybe the protagonist of Joyce's "A Little Cloud". 64.19; 542.33.

Chantacler or Chanticleer–cock in the Reynard (q.v.) cycle, "The Nun's, Priest's Tale", etc. The German rendering of a cock's crow is *kikeriki* ("kikkery key"). See Partlet. 584.21.

Chantry, Sir Francis (1782-1841)– English sculptor, made the statue of Grattan (q.v.) in Dublin. 533.16.

Chapelizod–environ of Dublin on the Liffey (q.v.). Its name is popularly derived from the chapel or tower of Isolde of Ireland (q.v.), hence all references to it are references to Issy (q.v.), who is the Chapel Perilous of the Grail Quest of FW.
    HCE's (q.v.) inn is in Chapelizod and parallels Shakespeare's (q.v.) Globe, likewise situated in an environ of a great city and on the city's river.

Chaplin, Charlie–English comedian. 166.14; 351.13; 467.26.

Charis, Charissima–in Greek myth the personification of grace and beauty, later any one of the three graces (q.v.). 561.22.

Charlemagne (742-814)–Holy Roman emperor, king of the Franks. 280.28; 310.20; 334.36; 338.26,32.

Charles II (1630-85)–king of England, known as the Merry Monarch. 138.33; 525.16-17; 539.22.

Charles III (879-929)—king of France, called "the Simple". †291.note 8—with Parnell (q.v.).

Charles, Martel (688-714)–Frankish ruler, grandfather of Charlemagne (q.v.). †63.33—with Ham; †64.13 —with Ham; 73.12.

Charley's Aunt–title and "character" in a long popular play. 183.27.

***Charlie,** 16.5; 271.left margin; 443.18.

***Charlotte–**Mr Wilder suggests Bernard Shaw's (q.v.) wife. As Lottie she surely has to do with Lot (q.v.). 59.12; 60.4-5; †62.34— with Lotta Crabtree (q.v.); 101.3; 113.16; 191.18; 238.2; 352.6; 434.15; †504.28—with Darwin; 561.15; 587.28.

***Charmadouiro,** La, 327.4.

Charmian and Iras–attendants on the queen in Shakespeare's *Antony and Cleopatra* (q.q.v.). 20.3; 527.18; 528.23.

Charon–ferryman of the Styx. †496.32—with Le Caron (q.v.).

Chart, D. A.–author of the book on Dublin in the Medieval Town Series. Joyce used it extensively. 541.4; 545.14; 551.32; 566.15; 593.31; 603.22.

***Charterhouse,** Elder, 137.21.

Chase, Charlie–American movie comedian. 494.15.

***Chattaway,** Mr I. I., 369.9.

Chatterton, Thomas (1752-70)– fabricator of the Rowley (q.v.) poems. See also *Ulysses,* 123/157. 573.34.

Chaucer, Geoffrey (1340-1400)– English poet. 245.35.

***Cheek, Doctor**–perhaps Sir John Cheke (1514-57), classical scholar, zealous protestant who was forced to embrace Rome and died of shame. 140.30.

***Cheekee**–see the above? 155.35.

Cheekspeer – see Shakespeare. 257.20.

***Cheels,** 106.19.

Cheops–pharaoh who built the Great Pyramid. 62.21; 553.10.

Chesterfield, Philip Dormer Stanhope, 4th Earl of (1694-1773)–the letter man. He was an excellent

lord-lieutenant of Ireland, beautified Phoenix (q.v.) Park by planting elms and erecting the Phoenix Monument in 1745. He also had much to do with promoting the "new style" of calendaring. 164.17 (chest of vialds); 553.19.

Chickspeer – see Shakespeare, Biddy Doran. 145.24.

***Chiggenchugger's,** 379.3.

Childe, Harold–title hero of Byron's (q.v.) poem. 423.8.

Childeric–three Frankish kings, the third was the last of the Merovingian dynasty. Chilperic—one Burgundian, two Frankish kings. 4.32.—see Eggbirth.

Childers, Hugh Culling Eardley (1827-96)–British M.P. for Pontefract, member of several of Gladstone's cabinets, supporter of Home Rule. See HCE, see Here Comes Everybody. †4.32—with HCE (q.v.); 32.18-19; 213.30-31; 481.22; 535.34; 598.36.

Childs, Samuel–tried in Dublin in 1899 for murdering his brother, Thomas, acquitted. 246.21.

***Chimepiece,** Mista–HCE as Master Humphrey's (q.q.v.) clock? 590.11.

Chimera–in Greek legend, monster with three heads, lion, goat, dragon. 67.8.

***Chimneys,** H. E. 141.20.

***Chimpden**–see HCE. There is no star in front of this in the first edition, but I realize I do not know why Chimpden, unless to remind us of our kinfolk the apes.

Chipps, Mr–schoolmaster in Hilton's novel. 371.11.

Chloe–Daphnis and Chloe,* a Greek pastoral romance, translated by George Moore (q.v.) in 1924. *Tale of Chloe,* novel by Meredith. Pope (q.v.) uses the name in "Moral Essays" to indicate Lady Suffolk, mistress of George II. 236.1.

Chopin, Frederic (1810-49)–Polish composer. 56.15; 582.28.

*Chrestien the Last, 245.28,29.

Chris-na-Murty–made up of Krishna, Jesus, Mary, Krisanamurti (q.q.v.). 472.15.

?Christansen, Adler – valet and Lord Alfred Douglas (q.v.) to Roger Casement (q.v.). 53.4.

Christies–London auction place. 130.31.

Christy Minstrels – black-faced troupe which came from America to London in 1857. Moore and Burgess (q.q.v.) were their rivals. 62.30-31; 224.20; ?515.29; †521.22 —with Tristram (q.v.).

Chummy the Guardsman–see Tommy Atkins. 210.8.

Chuff–see Glugg.

Churchill, Winston (1874-   )–English statesman whom Joyce thought of as First Lord of the Admiralty in the 1914-18 war. 587.16.

Cian–legendary Irish chief, father of Lug (q.v.). When his murderers tried to bury him, the ground rejected him seven times. 78.18.

Ciaran, St–see Ailbey. †484.23— with Declan (q.v.).

Ciardeclan–see Ciaran and Declan.

*Cicely–maybe the girl in Wilde's (q.v.) *The Importance of Being Earnest.* 224.21.

Cicero, Marcus Tullius (106-43 B.C.)–Roman orator, politician, character in Shakespeare's *Julius Caesar* (q.q.v.). 152.10; 182.9.

Cigarette–camp-follower in Ouida's (q.v.) *Under Two Flags.* †236.2— with Cynara (q.v.); 351.12.

Cincinnatus, Lucius Quintus–in Roman eyes, a type of old-fashioned integrity and frugality. Twice he was called from the plow (like Ulysses?) to serve his country and having served returned to the plow. 30.25; 139.5;

285.left margin; 307.left margin; 367.4; 456.8.

Cinderella–heroine of a fairy tale and a pantomime. For Joyce she is a girl with a split personality. I do not understand some of the following references. †224.30— with Helen (q.v.); †280.21—with Christine Beauchamp (q.v.); 331. 26; 440.27; 445.6 (ask unbrodhel —see Aschenbrödel); 551.9; †619. 17—with Rollo (q.v.); ?627.5— see Saltarella.

?Cinna – conspirator in Shakespeare's *Julius Caesar* (q.q.v.). 30.36.

*Ciondolone, Professor, 161.2-3.

Circe–enchantress who turned men into swine, an episode of *Ulysses.* 23.18; 129.8; ?319.6; 454.31.

Citizen, The–Michael Cusack (q.v.), the Polyphemus of *Ulysses* (q.q.v.). Citizen soldiers are members of the "Citizen Army" which rose at Easter, 1916. 338.4.

*Claffey's, 625.9.

*Clancartys–see Demetrius O'Flanagan McCarthy 27.25.

*Clancarbry, 144.5.

Clancy, Sheriff–Long John Clancy, mentioned in *Ulysses* as then sheriff of Dublin. 46.stanza 2.

Clanrickarde–famous family in Irish history, perhaps the Clanrickarde who fought Cromwell (q.v.). 367.32.

Clara, St (1194-1253)–founder of the Franciscan nuns. 226.10; 290.21.

Clarence, George, duke of (1449-78)–born in Dublin, lord-lieutenant of Ireland, married Isabelle Neville, character in Shakespeare's *Richard III* (q.q.v.). He is the only person in FW who really was "butt ended" (3.23). See George, Gorgias. 3.20; 191.6; ?266.12; 489.17.

Clarence and Avondale–see Albert Victor. The reference may include the river Avon and Avondale, Parnell's (q.v.) Wicklow estate.

Claribel–pseudonym of Mrs Charlotte Alington Barnard, composer of "Come Back to Erin". 232.16.

Clarke, Sir Edward (b. 1841)– English lawyer and politician, defended Wilde (q.v.). 558.20.

Clarkson, Willy–London maker of theatrical wigs. 625.3.

Claude, Jean (1619-87)–French protestant divine. 444.3; 509.30.

Claudesdales–probably Clydesdale, a kind of horse. 553.35.

Claudio–brother of Isabella (q.v.) in Shakespeare's (q.v.) *Measure for Measure*. He was, in a way, wrong-headed.   †121.1—with Claudius (q.v.).

Claudius–Roman emperor, 41-54. He was poisoned by his wife after disinheriting his son in favor of her son, Nero (q.v.). He introduced three new letters into the Latin alphabet, including ⅃, the consonanted V.   †121.1—with King Claudius and Claudio (q.q.v.).

Claudius–king of Denmark in Shakespeare's *Hamlet* (q.q.v.). See also Feng. The passage on 121 imitates G. C. Lichtenberg's description of Garrick (q.v.) acting Hamlet, which may be found in the *Variorum Shakespeare*. †121.1—with Emperor Claudius, Claudio; ?126.26; 444.3; 509.30.

Claudius, Appius–Roman statesman and author, correspondent of Cicero (q.v.). 581.22-23.

*Clausetter, Walther, 141.19.

Clays, Andrew – see Androcles. 468.32-33.

Clement–fourteen popes and two anti-popes. 154.20.

Cleopatra–Egyptian queen, character in Shaw's *Caesar* (q.q.v.) *and Cleopatra* and in Shakespeare's *Antony* (q.q.v.) *and Cleopatra*. Antony calls her his "serpent of

old Nile" and she dies by the serpent. In FW she has a number of cognate roles: 1) as Nile (q.v.), she and the Amazon (q.v.) are river nymphs; 2) as serpent and woman who embraces the serpent she is allied to Lilith-Eve (q.v.); 3) as a serpent she is one of the snakes or pagan deities that St Patrick (q.v.) catches (pp. 19-20) and thereafter she combines with him to make up the religious past of Ireland, pagan and Christian; 4) as a sow, princess of porkers, I guess she has to do with the sow goddess that Mr Graves is always going on about, but I confess I do not understand her place in the pig (q.v.) theme and I do not know why she ate a windowsill; 5) combined with Clio (q.v.) she defines history's muse and Joyce seems, therefore, to say that Clio is cunning past man's thought. This last is emphasized by Joyce's continual play with Nile and Nil. I take him to mean that Cleopatra, Nile and history, have cunning passages, are with difficulty explored and ultimately without meaning. The sources of the Nile are the lakes Albert and Victoria Nyanza (q.v.), which mean No Answer or such answer as may be suggested by a respectable, philoprogenitive king and queen abed. See also Dark Lady, Charmian.

19.31	nilloh
75.14	Nile
†91.6	Cliopatrick (the sow)— with Clio, Patrick (q.q.v.)
104.32	Cleopater
166.34	cleopatrician
198.1	ijypt
202.19	Nihil
†271.left	margin Cliopatria—with Clio (q.v.)
318.32	nihilnulls
328.22	Nile
332.29	nilly
364.21	Elin
493.5	nil
†10	seaserpents — with Julius Caesar (q.v.)

19	nihil
494.34	Nile Lodge (see Amazon)
†508.23	P. and Q., Clopatrick's —with Patrick (q.v.)
548.2	Impress of Asias (see Amazon)
598.6	Nil
627.30	Niluna (see Amazon, Moon)

Clery, Mr Martin and Mr Michael– see O'Clery. 520.3,15.

Clery's–Dublin department store. 459.8.

Clinker, Humphrey–title hero of Smollett's (q.v.) novel. 29.5-6,8.

Clio–muse of history; Joyce defines her by identifying her with Cleopatra (q.v.). †91.6—with Cleopatra and St Patrick (q.q.v.); 104.32; †271.left margin—with Cleopatra (q.v.).

Clive, Robert, Baron Clive of Plassey (1725-74)–victor over Surrajah Dowlah (q.v.) at Plassey, etc. 481.13.

Clodd, E.–see Tom Tit Tot. 69.29; 70.34.

*****Cloons,** 616.21.

*****Cloran,** Peter–same as Roche Mongan (q.v.). 40.16; 212.3.

?Cloten–character in Shakespeare's *Cymbeline* (q.q.v.) who does involve himself with clothes. 26.10.

Clotho–the spinning Fate. 152.9; 528.3.

Clotilda, St (d. 544)–wife of Clovis (q.v.) whom she converted to Christianity. 325.28.

*****Cloudia** Aiduolcis–cloud? Claudia? 568.10.

Clout, Colin–name adopted by Spenser in *The Shepherds Calendar* and *Colin Clouts Come Home Again*; rustic in Gay's (q.v.) *Shepherd's Week*; name of a poem of Skelton's. 49.26.

Clovis (466-511)–king of Salian Franks, husband of Clotilda (q.v.). 526.27.

Clytie–sea nymph, changed into the heliotrope, which is Issy's flower. †284.23—with Issy (q.v.).

Coats, Brothers–probably the thread-makers and also James and Andrew Coats who made an expedition to the antarctic in 1904. 325.26.

Cock Lane Ghost–a false ghost, investigated in 1763 by Samuel Johnson (q.v.). 118.13.

Cock of the North–George, 5th duke of Gordon (1770-1836)— raised the Gordon Highlanders, fought in Spain, Corsica, Ireland. Also a well-known bagpipe pipe. 482.27.

Cocker, Edward (1631-75)–reputed author of a famous *Arithmetick* who gave the phrase "according to Cocker" to the language. 303. right margin; 537.36.

*****Cocksnark** of Killtork, 353.11.

*****Cockshott,** Mr J. P., ?56.4-5; 524.14,16,34.

?Cockton, Henry–19th century author of *Valentine Vox* (q.v.) the *Ventriloquist* and *Sylvester Sound,* the *Somnambulist.* 56.4-5.

*****Codex** and Podex, Messrs., 185.3.

Coemghen and Coemghem–see Kevin. The "hen" and "hem" endings may refer to "hen" and "Ham" (q.q.v.); they may be misprints.

Cogan, Miles de–according to the Dublin Annals of 1177, he was governor of Dublin, defeated while fighting in Connaught. 516.12,20.

Cohen, Bella (Bello)–Circe (q.v.) in *Ulysses.* 368.10,12.

Coke, Sir Edward (1552-1634)– chief justice of England, opponent of Bacon (q.v.). ?409.35; 447.5.

Coldours–Cawdor—see Macbeth. 250.17.

Cole, King–nursery-rhyme character. †569.23—with Finn MacCool (q.v.); †619.28—with Finn MacCool (q.v.).

Cole, Kitty–see Kitty of Coleraine. 328.23-24.

Coleman–Dublin butcher (q.v.). ?†326.10—with Cuddy (q.v.); 443.27.

*Coll, 44.13.

Collars and Cuffs–see Albert Victor.

Colleen Bawn (Fair Girl)–Eily O'Connor, heroine of Boucicault's (q.v.) play which is based on *The Collegians* by Gerald Griffin, and was made into Benedict's (q.v.) opera *The Lily* (q.v.) *of Killarney*. Eily is poor but charming and the plot concerns efforts to part her from the hero, Hardress Cregan (q.v.). At one time she is believed dead, but is "resurrected". 39.23; 101.17; ?144.10; 224.11; 384.21; 385.1; 397.5; 438.34.

*Colleson–see Coilis. 129.35.

*Collier–maybe John Payne Collier (1787-1883), Shakespeare (q.v.) forger. 343.2.

Collins, Anthony (1676-1729)–English deist—see *Portrait of the Artist*, 230. 12.21.

*Collinses, 508.32.

*Collis–Latin "hill". "Amnist anguished axes Collis" parodies a mnemonic, sometimes used in teaching Latin feminines in the 3rd declension. Collis and Ward were Dublin solicitors. 256.25; 468.11; 602.20.

*Collopys, Saint, 457.2.

Colt, Samuel (1814-62)–American inventor of firearms. 84.24; 352.9.

Colum, Padraic–Irish writer. He wrote "as in wild earth a Grecian urn . . .". 68.35.

Columba, St (Ir. *Colum*) or Columkill or Crimthann (fox)–4th century Irish saint, head of the great monastery on Iona. See Raven and Dove for *columba* puns? 50.9-10; †120.2—with Columbus (q.v.); 122.26; 347.21; 409.27-28; †484.32—with Columbus (q.v.);

†496.30—with Columbus (q.v.); †615.2-3—with Columella (q.v.).

Columbanus, St (543-615)–fiery Irish saint and writer. 240.21.

Columbia, Queen–see Amazon. 548.2.

Columbine–see Harlequin.

Columbus, Christopher (1446-1506) –discoverer of America. See Raven and Dove. †120.2—with Columba (q.v.); 129.31; 409.15; †484.32—with St Columba (q.v.); †496.30—with St Columba (q.v.); 512.7; 513.16.

Columella, Lucius Junius Moderatus–lived in the 1st century A.D. and wrote on agriculture in *De re rustica* and *De arboribus*. 255.19; 281.5; 319.8; 354.26-27; †615.2-3—with St Columba (q.v.).

Columbkill–see Columba.

Comenius, Johann Amos (1592-1671)–humanist, born in Moravia, famous for prophecies, e.g. that the millennium would occur in 1672 and miraculous assistance would be given those who destroyed the pope. †155.34—with Arminius (q.v.).

Commodus, Lucius Aelius Aurelius –Roman emperor 161-92. ?3.14; 157.26.

?Comus–pagan god invented by Milton (q.v.), son of Bacchus and Circe (q.q.v.), waylayer of travellers whose faces he changed into beasts' faces. 409.12-13.

Comyn, Archbishop–St Lawrence O'Toole's (q.v.) successor to the see of Dublin. †130.21—with Newcomen (q.v.).

Comyn, Tutty–see Tut-ankh-amen. 367.10.

Conal–legendary Irish hero. In both cases he doubles with O'Connell (q.v.). †525.18; †625.12.

Conall, Gretecloke–see O'Connell. 553.14.

Conan–companion of Finn MacCool (q.v.). 19.25; †228.13—with Conan

Doyle (q.v.); 322.3—with O'Connell (q.v.).

Concanen, Matthew–minor 18th century hack, author of *An Essay Against Too Much Reading* (1728) in which he suggested Shakespeare (q.v.) had historians and grammarians to help him write his plays. 28.19.

*Concepcion, mother, 527.36.

Concessa–mother of St Patrick (q.v.). 327.24.

*Conchitas–Perhaps heroine of *La femme et le pantin*, by Pierre Louÿs, a temptress. 268.3.

Conchobar–king of Ulster in the Ulster cycle, uncle of Cuchulain (q.v.). 182.9; ?449.8.

Concrete Man–in *A Vision* Yeats (q.v.) calls Phase 20 "The Concrete Man", i.e. the man who dramatizes the Mask. Examples: Shakespeare, Napoleon (q.q.v.), Balzac. 285.note 5; 481.12.

Confucius or Kung tsze (478-550 B.C.)–Chinese sage. ?15.12; 35.36; 108.11; 131.33-34,35; 417.15; 485.35.

*Congan, 538.32.

*Coninghams, Lili–see Lily (q.v.). 58.30.

Conn–one of the Fianna. Such is the confusion of Irish heroes that I am not sure if this Conn is the same as Conn of the Hundred Battles who defeated King Eoghan (or Owen mor—q.v.) in the battle of Moylena. Conn's Half was the north of Ireland, Mug's the south. 51.12; 78.29; ?203.12; 475.6; 540.33.

Conn the Shaughraun–title character in a play by Boucicault (q.v.) which contains a wake at which the hero is resurrected. 289.24.

Connolly, James–founder of the Irish Socialist Party in 1896, one of the leaders executed by the British after the Easter rebellion in 1916. 303.9,12; 518.29.

Connolly, William–speaker of the Irish parliament in the 18th century. The Hellfire Club met at his house. 457.1.

*Connor, Laura, 507.29.

Conroy, Gretta–heroine of Joyce's story "The Dead". See Gretta Greene.

Constance–character in Shakespeare's (q.v.) *King John*. 71.29.

Constantine (?288-337)–Roman emperor who was converted to Christianity. 155.9; 442.5.

Consuelo–title heroine of a novel by George Sand (q.v.). She personifies moral purity amid temptation. 528.25.

Conways–pub in *Ulysses*. 214.20.

*Cooley-Couley, Madame–probably Anna Livia (q.v.) as wife of Finn MacCool (q.v.). 242.36.

*Coolie, Miss–probably Issy (q.v.) as daughter of Finn MacCool (q.v.). 330.18.

*Cooney, 194.29.

*Cooper, 59.5.

*Cooper, James Fenimore (1789-1851)–American novelist. See Hawkeye. 439.12.

Copaleen, Miles na–character in *The Colleen Bawn* (q.v.) and *The Lily* (q.v.) *of Killarney*. I have an idea there was an Irish journalist with some such name. 192.26-27; 246.19; 343.11-12.

Cope, Edward Drinker–American palaeoentomologist, authority on fossils. 98.30.

Copenhagen–Wellington's horse who was not white. See Marengo. 8.17; 10.2,13,21-22; 223.16; 388.17; 620.34.

?Copernicus, Nicholas (1473-1543) –Polish astronomer. 56.1.

Cophetua, King–made a beggarmaid his queen. 537.32.

Copperfield, David–title hero of Dickens's (q.v.) novel. †434.28— with David (q.v.), see also Uriah.

*Coppinger, Archdeacon – since there are lots of jokes about Coppinger and cradles, I wonder if he has to do with the incunabula man. The chartulary of St Thomas's Abbey was known as Coppinger's Register. 55.17-18, 30; 71.35; 211.20; 280.left margin; 294.note 1; 324.26; 329.3; 341.35; 369.11; 386.30; 390.12; 524.8,18; 525.1; 574.12-13,22; 575.6,24; 621.15.

*Corcoran, 504.20.

Cordelia–heroine of Shakespeare's *King Lear* (q.q.v.). In *Ulysses* (190/246) and in FW she is identified with Lir's (q.v.) lonely daughter, Finnuala (q.v.). At the very end, doubling with Anna Livia (q.v.), Cordelia returns to death and her father.

Coriolanus, Gaius Marcius–Roman hero, treated by Plutarch and Shakespeare (q.v.). Joyce uses him as a symbol of exile. 228.11; †354.33—with John Lane (q.v.)?

Cormac, MacArt–legendary king of Ireland. Under him, Finn MacCool (q.v.) led the Fianna. He was Grania's (q.v.) father. In Macpherson's "Temora" (q.q.v.) he is father of Roscranna (q.v.). 19.9; 329.18; 463.22.

Corneille, Pierre (1606-84)–French dramatist. 173.20.

Cornwall–preeminently Mark of Cornwall (q.v.), faintly the character in *King Lear* (q.v.); also a British official, secretary to the Irish post-office. Parnell's (q.v.) *United Irishman* accused him of homosexuality. Nobody won the ensuing libel suit, but Cornwall was dismissed. †260.note 1 — with Cromwell (q.v.); 419.17; 581.9.

Cornwallis–West, Mrs (b. 1865)— better known as Mrs Patrick Campbell, the actress. By a second marriage, Winston Churchill's mother was also Mrs Cornwallis-West. 157.33-34.

?Corot, Jean Baptiste Camille– French painter. 266.23.

Correggio (1494-1534) Italian painter. 435.8.

*Corriendo, Miss Corrie, 220.19.

*Corrig, Marcus of, 513.5.

Corrigan, D. J.–Irish doctor who discovered the ailment known as "Corrigan's Pulse". 214.23-24.

Corsair–Byronic(q.v.)hero. 600.11.

Corsican–see Napoleon.

Corsican Brothers–title characters, identical twins in a novel of Dumas père and a play of Boucicault (q.v.). Their names were Louis and Fabian Franchi. In FW they are identified with the Napoleon (q.v.) boys. †465.12 —with Frank (q.v.), 16; 561.6.

Cosgrove, William (b. 1880)–president of the executive council of the Irish Free State, 1922-32. 128.20.

Costard–clown in Shakespeare's (q.v.) *Love's Labour's Lost*. 464.30; 563.24.

*Costello, 132.13; 133.1-2.

*Costello, Hewitt, 135.29.

*Costollo, Odam–Adam? 254.25.

Cotterick–see St Patrick. 24.22.

Cotton, Edward–sergeant-major (late 7th Hussars), author of *A Voice from Waterloo*, which Mr Graham finds to be a source of the Museyroom episode. †9.8–with Creasy, Boycott (q.q.v.); 130.26.

Couhounin–see Cuchulain. 35.32.

*Courcy de Courcy, 370.22.

*Courtmilit's, 567.11.

*Cowley–maybe Luke Tarpey (q.v.), maybe Abraham Cowley (1618-67), English poet. 275.26; 378.16.

*Cox–domestic cook? 66.23.

*Coxon, Drummer, 39.9.

*Coyle, Jerry–see Jerry. 210.21; 370.21.

Coyle-Finn–Finn MacCool (q.v.). 330.17.

Crabtree, Lotta–19th century American soubrette. The reference may also include that crabtree under which the young Shakespeare (q.v.) passed out from drink. See Charlotte. 62.34.

***Craddock,** 98.31.

***Craig,** Pudge, 210.14.

***Craigs,** 51.28, 95.34, 96.24.

Crampton, Sir Philip (1777-1858)– Dublin surgeon who discovered in the eye of the ostrich a muscle which bears his name–see FW 162.32. He planted a famous pear-tree in Dublin. The Crampton memorial was known as "The Pineapple" and was on the site of the original Dublin Stone, erected by Olaf the White (q.v.). Its inscription is echoed 132.30. 204.36; 291.5.

Cranmer, Thomas (1489-1556)– archbishop who helped Henry VIII (q.v.) maintain his claim to be supreme head of the Church of England, character in Shakespeare's (q.v.) *Henry VIII.* 155.9.

***Crany's,** 105.32.

***Crawleys**–maybe just snakes, maybe the people in *Vanity Fair.* 288.note 6.

Crazier–see Drapier. 104.26.

Creasy, Edward Shepherd (1812-78)–author of *Decisive Battles of the World.* †9.8—with Cotton and Boycott (q.q.v.).

Cregan, Hardress–hero of *The Colleen Bawn* (q.v.) and *The Lily* (q.v.) *of Killarney.* 246.18.

Crippen, Dr–English murderer. 589.16.

?Crippled-with-Children and Dropping-with-Sweat–exiled Eve and Adam (q.v.). 102.29.

Crispin and Crispinian, Sts– brothers, Romans, martyrs, patrons of cobblers. Agincourt was fought on St Crispin's day—see *Henry V.* 491.6; 618.34.

Croce, Benedetto (1866-1952)– Italian philosopher. 511.31.

Crockard–see Pollard.

***Crocus,** 254.20.

Croesus–last Lydian king, richest man in the world. †231.18—with Joshua (q.v.); 564.5.

Croker, Thomas Crofton–author of *Fairy Legends of South Ireland* which contains "Three Pebbles on the Beach". †537.29—with Crockard (q.v.).

Crom Cruach–idol of ancient Celts. †22.14—with Cromwell (q.v.).

Cromagnon Man–a member of a race of the Old Stone Age. 20.7.

Cromwell, Oliver (1599-1658)– regicide, lord-protector of England. He planted protestants in Ulster and reduced Irish catholics with such fiendish cruelty that his time in Ireland was long known as "the curse of Cromwell". He remarked that the native Irish could go to hell or Connaught. I do not think I wholly understand the use of Cromwell in FW. I assume that he shares a number of "Oliver" (q.v.) references with Gogarty (q.v.) who seized the crown from Stephen Dedalus (q.v.) in *Ulysses.* The Irish called Cromwell's soldiers "Oliver's Lambs" (73.33).

9.2	Cromwelly
10.31	knollyrock
†22.14	cromcruwell — with Crom Cruach (q.v.)
39.7-8	Bold Boy Cromwell
44.13	Noll
	†in music Lord Olafa Crumple —with Olaf (q.v.)
†45.3	Lord Olofa Crumple— with Olaf (q.v.)
53.36	cramwells
64.10	allower
66.6	allover
68.15	Cromwell's

†74.4 Wulverulverlord (protect us!)—with Roland (q.v.)

†76.26 old knoll — with Old Knowell (q.v.)

88.21 Crumwall

105.35 All over

116.32 gromwelled

?132.22 Cromlechheight and Crommalhill

163.27 all over

206.35 allover

224.14 allover

†260.note 1 Cormwell's—with Cornwall (q.v.)

261.left margin Cronwall

299.9 Ollover Krumwall

301.note 3 allover

322.34 Ovlergroamlius

343.30-31 allaverred cromlecks

†347.10,32 Crimealian wall . . . Crummwiliam wall— with William III and William Joyce (q.q.v.)

350.6 olyovyover

353.34 wools . . . all over cromlin

†362.5 old nollcromforemost ironsides—with Old Knowell (q.v.)

†420.36 Crownd. Well — with Stephen Dedalus and Wellington (q.q.v.)

†422.31-32 Old Knoll—with Old Knowell (q.v.)

455.8 Iereny allover irelands

†499.23,28 altknoll . . . Oliver— with Old Knowell (q.v.)

500.6 Crum . . . Cromwell

512.17 cramwell

618.34 Nollwelshian

621.18 nolly

625.7 Wellcrom

Cronus–Titan who dethroned his father and was dethroned by his own son, Zeus (q.v.), god of harvests and time. 390.7; 415.21; 517.36.

Crookedribs is Eve–see *Paradise Lost* X, 884-885. 38.31.

Crooker–see Kreuger.

*Croona, 602.14.

Crosscann Lorn – "Cruiskeen Lawn" (little full jug), an Irish air. 89.10.

Crosse and Blackwell–English brand of preserves, etc. 448.8.

*Crostiguns, 177.9.

Croven, Godred–see Godred Croven. 262.note 3.

Crow–I have not listed them, but many refer to Robert Greene's (q.v.) "upstart crow" or Shakespeare (q.v.). There was a Crow Street Theatre in Dublin.

Crowhore, Croppy–probably refers to Banin's books, *Crowhore of the Billhook* and *The Croppy, a Tale of the Irish Rebellion.* 229.12.

Crown–see Stephen Dedalus.

Crozier, David R.–Shem (q.v.) is intended. Shaun calls him "David" (q.v.) to his (Shaun's) Jonathan; he calls him "Crozier" because Shem here plays the part of Simon of Cyrene and is invited to carry the Cross. There was also a primate of Ireland named Crozier. 464.3.

Cruden, Alexander (1701-70)– author of a Biblical concordance. 358.6.

*Crump, Henressy–Joyce's library contained *The Case of Mr Crump* by Lewisohn. 176.6-7.

Crusoe, Robinson–title hero of Defoe's novel and of an English pantomime. †65.15—with Peter Robinson (q.v.); †211.16—with Rogerson (q.v.); †243.31—with Monsignor Robinson (q.v.); 538.13; 619.24.

Cuchulain–hero of the Ulster cycle of Irish myths. The 11th *Britannica* says the name is pronounced "Coohoollin"; Mr Kelleher says it is pronounced "Coo-xull-in", taking x as the phonetic sign for the guttural ch. 35.22; 547.22.

*Cucullus, 248.16.

Cuddy–North Country name for donkey—see Ass. 20.27; †326.10 —with Coleman; 555.24.

Cullen, Paul, Cardinal (1803-78)– archbishop of Dublin. He was a bitter enemy of the Fenians and made himself unpopular with the Irish. Father James A. Cullen, S. J., was the original of Father Arnall in *Portrait of the Artist*. 33.2; 200.3; ?203.12; ?385.1; 440.9; 555.32-33.

Cullinan, T.–Cape colonist who acquired one of the richest diamond fields in the world. There are Cullinan diamonds in the British crown jewels. Also a 19th century Irish poet. 286.15.

*Cumbilum, 88.28.

Cummal or Cumall–Finn MacCool's (q.v.) father. 289.11; 334.15.

Cunina, Statulina, Edulia–Roman goddesses. The first presides over cradles. The second is the feminine form of the god to whom sacrifices were made when children were learning to stand. The third may be a mistake for Edulica, the goddess who supported weaned children with food. 561.9.

Cunningham, Martin–character in *Ulysses*, see Matthew Kane. I do not understand his use in FW, probably because I do not know enough about the real man. 387.28; 393.5; †467.33—with Ancus (q.v.).

*Cunningham, Minxy–wife of the above? 95.9; 433.19.

Cupid–Roman god of love–see Eros. 284.14; 445.22.

Curer of Wars–see Vianney. 440.10.

Curie, Pierre (1859-1906)–French physicist who with his wife studied radioactive elements. 138.12.

*Curley, Connie, 239.24.

Curll, Edmund (1675-1747)–English seller of mostly dirty books. "Curlism" became a synonym for literary indecency. Some of his books were *The Nun in her Smock, De Usu Flagrorum, John Ker of Kersland*. Pope (q.v.) attempted to make use of him and then pilloried him in *The Dunciad*. 159.30.

Curran, John Philpot (1750-1817)– Irish politician, lawyer, defended several United Irishmen, father of Sarah Curran (q.v.); author of "Cushla Machree". 93.32.

Curran, Sarah Philpot–Robert Emmet's (q.v.) sweetheart, the girl who was "far from the land where her young hero sleeps", and married, as a matter of fact, to a Major Sturgeon. †210.30—with Sarah and Saar (q.q.v.).

*Currens, Mrs, 550.32.

Currier, Master–Shaun (q.v.) as courier. 570.9-10.

*Curry, 295.18.

Cusack, Michael–the "Citizen" (q.v.) of *Ulysses*, a leading Fenian. †49.34—with Nicolas of Cusa (q.v.); 338.4; †550.30-31—with Tamerlane (q.v.).

Cush–son of Ham (q.v.), Ethiopia. 308.9.

Cuvier, Georges, Baron (1769-1832) –French naturalist. 606.27.

Cyclops–see Polyphemus.

Cymbeline – title character of Shakespeare's (q.v.) play. See Imogen, Posthumus. 292.25; 561.9; 607.10.

Cynara–subject of a poem by Dowson. †236.2—Cigarette (q.v.).

Cyril, St–he and St Methodius (q.v.) are the principal saints of the Eastern church. 159.30; 528.23 (liryc).

Cyrus–founder of the Persian empire. 263.7.

Cythera–see Aphrodite. 158.11.

Czerny, Karl (1791-1857)–Austrian pianist, composer of scales and exercises. 362.33.

D

Daedalus ("cunning craftsman")–fabulous artificer of antiquity, builder of the labyrinth for Minos (q.v.), son perhaps of Merope (q.v.), father of Icarus (q.v.). By wings of his own invention, he escaped his foes and thus became patron of makers. Sidney (q.v.) says: ". . . as the fertilest ground must be manured, so must the highest-flying wit have a Daedalus to guide him. That Daedalus . . . hath three wings to bear itself up into the air of commendation: that is art, imitation, and exercise."
  In *Portrait of the Artist* Stephen Dedalus (q.v.) invokes Daedalus to guide him, and in *Ulysses* (if I follow the plot) turns into Daedalus. I can't help feeling there are more Daedalus references than I have found in FW. 108.21; 179.17; 390.17.

*Daganasanavitch–maybe Dagon (q.v.). 278.23.

Dagda–the Zeus (q.v.) of the pagan Irish gods, father of Aengus (q.v.). 248.4; 596.2.

Dagobert (d. 639)–king of the Franks (q.v.). 35.12; 274.29; 394.18.

Dagon–national god of the Philistines, half man, half fish. 68.27; ?278.23.

Daguerre, Louis Jacques (1789-1851)–French inventor of the daguerreotype. 339.23.

Daisy–see Maggies.

*Dalems, Celana, Misses, 350.3; 351.30.

Daleth–not a person but the 4th letter of the Hebrew alphabet, meaning "door". 20.17.

Dalkey, king of–figure in an 18th century burlesque ceremony, held annually at Dalkey. He was called "His facetious Majesty, King of

Dalkey, King of Mugleins . . . Sovereign of the Illustrious Order of the Periwinkle and the Lobster". The English suppressed the ceremony. The Free State revived it. 87.25-26; 616.11.

*Dalough, St–partly St Kevin (q.v.). 39.9.

Dalton, John (1766-1848)–gave his name to a form of color-blindness. ?19.9; 248.22.

D'Alton, Edward Alfred–historian of Ireland. 572.36.

Daly's–Dublin club, founded 1750, popular with the literary. 42.35.

*Daly, Wardeb–*Ulysses*, 757/918: ". . . worse and worse says Warden Daly. . . ." 526.20.

Damon of Syracuse–Pythagorean (q.v.) celebrated for his disinterested friendship with Phintias who became Pythias. 103.9 (nomad); 350.13; 374.22; 578.34.

Dan–eponymous ancestor of the Danes (q.v.). Some "Dans" probably include Daniel, O'Connell, etc. 102.8; 139.22; 162.16; 199.14; 237.18; 317.14; 330.6; 355.21; 378.1; 466.20; 604.13.

Danaides–fifty daughters of Danaus, forty-nine of whom murdered their husbands, sons of Aegyptus (q.v.). They were punished in Hades by having everlastingly to pour water into a sieve. 94.14.

*Dandyforth–G. R. Sims wrote a play, *The Dandy Fifth*. 473.10.

Dane–the many "Danes" in FW refer to the Danish invaders and kings of Dublin; but since the historical Hamlet (q.v.) was one of these, I think a great many "Danes" refer to him or to his father. See Dean, Dayne, Dan.

*Danelly–Donnolly? 379.36.

Danelope–Dunlop (q.v.), Penelope (q.v.)? 359.14.

Dangerfield, Paul–the name by which Charles Arther (q.v.) is known throughout much of *The House by the Churchyard.* 80.8.

Daniel–in the Biblical book of Daniel, he was put in a lion's den and not eaten. See Susanna, Dan, O'Connell. 72.34; 160.18; 350.31; 354.3; 361.23; †435.15—with Danu, Dannyboy (q.q.v.); †468.33 —with O'Connell (q.v.); 523.17; 541.16.

Danis–see St Denis. 336.3; 617.6.

Dannyboy–refers to the words sometimes sung to "The Londonderry Air"—"Oh Danny boy, the pipes, the pipes. . . ." 51.33; †435.15 — with Daniel, Danu (q.q.v.).

Dannyman–sinister hunchback, agent of Hardress Cregan (q.v.) in *The Colleen Bawn* (q.v.). See also *Ulysses,* 626/743. 14.20; 621.7.

Dante, Alighieri (1265-1321)–Italian poet, also Mrs Riordan in *Portrait of the Artist.* See Beatrice, Rachel and Leah. 47; 59.5; 105.10; 205.2; 220.7; †229.4—with Daunt (q.v.); 251.23-24; 269.left margin; 337.30 (Donn, Teague); 344.6; 440.6; ?510.3; 539.6.

?Danton, George Jacques (1759-94) —one of the most conspicuous actors in the decisive episodes of the French Revolution. †81.7 (and Anton)—with Anton Hermes (q.v.).

Danu or Dana–Irish goddess of fertility and death. †7.12—with O'Connell (q.v.); 14.20; 79.15; 181.6; †386.22—with O'Connell (q.v.); †392.30—with O'Connell; †435.15—with Dannyboy, Daniel (q.q.v.); 448.31.

Daphne–river nymph, saved from the pursuit of Apollo (q.v.) when she was turned into a laurel tree. 203.30; †406.25—with Mab (q.v.); 556.18.

***Daradora**–perhaps Floradora. 434.7.

Darby and Joan–any attached elderly couple. See Derby. ?374.25; 454.32; 473.9-10.

***Darcy**–hero of *Pride and Prejudice?* 289.30; 333.8; 543.20.

***D'Arcy,** James–seems to be Shem (q.v.). See James and John.

***Dariou,** 257.7.

Darius–6th century Persian king, defeated at Marathon. †113.4— with Marius (q.v.); 138.27; 307. left margin.

Dark Lady–heroine of Shakespeare's (q.v.) sonnets, original (probably) of his dark Rosalines (q.v.—see also Rose) and of Cleopatra (q.v.). She has been variously identified with Mrs Davenant, Penelope Rich, Elizabeth I, Mary Fitton (q.q.v.), and, I am sure, with other ladies. In *Ulysses,* 194/252, Joyce follows Harris (q.v.) and makes Shakespeare-Fair Man-Dark Lady a triangle equal to Finn-Dermot-Grania or Arthur-Lancelot-Guinevere or Mark-Tristram-Isolde (q.q.v.). Unlike Harris, Joyce feels that Ann Hathaway (q.v.) was Shakespeare's muse and the Dark Lady "a darker shadow" of Ann, "two rages" which "commingle in a whirlpool".

I have hesitated about including the following references. For one thing, I am far from understanding the Dark Lady in FW. For another, I believe that FW is about Shakespeare and, therefore, I am sure to want to find the Dark Lady everywhere. All the same, I do think she's there. She may be the dark Isolde of Ireland, she may be a gipsy, she may even be a negress (see Ham). See also Fair Man, Mr W. H., Dark Rosaleen.

34.34; 59.2-4; 93.27; †114.10— with Lamp (q.v.); 121.27,31; 122.31; 136.31; 147.35; 148.4; 158.26; 223.28; 227.4 (Mary Fitton); 230.10; 251.11,24; 297.15; 328.28; ?355.9; 379.33; 403.29;

?450.18; †451.15—with Anna Livia; ?459.8; 493.35; †511.22—with Lettie (q.v.); 533.14; ?545.29; 563.13,15,16; 583.22.

Darthula–heroine of Macpherson's (q.v.) "Dar-Thula". She is roughly Deirdre (q.v.). 329.17.

Darwin, Charles (1809-82)–English naturalist. 252.28; 504.28.

Darwin, Erasmus (1731-1802)–English evolutionist and poet. †504.26-28—with Erasmus Smith and Charles Darwin (q.q.v.).

Dasent, Sir George (1817-96)–translator of the *Prose Edda*, etc. 578.14.

Dash, Sam–18th century Master of Revels at the balls at Dublin Castle. 210.26.

*****Dashe,** Miss, 523.21.

Dathi–last pagan king of Ireland. He was struck dead by lightning when crossing the Alps. 274.5.

*****Dattery,** Mrs, 550.32.

Daunt, William Joseph O'Neill (1807-94)–Irish novelist and historian, doubles with Dante (q.v.). 229.4; 373.32.

*****Dauran's** lord (Sniffpox), 60.33.

Dave–see David Garrick. 134.11.

Davenant, Mrs–wife of an Oxford vintner. He liked actors but never laughed. Aubrey (q.v.) says Shakespeare stayed with them and fathered Sir William D'Avenant. See Dark Lady. 60.2 (Death Avenue anent).

*****Daveran,** 146.8.

David and Jonathan–a type of loving friends. "The soul of Jonathan was knit with the soul of David and Jonathan loved him as his own soul." (1 Sam. 8). Shem and Shaun (q.v.) are David and Jonathan, knit perhaps but not exactly loving. Shem-David is Taff (q.v.), Shaun-Jonathan is Jonathan Swift (q.v.). †3.22,24 (tauftauf . . . nathandjoe)—with Taff, Swift, Nathan (q.q.v.); 8.23;

172.24,26; †177.20—with Browne and Nolan (q.v.); 192.22; †288.14 (saved and solomnones)—with Solomon (q.v.); †391.28—with Thomas Davis (q.v.); 412.5; †434.28—with David Copperfield (q.v.); 451.19; 462.8,17,30; 463.27,36; 464.3 (see Crozier); †464.36 —with Michael Davitt and Basil French (q.q.v.); †489.30—with Davitt (q.v.); 494.23.

Davis, Thomas (1814-45)–Irish nationalist, a poet of *The Nation*. †391.28—with David (q.v.).

Davitt, Michael (1846-1906)–leading Fenian, prominent landleaguer. He was always in and out of prison or Australia. Both references double with David (q.v.). †464.36—with French Devil (q.v.); 489.30.

Dayne–see Dean. 79.35; 593.14,23 (*bis*).

*****Deacon,** Daddy: Old Daddy Dacon/Bought a bit of bacon,/Put it on a chimney pot,/ For fear it would be taken. 257.14,21; 339.3; 348.23.

Dean–the word is more complicated in FW than you might suppose. Its most important and steadiest reference is to Dean Swift (q.v.) —see also Cadenus. But the Irish pronounce "Dean" as if it were "Dane" (q.v.); George Moore (q.v.) called himself Edmund Dayne (q.v.) in *Confessions of a Young Man* and he calls Yeats (q.v.) Ulick Dean (q.v.) in *Evelyn Innes*. I have not got the significance of these facts worked out, I merely state them. †211.2—with Draper (q.v.); †248.26—with Denis (q.v.); ?287.18; 288.19; 291.note 4; 368.21; 413.10; ?452.2; 460.31; 485.3; 494.19; †550.27—with Draper; 562.32.

Dean, Ulick–see Dean, Yeats. †337.36—with Dunn, Butt, Budd (q.q.v.).

Deane, Thomas–18th century Dublin architect. 552.11.

Deasy, Mr–schoolmaster, Nestor (q.v.) in *Ulysses.* 386.35.

Dea Tacita or Acca Laurenta— worshipped at Rome on Dec. 30 when offerings were made to the dead. According to Plutarch there were two Laurentas, confused: one, a mistress of Hercules (q.v.); two, the foster mother of Romulus and Remus (q.v.). 213.30.

*****Deblinite,** Philip–one of the Four (q.v.). 160.27-28,29.

Debora–Hebrew for "bee". In the Bible Debora was an Israelite heroine who encouraged her people to defeat Sisera. 415.4.

*****De Burgh**–family name of the earls of Clanrickarde (q.v.). †623. 23-24—with Struldbrugs.

Declan, St–see St Ailbey 484.23— with St Ciaran.

Dedalus, Stephen–hero of *Portrait of the Artist* where he is identified with Parnell, Satan (q.q.v.), Icarus (see Daedalus); and a protagonist of *Ulysses* where he is identified with Telemachus, Orestes, Hamlet, (q.q.v.). St Stephen (q.v.) was the first martyr. Stephen means "crown" and serves to tie Stephen Dedalus to the kings and princes, mostly uncrowned or dispossessed, in FW—notably Hamlet and Caliban (q.v.), etc. †43.32—with Parnell; 86.7; 152.25; †169.25—with Parnell (q.v.); 179.17; ?206.32; ?208. 33; 211.4; 230.24; 237.24; 252.15, 33; †289.30—with Parnell; 329. 29; 331.36; 366.28; 371.31; 385. 16; 392.17; 397.14; 399.7; †420.36 —with Cromwell (q.v.); 430.15, 18; 463.26; 474.31; 503.33; ?521.7; 549.20; 550.6 (in *Portrait*, Stephen identifies himself with Stephen's Green); 561.21; 587.9; 610.11,12.

Deever, Danny–title subject of Kipling's poem. He shot a sleeping comrade. 352.27.

Deirdre–the Irish Helen (q.v.), subject of plays by Synge and Yeats (q.q.v.). 449.8.

Dekker, Thomas (1570-1641)–English playwright, best known for *The Shoemaker's Holiday,* probable author (with Marston) of *Satiromastix* whose William Rufus (q.v.) has been identified with Shakespeare (q.v.). †620.7—with Van der Decken (q.v.).

Delacroix, Eugène (1798-1863)– French historical painter. 376.7.

*****Delandy**–maybe not a person but *delenda est Carthago.* 64.3.

Delaney, Patrick–Phoenix Park assassin, sentenced to life imprisonment, but released for testifying against Parnell (q.v.) at the Parnell Commission. Also perhaps Dr Patrick Delaney, a cleric, friend of Swift's (q.v.), who owned a place called Delville (43.26) outside Dublin. 43.33; 83.24; 84.8.

Delba, Madame–see Melba.

*****Delganey**–an Irish town. 334.8.

Delia–a name of Artemis (q.v.) who was born on Delos. In FW Delia is identical with the goddess, with Delia Bacon and Biddy Doran (q.q.v.).

†8.28	Delian alps—with Anna Livia (q.v.)
?116.30-31	sesquipedalia
147.11	Delia
180.5-6	Deal Lil–with Lily (q.v.)
?206.24	Deel
208.29	delia
266.1	bedelias
336.29	peckadillies
†349.22	Izodella—with Isabella la Catolica (q.v.)
†359.28	lhirondella (*bis*)—with Procne (see Philomela)
†415.2	Dehlia and Peonia (see Delia and Peona)
432.21	Dellabelliney
?475.9	daffydowndillies
?540.6	delited
596.28	dahlias
?615.4	and illyrical

Delia and Peona–Delia is the Moon (see Artemis) and Peona a loving shepherdess in Keats' "Endymion". See Delia above. 415.2.

Delilah–cause of Samson's (q.v.) downfall (Judges 26). 67.33; 523.16.

Delimata, Bertha–niece of Joyce's. 221.24-25.

Della Porta, Giovanni Battista (1538-1615)–Italian natural philosopher and playwright. His works include *I' Due Fratelli rivali.* See Pig. 9.35-36.

Delta or triangle–Anna Livia (q.v.) as river, as female sexual symbol. 119.19,21; 140.9; 194.23; 196, shape of the opening words; 197.22; †200.9 — with Melba; 210.9—with Altoid's (q.v.); 221.13; 229.23-24; 318.13; 465.3; 492.9; 568.32; 600.6; 614.25.

Delys, Gaby (fl. 1910-20)–French revue artist. 184.27; 351.23; 379.17-18.

*****Demaasch**–partly Joseph Maas (q.v.). 491.15.

*****De Marera,** 334.5.

*****De Mellos**–perhaps Greek "melody". 533.16-17.

Demeter and Persephone—known as "the two goddesses". See Persephone, see Kore. 508.31.

Demetrius–character in Shakespeare's *Antony and Cleopatra, Titus Andronicus* (q.q.v.) and *A Midsummer Night's Dream.* None of these seems specially to fit into place in FW. 319.5; 514.23.

*****Demidoff**–probably some member of the Russian family of Demidov. 329.23.

Democritus (b. 460)–Greek philosopher. 551.31.

Demosthenes (384-322 B.C.)–Attic orator and statesman. 542.18.

Dempsey, Jack–American heavyweight champion. †319.36—with Humpty Dumpty (q.v.).

Denis–a reference to "Denis Don't Be Threatening", the air to which Moore's (q.v.) "I've a

Secret to Tell Thee" is sung. †248.26—with Dean (q.v.).

Denis, St–patron of France. Decapitated in 280, he is usually represented carrying his head in his hands. Denis is the French form of Dionysus (q.v.). 43.30; 316.36; 336.3; 378.1; 617.6.

De Quincey, Thomas (1785-1859)–English writer. 285.note 6.

Derby, Ferdinand Stanley, 5th earl (1559-94)–as Baron Strange he was patron of Strange's Men, an Elizabethan theatrical company for which Shakespeare (q.v.) is thought to have acted. 39.32.

Derby, William Stanley, 6th earl (1561-1642)–a Shakespeare pretender. 180.15 (*bis*); ?325.6; 374.5; †473.9—with Darby (q.v.).

Dermot and Grania–Irish lovers. Dermot "of the love spots" was nephew of Finn MacCool (q.v.) and his greatest warrior. Finn was to marry Grania (daughter of Cormac, q.v.), but when she clapped eyes on Dermot, she loved him, drugged Finn, and eloped with Dermot. Finn gave chase, but the lovers, after many rather dull adventures, won to safety. Years later, Finn persuaded Dermot to go hunting and saw to it that he was killed by a magic boar. Then Grania and Finn were married. Grania has the same name in Irish as Grace O'Malley (q.v.). As Cormac's daughter she is the Misses MacCormack and MacKundred (q.q.v.). Dermot may sometimes include Dermot MacMurrough (see Eva MacMurrough) who brought the Anglo-Normans to Ireland; sometimes, as on 125.6, he includes Dermot, monarch of Ireland, who judged between Columba and Fintan (q.q.v.) in the matter of the psalter which Columba had copied. "To every cow, its calf." See Dark Lady, Arthur, Mark of Cornwall, Rowley the Barrel. 21.14,31 (redtom);

22.18 (dom ter); 58.11; 68.10,14; 105.3; 125.6,8; 137.2,3-4; 146.27, 29; 232.19-20; †291.24—with Adam (q.v.); 299.10-11; 306.28; 369.31; 375.29; 376.1; 495.18; †513.27,28; ?601.8.

*Derry, Chelly, 58-59; 484.33.

*De Razzkias–possibly Reszke (q.v.). 81.34.

Descartes, René (1596-1650)– French philosopher and mathematician. 269.note 2; 301.25; 304.27-28 (reborn . . . cards); 437.8.

Desdemona – heroine of Shakespeare's *Othello* (q.q.v.). 281.17.

Desosse, La–Paris dancer, painted by Toulouse-Lautrec (q.v.). 415.11.

D'Esterre, J. N.–man killed by O'Connell (q.v.) in a duel. *Esterre* is the Italian form of Esther (q.v.), if it matters. 52.29-30.

Destiny, Man of–Napoleon, Shaw (q.q.v.) play about Napoleon. 162.3; 334.7-8.

Deucalion and Pyrrha–sole survivors when Zeus (q.v.) destroyed the human race. They built a ship and floated to Mount Parnassus. To restore the race of men, they threw the bones of their mother earth, i.e. stones, over their shoulders. See Noah. Joyce described Anna Livia (q.v.) as "the Pyrrha of Dublin". 20.32; 179.9-10; 197.3; 199.21,35; 244. 17-18 (deff, coal lay on . . . pyress); †367.20—with Perry (q.v.); 538. 29; 548.28.

De Valera, Eamon (1882-)–Irish politician, known as "the long fellow". Henry Wadsworth must sometimes be comprehended in this last epithet. 4.4 (mathmaster); 41.12-13; 51.13; 82.13; ?82.17—see Ned; 257.8; 261.note 2; 287.1; 342.11; ?346.6; 347.26 —with Longaville (q.v.); 473.8; 478.23; 543.2; 626.31.

De Vere–see Oxford.

Devereux, Gipsy–Byronic protagonist of *The House by the Churchyard* by LeFanu (q.v.). He loves pure Lilias Walsingham (q.v.), courts her beside the Liffey (q.v.) and makes an extended comparison of Lilias and the Liffey; but his was a tarnished life and Lilias dies of grief instead of marrying him. See Lily. It has been suggested to me that Gipsy Devereux is also the Dark Lady, Penelope Rich (q.v.). Off-hand you would say this was starkly impossible, but she fits remarkably well into the context. 563.20.

*Devlin–name of a little Dublin stream. 3.35-36; 21.6; 24.25.

Devoy, John–a founder of the Irish Free State. 72.11.

Dewvale, Clod–see Duval. 457.11.

*Dhorough, St, 341.28.

Diana–Roman goddess of the moon, chase, chastity—see Artemis, Delia, Moon. 43.11; 112.34; 261. 11; 276.19; 476.1; †551.6—with Anna Livia (q.v.); 588.17 (di'); 613.36.

Diarmuid–see Dermot.

Diavolo, Fra–popular name of Michael Pezza (1771-1806), Italian brigand. Title hero of Auber's opera. 466.26-27; †553.13—with Father Mathew (q.v.).

Dick–see Richard III, Burbage, Rowan, Tierney.

Dick, Dirty–minor villain in *The House by the Churchyard* by LeFanu (q.v.). Dirty Dick's is a public house in London. 69.34.

*Dickens, Cardinal, 157.27.

Dickens, Charles (1812-70)–English novelist. 177.35; 434.27; 440.1-2; 610.3.

Dido–queen of Carthage who loved Aeneas (q.v.) and was left by him. 291.note 3; 357.15.

Didymus–means "twin", as does "Thomas". According to the apocryphal *Acts of Thomas*, Judas

Thomas was the twin of Jesus. 258.30.

*Dieudonney, Mr Q. P.–probably St Patrick, but both Jonathan and Nathaniel mean "gift of God". 369.10.

Digges–one of the family names of the Latouches (q.v.). 313.26.

Dignam, Patrick–see Duignan.

*Dijke, Kurt Iuld van, 100.31.

Dilke–possibly Sir Charles (1848-1910), Liberal politician—M.P. for Chelsea—who got into a Parnell-like (q.v.) scandal in divorce court. ?61.11; 90.4.

*Dillon–maybe Val Dillon of Ulysses, mayor of Dublin. 288.1; 519.8.

Dillon, Black–character in LeFanu's (q.v.) The House by the Churchyard. He is a blue-chinned, drunk, brilliant Dublin doctor who performs an operation that raises Sturk (q.v.), as it were, from the dead. Perhaps includes John Blake Dillon (1816-66), Irish M.P., nationalist. His son, John Dillon, was a Parnellite (q.v.) M.P. 219.23.

*Dinah–name sometimes given Kate. When she is a negro? In part it refers to the song, "Someone's In the House with Dinah". ?16.19; 141.29; 170.3; 175.35; 328.14.

*Dinamarqueza, 328.14.

Dinazad or Dinarzade–sister of Scheherazade (q.v.) in the Arabian Nights. 32.8.

*Ding Tams, 28.24.

Diogenes (b. 412 B.C.)–Greek philosopher who spent much time in a tub, and the rest of it searching with a lantern for an honest man. 184.17; 290.21; 307.left margin; 411.29; †421.26—with Guinness (q.v.).

Dion Cassius (b. 155)–Roman historian who wrote of Rome. †391.23—with Boucicault (q.v.).

Dionysius–two tyrants of Syracuse. Dionysius's Ear was a cave, shaped like an ear from which the slightest whisper could be heard. 70.36; 307.left margin.

Dionysus–see Bacchus.

Dis or Dis Pater–Roman name for Pluto (q.v.). 196.33-34.

Disraeli, Benjamin, first earl of Beaconsfield (1804-81)–English politician and novelist, opponent of Gladstone (q.v.). 27.1; 73.7; †100.19—with Bacon (q.v.); 373.27.

Diver, Jenny–girl in Gay's (q.v.) The Beggar's Opera. 39.33,34; 490.25-26.

Dives–rich man in Biblical parable, Luke, 16:19-31. 579.20.

*Divilcult, Mr Tellibly, 303.note 1.

Dix, Dorothy–one or more females who advised the love-lorn. 370.9.

*Dizzier, Sam–perhaps St Dizier, a French town whose local saint is St Didier, or perhaps Didier or Desiderius in the Gestes of Charlemagne (q.v.). 408.22-23.

*Dobbs, 480.30.

*D'Oblong–maybe Dublin and/or May Oblong, a Dublin whore of Joyce's time. 266.6.

*Dodd–perhaps any/or none of the following: 1) title of Tammuz (q.v.); 2) Dod's Parliamentary Companion; 3) Italian diminutive of Giorgio (q.v.); 4) Reuben J. Dodd of Ulysses. 191.23; 389.32; 413.25.

Dodderick, Ogonoch Wrack–see Roderick O'Connor (q.v.). 498.23-24.

Doddpebble, Miss–one of the washwomen, of "Anna Livia Plurabelle", turned into a stone. 620.19-20.

Dodgesome, Dora–Defence of the Realm Act. See Dora. 228.16.

Dodgson, Charles Lutwidge–see Lewis Carroll.

Dodwell, Henry (1641-1711)–Irish scholar, theologian, who gave up a scholarship to Trinity because of conscientious objections to taking orders. 212.33.

*****Dolando,** Deep Dalchi–Dear Dirty Dublin and what else? 570.3.

*****Doll**–Ibsen's Nora?'Joyce's Shakespeare's Tearsheet? (q.q.v.). The name is short for Dorothy, meaning "gift", and hence may refer to Pandora (q.v.). See also "Dot". Now and then Joyce may refer to the Dublin environ, Dollymount, which one book says was named for a celebrated beauty, Dolly Monroe, and another says was named for a beauty, Dorothy Vernon. 141.5; 166.12; 197.20; 210.23; 226.16,17; †246.26—with Dolly Gray (q.v.); 249.1; 266.18; 268.note 7; 294.note 1; 298.9,11; 327.25; 328.31; 365.12; 397.16; 430.34-35; 444.35; 451.1; 469.17; 492.8; 527.24 (see Idol); 562.6,7; 570.5; 575.24; 580.22.

Dolph–name given Shem (q.v.), from *adelphos*, Greek "brother". 286.25; 287.18; 304.26.

Domas, Garda–Thomas (q.v.) or twin. See Didymus. 258.30-31.

Domhall–"Donald a Domhnall", the air to which Moore's (q.v.) "I Saw Thy Form" is sung. 129.26.

Dominic, St–founder of the Dominican order. According to Giraldus the Irish saint, Domnoc or Dominicus (d. 664) introduced bees into Ireland. 261.20; 422.29; 580.5.

Domitian–Roman emperor, 81-96. 306.left margin.

Domovoj–Slavic soul of an ancestor, become a household god. 411.18.

*****Donachie's** – probably donkey (q.v.). 624.16.

*****Donahbella,** 585.24.

*****Donald,** Leathertogs, 71.24.

Donatus, Aelius–Roman grammarian and rhetorician. His *Ars*

grammatica was so popular in the Middle Ages that *Donet* came to mean a rudimentary treatise of any sort. 563.18.

*****Donawhu**–"don't know who"? Blue Danube? 76.32.

Donkey–see Ass.

Donne, John (1573-1631)–English poet. 261.16; 516.20; ?518.10.

Donnelly, Ignatius–author of *The Great Cryptogram*, 1888, a Baconian (q.v.) landmark. I am not sure that all the following Donnellys refer to Ignatius. 39.17; ?84.36; 281.note 3; 499.11-12; 518.30; 585.28-29.

Dooley, lipsyg – mostly P. F. Dunne's (q.v.) Mr Dooley, partly perhaps Kipling's Nangay Doola. See Hennessy. 10.5; †40.12—with Punch and Judy (q.v.); 107.19; 240.12.

*****Doolin**–perhaps Doolin or Doon of Mayence, subject of a French *chanson de geste* of the 14th century, reputed ancestor of Ogier the Dane. 332.10.

*****Doolin,** Dinah, 372.16.

Doolin, Larry–subject of an Irish ballad, a Dublin jaunting-car driver. †59.26—with Jerry (q.v.); 210.19.

Dora–Defence of the Realm Act. See Biddy Doran, Pandora, Riparia. 228.16; 443.5.

Doran, Biddy (named for Brigit, St Bridget, and for Pandora (q.q.v.), by way of Greek *doron*, "gift")–the guinea-hen (q.v.) who scratches on the dung-hill (see John Shakespeare) and produces the letter from Boston, Mass. (see Sally). FW 110-113 associates Biddy with Delia (q.v.), hence with Delia Bacon (q.v.), with Maggy (q.v.), and, less importantly, with Belinda and Lydia Languish (q.q.v.). As Delia Bacon she is at once Francis Bacon's (q.v.) cold, fatal victim, and his agent of resurrection. As Delia or

Artemis (q.v.) she is the moon (q.v.), worshipped as a guinea-hen on the Acropolis. If this explanation seems obscure, kindly go at FW 110-113 with Hawthorne's "Recollections of a Gifted Woman" in one hand and in the other, a classical dictionary, open at "Artemis". Below I have tried to list all available "hens" but there are a lot of circumambient chickens, poules, etc., unlisted and relevant. See also Anna Livia, Dora, Dot, Doll.

11.27	cearc (Ir. "hen")
12.17	a hin
†14.20	bliddy duran — with Pandora (q.v.)
38.18	old hens
39.33-34	red biddy
?36	Brigid Brewster (q.v.)
50.2	bidivil
55.11	hen
64.34	Hazel was a hen
66.23	Mrs Hahn
79.30	biddies
83.31	French hen
93.5	britgits
94.7	hen
110.21,22,23	Ahahn! ... hen ... kishabrigies
111.5	Belinda (q.v.) of the Dorans
7,33	Hane ... hen
112.2,8,27	hen ... auld hensyne ... Biddy Doran
119.23	hen
†123.16	ulykkhean — with Ulysses (q.v.)
124.23-24	Dame Partlet (q.v.)
128.32	henwives
†138.32-33	hahnreich the althe— with Henry VIII (q.v.)
151.12	hinn
199.30	hen
†200.12	hensmoker — with Moke (q.v.)
205.30,36	peahahn ... hennad
207.17	Then, then
220.21	hendrud
234.19	peahenning
†236.9-10	hin. A paaralone! A paaralone — with

	Pearl (q.v.) (*parelhoen* is Dutch for "guinea-hen")
†240.13	henesies—with Hennessy (q.v.)
?245.5	Hanoukan's
247.9	He nobit
?†254.31	hennin—with Helen (q.v.)
256.2,5-6	hen ... hen ... hen ... blessed brigid (see St Bridget)
273.note 3	Hoppity Huhneye ... hen
275.13,21	hen's ... hun
278.21	hen
299.note 1	Hen's
318.14	han in hende
321.26,27	hens ... biddy
336.17	hen
†350.7,8	hen ... Hanar—with Anna Livia (q.v.)
362.15	kenspeckled
364.36	handpicked hunsbend
†365.21	shenker—with Shem (q.v.)
370.2,9	hen ... then ... when
374.4	Ahem
379.23	henayearn
382.11	hen
393.23	mudhen
405.21	hencoop
420.8-9	handmud
427.36	Biddyhouse
432.6	henservants
†447.8	Henrietta's (q.v.)
452.32	guinea
†453.4	biddy moriarty (q.v.)
457.5	biddies
464.36	guidneys
478.15,32	moorhens ... doraphobian
479.5	guineagould
482.16,19	Hooshin ... hin ... Guiney
492.9	henpecked
495.9	henkerchoff
?497.20	Raheniacs (Raheny is an environ of Dublin)
518.26	Dorans
519.8	biddy
578.20	peahen
†583.17	rhean—with Rhea (q.v.)
584.20-21	hen of the doran's

586.21	hwen
†594.30	han . . . Sassqueehenna —with Susan, Queen, Anna Livia (q.q.v.) and a river (see Artemis)
?595.25	mudden
606.2,17	hanbath . . . hen
608.18	Alina (q.v.)
24-25	ohanthenth
615.10	hen
616.20	hun

*Dorans, Batteries, 372.31.

Dorcas–restored to life by St Peter (q.v.), Acts 9. 470.7.

*Doremon's, 433.4.

*Dorsan from Dunshanagan, 417.31.

D'Orsay, Alfred Guillaume Gabriel (1801-52)–French dandy, wit. 405.5.

*Dot, Sue–see Dots and Susanna. 210.25.

*Dots, Miss or Dot–see Doll. 238.1; 290.note 6; 296.25; 360.1; 444.35; 527.17; 532.23; 626.9.

Douce, Miss–siren in *Ulysses*, doubtless named for the Irish mountain. 208.29; 462.9.

*Dougal, Mr Jasper, 479.10.

*Dougherty's, 374.15.

Doughty, Charles Montague (1843-1926)–author of *Travels in Arabia Deserta, Adam Cast Forth, Mansoul, or the Riddle of the World*, etc. 363.21.

Douglas, Lord Alfred, "Bosie"–object of Oscar Wilde's (q.v.) love. The name Douglas means "dark glass". Wilde is so important a figure in FW that I feel sure Lord Alfred is hiding somewhere, maybe as Mr W. H. (q.v.). 355.9; ?†391.4—with Johnny MacDougal; †397.2—with Johnny MacDougal (q.v.); †536.22—with William Boyce; 588.1.

Dove–see Raven.

*Dowdy–plays on *The Decameron*. 435.9.

Dowlah, Surrajah–Indian prince, responsible for the Black Hole of Calcutta. 492.21.

*Dowling, 624.23.

Doyle, Conan (1859-1930)–English writer, creator of Sherlock Holmes (q.v.). He also wrote on spiritualism and produced a history of World War I in 6 vols. †228.13—with Conan; 617.14.

*Doyles–Joyce indicated that they refer to the Dail. "Doyle" comes from *dubh-ghall* or black foreigner, Dane (q.v.). They are usually connected with the Twelve (q.v.). 48.25; 142.26; 256.28; 574.9,32; 575.6 (Ann Doyle—doubtless Anna Livia, q.v.); 575.7,32 (Jeremy Doyle—see Jerry).

Doyne, Major–on the Whitechurch road near Willbrook (an environ of Dublin) is a statute which Major Doyne erected to the horse which carried him through the battle of Waterloo. 52.17; ?485.20.

Draco–Athenian law-giver, also a constellation. 343.2.

Dracula, Count–title and vampire of Bram Stoker's (q.v.) novel. 145.32.

*Dragon Man or Dragoman–seems to be the Man Servant and the Ass (q.v.). The word "dragoman" comes from Arabic *targun*. Targuns are explanatory paraphrases of certain Old Testament books. These mix in with Blake's (q.v.) targun, "The Marriage of Heaven and Hell", which is echoed on FW, 15: "I was in a Printing house in Hell, and saw the method in which knowledge is transmitted from generation to generation. In the first chamber was a Dragon-Man, clearing away the rubbish from a cave's mouth." 15.34; 112.7; 316.30; 479.9.32; 480.26; 577.1.

Drake, Sir Francis (1540-96)–English admiral. 390.8; 479.32.

Draper–see Drapier.

Drapier–pseudonym of Swift's (q.v.). A patent was granted to the Duchess of Kendal (the King's mistress) for supplying copper coins to Ireland. The patent was sold by her to William Wood (q.v.) for £10,000. In 1723 the Irish Parliament protested the transaction, and it was widely believed that the coins would be worthless. In 1724, Swift, in the character of a Dublin draper, published four letters against .Wood's halfpence. The letters caused such a stir that Swift became an Irish hero overnight, and the government was forced to abandon the project and compensate Wood.

Draper also takes in, at times, Shakespeare (q.v.) who, by one theory, spent his "lost years" as a draper's assistant, and AE (q.v.) who was for a time employed by Pim (q.v.) the Dublin draper.

40.15; ?104.26; †211.2—see Dean; †421.25—with Shem (q.v.); 422.1; 529.12; †550.24,27—with Dean (q.v.); †608.5—with AE (see Russell), 6 (*bis*).

Dreiser, Theodore–20th century American novelist. 55.23.

*Drewitt's–partly Druid—see Astrid. 279.note 1.

Dreyfus, Alfred (1859-1935)–French soldier, of Jewish parentage. He was condemned as a traitor on forged evidence; his subsequent rehabilitation convulsed French politics for many years. 78.21.

Dromios–low-born twins in Shakespeare's (q.v.) *Comedy of Errors*. 89.3; 598.2.

*Droughty–maybe Doughty (q.v.). 361.35.

*Drownings, the Mrs–Mrs Browning (q.v.)? 132.9-10.

*Drudge, 454.10.

Drughad, Reeve–probably *rive droite*. 197.1.

Druid–see Berkeley.

Dryasdust–prosy character to whom some of Scott's (q.v.) novels are addressed. 447.13.

*Drysalter, 512.2-3.

Dry Shanks–according to Brandes (q.v.), Charles Mackay tried to prove the Celtic origin of Shakespeare's (q.v.) name—i.e. *seac speir* or "dry shanks". 194.27 (dry yanks will).

Du Barry, Comtesse (1746-93)–mistress of Louis XV and a brand of American cosmetics. 461.2.

Ducrow, Andrew (1793-1842)–celebrated equestrian performer at Astley's (q.v.). Perhaps also the French general Ducrot (1817-82). 133.22.

Dudeny, Henry E.–English puzzle expert. 284.note 1.

Duessa–in Spenser's *Faerie Queene* (q.v.), she is the Catholic Church and Mary Queen of Scots (q.v.). †461.9—with Duchess of York and Duse (q.q.v.).

*Duff, 354.33; 467.17; 549.33; 566.21.

Duff, R. A. (b. 1878)–English cricketer. 583.34.

Dufferin, Lady (1807-67)–Sheridan's (q.v.) granddaughter, author of "Lament of the Irish Emigrant", which opens, "I am sitting on the stile, Mary". 93.30-31.

Dufferin and Ava, Frederick Temple Hamilton Blackwood, first Marquess, (1826-1902)–Indian viceroy, annexed Burma. 10.19.

*Duff–Muggli, 123.11.

Duffs, lucky–see Lindsays. 438.35.

*Duffy, 589.18.

*Duffy, Delores, 609.5.

*Duignan–in some lists Peregrine O'Duignan is one of the Four Masters (q.v.). Paddy Dignam of

Ulysses may also be included. 14.28; 324.33 (Mandig); 390.11.

Dulcarnons–not a person, but Arabic *Dhu'lkarnain* or "two-horned", or a dilemma. 276.left margin.

*Dulcey, 31.24-25; 226.17; †234.23 –with Dulcinea (q.v.).

Dulcinea del Toboso–the name Don Quixote (q.v.) gives to the peasant girl, Alonza Lorenzo, whom he elects mistress of his heart. †234.23—with Dulcey (q.v.).

Du Maurier, George (1834-96)– British artist and writer, author of *Trilby* and *Peter Ibbotsen* (q.q.v.). †494.20—with Mary (q.v.).

Dun, Sir Patrick–Dublin hospital. 40.35.

Dunboyne, Billy–mainly William III (q.v.) for whom they beat a big drum on the "Twalfth" in honor of the battle of the Boyne; but the reference seems also to include Billy Dunn, a character in *Heartbreak House*, whose supposed daughter, Ellie Dunn (q.v.), is at 211.35, followed line 36 by their creator, "swash". 211.34.

Duncan—murdered king in Shakespeare's *Macbeth* (q.q.v.). 479.34.

*Dunelli, El Don de–Donnelly (q.v.)? 84.36.

Dunhill–English tobacco and pipe sellers. 50.30.

Dunlop, John Boyd (1840-1921)– English inventor and manufacturer of tires and other rubber products. 29.3; 44.11-12; 58.3-4; 295.32; 350.14; 394.14; 395.6; 420.27; 437.6; 497.36; 584.13.

Dunn, Ellie–girl in Shaw's (q.v.) *Heartbreak House* whose heart is broken by Hector Hushaby (q.v.). See also Billy Dunboyne. 211.35.

*Dunne, 334.29.

*Dunne, Barnabas Ulick–name of the comedian who plays Butt (q.v.) in the televised performance of "Buckley and the Russian General" (q.v.). See Dean. 337.36.

Dunne, John–see Donne.

Dunne, Peter Finlay (1867-1936) creator of Mr Dooley (q.v.). He is doubtless comprehended in some Dunn or Dunne reference.

*Dunne, Promoter, 210.35; 213.34-35.

Dunnohoo, Theo–see The O'Donough. 439.19-20.

Dunstan, St (924-88)–Archbishop of Canterbury, statesman. 135.9.

*Durant, 243.11.

Duse, Eleanora (1859-1924)–Italian actress. 224.30; †461.9—with Duessa and the Duchess of York (q.q.v.).

Dusort, Pierre–the Stone of Destiny or Lia Fail. The reference here is to Johnny MacDougal (q.v.). 219.24.

Dutch–seems usually to refer to William III (q.v.).

Duval, Claude (1643-70)–noted highwayman, hanged at Tyburn. †457.11—with Claud Lightfoot (q.v.).

*Duzinascu–does not ask you? 64.32.

Dwyer, Michael–Irish rebel of the early 19th century. 600.18.

Dyas–Jupiter (q.v.) in the Vedas. 55.34.

*Dyer, 226.12.

Dyke, Betsy–wife of Thomas Moore (q.v.). Her name often turns up near her husband's songs. 528.32 (Tyke); 617.31.

*Dysart, 88.23.

E

E or ⊡ –Joyce described the first sign as "Earwicker, H C E by moving letter round" (Joyce to Miss Weaver, 24 March 1924). It is my impression that you could move the sign around till doomsday without getting a C or an H. To me it looks like an E or a W (as in William, q.v.?). Joyce said that the second sign means HCE interred in the landscape. (Joyce to Miss Weaver, 31 May 1927). He also explained (2 March 1927) that ⊡ is a Chinese letter-word, meaning "mountain", called "Chin", which is the common people's way of pronouncing Hin or Fin (see Finn). 119.17; 299. note 4.

E, wholebroader–HCE (q.v.). 51.19.

Eames, Emma–19th century American operatic soprano. 306. note 1.

Early, Jubal (1816-94)–one of the Confederate commanders at second Bull Run (Manassas). †84.2—with Jubal Cain (q.v.).

Earnshaw, Cathy–heroine of *Wuthering Heights*—see Brontë. †8.8— with Kate (q.v.).

?Earp, T. W.–20th century English writer. †191.20—with Earwicker (q.v.).

Earwicker–see HCE. See *A Wake Newslitter* No. 4, in which Mr Hart solves the question of the Earwickers of Sidlesham. Ear or Er is also a thunder god.

Earwig, Jacob–boots about the Swan (q.v.) in the play *Boots About the Swan* by Charles Selby. According to K. Sullivan, *Joyce Among the Jesuits*, p. 234, this play was put on at Clongowes Wood when Joyce was there in 1890. The song "Poor Old Joe" (q.v.) was sung on the same program. See Earwicker, Jacob, Moonshine. 63.34-35.

*East, Mother, 35.30.

Eates, Emma–see Eames.

*Ebahi-Ahuri, Professor, 165.28.

Eblis–Mohammedan Lucifer (q.v.). 11.5.

Ecclectiastes of Hippo–see St Augustine. 38.29-30.

Eccles, Solomon (1618-83)–London teacher of virginals and viols who destroyed his instruments when he became a Quaker. After helping Fox (q.v.) in the West Indies, he returned to England and relapsed into fiddling. His sons were all musicians and composers. I hope Eccles 'Street was named for this charming man. 514.15; 567.27.

Ecclesiastes–Greek rendering of Hebrew *koheleth* or preacher, author of a Biblical book. 29.16; 139.26; 242.11; 374.23; 514.14.

Eckermann, Johann Peter (1792-1854)–Goethe's (q.v.) secretary and Boswell (q.v.), author of *Conversations with Goethe*. 71.8-9; 356.2.

Edar, Ben–ancient name of Howth (q.v.), said to derive from Edar, a Daedanaan chief, buried on the hill. †7.28—with Heathcliff (q.v.); 326.18, etc.

*Eddems and Clay–Adam (q.v.), maybe Adam's hats. 278.note 7.

Eddy, Mrs Mary Baker (1821-1910)– founder of Christian Science. Joyce here plays on Aedes Christi or Christ Church, where Lewis Carroll (q.v.) lived. 482.1.

*Ede–see Eve. Possibly Kate Ede, heroine of George Moore's (q.v.) novel, *A Mummer's Wife*. 324.7.

Edison, Thomas Alva (1847-1931) –American inventor of the electric light, here combined with the Eddystone light house. 127.15.

Edmund, King–three Anglo-Saxon kings of England. One became a saint and martyr, one was called "Ironsides", all fought the Danes. Edmund is a bastard in *King Lear* (q.v.). Joyce says (*Ulysses,* 206-209/268-271) Edmund was suggested by Shakespeare's (q.v.) brother, Edmund. 61.29; 135.9; †256.11-12—with Burke (q.v.); †352.22—with Amundsen, AE (q.q.v.).

*Edward–in *Lear* (q.v.)? 136.33 (headwood).

Edward, Lord–see Fitzgerald. 88.31.

Edwards–brand of "dessicated soup", mentioned in *Ulysses,* 173/223. 26.31.

Edwards, Hilton–20th century Dublin actor, director. 569.28.

*Egan–"... a description of Shem-Ham-Cain-Egan, etc. ...." (Joyce to Miss Weaver 16 January 1924). I do not know for sure who this Egan is or where in FW. Maybe Patrick Egan, a Land Leaguer who went into perpetual exile in Paris, maybe Kevin Egan of *Ulysses.* †604.6—with Engels (q.v.).

Egan, Pierce (1772-1849)–English sporting writer, whose works include *Real Life in Ireland by a Real Paddy.* 447.23.

*Egari's, Isaac, 408.26.

Egbert or Ecgbert (d. 837)–king of the West Saxons. 4.32; 88.21.

Eggeberth, Haroun Childeric–HCE as Haround, Childeric, Egbert (q.q.v.). 4.32.

?Eglantine, Madam–prioress in Chaucer's (q.v.) *Canterbury Tales.* If not, a possible reference to John Eglinton (see Magee), as on p. 205/267 of *Ulysses.* 39.34.

Eglinton–see Magee.

*Egon, Equerry, 102.14.

Egypt, Little–dancer at a Chicago World's Fair. 551.30.

Egyptus–see Aegyptus. 263.6.

Eiffel, Alexandre Gustave (b. 1832)– engineer of the Eiffel Tower. 4.36.

*Eiffel, Holy Saint, †88.23-24–with Holly and Ivy (q.v.).

Eileen Aruna–Irish song. Joyce had a sister Eileen. 210.31; 620.5-6.

Einstein, Albert (1879-1955)– American mathematician, born in Ulm (see 100.36). 100.26; 149.28; 293.24; 305.6; †611.20 (Entis-Onton)—with Newton (q.v.).

Eithne–concubine of Cuchulain's (q.v.). 394.26.

Elbow–constable in *Measure for Measure.* 336.2.

*Elcock, Luke, 31.18; 329.26; 447. 12,14; 567.24.

Elders–in the apocryphal book of *Susanna* (q.v.), two ancient judges. When they were turned down by the young matron, Susanna, they accused her of being unchaste with a young man. Daniel (q.v.) unmasked their lies. In FW they are four (q.v.) Elders, who on 398-399 first proposition the woman and then accuse her falsely—see 598.22-23. For Joyce's extension of the story see also Sycamores, John Lane, Susanna Shakespeare. 24.12; 64.36; 219.22; 372.34; 428.3; 484.22; 552.20; 562.19-20; 568.27; 604.16.

Eleazar–character in Halevy's opera *La Juive.* 133.19.

*Elenders, 551.2.

Elgin, Lord (1766-1841)–British diplomat, art collector. 549.15.

Elijah–Hebrew prophet (1 Kings, 17 ff.). 156.26.

Eliot, George (1819-80)–pen-name of Mary Anne Evans Cross. See Liggen. †229.3-4—with St George (q.v.).

Eliot, Thomas Stearns (1888-)– American-born English poet. It is my opinion that "The Waste Land" would never have been written but for *Ulysses*, and that FW would never have been written but for "The Waste Land". Since I saw there is a large Grail theme in FW, I have been surer than ever that there is considerable covert reference to Eliot in FW, far more than I have indicated here, probably more than I have seen. Some "Tom" references may be to Eliot. Perhaps he is St Thomas à Becket. The references below are almost all unfriendly.

?19.33; †43.9—with Elliot (q.v.); 96.34 (possum); 191—this page is about Eliot, as Mr Wilder has pointed out, and its three paragraphs begin with Eliot's initials; 191.6,12 (possum), †191.20-21— with Tom, Hamlet (q.q.v.), 26 (possum); 275.21.

Eliphaz–one of Job's (q.v.) comforters. 244.35.

Elisha–Old Testament prophet (1 Kings, 19, etc.). 351.23 (*bis*).

Elizabeth–see Elizabeth I, Elizabeth Hall, St Elizabeth, Elizabeth Guinness, Gunning, Lamp, Lisa, Issy.

21.2	Lissom! lissom
23.23	lipth . . . lithpeth
53.5	liss
†90.10	bettygallaghers (see Gallagher Moon)
†94.30	beetyrossy—with Rose (q.v.) . . . bettydoaty
95.22	kissabetts
101.6	liss
†107.9	alphabetters — with Anna Livia (q.v.)
†111.6	Cheepalizzy's — with Chapelizod (q.v.), see also hen
147.11,30	Bett . . . lipsabuss
148.26	Liss, liss
156.34	Elissabed—see Queen Elizabeth
164.28	betteraved
176.24	bet
†183.13	alphybettyformed— with Anna Livia (q.v.)
?186.30	bethels

?187.26	Brown Bess (q.v.)
192.36	balbettised
†200.31	a lizzy a lossy—with Alice (q.v.)
†203.8	Alesse — with Alice (q.v.)
†208.20	alpheubett buttons— with Anna Livia (q.v.)
211.13-14	Betty Bellezza (q.v.)
†226.29	a lessle, a lissle—with Alice, Issy (q.q.v.)
232.35	elazilee
236.7	lissom
†237.9	alisten — with Alice (q.v.)
?241.27	koldbethizzdryel
242.5-6	wokingbetts
†245.9	lissaned — with Anna Livia (q.v.)
†256.33	nibulissa—with Nuvoletta, Issy (q.q.v.)
†270.20	Alis, alas—with Alice (q.v.)
276.note 6	lisplips
†note 7	A liss—with Alice (q.v.)
278.note 2	beth
?283.15	libs
286.left margin	bess
289.26	Lady Elisabbess
290.2	Liselle
†291.14	a nelliza . . . cliptbuss —with Anna Livia, Helen (q.q.v.)
297.32	bett
302.23	lib
?note 2	Lifp
325.7	bet
328.29,31	tha lassy! tha lassy . . . fiery quean—see Elizabeth I
†36	Elizabeliza — see St Elizabeth, Elizabeth I
329.11,36	bettest . . . bethhailey —see Elizabeth Hall
?337.34	bettle of the bawl
†340.6	Lissnaluhy
342.30-31	Bett . . . Bett
348.25	lyse
†26	lispias (with a girl in a song of Moore's q.v.)
358.24	bejetties

†359.32-33 Alys, Alysaloe—with Alice (q.v.)

?379.15 noiselisslesoughts

399.stanza 3 Lizzy

416.35 tetties

†420.10 Bauv Betty Famm (poor little woman)

†437.24 elizabeetons—with Elizabeth I, Mrs Beeton (q.q.v.)

†444.31 Annybettyelsas — with Anna Livia, Elsa (q.q.v.)

490.26,27 Better . . . redtetterday

†491.22 Lillypet—with Elizabeth II, Lily (q.q.v.)

†495.25-26 Elsebett . . . Gunning (q.v.)

497.20 bettlers—with Butler?

500.27 bet

508.7 bet . . . bet

525.24 lissy

?†528.13 Luz—with Luke Tarpey (q.v.)—see 526

†530.21 lizzyboy (reference seems to be to the Man Servant, q.v.)

†538.22 Lizzy and Lissy Mycock

?542.28 bethel of Solyman's

553.18 lisbing lass

†561.8 Halosobuth — Elizabeth I

†577.17 fryggabet—with Frygga (q.v.)

†583.21 bettyship—Elizabeth I

?22 jettyblack rosebuds—with Rose (q.v.)

586.11 bet

595.7-8 goodbett

†604.17 Strubry Bess—Elizabeth I

624.18 bet

Elizabeth, St–mother of John the Baptist (q.v.). Some references given under Elizabeth (q.v.) may include her.

Elizabeth I (1553-1603)–Queen of England, somewhat equivocal virgin (q.v.), muse of her poets who steadily identify her with the moon (q.v.), as Phoebe, Delia (q.q.v.), Cynthia, etc. Under Elizabeth (q.v.) I have indicated such references as I think belong to her. She ties to Elizabeth Hall (q.v.) because they both inspired the same poet—see Lamp and Lump. It must be remembered that Elizabeth was not always an ugly old queen (q.v.); she was even a baby and, as such, a character of Shakespeare's (q.v.), a reconciling babe.

Elizabeth II–the present Queen of England was called Lillybet when a child. †491.22 (Lillypet)—with Lily (q.v.); 561.24.

Elliot and **Fry**–London photographers. Like Atkinson (q.v.), they were pioneers in photography. Fry could, I suppose, include the cocoa-makers. Elliot certainly includes T. S. Eliot (q.v.) since the Grail is broken here. 43.9.

Ellis, Alexander (1814-90)–English philologist, mathematician, musician. 205.7.

Ellis, Henry Havelock (1859-1939) –English man-of-letters, anthropologist, sex student. See Havelok? 294.8.

*****Ellis, Madge**–see Maggies. 586.14.

*****Elly, Irmak**–*Irma* is Turkish for "river". 212.13.

*****Elmer,** 243.15.

El Monte de Zuma–see Montezuma.

Elpis–Greek "hope"; falsely believed to be the Christian wife of Boethius. 267.4.

Elrington, Thomas (1688-1732)– Irish actor. Swift (q.v.) mentions him in "Billet to the Company of Players". †55.36—with Elrington Ball (q.v.).

Elsa–heroine of Wagner's (q.v.) *Lohengrin*—see Swan. †444.31— with Anna Livia, Elizabeth (q.q.v.).

Elsie from Chelsea–once a popular song. 587.26.

Elsker–see Selskar Gunn. 388.6.

*Elters–Elders? 17.19.

Em, Fair–title heroine of a play that has been ascribed to Shakespeare (q.v.). Her situation is roughly that of Margareen (q.v.). †164.8—with Maggies (q.v.).

*Emery, 128.25.

Emilia–character in Shakespeare's *Othello* (q.q.v.) and in *The Winter's Tale.* See also Aemilia. 410.23.

Emma–see Lady Hamilton. 328.21.

Emmet, Robert (1778-1803)–Irish rebel hero, executed as a traitor. See Sarah Curran. ?13.33; 136.14; ?417.21.

*Ena, 94.14; 147.11; †278.note 3– with Stella (q.v.).

*Enders, Miss–probably the sender of the letter from Boston. See Anders. 412.23.

Endersen, H. C.–see Andersen. 138.16.

*Endles of Eons, Miss–possibly Mlle. D'Eon (1728-1810) who was also the Chevalier D'Eon, French political adventurer, famous for the mystery of his sex. 226.36.

Engels, Friedrich (1820-95)–Karl Marx's (q.v.) collaborator. 75. 31; 233.33; 519.1; ?†604.6—with Egan (q.v.).

Enghien, Duc d' (1772-1804)– Bourbon, executed by Napoleon (q.v.). 146.19,20.

Enobarbus–character in Shakespeare's *Antony and Cleopatra* (q.q.v.). 157.27.

Enoch–1) eldest son of Cain (q.v.); or 2) 7th in descent from Adam (q.v.) in the line of Seth (q.v.). 283.1; 357.30; 442.6.

Enos–son of Seth (q.v.). Enos Salts are a purgative. 30.16; 577.21.

?Enright–an IRA song, "Take It Down from the Mast, Irish Traitors", contains the line, "But we stand with Enright and Larkin . . .". 98.19.

Entis-Onton–approximate anagrams of Einstein and Newton (q.q.v.). 611.20.

*Entwhistle, Major Hermyn C.– there is a remote possibility that this includes Herman Melville (q.v.). 342.20.

Enver Pasha (b. 1881)–leader of the Young Turks. After an adventurous career, he was last heard of leading a revolt against Russia in the 1920s. 367.35; 582.12.

*Epiphanes, Reverend, of Saint Dhorough's–perhaps St Epiphanius (315-402), a Church Father who listed 80 heresies and had 5 tongues; or perhaps Antiochus IV or Epiphanes who served as a model for the Antichrist (q.v.). 341.27-28.

Ephialtes–see Outus. 493.23.

Erasmus, Desiderius (1466-1536)– Dutch humanist. 155.33; †301. note 5—with Eros (q.v.).

*Erchenwyne, 88.21.

Erebus–son of Chaos who begot Aether, Day, and Night on his sister. 239.30; 473.16.

Erechthonius–son of Hephestus, king of Athens, built Athena's (q.v.) temple on the Acropolis. When dead, he was worshipped in another temple on the Acropolis, the Erechtheum. 539.3.

*Ergastulus–maybe from Latin *ergastulum,* a slave's or debtor's prison. 532.12.

Eric–legendary Swedish king who controlled the direction of the wind by turning his magic cap. The word "eric" is the Viking word for a fine. 220.25.

Eric–the other man in Wagner's *Flying Duchman* (q.q.v.). 316.8; 530.21.

*Ericoricori, 623.1.

Erigena or Scotus, John (fl. 850)– mystic and philosopher. 4.36.

*Erminia, Regina–maybe the female form of Erminus, one of the eponymous national ancestors of the Teutons. 339.29; 391.1.

Ernest–non-existent character in Wilde's (q.v.) *The Importance of Being Earnest*. Maybe also the hero of Butler's (q.v.) *The Way of all Flesh*. 233.20; 452.7; 490.12.

Eros–Greek god of love—see Cupid. †40.13—with Oscar Wilde (q.v.); †301.note 5—with Erasmus (q.v.); 431.14.

Erskine, Harold–author of *Riddle of the Sands*. I am not sure but I think he was involved in the gun-running at Howth during the First World War. 596.5.

*Esa, 88.22.

Esau–see Jacob.

Escamillo–toreador in *Carmen* (q.v.). 350.22.

Escoffier–French gourmet. 59.29.

*Esellus, Hanner–since the ass (q.v.) is indicated, this probably has to do with Latin *asellus* and German *Esel*, both words meaning ass. 478.8.

Eset–seems to be Aesop, but Eset is also a form of Isis (q.v.). 29.13.

*Esme, 88.22.

Essatessa–see Stella and Vanessa. 278.note 3.

Essav–see Esau. 607.8-9.

Essex, Arthur Capel, 1st Earl of (1632-83)–popular lord-lieutenant of Ireland who prevented the grant of Phoenix (q.v.) Park to the Duchess of Cleveland. Later he was involved in the Rye House plot, was imprisoned in the Tower and cut his throat. Essex Bridge in Dublin was named for him, but is now called Grattan (q.v.) Bridge. I assume that Capel Street, Dublin, was also named for him. I do not understand the use made of him in FW. As Joyce says, he is indeed a dark horse (Ir. *capal*). He may be totally identified with the more famous Earl of Essex (see below) but I can find no evidence of this. See Arthur. In *Romeo and Juliet* (q.v.) Capulet is sometimes "Capel". 24.19; 51.27; 125.17; 161.29; †254-255—with Gautama, Artho (q.q.v.); ?291.26; †325.14—with Chapelizod (q.v.); 370.36; 446.24; 448.9; ?484.7; 487.31,32,33; 488. 3,28,33; 515.21; †521.4—with Robert Devereux, Earl of Essex (q.v.); 607.34; 608.7; †611.35—with R. Devereux, Earl of Essex (q.v.).

Essex, Robert Devereux, 2nd Earl of (1566-1601)–appointed lord-lieutenant of Ireland in 1599. Favorite of Elizabeth I (q.v.), the friend Bacon (q.v.) betrayed. It has been suggested that he was Hamlet and/or Mr W. H. (q.q.v.), and various other Shakespearean (q.v.) characters. Since the episode of Berkeley and the Archdruid (q.q.v.) seems to have to do with Bacon's "Colours (or pretenses) of Good and Evil", it is right that someone should be there in an "essexcoloured" suit. See Arthur Capel, Earl of Essex with whom this Essex doubles at least twice, perhaps always. 521.4; 611.35.

Esther–title heroine of a Biblical book, queen of the Persian, Xerxes. Esther is the Hebrew name for the planet Venus (q.v.) —see also Ishtar. Esthers, and variations—Essie, Hetty, Hester, etc.—are listed under Stella and Vanessa (q.v.).

*Esuan Menschavik–perhaps Esau (q.v.) who, like the Menscheviks, lost out. 185.34.

Eswurds–see Edwards. 26.31.

Ethelred or Aethelred the Unready –King of England, 979-1016. †439.36—with Ethelred Preston (q.v.).

Ethelwulf or Aethelwulf–King of the West Saxons. 88.22.

Euclid–Greek mathematician, 3rd century B.C. 155.32; 206.13; 283.24; †302.12—with Joyce (q.v.).

*****Eugenius**–name given Shaun (q.v.), meaning "nobly born". Possibly Eugene Schauman who shot General Bobrikoff (q.v.). 562.33; 572-573 (*passim*).

Eugenius–four popes. 154.20.

Euhemerus (fl. 300 B.C.)–Greek mythographer, author of *Sacred History*, a philosophic romance which asserts that the gods were originally human heroes and conquerors. 331.31.

Eulalina, St–martyred in Merida in 300. 430.36.

Eulenspiegel, Tyll–legendary prankster of 14th century Brunswick, title of a Strauss tone-poem. 208.9; 408.24.

*****Eulogia**, 527.12.

Euphemia – Greek for "well-spoken". See Jacqueline Pascal. 528.24.

Europa–raped by Zeus (q.v.) who was disguised as a bull. Most of Zeus's women are faintly indicated hereabouts. 208.19 (hayrope).

Eusapia–see Palladino. 528.14.

Eusebius–1) pope for 3 months in 309 or 310; 2) of Caesara (260-340), ecclesiastical historian with Arian (q.v.) leanings. The latter was noted for his *Canons* which harmonized the gospels. 409.36.

*****Eustache**, Mr–maybe just the eustachian tube. 361.11; 535.26.

Eva, Lady–see Eve MacMurrough. 288.15.

*****Evans**, 533.5.

Eve–see Adam.

Eveline–title and heroine of a story in *Dubliners*. 186.24; 222.32.

*****Evelyn**–John? 94.28.

Everallin–in Macpherson's "Fingal" (q.q.v.), the mother of Oscar (q.v.), who was grandson of Fingal. 228.4.

*****Evlyn**, Pomona–evil apple? 62.34.

*****Evora**–there is a seaport of this name in Portugal. When Tristram Amory (q.v.) landed at Howth, he fought on St Lawrence's (q.v.) day at "The Bridge of Evora" which crossed a small river, "The Bloody Stream". 623.27.

Ewe–see Rachel.

*****Exquovis**–Latin, "from wherever you like". 484.34.

*****Ex - Skaerer - Sissers** – probably Anna Livia (q.v.) as the tailor's daughter and Earwicker's wife—see Forficula. See also Nanny Ni Sheeres, 328.14. 375.25.

Eyeinstye–see Einstein. 305.6.

Eyesoldt, Mme. Gertrud–German actress, early 20th century. †222.27—with Issy (q.v.).

Eyolf–title character of Ibsen's (q.v.) *Little Eyolf*. 201.34.

Eyre, Jane–title heroine of Charlotte Brontë's (q.v.) novel. Note the references to two wives and Thornfield. 281.3 (faery).

Ezekiel–title and author of a Biblical book. 307.left margin.

F

F . . . A . . ., Mrs–sweet Fanny Adams. 59.4; †65.5—with Adam (q.v.).

Fabius Maximus (d. 204 B.C.)–known as "Cunctator" from his caution in war. 307. left margin.

Faerie Queen–poem by Edmund Spenser (who ought to be in FW but hasn't been found by me). The Faerie Queen is Elizabeth I (q.v.). 328.31.

*****Faherty**, Doctor, 25.5.

Fair–see Finn and Mr W. H.

*Fairbrother, 585.29.

*Fairlove–Mr W. H. (q.v.)? 300.28.

*Fairlys, 176.7.

Fairynelly–see Farinelli. 151.7.

Falconer, Father Flammeus– Messrs. John Falconer, the Dublin printers who burned the edition of *Dubliners*. 185.4.

Falstaff, Sir John–character in Shakespeare's two Henry IV (q.q.v.) plays and *The Merry Wives of Windsor*, a corrupter of youth. In 1 Henry IV he dies and is resurrected—see V,v, 112-113. 7.13; 366.30; 379.18; ?479.27.

Fama–in Classic myth the personification of rumor. 98.2.

Famm, Bauv Betty–*pauvre petite femme*. Does the reference include *Little Women*? See Elizabeth. 420.10.

Fand – Celtic goddess. 224.26; 315.28.

*Fanden–Norwegian word for "devil". 282.25; 516.19.

*Fanny–Anna Livia? Fanny Hill (q.v.)? 340.25,29.

*Fanny, Urinia–see Urania. 171.27-28.

Faraday, Michael (1791-1867)– English chemist and physicist. 542.33.

*Farber–pencil-makers? Faber and Faber? 65.32.

Fargo, William (1818-81)–American pioneer expressman, as in Wells-Fargo. 5.31.

Farinelli or Carlo Broschi (1705-82) –Italian male soprano. 151.7.

*Farley, Forrester–see Barley. 257.24.

*Farrel, Pat–see *Ulysses*, 127/163. 176.17.

Farrell–one of Dublin's sculptors. 552.12.

*Farrell, O'Mara, 270.left margin.

*Farrelly, Fiery, 13.13.

Farseeingetherich–see Vercingetorix. 54.3-4.

Farson, Negley (b. 1890)–American professional expatriate, author of *The Way of a Transgressor*. 171.4.

Fateha–not a person but *Fatiha*, a prayer found in the Koran. 235.2.

Fatima–daughter of Mohammed (q.v.). 205.31; 389.15.

*Fatmate, Mister–see Pig. Possibly Falstaff (q.v.)—see Epilogue to 2 Henry IV. 72.15.

Faust or Faustus–16th century magician who sold his soul to the devil, subject of works by Marlowe and Goethe (q.q.v.). 74.9; 83.29; †160.27,29—with William III (q.v.); 252.2; 288.9; 292.22; 356.1.

Fauxfitzhuorson–see Fitz-Warin. 529.20.

Fawkes, Guy (1570-1606)–English gunpowder plot conspirator, subject of a play, *The Fifth of November*, which has been ascribed to Shakespeare (q.v.). 177. 29; 193.19; 425.23; 514.33 (gaa . . . Fox); 545.31; †547.36—with Brer Fox (q.v.).

Fawnia–girl in Robert Greene's (q.v.) *Pandosto*, original of Perdita (q.v.)—"that which was lost"— in Shakespeare's (q.v.) *The Winter's Tale*. 547.7.

Fay, Frank and Willy–Irish actors. 526.17; 528.13,14; 569.35; 603.24.

*Fay, Varina–see Varina. 101.8.

Fearson–*Pearson's Weekly*. 359.27.

*Feeney's, 518.27.

*Feghin, Billey, 593.27.

*Feigenbaumblatt–Ger. "fig-tree leaf". 150.27.

*Feilbogen, Father Freeshots–Professor Sigmund Feilbogen was a Zurich friend of Joyce's. *Der Freischütz* is an opera of Weber's. In German "*Pfeil und Bogen*" is a bow and arrow. 464.29-30.

*Felicia–name given Issy (q.v.), apparently in reference to *felix culpa*. *Felicia* is an obscene book by Andrea de Nerciat. 347.35; 572.573 (*passim*).

*Felim the Ferry, 211.23-24.

Felix and Regula–patron saints of Zurich. 340.13,18; 610.8,10.

*Femorafamilla, 434.11-12.

*Fenella, 291.note 6.

Feng–original of Shakespeare's Claudius (q.q.v.) in Saxo Grammaticus (q.v.). 74.15.

Fenicia–see Phenitia.

Ferchios–character in Macpherson's "Fingal" (q.q.v.). 231.29.

*Ferdinand, penitent–characters in Shakespeare's *Love's Labour's Lost* and *The Tempest*. Both could be said to be penitent, but neither makes much sense in the context of FW. See Miranda. 535.8.

*Ferns, Flora–maybe the Irish town of Ferns. 212.9.

*Ferris–Fender, Mr W. K., 369.11-12.

Feste–fool in Shakespeare's (q.v.) *Twelfth Night*. Possibly allied to Festy King (q.v.) but I doubt it. 23.20.

*Festy, Pegger–Beggar (q.v.)? See Festy King. 91.1; 92.6; †149.7— with Maggies; 584.6.

*Ffogg, Boergemester "Dyk" of Isoles, 607.30-31.

Ffrench, Rev. Canon J. F. M.–his *Prehistoric Faith and Worship: Glimpses of Ancient Irish Life* (1912) was in Joyce's library and he may account for the ffrenches in FW. Canon ffrench collected Shelta and "batom" may be the Shelta word, *batoma* or policeman. 8.13; †296.note 1—with Percy French (q.v.).

Fiacre, St–7th century Irish saint. French hackney-coaches are called *fiacre* from the Hotel St Fiacre in Paris, where a man named Sauvage kept his vehicles. 81.11.

*Fiammelle la diva–*fiammella* is Italian "flame". 560.1-2.

*Fidaris–perhaps Brother Fidelis who tells how some clerks and laymen from Ireland, going to Jerusalem, went sailing on the Nile (q.v.) to Gizeh and thence to the Red Sea. Fidelis is quoted in Dicuil's *De mensura orbis terrae* (9th century). 202.8.

Fidele–see Fidelio. Name assumed by Imogen (q.v.) in *Cymbeline* (q.v.). 6.26.

Fidelio–title heroine of Beethoven's opera. Joyce also plays on the dirge for Fidele (q.v.) in *Cymbeline* (q.v.); he—she—like chimney sweepers comes to dust. †6.26— with Fidele (q.v.); 58.11.

Field, John (1782-1837)–Irish composer who developed the nocturne. 360.12.

Fields, Gracie–English singing comedian, 20th century. †584.11 —with William Grace (q.v.).

Fierceendgiddyex–see Vercingetorix. 66.12.

Fife, Thane of–see Macduff.

*Figura Porca, Lictor Magnaffica– see Pig? 463.5-6.

Findlater, Adam–19th century Dubliner who made his money as a grocer and spent it in civic restoration. The Dublin Presbyterian chapel in Parnell Square was restored by him and is called Findlater's Church. Finn MacCool also built a church, see Lund. 170.32; †214.11—with Finn MacCool (q.v.); †334.33—with Finn (q.v.); 420.35; 533.23; 588.10; †619.3—with Adam and Finn (q.q.v.).

*Fine's, 256.19.

*Finewell's, 80.7.

Fingal–Macpherson's (q.v.) name for Finn MacCool (q.v.) in the Ossian (q.v.) poems. Fingal, a Scottish hero in "Fingal" and

"Temora" (q.v.), crosses to Ireland and fights the Danes. "Fingal" or "fingall" is what the Irish called certain of the Norse invaders "the fair strangers". 22.10; 46.stanza 4 (see Boniface and Wilde); 72.7; 106.17; 215.14; 329.14; 469.15; 496.18; 596.36.

Fingal Harriers–an Irish Hunt. 480.34.

Finian or Findian of Clontard, St (470-548)–reformer of monasteries. Twelve (q.v.) of his disciples were known as the Twelve Apostles of Ireland. †372.29— with Browne (q.v.).

*Finlay, †506.9—with Finn Mac-Cool (q.v.).

Finn, Father–Jesuit author of boys' books. *Claud Lightfoot* and *Ethelred Preston* (q.q.v.) are two of his creations. 440.10.

Finn, Huckleberry–title hero of Mark Twain's (q.v.) novel. Joyce was probably interested in Huck Finn because of his name and because he and Tom Sawyer (q.v.) are "resurrected". Huck and Tom may be Shem and Shaun (q.v.), but Joyce makes little of this. Huck Finn is mentioned in FW rather than used. Bits of his language occur here and there— "fantods", "no slouch of a name", etc. ?25.33; 66.13; 68.6; 130.14, 15; 132.36; 137.12; 297.20; †346. 26—with Finn and Billy Budd (q.q.v.); 410.36; 454.7; 543.5; 616.1; 622.18.

Finn MacCool–giant hero (Boethius makes him fifteen cubits high) of the southern (or later or Fenian or Ossianic) cycle of Irish legend. Fallen, his head is the Head of Howth, his feet stick up in Phoenix Park, his body supports the city of Dublin. There is a tradition that he still lives underground and will come again, like Arthur (q.v.), at his country's need; daring men have sometimes penetrated his hiding place and spoken with him.

Finn was son of Cumal (q.v.), husband of Saar and Grania (q.q.v.), father of Ossian (q.v.), grandfather of Oscar (q.v.). Finn MacCool is sometimes said to mean "White Head", sometimes "White Hat". Throughout FW Joyce plays with Finn and other Irish words, *fionn* (white, fair, beautiful); *fion* (wine—see 5.9-12); *fiongal* (fratricide or murder). I believe the Irish pronounce Finn as if it were "Fewn"—hence he turns up in many "funerals" in FW.

Under Cormac (q.v.), king of Ireland, Finn led the Fianna or Fenians, a military body which went round being heroic. Finn was the wisest, most generous, most courageous of these heroes, and some say he was a poet, too. He had touched the salmon of wisdom with his thumb and had only to suck it to know anything at all. Finn was treacherously slain by the henchmen of his hereditary enemy Goll (q.v.). His dog was named Bran (q.v.). For the story of his love, see Dermot and Grania.

In FW Finn is the heroic, epic role of HCE (q.v.). References to him are so tightly woven with references to Tim Finnegan (q.v.) that the two can only be arbitrarily separated. See also King Arthur, Mark of Cornwall, Shakespeare.

Joyce told Dr Daniel O'Brien that FW was "about" Finn MacCool lying dying beside the Liffey, while history cycles through his mind (7.20-21?). Joyce told other people that FW was "about" other things. I doubt he ever absolutely lied, but I am sure he equivocated like crazy.

5.9,10,12 Mister Finn . . . Mister Finnegan . . . Mister Funn (includes the song "Mister Finagan", which is quoted 6.23)

6.13,27 Macool, Macool . . . finisky

7.9-10,15 Finfoeform the Fush . . . Finiche

9.28 Finnlambs

13.15 Finfim fimfim

15.25 fins

17.14,23 finnic . . . Finishthere

24.16 Mr Finnimore

25.31-32 Macullaghmore

28.12-13,34 Findrinny . . . Finn

32.6,23 finikin . . . few nutties

39.17 Finnish

42.11-12 fion . . . fion's

44.11 Phin

48.26 Fenn Mac Call

50.17 finsterest

53.1 fin

†55.5 Fennyana—with Anna Livia (q.v.)

58.28 Finner

65.33 Finny

68.11 son of a Coole

73.35 cumule

74.1 Finn . . . Finn

78.18 Finntown

89.30 Finn

95.18 fiunn

98.7 S.S. Finlandia

99.15 Hvidfinns

102.9, finickin . . . funickin

103.3 Fin

105.3,21 Fain Me Cuddle . . . Finns

†108.21-22 Fion Earwicker—see HCE

139.14 Finn MacCool

162.12 Fonnumag-ula

178.26 Finnados

203.9 Finn

†214.11 Finnleader—with Findlater (q.v.)

219.30 fern may cald . . . firn make cold

230.22 herselF, including

236.9 Fin

238.24 finnishfurst

240.23 Flinn the Flinter

†243.14 Hetman MacCumhal—with Hetman Michael (q.v.)

245.16 Finnyland

246.19 Finn

254.20 Finfinn the Faineant

277.3,4-5 Mogoul . . . fewnrally . . . fiannians

285.left margin Finnfinnotus of Cincinnati

297.4 Fin

309.21-22 Finnfannfawners

310.32 Culsen

313.27-28,30 fain make . . . finnence

314.1 finicking . . . funicking

319.3 fine me cowheel

325.12 finnisch

330.17 Coyle-Finns

331.24 fin

332.4,8 finnd . . . Fine again, Cuoholson

†334.33 Findlader's—with Findlater (q.v.)

340.24 Finnland

343.25 Foinn [foin is French argot for "tobacco"]

344.31 meac Coolp

352.29 finngures

354.6 Faun MacGhoul

362.12 finn

374.21 Finnish Make Goal

375.29 Fummuccumul

376.33 Fenn . . . Fenn . . . Fenns

380.10 finst

388.6 Fin

393.10 Finnan

420.25 Finn's

427.30 Fuinn

443.34 filmacoulored

†447.24 Fino Ralli—with Persse O'Reilly (q.v.)

†456.16 bloomancowls — with Bloom (q.v.)

481.13 Finnsen Faynean

488.14 Felin make Call

495.18,19,20 cawls . . . cool . . . Finnyking

499.18 Finnk

†506.9 Finlay's (q.v.)

510.24-25 Fyn's Insul

519.14 Finny . . . finny

521.33 Finnians

525.31 finn may cumule

531.28,33 finicking . . . child of Coole

532.2 Finn

553.23 Finmark's Howe

564.8 Finn

†569.23 Finncoole—with King Cole (q.v.)

32   finaly finaly
574.2   Finn Magnusson
†576.28   Big Maester Finnykin—
            with   Masterbuilder
            (q.v.)
578.6,10   Macfinnan's cool . . .
            finnoc in a cauwl
581.11   find me cool's
589.11   Finner
593.24-25   Foyn MacHooligan
596.4   fincarnate
600.10   Funn
607.4-5   MacCowell
614.14   Fennsense, Finnsonse
615.7   Finnius
617.6,11,16-17 Fintona . . . Foon-
            MacCrawl . . . Fing
            . . . Fing
     19,20,26 foon . . . fooneral . . .
            fooneral
618.1   MacCrawls—see   Mag-
            rath
†619.3   Finnlatter—with   Find-
            later (q.v.)
622.1   Coole
624.28-29   Captain Finsen makes
            cumhulments
626.17,23   Find Me Colours . . . fan
            me coolly

*Finneen, Dinny, 232.6.

Finnegan, Tim–character in an
anonymous ballad. See Finn
MacCool, see Tim. There are a
good many versions of the following:

Tim Finnegan lived in Walker Street,
An Irish gintleman, mighty odd;
He'd a bit of a brogue, so neat and
     sweet,
And to rise in the world, Tim carried a
     hod.
But Tim had a sort of tippling way:
With a love of liquor Tim was born,
And to help him through his work each
     day,
Took a drop of the creature every
     morn.
     Chorus
Whack! Hurroo! now dance to your
     partner!
Welt the flure, your trotters shake:
Isn't it the truth I've told ye,
Lots of fun at Finnegan's wake?

One morning Tim was rather full,
His head felt heavy and it made him
     shake.

He fell from the ladder and broke his
     skull,
So they carried him home, his corpse
     to wake.
They tied him up in a nice clean sheet,
And laid him out upon the bed,
Wid a gallon of whiskey at his feet,
And a barrel of porter at his head.
     Chorus
His friends assembled at his wake.
Missus Finnegan called out for lunch,
And first they laid in tay and cake,
Then pipes and tobaccy and whiskey
     punch.
Miss Biddy Moriarty (q.v.) began to
     cry;
"Such a purty corpse did yez ever see?
Arrah, Tim mavourneen, an' why did
     ye die?"
"Hold yer gob," sez Judy Magee.
     Chorus
Then Peggy O'Connor took up the job.
"Arrah, Biddy," sez she, "yer wrong,
     I'm sure."
But Biddy gave her a belt in the gob,
And laid her sprawling on the flure.
Each side in war did soon engage;
'Twas woman to woman and man to
     man;
Shillelah law was all the rage,
And a bloody ruction soon began.
     Chorus
Micky Maloney raised his head,
When a gallon of whiskey flew at him;
It missed, and falling on the bed,
The liquor scattered over Tim.
"Och, he revives! See how he raises!"
And Timothy, jumping up from bed,
Sez, "Whirl yer liquor around like
     blazes—
Souls to the devil! D'ye think I'm
     dead?"
     Chorus

3.31   Finnegan
†4.18   Bygmester Finnegan—
            with   Masterbuilder
            (q.v.)
5.10,12   Mister Finnagain . . .
            fined again
6.14   Fillagain's
15.26   Tim Timmycan timped
93.35   Timm Finn again's
102.9   finickin . . . finickin
105.21   Funnycoon's
121.15-16   kin again
176.17   Miliken's
221.27   Mr T. M. Finnegan

276.21-22	Tam Fanagan's
287.note 4	Finnican
321.17	Flammagen's
332.5	hinnigen
†337.28	Malster Faunagon—with Maltster (q.v.)
351.2	Fanagan's
357.35	Flannagan
358.19,23	win a gain was in again . . . Fenegans
375.16-17	Wimmegame's
394.15-16	Foehn again
415.15	Time Timeagen
496-497	quinnigan . . . Quinnigan's
499.13	Funnycoon's
503.10-11	Ealdermann Fanagan . . . Junkermenn Funagin
504.23	flamingans
531.26,28	Fullacan's . . . Finnegan
537.34	Fanagan's
580.19	Finnegan
594.4	kinagain
607.16	Finnegan's
608.32	Phoenican
628.14	Finn, again

Finnerty, King Saint–Finnachta Fledach ("the Festive"), king of Tara, 675-695. No saint he, Mr Kelleher says. 41.24.

Finn's Hotel–a Dublin hotel where Nora Barnacle (q.v.) was working when she met James Joyce. Mrs von Phul suggests that nothing fills up the blank on 514.18 so well as "Finn's Hotel" 330.24; 420.25.

Finnuala–"Lir's lonely daughter" in Moore's (q.v.) "Silent O Moyle". She was changed into a swan and condemned to wander and sing over the waters of Ireland until the coming of Christianity. Then she was restored to humanity and was old, old, sad and old. See Lir, Lear, Cordelia, Swan. ?226.5; 289.28; 548.33; 559.33; 600.31; 627.34.

Fintan MacBochra–the only Irishman to survive the flood. God preserved him that he might tell the early Christian saints the

story of Ireland's past. He spent centuries as an eagle, a hawk, and then became an otherworld god of wisdom, incarnate in the salmon that gave Finn (q.v.) his wisdom. †25.9—with Fintan Lalor (q.v.); 359.5.

*Finton, St–St Finton's Terrace is near Dublin. 617.6; 624.18.

Fion, Paustheen–an Irish air. 92.21; 95.17-18; 412.9.

*Fionia–maybe Fiona Macleod, female self of William Sharp (1855-1905), Scottish author of such works as *The Sin Eater.* 257.36.

First Gentleman of Europe–see George IV. 300.note 2.

First Murderer–Cain (q.v.), various Shakespearean (q.v.) characters. 460.6; 566.19.

Fish–in FW fish, all kinds of fish, are almost always HCE (q.v.). There are lots of reasons for this, but I think the main reason is that HCE is the Fisher King. At least some of the time he is. A fish is a symbol of Christ.

Fisk, Jim–American financier. Vanderbilt (q.v.) said, "Who's Fisk?" 180.30.

Fitton, Mary (1578-1647)–"A maid of honour with a scandalous girlhood", Stephen Dedalus (q.v.) calls her. She was Pembroke's (q.v.) mistress and a leading candidate for the Dark Lady (q.v.) of Shakespeare's (q.v.) sonnets. See also Mary, Penelope Rich, Mrs Davenant. †11.12—with Mr W. H.; †63.12-13—with Mr W. H. (q.v.); 227.4; 316.21,25 (Morya . . . fitten); 417.28-29; 504.21.

*Fitz, Funny, 211.14.

Fitzgerald, Lord Edward (1763-98) –conspirator of '98. He was a romantic, brave, not very bright youth who was betrayed by Francis Higgens (q.v.), captured by Major Sirr (q.v.), married to Pamela (q.v.). 88.31.

Fitzpatrick, William John (1830-95)–called "the modern Suetonius" (q.v.), authority on social life of past Ireland, author of *Irish Wits and Worthies, Including Doctor Lanigan* (q.v.). Probably also Samuel A. Ossory Fitzpatrick, author of *Dublin: A Historical and Topographical Account of the City* (1907) which, Mr Senn tells me, was used in FW. 133.27.

*Fitz Urse, Mr Lœwensteil, 97.5.

Five Bloods of Ireland–the O'Neils of Ulster; the O'Connors of Connaught; the O'Briens of Thomond; the O'Lochlans of Meath; the M'Murroughs of Leinster. See Four. 270-271.

*Flaherty, Paddy, 520.30.

*Flamming, 289.13.

Flanders, Moll–title heroine of Defoe's novel. See Mary. 204.22; 562.14.

*Flannigan, 504.23.

Flashnose or Flatnose–see Ketil.

*Flavin, 337.36; 460.27.

*Flebby, 304.right margin.

Fleischman–1) Martha Fleischmann, a Swiss girl for whom Joyce had a tenderness, *circa* 1919; 2) Helen Fleischman, Joyce's first daughter-in-law. See Butcher. 50.1.

Flemming, Elizabeth–Quaker missionary, committed to Dublin's Newgate in 1665. †542.23—with Elizabeth Fletcher (q.v.).

Fletcher, Elizabeth–18th century Quaker prison visitor. †542.23—with Flemming (q.v.).

*Fletcher–perhaps both Phineas Fletcher (1582-1650), author of *The Purple Island,* and John Fletcher (1579-1625). This last worked with Shakespeare (q.v.) on *Two Noble Kinsmen*—see Palamon. Various of his plays (with

Beaumont) are named or quoted in FW—*The Custom of the Country, The Knight of the Burning Pestle.* 312.36; 579.1.

Flinders, Polly–sat among the cinders in a nursery rhyme. Also Moll Flanders (q.v.). 562.14.

Flint, Captain–dead pirate in Stevenson's (q.v.) *Treasure Island.* See Billy Bones, Silver. 83.10.

Floh–German "flea". 248.17; 414.25; 417.17,29; 418.15; 458.32.

*Flood, Billy–see Billy. 14.18.

Flood, Henry (1732-91)–Irish statesman, associate of Grattan (q.v.). 202.17; 511.10; 514.32; 580.33.

*Florenza, aunt–influenza. 26.27.

Florestan–character in *Fidelio* (q.v.). †246.18—with Florestein (q.v.).

Florestein–rival of Thaddeus (q.v.) in *The Bohemian Girl.* †246.18—with Florestan (q.v.).

Florian, Jean de (1755-94)–French poet and fabulist. 385.11.

Florizel–young prince in *The Winter's Tale*–see Perdita. George IV (q.v.) corresponded with Mrs Robinson under this name. Florizel is the hero-prince of Stevenson's (q.v.) story *The Suicide Club.* 621.30.

Flukie of the Ravens–in the *Hauksbok*: "Floki, son Vilgerd, instituted a great sacrifice, and consecrated three ravens which would show him the way [to Iceland]; for at that time no men sailing the high seas had lodestones up in northern lands." 539.35.

Flute–bellows-mender. In Shakespeare's (q.v.) *A Midsummer Night's Dream,* he plays Thisbe who brought Pyramus to his death. See Phil the Fluter. 7.3; ?43.32; 224.20; 297.23; 343.36; 513.8; 520.20,27; 541.33; 590.1.

Fluvia–see Fulvia.

Flying Dutchman—see Vanderdecken.

Flynn, Father—the priest who broke the chalice in "The Sisters" in *Dubliners.* See Father Quinn? See Percival. 44.11 (dub him Lynn and Phin).

Fokes, Family—the Vokes Family, 19th century performers in musichalls and pantomimes, noted for agility and good-humor. 106.22.

Foley, John Henry (1818-74)—Irish sculptor. He made the Goldsmith and Burke (q.q.v.) statues for Trinity College and the O'Connell (q.v.) monument. 552.12.

Foli, Giovanni—name used by John McCormack (q.v.) in his early days in opera in Italy. 243.16; 397.12.

*Follettes, Flimsy, 193.23.

Fonar—bard in Macpherson's "Temora" (q.q.v.). 231.12.

*Foozle, Uncle and Aunty Jack, 496.2-3.

Ford, Ford Madox (b. 1873)—English novelist, editor of *The Transatlantic Review* who grew nervous over the prospect of publishing Joyce's "Mamalujo" (383-399) and called in Sisley Huddleston (q.v.) to vet it for obscenity. See Ellmann, 574. Joyce puts in Ford and Huddleston just where Anna Livia goes to the city and gets dirty. †203.7—with Huddleston (q.v.).

Ford, Henry—American car manufacturer. †364.16—with John Ford (q.v.).

Ford, John (1586-1640)—English dramatist, whose play *The Lover's Melancholy* was said to have been stolen from Shakespeare's (q.v.) papers. †364.16—with Henry Ford (q.v.).

Forficula—Latin "small shears or scissors", dim. of *forfex,* the typical genus of the earwig family. See HCE, Tailor. 18.11; 79.19; 310.10.

*Forstowelsy, Miss, 444.11.

Forsyte—as in Galsworthy. 290.10-11.

*Fortescue, filly—an ancient Irish poet was a *filé,* pronounced "fill-ee". 194.30.

Fortissa is Kate the Cleaner, Kate Strong (q.q.v.).

*Foster, 277.5; 490.23; 542.18.

Foster, Vere (1819-1900)—English philanthropist who aided Irish emigration during the famine. According to *Ulysses,* 705/848, he put out a "handwriting copybook". 172.1; 227.16; 280.17; 300.14.

Foughtarundser—fought and run? German *Vater unser* or "Our Father". 78.16.

*Foulke's—see Guy Fawkes. 545.31.

Four

They were not only opinionative, peevish, covetous, morose, vain, talkative, but incapable of friendship and dead to all natural affection. . . . Envy and impotent desires are their prevailing passions.

Gulliver's Travels

The four old men or historians of FW are Matthew Gregory, Mark Lyons, Luke Tarpey, and Johnny MacDougal (q.q.v.). Their first names come from the four evangelists (q.v.). Their surnames have not been satisfactorily explained, save for the obvious connection of St Mark and the Lion. Accompanied by the gray ass (q.v.), singing "One Keg of Beer for the Four of Us", they traipse in and out of the dream, at first mere shadows, but gradually coming clearer and developing individuality. At last they dominate two sections of FW (383-399, 475-528). In the first of these sections, the mating of Tristan and Isolde (q.q.v.) they are the Elders (q.v.) from the book of Susanna (q.v.), leering at the lovers through a shifting, frightening curtain of historical recollection. In their Elders or voyeurist phase they are frequently known as the Sycamores (q.v.), and as such spy on Adam's (q.v.) sexual fall in the garden, 203.21-22. In the honeymoon section they are also Mark of Cornwall, Swift's Struldbrugs (q.q.v.), and, being both male and female, are something like Tiresias, the peeping Tom of "The Waste Land". In their second section, the Four are more vigorous and come as Magi to the infant Yawn, over whom they hold an enquiry—half inquest, half seance.

Joyce does not prettify his senescent Four—they are always boring, repulsive, sinister—but he does leaven them. A crazy beauty hangs about the honeymoon section, and at the inquest their maunderings are disciplined by numerical significance. By this I mean that the old men are dominated by various implications of the number 4. 4 is a mystic number. Jung (q.v.) thought it more important in the racial unconsciousness than 7. 4 is the Pythagorean (q.v.) number of Justice: hence the Four often appear as judges. (The Elders were also judges.) They are also the Four Evangelists, (q.v.) each with appropriate creature; Four Masters (q.v.); Four Irish waves (see Rurie—there are only three waves except in FW); Four Provinces of Ireland—the ass is the missing fifth; Four compass points; Four Winds; Four dimensions, including time; Four elements; Paracelsus's (q.v.) Four parts of the human body; Four classical ages; Four ages of man, and doubtless many another Four as well. By rights, they should also be Four Viconian (q.v.) ages, but no one has been able to make this out.

The Four almost always stand in rigid order: Matthew, Mark, Luke, and John—Ulster, Munster, Leinster, Connaught—gold, silver, copper, iron—birth, marriage, death, rebirth. Each has the distinctive speech of north, south, east or west Ireland; each has pet phrases and obsessions by which he can be identified. Indeed Joyce lavished such finicky care on his Four that I wonder he had time for the rest of FW.

I do not know if the Four exist as characters in their own right or are a phase of HCE (q.v.). Early in the game, Joyce seems to have toyed with the notion of identifying the Four Old Men of Ireland with AE, Yeats, Shaw, George Moore (q.q.v.)—see *Scribbledehobble*, 104; though traces of them still hang about Four passages, the idea was abandoned. See also Joyce to Miss Weaver, 23 October 1923.

5.36	fore old porecourts
13.20	Four things
29.10	fourfootlers
57.4,8	forefarther . . . four of them
80.16-17	four hands of forethought
92.35-36	four justicers
94.24,31	four . . . four of them
111.17	four crosskisses
112.6-7	quad gospellers
121.36	the four
124.3,20	four . . . fourleaved
140.8	4
147.3-4	four courtships
175.25	four Shores
202.1	sparefours
214.33,35	four old codgers . . . four of them
219.22	four coroners
224.1	four gentlemen
282.20	four lovedroyd curdinals
?286.17	forewheel
325.31-32	quadrupede island
363.24	foursquare trust
367.8	Mask one. Mask two. Mask three. Mask four.
14,27	four avunculusts . . . fourdimmansions
368.5	fourlings

372.34   for eolders—see Elders

377.29,34 fore of them . . . Four ghools

384.4,7,10-11,14 four of them . . . four . . . four . . . four . . . four of us

385.27   four of them

386.14-15 four dear old heladies

387.15-16,17 four of us . . . four saltwater widowers

389.4,6,25,33 four trinity colleges . . . four grandest colleges . . . four of us . . . four of us

390.13-14 four middleaged widowers

393.31   four old oldsters

397.3,12-13 four . . . four confederates

422.4-5   four divorce courts

428.4   four

474.33   senators four

475.18   four claymen

476.13-14 quatyouare

503.18   four last winds

513.29,30,35 quobus quartet . . . fore . . . four wise elephants

522.34   quadroons

533.16   fourposter

555.20   four of them . . . quartan agues

557.1-2   four hoarsemen on their apolkaloops

560.24   fourlike

566.8   four seneschals

573.8   four excavators

574.19   four chief bondholders

581.22   carryfour

602.16   forecoroners

604.34   four wethers

621.5-6   four old windgags of Gustofairy

625.11   four

Four Evangelists–Saints Matthew, Mark, Luke, and John are the Four (q.v.) old men, Matthew Gregory, Mark Lyons, Luke Tarpey, Johnny MacDougal (q.q.v.). As in medieval art, as in the Book of Kells, they are often accompanied by or identified by their beasts (see Ezekiel, 1:10; Revelations 4:7): man or angel, lion, ox or calf, eagle. As in much art they are surely argus-eyed (see *Purgatorio*, xxix, 95). In the Evangelist context, the ass (q.v.) is Christ, a disguised Christ as at Emmaus.

†13.20   Mammon Lujius—with Mammon (q.v.)

122.28   Matthew

223.30-33 matthued . . . mark . . . luked . . . johntily

245.29-30 matt . . . mark . . . luked . . . johl

253.12   symethew, sanmarc, selluc and singin

256.21   Mattatias, Marusias, Lucanias, Jokinias

257.14-15 (Luke in the 100 letter word)

285.14-15 madahoy, morahoy, lugahoy, jogahoyaway

290.note 3 Mamalujorum

325.32   madhugh, mardyk, luusk and cong

367.16   maddened . . . morgued . . . lungd . . . jowld

377.31-33 Mr Justician Matthews . . . Mr Justician Marks . . . Mr Justician Luk de Luc . . . Mr Justinian Johnston-Johnson—see Justinian

396.34   mummurrlubejubes

397.3,11,30 Mat and Mar and Lu and Jo . . . Mamalujo . . . M.M.L.J.

398.4   Mamalujo

†399.31   Mattheehew, Markeehew, Lukehew, Johnheehewheehew—with Mr W. H. (q.v.)?

†36   john . . . john . . . johnajeams—with James and John (q.v.) and Shakespeare's (q.v.) "John O'Dreams"

428.3-4   luking . . . marking . . . jornies . . . matts

476.32   mamalujo

†528.12-13 Magda, Martha . . . Luz . . . Joan (see Martha and Mary, Magda, St Joan, Elizabeth)

541.15-16 matt . . . mark . . . Luc

554.10	Mattahah! Marahah! Luahah! Joahana-hanahana'!
559.22	Matt
564.2	Mark
590.23	johnny
598.22	Mildew, murk, leak and yarn
609.6-8	Mata . . . Matamaru . . . Matamaruluka . . . Matamarulukajoni — with Mata (q.v.)
614.28	"Mamma Lujah"
29-30	Matty, Marky, Lukey or John-a-Donk

Four Masters–*The Annals of the Four Masters* was compiled in the Franciscan monastery of Donegal by Michael Conary, and Peregrine O'Clery, and Ferfesa O'Mulconry (q.q.v.) in the 17th century. The work begins with the arrival in Ireland of Caesair, granddaughter of Noah (q.v.), contains the information that Hamlet (q.v.) fought at Dublin, and comes down to 1616. Michael O'Clery (q.v.) made a catalogue of the kings of Ireland, genealogies of the Irish saints, the *Martyrology of Donegal* and the *Book of Invasions*. Joyce's Four (q.v.) are the Four Masters collectively, not individually. See Duignan.

14.28	farfatch'd and peragrine . . . clere
21.29	four owlers masters
91.20	four of Masterers
95.27	fourbottle men, the analists
123.1	fourlegged ems
184.33	four masters
256.21	Four Massores
305.31	Foremaster's
373.8	Waves (q.v.)
384.6,8	four maaster waves of Erin . . . four waves (see Waves)
385.7,35	four waves . . . O'Clery (see Waves)
386.20	O'Clery's
390.15-16	four of the Welsh waves
391.7-8	four maasters
392.19-20	perigrime

394.17	five fourmasters
395.6-7	foretyred schoonmasters
398.1,15,16	Conry . . . Peregrine and Michael and Farfessa and Peregrine
424.29	four waves
477.2,13	masters . . . quartermasters
479.29	fourmaster
482.12	O'mulanchonry
530.3,15	Mr Michael Clery . . . Mr Martin Clery
533.20-21	O Clearly

*Fox–there are a great many foxes in FW. I do not list them and cannot usually tell whether or not a person is indicated. Parnell (q.v.) carried on with Mrs O'Shea (q.v.) under the name of Fox. In *Ulysses*, 191/247, Christ and Shakespeare (q.v.) are compared to a fox. Ulysses (q.v.) himself was called by Shakespeare (*Troilus and Cressida*, V,iv,12) "that same dog-fox"—cf. FW 30.30? If, as seems to me unlikely, "The Mookse and Gripes" really is about the Fox and the Grapes, Mookse (q.v.) would doubtless link up with Fox. See Reynard, Brer Fox.

Fox, Brer–character in the *Uncle Remus* (q.v.), stories by Joel Chandler Harris (q.v.). The use Joyce makes of him on 574-575 is not wholly clear to me, but I think that Brer Fox is the wily Ulysses-Bloom (q.q.v.) who tells his wife that hereafter he "will breakfast in bed". See Fox. 245.9; 574.4; †574.36—with Guy Fawkes (q.v.); 575.11,29,30.

Fox, George–founder of the Quakers. 289.note 5.

*Fox-Goodman–the name is always used in a context which suggests a peal of bells and/or a church. The reference may be to Bloom, a foxy-grampa, whom Joyce described as a "good man". See Fox. 35.30; 328.26; 360.11; 369.8; 511.9; 515.2; 557.13-14; 603.32; 621.35.

*Fox-Goodman, Fauna, 212.9-10.

*Foyle, Josephine, 212.13.

Fram–not, so far as I know, a person, but the ship *Nansen* (q.v.) used to attempt the North Pole in 1893-96. 312.7; 317.9; 596.7.

*Francie–Festy King's (q.v.) pig, perhaps named for St Francis (q.v.), perhaps for Francis Bacon (q.v.). Is Francie identical with the sow Cliopatrick (see Cleopatra, Clio, St Patrick)? One would give much to know. See Pig. 86.27; 420.9.

Francis of Assisi, St (1181-1226)–founder of the Franciscan order, devoted to animals. ?†86.27—with Francie and Francis Bacon (q.q.v.); 226.9; ?420.9; 433.1; 440.20-21.

François de Sales, St (1567-1622)–patron of writers. †212.15—with Macleay, Xavier (q.q.v.).

Fran Czeschs–see Schaurek.

Frank, Francis–a name of Shaun's (q.v.). It ties him, I think, to Francis Bacon (q.v.). See also Kevin, Free. 48.23-24 (see Frank Smith); †62.15-16—with Abel (q.v.); 70.5,10; 86.27; 121.3,7,20; 127.29; 134.26; 183.19; 198.18; 220.12; 226.9 (see St Francis); 282.8; †289.10—with Ben Franklin and Ben Jonson (q.q.v.); 302.31; 303.30; ?312.7; 315.36; 332.8; 343.28; ?372.8 (see Ben Franklin); 388.18; 405.23; 410.21; 413.30; 420.9; 433.1 (see St Francis); 440.20-21 (see St Francis); 452.15; 465.12; 478.17,19; ?521.23,24 (see Frank Power); 533.15; 557.20; †562.23—with Kevin (q.v.); 606.20 (see Ben Franklin); 615.13.

Franklin, Benjamin (1706-90)–American diplomat, statesman, scientist. Just before the American revolution, he visited Ireland to recruit Irishmen to fight England. I think he is connected with a good many of the Frank and Francis Bacon (q.q.v.) references.

†289.10—with Ben Jonson (q.v.); 372.7-8; 606.20.

*Fred–Watkins (q.v.)? 330.4.

Freda–see Fred Watkins. 588.2.

Free–the word has many uses in FW, but not infrequently Joyce uses it to refer to Frank (q.v.). When it occurs, as it often does, in the neighbourhood of "will", I take "free" and "will" to refer to Bacon and Shakespeare (q.q.v.).

French, Basil–character in Henry James's "Julia Bride" (q.q.v.) of whom Julia was "proud". †464.36 —with David and Davitt, French Devil (q.q.v.).

French Devil–Jean Bart (1651-1702), a brave French sailor. †464.36—with Davitt, Basil French (q.q.v.).

French, John Denton Pinkstone, 1st Earl of Ypres (1852-1925)–commander of the British Expeditionary Force in France and Belgium, 1914-1915—note Hill 60, 7.33; Irish lord-lieutenant, 1918-21. 8.11.

French, Percy–at the turn of the century, a writer of popular songs and an entertainer in Dublin. He wrote "Abdul the Bulbul Amir", "Phil the Fluter", "Slattery's Mounted Foot" (q.q.v.), "Are You Right There, Michael", "The Mountains of Mourne," etc. †296.note 1—with ffrench (q.v.); 495.3,27.

Frere, John H. (1769-1846)–English writer of light verse. See Hood. 487.21.

Freud, Sigmund (1856-1939)–psychoanalyst. 115.23; 299.2-3; 337.7; 411.35-36; †460.20—with Jung (q.v.).

Frey–Norse god of fertility, peace. 211.4; 231.13; 335.15; 356.17.

*Frick's Flame–*fric* is French argot for "money" and its flame may be a mercenary woman. 537.30.

Frida, Freda, etc.–Joyce to Miss

Weaver, 8 August 1928: "These are 29 words for 'Peace' taken from or modelled on the following tongues and variations (German, Dano - Norwegian, Provençal, French, Greek, French variations, Malay, Echo, Gipsy, Magyar childrens, Armenian, Sengalese, Latin variation, Irish, Diminutive, N. Breton, S. Breton, Chinese, Pidgin, Arabic, Hebrew, Sanscrit, Hindustani and English). . . . This word was actually sighed around the world in that way in 1918." 470-471.

Friday–Robinson Crusoe's (q.v.) native friend. 211.16.

Frith, William Powell (1819-1909)– English painter who painted Swift and Vanessa (q.q.v.). 358.36.

*Fronces–maybe Peaches Browning (q.v.), born Frances Heenan, maybe Francie (q.v.). 527.17.

Frou Frou–Title of Meilhac and Halevy's opera. I have never found out whether Frou Frou is a person or not. 127.17; 236.12-13; 510.35.

Fruit–because of the nature of its perilous theme, FW is bound to abound in fruit which as often as not is feminine. I do not pursue the subject, but I can report that Moore (q.v.) Park is an apricot, Barbarossa a grape, Isabel and Georgia peaches. By times, however, I suspect that the fatal fruit of FW is the earth-apple or the potato.

*Frullini, Romiolo, 531.21.

Fry, Elliot, Atkinson–see Elliot and Fry.

*Fry, Paul–Paul Pry? See Elliot and Fry. 43.9.

*Fry, Mr, 342.10; 413.35.

Frygga–Odin's (q.v.) wife. †577.17 —with Elizabeth (q.v.).

*Fudgesons, Fidge, 257.36.

Fugger's News Letter–a collection of letters, 36,000 pages of m.s., sent by agents mostly to Count Edward Fugger, from 1568-1605, written in Italian, German, Latin, dog-Latin. 97.32.

Fulke Fitz-Warin–in From Ritual to Romance, p. 181, Miss Weston (q.v.) mentions Histoire de Fulke Fitz-Warin. I believe he is an outlaw. 529.20.

Fulvia–first wife of Mark Antony (q.v.). In Antony and Cleopatra (q.v.) she is an off-stage character, the wife left at home, as Shakespeare (q.v.) left Ann Hathaway (q.v.). †546.30,35; †547.5–both with Anna Livia (q.v.).

*Fumadory, 395.10.

*Fung Yang, 109.6.

Furey, Michael–see Bodkin.

Furies–see Bodkin.

Furlong, Thomas–19th century Irish poet. 71.35.

Furniss, Father–author of Sight of Hell (1861), a book for scaring children. 289.13.

Furphy–according to Brewer's (q.v.) Phrase and Fable, in World War I, Australian latrine buckets bore the name of their manufacturer—Furphy. A "furphy" is, therefore, "a latrine rumor". 65.22.

*Futter, Canon–anything more than cannon fodder? 9.19-20.

*Futtfishy the First–see Fish. 480.16-17.

Fynlogue or Finnloga–father of St Brendan (q.v.). 327.3.

Fyrapel, Sir–the leopard in the Reynard (q.v.) cycle. 483.15.

G

Gabler, Hedda–title heroine of Ibsen's (q.v.) play. 540.24.

Gad–1) Semitic god of fortune; 2) seer at David's (q.v.) court; 3) Israelite tribe. 219.15; 246.5; 284.29; 597.9.

Gage–"Gage's Fane" the air to which Moorc's (q.v.) "'Tis Believed That This Harp" is sung. 600.15.

Gainsborough, Thomas (1727-88) –English painter. 260.24.

Galahad–perfect knight of Arthurian (q.v.) legend, a Grail knight—see Gawain, Percival. 389.23.

Galatea–1) a nymph loved by Polyphemus (q.v.) and slain by him because she loved Acis; 2) Pygmalion's statue which Venus (q.v.) animated. 32.12; ?547.32.

Galen, Claudius (b. 130)–most celebrated of ancient medical writers. 424.7.

Galeotto–Italian form of Galehoult, who in Old French prose romances brings Lancelot and Guinevere (q.q.v.) together, hence a pandar —see Ruffin. In *The Inferno* (v. 137) Paola and Francesca are said to have been brought together by reading of Lancelot and Guinevere. "A Galeotto was the book and he who wrote it." †251.25—with Galileo (q.v.).

Galileo (1564-1642)–Italian astronomer. †251.25—with Galeotto (q.v.); 583.8.

Gall, Franz Joseph (1758-1828)– Austrian anatomist, founder of phrenology. ?46; 364.15.

Gallaghers, Betty–two moons and Elizabeth I (q.v.) as Moon (q.v.) goddess—*gealach* is Irish "moon". See 256.36. 90.10; 502.14; 524.29.

*Galloper, Troppler, 48.27.

*Gallus–name of various prominent Romans. Latin for domestic cock. 256.2; 594.30.

Gallus and Magnus, Sts–connected with the Abbey of St Gall where they keep facsimiles. 484.35.

Gallus, Cornelius–according to Brewer, died while kissing his wife's hand. 377.21.

Gama, Vasco da (1469-1524)–Portuguese navigator. 512.15.

Gambrinus, Gaudio – mythical Flemish king, credited with brewing the first beer. 134.6.

*Gamellaxarsky,Abdullah–gamellax is Norwegian for "old salmon". See Fish. 34.2-3.

Gamp, Sairy—midwife in *Martin Chuzzlewit* (q.v.). She carried a large umbrella, which is why midwives and umbrellas are called gamps. 57.23; 449.14.

*Gamuels, 318.22.

Gamut–see Rainbow.

Gandhi, Mohandas Karamchand (1869-1948)–Hindu nationalist, assassinated. 276.17; 289.2.

Gandon, James–18th century Dublin architect. He designed the Custom House, the east front of the Parliament House, and the Four Courts. 552.11.

Ganymede–beautiful youth who was carried off by an eagle and became a cup-bearer on Olympus. Name assumed by Rosalind (q.v.) in *As You Like It*. 269.18; 583.11.

Garcielasso–see Vega.

*Gardiner, Master–Adam? 133.23.

Gargantua–Rabelais' gigantic hero. 319.26.

Garrick, David (1717-79)–English actor and theatrical manager. 55.35; 134.11.

*Garry–Jerry (q.v.)? 215.3.

*Garrymore–Barrymore? 583.11.

*Garterd, Miss, 423.35.

*Gascon Titubante or Tegmine-sub-Fagi–probably a made-up name for HCE. *Titubent* means to reel with drink. *Tegmine-sub-Fagi* plays with the first line of Virgil's (q.v.) first eclogue, *sub tegmine fagi.* 403.20-21.

*Gaspey Otto and Sauer, 485.3.

Gatling, R. J.–American inventor of a machine gun which by 1870 was adopted by nearly every civilized country. 246.21; 377.6.

*Gattabuia and Gabbiano's, 424.10.

Gaudyanna–the Spanish river Gaudiana, including Anna Livia and Anne Whitefield (q.q.v.). †294.29.

Gaunt, John of–Shakespeare's time-honored Lancaster (q.v.) who dies in *Richard II* (q.v.). 121.4; ?381.13.

Gautama, Siddhartha, Buddha– 5th century founder of Buddhism. A number of the following references include Billy Budd (q.v.). See also Arthur. 25.25; 59.7; †60.19—with Moody and Sankey (q.v.); 234.14; †254.36—with Artho (q.v.); 277.left margin; 338.13; †347.9—with Wellington; 544.24; 602.27; 620.3.

Gawain–nephew of King Arthur (q.v.), knight of the Round Table, Grail knight—see Percival. 398.6.

Gay, John (1685-1732)–English poet and playwright, author of *The Beggar's Opera.* See Peachum. 179.8; 236.30.

Gay Socks–see Guy Fawkes. 193.19.

*Gaylord, 198.4.

Ge, Gaea, Gaia–Greek earth goddess, called Tellus (q.v.) by the Romans. 256.36; 257.5,6; 297.1; 411.15.

*Gedankje, Dr, 150.11.

Gelchossa–minor female in Macpherson's "Fingal" (q.q.v.). 228.14.

Gelert–faithful dog, wrongly slain in a Welsh story. His grave is called Bethgelert (q.v.). 177.22.

Gellius, Aulus (130-180)–Latin grammarian. 255.19.

Gemellus–Latin "twin". 90.18.

Gemman–Christian filé who taught St Columba (q.v.). 202.20.

*Gemuas, the two, 358.32.

Genesius, St–I was told by a playwright that he is patron saint of actors, but *The Listener* says St Blaise (q.v.) is. 219.21.

*Genevieve, 266.27.

Genghis Khan (1162-1227)–Mongul conqueror. †24.35—with Guinness (q.v.); †593.29-30—with Guinness (q.v.).

*Gentia Gemma, 92.25.

*George–the name begins as Georgia, USA (named for George II), and more often than not it keeps this meaning and is associated with Shaun who, like Peter Sawyer and Giorgio Joyce (q.q.v.), is always about to go off and make his pile, in spite of undesirable parents, in the New World. George means a husbandman and on p. 3 is the plebeian, opposite Patrick or patrician. George also refers by times to Gorgias, George Duke of Clarence, George Moore, George B. Shaw (q.q.v.). Below I give the Georges which I can't absolutely assign. 3.20; 11.15; ?102.7-8; (see G. Moore); 140.30; 181.9; 303.17; ?327.30; 385.36; 406.7; 458.25; 492.34; 562.29; 563.30; †599.18 (G. Moore?).

George–here, I think, Mrs Yeats (q.v.) because of *A Vision.* 179.31.

George, St–patron of England. St George's channel is a strait joining the Atlantic and the Irish sea between Wales and Ireland. 3.20; †229.3-4—with George Eliot, perhaps with Moore and Shaw (q.q.v.); 324.31; 492.34.

George IV (1762-1830)–king of

England and Ireland, known as the First Gentleman of Europe. On the occasion of a visit to Ireland, the town of Dunleary was renamed Kingstown. (See Lear). The Free State renamed it Dunleary. See Florizel. 300.note 2; 428.19; 558.17.

George, Royal–British war ship that sank with 800 persons in 1782. The accident was caused by a leak below the waterline and by incompetent shifting of cargo. The Royal Gorge is a canyon in Colorado. 151.29.

Geryon–monster killed by Hercules (q.v.). 594.7.

*Geyser, Soapy–probably Mark Lyons (q.v.). 305.note 3.

Ghost–often as not, King Hamlet (q.v.).

*Giacinta, 615.3.

Gibbon, Edward (1737-94)–historian. 504.29; 531.1.

*Gibsen's–partly Ibsen (q.v.), referring to tea in *Love's Comedy.* 170.26.

Gide, André (1869-1949)–French writer, apologist for homosexuality. I am not sure all these references are to him. †345.22— with Guinness (q.v.); 346.9; 347. 27.

Gideon–liberator, reformer, judge of Israel (Judges, 6-8). 325.27.

Giedion-Welcker, Mrs Carola— Zurich friend of Joyce's in the '30s. 603.15,17.

*Giglamps–probably Matt Gregory (q.v.). 305.note 3.

Gilbert, J. T.–19th century author of an entertaining history of Dublin which Joyce used in FW. Stuart Gilbert may be included. †573.14—with W. S. Gilbert (q.v.).

Gilbert, Sir W. S.–writer of librettos for comic operas. See Sullivan, D'Oyly Carte. One of these operas is *Trial by Jury.* †573.14—with J. T. Gilbert (q.v.).

Gilbey–kind of gin. †406.33—with Quilbhe (q.v.); 558.2.

Gilda–heroine of *Rigoletto* (q.v.). 147.12.

*Giles, Farmer, 240.31.

Giletta of Narbonne–original of Shakespeare's Helena (q.q.v.) in *All's Well*; she is in a story from *The Decameron,* as retold by William Painter in *The Palace of Pleasure.* †391.21—with Juliet (q.v.).

Gill–Dublin publisher and bookseller. 440.14-15.

*Gill, Gilly–name given at times to HCE's (q.v.) slanderer, the Cad (q.v.). He is probably identical with Magrath and the Man Servant (q.q.v.), for *gill* is Gaelic for boy, servant. According to Brewer (q.v.), Gilly, Magrath, and Toller (q.q.v.) were giants. Gilly was Swedish, 8 feet, 10 inches tall. Mr Atherton suggests Gill has to do with Hogg's (q.v.) Gilmartin who is the Devil in *Confessions of a Justified Sinner.* I throw in the following snippets, not knowing that they apply: a gill is a ravine with a stream in it; *giolla* is Irish for "boy"; *gile* is Irish for "brightness"; *giall* is Irish for "hostage"; *geille* is Irish for earwig; Shakespeare (q.v.) had a brother, Gilbert (q.v.); Gille was an Ostman bishop of Limerick and Ireland's first papal legate. 36.35; 37.8; 54.29; ?72.29 (guilphy); 227.30; 244.23; 254.36; 267.7; 278.26; 305.9; 312.29; 354.13; 382.9; 518.9; 524.28; 578.6; 617.19.

*Gillia–apparently with wife of Gill (q.v.), seems to be Lily Kinsella (q.v.). 572.35; 573.16.

*Gilligan, 421.32; 622.22.

*Gilligan-Goll–probably Gill and Goll (q.q.v.). 370.22.

*Gillooly, 178.16.

Giovanni, Don or Don Juan– Spanish hero, subject of Mozart's (q.v.) opera, Byron's (q.v.) poem, and, under the name of Tanner (q.v.), hero of Shaw's (q.v.) *Man and Superman*. Moreover it is the subject of Kierkegaard's (q.v.) *Either/Or*, at least one of the main subjects. Joyce's version of him may be found in III,ii where Shaun-Jaun (q.q.v.) preaches to a mob of titillated maenads and fails with his own true love. See Anne Whitefield, Ottavio, John McCormack.   †211.32 — with Joseph Vance (q.v.); †281.left margin—with Don John (q.v.).

Girofle and Girofla–twin sisters in Lecocq's opera. 129.30.

Gisela–when Rolf Ganger (q.v.) got most of Normandy from Charles the Simple (q.v.), he also got Charles's daughter, Gisela. *Giselle* is a ballet. 352.31.

Gish, Lilian and Dorothy–American movie stars. 80.33.

Gissing, George (1857-1903)–English novelist. 527.8.

***Gizzygay**, 451.30.

Gladstone, William Ewart (1809-98)–British prime minister, "The Grand Old Man", "The Grand Old Spider" (Parnell's, q.v., phrase), "William the Conqueror" (q.v.), "The People's William". Certain cheap French wines were called "Gladstone"; there was a Dublin actor named Gladstone.
   In FW much is made of Gladstone's persistence in uplifting fallen girls—see Peter Wright—and of his somewhat equivocal love affair with Irish Home Rule. Since, at last, he helped bring Parnell down, Joyce associates him with Pigott (q.v.). Gladstone's avocation was felling trees and all the "woodman spare" passages refer in part to his felling of Parnell and also to his passion for fallen women, since in Elizabethan slang a "woodman" was a wencher. See Sir Arber.
   In *Ulysses*, 201/262, Gladstone

is identified with Shakespeare (q.v.), and they may both contribute to William's (q.v.) "short-fingeredness", FW 31.16. Gladstone had only nine fingers, and Shakespeare's bust, in the 18th century, was lacking some fingers.

31.30,32	pebble . . . cheerycherrily . . . cladstone
41.35	Primewar Glasstone
61.13	gladsome
72.27	glatt stones
77.34	glasstone
146.34,35	gravestone . . . Garnd ond mand
?169.30	gleetsteen
†170.32	Gladstone's — with Gluckstein (q.v.)
221.34,35	Grabstone . . . *General Orders Mailed*
261.16	Glattstoneburg
†321.8	Glasthule Bourne—see Browne, Bourne
332.20	gronde old mand
†334.6,11,13-14	Mr "Gladstone Browne" . . . ground old mahonagyan . . . glance down his browen—with Browne (q.v.).
336.34	wilom eweheart
337.16	billy (q.v.)
352.24	grand ohold spider
365.11	gladyst tone
373.28	Gladstools
393.18	Gallstonebelly
438.14	Gloatsdane's
468.29-30	grand old manoark
536.20	glad stein
537.1	gladshouses
607.35	Grand old Manbutton
624.27	Grand owld marauder

***Gladys**, †365.11–with Gladstone; 470.17.

Glamours–Glamis–see Macbeth. 250.16.

***Glassarse**, Tom Bowe–"glass-house" is slang for a military prison. 27.1.

Glendalough, lord of–see St Kevin. 248.30.

Glideon–see Gideon.

Glimglow, Miss–the lamp (q.v.) in

the Earwicker's (q.v.) bedroom. 585.5.

Glinka, Michael Ivanovich (1803-57)–Russian composer of *A Life for the Czar* (341.17). 360.12 (clinkars).

Glintylook, buyshop of–see St Kevin. 130.33.

Gloatsdane–Gladstone (q.v.).

***Gloria,** Mrs–perhaps Old Glory since the USA is indicated. 228.19-20.

Glover–I have not listed these but they refer to John Shakespeare (q.v.) who was a glover and perhaps to William who was (perhaps) his apprentice.

Gluck, Alma (1884-1938)–Russian-born American soprano. 200.8-9.

Gluck, Christoph (1714-87)–operatic composer. 360.9-10; ?569.4.

Gluckstein and Salmon–owners of the Lyons Corner Houses in England. †170.32—with Gladstone (q.v.).

Glue and Gravy–the Blue and the Gray. See Grant. 30.18-19; 97.20-21; 329.8-9; 375.3; 412.5; 537.13.

***Glugg** and Chuff–parts played by Shem and Shaun (q.v.) in "The Mime of Mick, Nick and the Maggies" (q.q.v.). To the Irish a "glugger" is an addled egg or *ugh.* 219-259 (*passim*).

Glwlwd of the Mghtwg Grwpp–character in "Culhwch and Olwen" in *The Mabinogion.* 482.13.

***Gnoccovitch,** Gnaccus, 159.28.

Gobbo, Launcelot and his father Old–comics in Shakespeare's *The Merchant of Venice.* In Italian *gobbo* is "humpback" and on FW 623 it refers back to "Lord", line 4; humpbacks were once called "lords" from Greek *lordos* or "crooked". 319.20; 455.26 (with the Globe Theatre); 603.25; 623.12.

***Godard,** 185.21.

Godfrey–one of the Nine Worthies. 550.2.

Godfrey, My Man–title character of a pretty funny movie, starring William Powell and Carol Lombard. †378.35—with Michael Gunn and Adam (q.q.v.).

***Godolphin,** Jerry (q.v.) or the lad in the Hoy's Court. Shem (q.v.) is indicated. Mr Atherton and Mrs Jarrell identify the lad with Swift (q.v.) who was born in Hoey's Court, Dublin. 555.32; †563.25-26 (see Sidney Godolphin).

Godolphin, Sidney, Earl of (1645-1712)–financial genius, British statesman, Lord of the Treasury. Into England he introduced the Godolphin Arab from which all pedigreed race horses are descended. 300.28; 563.25-26.

Godred Croven–Norse king of Dublin, conqueror of the Isle of Man. 7.19; 262.note 3.

***Goerz** from Harleem, 577.22.

Goethe, Johann Wolfgang von (1749-1832)–German poet, playwright, novelist, philosopher. 71.26; 229.3; 251.26; 344.5; ?352.11; 389.23; ?480.36; 510.11; 539.6; 596.36.

Gog and Magog–represent the nations of the earth that are deceived by Satan (q.v.)—(Rev. 20). In legends of Alexander the Great, Gog and Magog are enemies that he sealed behind a great wall in the Caucasus. In *The Faerie Queene* (q.v.) Gogmagog is the chief giant of Albion. There are statues of them both in London. 6.19; 25.23; 71.26; 73.6; 222.14; 246.5-6.

Gogarty, Oliver St John (d. 1957)–Irish eye, ear, nose, throat doctor, writer, original of Malachy "Buck" Mulligan (q.v.) in *Ulysses.* Joyce cannot create an enemy who is not in large measure Gogarty. Oliver Gogarty is the priest, hero of George Moore's

The Lake. See also John, St John, Oliver, Antinous, Claudius. 498.17.

Golazy, pere–see Pergolesi. 360.7.

Goldsmith, Oliver (1728-74)–Irish writer. See Hardcastle, Whang. 56.30 (Mr Melancholy Slow–see "The Traveller", line 1); †256.12-13—with R. B. Sheridan (q.v.); ?†322.34—with Cromwell (q.v.).

Goldylocks–heroine of "The Three Bears". 615.23.

Goliath–the giant David (q.v.) slew (1 Sam. 17). 8.20; 491.1.

Goll (one-eyed)–hereditary enemy of Finn MacCool (q.v.). Finn kills him and is killed by his followers. 240.13; 354.13; †370.22—with Gilligan (q.v.); 512.1.

*Gollovar, Gorotsky–suggests Gulliver, Goll, Oliver, Lover, maybe Corot and Trotsky (q.q.v.). 294.18.

*Gomez–maybe "that matador Gomez", *Ulysses*, 740/895. 545.32.

Goncourt, Edmont Huot de (1822-96) and his brother Jules (1830-70)–French authors, collaborators. 89.17.

*Gondibert–possibly the title hero of an unfinished epic by Sir William D'Avenant, 1651. 57.25.

Gonne, Maud (Madame MacBride) –*Ulysses*, 44/53: "Maud Gonne, beautiful woman." She was an Irish revolutionist, Yeat's (q.v.) muse, celebrated by him as Leda (q.v.—see also Swan) and as Helen (q.v.). She played Cathleen Ni Houlihan in Yeats' play. In FW she is linked to the Gunnings and Gunn (q.q.v.). Many instances of "gone" may refer to her which are not listed below.
8.8,9 (mistress Kathe . . . goan); 10.22; ?72.25; 75.18; 95.6; 141.6; 159.10; 204.27; 263.17,18; 280.6, 10; 292.12; 297.4; 306.note 2 (ter); 376.17; 398.6,22; 399.stanza 4; 451.3; †508.28—with the Gunnings (q.v.); †512.18—with Anna Livia (q.v.); 526.26; 540.30; 546.32; 596.15; †598.9 (*bis*)—

with Gunning (q.v.); †625.32—with Gunn (q.v.).

*Gooch, Gwendolyn, 609.4-5.

Gooch, Reeve–*rive gauche*. 197.1.

Goodfellow–see Puck.

Goody Two-Shoes–18th century children's story, maybe by Goldsmith (q.v.). 14.4.

Goose, Mother–wrote all the nursery rhymes. Maybe Nora Barnacle (q.v.). 242.25; 353.27; 449-450; 623.3-4.

*Gophar, 325.26.

*Gopheph, 125.17-18.

*Gordon–General? 373.20.

Gordon, gay–see Lindsays. 438.36.

Gorgias–title character of a dialogue of Plato's (q.v.), a false rhetorician whose art Plato calls ignoble. *Gorgias* contains the famous comparison of the ignorant soul to a leaky barrel (510.17-18). I think it lies behind the concept of Shaun (q.v.) as a barrel, leaking hot air, as he floats down the Liffey (q.v.), FW III,i,ii. Gorgias may double with a lot of Georges (q.v.).

Gorgons – snaky-haired sisters whose gaze turns men to stone. 102.7-8.

*Gorham, see Roe. 277.note 4.

Gorky, Maxim (1868-1936)–pseudonym of Alexi Maximovich Peshkov, Russian writer and revolutionary whose works include *The Mother*. 132.35.

Gorman, Herbert–a Joyce biographer. *The Martyrology of O'Gorman* was a medieval Irish book. 235.29; †349.25—with O'Gorman (q.v.); 407.1.

Gormleyson, Sitric or Cedric Silkbeard–son of Gormfhlaeth, who by her prodigal life left Sitric (q.v.) in doubt of his male parent. 348.18.

Gosse, Edmund–English man of letters who compared *Ulysses* to the works of de Sade (q.v.)–see Ellmann, 542. 325.16.

Gottgab, Mr–seems to be St Patrick (q.v.) but see also Dieudonnay. 490.8.

Gough, Sir Hugh (later Lord)–won the battle of Gujerat in 1849, which gave the English possession of the Punjab. His statue stands in Phoenix Park. I do not really understand Joyce's references to him. 211.25; 271.29; 334.18; 357.31; 375.17; 616.22.

Gould, Jay (1836-91)–American financier. 140.15; 327.28.

*Gow–anglicization of Irish *gabhe* or "smith" (q.v.). 356.3.

*Gowan–could it be Gowan Stevens of *Sanctuary*? Temple is 398.14. 398.5; 624.8.

Gracchi–Tiberius and Caius Gracchus, Roman politicians. Their mother, Cornelia, said her children were *her* jewels. Their family name was Sempronius. See also Titus Andronicus. 128.15; †614.1 —with Gripes (q.v.).

Grace–Anne means "grace"; therefore, a great many "graces" refer to Anna Livia (q.v.). It can also refer to the story "Grace" in *Dubliners* or to William Grace, Grace O'Malley, Grania, Gracehoper (q.q.v.). 7.6; 24.10; 57.23; 69.28; 71.19; 83.23; 89.11; 95.4; 105.27; 115.20; 118.10; 141.2; 144.26; 146.30; 161.4; 186.31,35; 201.32; 213.21; 214.18; 227.25; 240.32; 242.9; 252.20; ?260.left margin; 273.19,note 6; 291.9; 312.27; 317.36; 318.1; 329.30; 356.7; †361.21—with William Grace; 377.30; 384.9,16; 387.15, 34; 391.2,22; 393.15; 395.21 (*bis*), 24; 406.26; 408.36; 413.3; 419.6; 424.14; 427.29; 428.16; 465.17; 509.30; 512.28; 550.35; 561.14, 17; 568.25; 570.6; †577.3—with Swan (q.v.); 584.11 (William Grace); 597.9; 603.1; 607.34; 614.1; 623.11.

*Grace, Pointer the or Pastor de–probably the pope. 289.21; 329.30.

Grace, William Gilbert–the hero, the Babe Ruth, of 19th century cricket. I think he doubles usually with William Shakespeare (q.v.). See also William, Grace. 25.36; ?71.19; 160.2-3; 337.1; 583.28; †584.11 — with Gracie Fields (q.v.); 607.34.

Gracehoper–see Ondt, Grace.

Gramont, Comte de–subject of *Mémoires de la vie du Comte de Gramont* (1713) by Anthony Hamilton (q.v.). Gramont married the Irish beauty, Elizabeth (q.v.), La Belle, Hamilton (q.v.). 137.36.

Granby–Dublin actor, mentioned by Fitzpatrick (q.v.). 569.36; 570.1.

Grand Old Man or G.O.M.–see Gladstone.

*Grande, Ciliegia–the Grande is a river, *ciliegia* is Italian "cherry". 207.12.

Grania–see Dermot.

Grant, Ulysses S. (1822-85)–18th president of the United States, leader of the Union Army in the Civil War—see Glue and Gravy. His opponent was R. E. Lee (q.v.). I do not really understand what Joyce does with him in FW. The fact that his name was Ulysses may matter. He seems to represent freedom, is perhaps a negro and representative of the dark people's rise against the white. This is the more likely as the Irish called "blue men" the Moors who were captured in Spain by the Vikings and brought to Dublin. Joyce's joke about "pillfaces" (78.27) derives from the Pill which was then the little harbor of St Mary's Abbey where the Bradogue entered the Liffey. See Ham. †4.35—with Joyce (q.v.); 78.24,25,28,29; 116.32; 273.20-21; ?301.note 5; 336.21; 361.30; ?463.13; 466.22; †513.28—with

Grania (q.v.); 515.14; ?566.32; 581.26; ?605.7.

Granu or Grana Wail or Uile—see Grace O'Malley.

Granville, John Carteret, Earl of (1690-1763)–popular lord-lieutenant of Ireland, friend of Swift's (q.v.). 553.26.

Grasshopper–see Ondt.

Grattan, Henry (1746-1820)–Irish statesman who worked for a separate parliament and moderate reforms for Ireland. Flood's (q.v.) name is popularly associated with his. Essex (q.v.). Bridge was renamed for Grattan. 202.17; 580.32.

Gray, Dolly–as in "Goodbye Dolly Gray". 228.13; 246.26.

Gray, Dorian–hero of *The Picture of Dorian Gray* by Oscar Wilde (q.v.). 186.8; 257.6.

Gray, Dwyer (d. 1888)–Irish nationalist, editor of the *Freeman's Journal*. Joyce associates him with the gray ass (q.v.). Is it an Irish joke? 214.33; 398.2; 602.14.

*Gray, Grogram–the ass (q.v.). See also Dwyer Gray. 399.stanza 2; 609.10.

Gray, Thomas (1716-71)–English poet. 192.34.

Great Harry, The–or Henry Grace a Dieu, a great ship of Henry VIII's (q.v.) navy, burnt in 1553. The reference is to Henry himself since Shaun (q.v.) is here leaving the Church. 431.26.

Great White Caterpillar–see Oscar Wilde.

Green, Hetty (1835-1916)–American capitalist. 471.13.

*Greene, 277.note 4—see Roe; 377.5; 381.13.

Greene, Gretta–Joyce to Stanislaus Joyce: "Having eloped with my present wife in 1904 she with my full consent gave the name of Miss Gretta Greene which was quite good enough for il cav.

Fabbri who married us. . . ." This accounts for Joyce's calling Nora "Gretta" in "The Dead". Since Gretta is a form of Margaret, it also accounts for the pairing of Maggie and Father Michael or Michael Bodkin (q.q.v.) in FW. 67.31-32; 94.1; 212.10; 533.19.

Greene, Leticia or Lettice–in 1608 Thomas Greene and his wife Leticia lived at New Place, Stratford-on-Avon, and had a son named William. I fancy Joyce read some book in which Leticia Greene played an important part in Shakespeare's (q.v.) life. 20.24; 43.28,29; ?68.6; 161.30; 184.25; 203.29; 229.21; 251.30; †267.1,2 —with Leda; 284.23; ?340.18; 344.11,12; †415.3 (see Plussiboots); †511.22—with Dark Lady (q.v.); †540.23—with Lady from the Sea (q.v.); †542.29—with Lucrece (q.v.); 548.1; 603.17; ?620.10-11 (let us . . . Rathgreany).

Greene, Robert (1560-92)–English writer who died of a surfeit of food and Rhenish wine—see 406.20. In *A Groatsworth of Wit Bought With a Million of Repentance* (q.v.) he did not, as Stephen Dedalus (q.v.) says he did, call Shakespeare or Hamlet (q.q.v.) "a deathsman of the soul" (*Ulysses*, 185/239). That was what he called "lust", but he is generally thought to speak of Shakespeare when he says: "Yes, trust them not: for there is an upstart crow (q.v.), beautified with our feathers that with his *Tiger's heart wrapt in a player's hide* supposes he is as well able to bombast out a blank verse as the best of you; and being an absolute *Johannes fac totum*, is in his own conceit, the only Shakescene in a country." To my mind this accuses Shakespeare of stealing other men's work, an accusation pretty well rampant in FW. Shakespeare held no lasting grudge, however, and went on to base *The Winter's Tale* on Greene's *Pandosto*—see Fawnia. See also Jekyll and Hyde. 88.15; 193.10; 360.30; 406.19; 411.24; 412.11,33.

Greenwood, Sir George, K.C., M.P. –believed that Shakespeare (q.v.) the actor was distinct from the poet, had a long controversy about it with Andrew Lang (q.v.). Greenwood's book is, *The Shakespeare Problem Restated.* Lang's is *Shakespeare, Bacon, and the Great Unknown* (1912). ?74.9-10; 335. 32-33; 450.33.

Gregory, Matthew–first of the Four (q.v.). Among other things he is the number 1, the first letter of the Hebrew alphabet, St Matthew (see Four Evangelists), the province of Ulster and various towns in that province, also the red hand of Ulster; he is also north and the north wind, the element of fire, the Golden age, and birth. He lives at Bothersby North; his road is the North Umbrian. See also Four Masters. †67.17—with Mutt (q.v.); 99.21; †184.34—with Father Mathew (q.v.); 214.34; 366.8,13; 368.33; 384.7,8,10-11; 385.19; 386.13; 388.30; 392.14,16,19; 393.4; 397. 2,5,6; 398.1-2; 405.4; 466.28; 475.23-24; 476.3-4,25; 477.20; 482.27; †520.16—with Father Mathew (q.v.); †533.21—with Pope Gregory I (q.v.); 573.8,28.

Gregory I, Pope–ordered the making of the collection now known as the Gregorian Chant. †533.21 —with Matthew Gregory (q.v.).

Gregory VII–see Hildebrand.

Gregory XIII, Pope–in 1582 modified the Julian (q.v.) Calendar. The modification was adopted in England in 1752 and was known as "New Style". See Chesterfield. 553.16-17.

Gregory, Pope–sixteen popes and one anti-pope. 154.21; 156.21; 605.30.

?Gregory, Lady Augusta (1852-

1932)–Irish writer. I can't help feeling there is more of her than I have found in FW. Could she have some relation to Matt Gregory (q.v.)? 303.13-14.

*Gretched–see Maggies. 538.24.

Gretta–see Gretta Greene.

*Grex's–Latin "flock". 170.34.

Grey One–see Badbols. 376.27.

*Grey, Rhoda, 583.18.

Grieg, Eduard (1843-1907)–Norwegian composer who set Ibsen's *Peer Gynt* (q.q.v.) to music. 279. note 1.

Griffin, Gerald (1803-40)–Irish author of *Talis Qualis* and *The Collegians* which was the basis of Boucicault's *Colleen Bawn* (q.q.v.), which was the basis of *The Lily of Killarney* (q.v.). 450.14.

Griffith, Arthur (1872-1922)–one of the founders of the Irish Free State. 307.9; 358.22.

Griffith's Valuation–played a part in the struggles of the Land League. It means: "a rent reduced to the government rating valuation of the farm". 41.34; 619.4.

Grimaldi, Joseph (1779-1837)– most celebrated English clown. Because of him clowns are called "Joey". 55.35.

*Grimes, 370.20.

Grimm, Jacob and Wilhelm–19th century German philologists and mythologists, best known for their fairy tales. Jacob Grimm formulated "Grimm's Law" which deals with the shift of consonants. 206.2-3; 330.6; 335.5; 378.28; ?†388.31—with Saxo (q.v.); 414. 17; †448.24—with Isengrim (q.v.).

Grimshaw, Bragshaw and Renshaw–*Grimshaw, Bagshaw*, and *Bradshaw* was a farce performed at the Haymarket, 1856. I think G. B. Shaw (q.v.) is indicated. 132.10.

*Grimstad, 602.35.

Gripes–see Mookse.

Grissil or Griselda–type of long-suffering fortitude. 410.9.

Gristle, Madam–see Steevens. 40.34.

Grose, Captain Francis–author of *A Classical Dictionary of the Vulgar Tongue*, which was in Joyce's personal library and, as shown in *A Wake Newslitter* No. 7, November 1962, used for FW. 158.7.

Grotius, Hugo (1583-1645)–Dutch statesman, author of *Adamus exile*, etc. 415.25.

Grouchy, Marshal (1766-1847)– marshal of Napoleon (q.v.), fought at Waterloo. 8.22.

*****Grouseus,** Saint–St Grouse's Day is the start of the grouse season in England. 449.27.

*****Growley,** Garda, 197.7.

*****Grum,** 65.20,23.

Grundy, Mrs–muse of disapproval. 413.21.

*****Gudfodren,** Priest–God the Father. More? 326.24.

Guelphs and Ghibellines–warring factions in 13th century Italy. It is inaccurately said they were named for Guelph and Gibel, rival brothers of Pistoia. 31.32; 567.36.

*****Guglielmus**–probably Shakespeare (q.v.). See also William. 573.24.

*****Guglielmus** Caulis–probably William III (q.v.). See also William. 553.14.

Guido of Arezzo–11th century musician. He introduced the names of the first six notes of the scale, first made use of the lines of the staff and the intervals between them, and probably introduced the F Clef. ?83.15 (languidoily); 260.24-25.

Guinea-hen–see Artemis, Biddy Doran. To the Elizabethans, a guinea-hen was a whore.

Guinevere–King Arthur's (q.v.) queen, Lancelot's (q.v.) mistress.

See Jinnies. 28.1; 285.left margin; 318.5; 389.23; †433.6—with Kevin (q.v.).

Guinness–Dublin's great brewing family and their beer. The firm was founded in the 18th century and became prosperous in the time of Benjamin Lee Guinness (1798-1868) when its beer was first exported. B. L. Guinness restored St Patrick's cathedral, Dublin. His sons, Sir Arthur Guinness (later Baron Ardilaun) and Edward Cecil Guinness (later Baron Iveagh), carried on their father's business and his philanthropies. Today the Guinness brewery, which is on the Liffey, is one of the largest in the world. Its slogan is: Guinness is Good for You. Guinness beer is made of Liffey water.

Joyce associates the Guinnesses with Noah (q.v.), see letter to Miss Weaver, 15 November 1926. Here is another mention of Guinness which the reader can worry out for himself—Joyce to Miss Weaver, 13 January 1925: "I cannot find anything at present about Noah's wife (the medieval figure of the mystery plays is one of the models for Anna Livia) Elizabeth, afterwards Lady Guinness, but . . . I wondered what the Irish word for Guinness's vineyard beverage would be. It is *lin dub* or *dub lin*." See Gunn. 4.24; 6.27; 9.18; 16.21; †24.35 —with Genghis Khan (q.v.); 29.3,4 (yardalong . . . ivoeh); 35.15; 44.12; †64.33—Noah Beery (q.v.); 71.4; 90.13; 99.3; 106.30; 140.1 (Benjamin's Lea); †141.6— with Maud Gonne?; 190.17; 212.1; 272.27; †285.left margin—with King Arthur (q.v.); 299.30; 307.1; 309.13; 325.4; †333.17—with John (q.v.); 345.22-23; †361.5— with King Arthur; 383.3; 407.4 (ardilaun); 407.27,28; 408.28; 414.12; 420.22; †421.26—with Diogenes (q.v.); 443.32; 498.14 (ordilawn); 510.13; †549.34—with

Noah (q.v.); †593.29-30—with Genghis Khan (q.v.); †621.7-8—with St Anthony (q.v.) and Arcturus.

Gulliver, Lemuel–narrator of Swift's (q.v.) *Gulliver's Travels.* 173.3; 294.18; †453.13—with Boliver (q.v.); †464.13—with Shem (q.v.); 620.13-14.

*Gundhur Sawab, Lightnints, 351.32.

Gunn, Michael (1840-1901)–manager of the Gaiety Theatre, South King Street, Dublin, where Christmas pantomimes were annually produced, husband of Bessie Sudlow (q.v.), father of Selskar Gunn (q.v.). In FW Gunn is identified with HCE (q.v.) as the creator who produces the pantomime which is human history. Gunn-HCE has obvious affinities with Shakespeare, as Shakespeare is seen by Stephen Dedalus (q.v.) in the "Scylla and Charybdis" section of *Ulysses.*

Many of the folk tales and nursery rhymes which occur in FW are also pantomimes. Some of them are "Red Riding Hood", "Cinderella", "Goody Two-Shoes", "Dick Whittington", "Humpty Dumpty", "Ali Baba", "Three Bears", "Sinbad the Sailor", "Sleeping Beauty", "Babes in the Wood", "Robinson Crusoe" (q.q.v.). See Mr Atherton's *The Gist of the Pantomime* (*Accent*, Winter, 1955).

I have a hard time separating Gunn, Gonne, Gunning, Guinness (q.q.v.) and sometimes understanding why they should melt into one another.

8.11,14 gunn . . . Crossgunn
25.21-24 game old gunne . . . G.O.G. . . . duddand-gunne
†44.12 Gunn or Guinn—with Guinness (q.v.)
65.11 popguns
?67.16 guntinued
104.20,24 Duddy Gunn . . . Hobe-gunne

116.15 oldowth guns
†220.24 Mr Makeall Gone—with HCE (q.v.)
242.10 gunnfodder
257.34 Gonn . . . Gunnars
†263.18 Gunne's—with Maud Gonne (q.v.)
331.1 poppa the gun
343.23-24 gunnong
350.33 agun
352.23 bragadore-gunneral
?368.1-6 guns . . . guns . . .guns . . . guns
?379.10 gunnell
†387.35 gunfree—with My Man Godfrey (q.v.)
434.10 gun's
481.19 Gun, the farther
†497.17 gunner—with Gunnar
†510.13 Gunner—with Gunnar (q.v.)
531.4-5 Master's gunne
†588.11 gunner
590.24 gunne
†596.15 Gunnar of The Gunnings, Gund—with Gunnar, Gunnings (q.q.v.)
†598.9 goning at gone—with Gunnings, M. Gonne (q.q.v.)
622.23 guns
†625.32 gunne — with Gonne (q.v.)

Gunn, Selskar–son of Michael Gunn and Bessie Sudlow (q.q.v.), friend of Joyce's. I don't know why he turns up in FW with Pervenche (Fr. periwinkle) who seems to be his female partner. She is listed here. 28.26-27; 223.7; 238.23; †281.14-15—with Venus (q.v.); 388.6; 580.17-18; 626.19.

*Gunnar–may usually be Michael Gunn (q.v.) with whom he surely doubles a good deal. Gunnar is Brynhilda's husband in the *Nibelungenlied.* 177.18; 257.34; 497.17; 510.13; 588.11; 596.15.

Gunning, Elizabeth and Maria–beautiful 18th century Irish sisters who took London by storm. Maria married Lord Coventry. Elizabeth married the Duke of

Hamilton and later the Duke of Argyll. See Elizabeth, Mary.

Also Elizabeth or "Gunnilda" Gunning (1769-1823), niece of the above. All the Gunning references in FW take in this girl as well as her more successful aunts. The great Gunning scandal may be found in Horace Walpole's (q.v.) letters to the Misses Barry, 1790-91. Miss Gunning wanted to marry Lord Blandford, who was going to be the 4th Duke of Marlborough (q.v.). She and her mother cooked up a plot to this end, forged letters, perjured themselves, and had the town in a tizzy. They were unmasked, disowned by their father and husband, General Gunning, and retired to the Continent. Walpole casts the affair in terms of war; he calls the girl Miss Charlemagne or The Infanta (q.v.); he describes a Gillray print called "The New Art of Gunning" in which Miss G. is "astride a cannon . . . firing a volley of forged letters at the Castle of Blenheim, and old Gertrude . . . lifting up her hoop to shelter injured innocence, as she calls her". (Cf. FW, 8.29-36). Since the above is echoed in the "Museyroom" episode of FW, the various "Gunns" and the whole

war of Wellington and the Jinnies (q.q.v.) may be thought of as paralleling Gunnilda and Marlborough (q.v.). The Gunnings are next to impossible to separate from Maud Gonne (q.v.). That is understandable for they are beauties all, their weapon sex; but I do not know why Joyce ties them up with Michael Gunn (q.v.).
†8.11,14—with Michael Gunn (q.v.); 376.18; 495.25-26; †508.28 —with Maud Gonne (q.v.); 567. 11; 596.15; 598.9.

Gutenberg, Johann (1398-1468)– German printer. 20.7.

*****Gwen,** 406.11.

Gwenn du Lake–see St Kevin. 433.6.

*****Gwyfyn,** 418.28.

Guy's Hospital–in London. †545.31 —with Guy Fawkes (q.v.).

*****Gygas**–perhaps just *gigas*, Greek "giant"; or Gyges, Lydian king. 36.13; 494.23.

Gynt, Peer–Norwegian folk hero, hero of a play of Ibsen's (q.v.). 75.29; 311.29; 365.6; †369.10— with Frank Power (q.v.); 389.23; 445.24.

H

Haakon–several Norwegian kings. 322.16.

Haarington, King–see Sir John Harington. 447.9.

Habakkuk–Old Testament book. 116.32.

*****Hackett,** Lictor–probably not a person. In Roman antiquity a lictor was an officer who carried the fasces—a kind of hatchet. 197.6.

*****Haddocks** Roche–maybe St Peter (q.v.). See Fish. 34.9.

Haensli and Koebi–Swiss-German

diminutives of John and James (q.v.). 163.5-6; 487.10.

Hafiz–pen-name of Shams-ad-din-Mohammed (d. 1388), Persian poet. 595.3.

Hagaba–see Hagar, Hecuba. 276.9.

Hagar or Hagaba–Abraham's (q.v.) concubine, mother of Ishmael (q.v.). Gen. 16. †276.9—with Hecuba (q.v.); 530.34.

Haggispatrick–see St Patrick.

Hahn, Mrs–Biddy Doran (q.v.). Perhaps also Mme Blavatsky (q.v.), née Hahn-Hahn. 66.23.

Haines–young Englishman in *Ulysses*. 416.1.

*****Hajizfijjiz**–maybe Hafiz or Hodges Figgis (q.q.v.) a Dublin bookstore. 347.19.

Hal–see Harry.

*****Haliday**–may be one of two people: 1) Charles (1789-1866) who wrote *The Scandinavian Kingdom of Dublin*; or 2) William (1782-1812) who translated Keating's *History of Ireland*. ?264.4; 573.2.

*****Hall**–Shakespeare's (q.v.) daughter Susanna (q.v.) married Dr John Hall (q.v.) and had a daughter Elizabeth (q.v.). The following may refer to some or all of these, to someone else altogether, or not to a person at all. The word "hall" is a most common word, but it is not much used in *Ulysses*. 4.15,16; 25.14; 28.1; 49.9; 64.5; 72.14; 74.9; †77.2—with Lot (q.v.); 78.3,8; 92.3; 107.36; 117.16; 122.8; 125.13; 133.24; 137,25; 146.14 (all); 215.36; 237.27, †35 —with Heloise (q.v.); 310.23; 324.9; 360.23; 364.22; †377.7— with Shelbourne Hotel; 379.34; 405.25; 421.12; 429.29; 435.35; 468.15; 478.13-14; 497.25; 498.7; 510.14; 511.12; 544.3; 547.29; 549.15; 565.2; ?602.13; 609.18; 613.2.

Hall, Elizabeth (1608-70)–daughter of Dr John Hall and Susanna Shakespeare Hall (q.v.), granddaughter ("niece", q.v.) of William Shakespeare (q.v.). Her first husband was Thomas Nash (not *the* Thomas Nash, but see him), her second Sir John Bernard or Barnard. According to *Ulysses*, 192-193/249-250, Elizabeth inspired Shakespeare's late heroines and was "Lizzie, grandpa's lump (q.v.) of love" (*Ulysses* 210/273). In FW Lizzie is identified with HCE's (q.v.) daughter Issy (q.v.), whose name is often spelled "Izzy". She is the very young girl loved by an older man, who

loses her to a younger man—as Marina, Perdita, Miranda (q.q.v.) are lost. See also Alice, Dark Lady.

Lizzie is also steadily identified with Elizabeth I; together they make up the Muse of Elizabethan poetry. References to Elizabeth Hall will be found under Elizabeth (q.v.). I think that all Elizabeths are Lizzie.

Hall, Mrs Susanna Shakespeare–see Susanna, see Hall.

Hall and **Knight**–writers of a series of mathematical textbooks for schools. 283.26 (allanights).

Hallam, Arthur (1811-33)–Victorian charmer, subject of Tennyson's (q.v.), "In Memoriam". 40.14 (epickthalamorus). ?256.11.

Halley, Edmund (1656-1752)–English astronomer who observed the great comet of 1680 which bears his name. 54.8; 90.4.

*****Halligan,** 622.22.

*****Halpin,** Martin, 266.note 2.

Ham (warm)–sometimes the second, sometimes the third son of Noah (q.v.)—see also Ham, Shem, Japhet. Ham saw his father naked in a drunken sleep and Noah said, "Cursed be Canaan (q.v.), a servant shall he be unto his brethren". (Gen. 9:25). Outcast, Ham became father of Cush (q.v.) or Ethiopia, Egypt, and the negro race. The Egyptians called him *Khem* or black. As dispossessed, Ham ties to Hamlet (q.v.), from whom I am frankly unable to disentangle him, also to Caliban, Havelock, Ishmael, Cain (q.q.v.). As servant, he is identical with, or strongly linked to, the ass, the Man Servant, (q.q.v.). He is moreover connected with Francis Bacon (q.v.) in a way I see but do not understand. See also pig.

10.25	warm
†31.24	hamlock—with Hamlet (q.v.)
37.4	ham

†39.17   Packenham's (q.v.)
†40.11   beham (see Man Ser-
         vant)
†41.14   shinkhams—with Ba-
         con (q.v.)
†41.18   hamlet (q.v.)
?43.2,5 hamalags . . . hammer-
         smith
49.22   ham
?55.15   tam, homd, and dicky
         (see Tom, Dick,
         Harry)
?58.30   Lili Coninghams (q.v.)
64.7   hammering
†9   Mullingcan Inn—with
         Cain, Mulligan
         (q.q.v.)
†13   martiallawsey — with
         Charles Martel (q.v.)
†73.9   Wholyphamous—with
         Polyphemus (q.v.)
76.5   ham
79.1   ham
†81.30-32 let . . . hum . . . him—
         with Hamlet (q.v.)
†82.9-11 Let . . . him . . . ham—
         with Hamlet (q.v.)
?90.24   Multifarnham
93.8,15 rawdownhams . . .
         hames
124.13   Him
125.12   with amother
170.24,25 Sham . . . sham—with
         Shem (q.v.)
†177.21 hambone—with Ham-
         let (q.v.)
181.36   Hamis
187.22   Tamstar Ham of Ten-
         man's thirst
229.1   harm
247.14   hamo
253.24   ham
264.9-10 Canaan the Hateful
         (q.v.)
†286.29 kisshams—with Shem
         (q.v.)
309.34   hamshack
310.19   hummer
316.25-26 hammer
†317.10 Hombreyhambrey —
         with Humphrey
         (q.v.)
16   ham
?318.16-17 Tham the Thatcher

21   backonham—with Ba-
         con, Buckingham
         (q.q.v.)
319.23   hem
320.9   hamd
322.35   ham
?†351.16 Paddy Bonhamme
         (q.v.)
?355.28,31 hangsters . . . Khum-
         mer-Phett
357.7   hamid
†359.22,27 a ham . . . a ham . . .
         Lets—with Hamlet
?363.5   humm
†364.19 let him be asservant to
         Kinahaun — with
         Hamlet, ass (q.v.)
†31   abery ham — with
         Abraham (q.v.)
368.15   hemmer and hummer
?371.10,11,21,23 Himhim. Him-
         him . . . himmed . . .
         humming . . . hem
376.16   unclish ams
404.6,20 hummers . . . ham-
         mered
421.19-20 mentioningahem
422.18,33 Aham . . . hem
?431.5-8 ham . . . hom . . . hem
         . . . hom
455.7   bonhams (q.v.)
?468.10-11 Hammisandivis
489.15   ham
493.16-17 whem . . . whom . . .
         wham . . . whim . . .
         whumember
497.33-34 Halfa Ham
†518.28 barbarehams — with
         Barham (q.v.)
?†538.33 Gothamm
547.25   hemselves
565.34   hammers
†584.2   blackhams (q.v.)
†586.35-36 ham . . . ham—with
         Anna Livia (q.v.)
†587.1   him—with Anna Livia
         (q.v.)
?597.28 mahamayability
613.12   hottyhammyum
623.12   hamage

Ham, Shem, Japhet–sons of Noah
(q.v.) who repopulated the world
after the flood. Shem (q.v.) is

Shem-Ham, often appearing as Sham. See Ham.

†3.25	Jhem or Shen—with John Jameson (q.v.)
29.33	hamissim of himashim
63-64	homp shtemp and jumphet
87.10	Sam, him and Moffat
†114.18-19	semetomyplace and jupetbackagain from tham Let Rise till Hum Lit—with Hamlet (q.v.)
†143.23	Jeff . . . Ham—see Jeff
†168.5-6	Mac Jeffett—see Jeff
170.24-25	Sham . . . sham . . .sham
189.31	jophet
275.20-23	shame, home and profit . . . ham
297.8-9	seam hem and jobote
317.28	himshemp
351.26-27	sham! hem! or chaffit!
365.21	dhamnk me, shenker, dhummk
406.31-32	some hame and jaffas
422.33-4	mem and hem and the jaquejack
†531.18-19	shims . . . hanis . . . juppettes—with Mrs Jupp (q.v.)
552.8-9	Hams . . . Shemites
582.10	shame, humbug and profit
583.18	japets

Hamazum, Mrs–see Amazon. 494.35.

Hambledon–18th century cricket club. 584.18; 586.11.

***Hamid** and Damid, 357.7.

Hamilcar Barca (b. 270 B.C.)– Carthaginian general, father of Hannibal (q.v.). 192.6.

Hamilton, Anthony (1646-1720)– author of *Mémoires de la vie du Comte Gramont* (q.v.). †138.1— with both Sir William Hamiltons (q.q.v.).

Hamilton, Edwin (1849-1919)– Dubliner, wrote libretti for several pantomimes, including *Turko the Terrible* (q.v.). 513.21.

Hamilton, Elizabeth–see Gramont.

Hamilton, Emma, Lady (1761- 1815)–Nelson's (q.v.) mistress, mother of Horatia (q.v.). 328.21.

Hamilton, William Gerard, "Single Speech" (1729-96)–Irish M.P., made a brilliant maiden speech in Parliament, said never to have spoken again. †138.1—with Anthony Hamilton and Sir William R. Hamilton (q.q.v.); 299.22-23; ?584.18.

Hamilton, Sir William Rowan (1805-65)–Dubliner, mathematical genius. He discovered quaternions. †138.1—with Anthony Hamilton and Sir William G. Hamilton (q.q.v.); 285.10; 300. 27-28 (rovinghamilton).

Hamiltons, haughty–see Lindsay. 438.36.

Hamlet, King–a ghost in *Hamlet* (see Prince Hamlet), a role played by Shakespeare (q.v.). Many "Hamlets", listed under the Prince, refer to the king. He and his brother Claudius (q.v.) are a prime example of *der bestrafte Brudermord*, a theme omnipresent in FW. See also Knowell, Tiberias, Claudius.

Hamlet, Prince–title character in Shakespeare's (q.v.) play, role assumed by Stephen Dedalus (q.v.) in *Ulysses* and by Shem (q.v.) in FW. Joyce felt Prince Hamlet to be an incomplete person, always a son, never a father.

Many uses of "Dane" (q.v.) in FW refer to Hamlet (see also Woeful Dane's Bottom), not only as a Shakespearean character but also as an actual Danish invader of Ireland. *The Annals of the Four Masters* (q.v.) quotes a stanza by the Irish queen Gormfhlaith lamenting the death of her husband Niall Glundubh (q.v.) at the battle of Ath-Cliath (Dublin) in 919. His slayer is Amhlaith or Hamlet. Other authorities say Nial was killed by Sitric (q.v.) whose son Olaf (q.v.) is a prototype of Hamlet and of Havelok (q.v.). The author of "Hamlet" in the 11th *Britannica* (which by all means see) thinks Olaf and Hamlet may be one and the same and that the deed of Sitric, the father, was confused with that of Olaf-Hamlet, the son. In FW Joyce means Hamlet when he says Olaf, as on 294.8-9: "Olaf's lambail", meaning Lamb's (q.v.) tale of Hamlet.

In FW Hamlet is scarcely to be distinguished from Ham (q.v.). This is not odd when you consider they were both—like Stephen Dedalus—dispossessed, and that in *Ulysses*, 208/268, Joyce calls Hamlet "the black prince" (q.v.). See also Havelock, Bacon, Beggar, Claudius, Ophelia, Kersse, Hamnet Shakespeare, Pig. I may say that I am far from seeing all round the use of Hamlet in FW.

6.30-33	Him . . . let . . . Hom . . . Hum
17.23	Let erehim
†31.24	hamlock
†41.18	hamlet
59.31	homelette
72.8	Let Him
†77.14	Dane to pfife—with Macduff (q.v.)
79.35	King Hamlaugh's
81.30-32	let him . . . him
82.9-10	Let . . . him . . . ham
84.32-33	Hamlaugh
93.8	rawdownhams
102.20	let him
114.19	tham Let . . . Hum Lit —with Ham, Shem, Japhet (q.v.)
†129.92	Hanno O'Nonhanno— with Hanno (q.v.)
143.7	camelot prince of dinmurk
?147.3-4	Let them . . . Let them
†191.20-21	to let him tome—with T. S. Eliot (q.v.)
192.35	let him
193.11	hammet
†201.8,30	Dane . . . Olaph lammet —see Olaf
230.7	omulette
258.10	let him
359.22,27	a ham . . . a ham . . . Lets
364.19	let him (see Ham, Ass)
385.16	mad dane
409.3	let him
418.1	Let him
†18	Moyhammlet—with Mohammed (q.v.)
465.32	hamlet
†530.14	halmet—with Hal (q.v.)
536.3	Let . . . him
585.36	Let . . . himself
586.18	homelet

*Hamman–maybe Ham (q.v.) or Haman in *Esther* (q.v.), but neither fits. 205.30.

Hammeltones, Simperspreach— see William Gerald Hamilton. 299.22-23.

Hammerfast–not a person but Hammerfest, Norway, the most northern town in Europe. 46.

Hammurabi (1955-1913 B.C.)– Babylonian king who formulated an early code of laws. 139.25.

*Hanandhunugan's, 6.20.

*Hanar–maybe Anna Livia and hen (q.q.v.). 350.8.

Hand, Robert–the other man in Joyce's *Exiles*—see Rowan, Bertha. I am not sure these references are to him. ?244.6; 404.16; 407.23-25 (*passim*).

Handel, George Frederick (1685-1759)–English composer. 295.28.

*Hands, Nancy–a name for Anna Livia (q.v.). 244.20; 376.24; 382.27.

Handy, Andy–see Rooney.

*Hanigan, 332.4,5.

Hannibal (b. 247 B.C.)–Carthaginian general, son of Hamilcar (q.v.). He crossed the Alps and harried Rome. 81.3; 132.6; 274.9; 538.10.

Hanno–several Carthaginian soldiers and rulers. The first reference below is to Hanno, the Carthaginian navigator (fl. 500 B.C.)

who wrote an account of a voyage along the west coast of Africa. Inscribed on a tablet in the Phoenician tongue, it was hung in the temple of Melkarth (q.v.). †123.32—with Hamlet (q.v.); 182.20.

Hanny, Joe–Johann or John (q.v.). 455.11.

*Hanoukan's–hen (q.v.)? 245.5.

Hanover, House of–English royal house which turned into Windsor. 388.17.

*Hans, Dirty, 209.26.

Hans the Curier–Shaun or John (q.q.v.). Perhaps also Hans Curjel, director of the Corso Theatre in Zurich, whose daughter, named Lucia, drew the pictures on FW 308. 125.14.

Hansard–official report of the proceedings of the House of Commons. 98.28.

Hansel and Gretel—children in a fairy-tale and a pantomime. See Gretta. 105.15; 551.9; 618.2-3.

*Hansen–see Hensen. 529.25.

Hansen, Mr Hurr–the Eberfeld Calculating Horse (108.15-16), Clever Hans. See John. 602.31; 603.16.

Hanway, Jonas (1712-86)–English traveller, the first man to carry an umbrella in London, for which he was stoned. He wrote against tea - drinking.　†449.14 — with James (q.v.).

*Hanzas Khan, 497.34.

*Hapapoosiesobjibway – HCE's (q.v.) Indian name which must surely mean Haveth-Papooses-Everywhere. 134.14.

Hapsburgs–family to which the imperial dynasty of Austria belonged. 557.6.

Harald Fair Hair or Haarfager (850-933)–Harold I, first king of Norway. He annexed Scottish islands. See Harold. 134.27; 169.16; 324.28; 610.3.

Harald Gray Cloak or Graafeld–Harald II, grandson of the above. With his brothers he ruled the west of Norway, was murdered in 969. See Harold. 567.18.

Harald Harefoot–King of the Saxons, 1035-1040. 444.5.

*Haraldsby, 139.34.

Hardcastle, Mr, Mrs, Kate–characters in Goldsmith's (q.v.) *She Stoops to Conquer, or The Mistakes of a Night.* See Lumpkin, Miss Bulkeley. 538.31-32.

Hardicanute (1019 - 42)–son of Canute (q.v.), King of England. He was cruel, treacherous, and fought for the throne with his half-brother Harold. 325.23.

*Harding–president? 273.23-24.

*Hardmuth–Hardtmuth the pencil-maker? 42.27.

Hardress–see Cregan. 246.18.

Hardy–seems to include Thomas (1840-1928), English novelist, and Nelson's (q.v.) "kiss me, Hardy". 199.24; 202.23; 333.22.

*Hare, uncle, 466.30.

Harington, Sir John (1561-1612)– English courtier, author of *Metamorphosis of Ajax,* a work on water-closets. He served in Ireland with Essex (q.v.) and wrote a book about Ireland. 266.12; †447.9—with Harrington (q.v.).

Haristobulus–see Hyrcan. 219.26.

Harlequin and Columbine–pantomime characters. 48.27; 221.25; 360-361; 455.28; 527.26-27.

Harley–hero of Mackenzie's *Man of Feeling,* whose sensibility was so exquisite that he died when his love accepted him in marriage. †426.12—with William Harvey (q.v.).

Harmsworth–see Northcliffe.

*Harnett, Sheilia, 176.3.

Harold II, last of the Saxons (1022-66)–English king, defeated and slain at the battle of Hastings, fighting William (q.v.) the

Conqueror. I think that all Harolds and Haralds (q.v.) are identified with him, but I do not exactly understand his significance to Joyce. 5.6; 9.11-12; 30.14.33; †31.8-9—with Humphrey (see HCE); 324.28; 375.6.

Harold, Bluetooth (940-986)–Danish king whose baptism marked Denmark's conversion to Christianity. See Harold II. 387.8; 403.24.

*Harriman–maybe the American railroad fancier, Edward Henry Harriman. 289.note 6.

Harrington–William O'Connor (q.v.) wrote *Harrington: A Story of True Love* (1860), which is in praise of Delia Bacon (q.v.). †289.note 6—see Harry, Harriman?; ?330.34; †447.9 —with Harington (q.v.).

Harriot, Thomas (1560-1621)–English mathematician. 301.17.

Harris, Frank–biographer of Shakespeare and Wilde (q.v.). Along with Brandes and Lee, he is one of Joyce's principal sources for Shakespeare. The distinction between the names Harris, Horace, Horus (q.q.v.) is not so clear to me as it ought to be. †326.32; 511.20 (airs).

Harris, Lord – 19th century cricketer. 584.1.

Harrods–London department store which probably always doubles with Herod (q.v.). 127.11; †159.15 —with Hope Bros. (q.v.); 536.35.

Harry, Hal–"Harry" or "hairy" sometimes means Esau (see Jacob), and sometimes one or more of the King Henrys of England. Henry IV, Henry V, Henry VI, Henry VIII (q.q.v.) are all Shakespearean (q.v.) characters. See also Henry II. 28.3 (*bis*), 25; 71.15; 93.7; †110.17 —with Aristotle (q.v.); 117.16-17 (see Henry VIII); 176.20; 187.19-20; 224.12; 233.31; 234.4; 289. note 6; 300.10; 316.5 (see Henry

II); 358.20; 373.17; 396.16; 410.2; 414.31; 416.1,2; 440.36; 441.4; 454.19; 484.21 (see Henry II); 511.22 (*bis*), 24 (*bis*); 535.5; ?538.18; 546.10 (see Henry II); 557.10; 576.6 (see Henry VIII); 578.7; ?583.28; 584.1 (see Lord Harris); 616.14; 621.24.

Harry the Minstrel or Blind Harry (b. 1470)–Scottish poet. †484.21 —with Henry II (q.v.).

Hart, Bill–American Shakespearean actor and movie hero of silent pictures who played in westerns. 275.14.

Hart, William and Joan–Joan was Shakespeare's sister. Her Hart descendants are alive to this day. The rest of the Shakespeares founded no enduring lines. 11.26; 37.11; 83.5; 547.4.

*Harte, Eva–see Eve. 251.28.

*Hartigan, Hurricane–perhaps Harrigan and Hart, Irish-American comedians and song-writers. 210.16.

Harun Al-Rashid or Harun the Orthodox (763-809)–fifth of the "Abbasid" caliphs of Bagdad, best known to western readers from the *Arabian Nights* in which he goes about disguised. 4.32; 33-34; 358.28.

Harvey, Bagnal–hanged for his part in the Irish rebellion of '98. 471.33.

Harvey, William (1578-1637)–English doctor, discoverer of the circulation of the blood, which lost him all his patients. †426.12 —with Harley (q.v.).

Hasculf–last Danish ruler of Dublin, defeated and slain by the Anglo-Norman invaders. 516.19.

Hasdrubal–son-in-law of Hamilcar (q.v.). He was beheaded and his head thrown into his brother Hannibal's (q.v.) camp *pour décourager les autres.* 192.16.

*Hatchett, Lifetenant-Groevener, 325.1.

Hathaway, Ann–Shakespeare's (q.v.) wife—see Anne Whateley. Since I think FW is about Shakespeare, I think that all the Ann references in the book are references to her. See Anna Livia. ?26.35; ?68.25; 113.18,20 (Add dapple inn . . . whatholoosed); 114.16-17; 116.36; 117.19; 170.20; †230.14-15—with Casanova, see also Casanuova; ?243.2; 411.27-28; 623.34.

*****Hatta**–name of an Anglo-Saxon messenger in *Through the Looking-Glass*, see Alice. †383.36—with John (q.v.).

*****Haught,** Ellishly–maybe just "hellishly hot". 289.14.

Haun–see John.

Haussmann, Baron (1809-91)–leading spirit in the rebuilding of Paris. He laid out parks, new streets, new sewers, water supplies, bridges, etc. 129.16; 205.35.

Havas–foreign news agency. 421.32; ?593.18.

Havelok the Dane–*The Lay of Havelok* is a 14th century verse romance, which has much in common with the pre-Shakespearean Hamlet (q.q.v.). Of royal birth, Havelok's throne is usurped; he escapes to England where he serves as a scullion and in time triumphs over all obstacles. See Man Servant, see Olaf. 15.31; †556.23—with Man Servant (q.v.).

Hawk, The–James Stephens, the Fenian leader. 91.29.

Hawker, Harry–fell into the sea on 18 May 1919 while on a transatlantic flight. 158.34.

Hawkeye or Natty Bumpo–hero of Cooper's (q.v.) *Leatherstocking Tales*, which include *The Last of the Mohicans*. 106.24.

Hawkins, Sir John (1532-95)–British admiral, explorer of the New World, popularly supposed to have brought the first potato plant to Ireland. See Raleigh. 316.27-28; 542.1.

Hawthorne, Nathaniel (1804-64)–American novelist, author of *The Scarlet Letter*, *The House of the Seven Gables*, "Recollections of a Gifted Woman", etc. See Delia Bacon. 135.2-3; 160.6; 204.20; ?326.13; 357.32.

*****Haycock,** 136.14.

Haydn, Franz Joseph (1732-1809) –Austrian composer. His "Creation" is based on *Genesis* and *Paradise Lost*. †482.17—with Haydon (q.v.).

Haydon, Benjamin Robert (1786-1846)–English historical painter. Joyce was probably thinking of "The Curse of Adam". †482.17—with Haydn (q.v.).

Hayes, Conyngham, Robinson–Dublin chemists. 434.12.

Hayes, Bully–American, pirate who flourished in the Pacific islands in the 1860s and '70s. Hack novelists turned him into a Robin Hood. Perhaps, Dan Hayes, an 18th century Limerick buck. An old Irish play-bill (often quoted) read: "*The Tragedy of Hamlet* by the celebrated Dan Hayes of Limerick." 210.16; 289.14.

*****Hayre,** Cattie, 239.24.

*****Hazel**–see hen. Maybe something to do with Hazelhatchery on the Liffey. 64.34.

*****Hazelton,** Secret Speech–perhaps W. G. Hamilton (q.v.). 515.12.

HCE–hero of FW—see Here Comes Everybody. His full name is Humphrey Chimpden Earwicker, but he is usually called Humphrey (or some variation) in reference to his humped back (see Gobbo, Pukkel) and to Humpty Dumpty (q.v.); or he is called Earwicker (q.v.) because, it is said, of the earwig, a small unpleasant insect —see Forficua, see Persse O'Reilly, Jacob Earwig. The initials,

HCE, occur thousands of times in FW, and indeed the word "he" is meant to remind us that our hero is always present.

HCE is the Macrocosm, Here Comes Everybody, and the Microcosm, Humphrey Chimpden Earwicker, an innkeeper of Chapelizod (q.v.), which is a suburb of Dublin, on Dublin's river, the Ann Liffey (q.v.). At his inn the dramas of human history are presented with HCE, a jack of all trades, serving now as playwright, now as producer—actor—audience—whatever is required.

The basis of all plays is the mystery play of Adam and Eve (q.v.). HCE's great role is Adam ybounden, one-eyed, grousing, stammering, defending—a hump of guilt, like Christian's, on his back. Then suddenly he is up and abroad, disguised as this man, that man, everyone, nobody. The old Adam does not die, not even when the new Adam comes to replace him. HCE is no featureless abstraction with the word "Everyman" pinned to his coat, but at once a real character and a burst of vitality, conceived in comedy, executed in admiration. See Here Comes Everybody, Shakespeare, Howth.

I HCE

32.14	H.C.E.
39.6	finish ek
95.12	H₂CE₃
119.18	hecitency Hec
198.8	H.C.E.
199.24	Hek
264.3	ech
281.1	hce che cch
291.note 1	hce . . . hce
332.3	hec
377.3	Hecech
411.18	Hek
420.17-18	Hek . . . Hek
484.20	Hekkites
546.23	hek
577.23	hekhisway
584.5	hek
623.9	ech

II Humphrey Chimpden Earwicker

24.7	Unfru - Chikda - Uru-Wukru
†30.14-15	Harold or Humphrey—with Harold II (q.v.)
32.16	Chimbers
33.30	H. C. Earwicker
36.12	H. C. Earwicker
46.2	Chimpden

III Humphrey

†6.30,32,33	Him . . . Hom . . . Hum — with King Hamlet (q.v.)
17.9	hunfree
22.28	trihump
*23.20	Homfrie Noanswa—with Nyanza (q.v.)
29.5-6	humphing
30.32	Humphrey
†31.8-9	Haromphreyld—with Harold II (q.v.)
†32.14-15	Haromphrey . . . Dook Umphrey—with respectively Harold II and Duke Humphrey (q.q.v.)
42.18	humps
46.33	Humpharey
52.23	Humphrey's
53.9	humphriad
62.28	humping
70.13	Humphrey's
72.13	Humborg
74.16	Humph
77.34	honophreum
97.3	Humfries
101.35	hungray
134.34	Humphrey's
173.22-23	Mr Humhum
196.33	Humphrey
198.29	Humber
199.32	Hum
200.32	Humpy's
203.6	Humphrey's
220.24	Hump
242.22	Hump
254.14	Humph
270.13	Humphreystown
275.note 4	Humphrey's
312.13	Hump! Hump.
†317.10	Hombreyhambrey—with Ham (q.v.)
325.28	Humphrey

327.33	Humpopolamos
328.34	crihump
†375.5-6	Hunphydunphyville'll — with Humpty Dumpty (q.v.)
390.32	humple
430.7	sir Humphrey
484.9	Humphrey
492.29	humpbacked
525.19	Hump's
572-573	Honuphrius (*passim*)
582.26	Humphrey
584.18	hump
585.22,30,32	Humperfeldt . . . Humbo, Humphrey
602.24	perhumps
616.36	Mr Stores Humphreys

IV Earwicker

17.34	earwig
18.11	Forficules (q.v.)
20.23	eerie whig's
21.1	norewhig
28.15	Airwinger's
30.19-20	Earwickers of Sidlesham
31.11,28	earwuggers . . . earwigger
34.13-14	Southron Earwicker
35.21	The Earwicker
42.31-32	airwhackers
47.16,17,18	Earwicker . . . earwigs . . . earwigs
48.28-29	Eyrawyggla
59.27	Irewaker
70.35	Earwicker
73.3-4	Earwicker . . . Messrs or Missrs Earwicker
79.2,3,5	wugger . . . whiggissimus . . . Massa Ewacka
16,19,33	earwigs . . . frockful of fickles . . . her weaker
83.6	wick's ears
84.27	her whacking
91.11	earbig
98.28,29,32	earwag . . . e'er a wiege ne'er a waage
107.2	Mirsu Earwicker
†108.21-23	ear of Fionn Earwicker . . . wicker—with Finn (q.v.)
119.16-17	Earwicker
134.16	Eelwick
149.13	wag on my ears

164.29	earwig
173.9-10	earwaker's
175.25-26	Eirewhiggs
†191.20	earps brupper—with Earp (q.v.)?
193.13	wig in your ear
221.28	hairwigs
238.31	Eer's wax
243.17	lugwags
246.7	periwig
255.5	erewaken
301.8	Erewhig
311.11	wickser in his ear
312.16	earpicker
320.26-27	ire wackering . . . eyewinker
321.17	Irinwakes
327.32-33	Eriweddyng
351.25	earwakers
359.26	Eeric Whigs
360.32	eeriewhigg airywhugger
?367.33	eyriewinging
375.19	wecker your earse
378.7	Rrwwwkkkrrr
382.25	wakes of his ears
390.4-5	earing his wick
414.36	wigeared
421.12	Ereweaker
434.11	here Mr Whicker
435.19-20	Stick wicks in your earshells
†445.36	Aerwenger's—with AE (see Russell)
467.28	weaker our ears
485.21	esquire earwugs
491.30	Mr Hairwigger
496.12,15	Mr Eelwhipper . . . ears did wag . . . Eire wake
520.6	earwanker
539.4-5	Nearwicked
559.25	beer wig
560.15	airwaked
568.26	Ear! Ear! Weakear
579.25	earwigger's
581.6	Eyrewaker's
593.15	Eireweeker
615.16	uhrweckers
619.12	herewaker
622.32	ear, wiggly
625.2-3	beardwig
17	wick dear

*Head-in-Clouds—a giant? 18.23.

*Healy, Billy, 608.8.

Healy, Timothy Michael (1855-1931)–Irish nationalist politician who ratted on Parnell (q.v.) and did much to guide the Free State in its early days. By his friends, he was called "Tiger Tim" (q.v.), by his enemies "Healy the Hound". His house in Chapelizod (q.v.) was known as Heliopolis. When he was Governor-General of Ireland, Dubliners called the Vice-Regal Lodge "Uncle Tim's Cabin". All these names and jokes get into FW, but I sometimes think I may confuse Tim Healy with a 19th century Dublin bishop named Healy. See also Tim. 24.18; 73.19; †176.12—with Ali Baba (q.v.); †291.8—see Tim; †329.34—with Mary (q.v.); 435.30; †622.7—with Uncle Tom (q.v.).

*Heaton, 552.12. 306.3.

*Heavyscuisgardaddy – HCE. 306.3.

Heavystost's – see Hephaestus. 514.11.

Hebeneros–see Hebe, Nero, Eros? 346.4.

Heber and Heremon–sons of Milesius, a legendary invader of Ireland. The island was divided between them, they quarrelled, and Heber was killed. Heremon became king of Ireland and founded the royal lirte that ended with Roderick O'Connor (q.v.). †14.35-36—with Ahriman and with Esau (q.q.v.); 271.19-20; 394.29; 604.4.

Hecate–in Greek myth, goddess of the moon and night, of childbirth, of magic, and of the underworld. Also a character in *Macbeth* (q.v.). 273.17.

Hector–Trojan hero in the *Iliad* and in Shakespeare's *Troilus and Cressida* (q.q.v.). 255.16.

Hecuba–queen of Troy, wife of Priam (q.v.) in the *Iliad*. †276.9 —with Hagaba (q.v.).

Hedwig–girl in Ibsen's (q.v.) *The Wild Duck*. 274.17.

*Heenan, 466.29.

Heeny, Bill–see Bellini. 360.7.

Heep, Uriah–character in *David Copperfield* (q.v.). †434.29—with Uriah the Hittite (q.v.).

*Hegan, 67.16 (he guntinued).

Hegel, Georg (1770-1831)–German philosopher. 12.21; 416.33; 604.6.

Hegesippus–1) Athenian orator of Demosthenes's (q.v.) time; 2 early Christian writer (fl. 150-180); 3) supposed author of a free Latin adaptation of the *Jewish War* (fl. 4th century). 38.16.

Heidelberg Man–Man of the Old Stone Age. 18.23; 37.1.

Heidsieck–brand of champagne. 35.9; 372.35-36; 373.7; 451.26; 462.10.

Heighland, Gordon–Scottish Infantry regiment, the Gordon Highlanders. 392.34.

Heinz–brand of American canned goods. 581.5.

Helen–character in Homer, Shakespeare (q.q.v.), and (as Mrs O'Shea, q.v.) in *Ulysses*. A "hennin" is a French medieval spire-shaped head-dress. See Nelly. †254.31—with hen (q.v.)? †291.14 —with Elizabeth (q.v.).

Helena–girls in Shakespeare's (q.v.) *All's Well That Ends Well* and *A Midsummer Night's Dream*. Shakespeare lived in the parish of St Helena in London. See Giletta. 71.29.

Hellogabalus–Roman emperor, 218-222. He was cruel, profligate and made the worship of the sun-god paramount at Rome. 157.26.

Helios–Greek sun-god. 67.10.

Helmholtz, Hermann Ludwig Ferdinand von (1821-94)–German scientist who wrote on color-vision in *Physiological Optics*. 611.28.

Heloise–see Abelard.

*Helmingham, 88.21.

*Helusbelus – Elizabeth   (q.v.)?
594.23.

Helvétius, Claude Adrien (1715-71)
–French freethinker. In *De
l'Esprit* he treats the Bible in a
derisory manner. †4.21 — with
Leviticus (q.v.).

Hemans, Felicia Dorothea (1793-
1835)–English poetess, buried in
Dublin. 397.31.

Hen–see Guinea-hen, Biddy Doran,
Artemis.

Hengest and Horsa–brother chief-
tains who led the first Saxon
invaders of England. 63.22;
143.22-23; 214.12; 272.17; 325.17.

Hengler, Albert–proprietor of a
circus, which according to *Ulysses*,
680/816, performed at the Rotunda in Dublin. 307.8; 529.34.

Hennessy–a brand of brandy.
176.6.

Hennessy–friend of Mr Dooley
(q.v.). 10.4; 240.13; 325.8-9.

Hennu–name sometimes given
Osiris (q.v.) in *The Book of the
Dead.* Hennu is Lord of Tattu
(q.v.). 479.33.

*Henrietta–street in Dublin.
†447.8–with hen (q.v.).

Henry II (1133-89)–king of England who, with the blessing of the
Pope (or not, as modern scholars
have decided), took over Ireland.
He gave Dublin to Bristol as a
colony.   Pseudo-Shakespearean
(q.v.) character–see Ireland. See
Harry. 316.5; †484.21 (bland
Harry)—with Harry the Minstrel
(q.v.); 539.32-33; 545.23; 546.10
(Enwreak us wrecks).

Henry VIII (1491-1547)–king of
England, Shakespearean (q.v.)
character. See Anne Boleyn,
Elizabeth I, Great Harry. 93.4,7,
8; 117.16-17; †138.32-33—with
Hen (q.v.); †307.14—with Sir

Henry   Tudor   (q.v.);   455.13;
539.33; 576.6; 578.7.

*Henson or Hansen, 446.30; 529.25.

Hephaestus–Greek god of fire,
identified with Vulcan (q.v.).
514.11.

Heppy–two Egyptian gods. 416.1;
443.10.

Hera–wife of Zeus (q.v.). The passage on 208 parodies the *Iliad*,
XIV. A lot of Zeus's women are
buried in it. See Hero? 117.2;
208.2 (Werra); †415.11-12—with
Ra (q.v.); †457.13—with Tethra
(q.v.).

Herbert–see Pembroke.

Hercules–chief national hero of
Hellas. The role of Hercules is
performed by Moth (q.v.) in
Shakespeare's   (q.v.)   *Love's
Labour's Lost.* The sign of the
Globe Theatre was Hercules with
the world on his back. He is
joined with goats in FW because
the Globe was not infrequently a
house of tragedy. 16.4; 81.3;
128.36; 487.15; 492.5; 570.17.

Here Comes Everybody–see HCE,
Childers. *Punch* 9 May 1885,
"Essence of Parliament": "Chil-
ders brings in budget. Always
a little self-important—H-ere
C-omes E-verybody Childers, as
Gibson fills up his initials. Tonight
bursting with importance and a
Deficit of Fifteen Million."
Punch, 12 Dec. 1885:

T-by, M.P.: . . . How's H. C. E.
today? He doesn't look so like H-ere
C-omes E-verybody today. . . .
Mr. H. C. E. Childers. No, Toby. I
confess it's broken me down a little.
After all I have done for the country.
. . . I strengthened its Navy, reformed
its Dockyards, made its Budget, and
now in my old age Pomfret deserts me.

Heremon–see Heber.

Hermann and Dorothea–title
characters of a poem by Goethe
(q.v.). †283.28-29—perhaps with
Herman Melville (q.v.), certainly
with Rhea (q.v.).

Hermes–see Hermes Trismegistus, Mercury.

***Hermes**, Anton–Hermes Trismegistus? 81.7.

Hermes Trismegistus–to the Egyptians he was Thoth (q.v.), god of words and wisdom, author of sacred or Hermetic books. In the middle ages "hermetic" was applied to a hodgepodge of Neo-Platonic, cabbalistic, alchemical literature which sought a substitute for Christianity. These books were called *Tables of Emerald* and were said to date from before the flood. They taught, among other things, that "That which is above is reflected in that which is below".
According to Joyce (to Miss Weaver, 14 August 1927), Shaun (q.v.) is Trismegistus in III,ii. Here and elsewhere Shaun is also Hermes as messenger, god of roads, master-thief, for he has stolen the letter and pretends it is his own. In III,i,ii Shaun is, of course, also Don Giovanni, John McCormack, and Antichrist (q.q.v.), etc. 263.22.

?Hermia – Girl in Shakespeare's (q.v.) *A Midsummer Night's Dream*. 207.18 (her mealiebag).

?Hermione–queen in Shakespeare's (q.v.) *The Winter's Tale*. See Perdita. 14.8.

Hero – heroine of Shakespeare's (q.v.) *Much Ado About Nothing*. Listed under Hero and Leander (q.v.). See also Claudio, Beatrice, Benedick, Phenitia.

Hero and Leander–lovers in classical story and a poem by Marlowe. The Leander is a British rowing club. In FW, Hero is so well confused with Shakespeare's Hero (q.q.v.) that I have not tried to separate them. 68.25; ?74.3; 117.2; 135.17; 146.24; 203.13; 249.14,19; 328.19-20,25; ?384.23; ?394.33; 398.5,29; 466.14; 487.31.

Herod–the Biblical Herod ruled from 4 B.C. to A.D. 39. †13.20— with Herodotus (q.v.); †127.11 with Harrod's (q.v.); 260.note 1; 520.5; †536.35—with Harrod's (q.v.).

Herodotus (484-425 B.C.)–Greek historian. †13.20—with Herod (q.v.); 275.note 5; 410.2; 614.2,35.

Herrera y Tordesillas, Antonio de –wrote *General History of the West Indies*. 512.18.

Herrick, Robert (1591-1674)–English poet. 30.21.

***Herrington** – see Harrington? 101.14.

***Hersy**–heresy? 355.15.

Hertz, Heinrich Rudolph (1857-94) –German physicist who discovered the phenomenon known as "hertzian waves". 232.10; 331.23; 460.25.

Hesperus–personification of the evening star. 245.23; 306.27; 538.23.

Hester–see Stella.

***Heterodithero**, 221.31.

Heth–Phoenician name for the Letter H—as in HCE (q.v.). 452.13; 623.34.

Hetty, Jane–see Stella. 27.11.

Heva–see Eve.

***Hewit**–in 1803 Robert Emmet (q.v.) lived under the name of Hewitt at a Mrs Palmer's at Harold's Cross. Maybe. 42.4; †135.29—with Costello (q.v.).

Hiawatha–Indian hero of Longfellow's (q.v.) poem. 600.8.

Hibbert, Robert–19th century liberal who endowed a lectureship. †388.29—with Mother Hubbard (q.v.).

Hickey's–second hand bookseller on Bachelor's Walk, Dublin. 286.10.

***Hicks**, 49.27; 64.6; 67.19,20; 423.11; 454.15.

***Hickstrey**–see Hicks. 64.6.

*Higgens–hero of Shaw's *Pygmalion* (q.q.v.)? 604.6.

Higgens, Francis, "the Sham Squire"–betrayer of Lord Edward Fitzgerald (q.v.). 517.27.

*Highfee the Crackasider, 418.2.

Hilarion, St (290-371)–abbot who first introduced the monastic system into Palestine. The Roman Hilaria is also meant here. 361.30-31.

Hilary–one of the twins (see Shem and Shaun) in the Prankquean episode, FW 21-23. Mr Tindall has pointed out Bruno's (q.v.) motto "*In tristitia hilaris hilaritate tristis*" as the source of the names Tristopher (q.v.) and Hilary. Hilary ties onto Joy (or Joyce), Isaac, Shandy, etc. 21-23 (*passim*); 520.27 (hill ar yu).

Hilda–heroine of Reyner's opera, *Sigurd.* 147.12.

Hildebrand   (1020-85)–became Pope Gregory VII. He tried to magnify the power of the papacy and force the Emperor Henry IV to do penance. †155.36—with Alday (q.v.).

*Hill–probably HCE as Howth (q.q.v.). 82.32.

Hill, Fanny–*Fanny Hill, or the Memoirs of a Woman of Pleasure*, by John Cleland, 1750. 94.9-10; 204.8,13.

Hillel–Jewish rabbi and scholar who lived in Jerusalem at the time of Herod (q.v.). 350.3; 499.8.

Hillman Minx–English car. 376.3.

Himana–see Aminah. 309.26.

*Himmyshimmy, Mr–HCE (q.v.)? 173.27.

Hind Horn–ballad hero. 403.25-26.

*Hing the Hong–see *Ulysses*, 210/274. 206.3.

*Hinnessy, hiena–see Hennessy. 10.4,5,7.

Hippolyta–see Amazon.

*Hips and Haws–see Hughes? 257.11.

*Hitchcock, "Ductor", 44.2; 363.2-3.

Hitler, Adolf–German dictator. 191.7; 410.8 (hikler's).

Hobbs, Jack – 20th century cricketer. 584.15.

Hobson, Thomas (1544-1630)–Cambridge-London carrier who would hire horses only in turn and gave us the expression "Hobson's choice", meaning "this or nothing". Possibly also Bulmer Hobson who advocated an Irish uprising in 1915. 63.2; 432.35.

*Hodder's–probably just the Yorkshire river. 537.36.

Hodge–English steamboat service between Ireland and Holyhead. 138.11.

*Hoel–maybe the 11th century Duke Hoel of Brittany, or the father of Isolde (q.v.) of the White Hands, or the hero of Meyerbeer's (q.v.) opera, *Dinora.* 143.15.

*Hoet of the rough throat, 254.29.

Hog–see Pig.

Hogam–Ogham writing. 223.4.

*Hogan–perhaps Rev. E. Hogan who collected *Bearlagair Na Saer* words—see Macalister's *The Secret Languages of Ireland,* 226. 98.30.

Hogan, John (1808-58)–Irish sculptor who made the statue of O'Connell (q.v.) which stands in the City Hall, Dublin. 552.13.

Hogarth, William (1697-1764)–English painter. 435.7.

Hogg, James (1770-1835)–"The Ettrick Shepherd", a Scottish writer whose *Confessions of a Justified Sinner* (which reads like one of Hawthorne's shorter works) is used in FW. See Pig. 69.19; 366.26; 487.7; 533.35.

Hokmah–Hebrew for "divine wisdom". 32.4.

Hokusai (pronounced "hock sigh") –18th century Japanese artist. 36.4; 548.9.

Holly and Ivy–they are Mary and Eve, the second and the first Eve (q.q.v.), and they occur in a Christmas carol which began pagan. Ivy is sometimes associated with Parnell (q.v.), but not usually in the Holly combination. On p. 27 the Holly and Ivy are identified with the Esthers (q.v.), but I can't see that Joyce keeps it up. 5.30; 27.13,15; 31.25,32; 58.5,6; 59.9; ?88.23-24; 138.25; 147.10, 11; 152.3; 163.10-11; 167.35; 236.13-14; 265.17; 291.9,11; 421. 6-7; 465.13; 485.21,22; 502.2,4; 505.3; 556.3; 588.17; ?616.32 (icy).

Holman, Libby–night-club singer of the jazz era. 200.12.

***Holmes**, 276.note 2.

Holmes, Oliver Wendell (1809-94)– American author of *The Autocrat of the Breakfast Table* and of *The Professor at* the same. †458.23— with Harmsworth (q.v.).

Holmes, Sherlock–Conan Doyle's (q.v.) detective. 165.32-33; †534. 31—with Lorcan Sherlock (q.v.).

***Holmpatrick**, the lady, 31.31.

***Holohan**, Dan, 147.30.

Holt, Joseph–rebel of '45. 97.2; 315.31.

Holwell, Zenaphiah–leader of those imprisoned in the Black Hole of Calcutta. See Dowlah. 492.18.

Home, Daniel Douglas (1833-86)– Scottish spiritualist who inspired Browning's "Mr Sludge" (q.q.v.). 536.12 (Hone).

Homer–Greek epic poet from whom Shakespeare and Joyce (q.q.v.) borrowed heavily. It probably mattered to Joyce that he was blind and impersonal. †21.13— with B. Vanhomrigh (q.v.); 34.12, 16; 129.23; 306.left margin; †314. 23-24—with Vanhomrigh (q.v.); †351.9-10—with O. Khayyam

(q.v.); 445.32; †481.21 (re humeplace)—with Surgeon Hume (q.v.); 515.24.

***Homin**, 24.34.

***Hone**–maybe William Hone (1786-1842)—English author of political and religious burlesques. 382.21.

Honorius–four popes and one antipope. 154.36.

Honuphrius–see HCE. The Honuphrius passage parodies M. M. Matharan (q.v.), *Casus de matrimonio fere quingenti quibus applicat et per quos explicat sua asserta moralia circa eamdem materiam.* Parisseis, 1893. 572-573 (*passim*).

Hood, Thomas (1799-1845)–English writer of light verse. Charles Lamb (q.v.) beat Joyce to this pun, as to the remark about the Catholic Church being founded on a pun—see Frere. 487.21.

Hookback, Dook–see Richard III, Luke Plunket, HCE. 127.17.

***Hooligan**, 622.22.

***Hooper**, 255.9.

Hoover, Herbert (1874-)–31st president of the U.S. 376.6,14,15.

?Hope, Anthony–19th century English novelist. The reference here is to the commonface of *The Prisoner of Zenda*. †159.15—with Hope Bros. (q.v.).

Hope, Brothers–London department store. †159.15—with Anthony Hope and Harrods (q.q.v.); 461.7.

***Hopeandwater**, Dora Riparia– the Dora Riparia is a North Italian river; *deoc an doruis* is "good vernacular for a small whisky" or a stirrup cup. See Dora, Pandora. †211.10—with Pandora (q.v.); 462.7.

***Hopely**, 280.3.

Hopkins and Hopkins–jewelers of O'Connell Street, Dublin. 26.2.

***Hopsinbond**, Mr, 510.35.

Horace–Roman poet, quoted in FW. 307.left margin.

Horace–see Horus.

*Horan, Paul–see Cloran. ?20.10; 49.15.

Horatio–see Horus.

Hore-Belisha–see Belisha.

*Horizon, Miss, 340.28-29.

Horkos–according to Hesiod, the Greek god of oaths.

Horn, Dr–of the maternity hospital in *Ulysses*, "Oxen of the Sun". I think he occurs here because Shaun (q.v.) is, among other things, in III,i,ii, a child moving through nine months in the womb. †403.26–with Hind Horn (q.v.).

Horner, Jack–nursery-rhyme character. See John. 465.4; 623.3.

Horniman, Miss–English lady who subsidized the Abbey (q.v.) and other theatres. 377.15-16; 540.22.

Horrocks–Lancashire firm which weaves sheets, etc. 326.1—see Horus; 491.32.

Horus and Set–Egyptian gods. Egyptian myth has an elder and younger Horus, both beneficient; the younger is more important. He was son of Isis and Osiris (q.v.); he avenged his father's death by overcoming the murderer, Set or Seth. Horus and Set fought three days, and though Set threw excrement at Horus, Horus emasculated Set. Horus was a sun-god, Set a god of malignant darkness, pictured by the Egyptians as an onager or ass (q.v.). The Norwegian Captain episode (FW 309-333) parallels in some fashion the Horus-Set battle. Kersse (q.v.) appears to be Horus, the Norwegian Captain (q.v.), Set. Horus has, I think, an affinity with the Horatio of *Hamlet* (q.v.). †29.27-28—with the Biblical Seth (q.v.); 72.6; 105.28-29; 135.22,23 (horse . . . set); 241.11 (*bis*); 311.25; 312.3; 313.4; 319.21; 322.25; 324.15;

325.13; †326.1,32 — with Horrocks, Toler, Harris (q.q.v.); 328.34; 360.16; 416.1,2; 455.6; 499.19; 616.26.

Hosea–first of the minor prophets of the Old Testament. 553.35.

Hosty–the personification of Vico's (q.v.) plebe, eternally in revolt against the patrician. He is probably Shem (q.v.). See *The New Science*, trans. Bergin and Fisch, sections 549, 611, 638, 686. Joyce's picture of the class-struggle is almost pure Vico. Others have pointed out that Hosty is also, by virtue of his name, the host of the inn, and the sacrifice. 40.21; 41.5,8; 44.8, 15 (ter); 45 (*bis*); 46; 48.31 (Osti-Fosti); 162.12; ?166.18; 167.34; 202.18; 211.20; 315.10; 317.32; 335.12-13; 338.7; 364.6; 371.9 (Ostia, *bis*), 25; 372.23; 373.9; 378.32; 497.26; 518.16; 523.27; 566.1; 580.36.

Hotchkiss–machine gun. 523.14.

Hotten, J. C.–compiled *The Slang Dictionary*, 1st ed. 1859 and many subsequent editions. It contains the story of Who Struck Buckley (q.v.). 117.30.

Houdini, Harry (1874-1926)–American magician who specialized in escapes from locked places. 127.11.

House, Edward M., Colonel (1853-1938)–American diplomat, President Wilson's adviser. 600.17.

*House, son of Clod, 70.34.

Houyhnhnms–Swift's (q.v.) well-bred horses. See Yahoo, Gulliver. 15.13-14.

Howarden–Hawarden, Gladstone's (q.v.) country place. 242.33.

?Howe, Richard Howe, Earl (1726-99)–British admiral, Irish peer. 18.12; 26.23.

*Howells–William Dean? 205.4; 260.17.

*Howitts–possibly William and Mary Howitt, authors of *The Book*

of the Seasons, 1831, a work dealing with spiritualism and priest-
craft. Their son Alfred explored
Australia and the Howitt mountains are named for him. 15.24.

Howth
Howth settled for slumber tired of
long days, of yumyum rhododendrons (he was old) and felt gladly
the night breeze lift, ruffle his fell of
ferns. He lay but opened a red eye
unsleeping, deep and slowly breath-
ing, slumberous but awake.
                              Ulysses, 372/494

(Pronounced, Joyce says,
Hoaeth) – derived from *hoved*,
Danish word for "head". Howth
head is a rocky hill, nine miles
north of Dublin, and forming the
northern horn of Dublin Bay.
Old geographers thought Howth
an island, but the isthmus of
Sutton joins it to the mainland.
Howth Castle was long the domain
of the St Lawrence (q.v.) family
and associated with such diverse
characters as Swift and Grace
O'Malley (q.q.v.).
   Howth was anciently called Ben
Edar (q.v.) and was called a
mountain as late as 1652. This
heather-covered hill (where Leopold Bloom kissed Molly among
the rhododendrons) is a good deal
more than landscape in FW. A
hill or mountain is masculine as a
river (see Liffey) is feminine.
Howth is humpy, one-eyed HCE
(q.v.), or rather his head, as he
lies, a sleeping giant buried in the
landscape.

*Hubba, 477.10.

Hubbard, Mother–nursery-rhyme
character. †388.29—with Hibbert
(q.v.).

Hubert, St–patron of the chase.
†6.7—with Herbert (see Pembroke); 31.25; 376.6.

Huddleston, Sisley–Paris acquaintance of Joyce's. †203.6-7—with
Ford Madox Ford (q.v.).

*Huddy–seems to be HCE (q.v.).
Possibly a reference to the

Huddys, a family in the Joyce
country, notoriously murdered in
Land League days. 257.8,18.

Hudibras–title character in a poem
by Samuel Butler (q.v.), satirizing
the Puritans. Butler spends forty
lines on the beard of Hudibras.
He also satirizes the Puritan dislike of bear-baiting. See Bear.
357.7; 373.29.

Hudson–American river, brand of
English soap. 212.24.

Huey, Myramy–personification of
the rainbow, made up, I think, of
Willie Hughes and Mary Fitton
(q.q.v.). See also Seven. 63.12-13.

*Huffsnuff – from context, Mark
Lyons (q.v.). 124.35.

Huggins–short for Hugh (q.v.).
376.23.

Hugh–see Mr W. H.

*Hugh, Lord, the Lacytynant,
388.33.

Hughes, Father Matt–see Father
Mathew. 330.5.

Hughes, Willie–see Mr W. H.

Huginn and Muninn–Mind and
Memory, Odin's (q.v.) raven
messengers in the Eddas. 327.36.

Hugo, Victor (1802-85) French
writer. †211.18–with Hugonot
(q.v.); ?291.4.

Hugonot, Victor–sold ties on a
Dublin quay. In FW "huguenot"
and variations can also refer to
Meyerbeer's (q.v.) opera or to the
Mountjoy (q.v.) family, Huguenots, with whom Shakespeare
(q.v.) lived in London. †211.18—
with Victor Hugo (q.v.).

*Hull, 518.35.

Hullespond, Huppy–see Leander.

*Hulme–T. E.? †310.24—with Wild
Man from Borneo; 378.4; 594.13.

Humboldt, Friedrich Heinrich
Alexander, Baron von (1769-
1859)–German naturalist, author
of *Kosmos*. 588.33.

Hume, David (1711-76)–English

philosopher, historian, political economist. Knowing nothing about his philosophy, I find it nearly impossible to keep him and Surgeon Hume (q.v.) straight. 97.24; 261.5; 450.13; 606.16.

Hume, Surgeon – 18th century, house-building Dublin doctor. See David Hume. ?43.1; 80.18; 443. 19; 481.21.

*Humme the Cheapener, Esc – HCE (q.v.). 29.18.

Humpheres Cheops Exarchas – HCE (q.v.). See also Humphrey, Cheops. An exarch was a Byzantine viceroy, also an officer in the Eastern church or the head of the Bulgarian church. 62.21.

Humphrey–see HCE.

Humphrey, Good Duke – HCE (q.v.). Humphrey, Duke of Gloucester (1341-1447), was called "Good" because he patronized letters. "To dine with Duke Humphrey" means to go without dinner. He is a character in Shakespeare's *2 Henry IV, Henry V, 1 and 2 Henry VI* (q.q.v.). A lost or never existing play, *Duke Humphrey, a Tragedy,* was attributed to Shakespeare in 1653. 32.15; 405.17-18; 441.7 — with Jukes (q.v.).

Humphreys, Henry–author of *The Justice of the Peace in Ireland* (4th ed., 1877). 134.34; †275.note 4—with HCE (q.v.).

Humpty-Dumpty–nursery-rhyme character who fell off a wall and could not be put together by all the king's men (q.v.) because he was an egg. He also appears in *Through the Looking-Glass*—see Alice—and lectures on "portmanteau" words. In FW Humpty is almost always HCE (q.v.) because of the similarity of Humpty and Humphrey, because HCE has a hump on his back. Humpty is also John Shakespeare's (q.v.) dump, the fallen cosmic egg from which human drama is created.

12.12; 44.in music; 45.1; 97.26; 106.20; 129.18; 184.14; 219.27; 230.5; 242.22; 314.8-9,16; 317.24; 319.36; 351.21; 352.15; 363.24; 372.19; 373.6; 374.34; 375.5-6; 386.8; 415.14-15; 455.24; 496.6-7; 550.36; 567.12; 589.17; 606.34; 619.8-9; 624.13; 628.11.

*Hungaria, Margrate von–see the Maggies? 460.26.

Hunker, Mr–see Hunter. 65.17.

Hunks, Old–blind, baited bear (q.v.), contemporary of Shakespeare's (q.v.). See Man Servant. 94.10; 373.17; 408.3.

Hunter, Mr–Joyce's name for a man who was to be one of his Dubliners. He finally became Bloom (q.v.). 65.17.

*Hunter, Paco, 286.left margin.

Huntley and' Palmer – English brand of cookies. 263.note 1.

Huon of Bordeaux–hero of a 13th century French *chanson de geste.* 202.23.

*Hurtreford, first lord of–plays with the Ford of the Hurdles (Dublin) and some one of the earls of Hertford, perhaps the 18th century lord-lieutenant of Ireland, perhaps with the 3rd marquess, original of Thackeray's (q.v.) Marquis of Steyne. 353.23.

Hushaby, Hector and Hermione– characters in Shaw's (q.v.) *Heartbreak House.* See Ellie Dunn. 211.35.

Huss, John (1373-1415)–Bohemian reformer. 267.5; 589.33.

Huster–see Stella. 184.22.

Huxley, Thomas Henry (1825-95)– English philosophical writer. He battled against religion, supported Darwinism. Of him, the Rev. W. S. Lilly wrote in 1886: "Morality in Professor Huxley, I can well believe, is strong enough to hold its own. But will it be strong enough in Professor Huxley's grandchildren?" 253.4 (husky).

*Hwang Chang, 130.35.

*Hwemwednoget, 243.3.

Hyacinth–youth beloved of Zeus and Apollo (q.q.v.). He preferred Apollo and was killed by Zeus. Apollo changed him into a flower. Because the name first occurs in a passage full of Wilde (q.v.) refer- ences, I imagine Joyce associates Hyacinth with Lord Alfred Doug- las (q.v.) to whom Wilde wrote: "No Hyacinthus followed Love so madly as you in Greek days." See Hyacinth O'Donnell. 86.15; 87.12,32; 118.28,29; 335.6; 563. 16; 603.28.

*Hyam Hyam–possibly the brand of men's trousers mentioned in *Ulysses.* 455.23.

Hyde, Mr–see Jekyll.

Hyde, Douglas–Irish scholar, writer, politician. I do not see that he specially fits into the Jekyll and Hyde (q.v.) context, but it is impossible that he should not be in FW.

Hydra–one of the labors of Her- cules (q.v.) was to kill this many- headed monster. 36.7.

Hymen–in classical myth, the god of marriage. 446.4.

*Hynes–Joynes, 370.21-22.

Hyphen–see Hymen.

Hyrcan and Aristobulus–warring brothers. John Hyrcanus II was high-priest of the Jews from 78-40 B.C. His brother Aristo- bulus was always trying to unseat him. 219.26.

I

Iago, St–St James (q.v.) of Com- postella to whose shrine pilgrims flocked in the Middle Ages, wear- ing scallops or cockleshells in their hats. Since the reference to St Iago occurs in a Shakespearean (q.v.) quotation, I assume that the cocklehat is also the cuckold hat of Ancient Iago (q.v.). 41.2.

Iago–the Ancient in Shakespeare's *Othello* (q.q.v.). It is the Spanish form of James (q.v.). See St Iago. I have listed below a good many "Ancients", some of which may merely mean extremely old or refer to another Ancient, Pistol (q.v.). ?19.33; †412.2—with St Iago (q.v.); ?270.17; 281.21; †343.23—with Ondt (q.v.); 357.8; 564.29; ?624.1.

*Iar-Spain, queen of–*iar* is Irish for "west". 50.20.

Ibbetson, Peter–title hero of a novel about "dreaming true" (as in "The Brushwood Boy", q.v.) by George Du Maurier (q.v.). A note in *Scribbledehobble*, 103, sug- gests that Joyce may have

thought the book was called *Peter Ibsen.* †535.19—with Ibsen (q.v.).

Ibdullin – father of Mohammed (q.v.). See Himana. 309.25.

Ibn Sen–see Avicenna. †488.7— with Ibsen (q.v.).

Ibrahim, Alibey – see Abraham. 346.5.

Ibsen, Henrik (1828-1906)–Nor- wegian dramatist and poet whose influence on all Joyce's work is of first importance and has been very badly understood. 170.26— with Gibsen (q.v.); 378.25; †488.7 —with Ibn Sen (q.v.); 523.34; †535.19—with Peter Ibbetson (q.v.).

Ichabod (inglorious)–name that the wife of Phineas gave her child, saying, "The glory has departed from Israel." (1 Sam. 6). 116.32.

*Ida Ida–a goddess in Hindu myth and wife of Manu (q.v.) who is Adam and Noah (q.q.v.). Gilbert and Sullivan's (q.v.) Princess Ida was a baby bride. 29.27; 211.35; 227.14; 276.note 4; 379.15; 504.22

Idol or Idola–in Bacon's (q.v.) *Novum Organum,* Idols are the fallacies or errors to which the human mind is peculiarly prone. In FW HCE's (q.v.) daughter, Issy (q.v.), is a highly erroneous girl. 325.25; 395.2; 455.3; ?465. 13; 527.24.

*Iggri, 193.17.

Ignatius, St–see Loyola.

Igor early Russian king, Oleg's (q.v.) successor. Another Igor is hero of the *Tales of Igor,* oldest Russian medieval epic. 353.19.

Igraine–mother of King Arthur (q.v.), an adultress. 19.23.

*Ilma–Mr Thompson says, Russian for "elm". 621.9.

*Immaculatus, 191.13.

Imogen–heroine of Shakespeare's *Cymbeline* (q.q.v.). See Posthumus, Cloten, Fidelio. †6.26—with Fidelio (q.v.); 251.17; 300.left margin; 331.30; 443.2; 547.35; 563.4 (images).

Indian Boy – offstage character, cause of contention between Oberon (q.v.) and Titania (q.q.v.) in *A Midsummer Night's Dream.* See Willie Hughes. 403.25.

Indra–in Hindu myth, god of the clear sky, greatest of all Vedic gods, lord of the thunder and the elements. 60.21; 223.7; 573.1.

Inexagoras–see Anaxagoras. 155. 32-33.

Infanta–see Gunning. 166.22-23; 211.22.

*Inge, Payne, 370.3.

*Ingelsant, Penelope–maybe the stay-at-home wife of *Ulysses,* Penelope (q.q.v.). 212.10.

*Inglis, William–perhaps one of the English King Williams (q.v.), perhaps Shakespeare (q.v.), perhaps Sir William Inglis (1764-1835), officer in the Peninsular war, later governor of Kinsale and Cork, perhaps the 18th century Gaelic poet, Father William Inglis of Cork. 543.17-18.

Ingoldsby, Thomas–*nom de plume* of Barham (q.v.) when he wrote *The Ingoldsby Legends.* 156.3.

Ingram, John Kells (1823-1907)– Irish economist, poet, author of "The Memory of the Dead", which begins: "Who fears to speak of '98?/Who blushes at the name?" 93.29 (Sean Kelly's anagrim).

Ingram, Rex–American actor who played "de Lawd" in *Green Pastures.* 568.35.

Innocent–thirteen popes and one anti-pope. The first reference below is to Pope Innocent III who was opposed by the anti-pope, Anaclete (q.v.). 13.29; 152. 2; 483.21.

Insull, Samuel (1859-1936)–American promoter of utilities, had a great fall. 510.25.

*Intelligentius, Brother – Shem (q.v.) is indicated. 464.16-17.

Io–girl loved by Zeus (q.v.) and turned into a heifer by jealous Hera (q.v.). 305.right margin; 583.10; 585.5.

Iosa–Jesus in Gaelic. 562.25.

Iosal–in the Ossianic (q.v.) poem "The Fiona", Iosal is a character so heavy and unwieldy that it took 100 men to lift him. 408.6

Ipanzussch–see Averroes. 488.7.

*Ipostila, Mona Vera Toutou– perhaps as Stuart Gilbert suggests, "the one true Catholic . . . and Apostolic church". 449.10-11.

Ireland, Mr–HCE (q.v.) as Ireland, but he is of course a foreigner, a false Irishman, as William Henry Ireland (1777-1835) was a false Shakespeare (q.v.). Ireland forged two "Shakespearean" plays, *Vortigern and Rowena* and *Henry II* (q.q.v.). 608.14.

Irelly, Parasol–see Persse O'Reilly.

Iremonger–English cricketer. 584. 5.

Irena–in Spenser's *Faerie Queene* (q.v.), Bk. V, personifies Ireland, oppressed by Grantorto and righted by Sir Artigal. 14.30; 23.19.

Irenaeus, St–2nd century Bishop of Lyons. 23.19(?); 254.10.

***Ireton** – possibly Henry Ireton (1611 - 51) — Cromwell's (q.v.) general. 480.8.

Iris–personification of the rainbow in Greek myth and FW. *Iris* is the Irish word for "faith". See Seven. 285.27; 318.34; 354.25; 489.31; †493.28—with Isis (q.v.); 528.23; 612.20.

Iron Mask, Man in the–a mysterious political prisoner of Louis XIV's. The Malay word for "man" is *oran*. 390.10.

Irons, Ezekiel (Ezekiel means "God strengthen you")–sexton in Le-Fanu's (q.v.) *The House by the Churchyard*. Here he is one of the Four (q.v.). 27.23.

Irving, Edward (1792-1834)–Scottish minister who founded a sect known as the Irvingites. The actor Henry Irving may also be included here. 491.7.

Isa–the Hindu Ceres (q.v.). †226.4 —with Issy and Isa Bowman (q.q.v.).

Isaac–only child of Abraham and Sarah (q.v.), born when his parents were 190 (Gen. 17). He married Rebecca (q.v.) and begot Jacob and Esau (q.v.). Isaac is Hebrew for "laughter" and is so used- throughout FW. Blind old laughter on p. 3 seems to me to be Joyce himself. †3.23–with Isaac Butt (q.v.); 11.35; 58.4; †76.28—with Isaac Walton (q.v.); 104.22 (Ik); 106.28; 253.35; 307. left margin; †483.20—with Mick and Nick (q.v.), 25 (ike); ?621.19.

Isabel–see Issy.

Isabella–heroine of Shakespeare's (q.v.) *Measure for Measure*. More Isabels, Issies (q.v.) than I have

listed may refer to her, especially when they occur with angels or Angelo's (q.v.). See also Claudio, Marianna, Vincentio. 257.1 ; 556.5.

Isabella la Catolica–Queen of Castile, married Ferdinand of Aragon, patronized Columbus (q.v.). †349. 22 — with Issy, Delia Bacon (q.q.v.).

Isaiah – greatest Old Testament prophet, a book of the Old Testament. 269.31.

Isengrim–wolf in the Reynard (q.v.) cycle. 244.21; †448.24— with Grimm (q.v.).

Ish–see Adam and Eve, Issy.

Ishmael–son of Abraham (q.v.) and his concubine, Hagar (q.v.). Mother and son were cast out by Abraham at Sarah's request. 258.13,16,17.

Ishtar–Babylonian fertility goddess, earth mother, the planet Venus (q.v.). See Esther, Issy, Astarte, Tammuz. †69.14—with Stella and Vanessa (q.v.); †295.1-2—with Stella and Vanessa, Issy (q.q.v.).

Isis and Osiris–chief goddess and god of ancient Egypt, brother and sister, husband and wife. See Horus. †26.17—with Issy (q.v.); 105.29 (Oldsire); 135.22 (O sorrow); 278.left margin (*bis*); 350.26; 470.15-20; 479.33 (Hennu, q.v.); 486.14,24 (lord of Tuttu —see Hennu); 491.13; 493.28,31; 566.29; 601.5; 620.32.

Ismene–daughter of Oedipus (q.v.), sister of Antigone. 54.16.

Isolde of Ireland–see Issy.

Isolde of the White Hands–Issy's (q.v.) double or mirror self. She has not been properly separated from the other Isolde, but maybe somebody will come along and do it. I think that all references to "Blanche" and some references to "White" are references to her. She was the princess of Brittany whom Tristram (q.v.) married, although he loved Isolde of Ireland. 145.1; 164.28; 527.21; 571.15.

Israfel–in the Mohammedan religion, the angel of music who is to sound the trumpet on the day of resurrection. 49.23.

*Issossianusheen, 267.19.

Issy, Izzy, Isabel, Isolde–daughter of Anna Livia and HCE (q.q.v.), ingenue lead of FW. Issy is a triumph of female imbecility, sister to Gertie MacDowell and Willie Baxter's baby-talk lady: "Nothing under her hat but red hair and solid ivory . . . and a firstclass pair of bedroom eyes, of most unhomy blue. . . ." Issy is known to us mainly by her monologues, which are nervous, coy, bare of content, morals or amiability; yet she is a type fatally attractive to men. In much of FW, Issy is cast as Isolde of Ireland (q.v.), turning from the aging Mark of Cornwall (q.v.) to the young virile Tristram (q.v.), but she is also often the bone for which warring brothers (Shem and Shaun, q.v.) contend. She sustains the role of Isolde—"one of romance's fadeless wonder-women" very fairly, for few wonderwomen are endowed with anything more (more is not needed!) than immense sexual attraction. Issy is not, then, a charming or coherent talker. Conversation is a civilized art and she is at once below and above civilization. Joyce has lots of fun with her wonderful pretensions to humanity, her gush of erotic inanities; but he never forgets she is a deadly female and he never makes her vulgar—she is too near nature to be vulgar.

Issy melts into all the temptresses in FW. She is the desire that lures her father, HCE,— lures every man—up the dark, dream garden path. Her mother casts a cool eye on her: Issy is her mother's past and future; when she is no longer an object of masculine attention she will make up her "myriads of drifting minds" in one, die a death, and become her mother. Mother and daughter may be confused in men's minds, but they are distinct in personality and in the rhythm of their speech. Issy (she is often comprehended by the syllable "is") represents the bewilderment of diverse temptation that leads man to his fall: Anna Livia is the unity that calms and heals. That these two principles make up Woman I have from no less an authority than D. H. Lawrence (q.v.), writing on Hester Prynne (q.v.).

In the note to the Maggies (q.v.) the psychological basis of Issy's diversity is explained. Here it is enough to say she is a multiple or dissociated personality, like Morton Prince's Miss Beauchamp (q.q.v.), or like Dante's Rachel and Leah (q.q.v.). By other mechanisms she is also the Seven Rainbow Girls (q.v.), and the Twenty-nine Leapyear Girls (q.v.). I believe her also to be very much Shakespeare's grand-daughter, Elizabeth Hall (q.v.). See also Eve, Ish, Isis, Idol, Isabella, Mildew Lisa, Chapelizod, Felicia.

3.18,22,24	isthmus . . . penisolate . . . †venissoon —with Venus (q.v.) . . . †vanessy—with Vanessa (q.v.)
4.14	Iseut
†7.4,33	issavan essavans—with Vanessa (q.v.)
†26.17	Isid—with Isis (q.v.)
29.1	is told
†69.14	Isther Estarr — with Stella, Ishtar (q.q.v.)
75.23	Ysit
†80.36	Issy-la-Chapelle—with Chapelizod (q.v.)
87.29	Isod's
93.19	belles
104.22	Icy Siseule
113.19	Ysold

117.2	insult the fair	325.25	Idyall (see Idol)
137.36	La Belle—see Gramont	†346.5	Bella Suora—with Sarah (q.v.)
144.12	belle		
146.7	isabeaubel	†349.22-23	Izodella the Calottica —with Isabella La Catolica, Delia (q.q.v.)
148.11	I sold		
159.18	I'se		
176.28	belles		
194.26	belles	351.30	belle
203.9	Izod	†361.22	Isas Boldmans—with Isa Bowman (q.v.)
209.24-25	Isolabella		
210.12	Isabel	372.1	belles
212.17	Izzy	379.23	icy
213.18	Belle	383.30	Usolde
220.7	Izod	384.22,31	belle . . . Isolamisola
†222.27	eyesoult—see Eyesoldt	388.4	Tuesy
223.11	Isot	†394.20,30	issle issle . . eyesolt of the binnoculises — with Lisa (q.v.)
224.28	bellas		
†226.4,6-7	Isa . . . I solde—with Isa Bowman (q.v.)		
		395.2	Idoless (see Idol)
†232.11	venicey—with Venus, Vanessa (q.q.v.)	396.31	chapelledeosy (see Chapelizod)
234.26	Yimissy	398.17,18,29	Miss Yiss . . . Doelsy . . . Iseult la belle (Swift, q.v., called Vanessa, q.v., "Missessy")
235.28	I sold		
237.8	dumbelles		
†238.3,4	isaspell . . . ishibilley —the first with Isa Bowman (q.v.), the second with Ish, Billy (q.q.v.)		
		399.stanza 2	(acrostic) O ICY
		†stanza 2	Lizzy—with Elizabeth—see also Susanna
246.20	la bella. Icy-la-Belle		
†251.31	I is a—with Isa (q.v.)	431.15	Izzy
†256.33	nibulissa—with Nuvoletta (q.v.), Lizzie (see Elizabeth)	433.3	is a bell
		444.34	isod
		446.7	isabellis
†257.1,2,20	Izzy . . . Fain Essie . . . Missy Cheekspeer— with respectively Isabella, Vanessa, Shakespeare (Elizabeth Hall), q.q.v.	†449.4	Vanissy—with Vanessa (q.v.)
		451.30	Gizzygay
		?†453.26	alloyiss—with Heloise (q.v.)
		457.27	Tizzy
261.note 2	Izalond	459.6	Issy
262.note 2	Dozi	†461.2	Vanisha—with Vanessa, Ish (q.q.v.)
265.13	Izolde		
272.13	missy	462.15	Isley
279.note 1	Isabella	465.18	Idos
†280.23	Soldi—with Sally (q.v.)	471.7	Dizzier
		478.1	I see
?†284.23	bissyclitties—with Clytie (q.v.)	482.29	I see
		484.5	eyesalt
289.28	Isolade	486.17,20	I see . . . isoles
†290.2,18	belle of La Chapelle . . . Liselle (see Elizabeth) . . . iselands . . . miss	490.11	I see
		500.21,22,25	Sold. I am sold . . . I sold . . . Isolde
		501.4	Iss
291.5	inseuladed	502.9	Icecold

512.3	Izod
†513.25	Lillabil Issabil—with Lily, Billy (q.q.v.)
515.2	belle
†525.24	lissy—with Elizabeth (q.v.)
†527.21,24	Isacapellas? Ys? . . . idoll—with Chapelizod, Idol, Doll (q.q.v.)
29,30	ishebeau . . . reinebelle (see Seven)
561.16	cissiest
562.18	I see
563.19	I see and see
566.23	infant Isabella (see Infanta)
571.12	Ziod
580.18	Isad Ysut
583.3	I see
584.29	belle
588.24	Izzy's
†605.12	Yssia and Essia—with Stella (q.v.)
607.31	Isoles . . . Eisold
616.32	icy
†624.18	bet (backward is Teb or Tib, short for Isabel)—with Elizabeth (q.v.)

*Isthmon, 17.21.

Ita, St—early Irish female saint who wrote religious poetry. 94.12; 147.12.

Ivan the Terrible or Ivan IV (1560-84)—first tsar of the Russians. †138.17—with John Bull (q.v.); 353.24.

Ivanhoe–title hero of Scott's (q.v.) novel. 178.1.

Ivor or Ivar—brother of Olaf the White (q.v.), Danish ruler of Dublin, slain fighting Brian Boru (q.v.). 4.31; 12.31; 19.23; 100.25; 255.15-16; 327.28; ?387.9.

Ivy–see Holly.

Ixion–king of Lapithae who murdered his father-in-law and ended up chained to an ever-rolling wheel in the air. 346.13; 377.24; 604.15.

Izod–see Issy.

Izodella–see Isabella la Catolica, Delia.

Izzy–see Issy, Lizzy.

J

Jabal–see Jubal.

Jabberwock–a poem and a mythical monster in *Through the Looking-Glass*—see Alice. 565.14.

Jack–see John.

Jack and Jill – nursery-rhyme characters. 141.9; 211.15; 290. note 2; 318.10-11; 462.6.

*Jack, Laughing–jackasses? 95-96; 153-154; 330.22.

Jack the Giant Killer–character in a nursery-tale and in English pantomime. 307.note 1; 615.25; †624.10—with Jove (q.v.).

Jack the Ripper—name assumed by an unknown man who claimed to have committed a revolting series of murders in London in 1888-89. The name is frequently applied to Shaun who as St Kevin, Bacon, Swift (q.q.v.) is also a lady-killer. 179.8; 361.27-28; 466.13-14; †511.35 — with Jung (q.v.), 36; †589.15—with Jekyll (q.v.); †611.1—with John (q.v.).

Jacko–see Jack and La Fontaine. 414.17.

Jackson, Thomas Jonathan, "Stonewall"–American Confederate general. †10.2—with Wellington (q.v.); 291.19.

Jacob and Esau–twin sons of Isaac and Rebecca (q.q.v.). It was prophesied that they would be two nations and the elder would serve the younger—see Ham. Esau ("Hairy"—see Harry) was first-born, Jacob ("Supplanter") came clutching his brother's heel. Esau was a hunter, who like Abel (q.v.), pleased his father with gifts of meat, Jacob was a farmer like Cain (q.v.). When Esau was starving he sold his birthright to Jacob for a mess of pottage (see Jacob's biscuits). On Rebecca's advice, Jacob put on a goat skin, carried venison to blind Isaac, who said, "The voice is Jacob's voice, but the hands are the hands of Esau", and gave his blessing to Jacob. Later, Jacob went into exile, slept on a stone in Bethel (traditionally it became the Stone of Destiny, the Stone of Scone, the Lia Fail); he dreamt of a ladder reaching up to heaven, wrestled with an angel, married Rachel and Leah (q.v.). (Gen. 25 ff.) The use of these twins in FW is extensive. Shem and Shaun (q.v.) switch the roles around, but Shem is usually Jacob (a form of James, q.v.) and Shaun is Esau. 4.11; †14.36—with Ahriman and Heremon (q.q.v.); 89.13,15; 93.17; 111.4; 169.13; 201.34; 246.30-31; †289.5—with Cain and Aesop (q.q.v.); 300.12; 303.16; 307.left margin; 359.17; †366.36—with Jacques (q.v.); †414.17—with La Fontaine, Aesop (q.q.v.); 420.30; 433.20; 483.19; †487.10,22—with Jones (q.v.); †542.30—with Jacob's Biscuits (q.v.); †547.23—with Ajax (q.v.); 563.24; 607.8-9.

Jacob's Biscuits–manufactured in Dublin where they rank second in importance only to Guinness (q.v.) beer. In FW they are sometimes the mess of pottage which Jacob (q.v.) sold Esau. Pottage is also grain, the basis of alcohol. 26.30; 138.14; 542.30.

*Jacobus a Pershawn–doubtless partly Jacob-James (q.q.v.). 449.15.

Jacques–melancholy character in Shakespeare's (q.v.) *As You Like It*. He doubles always with James (q.v.). I think that Jacqueson's Island (245.24) is Jackson's Island

in *Huckleberry Finn* (q.v.). See Rosalind. 245.24; 253.35; 335.34; †366.36—with Jacob (q.v.); †422.33-34—with Jack (see John).

Jaggard, William – Elizabethan printer, printed *The Passionate Pilgrim* (1599) in which two sonnets of Shakespeare's (q.v.) appeared and many poems wrongly attributed to Shakespeare. He also had a hand in printing the First Folio. See Butter, Pavier, Thorp. 481.36.

Jambaptistae–see Vico, John the Baptist. 287.24.

Jambuwel–see John Bull. 366.20.

James I (1566-1625)–king of Great Britain and Ireland. Since Joyce puts all the kings and queens of England into FW, James I and James II, for that matter, must be comprehended in some "James" references, but I have not spotted them. Shakespeare (q.v.) was one of James I's "men", and there is a tradition that the poet and the king exchanged letters now lost.

James the Little–one of the twelve (q.v.) apostles, often called the brother or cousin of Jesus. Here he is given the name of Stephen (i.e. "crown") as James Joyce gave himself the name of Stephen Dedalus (q.v.). 211.4.

James and John–Shem and Shaun (q.v.), the Earwicker twins. Maybe there is some distinction between James-John and Shem-Shaun, but I have not observed it. See also Jacob, Jacques, Iago, Jim, Jameson, James Joyce, John Joyce, Jack, Jonathan, Jaun.

7.35-36	upjook . . . jamey
21-23 (*passim*)	jiminies
39.21	jimmy o'goblin (jemmy o'goblin is English slang for a sovereign)
53.7	jauntyjogging
59.25	jauntingly
121.18	jims
125.14	Hans the Currier (q.v.)
126.19	Jockit Mic Ereweak
163.5,6	Haensli . . . Koebi (q.v.)

168.11	jack
169.13	Jem . . . Jacob (q.v.)
172.5,7	Johns . . . Johns
176.26	pyjamas
181.27,30	Jymes . . . jymes
184.2	jas
188.28	johnjacobs—see Jacob
193.9,35	ghem . . . jimjams
197.26	jackalantern's
†211.6,15	Sunny Twimjim (see Sunny Jim) . . . Jack
215.18	Joe John
216.1	John
†222.7-8	Joan Mock-Comic . . . Jean Souslevin—with Joan of Arc?, John McCormack, John Sullivan (q.q.v.)
225.34	jauntings
238.18	bejimboed
243.8	jackticktating
†245.24	Jempson's . . . Jacqueson's—with Jacques (q.v.)
†253.35	jacquemin — with Jacques (q.v.)
268.7	jemmijohns
274.22	jackhouse
278.13	Johnny Post
†281.left margin	Dons Johns—(q.v.)
303.16	Jacoby
†307.5	Brother Jonathan (q.v.) —see also Swift
20	Jimmy Wilde and Jack Sharkey (q.q.v.)
308.28	jake, jack
330.22	Laughing Jack (q.v.)
†335.34	jollyjacques (q.v.)
†347.29-30	johnny dann sweept— with Swift (q.v.)
349.23	Jan of Nepomuk?
†359.28,34	jaunty . . . Mount Saint John's—with Swift, Wellington (q.q.v.)
360.4	jemcrow, jackdaw (see Crow)
†366.35-36	Joh Joseph's . . . Jacq Jacob's—with Joseph, Jacques (q.v.)
†373.25-26	johnsgate . . . jameseslane—with John Lane (q.v.)
†383.36	hattajockey—with Hatta (q.v.)

†399.36	john . . . john, johnajeams—with John-adreams (q.v.)
†422.33-34	jacquejack—with Jacques (q.v.)
†408.33	John's Lane (q.v.)
†423.1	jameymock farceson— with Macpherson
†428.20	Jonnyjoys—with John Joyce (q.v.)
429.13	Jaun—see Juan
†28	januarious — with St Januarius (q.v.)
†430.10	jaonickally—with Nick (q.v.)
430.441 (passim)	Jaun (see Don Giovanni, John McCormack)
†433.8-9	jocosus inkerman militant — with James Joyce, Shem the Penman (q.q.v.)
447.22	Jno Citizen . . . Jas Pagan
448.32,34	John . . . Jaun
†449.14	Saint Jamas Hanway— with Jonas Hanway (q.v.)
15	Jacobus a Pershawn (q.v.)
†453.14-15	Jaun Dyspeptist—with John the Baptist (q.v.)
33	Johannisburg
†454.9,16	Jaunathaun . . . Jaun— with Jonathan, Swift (q.q.v.)
455.11,31	Joe Hanny's . . . jacknife
456.6	jemes
†457.36	Jaunick — with Nick (q.v.)
458.13	Joke
459.27	Jack
460.27	Jack
461.31,33	Jaime . . . Juan . . . Juan (see Juan)
†462.28	Jaunstown—with Ben Jonson (q.v.)?
†463.29	jeenjakes—with Rousseau (q.v.)
27	jonnythin (see Jonathan)

†465.4 Jackot the Horner—with Jack Horner (q.v.)

†466.14 jac jac jac—with Jack the Ripper (q.v.)

469.29 Jaun the Boast's

†470.24,33 Jaun . . . Juan Jaimesan —with John Jameson (q.v.)

†471.14 Jawjon Redhead—with Rousseau (q.v.)

35 Haun

472.11,14,20 Hauneen . . . Haun . . . Haun

473.3,10,21 Janyouare . . . Juhn . . . Haun

474.13,23 Yawn . . . Yawn

476.19 Yawn

477.3,27 Yun . . . Yawn

485.33 Jackinaboss

487.4 Upjack

†10,22 Jake Jones . . . jokeup —with Jacob (q.v.)

?497.34 Hanzas Khan

513.7,9 Jorn . . . Jambs

†521.13-14 Jones's lame or Jamesy's gait—with John Lane (q.v.)

535.1,3 jackadandyline . . . jackery (jack-a-dandy is rhyming slang for brandy)

†540.27-28 Jock Shepherd . . . Jonathans, wild—with Jack Shepherd and Jonathan Wild (q.q.v.)

542.34 jaunted

543.20 darsy jeamses . . . drury joneses

†547.23 Highjakes—with Jacob, Ajax (q.q.v.)

581.11 highjacking

587.4,5,19,24,30, Jimmy d'Arcy
35,36 . . . Jimmy . . . Jimmy MacCawthelock . . . Jimmy . . . Jocko Nowlong (see Nolan)

588.6,13 Jamessime, Jimmy

†589.15 jackill—with Jekyll and Jack the Ripper (q.q.v.)

?590.17 Nuah-Nuah (Haun?)

603.16 Hans

†611.1-2 Jockey the Ropper . . . Jake the Rape—with Jack the Ripper (q.v.)

*James, Mr Dame–see James and John. Since Joyce quotes from "Julia Bride" and mentions Vereker (q.q.v.) it is reasonable to assume that some "James" is a reference to Henry James. Maybe this. 387.7-8.

Jameson, John and Sons–Irish whiskey, known as "J.J. and S." or "J.J.". In FW it is almost always doubled with James and John (q.v.). It was Joyce's favorite whisky. He said: "All Irish whiskies use the water of the Liffey (q.v.); all but one filter it, but John Jameson's uses it mud and all. That gives it its special quality." †3.25 — with Ham, Shem (q.v.); 42.5 (gee and gee); 83.3; 126.16-17; 229.23; 305.17; 308.24; 333.16; 382.4; 424.27; 470.33; 523.16 — with Samson (q.v.).

Jan of Nepomuk–patron saint of Bohemia. See James and John. 349.23-24.

Jane, Ginger–of the British Museum —oldest complete human body in the world. †59.26—with Jane Carlyle (q.v.).

Jansen, Cornelis (1585-1638)– Bishop of Ypres, father of the religious revival within the Catholic Church, known as Jansenism and condemned as heresy. †173.12 —with Jesus.

Januarius, St–patron of Naples, martyred in the 3rd century. His blood liquefies twice a year in the cathedral at Naples. †429.28—with John (q.v.).

Janus–Roman god of the doorway, represented with two heads which face in opposite directions. Frazer finds him identical with Jupiter (q.v.). HCE (q.v.) is often a janitor. See Porter. 133.19; 272. 16; 542.16.

Japhet–see Ham. Japetus is a satellite of Saturn (q.v.).

*Jarama, 602.13.

Jargonsen–see Jorgensen.

Jarndyce–several characters and the great Chancery suit, *Jarndyce vs Jarndyce* in Dickens's (q.v.) *Bleak House*. 582.11.

Jarry, Alfred – eccentric French dramatist, Joyce's contemporary. He doubles with Jerry (q.v.). 222.31; 463.12.

*Jasminia Aruna, 613.34.

Jason–leader of the Argonauts in the quest of the golden fleece. Legend says he ultimately came to Ireland. See Jotalpheson. 89.34 (*bis*); †123.26—with Jesus.

Jaun–name assumed by Shaun (q.v.) when he plays Don Juan (q.v.) in III,ii. See also James and John.

Jeames de la Pluche–*The Diary of*, by Thackeray (q.v.). †177.30—with Shem (q.v.).

Jeff–see Mutt.

Jehoshaphat–good king of Judah (1 Kings 15). 255.12.

Jehovah or Yahweh–God of Israel. The name has been derived from *hawah*, "to sink down or fall". 35.33; 405.20; 478.11 (yav hace).

Jehu–king of Israel (2 Kings 9-10) whose name came to mean a fast and furious driver. 53.8; 346.7; 469.9; †563.7—with Jerry (q.v.).

Jekyll, Dr and Mr Hyde–title characters in Stevenson's (q.v.) novel. Dr Jekyll, conscious of the duality of good and evil within him, creates a separate personality, Mr Hyde, to absorb all evil. Hyde grows strong and commits revolting crimes. Jekyll kills them both. Some one of the "Hyde" references in FW almost certainly must include Douglas Hyde (q.v.). Perhaps some of them also include Shakespeare (q.v.) that "tiger's heart, wrapped in a player's hide".— see Robert Greene. 66.17; 150.17-18; 186.30; 208.11; 211.31; 374.21; †589.15-16—with Jack the Ripper (q.v.); 603.15.

Jellyby, Mrs–character in Dickens's (q.v.) *Bleak House*. 6.2.

Jenkins, Robert (fl. 1731-45)–one of the causes of war between England and Spain in 1739. He claimed a Spanish commander cut off his ear while illegally aboard Jenkin's ship. The war was known as "The War of Jenkins' Ear". 485.21.

Jenner, Edward (1749-1823)–English doctor, discoverer of vaccination. 84.18.

*Jennings–see Jinnies. 271.19.

Jenny–see Jinnies.

Jeremiah–last pre-exilic prophet whose book in the Bible is known for bitterness and gloom. All Jerry (q.v.) references include Jeremiah. 229.32.

Jeremias–see Jerry. 572-573 (*passim*).

*Jermyn–maybe "German". 625.2.

*Jeroboam, Gubbs, 558.15.

Jerome, St (340-420)–translator of the original Vulgate. See St Mowy. 124.35 (see Four); 252.11.

Jerry–see Kevin.

Jervis, Sir Humphrey–a Dublin hospital. 40.35.

Jeshuam–Jesus and Joshua (q.v.), for whom the sun stood still (Joshua 10:13), and Jeshurun, a symbolic name for Israel. 452.35.

*Jess–maybe the heroine of Spohr's opera, *Jessonda*. 147.12.

Jesse–father of David (q.v.). Perhaps also—though it makes no special sense—Jessica in Shakespeare's (q.v.) *The Merchant of Venice*. †34.29—with Jesus; 236.17; 502.3,7; †612.33—with Jesus.

Jessup, G. L.—English cricketer. 583.33.

Jesus Christ–see Mary, Joseph, Judas, Twelve, Antichrist. 33.29; †34.29—with Jesse (q.v.); †38.32 —with Josephine (q.v.); †91.19— with Lloyd George (q.v.); †111.14 —with Christine Beauchamp?; 120.21; †123.26 — with Jason (q.v.); 154.19; 172.23; †173.12— with Jansen (q.v.); 192.36; 267. left margin; 296.10; 300.29; 301. 9; 342.18; †349.20—with the Russian General (q.v.); 349-350; 365.24; 375.5; 384.15; 393.2; †395.32—with Joyce (q.v.); 398. 32; 408.6 (see Iosal); 412.36; 450.25; †464.32—with Turgesius (q.v.); †472.15 — with Mary, Krishna, Krisanamurti (q.q.v.); †477.22 — with Lucifer (q.v.); †480.15,16—with Jeyses (q.v.); 481.6,9; 482.1; 500.14,15; 518.36; 535.25; 562.25; 596.6,34; †612.33 —with Jessie; 620.17 (cries tis —see Julius Caesar).

Jeyses' Fluid–disinfectant used in England. †480.16—with Jesus.

Jezebel–wife of Ahab (q.v.) in 1 Kings 16. A generic name for an abandoned woman who uses cosmetics. 192.25; 210.12; 562.3.

Jilian of Berry–a barmaid in a song from *The Knight of the Burning Pestle* (see Fletcher), and St Julian of Berry, patron of hospitality. 406.24-25.

*Jilke, Jarley–maybe Dilke (q.v.). 61.11.

Jim the Penman–the real Jim the Penman was James Townshend Saward who from 1831 to 1856 forged £100,000 worth of checks He was a respectable barrister. *Jim the Penman* is a 19th century play by Sir Charles Young. A skilled American counterfeiter, Emanuel Ninger, was also "Jim the Penman". See Shem.

Jimmy or Jim–see James. According to Samuel Lover (q.v.) Irish idiots are called "Jimmy" as we say "Tom" Fool.

Jingle, Alfred–confidence man in Dickens's *Pickwick Papers* (q.q.v.). His speech, based on free-association, was said by Wyndham Lewis (q.v.) to be a precursor of the interior monologue. In Lewis's *The Lion and the Fox,* he mentions a Mr Jingleboys, an Italianate Englishman in a play of Beaumont's, but then Lewis thinks Shakespeare and Falstaff (q.q.v.) are women. 275.note 6; 416.8; †466.18—with Joyce (q.v.).

Jinnies or Jennies–two (q.v.) girls with whom HCE (q.v.), as Wellington (q.v.), is at war in the Museyroom episode (FW 8-10). Plainly enough, they are the "Cherry Jinnies" or "Dear Jenny" who the Duke told to publish and be damned. Beyond this, I really do not understand the Jinnies. They may sometimes be young jenny-asses. Jinny may also be short for Virginia, Guinevere (q.v.). 8-9 (*passim*); 93.7; 97.35; †273. left margin—with Jill (see Jack and Jill); ?278.12; 327.10; †359.35—with Jenny Lind (q.v.); 457-458; 461.16; 490.25-26; 526. 17; †576.36 — with Magdalene (q.v.).

Joachim of Floris (1145-1202)– Italian monk who, in *Expositio in Apocalypsin* divides history into: 1) the age of Law or the Father; 2) the age of the Gospel or the Son; 3) the age of the Holy Ghost where all ends. The reference here is also to John the Baptist (q.v.), come to bring tidings of a new era and to Joachim, Mary's (q.v.) father. 214.11.

Joan of Arc, St (1411-31)–French saint, Maid of Orleans, title heroine of a play of Shaw's (q.v.), character in Shakespeare's (q.v.) *I Henry VI*, where she is called La Pucelle. If, as I think, FW is about Shakespeare, these references may include his sister, Joan—see Hart. 29.8; 202.17-18; †222.7—with John McCormack (q.v.); 223.20; 233.21 (jaone-ofergs)?; ?323.7; †528.13—with St John (q.v.); ?607.13.

Job–title character of an Old Testament book. 181.30; 282.1; 307.left margin; 563.7.

Jocasta–mother and wife of Oedipus (q.v.). †63.30-31—with Joyce (q.v.).

Joe–fat boy in *Pickwick* (q.v.). 171.24.

*Joe, Old–the Man Servant (q.v.). "Poor Old Joe" was sung at an entertainment when Joyce was at Clongowes—see Jacob Earwig. 170.3; 184.2; 199.29; 230.3-4.

John–see James.

John-a-dreams–see *Hamlet* (q.v.), II,ii, 595. 61.4; †399.36—with James and John (q.v.).

John, Crazy-Headed–Russian folk ballad, Chaliapin's best-selling record in the '30s. Yeats's (q.v.) Crazy Jane may also be comprehended. See John 513.7.

John, Don–villainous brother in Shakespeare's (q.v.) *Much Ado About Nothing*. See John and Don Giovanni. †281.left margin—with Don Giovanni (q.v.).

John, St, the Evangelist–see Four Evangelists, Johnny MacDougal.

John the Baptist–forerunner of Christ. His day is June 24. See John, Vico. †287.24—with John and Vico (q.q.v.); †453.14-15—with Jaun (q.v.); 473.10.

Johnson, Esther–see Stella.

*Johnson, Father, 440.8.

Johnson, Samuel (1709-84)–English lexicographer. His wife, Tettie, may occur at 192.36. See Boswell. 192.35.

*Johnston-Johnson, Mr Justinian–Johnny MacDougal (q.v.) is indicated. †377.32-33—with Justinian (q.v.).

Jonah–title character of a book of the Old Testament. †245.12—with Juno (q.v.); 323.7; 358.24-

25; †431.12—with Jones (q.v.); †434.27—with Adonis (q.v.); 463.31; †529.23—with ass (q.v.); †536.32-33—with John Whalley and Mark Lyons (q.q.v.).

Jonas–see Jonah and Adonis. 434.27.

Jonathan–see David, John, Swift.

Jonathan, Brother–the reference is to prohibition (dryness) in the United States (whose symbol used to be Brother Jonathan rather than Uncle Sam) and to sexual prohibition (dryness) in Jonathan Swift (q.v.). 307.5.

*Jones–generally Shem (q.v.), while Shaun is Smith. The name may refer now and then to William Jones who, by climbing a ladder, caused Christine Beauchamp's (q.v.) personality to split. 48.24; 149.10; 275.note 5 (see Boy Jones); †431.12 — with Jonah (q.v.); †487.10—with Jacob (q.v.).

*Jones, Boy–maybe the boy who kept getting into Windsor Palace in Victoria's (q.v.) time, maybe a Welsh Fusilier in Graves' *Goodbye to All That* who committed a nuisance like the Russian General (q.v.). 275.note 5.

Jones, Casey–hero of an American railroad ballad. 368.27,28 (K.C. jowls).

Jones, Frederick E. "Buck" (1759-1834)–manager of the Crow Street Theatre in Dublin. His name is preserved in Jones Road which leads to his mansion, Clonliffe House. 210.17; ?543.20.

Jones, Jenny–female in *Tom Jones*. See Jinnies. 576.36.

Jonson, Ben (1572-1637)–English poet and playwright, known as "The Brick-layer". His *Underwoods* (q.v.), *Every Man In and Out of His Humour, Sejanus* are in FW, and there may be Jonson references that I have missed. See Knowell, Tiberius, Shakespeare. The poem Jonson wrote for his little son who died in the plague is quoted at 289.10. He—and Joyce after him—puns on Benjamin's meaning "of the right hand". See also Benjamin. 38.2; 229.7; †?248.30—with Benedict (q.v.); †289.10—with Franklin (q.v.); 299.note 1; ?302.28; 457.29; †462.28—with Jaun; †606.14 —with Franklin (q.v.).

?**Jordan,** Mrs Dorothea (1762-1816) –Irish actress, mistress of William IV (q.v.), by whom she had ten children. She played Phoebe (q.v.) in *As You Like It*, Rosalind, Imogen (q.v.), but her specialty was "breeches" parts, as that of William (q.v.) in *Rosina* (q.v.). 210.30.

*****Jordan's,** 480.2.

Jorgenson, Jorgen (b. 1780)–Dane who joined the British navy, spied for Britain. After an adventurous and not undistinguished career, he fell on evil days and was transported to Van Dieman's Land for pawning somebody else's furniture. There he wrote a number of books, including a vocabulary of aboriginal words. 621.22.

*****Jorum**–perhaps not a person. 316.19.

Joseph–see Gen. 37 ff.—a skilful interpreter of dreams, owner of a coat of many colors and an impregnable chastity. See Potiphar's wife. He was also victim in a brother-battle. 208.17; 307.left margin; ?460.36.

Joseph, St–husband of Mary (q.v.). 274.left margin; 365.24; 460.36; †485.32—with Adam (q.v.).

Josephine and Marie Louise – Napoleon's (q.v.) first and second wives. They are the subject of an unpublished play, *A Royal Divorce* by W. G. Wills (q.v.). Mr Atherton has seen this play and feels it contains little that matters in FW. In FW I think the two women are a fairly unimportant aspect of the two (q.v.) temptresses, and I think the "Royal Divorce" is used to indicate the splitting of the female personality —see the Maggies—see also *Henry VIII*, Shakespeare's (q.v.) "Royal Divorce". †38.32—with Jesus; †223.2—with Mary Lamb (q.v.); †243.35 — with Maas, Mario (q.q.v.); †246.17—see preceding entry; 365.29-30; 388.8.

Josephs, Luiz-Marios—see Josephine, Joseph Maas, Mario. 243.35.

Joshua–title character of the 6th book of the Old Testament. Joshua was son of Nun (q.v.) and one of the Nine Worthies. 4.20; 53.22; †231.18 — with Croesus (q.v.); 452.35 — see Jeshuam; 550.2.

Jotalpheson, Jason (q.v.). See Macalister, *The Secret Languages of Ireland*, 90-91. 89.34.

Joule, James P. (1818-89)–English physicist. 315.11.

Jousse, Marcel–author of *Language as Gesture*. I am not sure if it is a book, or a series of articles. 229.26; 468.5; 531.36; 535.3; 568.8.

Jove–poetic equivalent of Jupiter (q.v.), chief Roman god. See also Zeus. 50.32; 80.28; 181.8; 231.23; 351.35; 472.15; 583.8; †624.10— with Jack the Giant Killer (q.v.).

Joyce, Giorgio–James Joyce's son, now living in Munich. His name can be made out on p. 3 of FW from l. 20 "gorgios" and l. 23 "isaac" (q.v.v.). I am not competent to disentangle Giorgio from other George (q.v.) references. It may be that all references to the state of Georgia—the New World—are references to Giorgio.

Joyce, Helen—see Fleischman.

Joyce, James (1882-1941)—is, I think, intended, in all words which express joy—thus he is the blind old Isaac (q.v.) of p. 3 of FW. Perhaps he is also present in sorrow words, but I have not attempted to list the joys and sorrows. Certainly he—or a self he once was—is indicated in all James-Shems (q.v.), and in all Stephen Daedalus (q.v.) references. 3.23,25 (isaac . . . Jhem or Shen); 15.7; 27.2; †63.30-31—with Jocasta (q.v.); 68.2; 94.1; 113.36; 161.16; 180.7; †192.35—with Johnson (q.v.); †211.6—see Sunny Jim, see Bodkin; 244.29; 245.21; †302.12 — with Euclid (q.v.); 310.31,33; 384.24; †395.32 —with Jesus; 414.23; 443.11; †466.18—with Jingle (q.v.); 485. 13; 495.20; 563.2; 583.17; 598.25.

Joyce, John–James Joyce's father, his creation as Simon Dedalus in *Ulysses*, and probably as HCE (q.v.) in FW. See James and John, John Shakespeare. This is the explanation of the John Joyce reference, 428.20: someone sent Joyce a throwaway saying that the pleasure steamer JOHN JOYCE would sail on 3 hour cruises from Dun Laoghaire (see Lear), weather and other circumstances permitting. (Joyce to Frank Budgen, 9, 20 Sept. 1937.) Joyce finally decided the ship was a phantom. I fancy it was a pleasant practical joke. I don't think many John references in FW have to do with him.

Joyce, (John) Stanislaus – James Joyce's brother, now dead. See James and John. He is identified with Shaun (q.v.). †237.11—see Stainusless; 277.note 5; 463.14.

Joyce, Lucia Anne–James Joyce's daughter who went mad. If indeed she is comprehended in the Lucys of this book, I do not understand them. See St Lucy, Lucan, Sir Thomas Lucy. †155.25 —with Lily (q.v.) (lucciola is It. "firefly"; *luccio* is It. "luce"—see Sir Thomas Lucy); †157.24—with Nuvoletta (q.v.); †203.26—with Lycidas, Wordsworth's Lucy (q.q.v.); 262.16 (plays on the Requiem Mass—*lux perpetua luceat eis*); †295.33—with Lucifer;

†327.5—with Lamp (q.v.); ?†478. 13-14—with Hall (q.v.).

Joyce, Mary—see Murray.

Joyce, Patrick–an Irishman who called himself Dr Achmed Borumbored and masqueraded as a Turkish doctor with such success that he became the lion of Dublin society in 1790 and persuaded the government to help him finance a magnificent Turkish bath in Dublin. Joyce calls him "Hairductor" because, according to Sir Jonah Barrington (q.v.), his attraction lay in his hair. The Germans address anyone with a doctor's degree with *Herr Doktor*. See also Ahab. 492.22-23.

Joyce, William, "Lord Haw Haw" (1906-46)–I have checked dates and James Joyce could not have known that William Joyce was going to be Lord Haw Haw. If the dates had been right, I would have accepted the identification. I include it as a horrid warning and because James Joyce dearly loved a coincidence. 347.32-33.

Juan, Don–see Don Giovanni.

Jubal and Tubal Cain–Jubal was "father of all such as handle the harp and organ". Tubal was "instructor of every artificer in brass and iron". (Gen. 4.) Their brother Jabal was father of those who live in tents and have cattle. 13.12; 66.29; †84.2—with Jubal Early (q.v.); †305.14.19—with Cain. Kean (q.q.v.); 338.17; 445.34-35; 463.17; 466.18.

Judas–the disciple who betrayed Jesus. 193.9; 492.5-6; 575.36.

*Judd, 441.24.

Juggernaut–title of Krishna (q.v.), also the idol of the god at Puri, annually dragged in a great car beneath whose wheels devotees threw themselves. 342.13-14.

Jugurtha–king of Numidia, 2nd century B.C. He said Rome was "a city for sale, and doomed to perish as soon as it finds a purchaser". 403.24-25.

Jukes and Kallikaks – American families, known for their hereditary physical and mental degeneracy. I cannot imagine why Joyce often associates them with Wellington who Charlotte Brontë (q.v.) and I consider a Man of men. 33.24; 137.11-12—with Wellington (q.v.); †162.4—with Wellington (q.v.); 295.note 1; †367.18 —with Deucalion (q.v.); 375.4; 456.31.

Jukoleon–see Deucalion and see Jukes. 367.20.

Julepunsch–see Punch and Judy. 594.35.

*Jules–see Coppinger. *Jules* is French argot for "chamber-pot". 386.30.

Julia – heroine of Shakespeare's (q.v.) *Two Gentlemen of Verona*. See Sylvia, Valentine, Juliet. I am by no means sure that all the following references are to her. †207.24 — with Julius Caesar (q.v.); 242.14; 426.4; ?430.36; ?465.2—with Julia Bride (like Julia, a jilted girl); 502.24.

Julian of Berry, St–see Jilian of Berry.

*Julie and Lulie–see Julia, Two. 502.24.

*Juliennaw–Julianna. 430.36.

Juliet–see Romeo.

Julius Caesar (100-44 B.C.)–Roman general and dictator, subject of plays by Shakespeare and Shaw (q.q.v.). In FW the episode of "Burrus and Caseous" (q.v.) mocks a Preface which Shaw did not write for Shakespeare's *Julius Caesar*. See also Cleopatra, Mark Antony. 150.9; 161.36; 162.1; †207.24—with Julia (q.v.); 271.3; 281.23; 306.left margin; †493.10 —with Cleopatra; 540.23; 549.25; †553.17—with Juliet (q.v.)—the reference is to the Julian Calendar.

Jung, Carl Gustav (1875-1961)– Swiss psychiatrist. 112.4; 115.22; 170.30; 268.note 3; ?348.13; 416. 9; †460.20—with Freud (q.v.); †511.35—with Jack the Ripper (q.v.); 586.11.

Jung, Johann Heinrich (1740-1817) –friend of Goethe's (q.v.), author of *Heinrich Stillings Jugend*. 318. 9-10.

Juno–chief Roman goddess—see Hera. See Paycock? 87.5; 203.20; †245.12—with Jonah(q.v.); 538.1.

Jupiter – chief Roman god — see Zeus, Stator. ?152.14 (Joe Peters); ?159.22-23; 241.34-35; 342.14; 390.22-23; 426.21; 451.36.

Jupp, Mrs – elderly, disreputable landlady in Butler's *Way of All Flesh*. †531.19—with Ham, Shem, Japhet (q.v.).

Jurgen–title hero of J. B. Cabell's novel. Chapter 22: "And time . . . came in with Jurgen since Jurgen was mortal. . . ." 35.28.

Justine–title heroine of a novel by de Sade (q.v.). 445.14.

Justinian – (527-65) — Byzantine emperor. †377.32—with Johnny MacDougal (q.v.).

Justius–Shaun (q.v.) or Justice in a debate of Justice and Mercy. See Mercius. 187.24.

Jute–see Mutt.

K

*Kaempersally, Mr Deaubaleau Downbellow–see W. W. Kelly. ?332.18; 383.33-34.

*Kahanan–possibly Kinahan and Co., Dublin distillers. 108.17.

Kain–see Cain.

Kali–goddess of death and destruction in Hindu myth. 5.16.

Kalidasa–most illustrious Sanscrit

writer of the 2nd epoch, author of *The Little Clay Cart*—see FW 186.23. 187.7.

Kamen, Navellicky–see Navellicky.

*Kane–always Cain (q.v.), but I don't know why. It may have something to do with Matthew Kane (Martin Cunningham), q.q.v. The oft-occurring form "Kanes" is, of course, an anagram of "snake". 421.5; 448.3; 455.18; 516.23; 536.27.

*Kane, Ebell Teresa–Able to raise a Cain—see FW 47. See Cain, Abel, Teresa. 491.16.

*Kane, Karmalite, 211.29-30.

Kane, Matthew–original of Martin Cunningham (q.v.) in *Ulysses*. He and Ned Thornton (q.v.) were cronies of John Joyce (q.v.). He died by drowning. 63.7.

*Kanel, Katty–a contributor to *transition* was named Kathleen Cannell. I have a vague idea that Lucia Joyce (q.v.) had a friend named something like this. 212.7.

*Kang the Toll–HCE. Possibly pigeon English for the Tall King. 52.25.

Kant, Immanuel (1724-1804)–German philosopher. I have never read Kant, but I think Joyce is playing with him, 229.36. Kant defined Time as a form of the inner sense, as Space is a form of the outer. 64.13-14; ?77.22; 109.1; 286.26; 297.9; 414.22; 416.13; 432.32; 440.17 (Manoel Canter).

Kapp and Peterson–Dublin pipe and tobacco makers. 221.9.

Karenina, Anna–title heroine of Tolstoy's novel. †331.25—with Anna Livia (q.v.).

Karlikeevna, Nana–includes Anna Livia, Anna Karenina, Nana (both Zola's girl and the Sumerian goddess of love) (q.q.v.). In Russian tradition *Karliki* were spirits who fell into the underworld and became dwarves. 331. 25.

*Karrs and Polikoff–maybe Carson, maybe Alphonse Karr, author of *Voyage Autour De Mon Jardin*, which was in Joyce's library, maybe Private Carr of *Ulysses*— see all these people, but I bet it will turn out to be a well-known men's store in Dublin. 339.14-15.

*Karssens, Lotta–doesn't seem awfully likely to be Sir Edward Carson (q.v.). 241.33.

Kat Kresbyterians–see St Patrick. 120.2.

Katachanka–Mohammed's horse (q.v.). 24.23.

Kate (Mrs Tam O'Shanter, q.v.)– ties in with Kate the Cleaner and Kate the Shrew (q.v.) as a Mrs Caudle (q.v.). †116.22—see the two Kates following.

Kate the Cleaner

. . . the generations for 700 years fought for the liberation of beautiful Cathleen ni Houlihan, and when they set her free she walked out, a fierce vituperative old hag.

George Russell to Lady Gregory.

Kate (Gr. *kathairein*, to clean) is the Earwicker's female servant. Cleaning, cooking, dancing, delivering curtain lectures and conducting tours of the Wellington (q.v.) Museyroom are her principal occupations. Sometimes she is called Dinah, sometimes Countess Cathleen (q.q.v.), which makes her Cathleen ni Houlihan or Ireland, a domestic terror. She is also Shakespeare's (q.v.) Kate the Shrew, grown older. According to Brandes and Stephen Dedalus, Ann Hathaway (q.q.v.) inspired Shakespeare's shrews, and in FW Kate appears to be HCE's (q.v.) first or deserted wife. Her exact relation to Anna Livia and to the Hen (q.q.v.) is not clear to me. Kate also appears as HCE's widow, raking muck about "her weaker" who turned his face to the wall, meaning he died or engaged in creative work. The word "tip" is associated with her because she is a muckraker who tips rubbish into a rubbish tip. See Varians, Mrs Caudle, Mrs Jupp, Kate Strong, Katty Lanner. 8.8; 27.31; 40.11 (*katya* is Sanscrit for "poet", I think I remember); †79.27,33—with Kate Strong (q.v.); 93.22; 113.21; †116. 22—see Kate above; 141.30,33 (Tok . . . Tik); 142.2,7 (Tuk . . . Tuk); 211.19; †221.12—with Rachel and Leah, Varians (q.q.v.); 239.18,21; 245.34; 330.35; 333.7; 334.28 (*bis*); ?335.19 (*bis*); †380. 1-2—with Varians (q.v.); 394.28; 421.4; 423.12; 431.3; †448.10— with Countess Cathleen (q.v.); †451.17—see Varians; 530.32-33; †531.15-16—with Katty Lanner (q.v.); 538.22; 556.32; 566.11; †572.27-28,32—see Kate Strong; †573.27—see Kate Strong; 601.32.

Kate the Shrew–heroine of Shakespeare's (q.v.) *The Taming of the Shrew*. See Kate the Cleaner.

Kavanaugh, Arthur MacMorrough (1831 - 89)–Irish politician, descended from the kings of Leinster, M.P., philanthropic landlord, married Frances Mary Leathley who may be "leathered" 380.22. †380.22—with Art Mac Murrough (q.v.).

Kavanaugh, Thomas Henry–English leader in the Indiań Mutiny. 492.28-29.

Kayenne, Homard–see Khayyam, Homer. 351.9-10.

*Kay O'Kay, Cardinal, 282.23.

Kean, Edmund (1787-1833)–Shakespearean (q.v.) actor. †273.left margin—with Cain (q.v.); †305. 18-19—with Cain and Jubal Cain (q.q.v.).

Keeper–the word has a number of meanings in FW. It sometimes refers to HCE (q.v.) as Innkeeper; it turns up occasionally in "Am I my brother's keeper?" contexts— see Cain; but it is usually applied to the Abel-playing Shaun, who keeps the letter from Boston,

Mass. I think the title "Keeper" ties Shaun-Kevin to the Lord Keeper, Francis Bacon (q.v.) (who was so called even when a child by Elizabeth I, q.v.). What Bacon and St Kevin (q.v.) have in common is that each was deathly cold to a female—see Biddy Doran. †110.32—with Kevin; 320.35; 362.19; †370.8 — with Kevin (q.v.); 418.14; 464.25; 482.22; 498.2,6; †565.15 — with Kevin (q.v.); 566.6,11; 606.8.

Kehoe, Donnelly–ham and bacon (q.q.v.) curers of Dublin. 39.17; 318.21; 379.36.

*Kelly, †33.24–with Kallikaks (see Jukes); 193.24; 370.20; 372.15.

Kelly, Kitty–"Pretty Kitty Kelly", a song. See Kate? 361.15-16.

Kelly, Michael (1762-1826)–Dubliner, actor, singer, composer. A friend of Mozart's (q.v.), he sang in the first performance of *The Marriage of Figaro*. 199.28 (Chelli Michele's); 407.16.

*Kelly, Moll, 299.27.

Kelly, Sean–John Kells Ingram (q.v.). 93.29.

*Kelly, Terry per Chelly Derry, 484.33.

*Kelly, Thaddeus, 456.30.

Kelly, W. W.–manager of the Evergreen Touring Company of Liverpool which toured the British Isles before 1914 with *A Royal Divorce*—see Napoleon, Josephine, Henry VIII. Mr Atherton tells me that a real white horse was brought onto the stage. †32. 29—(Mr Wallenstein Washington Semperkelly's)—with Washington, Wallenstein (q.q.v.); 365.30; 383.33-34 (Mr Deaubaleau Downbellow Kaempersally).

?Kelvin, William Thomson, Baron (1824-1907) – British physicist. 155.33.

Kempe, Will (fl. 1600)–English comic actor and dancer, actor until 1599 in Shakespeare's (q.v.)

plays. Brandes (q.v.) had a theory that Shakespeare disliked Kempe for spoiling his plays with ad libs. I think Joyce puns on Kempe's name, when in *Ulysses* (212/276) he calls Mulligan (q.v.) "a lubber jester, a wellkempt head". 13.7,8 (blotchwall . . . innkempt).

*Kennealey, 71.36.

Kennedy–Dublin baker. 7.11; 317. 1-2; 498.19.

Kennedy, Stoddart, Rev.–British chaplain who distributed cigarettes to the troops in the first World War, known as "Woodbine Willy". See Will. 351.12.

*Kenny, 193.24; 332.33.

?Kent–character in Shakespeare's *King Lear* (q.q.v.). 359.19; 584.6.

*Keogh, 193.24; 349.3; 350.18; 379. 36; 448.3.

*Keowns, Laura, 205.9-10.

Kersse the Tailor–Joyce's father had a story about a hunchbacked Norwegian Captain (q.v.) who ordered a suit from a Dublin tailor, J. H. Kerse of 34 Upper Sackville Street. The finished suit did not fit and the Captain and Kerse had a long verbal row about it (Ellmann, 22). This story is doubtless the basis of the "Norwegian Captain" episode in FW II,iii, but knowing the plot does little to clear up Joyce's story for me. I get the impression that the Captain is castrated and that Kersse is a female or turns into a female. Here is another mad possibility: In 1940 T. F. Healy in *The American Mercury* declared that Hamlet (q.v.) is an Irishman whose character is largely based on an Irish tradition that the Hamlets were a family of Irish tailors. The Norwegian Captain is, of course, a character in *Hamlet* and his episode has a certain likeness to the rude Ur-Ur-Ur Hamlets from which Shakespeare's play evolved. See also Starveling? It has been suggested Kersse is the Celtic form of Persse, as in Persse O'Reilly (q.v.). 23.10-11; 37.10; 85.33; 137.22; 180.11; 311.7; 312.15; 313.7; 317.22; 319.27,29; 322.1,5, 17,18,19; 328.4; 339.6; 372.3; 404.32; 510.32; 575.24; 594.36; 623.11.

Ket, Robert (d. 1549)–English rebel. 151.14.

Ketil Flatneb–one of the Viking conquerors of Dublin. 73.8; 332.2; 549.13.

Kettle, Galorious–Mark Lyons (q.v.) as the magic cauldron of Dagda (q.v.), one of the four magic objects, brought to the battle of Mag-Tured. 219.24.

Kettle, Lawrence–proposed a new electric supply scheme for Dublin. 307.9.

Kettle, Tom – Irish nationalist, helped found the Free State. 122.7; ?307.9; ?340.31; 362.10.

Kevin and Jerry – names given Shaun and Shem (q.v.). Kevin's name comes from St Kevin, one of Shaun's most important roles in FW. St Kevin (d. 618)—Irish Coemghin, see Coemghem—was an eremite who lived for seven years as a solitary in the valley of Glendalough in Wicklow. He spent his nights in a cave—St Kevin's bed, a popular tourist attraction—and his days in a hollow tree by the shore of the lake. Thither, according to legend, a young woman named Cathleen (q.v.) followed him for love, and when he spurned her charms she drowned herself. This is why Kevin is often called "Frank" or "Keeper" (q.q.v.), names which tie him to Francis Bacon (q.v.)—both of them killed a female creature with cold. Kevin and Cathleen have been the subject of a good deal of Irish poetry, some serious, some not. The legend is the basis of George Moore's (q.v.) *The Lake* (see FW 605-606) in which the priest, or Kevin figure, is called Oliver

Gogarty (q.v.). Shaun-Kevin is a Gogarty figure.

Jerry is the Ass (q.v.) and the Biblical Jeremiah (q.v.). According to a legend (mentioned by Thomas Lover) St Kevin was wisest of the saints because he went to school to Jeremiah, and Shem is always teaching Shaun. Joyce contrasts the frigid, cheap lithograph of a St Kevin (who resists temptation, or rather, turns it to practical use) with St Patrick (q.v.), and Shem (who sins and deeply repents).

15.7-8,16	jerrybuilding . . . Kevanses . . . Kerry
27.5,9	Kevin's . . . Jerry
40.36	Saint Kevin's
41.3	jerrywangle
59.16-17, 18,21, 23,25, 26	Sevenchurches . . .Glintalook . . . thankeaven . . . O'Dea (cf. 210.14) . . . jauntingly . . . Lorry
64.23-24	astrollajerries . . . Keavens
†110.32	keepy little Kevin— with Francis Bacon, Keeper (q.q.v.)
130.33	buyshop of Glintylook
150.20-21	Jericho . . . Cavantry
210.14,21	Kevineen O'Dea . . . Jerry Coyle
?215.3	Garry
†222.31	jarrety — with Jarry (q.v.)
225.34	Jerry
†229.32	jeeremyhead — with Jeremiah (q.v.)
†234.10,20	mookst kevinly . . . kerilour kevinour—with respectively Mookse and Lewis Carroll (q.q.v.)
246.36	Jeremy
248.30	lord of Glendalough
257.6	jeerilied
265.note 2	jerryhatted
274.22	jerry
†278.note 1	jarry—with Jarry (q.v.)
283.28	jerrybly
286.27	Kev
288.note 5	jerried
300.15	P. Kevin

302.24-25	jirryalimpaloop
†303.15,17	Kev . . . Georgeous, Kevvy—with George (q.v.)
333.2	thingajerry
†370.8	Jeremy Trouvas to Kepin O'Keepers — with Francis Bacon, Keeper (q.q.v.)
†382.11,21	Kaven's . . . Larry's— with St Lawrence O'Toole (q.v.?)
?383.36	kemin
†433.6	Gwen du Lake—with Guinevere (q.v.)?
458.15	Jer
†463.12	jarry—(q.v.)
470.18	anjerichol
†482.18	Kevin . . . Evan Vaughan —with Thomas Vaughan (q.v.)
483.5	Kevin
489.14	Venerable Jerrybuilt (Vanderbilt?)
547.18	Kevin's
†555.28,32	Kevin Mary . . . Jerry Godolphing (see Godolphin)
†562.23	Frank Kevin — with Francis Bacon —see also Frank
†563.7	Jerry Jehu—see Jehu
36	kerryjevin
565.10,15	jerry . . . keve
575.25,26,32	jerrykin . . . jarry . . . Judge Jeremy Doyler —see Doyle
601.18-19	Keavn! Keavn . . . Keavn
602.9	Coemghen
603.34	Coemghem
604-606	(passim)
606.4	Saint Kevin

Kevin, St see Kevin.

Khayyam, Omar (d. 1123)–Persian astronomer, poet. *The Rubaiyat*, a translation of some of his quatrains, was made by Edward Fitzgerald. 122.16,19 (O'Mara); ?312. 6; 319.34; †351.9-10 (Homard Kayenne)—with Homer (q.v.).

Kickham, Charles Joseph – Irish author of *Knocknagow.* 208.31.

*Kidballacks, 315.28.

Kidd, Captain (1645-1701)—English pirate. These references may include Thomas Kyd (q.v.). 69. 19; 403.27; 587.5.

*Kieran, Teasy, 212.8.

Kierkegaard, Soren (1813-55)– Danish philosopher whose *Either/ Or* is rather important in FW— see Don Giovanni. 201.31; 246.1; 388.2; 596.31; 600.20.

Kilbride–a place on the Liffey (q.v.). Here the reference seems to be to Henry VIII (q.v.). 576.6.

Killorglin, Goat King of–Killorglin, Co. Kerry, holds a Puck Fair at Lammas. A male goat, called Puck, is king of the fair, is paraded, wreathed, driven out. 87.26.

*Kimmells, 19.8-9.

King–I believe that all or most "Kings" have reference to Shakespeare's having played "kingly parts" on the stage. See King's Men. See Williams I, II, III, IV.

King, Sir Abraham Bradley–lord-mayor of Dublin, 1820-21. 294.24; 421.5-6.

*King, Festy–appears to be Shem, but I do not understand him. His surname may come from Porcius Festus, procurator of Judea, before whom St Paul (q.v.) was brought (Acts, 25,26) or to the title hero of a cosmic poem by P. J. Bailey (1839). He is identical with Pegger Festy. Festy may tie to Feste (q.v.) of *Twelfth Night.* I doubt all the foregoing. 85.23; 86.7,13 (Tyking-fest); 93.1; 212.1; 231.12.

*King, T. C., 495.12.

King Kong–a big ape. 32.2.

King's Men–Shakespeare's (q.v.) acting company, under the patronage of James I (q.v.). See also Humpty Dumpty, Queen's Men, Strange, M. Gunn. 47.last stanza; 219.27-28; 343.22; 567.17.

*Kinihoun–perhaps Kinahan and Co., Dublin distillers. See Kahanan. 108.17; 364.19.

*Kinsella, 133.2; 549.19.

*Kinsella, Lily – see Lily, Mrs Magrath. 205.11; 572.33,35 (Gillia); 573.16; 622.3.

Kish–father of Saul (q.v.). 164.12; 512.8.

*Kissilov's, 532.22.

*Kitty–maybe Kate or Kitty O'Shea (q.q.v.) or maybe the scullery maid in Townley's *High Life Below Stairs* (1759). She wanted to know who wrote "Shikespur" (q.v.). 239.18; 243.17; 340.31.

Kitty of Coleraine–subject of an Irish ballad who broke a pitcher of buttermilk and was comforted by a kiss from a nice young man. It is also the air to which Moore's (q.v.) "When Daylight was yet Sleeping" is sung. 210.33; 328. 23-24.

*Kitty the Beads–obviously Kate (q.v.), but why beads? 530.32-33.

*Kjaer, Hjalmar, 284.note 4.

Klee, Paul (1879-1940)–German painter. 511.30.

*Kleinsuessmein, Kitzy, 330.23-24.

Knickerbocker, Father–humorous name for New York City. The name comes from Harman Jansen Knickerbocker (1650-1720), whose name was used by Washington Irving. 139.6; 442.8-9; ?549.4.

*Knight–I make no attempt to deal with the problem, but some instances of "knight" in FW are clearly to the Grail Knight. 201. 13; 225.17; 559.36.

Knight, E. H.–manager of the Euston Hotel, London — see Joyce to Miss Weaver, 20 January 1926. 245.32.

Knittrick Kinkypeard–see Sitric. 353.14.

Knopf–American book publisher. 52.27.

Knowell, Edward–young Knowell (q.v.) in *Everyman in His Humour* by Ben Jonson (q.v.), a model youth. 191.15,23 (well known . . . teddyfy).

Knowell, Old–it is known that Shakespeare (q.v.) acted in Ben Jonson's (q.v.) *Everyman in his Humour* (FW 502.7,21) and the role of Old Knowell is usually assigned to him—for no special reason—just as Tiberius (q.v.) in *Sejanus* (q.v.) and Adam (q.v.) in *As You Like It* are assigned.

13.13-14	well known . . . old . . . W.K.O.O.
†76.26	old knoll—with Cromwell (q.v.)
126.26	well known
†257.15	stow well—with Stow (q.v.)
344.6	well know
†351.1	nowells — with Nolan (q.v.)
†362.5	old noll—with Cromwell (q.v.)
†422.31-32	Old Knoll—with Cromwell (q.v.)
434-435	well known
†499.23	altknoll — with Cromwell (q.v.)
503.8,12	wellknown . . . W.K.
575.19	wellknown

*Knox, Myles, 567.1.

Knox, Robert–the anatomist who bought from Burke and Hare (q.v.). 342.2; 443.15; 596.20.

?Ko-Ko–of *The Mikado*. Ko-Ko is Chinese for "elder brother". 36.20.

*Koombe, Haryman of, 390.31-32.

Kore–see Persephone. 202.35; 203.23; 220.19; ?225.26; †363.3—with Cora Pearl (q.v.).

*Kornalls, Tanah, 351.22.

*Kostello, Panny – see Costello. 334.3.

*Koy, Pat–possibly Pat Hoy, a friend of Joyce's. Here one of the Four (q.v.). 27.27.

Krafft-Ebbing, von, Baron Richard (1840-1902)–German neurologist, wrote on sexual perversion. 290.28.

*Krasnapoppsky, 404.24-25.

Kreuger, Ivar and Toll–a firm of crooked match-makers. 221.28-29.

Krisanamurti–Indian "sage" of the early 20th century. †472.15 —with Jesus, Mary, Krishna (q.q.v.).

Krishna–an incarnation of Vishnu (q.v.); god of fire, storm, lightning in Hindu myth. 80.20; 215.2; †472.15—see Krisanamurti.

*Kristansen–see Christansen. 53.4.

Kropotkin, Peter Alexeivich, Prince (1842-1921)–Russian author and revolutionary. †81.18—with St Patrick (q.v.)—see also Crow.

Krupp–German munitions makers. 10.13; 323.5

Krylov, Ivan (1768-1844)–Russian writer of fables. 159.14.

*Kund, 201.33.

Kung–see Confucius.

*Kunut, holymaid of, 390.31.

Kyd or Kid, Thomas (1558-94)– English dramatist who probably wrote an Ur-*Hamlet* (q.v.). See Kidd. 05.00; 69.19.

L

*Laccorde, 222.2.

*Lacey, Kicky–see Two. 238.23.

La Chaise, François de (1624-1709) –confessor to Louis XIV (q.v.); the Paris cemetery Père-la-Chaise is named for him. 76.36.

Lacy, Hugh de (d. 1242)–first earl of Ulster, Henry II's (q.v.) governor of Dublin. 388.33.

Lady from the Sea–Ibsen's (q.v.) heroine, Ellida Wangel. †540.23 —with Lettice Greene (q.v.).

Lady of the Lake–Ellen Douglas, heroine of Scott's (q.v.) poem. Lady of the Lake is an old term for "whore". 465.36.

La Fayette, Marie Joseph Paul Yves Roch Gilbert De Motier, Marquis de (1757-1834)–French general who aided the American colonies in the Revolution. It has been suggested to me that the Abraham (q.v.) references on p. 26 include Abraham Lincoln (q.v.) and Lafayette refers to Lafayette Square in Washington. 26.16; †126.25—with Anna Livia (q.v.).

La Fontaine, Jean de (1621-95)– French poet and fabulist. †414.17 —with John (q.v.).

Lagener–anagram of General—see Buckley. 390.4.

*****La Gilligan,** Wildrose–perhaps a reference to Gill or to Lily Magrath (q.q.v.). See Rose? 229. 11.

Lagrima and Gemiti–Italian tears and groans. 290.27.

*****Lajambe,** Folletta–see Two. 422. 33.

Lalage–woman friend of Horace (q.v.). 229.10.

Lallah Rookh–title and heroine of Moore's (q.v.) poem. 184.16.

*****Lally**–blankest ignorance would be better than my guesses about Lally. Lally is always (bar p. 67) associated with the Four (q.v.) and might, therefore, be the ass, but I have no proof of this. The Four, as Elders (q.v.) are also associated with Susanna (q.v.), which is Hebrew for "lily". Lally certainly melts into Lily (q.v.) on pp. 96, 396, but I really do not know why Lily should be keeping the peace between the Elders. The Lally references in *Scribbledehobble* (pp. 16, 56, 82) suggest

a male. On FW, 67, Lally may be a policeman which would tie him-her to the Man Servant (q.v.) who is a constable, but a "special" is also a paramour. 67.11,23-24; 94.26; 96.4,19,20,23 —see Lillytrilly; 387.19; 390.3; 394.18; 396.25-26; 397.34.

Lalor, James Fintan–19th century Irish nationalist. The Fintan Lalor Fife Players make recordings. †25.9-10.

?Lamb, Lady Caroline (1785-1828) –Melbourne's wife, Byron's mistress. 527.5.

Lamb, Charles and Mary–authors of *The Adventures of Ulysses* (1808), which Joyce said he used instead of Homer (q.v.) for *Ulysses,* and of *Tales from Shakespeare* (1807). In FW Joyce seems very nearly to assume that Mary was sole author. †70.7—with Shakespeare (q.v.)?—see Will; 91.32; †201.30 — with Hamlet (q.v.)—see also Olaf; 223.1,2; 294.4,9; 350.24; †358.15—with Merlin (q.v.); †440.18—with Liddell (q.v.); 464.35; 486.1; 502.36; 529.32.

*****Lambel,** 595.6.

*****La Mesme,** Trina–three in one. The old French form of *la même* is *la mesme.* 212.12.

Lamfadar–see Lug.

Lamp and Lump–in FW the lamp is the Moon (q.v.) except in III,i,ii where Shaun as Moonshine (q.v.) carries it as the lamp of the man in the moon. I believe that lamp-moon is Elizabeth I (q.v.) as moon goddess and muse of her poets. The lump (which is very often associated with the lamp) is Shakespeare's (q.v.) granddaughter, Elizabeth Hall (q.v.), "Lizzie, grandpa's lump of love". (*Ulysses,* 210/273.) According to Stephen Dedalus (q.v.)—*Ulysses,* 192-193/249-250—Lizzie was the muse who came to Shakespeare "when the shadow lifts" and inspired his last plays — see Marina, Perdita, Miranda. The shadow is, of course, the Dark Lady (q.v.) who is scarcely to be distinguished from Ann Hathaway (q.v.) — *Ulysses*, 194/252. Shakespeare's queen and his granddaughter are joined by name and by having inspired (in part) the same poet. In *Henry VIII*, Elizabeth I is also a reconciling babe.

"The gloom hath rays, her lump is love", Shaun (q.v.) says—FW 411.27-28. Light is born of darkness, Elizabeth Hall is Ann Hathray's daughter's daughter; Lizzie is a lamp and a lump of sin or a hump such as HCE (q.v.) carries on his back. See Susanna. 10.27,35; 19.31; ?21.10; 33.10; 65.4; ?68.35; ?88.33; 94.17; 100. 19; †106.20 — with Humpty Dumpty (q.v.); 114.10-11; 127. 15; 137.1; 164.20; 170.36; 178.28; 182.11; 190.33; 198.31; 206.11; 245.5; 248.19; 252.17; 270.1,2; 277.2-3; 290.22; 294.25; 299.17; 318.14; 321.4; 323.23,28, 32; 324.13; †327.5—with Lucia Joyce or St Lucy (q.q.v.); 330.2; 332.17; 352.20; 362.22; 363.24; 374.6-7; ?404.13; 411.28; 418.19; 427.15,16; 438.30-31; ?445.4; 447. 21; 455.8; 509.31; 511.12; 514.34; 549.15; 560.19; 578.18; 580.27; 583.31,33; 585.5; †595.19—with Anna Livia (q.v.); 612.33; 613.1 (*bis*); 621.5.

Lampi, Toni–see Lumpkin. 323.32.

Lancaster–see York.

Lancelot of the Lake–knight of King Arthur's (q.v.), lover of Guinevere (q.v.). 285.1.

Lancey, Pobiedo – Luke Tarpey (q.v.) as the spear of Lug (q.v.) which was one of the four magic objects brought to the battle of Mag-Tured. 219.24.

*Landauner, Lady Victoria–carriages? 568.6.

Lane, Sir Hugh (1875-1915)–Irish art collector, nephew of Lady Gregory (q.v.). He offered a number of splendid paintings to the city of Dublin, but because Dublin dragged its feet, he gave them to the Tate. When he went down on the *Lusitania*, he left a will which again gave the pictures to Dublin, but a legal flaw let the Tate keep them. A celebrated controversy followed in which Lady Gregory and Yeats (q.v.) took part. He may always double with John Lane (q.v.). 79.27; 242.7.

Lane, John–of Sheep's Street (148. 10), Stratford-on-Avon. He was brought to the Consistory Court in Worcester for having said Mrs Susanna Shakespeare Hall (q.v.) "had the runninge of the raynes" at home (cf. FW 99.3) and that she "had bin naught with Rafe Smith (q.v.) at John Palmer's". Lane did not appear in court and was excommunicated. In FW he stands for false accusation and pruriency. See Elders, Susanna, Sycomore. John's Lane is a Dublin Street. John Lane is the British publisher who published *Ulysses* in England. 34.23; 51.8; †79.27,35 — with Hugh Lane (q.v.); ?84.8,19; †93.27 — with Dark Rosaleen (q.v.); †95.21— with Sycomore (q.v.); ?107.34; 116.34; 139.23; 141.4; 148.10; †242.7—with Hugh Lane (q.v.); ?244.8; 330.2; †354.33 — with Coriolanus (q.v.); 355.15; †365. 23-24—with Rosaline (q.v.); †371. 33-34—with Rosaline and Rachel (q.q.v.); †373.25-26—with James (q.v.); 408.33; 436.9; †444.29— with Rosaline; ?491.15,30; ?510. 11; 521.13-14; 544.30; ?568.22; 578.27; 618.9.

Lane, Rosa–the "dark Rosaleen" (see Rosaline, Rose) of Mangan's (q.v.) poem. She is Ireland. 93.27.

Lang, Andrew (1844-1912)–Scottish translator of Homer (q.v.), man of letters. I am quite sure that Lang is referred to on p. 335.32, as the author of *Shakespeare,*

Bacon, and the Great Unknown, 1912; but I am not sure he is intended in any other of the references listed below. At the same time, it is my impression that the "langs" of FW are a bit obtrusive unless Joyce is punning on something. See Greenwood. 21.5; 73.1; 202.22; 244.25; 305. 29; 315.32; 335.32; 338.20,22,35-36; 353.31; 414.26; 415.12,24; 484.25; 595.4.

*Langley–perhaps Francis Langley, builder and proprietor of the Swan (q.v.) theatre, who, along with Shakespeare (q.v.), Dorothy Soer and Anne Lee, gave sureties to keep the peace against William Wayte in 1596. 50.6,14.

Languish, Lydia–heroine of *The Rivals* by R. B. Sheridan (q.v.). She is of interest to Joyce because she wrote herself letters and lived in a world of female illusion, in love with an imaginary ensign. 96.11; 111.23; 232.21; 236.2; 294.20; 465.2; 508.34; 528.10,14.

*Lanigan, Meetinghouse–see Fitzpatrick? 354.17.

Lankystare–Lancaster and Cassius (q.q.v.). 465.33.

Lanner, Katty–Dublin soubrette— see *Ulysses,* 560/677, 730/881. 27. 19; ?292.23; †531.15-16—with Kate (q.v.).

*Lannigan–"Lannigan's Ball" is an Irish ballad. 377.6.

*Lanno, Bruni–see Browne and Nolan. 373.16.

Laoghaire (pronounced "Leary")– High King of Ireland in 432, who forbade St Patrick (q.v.) to light the Paschal fire at Slane. When Patrick vanquished the king's druids (q.v.), Laoghaire became a Christian. He was responsible for the first Irish code of laws, the Senchus Mor. In FW he is always, after some fashion, linked or combined with Shakespeare's King Lear (q.v.). 398.23; 610.9; 611. 33; 612.4,6,9-10,12,35.

Laotse–Chinese teacher, founder of Taoism, lived in the 6th century B.C. 208.30; 242.25-26.

Lapidous–see Lepidus. 271.6.

*Lapole, 390.11.

Lapoleon–see Napoleon, 388.16.

*Lappin, Ena–see Ena. 212.8.

*Laraseny, sergeant–maybe the Superintendent Laracy, *Ulysses,* 571/686. 618.31.

Larbaud, Valery – French critic, friend of Joyce's. 178.28.

Larchet, John F.–orchestra leader at the Abbey (q.v.), starting in 1908. 222.2.

Larkins, James–founder of the Irish Socialist party which met at Dublin's Liberty Hall. ?346.29; 582.19.

*La Rosa, Shadow–see Rose. Maybe a reference to the ballet, *Spectre de la Rose.* 495.24.

L'Arronge, A.–German dramatist of the late 19th century. 203.27.

Lasso, Orlando (1530-94)–Belgian composer. 279.note 1.

*Laterza, Una Bina–1, 2, 3. 212.12.

Latimer, Hugh (1490-1555)–English bishop, promoter of the Reformation, burned at the stake under Bloody Mary. 388.32,33.

Latouche–great banking family of Dublin. 450.36.

*Latouche, Luperca–see Two and see Lorette.

Laud, William (1573-1645)–English archbishop. ?483.34.

*Launer, 292.23.

Launfal, Sir – Arthurian (q.v.) knight, hero of a 15th century poem. 325.14,15.

Laura–Petrarch's (q.v.) beloved. 203.30 (laurals); 327.15; ?359.14; †548.10—with Annie Laurie and Anna Livia (q.q.v.); 561.19.

*Laura, Fountainoy, 212.14.

Laurens, Henry (1724-92)–American statesman, or his son John (1754-82)—Revolutionary War officer, "The Bayard of the Revolution". Laurens Co., Ga., whose capital is Dublin, was named for one of these. In all cases Laurens doubles with St Lawrence O'Toole and the St Lawrences (q.q.v.) of Howth. 3.20; 5.3; 613.15; 616.34.

*Lauretta–maybe Laurette Taylor who played in *Peg o'My Heart*—see Peg. 359.14.

Laurie, Annie–subject of a Scotch song. †38.21—with Anna Livia (q.v.); †548.10—with Anna Livia, Laura (q.q.v.).

*Lautrill, 81.14.

Laval, Pierre (1883-1945)–French politician who wore regrettable ties. 51.7.

Lavater, Johann Kaspar (1741-1801)–Swiss poet and physiognomist. 260.22.

Lavery, Sir John–20th century portrait painter. 134.3.

Lavinia–heroine of Shakespeare's *Titus Andronicus* (q.q.v.). She suffered the fate of Philomela (q.v.). Lavinia is also the wife of Aeneas (q.v.) and heroine of Shaw's *Androcles* (q.q.v.) *and the Lion*. 40.11; †275.12—with Anna Livia (q.v.); 327.12.

*Lawless, Eddy–perhaps Emily Lawless. 210.33.

Lawrence O'Toole, St–patron of Dublin. I imagine there is more of his life and legend in FW than has yet been found. All I know of him is that he was Dublin archbishop at the time of the Anglo-Norman invasion, and that he died at Eu in Normandy. Many references below are to places named for the saint. He doubles with Laurens (q.v.) and the St Lawrence (q.v.) family of Howth. He seems almost to make a pair with his contemporary, St Thomas à Becket (q.v.). Joyce

may playfully associate his name with D. H. Lawrence (q.v.). 5.3; 19.28; 22.12,19; 24.1-2; 53.29; 59.7; †77.2—with Lot (q.v.); 86.23; 138.26; 179.12; 180.14—here one of the Four (q.v.), Luke Tarpey (q.v.) as Dublin; 228.25; 235.19; 264.26; ?382.21; 388.14; 419.24; 433.5; 510.18; 517.35; 519.5; 534.36 (with the Larry who was stretched?); 569.6; 601.28; 613.15; 616.34; 617.12-13.

?Lawrence, D. H.–20th century novelist. See St Lawrence O'Toole.

Layamon (fl. 1200)–author of a "Brut"—see Brutus. 254.6; 359.17.

Lazarus–raised from the dead by Jesus (John 11). 41.2; ?209.3; 398.26; ?429.18.

Lazenby's–a pickle-making firm. 405.26.

Leah–see Rachel.

Leander–see Hero.

Lear, Edward (1812-88)–English artist and humorist. He may be present in all "Lears". I am not sure. 65.4.

Lear, King–hero of Shakespeare's (q.v.) play. Sometimes in FW he represents a foolish fond old man, sometimes ruined majesty. Not till the last pages of the book when Anna Livia (q.v.), like Cordelia (q.v.), returns to a mad feary father who is death, do you realize that for Joyce Lear is at once Shakespeare's character and Lir (q.v.), the sea. See also Laoghaire, Finnuala.
I would also draw the reader's attention to the end of the last piece in *Our Exagmination*: ". . . is there really in your work some ass pecked which is Uncle Lear?" 65.4; ?93.33; †139.21-22—with Ossian (q.v.); ?191.20 (itt*le ear*ps) —with Earp, Earwicker (q.q.v.); ?197.34; †234.30 — with Liber (q.v.); 331.32; 367.12; †381.12— with Lanty Leary (q.v.); ?391.7

(yearl); 398.23; 428.18; ?442.29; 567.5,6; 570.24,25; †582.35—with Larry Twentyman (q.v.); 590.2; 596.12; 610.9; 611.33; 612.4; 627.26 (bleary); 628.2 (feary).

Leary, Dan–the town of Dun Laoghaire (pronounced Leary), for a while called Kingston, but not after the founding of the Free State. See King Lear, George IV. 367.12; 428.18.

Leary, Lanty–a hero of Samuel Lover's (q.v.). 81.12.

Leary, Paddy–subject of the song "Off to Philadelphia". 93.33.

*Leas–Leah? 466.6.

Leaverholma – see Leverhulme. 517.19-20.

Le Caron, Henri (1841-94)–the *nom de guerre* of Thomas Miller Beach, a British spy, who went to America, fought gallantly in the Civil War, infiltrated the American Fenians, whose plans for invading Canada he betrayed. At the Parnell (q.v.) Commission, he testified for *The Times*. The Italian form of Charon (q.v.) is *Caron*. 496.32.

Lecky, William Edward (1838-1903) –Irish historian. His *History of European Morals* was in Joyce's library. 276.16; 438.26; 551.6.

L'Ecluse, N. D. (No Date?)–see Lenclos. 520.19.

Leda–visited by Zeus (q.v.) in the form of a swan, she gave birth to Helen (q.v.), Clytaemnestra, Castor and Pollux (q.v.). See Maud Gonne, Swan. †204.10 — with Aida; 208.18; 266.27; 267.1; 272. 2; 279.note 1.

Le Decer–14th century mayor of Dublin. 139.36.

Ledwidge Salvatorious–see Muggleton, Ludwig. 538.3.

*Lee–some such reference surely includes Sir Sidney Lee whose book on Shakespeare (q.v.) has been shown to be a source of *Ulysses.*

I think it is also very important to F.W. 250.22; 583.1.

Lee, Gipsy–avenger in the play *Maria Martin or the Murder in the Red Barn*. 210.7.

Lee, Robert E. (1807-70)–American confederate general. See Grant. †133.21—with Wellington (q.v.); 338.27; ?513.28; 516.9; 581.27.

*Leech, bishop, 302.1.

LeFanu, Joseph Sheridan (1814-73) –Irish novelist. His novel of Chapelizod, *The House by the Churchyard* is much mentioned in FW, but its use is mostly decorative. I believe that in Joyce's mind the title of the novel combined with a statement of Charles Gilden's, made in the 17th century: "I have been told that he [Shakespeare] writ the scene of the ghost in *Hamlet*, at his house which bordered on the Charnel House and Church-yard." See also *Uncle Silas*, Gipsy Devereux, Stark. 213.1; 265.4.

*Le Febber, Raoul–may be the French poet and Shakespearean (q.v.) critic Raoul Le Fevre. 372. 9-10.

Leftus, Adam–see Loftus. 246.28.

*Legge, 127.8.

*L'Eglise, Madame Gabrielle–see Delys? 184.27.

Leibnitz, Gottfried Wilhelm (1646-1716)–German philosopher. 416. 29.

Leif Ericsson (fl. 999-1000)–Scandinavian explorer, first known European to reach "Vineland" in North America. 316.27; 326.30-31; 506.8; 580.13.

Leland, Charles – 19th century author of a poem about the Flying Dutchman (q.v.). 311.5.

Leland, Charles Godfrey – discovered Shelta in 1876 on a road near Bath. 487.31.

Lelia–title heroine of a novel by

George Sand (q.v.). †340.22— with Lily (q.v.).

?**Lelong**, Jacques (1665-1721)– French priest, bibliographer, began a valuable *Bibliothèque historique de la France*. 371.33.

Le Monade, Prince–lemonade to be eaten with shortbread. 236.3.

Lenclos, Ninon de (1615-1705)– indestructable French courtesan. 153.4-5; 520.19.

*****Lenfant**–perhaps the Major Lenfant who designed Washington, D.C. 545.36.

Lenin, Nikolai (1870-1924)–Russian revolutionary. 271.left margin; 351.28.

Lennon, Judge Michael–Dubliner who attacked Joyce and his family in the *Catholic World*. See Ellmann, 655, 717. 179.2; 513.8.

Leo–thirteen popes. The reference on 155.7,8 is to Leo IV (847-55) who fortified the Vatican, thereafter known as the Leonine City. 153.34; 155.6,7; 544.24.

Leo–often refers to Mark Lyons because the lion is the heraldic beast of St Mark (q.v.).

Leodegarius Sant Leger–St Leodegarius or Leger led a revolt against the French crown in 675. The St Legers (q.v.) are an Irish family (*Ulysses*, 175/226) and a horse-race (*Ulysses*, 485/615). 498.3.

Léon, Paul–Russian friend and helper of Joyce, killed by the Germans. †246.16—with Napoleon; ?272.26.

Leonard, J.–Dublin chemist. 549.2.

Leonidas–Spartan king, commanded at Thermopylae. 307.left margin.

Lepidus–triumvir with Octavius and Mark Antony (q.q.v.), character in Shakespeare's *Antony and Cleopatra* (q.q.v.). 271.6.

Leporello–servant to Don Giovanni (q.v.) in Mozart's (q.v.) opera. 172.23.

*****Lerck**, Letty–Lady Luck? Letty Greene (q.v.)? 203.29.

Lesbia–the name under which Catullus (q.v.) celebrated Clodia (q.v.). "Lesbia hath a beaming eye" is the air to which Moore's (q.v.) "Nora Creina" is sung. 116.28-29.

Lescaut, Manon–title heroine of a novel by Abbé Prévost (q.v.). Manon seduces a youth who is studying for the priesthood. She is also subject of an opera by Massenet. †203.21—with Anna Livia (q.v.); 433.4.

*****L'Estrange**, 17.33.

Letty–see Leticia Greene. I am not sure all Letties refer to her.

*****Leven**, Litty fun Letty fan–see Letty Greene? 184.25.

Lever, Charles (1806-72) – Irish novelist. †93.34—with Samuel Lover (q.v.).

Leverhulme, William H., first viscount (1851-1925)–British soap magnate. His soap is called "Sunlight Soap" and he built a model town for his workers, called Port Sunlight. 517.19-20; 594.13.

*****Levey**, 50.14.

Levi-Brullo–see Lévy-Bruhl. 151. 11.

*****Levy**, Hannah–with Anna Livia (q.v.). 273.11.

Lévy-Bruhl, Lucien (1857-1939)– French anthropologist whose special interest was the primitive mind. 150.15; 151.11,32-33.

*****Lewes**, Mise of–possibly Mr Lewes who played Young Marlowe in *She Stoops to Conquer*. See Miss Bulkeley. 87.20.

Lewis, (Percy) Wyndham (1884-) –English novelist who attacked *Ulysses*. Various of his works are mentioned in FW—*Time and Western Man, Cantleman's Spring Mate*, etc. 56.29; 236.6 (Luisome); †440.9—with Percy Wynns (q.v.).

*****Leytha**, Liane, 212.11.

Liam–see William.

***Liane**, Leytha, 212.11.

Liber, Father–Italian counterpart of Dionysus (q.v.). He was worshipped in fertility rites which included leaping and dancing high. "Liber" is Bog Latin for *ler* or "sea". 226.24; 234.30—with Lear (q.v.); 250.19,20,21.

***Licking,** Lezba, 212.10-11.

Liddell–see Alice in Wonderland.

Liddlelambe, Mary – see Mary Lamb, Alice Liddell. 440.18.

***Liebsterpet,** 133.8-9.

Liffey–see Anna Livia.

Ligger–when George Eliot's (q.v.) identity was unknown, a table rapped in Nuneaton and said that George Eliot was "Liggers". This was interpreted locally as a reference to a Mr Liggens, who basked for some time in admiration. 228.27; 390.5.

Lightfoot, Claud – hero of some boys' books by Father Finn (q.v.). †457.11 — with Claude Duval (q.v.).

Lilith (from Hebrew *lilatu* or night) –female demon of Jewish folklore, a sort of vampire. In Rabbinical literature, she was the first wife of Adam (q.v.), deposed by Eve; according to another tradition, she married Satan (q.v.) and gave birth to Cain (q.v.). She is obviously present in all "Lily" references, but the use made of her in FW is unclear to me. There are certainly hints that HCE (q.v.) had a wife before he married Anna Livia (q.v.). See Lily.

Lillytrilly–Danish *Lille-Trille* or Humpty Dumpty (q.v.). See Lily, Lally. 96.4; 189.23.

***Lily**–the confusions of this character in FW have not been wholly resolved for me. She must, one would think, have to do with Lilith, she is certainly Mrs Magrath (q.v.), she is called (for what reasons?) Lily Kinsella

(q.v.). None of this has much bearing on the fact that she seems to me to be identical with, or strongly connected with Susanna (q.v.), for in Hebrew Susanna means "Lily". See Lily of Killarney, Lally.

22.8	lilipath (Liliput)
30.13-14	Lili O'Rangans (see Orange)
†32.11	Rosa and Lily Miskinguette—with Rose, Mistinguette (q.q.v.)
35	The Lily (see Lily of Killarney)
†34.33	lilyth—see Lilith
52.3	Lili and Tutu (see Tutu)
58.30	Lili Coninghams (q.v.)
?†59.7	lallance—with St Lawrence O'Toole, Shakespeare?
66.36	Lily boleros
68.26	lills
75.17	lililiths
?78.4	lethelulled
89.36	Leally and tululy
96.4	Lillytrilly (q.v.)
100.21	lollike
†155.25	lucciolys—with Lucia Joyce (q.v.)
176.36	lullobaw's
†180.5-6	Deal Lil—with Delia (q.v.)
198.5	lille
200.12,13	lilyhung
205.11	Kinsella's Lilith
206.4	Lilt a bolero
212.13-14	Snakeshead Lily
241.4	lilithe
†242.28	Avenlith (q.v.)
?244.4,22	lolave . . . lolling
246.18	lily of Bohemey—with the Bohemian Girl
†251.25	Galilleotto — with Galeotto (q.v.)
273.21	lilt
†284.24-25	Aysha Lalipat—with Aysha, Anna Livia (q.q.v.)—and also of course Liliput
291.21	lilying
295.5	lil
298.24	cosin Lil
304.23	lollypops

306.note 4 Lily
310.18,21 lall . . . lill
318.4   lilady
324.25   Lull
326.3-4   lollies off the foiled
331.27   lil lolly
332.1   lil
333.30   lillabilla lullaby
338.2   saillils of the yellavs
            (Joyce left a note
            saying he associated
            lilies of the valley
            with his wife)
†340.22   lelias on the fined—
            with Lelia (q.v.)
352.21,22   lolly . . . lilly
365.12   lolly
366.25   liliths oft I feldt
369.36   lull
†373.3   Lilly Tekkles (q.v.)
   34-35   allalility—with Anna
            Livia (q.v.)
396.25-26   lally . . . lolly . . . lelly
            . . . lilly. See Lally
422.32   liliens of the veldt
†428.8   Slyly—with Sally (q.v.)
?430.33   kindlily
433.13   linen of Killiney (see
            Lily of Killarney)
434.18   point a lily
436.33   lilylike
450.24,29   lilt . . . lillabilling of
            killarnies (see Lily of
            Killarney)
459.23   loveliletter
†491.22   lillypets—with Eliza-
            beth II (q.v.)
502.24   Julie and Lulie (q.v.)
?512.1   Lollgoll
†513.25   Lillabil Issabil—with
            Issy (q.v.), see also
            Bill?
†525.14   Lalia Lelia Lilia Lulia
            . . . Lola Montez
            (q.v.)
543.14   lilies on the veldt
?†547.11   Tollollal — with Lot
            (q.v.)
548.20   lilienyounger
†561.19,24 lillias . . . lilybit—with
            Elizabeth (q.v.)
†563.20   Lylian—see Lilias Wal-
            singham
566.6   lilygem
?572-573   Gillia (passim)

†583.9   lyly (q.v.)
618.4,16   Lily Kinsella (q.v.) . . .
            Lily
621.24   lil

Lily of Killarney—Benedict's (q.v.)
opera, based on The Colleen Bawn
(q.v.). See Lily.

Lincoln, Abraham (1809-65)–16th
president of the United States.
He doubles with Abraham (q.v.).
?26.16,19-20; 78.15.

Lind, Jenny (1820-87)–"the Swedish Nightingale", which ties her
to Philomela (q.v.). †359.35—
with the Jinnies (q.v.); †360.2—
with Florence Nightingale (q.v.).

Lindley and Murreys–see Lindley
Murrey. 269.29.

Lindsays–see "Battle of Otter-
bourne": "He chose the Gordons
and the Graems,/With the Lindsays, light and gay. . . ." 438.35,
36.

Lindundarri, Cardinal–Matt Gregory (q.v.) as Londonderry. 180.
13-14.

Lio the Faultyfindth–see Pope Leo.
153.34.

Lion–I have not listed lions, but
they are of some importance.
Joyce called FW I,iv "The Lion".
Lions can be Mark Lyons, Tristram of Lyonesse, the lion played
by Snug (q.v.) the joiner, one of
the Pope Leo's, England—all of
which see. See also Noble.

*Lionel, false–perhaps the hero of
Martha (q.v.). 241.32.

Lipoleum–see Napoleon.

Lipton, Sir Thomas (1850-1931)–
English tea magnate and yachting
enthusiast. 288.15; 541.28.

Lir (M.Ir. ler, Ir. lear, W. llyr, "the
sea"). To the Tuatha De Danaan,
he was the sea and his son
Mananaan MacLir the sea god.
One of the "Three Sorrows of
Story-Telling" is "The Fate of
the Children of Lir". Lir's three

sons and one daughter were changed by a wicked step-mother into swans and forced to wander the waters of Ireland, singing the most beautiful songs, until the coming of Christianity. When Christianity came and they were restored to humanity they were unbelievably ancient and desired only to die. In the legendary history of Britain, Lir became King Leir, and, by way of Geoffrey of Monmouth, he became Shakespeare's *King Lear* (q.q.v.). "Lir's lonely daughter", Finnuala (q.v.), is the subject of Tom Moore's (q.v.) song, "Silent O Moyle". That Joyce associates this swan-maiden with Cordelia (q.v.) may be seen from *Ulysses*, 190/246. At the end of FW Anna Livia (q.v.) dies as swan and Cordelia.

Lise, Mildew–*Mild und leise* are the opening words of the *Liebestod* in Wagner's (q.v.) *Tristan und Isolde* (q.v.). In FW they become a name for Issy, which ties her to Elizabeth Hall (q.v.). Isolde leaves the older Mark of Cornwall for the younger Tristan; so Shakespeare's (q.v.) late heroines (inspired by Elizabeth Hall) leave their fathers for younger men. See also Dark Lady. 18.2; 40.17; †41.3-4—see Lisa O'Deavis; †57.27,28; ?87.20; ?221.11; 304.3 (Formalisa. Loves deathhow); ?372.28; 388.4 (see Niece); 398.10; ?416.9; 424.28.

Liselle–see Elizabeth.

Liszt, Franz (1811-86)–Hungarian composer. 508.34.

?Little, Brown – American publishers. 114.31.

Little Old Man–in certain fertility rites, the last sheaf. 40.1.

*Little on the Green–improbable, but maybe "little George upon the Green" in Suckling's, "A Ballad Upon a Wedding". 15.8.

*Littleton–as in Coke (q.v.) upon? 435.4.

Livia or Livy–see Anna Livia.

Livingston, David (1813-73)–Scottish missionary, African explorer. 283.17-18.

Livius–see Livy.

Livy or Titus Livius (50 B.C.-A.D.17)–Roman historian. 260. 21,25.

Lizzie–see Elizabeth Hall.

Lloyd George (1863-1945)–British Prime Minister who loosed the Black and Tans. †91.19—with Jesus; ?533.35.

Lloyd's of London–insurance company. 326.19; 373.4; 413.5; 590.5; 609.3.

*Lludillongi–maybe Lord Mayor of Dublin, Val Dillon of *Ulysses*. 519.8.

Llyn–part of Dublin. See Father Flynn. 44.11.

Lob–another name of Puck (q.v.). 297.15.

Lochlaun or Locklaun–not a person, but the Irish name for Norway. 268.note 6; 370.28.

Lodenbroke the Longman–see Ragnar Lodbrok. 373.29.

*Lodewijk–see Ludwig, Lewis Carroll. Perhaps it is also the name —Lodowick—that Duke Vincentio (q.v.) assumes in Shakespeare's (q.v.) *Measure for Measure*. 361. 21.

Lodge, Thomas (1558-1625)–English playwright and miscellaneous writer. His *Rosalynde* (see Rosalind) furnished the story for Shakespeare's (q.v.) *As You Like It*. Fleay suggested that he collaborated with Shakespeare in writing *2 Henry VI* (q.v.). Lodge reference may also be to Sir Oliver Lodge, physicist, spiritualist. ?160.7; 574.17.

Loewy-Brueller–see Lévy-Bruhl. 150.15.

Loftus, Adam (1533-1605)–Archbishop of Armagh and Dublin, lord chancellor of Ireland. He suggested the establishment of Trinity College, Dublin, to Elizabeth I (q.v.). He always doubles with Adam (q.v.). 246.28; 549.33.

*Log Laughty, 531.4.

Logan, James–Irish botanist for whom a family of Australian undershrubs are named. 450.9,31.

Logue, Cardinal–condemned *The Countess Cathleen* (q.v.) as heretical though he hadn't read it. 440.4.

Loisy, Abbé Alfred Firmin–French theologian, excommunicated in 1908. 516.9.

Loki–Norse god of mischief and evil. He contrived the death of Balder (q.v.). 51.26; 221.9; 237. 22.

Lokman–probably Luqman whose name is the title of Sura 31 of the Koran. He remonstrated with his son for not being respectful to his parents. 367.1.

*Lona the Konkubine, 284.note 4.

Lonan–see Onan. 24.34.

*Long, 88.31; 127.7.

Long, John–English publisher who refused *Dubliners*. 356.20.

Longaville–one of the young men who give up women in Shakespeare's (q.v.) *Love's Labour's Lost*. 347.26.

*Longeal of Malin, 525.29.

Longfellow–occasionally the American poet—H. W. (1807-82)—but more often a reference to De Valera (q.v.) whom the Irish called "the long fellow". See De Valera for listing.

*Lonni, Brani–see Browne and Nolan. 373.16.

*Loomis, Francist de, 372.10.

Loos, Joe–British band-leader. See Job. 448.22.

Looshe, Lesbia–Moore's song "Nora Creina" opens "Lesbia hath a beaming eye". The French for "squint" is *louche*. Lucia Joyce

(q.v.) had a squint. 93.27-28; 348.26.

Loper de Figas–see Lope de Vega. 440.17.

*Lorcans, 518.11.

*Lorcansby, 448.19.

Lord-Mayors of Dublin–this list of Lord-Mayors in chronological order was compiled by Mr Atherton from two editions of Thom's (q.v.) *Dublin Directory*, 1851, 1951. Of his list, Mr Atherton writes:

Joyce introduces into FW the names of 200 Lord-Mayors of Dublin, beginning with Mark Quin who was Mayor 1697-98. With the exception of Bartholomew Vanhomrigh, Daniel O'Connell, Dwyer Gray, Lorcan Sherlock and Alfred Byrne (q.q.v.), he seems to ignore their Christian names. Surnames are introduced into passages where HCE (q.v.) is present as chief magistrate (e.g. 623.15; 495.29-30). Some Lord-Mayors had names ending in "son". These are usually named without the last syllable, probably because the mayor is a father-figure. For the same reason "Mac" is usually omitted. Another group of names omitted is that of Mayors with non-Irish place names; "ham" and "ton"—both Saxon for towns—are usually omitted, e.g. 47.5, Billing for Billington.

Mayors' names are often combined into such a group as "Knox-atta-Belle" (139.35); other names are used as verbs: boltoned, sankeyed, murrayed, etc. Often they are combined with three or four other allusions, and are just one of Joyce's many ways of adding extra layers of significance to his text. Sometimes Mayors add point to the text, as on 548.35: "her aldritch cry", for Anna Livia (q.v.) is crying out that the Lord-Mayor is assaulting her—see also 536.12.

My list is not complete with the naming of every Mayor. Some Mayors come in dozens of times. It is noticeable that when common words happen to be the names of Mayors, they are carefully avoided in those parts of the text where they would not be fitting. (†indicates: not found.)

Quin	305.20
Forest	306.21
*Desmyniers	
Reader	120.13
Totty	125.11; 281.left margin; 327.7
*Deay	
Allen	57.13; 618.23.
Brewster	29.4-5; 71.8
Smith	48.24, etc.
?Lovet	231.12 (Lovvey)
Eastwood	160.12 (East—surrounded by names of trees)
?Lowther	460.11 (louther)
Best	414.35; 96.5; 72.2; 539.8, etc.
Ram	28.36; 208.4; 256.7; 396.15; 490.4; 624.14
Knox	†139.35—with Bell; 342.2; 567.1; 596.20
?Castleton	21.13, etc.
Hacket	197.6
?Creagh	51.28
?McDermott	21.14, etc.
*Otrington	
Mitchell	13.9; 147.6; 281.note 4
Rogerson	211.16
?Blackhall	549.5
Watts	321.9
?Billington	47.5 (Billing); 436.27 (billing)
Van Homrigh	623.16-17 (see Van Homrigh)
?Rainford	74.17 (raindrips to Rethfernhim)
?Walton	508.15 (Walty)
Bell	†139.35 — with Knox; 552.23, etc.
Page	108.31; 115.3, etc.
?Stoyte	443.30; 619.32 (Stout)
Gibbons	504.29
?Burton	293.note 2
?Pearson	359.27
*Fownes	
Forest	306.21; 257.24
Eccles	179.27; 514.15; 567.27
Gore	128.22; 348.21; †606.19 — with Knox

Cook	79.7; 199.15; 269.22, etc.
Barlowe	553.20
?Stoyt (see above)	
Bolton	548.5
Barkey	552.9
Quail	244.30; 547.21
?Wilkinson	90.11; 464.19
?Forbes	614.7 (Forbeer)
?Curtis	106.12 (note the magistrate reference)
?Dickson	610.3 (dickhuns)
Porter	72.3; 106.32; †122.10 — with Roe; 560.24, etc.
?Reyson	365.29 (reyal); 550.32.
Kane	63.7; 211.30; 448.3; 491.16; 516.23; 536.27
?Empson	175.11 (Emp)
Whitwell	536.25
Burrows	565.36
Page (see above)	
Verdoen	4.4 (Verdons)
Pearson (see above)	
Nuttal	550.14
French	50.9; 83.31; 146.20; 192.15; 246.32; 498.1, etc.
Howe	18.12; 26.23; 315.20; 553.23
Kane (see above)	
Grattan	202.17; 580.32
?Somerville	473.5 (summer)
Walker	473.3; 394.12; 376.30; 555.24, etc.
?Maccarroll	294.7 (carollaries)
Falconer	185.4
Cooke (see above)	
Aldrich	548.35
Walker (see above)	
Cooke (see above)	
White	29.15; 269.note 4; 334.15, etc.
Walker (see above)	
?Ribton	437.8 (rib), etc.
Ross	314.34; 340.35, etc.
Adamson	28.32 (see Adam)
Taylor	61.28; 365.33
Cooke (see above)	
Burton (see above) 595.18	
Murray	63.27; 227.29, etc.

Baillie   85.26; 317.30; 480.
                 18, etc.
Hunt   355.16; 530.24,25;
                 594.7; 603.32, etc.
?Forbes (see above)
Meade   286.7; 496.11 (meid,
                 with nogent for
                 Nugent)
Crampton   291.5, etc.
Tew   295.30; 538.21
Hamilton   138.1; 274.9; 438.
                 36, etc.
Allan   57.13; 618.23
?Rossell   122.16; 250.3; 286.
                 14   (rosseculli-
                 nans); 465.30
?Forbes (see above)
?Geale   352.31 (gayl)
Taylor (see above)
Sankey   533.20
*Fetherston
?Barton   247.10 (Barto no)
?Blackhall (see above)
*Reynolds
?Booker   111.32 (boucher)
French (see above)
Lightburne   549.4
Hart   339.8 (with Hunt,
                 Bell, Ross)
*Emerson
Bevan   618.14 (bevyhum)
Dunn   518.10
King   294.24; 421.6; 495.
                 12; 499.15, etc.
Hamilton (see above)
?Swettenham   37.2 (Sweatagore—
                 with Gore)
*Darragh
Warren   574.4
Green   15.8; 45.9, etc.
Horan   49.15
Shiel   159.1 (shieling)
Rose   495.24; 548.24, etc.
*Howison
Sankey (see above)
Carleton   622.29 (with Hart)
James   386.26; 387.8; 521.
                 14, etc.
Moncrieff   536.12
*Worthington
Reed   94.6; 385.6; 398.30;
                 433.9; 442.34
Fleming   43.4; 622.34
Andrews   328.5; 393.5; 468.
                 32; 471.34

Sutton   17.11; 533.30; 587.
                 23
Thorp   4.27
Poole   164.4
*Hutton
Jenkin   485.21
Vance   211.32; 539.19
*Pemberton
?Trevor   192.12 (trevi)
Darley   137.3
?Stamer   252.36; 467.19; 511.
                 8; 547.26
Hone   382.21; 536.12 (with
                 Moncrieff)
Archer   63.13; 80.9; 440.4
King (see above)
Cash   133.13; 538.16
*Beresford
Shaw   132.10; 263.7; 378.
                 24
*Bloxham
Allet   43.3; 119.31; 178.6;
                 260.29
?McKenny   193.24; 332.33 (both
                 Kenny)
Stamer (see above)
King (see above)
James (see above)
Fleming (see above)
Smyth   178.22
Jones   210.17; 487.10; 521.
                 13, etc.
Abbot   539.27
?Tyndall   468.28 (tisdall)
Nugent   24.26; 496.10
Montgomery   426.11; 525.7; 543.
                 28
West   105.7; 274.13; 523.
                 25, etc.
?Harty   547.4 (hartyly)
*Whelan
Archer (see above)
*Whiteford
*Perrin
Morrison   192.4
?Hodges   138.11; 285.6
Warren (see above)
Hoyte   536.14
?Brody   356.18 (brodhe)
Jones (see above)
O'Connell   468.33, etc.
Roe   122.12; 277.note 4;
                 394.18; 397.36;
                 543.33

O'Brien   70.7; 270.31; 370.
                 21; 385.15
Arabin   553.35
Keshan   534.30 (keshaned)
?Staunton   423.24 (staun)
Dunne   210.35; 337.36
O'Brien (see above)
*Reynolds (see above)
Guinness   35.15, etc.
D'Arcy   587.4
Kinahan   364.19
?McDonnel   39.17; 281.note 3;
                 585.28 (all Don-
                 nelly)
Boyce   536.22
Farrell   176.17; 270.margin;
                 547.24; 552.12
Atkinson   43.10
?Moylan   25.27; 628.3
Vereker   536.17
McSwiney   535.20
Barrington   536.32
Mackey   106.11
Joynt   15.7
Carroll (see above)
?Purdon   445.17   (papapar-
                 don)
?Bulfin   445.24 (bullin)
Durdin   548.6
Mackey (see above)
Brooks   264.6; 440.29, etc.
McSwiney (see above)
Owens   294.21; 574.1; 574.4
                 (with Warren)
Tarpey   214.34,   etc.   (see
                 Luke Tarpey)
Barrington (see above)
Dwyer Gray   214.33; 228.13; 371.
                 7, etc.
Moyers (see above)
?Dawson   496.2 (Daw)
Meagher   61.13,22;   211.11;
                 214.4; 508.15
O'Connor   271.1; 317.31; 380.
                 12,33; 381.25
Sullivan   142.26; 581.4, etc.
Sexton   148.8; 230.11; 416.
                 13; 511.8; 552.23
Kennedy   7.11; 317.1; 498.19
Meade (see above)
Shanks   144.33; 471.21; 538.
                 28; 578.1
Dillon   288.1; 586.15

?McCoy   139.24; 157.21; 354.
                 33; 431.4; 433.29
                 (all "coy")
Tallon   549.3   (tallon-
                 kindles); 606.30
Pile   130.4; 211.5; 548.
                 26; 624.30
Harrington   266.12; 289.note 6
                 (Harring)
?Hutchinson   337.7; 543.11 (both
                 "hutch")
?Nannetti   567.15 (Nanetta)
O'Reilly   44.14,24; 616.1, etc.
?Coffey   43.8 (Coffee)
Doyle   142.26; 574.9, etc.
Farrell (see above)
Lorcan Sherlock 534.31
Gallagher   8.25, etc.
O'Neil   550.31
Alfred Byrne   289.13; 568.32

Lorelei–in German folk-tale and
Heine's song, a siren of the Rhine.
I think Joyce may include Lorelei
Lee. 201.35.

*****Lorette**, Lupita–see Two. Legend
says St Patrick (q.v.) had two
sisters, Lupita and Darerca, who
were sold into slavery in Ireland.
I have a vague recollection of
another legend in which by accident? design? he caused the death
of one or both sisters who had
become whores. 67.33; 444.28,36.

Loritz, errol – see St Lawrence
family. 312.19.

Lorne, Crosscan–see Crosscan.

Lorrequer, Harry–title hero of
Lever's (q.v.) novel. 228.21.

*****Loryon** the comaleon, 136.27.

Lost–see Perdita.

Lot, his wife and daughters–escaped
the destruction of Sodom and
Gomorrah, but Mrs Lot looked
regretfully back (as do the
Twenty-nine on 470) and turned
into a pillar of salt. Lot's daughters, believing their father the one
man left alive, got him drunk,
lay with him, and bore him sons
(*Genesis*, 19). 39.33 (blotto); 62.9,
11, ?†34—with Lotta Crabtree
(q.v.); 63.22; ?65.17 (tolloll);

†77.2—with St Lawrence O'Toole (q.v.); 117.6,36; 191.18—with Charlotte (q.v.); 249.36; 257.35; ?302.10; 307.left margin; 321.17; 364.35; 379.26; 388.14,15; 436.24; 470.14 (lothleid); ?492.2; 509.31; 518.18; 535.4; ?547.11; 561.15— see Lottie; ?567.34-35; 568.7; 570.17; 579.24; 582.3; 586.24; 596.12; 599.21.

Lothario – heartless libertine in Rowe's (q.v.) *The Fair Penitent.* *263.note 4—with Luther (q.v.).

*Lottie–maybe one of Lot's (q.v.) daughters. See also Charlotte. 561.15.

*Loughlins–maybe Lochlaun or Norway. 541.18.

Louigi–Luigi, fashionable London restaurateur. 59.29.

Louis XIV "The Sun King" (1638-1715)–king of France—see Solsking. 607.28.

Louise – title heroine of Charpentier's opera. 147.12.

*Louise, Queen – maybe Marie Louise (see Joséphine), maybe the queen of Prussia (1776-1810). 102.10.

Loundres, Henry de–Irish viceroy and Archbishop of Dublin in 1213. 543.18.

Lousadoor, baroun–see Lucifer. 107.36.

*Love, Amos–just a pun? 372.9.

*Lovel–I don't think it's Lovel our dog. 226.5; 237.9; 361.9.

?Lovelace, Richard (1618-58)–English poet. Hero of Clarissa? 350.14; 527.35.

Lover, Samuel (1797-1868)–Irish novelist and song writer. †93.34— with Lever and Sam Weller (q.q.v.).

*Lovvey, googlin, 231.12.

*Lowe, Sir Hudson – Napoleon's (q.v.) keeper on St Helena. 343.17.

Lowe, Oliver–ferocious magistrate in LeFanu's (q.v.) *The House by the Churchyard.* 34.9.

*Loyd–perhaps Constance Lloyd or Mrs Oscar Wilde (q.v.). 326.19.

Loyola, St Ignatius (1491-1556)– founder of the Society of Jesus. 186.13; 228.11; 433.1; 451.19.

Luath–dogs belonging to Cuchullin and Robert Burns (q.q.v.). Luathan is Bog Latin for "bird". 244.30.

Lubbock–see Avebury.

*Lucan–an environ of Dublin on the Liffey. Two earls of Lucan may possibly have interested Joyce: 1) Patrick Sarsfield, one of the Wild Geese, fought under James II (q.v.), died in 1693 in France, saying "O that this were for Ireland!"; 2) G. H. Bingham who commanded a division of British cavalry at Balaklava. I feel, however, that I am missing the point of the Lucan references. It may be that they sometimes refer to Sir Thomas Lucy (q.v.). 253.32; 452.29; 620.8.

Lucan, Charley–apparently a combination of (1) the Roman poet Lucan (39-65), author of the *Pharsalia*, and (2) Charles Lucas (1713-71) an advocate of the principles of Molyneux and Swift (q.v.), whose pamphlets made him so obnoxious to the government that he was voted an enemy to Ireland. 419.36.

Lucas, Charles–see Charley Lucan. 184.34-35 — with Luke Tarpey (q.v.); 419.36.

Lucia–see Lucia Joyce.

Lucifer–in Greek "lightbearer", a name given originally to the morning star, Venus (q.v.). Through a mistranslation of Isaiah, 14:12 the name became that of Satan (q.v.) before his fall. See Mick and Nick. 35.11; 69.12; 107.36; 140.5; 182.5; 183. 16; 239.34; 250.34; 257.27 (in the 100-letter word); †295.33—with Lucia (q.v.)?; †354.32; 378.17; 439.7; 505.32-33; 621.3.

*Lucille, 247.36.

Lucretia or Lucrece–Roman lady who was raped by Sextus Tarquinius (q.v.); having exacted an oath of vengeance from her menfolk, she stabbed herself. Subject of a poem by Shakespeare (q.v.). 277.note 2; 542.29.

Lucretius (98-55 B.C.)–Latin poet who went mad from a love-potion made of Spanish fly. 306.left margin.

Lucy–Wordsworth's young friend. †203.26—with Lycidas and Lucia Joyce (q.q.v.).

Lucy, St–patron of eyes. See Lucia Joyce.

Lucy, Sir Thomas (1532-1600)– Warwickshire squire, magistrate. Nicholas Rowe (q.v.) says he prosecuted (jailed and whipped) Shakespeare (q.v.) for poaching his deer. (Some say the deer was shot for Shakespeare's wedding.) Shakespeare aggravated the offense by writing a ballad against Sir Thomas, and had then to leave Stratford, go into exile. One extant version of the ballad deals with the morals of Lady Lucy and the cuckolding of Sir Thomas; the other harps at length on the fact that Lucy was pronounced "lousy" (see *Ulysses*, 213/277). I think this second effort is paralleled by "The Ballad of Persse O'Reilly" in which HCE (q.v.) is confounded with an insect, the earwig.

It is also believed (disbelieved) that Shakespeare satirized Lucy in *The Merry Wives of Windsor* by giving Justice Shallow (q.v.) a dozen white luces on his coat-of-arms. Lucy had luces on his arms. The luce is a pike, *Esox lucius*, which at 525.12 I take to be a reference to Sir Thomas; "pikes" at 31.2; 420.11; 450.16; 570.4; 623.14 may or may not refer to him. Sometimes I think he ties up with the Lucan (q.v.) references, sometimes I don't. When it comes to the word "Lucy"

I am likewise of two minds, but I shove in the references for what they are worth, taking only 525.12 to be certain. See also Lucia Joyce.

24.6; †155.25—with Lucia Joyce (q.v.)?; 283.10; †295.33—with Lucia Joyce and Lucifer (q.q.v.); 297.17; 324.32; 381.33; 452.29; 516.9; 525.12; 545.33; 555.17.

Ludwig (born Ledwidge), William (1847-1923)–Irish baritone. See also Lodewijk. 243.17; †361.21— with Lewis Carroll (q.v.); †538.3 —with Muggleton, Lewis Carroll (q.q.v.).

Lug or Lugh (a lug is an ear)–Gaelic sun-god, leader of the Tuatha De Danaan, known as *Lamhfada* (long-armed) and as *Lugaid*. 11. 23; 44.11; 79.21; 130.4; 162.26; 305.right margin; 416.34; 507.12; 594.19; 597.1.

*****Luis**, 384.19.

Luke, St–see Four Evangelists, Luke Tarpey.

Lully, Jean Baptiste (1633-87)– Italian composer. †96.19—with Lally (q.v.).

Lump–see Lamp.

Lumpkin, Tony–character in Goldsmith's (q.v.) *She Stoops to Conquer*. 323.28,32; 324.13.

Lums, Sally–kind of cake. 249.35.

Luna, Conte de–villain of *Il Trovatore*, Verdi's (q.v.) opera. 465.21.

Lund–not a person; the cathedral in Lund, Sweden, built by Finn MacCool (q.v.) at the request of St Lawrence. If St Lawrence did not guess Finn's name by the time the church was built, Finn would get the saint's eyes. St Lawrence guessed, as the last stone was put in place. Finn tried to pull the church down, but was changed to a stone and stands there to this day. Mr Clive Hart has seen him. 137.9-10.

Luney, Shuley–"Shule Aroon", the

air to which Moore's "Alone in Crowds" is sung. 49.6.

*Lung, Tum, 578.6.

*Luntum, 12.5.

Lupton, Mrs Tummy–Anna Livia (q.v.) as tea, I guess. See Lipton. 257.13.

Luse–louse. 414.25; 417.18,29; 418. 15; 458.33.

Luther, Martin (1483-1546)–German religious reformer. 71.27; †263.note 4—with Lothario (q.v.); 536.36; 582.33.

*Lutran, 110.8.

Luttrell, Henry (1655-1717)–betrayed Limerick to De Ginkell (see Athlone). He was murdered while riding through Dublin in a sedan chair. 81.14; 262.16; 534.9.

?Luvvah–a male spirit in Blake's (q.v.) Four Zoas (q.v.). 369.19.

Lycidas (Edward King)–title character of Milton's (q.v.) poem, which is echoed here. †203.26—with Lucia Joyce, Wordsworth's Lucy (q.q.v.).

Lydia–see Languish.

Lylian–see Lilias Walsingham. 563. 20.

Lyly, John (1554-1606) – English author. See Lily. 583.9.

Lynch–word of doubtful origin. One possibility is James Lynch Fitzstephens, Mayor of Galway, who condemned his own son to death. Lynch is a character in Portrait of the Artist and Ulysses. 495.11; 545.32.

Lynch, Anne–Dublin brand of tea —see Ulysses, 659/788. In all cases Anne Lynch doubles with Anna Livia (q.v.). 293.25; 325.4-5; 392.32; 406.27; 506.34-35.

Lyons, Lady of–Pauline Deschappeles, heroine of a play by Bulwer Lytton. Also Lyons Corner Houses, English restaurants. See Lion. 449.11.

Lyons, Mark–second of the Four (q.v.)—see also Four Evangelists. His surname comes from the heraldic associations of the Lion with St Mark. He is the province of Munster and various places in Munster; south and the south wind; the number 2 and the second letter of the Hebrew alphabet; the element air; the silver age; Joyce's second age or marriage. He lives at Poors Court, Soother; his road is the Fivs Barrows; and—though I don't know why—he asks most of the questions in the "Yawn" section. At times—perhaps at all times— he is indistinguishable from Mark of Cornwall (q.v.). 184.34 (see Noble); 214.34; †290.6-7 — see Macbeth; 368.33; 384.8,11; 385. 19; 387.14; 388.10,34; 391.14; 397.21; 398.2; 405.4; 475.24-25; 476.26; 480.11; †483.17—with Mark Antony, Antonio (q.v.q.); 519.24,33; 520.13; 533.20; 564.2; 565.8; 573.8,28.

Lyons, Mrs–see Mark Lyons.

M

Maas, Joseph (1847-86)–English tenor who sang, among other things, Des Grieux to Marie Roze's (q.v.) Manon (see Lescaut). 165.2; 203.31; †243.35—with Josephine (q.v.); †246.17—with Josephine (q.v.); ?384.6; 391.8; 491.15.

*Maassy, Muriel – probably the Dutch river. 212.8.

Mab, Queen–in Romeo and Juliet (q.v.), the fairies' midwife, elsewhere Titania (q.v.); Title of a poem of Shelley's (q.v.). Mavrodaphne is a modern Greek wine. 379.18; †406.25—with Daphne (q.v.).

McAdam, John L. (1756-1836)– Scottish inventor of macadamized roads. 80.1; †469.20—with Mac-duff.

*McAdoo–I really don't think this is Cleveland's Secretary of the Navy or Wilson's Secretary of the Treasury. The name always occurs in Shakespearean (q.v.) passages, and in the First Folio, the play is *Much adoo about Nothing*. On 290 the reference is to Johnny MacDougal (q.v.) and may intend a reference to Dr John Hall (q.v.). 227.33; 290.9

Macaires, Colly–maybe Robert Macaire, a typical villain of French comedy, from the play *Robert Macaire* by Lemaître and Anber, 1845; or the murderer of Aubrey de Mouldicher in old French legend. 65.4.

*MacAlister, 370.21.

MacAlpin, Molly–the air to which Moore's (q.v.) "Remember the Glories of Brian the Brave" is sung. 338.28-29.

*MacArty, Basilius O'Cormacan–doubtless an ancient Irish king—see McCarthy Cormac? 463.22.

*Mac Auliffe–Matt Gregory (q.v.) as the first letter of the Hebrew alphabet, Aleph. 290.6; 427.4.

*MacAuscullpth, Owllaugh the Thord—Olaf? Thor? 532.8-9.

Macbeth–title hero of Shakespeare's (q.v.) play. 250.16 (Glamours), 17 (Coldours . . . Lack breath), 34; †290.6-7 (Mark Lyons, q.v., as the second letter of the Hebrew alphabet, Beth); 302.note 1; 347.3-4; 412.21.

MacBlakes–see Blake. 409.23.

MacBruiser, O'Bryan–see Brian Boru. 376.8-9.

MacCabe, Edward–19th century Dublin Archbishop and Cardinal. 33.2; 200.3-4.

McCarthy–made up to two people: 1) when Roderick O'Connor (q.v.) was fighting the Anglo-Normans, one of his allies, Dermot Mac Carthy, deserted to the enemy; 2) when Parnell was disgraced in divorce court, most of his followers were led away by Justin M'Carthy (1830-1912). 381.2.

McCarthy, Demetrius O'Flanagan—subject of a song. He took the floor at Enniscorthy. 27.25; 463. 22.

MacCarthy, Denis Florence (1817-82)–Irish poet. 200.34-35; 231.15; 232.6; 452.9.

*MacCawley, Mic Mac Magnus–I think the micro- and macrocosmic son of Cool or Finn MacCool. The reference may also be to Lord Macaulay whose works are quoted in FW, and whose account of Bacon's (q.v.) death is basic to an understanding of Biddy Doran (q.v.). 25.36.

*MacCawley, Mrs, 392.8.

*Macclefield's, 381.14.

*MacClouds–Macleods? 519.7.

MacCool, Finn–see Finn.

McCormack, John (1884-1945)–Irish-born tenor who went to America, made his pile, became an American citizen and a Papal Count. It is evident from Joyce's letters (to Miss Weaver, 14 August 1927, 23 October 1928) that McCormack was a principal model for Shaun-Jaun (q.v.), especially in III,i,ii. Shaun-Jaun sings McCormack's favorite songs; both are strongly identified with Don Giovanni (q.v.), indeed Mc-Cormack was known as "Giovanni" in the musical world; according to McCormack's wife, Lily (q.v.), her husband was, like Shaun-Jaun, a great child who ate and ate—food, drink, violins, motor-cars, toy trains, chalices, yachts, Rodins—and grew heavier and heavier and heavier, a kind of wonder of the sheerly material; again, like Shaun-Jaun, Giovanni McCormack was—until his voice went—a peerless spellbinder, so peerless that Woodrow Wilson begged him not to go into the army, but stick on the home-front "to keep the fountains of sentiment flowing". Anyone who wants to know what Shaun-Jaun looks like, should turn to the pictures in Mrs McCormack's book, *I Hear You Calling Me* (Milwaukee, 1949). As the King's Post, Shaun's uniform owes, as Mr Atherton has shown, much to Sean the Post (q.v.), but spiritually it is the uniform of the divinely complacent McCormack as Papal Count. See Foli. †227.7—with St Joan (q.v.); 243.16; 397.12; 450. 25.

MacCormack Ni Lacarthy, Miss–Grania (q.v.), daughter of Cormac (q.v.)—see MacKundred. 137. 2.

Mac Courther, Tennis Flonnels–see Denis Florence MacCarthy. 452.9.

MacCrawls–see Magrath. 618.1.

Maccullaghmore–see Finn Mac-Cool. 25.31-32.

MacCumhal, Hetman–Finn Mac-Cool (q.v.), perhaps also Hetman Michael (q.v.) of *Jurgen* (q.v.). 243.14.

*****MacDollett,** McAdoo – Johnny MacDougal (q.v.) as the 4th letter of the Hebrew alphabet, Daleth. See McAdoo. 290.9.

*****MacDonagh,** Thomas – executed for his part in the Easter Rebellion. An uncertain identification. 490.6.

?MacDonald, John, M.A.–author of an account of the Parnell (q.v.) Commission which Joyce used in FW, I,1v. ?†87.12—see O'Donnell.

MacDonnell, Sorley Boy (1505-90) –chieftain of Ulster who fought his neighbors and Elizabeth I (q.v.). 16.5; 499.22,24.

MacDougal or Mac Dougall, Johnny –the fourth and somehow most important of the Four (q.v.). He is always a little separate from the other three, and because he

is an Elder (q.v.) and named John, he is probably closer to John Lane and John Hall (q.q.v.) than the others. Moreover since he is named John (q.v.) and his ass (q.v.) is Shem (q.v.), he is in some manner Shaun (q.v.). Johnny is the province of Connaught and towns in that province; west and the west wind; the element water; the iron age; Joyce's fourth age, rebirth; the human bottom, according to the geography of Paracelsus (q.v.). He lives at Moherboher or Bohermore (*boher* is Irish "road") to the Waste and his road is the Bower-Moore. (See Moore, Four.) His heraldic beast is the eagle. See Walker, Four Evangelists, Four Masters. 184.35 (Padre Aguilar); 210.13; 214.36; ?†290.9—with John Hall—see Mac Adoo; 368. 33-34; 384.14; 386.6,12; 387.15; 389.17-18; 391.4,5; 397.2; 398.2 (Podex); †399.36—with James and John, John - a - Dreams (q.q.v.); 405.5-6; 475.29-30; 476. 27-28; 482.9,11,14; 521.10; 526. 18; †533.21—with Bach (q.v.); 573.8,28; 590.23.

MacDuff–the Thane of Fife in Shakespeare's *Macbeth* (q.q.v.). †77.14—with Hamlet (q.v.); 250. 34; 302.note 1; 411.11; †469.20,21 —with McAdam (q.v.).

*****MacDyke,** Dirty–in the context, the Dick of Tom Dick Harry. 8.27.

*****MacElligut,** Mr–perhaps P. Mac-Elligott of Limerick who discovered *Bearlagair Na Saer* (Vernacular of the Masons) in 1808. 365.26.

*****McEndicoth,** 277.note 4 (see Roe).

*****MacFarlane,** 180.10.

MacFarlane's Lament is the air to which Moore's (q.v.) "Shall the Harp Then Be Silent" is sung. 100.3.

*****MacFarlane,** Poor Piccolina Petite–seems connected with Santine's novel *Picciola* (1836) in which a prisoner saves his reason by tending a poor little flower who turns into a beautiful dream girl. 210.10.

*****MacFearsome**, Shrove Sundy, 227.31-32.

*****MacFewney**, MacGarath O'Cullagh O'Muirk–obviously Magrath (q.v.). 622.4-5.

*****Mac Gale**, Gush, 87.17.

*****MacGarry**, Moth, 526.23–24.

*****Mac Garvey**, 176.18.

McGee, Thomas D'Arcy (1825-68)– one of the poets of *The Nation*. 231.14 (horsery megee).

*****MacGhimley**–Luke Tarpey (q.v.) as the third letter of the Hebrew alphabet, Ghimel. 290.7.

McGinty–as in "Down Went". 366.32.

*****MacGolly**, Jolly–probably Johnny MacDougal (q.v.). 395.3.

*****McGree**, Graw–maybe Magrath (q.v.). 488.36.

*****MacGregor**, Father–Matt Gregory (q.v.)? 520.4,10.

McGuckin, Barton–Dublin tenor of Joyce's time. 180.8.

*****MacGuiney's**, 381.19.

*****Mac Gurk**, Mr–possibly the "Professor of Moral Philosophy", mentioned in Gogarty's (q.v.) *As I was Going Down Sackville Street*. 365.24-25; 378.25-26.

*****Mac Gusty** – probably Johnny MacDougal (q.v.) as the sense of taste. 305.note 3.

*****Mac Hamilton**, Hannibal – see Hannibal. 274.9-10.

MacHammud – see Mohammed. 156.22.

Machiavelli, Niccolo (1469-1527)– Italian statesman and author. 89.6-7; †182.20—with Nick (q.v.); 251.26-27.

*****Machonochie**, Middle, 228.1.

*****MacHooley**, Tulko, 125.4.

MacHooligan, Foyne – see Finn MacCool. 593.24-25.

Machree, Mother–Irish song. 397. 12; 542.20-21.

Machree, Widow–humorous poem by Lover (q.v.) in which the speaker advances reasons why the widow should marry him. 399.stanza 3; 456.35.

*****MacIsaac**, 227.33.

Mac Jeffet–see Japhet. 168.5-6.

*****MacJobber**, 178.22-23.

*****MacKenna**, 589.18.

*****Mackenzie**, Andy, 210.21-22.

MacKenzie, Miss–probably Trollope's (q.v.) title heroine, a middle-aged heiress, wooed by middle-aged men. 65.12.

Mack Erses's Dar–see Kersse. 575. 24.

*****Mackeys**–see Maggies. 106.11.

*****Mackinerny**, 264.left margin.

*****MackPartland**–see Mike Portlund. 67.25.

McKraw, Massach–see Magrath, Masoch. 284.note 4.

MacKundred, Ineen MacCormick MacCoort MacConn O'Puckins–Grania (q.v.). Mr Kelleher explains it thus: *inghean Cormaic mic Airt mic Cuinn Cétchatatch* or daughter of Cormac (q.v.) son of Art son of Conn (q.v.) of the Hundred Battles. I think Kundry, the saintly-siren girl of *Parsifal* (q.v.), may be included. See Miss McCormack. 376.1-2.

*****Macleay**, Marie Xavier Agnes Daisy Frances de Sales–all saints' names—see Xavier, François de Sales. 212.14-15.

*****MacLeish**–Archibald? Daniel Maclise (1806-70), Irish illustrator? 461.23.

Mac Loughlin, The – see Five Bloods. 271.1.

Mac Mahahon, Bernesson–see MacMahon, Man Servant. 340. 17.

MacMahon, Marie Esmé Patrice Maurice de, duke of Magenta (1808-93)–French marshal and president of France. He was descended from an Irish wild goose. He commanded a division in the Crimean war whose assault led to the fall of Sebastopol. The Man Servant (q.v.) is probably named Maurice Mahan, but I am at a loss to explain the connection, if any. 99.28; 254.3-4; 340. 17; 529.16.

*MacMannigan, Miss of Mrs, 523. 18.

Mac Milligan's daughter–see Alice Milligan. 133.26.

MacMurrough, Art–14th century king of Leinster who successfully fought off forces of Richard II (q.v.). 378.13-14; †380.22—with A. M. Kavanaugh (q.v.).

MacMurrough, Eva–daughter of Dermot MacMurrough, King of Leinster, who persuaded Henry II (q.v.) to send Strongbow (q.v.) to Ireland. Eva was married to Strongbow amid slaughter and carnage. 288.15.

*Mac Namara, Paddley, 325.23.

Mac Namara, The–see Five Bloods. 271.1-2.

MacNeill, John Gordon Swift (1849-1926) – Irish politician, writer. 450.6.

*Mac Noon, Andy, 72.1; 228.4.

Macoghamade–see Ogma. 89.30.

*MacPacem, Nerone, 212.4.

MacPerson–see James Macpherson. 123.25.

Macpherson, Aimee Semple – American female evangelist. She created a sensation in the 1920s by disappearing for a time with a man. 335.30; 351.33.

Macpherson, James (1736-96)– Scottish "translator" of the Ossian (q.v.) poems, whose hero is Fingal or Finn MacCool (q.q.v.).

123.25; 294.13; †423.1 – with James (q.v.).

Macrobius, Ambrosius Theodosius (fl. 395-423)–Roman grammarian, philosopher, author of *Somnium Scipionis.* 255.20.

*MacShane, Mistro Melosiosus MacShine–seems to be Shem (q.v.). 80.32; 437.33.

*MacSiccaries of the Breeks, 228. 2; 586.29-30.

*Macsorley, Fish hands, 408.25.

Macswiney, Terence – mayor of Cork, died in the 1920s on a hunger-strike in Brixton Prison. 535.20.

Mad Hatter–in *Alice in Wonderland* (q.v.). Joyce was so called by his schoolmates. 82-83.

*Madden–three characters in *Ulysses*: Mr Justice Madden; O. Madden, a jockey; William Madden, medical student. Sir Frederick Madden was an Irish palaeographer. 232.18; 240.12; 367. 16.

*Madison–James? 25.4.

Madonagh–see MacDonagh.

Maeterlinck, Maurice (1862-1911)– Belgian-French dramatist. 417.4.

?Maeve–a queen in Irish legend. 326.19.

Magda–English title and heroine of Sudermann's play, *Heimat*, 1893. The name always doubles with Maggies (q.v.). ?129.4; 139.32; ?436.12; †528.12 — see Four Evangelists.

Magdalene, St Mary–the penitent whore whose seven devils were cast out by Jesus. In FW the seven (q.v.) devils are, among other things, the multiple selves of a dissociated personality. See Maggies, Olona.

*Magee–I make no sense of John Eglinton in this passage, but he must be somewhere in FW. See Eglantine. 27.20.

Magellan, Ferdinand (1480-1521)–

first circumnavigator of the globe. 358.14; 512.5.

*Magennis, Mor–perhaps the Mrs M'Guinness of *Ulysses*, 217/282. 497.27.

Maggi–brand of dried Swiss soup. Perhaps in this context alphabet soup. †211.22—see Maggies.

Maggies–in FW Maggy (who gets the letter from Boston) and the Maggies are, I think, the singular and the plural state of the same thing, as the seven (q.v.) devils were the plural state of the singular Magdalene (q.v.), and the multiple selves were the plural state of the singular Christine Beauchamp (q.v.). At bottom—if there is a bottom to anything in FW—Maggy is Joyce's earlier heroine, Gretta Conroy (see Gretta Greene) who is Nora Barnacle. I may add that I am not sure of this.

　　See Margaret, Majesty, Gretchen, Magda, Pearl, Daisy, Onion, Peg, Grace O'Malley(?) and all those listed below with whom the Maggies combine.

7.32	maggy seen all (see Wall)
11.24	midgers and maggets
22.7	madesty
†27.20	whirligigmagees — with Magee (q.v.)
31.10	maggers
39.13	maggies
48.23	maggies
54.21,23	Maggis . . . Meggeg
†57.27	maugdleness — with Magdalene (q.v.)
66.19	Maggyer
67.31-32	magretta
†94.16	amygdaleine — with Magdalene (q.v.)
102.7	Pearlfar
106.11,23	Mackeys . . . Maggiestraps
111.11,15,16	Maggy . . . Muggy . . . Maggy
112.28	midget madgetcy (see Biddy Doran)
113.10,19	(in 100-letter word) . . . tentpegs

116.8,24	Margaret . . . Maggy's
120.17-18	maggers . . . majesty
†123.21	Neomugglian—with Muggleton (q.v.)
129.4	magd
139.10	pearly
142.30	maggies
†143.2	Peck-at-my-Heart—see Peg O'My Heart
35	pig . . . pigaleen (see Pig)
145.2	maggis
?149.7	pegged — see Pegger Festy
153.7,36	purliteasy . . . maudelenian — see Pearl, Magdalene
158.2	daisy's
159.13	tear . . . tear . . . tear
†164.8	M—with Fair Em (q.v.)
14,19-20	Margareen . . . Margareen . . . Margareena . . . Margareena
165.14,22	Marge . . . Marge
166.1,5,30	Margees . . . Marge . . . Margareena
171.25	magyansty
176.4	Moggie's
186.28	Mergyt
190.5	onions
199.12,15,26	purling . . . maggias . . . peg
202.8	perils
208.22-23	clothespeg
211.7-8	Olona Lena Magdalena (q.v.)
†22	Maggi — with Maggi (q.v.)
215.19	markets
219.31	Maggies
†225.26	pearl—with Cora Pearl (q.v.)
32	tears
226.1	pearlagraph . . . pearlagraph
228.5	maggoty mag
232.5	Mag
†236.9-10,21	paaralone . . . paaralone . . . purly—with Biddy Doran (q.v.)
237-238	magdelenes (q.v.)
242.17	rhainodaisies
247.21	margary
249.12	uniomargrits (see onion)
267.20	mag

272.9 daisy
273.note 6 Maggy . . . Maggy
276.15 pearls
278.note 6 modesties
280.14,20 maggy . . . mabby
281.6,14 la marguerite . . . Mar-
garitomancy
289.20 murty magdies
290.3 peg-of-my-heart (q.v.)
291.5 peggy
301.15 waggy
302.7-8 wiggywiggywagtail . . .
yaggy
†335.31 grace so madlley—with
Grace O'Malley (q.v.)
337.18 inmaggin
†338.28-29 Mollies Makehalpence—
with Molly McAlpin
(q.v.)
342.2 Dmuggies
†352.8 mairmaid maddeling—
with Maid Marian
(q.v.)?
354.27 magpyres
†363.3 upsadaisying Coras
pearls—see Cora Pearl
36 Meggy Guggy's
364.9-10,12 merging . . . mergers
. . . marchers
369.30 Madges Tighe
?376.18 Gormagareen
379.30 your Meggers
†387.19 Fair Margrate . . . Swede
Villem—see Margaret
and Sweet William,
see William
†394.35-36 peril-whited—with
Pearl White (q.v.)
399.stanza 2 pearl
†406.7 onion (Margareter, Mar-
garetar, Margarasti-
candeatar)—with
Margaret Anderson
(q.v.)
413.2,17,24 peg . . . tears . . .
maddlemass
420.7 madges (Madge is 18th
century for the female
organ)
434.16 Marie Maudlin (see Magdalene)
436.12 nursemagd
†451.3 madamaud—with Maud
Gonne (q.v.)

453.19 miry lot of maggalenes
(see Magdalene)
456.23 oinnos
†458.10 sester Maggy — with
Esther (q.v.)
18 magginbottle
459.4 nurse Madge
†460.26 Margrate von Hungaria
—with St Margaret of
Hungary (q.v.)
461.28 Mag
462.11 pearlies
478.7,9,12,17 maggers . . . Magis
. . . majestate . . .
Magis
†490.32 pool Pegeen—with hen
and pig (q.q.v.)
495.30 mergey margey magis-
trades
496.23 mirgery margery
504.36 pegging
506.22 onions
508.19 peggylees
†528.12 Magda — see Four
Evangelists
532.1 meg of megs
†537.34 Mons Megs (q.v.)
†538.24 gretched—see Gretchen
540.22 mansiemagd
549.20 peurls
†556.12 queenly pearl — with
Queen Margaret (q.v.)
561.15 daughterpearl
?562.21 maggots
†576.25,36 perils . . . magdalenian
jinnyjones—see Jin-
nies, Jenny Jones
577.16 peg
579.17 Peg
586.6-7,9,12,14,15 Maid Maud . . .
Madeleine . . . maud-
lin . . . maggies . . .
Madge Ellis Mag Dil-
lon
†594.11 Morkret Miry — with
Mary (q.v.)
615.3,13,31 Margaret . . . majesty
. . . margarseen oil
623.16 magyerstrape

Maggy and Michael–a possible explanation of the association of
these two is given under Gretta
Greene (q.v.). See also Maggies.

Maginn, William (1793-1842)–

Irish poet, journalist, author of *Homeric Ballads*, *Shakespeare Papers*. He drank himself to death. 302.11; 458.18.

*__Magnall__, Chudley, 88.24.

*__Magnes__—possibly the Athenian writer (fl. 460 B.C.). 375.28.

*__Magnus__, General Sir A. I., 329.5.

*__Magnus__, Spadebeard, 480.12.

*__Magnusson__—E. Magnusson, with William Morris (q.v.), translated the *Heimskringla*. The *Magnussaga* is an Icelandic saga. †574.2 —with Finn MacCool (q.v.).

*__Magories__, Johnny—*Ulysses*, 172/ 222: "If you didn't know risky putting anything into your mouth. Poisonous berries. Johnny Magories." 395.3; 397.25; 454.15.

*__Magory__, L'arty—possibly Lady Gregory (q.v.). 303.13-14.

*__Magrath__—one of FW's mysteries. I think he is the Cad with a Pipe, Gill, Snake, Satan (q.q.v.), but I can't prove it. He is certainly HCE's (q.v.) enemy and traducer, Anna Livia's (q.v.) particular hatred. He seems to be married to Lily Kinsella (q.v.); his servant is Sully (q.v.) the Thug. Magrath is perhaps meant for the Druid Mog-Ruith who made a great wheel which ran around the sky. The Magraths were hereditary custodians of Patrick's (q.v.) Purgatory. Magrath may be identical with some or all of the Magraths which follow this entry.

?4.4   Malachus Micgranes
145.22   Magrath
212.3   Master Magrath (q.v.)
243.3   magrathmagreeth (Irish *mo grádh mo chroidhe* or "love of my heart" —see also 488.36)
†284.note 4 Massach McKraw—with Masoch (q.v.)
296.note 3 Thargam
323.21   Mecckrass
353.10   my grafe
377.4   Mawgraw
?448.10   muckrake

488.36   Graw McGree
495.3   Magrath's
511.2   Magraw
572-573   Magravius (*passim*)
615.16,30 Mucksrats . . . me craws
618.1   MacCrawls
622.4   MacGarath O'Cullagh O'Muirk MacFewney

__Magrath__, Cornelius (1736-60)—Irish giant who was exhibited on College Green in Dublin and was befriended by Bishop Berkeley (q.v.). 98.9.

*__Magrath__, Mr Danl "Caligula" (q.v.), 60.26; 494.26.

__Magrath__, Master—Irish greyhound, won the Waterloo Cup in 1869; subject of a song. See Magrath. 212.3.

*__Magrath__, Mrs—see Magrath, Lily Kinsella. "Mrs Magrath" is an Irish song about a mother whose son has lost his legs in war. 204.34.

__Magravius__—see Magrath.

*__Magreedy__ prince of Roger—the actor Macready? See Roger. 373. 14-15.

*__Magtmorken__, 378.14.

__Maguires__, Molly—Irish secret society. 92.1-2,3-4.

__Mahaffy__, Sir John Pentland (b. 1839)—Irish classical scholar and wit, who said Dublin was where the possible was the improbable and the improbable, the inevitable. 110.7.

*__Mahamewetma__, 297.30.

__Mahan__, Mahon—see Man Servant (q.v.). See Playboy.

*__Mahony__—possibly Father Prout (q.v.). Man Servant (q.v.)? 133.2.

*__Maistre__—probably either Joseph de Maistre (1754–1821), French diplomat who wrote in praise of the hangman; or his brother Xavier (1763-1852), author of *Voyage autour de ma chambre*. 177.30.

__Majesty__—see Maggies, see Elizabeth I? James I?

Makefearsome–see James Macpherson.

Malachy II–predecessor of Brian Boru (q.v.) as king of Ireland. In 966 he fought the Dublin Danes. It was he who "wore the circle of gold,/That he won from the proud invader". 32.1; 151.24; †473.7— with Moloch (q.v.).

Malachy, St (1095-1148)–archbishop of Armagh, supposed author of *Prophecy Concerning the Future Roman Pontiffs*. 155.34.

Malakoff–fortification near Sebastopol, named for a drunken Russian soldier who opened a blind pig there. Stormed 1859. 339.11.

Malbruk–see Marlborough. 73.13.

*__Maldon__, Don, 94.2.

Malherbe, François de (1555-1628) –French critic. 478.9.

*__Malkos__, 512.22.

Mallon, John–Superintendent of the Dublin police at the time of the Phoenix Park assassinations. 34.3.

*__Mallon__, Tom–Tom Malone (q.v.)? 94.2.

*__Mallowlane__, 491.15.

*__Malone__, Thom–Thomas Malone Chandler is the hero of "A Little Cloud". 215.33; 256.11 (Halome); ?331.12.

Malorazzias–not a person, but *Malorusskij*, the dialect of the Ukraine. 338.22-23.

Malory, Sir Thomas–15th century author of *Morte d'Arthur* (q.v.). 229.10.

Malpas, Colonel–erected an obelisk on Killiney Hill, called thereafter Malpas High Hill. 81.15; 577.23.

Malthos–in Macpherson's "Temora" (q.q.v.), an Irish rebel warrior against whom Fingal (q.v.) fights. 231.28.

Malthus, Thomas Robert (1766-1834)–English economist. 585.11; 604.7.

Maltster–HCE (q.v.) as a brewer of beer, also Guinness (q.v.), also Willy Shakespeare (q.v.) who brewed a peck of malt during a famine. 3.25; ?231.28; 319.9; †337.28—with Finnegan; 338.1.

Mammon – Aramaic word for "riches" which, in the Middle Ages, became the name of the devil of covetousness. Milton (q.v.) revived the use in *Paradise Lost*. †13.20—with Four Evangelists (q.v.); 205.11; 535.6.

Mandig–see Dignam.

*__Mandrake__, Minucius–see Mencius? 486.13.

Manet, Edouard (1832-83)–French painter. 272.5.

*__Mangain's__, Mrs, 434.15.

Mangan, James Clarence (1803-49) –Irish poet, author of "Dark Rosaleen" (q.v.). Joyce wrote an essay about him. See Mann (q.v.) in the Cloack. 184.36; 211.1.

Mani (b. 527)–Persian heretic. In Scandinavian myth, *Mani* is the moon (q.v.). 472.20.

*__Manlius__, Publius–maybe HCE (q.v.). as Man of the Pub. 336.22.

Mann in the Cloack–Mangan (q.v.) was known as "The Man in the Cloak". He died of cholera morbus. *La cloaque* is French argot for "brothel". See also O'Connell (q.v.). 211.1.

Mann, Thomas (1875-1955)–German-American novelist. See Castorp (q.v.). 310.20.

Manners–see Rutland.

*__Manning__–all may be the Cardinal –see below. 182.25; 911.27.

Manning, Henry Edward (1808-92) English Cardinal. 282.21.

*__Manning__, Michael M., 31.19; 447. 12,14.

*__Manning__, Morty–mortemain? 329. 24.

Man o'War–American race horse. †525.32—with Manu (q.v.).

Man Servant–the Earwickers have two servants, Kate (q.v.) and a curate at the bar. He is "most mousterious" (15.32-33), meaning primitive (Mousterian), a servant-monster like Caliban (q.v.)—see also Dragon Man—and mysterious. He goes by certain names —Old Joe, Maurice (Moor), Behan-Beham (see Ham)—which are names of the dark races in their servitude. On the other hand, he is called Constable Saxon (and variations) and described as "butterblond". I assume therefore that he represents any subject race—black Ham, servant to white brothers—white Saxon Harold (q.v.), servant to Norman William (q.v.). The Irishman, Stephen Dedalus, describes himself as servant to England, the Saxon—*Ulysses*, 22/24. In the "Mutt and Jute" (q.v.) episode (16-18) the Man Servant is Mutt.

Another name of the Man Servant is Mahan or Mahon—"a quhare soort of a mahan" (16.1). A queer sort of man he seems to the conqueror: subject races are always queer, they smell funny, they are half animal. A queer sort of "mahan" means, at the same time, a queer sort of animal, for "mahan" and "mahon", so Mr Kelleher says, are anglicizations of the Irish *Mathglamhain* or "bear". (*Art* is also from an Irish word for "bear", but I don't think Joyce uses it so.) Mahan-as-bear fits, of course, neatly with the fact that the Man Servant is also Sackerson, the bear at the Paris Gardens on the Bankside—see *Ulysses*, 186/240—see also Hunks. (The bear theme in FW should be looked to.) Since I think FW is about Shakespeare (q.v.), I am delighted to find the Man Servant associated with both Caliban, the red Indian, and the baited bears of the Bankside. The form of Behan at 333.15, "behomeans", is nearly an anagram of "Bohemians" and reminds us of the

Bohemian bear in *The Winter's Tale*. For what it is worth, a note on p. 178 of *Scribbledehobble* reads: "Lizzyboy (bear)"—see FW, 530.21.

Readers of FW know that it contains many a reference to "bear". I have not listed these unless they are queer bears, walking more or less like men. Other bear references will be found under many of the people I ask you to q.v.

Teutonic words for "bear"—e.g. Danish *björn* (q.v.), Dutch *beer*—all come from "brown", the bear's most common color. (The bear, like subject races, may, of course, be brown, black, or white.) Thus there are many "Bruins" (q.v.) in the Browne and Nolan (q.v.) theme. I don't know why anymore than I know why Brian Boru (q.v.) and Bruin often go together. Speaking of Bruin, who is in the Reynard (q.v.) cycle, it may be significant that the cycle originated in Flanders, for Joyce surrounds—or planned to surround—the Man Servant with Flemish words—see letter to Miss Weaver, 24 September 1926.

An obvious and important association is that of bear and the Russian General (q.v.). (What, by the way, is the Russian word for "bear"?) The Russians are not notably a subject people, but the General is brought down from greatness by Buckley (q.v.). In Vico (q.v.) and FW no one stays a tyrant or a slave forever; they do not become free men, they just swap roles. In his fall, the Russian General is a baited bear—339.26-30, 340.17-24. Less importantly, bears are associated with Wall Street pessimists, with *boers*, Boers, boors, Bern (q.v.), Switzerland, and with female bears, Ursa Major and Artemis (q.v.).

There is plainly much to be worked out about the Man Servant, but I really do not think this note is too heavily weighted with bear. Hibernating, waking, the bear makes a very fair symbol of resurrection, personal or national; Bruin is always the gull in Reynard stories; the bear can be made to dance and ride a bicycle; he walks upright and on all fours, exemplifying inferior races which seem half-bestial to their masters.

The Man Servant represents not only the subject races of modern history, but the more primitive races of pre-history. He is "mousterian" and in the Mousterian period, Neanderthal man was giving up the ghost. More than that, the Man Servant as bear represents, I think, that most subject of all kingdoms, the animal. The bear was here on earth before man, just as the Utah Indian (16.10) was on the American continent and Caliban in Bermuda before Prospero or Trinculo-Stephano came to outsmart him. The Man Servant is not only subject, he is dispossessed, and as dispossessed ties onto one of the great themes of FW, a theme which includes the Irish, ass, St Patrick (when he was a slave with four masters, q.v.), Esau, Ham, Hamlet, Havelok (q.q.v.), and even Adam (q.v.), dispossessed of Eden and become a toiler. See also Playboy, MacMahon, Belchum.

15.30,35 be he . . . Comestipple Sacksoun
16.1 mahan
27.31 Behan
†40.11 beham — with Ham (q.v.)
63.35 Maurice Behan
?97.5 Mr Loewensteil Fitz Urse's
99.28 MacMahon (q.v.)
110.2,3 Brien . . . bearspaw (see Artemis)
30 sunseeker (see Seekersen)
141.27 ole Joe (see Joe)
170.3 jo
175.35,36 old Joe . . . old Joe

?184.2 jos
199.29 old Jo Robidson
201.24 mahun
212.2-3 O. B. Behan
221.6 Saunderson (Mr Knut Oelsvinger . . .)
230.3-4 owld jowly
245.33 Watsy Lyke
254.24,25,26 old Joe, the Java Jane . . . Mahun Mesme (*mesme* is Old French for *même*)
255.15 Bearara Tolearis (the Pole Star is in the Little Bear)
?284.note 4 Braham the Bear
?321.23 Odorozone
333.15 behomeans
334.11 "ground old mahonagyan" (see Gladstone, Nolan)
340.17 Bernesson Mac Mahon (see MacMahon)
†20-21 Bruinoboroff . . . grizzliest — with Brian Boru (q.v.)
353.12 Ussur Ursussen
370.30 Sockerson boy
371.6,16 siegguldson . . . sockson
?412.18 teom bihan
429.31 comestabulish Sigurdsen
430.7 the bear, the boer, the king of all boors, sir Humphrey (q.v.) his knave
471.30 Sickerson, that borne of bjoerne (note Joe)
31 Ursulinka (see Ursula)
511.20 suckersome
†529.16 O'Bejorumsen or Mockmacmahonitch—with MacMahon (q.v.)
†530.20 Roof Seckesign van der Deckel—with Vanderdecken (q.v.)?
21,22 Sickerson, the lizzyboy, Seckersen magnon of Errick . . . Sackerson (see Lizzy)?
?539.30-31 Allbrecht the Bearn
†556.23 Wachtman Havelook— with Havelok (q.v.)
566.10 boufeither Soakersoon
572-573 (*passim*) Mauritius

586.28   patrolman Seekersenn (q.v.)
588.31   behanshrub
608.10   Sigurd Sigerson
616.3   Eirinishmhan

Mantuanus, Baptiste–Renaissance poet, writer of Latin eclogues used in provincial schools in Shakespeare's (q.v.) time. See *Love's Labour's Lost,* IV, ii, 89-90: "good old Mantuan". 113.2.

Manu–the Adam (q.v.) of Indian myth. 25.16; 179.23; 344.17; 364.33; †525.32—with Man o'War (q.v.); 616.30.

Mara – a devil who tempted Gautama (q.v.) when he was fleeing temptation. Mara offered the kingdoms of the earth. 62.5.

***Marcella**–midget queen, *Ulysses,* 620/736. 112.28.

***March,** 442.15.

March Hare–character in *Alice in Wonderland* (q.v.). 210.15.

***Marchison,** Pat, 58.32.

Marcion–2nd century heretic who believed in two Gods. 192.1.

Marcon–see Marcion.

Marconi, Marchese Guglielmo (1874-1937)–Italian inventor of a system of wireless telegraphy. 407.20; 408.16.

Marcus Aurelius Antoninus (121-180)–Roman emperor, stoic philosopher. 132.19; 306.left margin.

***Marcus** of Corrig–Mark of Cornwall? Mark Lyons? (q.q.v.). 513.5.

Mardred–Mardrus, Modred (q.q.v.). 517.11.

Mardrus, J. C.–French translator of the *Koran* and the *Arabian Nights.* 374.12; ?†517.11—with Modred (q.v.).

Marengo–Napoleon's (q.v.) horse. See Copenhagen. 223.16.

Margaret–see Maggies.

Margaret and Sweet William–lovers in an old English ballad. See Maggies, William. 387.19.

Margaret, St–virgin martyr of Antioch whose feast is July 20. The Greeks call her Marina (q.v.). 146.12.

Margaret, Queen – character in Shakespeare's *Henry VI* and *Richard III* (q.q.v.). See Maggies. 556.12.

Marge, Margery, Margareen—see Maggies.

***Margrate** von Hungaria–perhaps St Margaret of Hungary who received the Stigmata. See Maggies. †460.26.

?Margutte–according to Brewer, a 10 foot high giant who died laughing on seeing a monkey pulling on his boots. The incident is referred to at 74.10.

Maria–character in Shakespeare's (q.v.) *Twelfth Night.* See Mary. 214.18.

Maria-Theresa   (1717-80)–Archduchess of Austria, Queen of Hungary and Bohemia. 538.1-2.

Marian, Maid–Robin Hood's sweetheart. See Mary 257.6-7; 276.note 2; †352.8—with Maggies (q.v.).

Mariana–girl who pines in a moated grange in Shakespeare's (q.v.) *Measure for Measure,* and was taken, in mistake for Isabella (q.v.) by Angelo (q.v.) by night. Also France. †102.28-29; 625.1—both with Anna Livia (q.v.).

***Marianne**–perhaps the above, but from context she seems to be the Mary of William and Mary—see William III, Wilkins. †106.17—with Anna Livia (q.v.) and Marina (q.v.).

Marie Louise–see Joséphine.

***Maries,** Two. See Mary. 126.30.

Marina–heroine of Shakespeare's *Pericles Prince of Tyre* (q.q.v.), so named because she was born at sea. Stephen Dedalus (q.v.), however, calls her "a child of storm" (*Ulysses,* 193/250). See Miranda, Perdita, Elizabeth Hall, Wilkins.   ?†102.28-29 — with

Mariana (q.v.); ?†106.17 — see William and Mary, Marianne; 162.16; 163.1 (arinam); †502.36 —with Mary Lamb (q.v.); 607.1.

Mario, Giuseppe, Count of Candia (1810-83)–most famous Italian tenor of the 19th century. †243.35 —with Marie Louise (q.v.); †246.17—with Marie Louise; 407.16; 408.11; 540.24.

Marius, Gaius (155-86 B.C.)–Roman general who drove the barbarians from Rome. †113.4—with Darius; 307.left margin.

Marivaux, Pierre Carlet de Chamblain de (1688-1763) – French novelist and dramatist who created a fantastic style, "an introduction to each other of words which have never made acquaintance, and which think they will not get on together". He also translated Homer (q.v.). 186.1-2.

Mark of Cornwall–uncle of Tristram of Lyonesse (q.v.), king. In some versions of the story of Tristram and Isolde (q.v.), Mark is a good man; in others, a cruel, crafty one. In all versions he is an older man who loses a young woman to a young man, playing in the triangle the same role as King Arthur, Finn MacCool, Shakespeare (q.q.v.). Mark is a character in Wagner's (q.v.) opera —see Mildew Lisa.
I would give a good deal to know if all "Marks" in FW refer to Mark of Cornwall. I would like to know his relation to Mark Lyons (q.v.), and to the Four (q.v.) who are certainly Mark in II,iv. I do not know if all of the following references are to Mark of Cornwall. See also Mark Twain.
?14.22; 17.1; †21.18—with Swan (q.v.); 22.5,29; 23.23; ?25.16; 76.8; †91.13—with King Arthur, Melkarth (q.q.v.); 96.5,6; 101.9; 135.1; 249.3; 266.9; 292.4; 298.6; 305.32; †318.29; 336.23; 348.24; 363.15; †372.4—with Moke, Swan

(q.q.v.); 376.16; 378.13; 380.4; 383.13,15,20,26; 388.2; 403.18; 423.3; †425.29 — with Mark Twain (q.v.); 442.18; 444.35; 446.17; 448.34; 464.3; 480.11; 491.17; 504.1-2 (backwards — cram is Ir. "trec"); 506.24; ?513.5; 515.3; 525.19,28; 564.2; 567.12; 585.15; 608.1; 621.18,20.

Mark, St–see Four Evangelists, Mark Lyons, Mark of Cornwall.

Markarthy – Mark of Cornwall, King Arthur, Melkarth (q.q.v.). 91.13.

Marlborough, John Churchill, 1st Duke of (1650-1722) – English general, subject of a French song. In 1690 he captured Cork and Kinsala for William III (q.v.). Some of the references include the 4th Duke (see Gunning) and the 7th Duke, an Irish viceroy. 57.35; 73.13; 105.8; 132.22; 569.14-15.

Marley–dead of course in Dickens's (q.v.) *A Christmas Carol.* †245.28 —with Mary Queen of Scots (q.v.); 365.29-30—see Joséphine.

Marlow–hero of Goldsmith's (q.v.) *She Stoops to Conquer.* 148.24.

Maron–4th century churchman whose followers were sometimes heretics, sometimes not. Joyce uses the Maronite ritual on FW 470. (Joyce to Miss Weaver, 8 August 1928.) 470.14.

Mars–Roman god of war, planet. See Ares, Bellona. †40.10—with Martha; 64.13; 134.12; 263.left margin; 353.2; 366.30; 494.12; †518.2—with Moses (q.v.).

Marsh, Narcissus (1638-1713)–protestant archbishop of Dublin and Armagh, founded the Marsh library in Dublin where Stephen Dedalus (q.v.) read. †212.31-32— with Narcissus (q.v.); 349.3.

Martha and Mary—represent the active and the contemplative lives (Luke 10)—see Rachel and Leah. 9.33; †214.23—with St

M. M. Alacoque (q.v.); 528.12; 529.11-12.

Martin, St–patron of drinking, jovial meetings, reformed drunks. His day is November 11, which is, I think, the leading contender for the date on which FW takes place. Sheelmartin lies between Dublin and Howth. 328.24; 419.8; 434.32; 517.34; 624.21.

*Martinetta, Mrs Magistra, 89. 20.

Marx, Karl (1818-83) – German socialist. 83.10,15; †365.20—with Mookse (q.v.).

Mary, Virgin–mother of Jesus. Joyce's own mother was Mary Jane Murray (q.v.), and his little boy naughtiness was doubtless in full play when he gave Mrs Bloom (q.v.) the name of Molly. A lot of the Marys listed below do not refer predominantly to the Virgin (q.v.) but I take her to be somehow present in every use of the name. See also Mary Shakespeare, Mary Fitton, Mary Lamb, Magdalene, Mariana, Marina, Miriam, William and Mary (Wm. III). 6.11; †27.12,15 — with Holly (q.v.); 53.30; †63.27—with Murray (q.v.); 81.28; †93.35—with Molly Bloom (q.v.); 126.30; †162. 16—with Marina (q.v.); †163.1—with Marina (q.v.); 177.2,6; 198. 8; 206.6 (12th century Dublin church); †208.35—with Murray (q.v.); 214.18; †227.17-18,29—with Murray (q.v.); 241.16; 244. 14-15; 264.note 3; 274.left margin; 300.12 (*bis*); 309.36; †316.21, 25—with Mary Fitton (q.v.); †329.34—with Healy (q.v.); 340. 28; †370.6—see Carey, Mather; 376.35; 404.34; 411.20; †435.30—with Healy (q.v.); 440.18—with Mary Lamb (q.v.), 36; †450.25—with Molly Bloom (q.v.); †472.15 —with Jesus, Krishna, Krisanamurti (q.q.v.); 492.31; †493.6—with Maya (q.v.), 7; †494.20—with Du Maurier (q.v.); 495.34; 502.22 (*bis*), †33,36—with Marina,

Mary Lamb; 503.15; 508.20; 524.21,26; †561.21 (*bis*)—with Bridget (q.v.); †562.12 — with Bridget (q.v.); †588.17 — with Holly (q.v.); 604.10.

Mary, Queen (1867-1953)–queen of George VI, born Princess May (q.v.) of Teck. See Albert Victor. 201.10; 208.34; 209.5.

Mary Queen of Scots (1542-87). †245.28–with Marley (q.v.).

Masaccio (1401-28)–Italian painter. 435.9.

Masoch, L. von Sacher (1835-95)–Austrian novelist. †284.note 4—with Magrath (q.v.).

Masons, Mutther–Freemasons, and *Bearlagair Na Saer* (Vernacular of the Masons). 223.5.

Massine, Leon–choreographer of the Russian Ballet. 219.17.

Masterbuilder–(*Bygmester* in the original)—Ibsen (q.v.) play in which the Masterbuilder, Halvard Solness (q.v.), rises from moral death by climbing, at the behest of a young woman from the hills, a tower which he has built. He falls from this tower, blasted by the God he has defied. The play is probably the most important source of the sexual symbolism of FW. See Hilda Wangel, Aline. †4.18—with Tim Finnegan (q.v.); 58.16; 62.3; 77.3; †111.21—with Billy (q.v.); 274.11; 296.7—with Billy (q. v.); 309.25; 324.27-28; 337.18-19; 377.26; 530.32; †576. 18,28—with Tim Finnegan (q.v.); †607.30-31—see Ffogg; 624.11 (soleness . . . bigmaster).

Masters–see Four Masters.

Mata–seven-headed tortoise, born of Eve (q.v.) and the serpent, who hollowed out the Boyne valley. The men of Ireland killed it and its ribs washed out to sea, then came ashore at Dublin where they were used to build the hurdleford. †609.6-8—with Four Evangelists (q.v.).

Matharan, M. M.–see Honuphrius. 572.19.

*****Mather**–a magician who put Tantric symbols on Yeats's (q.v.) forehead so he would see visions —cf. FW 486. I guess the references could include Cotton and Increase. 89.26; 146.5; 268.left margin; 288.8; 296.21; †370.6— with Mother Carey (q.v.); 389.6.

Mathew, Father Theobald (1790-1856)–Irish temperance advocate. †184.34 — with Matt Gregory (q.v.); †263.5-6 — with Tibbs (q.v.); 330.5; 443.28; †520.16— with Matt Gregory (q.v.); †553.13 —with Fra Diavolo (q.v.).

Mathurin, St–patron of fools. 335. 34-35.

*****Matieto,** la, 257.7.

*****Matrosenhosens**–*matrosen* is German "sailors", *hosen* is "trousers". 133.16.

Matthew, St–see Four Evangelists and see Matt Gregory.

Maturin, Charles Robert (1782-1824)–Irish novelist, dramatist. His best-known novel is *Melmoth the Wanderer* (1820) which is about a man who sells his soul to the devil and wanders thereafter miserably about Europe. Oscar Wilde (q.v.) called himself Sebastian Melmoth (q.v.) after his release from prison. 549.23.

*****Maucepan,** Susy–see Susanna, Mary? 562.14.

Maud–heroine of a Tennyson (q.v.) poem (1855). The reference may include Maud Gonne (q.v.). 253. 17.

Maule–wizard and his descendants in Hawthorne's (q.v.) *The House of the Seven Gables*. See Pyncheon. 437.31.

Maunsel–Dublin firm which was to have published the edition of *Dubliners* which the printers burned. 185.1-2.

Maurice, St–martyred with his entire Roman legion. In *Stephen Hero,* Stanislaus Joyce (q.v.) is called Maurice. †123.4 — with Meurice (q.v.).

Mauritius – see Man Servant. Maurice means "Moor" (q.v.).

*****Mauser,** Misma–cat? 568.1.

Mauser, Paul (b. 1838)–German inventor of a repeating gun. 354.12; 312.2.

*****Max**–perhaps Max Beerbohm (b. 1872), writer and caricaturist. I have always had an idea that part of the Museyroom episode might be based on a cartoon of his. 10.3,18; 248.34; 415.13.

Maxim, Sir Hiram (1840-1916)–gunsmith. 176.25.

*****Maximilian**–I cannot choose between all the noble Bavarians, Holy Roman Emperors, Mexican Emperors, etc. 607.2-3.

Maximus–four Roman emperors. 88.22.

Mayors of Dublin–see Lord-Mayors.

Maxwell, James Clerk (1831-79)–British physicist. 130.11.

*****Maxwelton,** Bareniece–wife of the Cad (q.v.). Her name seems to have something to do with "Maxwelton's Braes". See Niece? 38.9.

May, Princess of Teck–see Queen Mary.

Maya–mother of Gautama (q.v.). See †317 in Mr Connolly's *The Personal Library of James Joyce*. 59.14; †234.13 — with Queenie (q.v.); †493.6—with Mary and Anne (q.q.v.).

Mayhew, Thomas (1592-1683)– early settler and grantee of Martha's Vineyard. 549.25.

*****Mazourikawitch**–Chopin? 437.29.

Mazzaccio–see Masaccio.

Mazzini, Giuseppe (1805-72)–Italian revolutionary. 173.15.

*****Meade**–see Meath? 18.22; 41.10; 95.7; 336.7.

Meade, Joseph–lord-mayor of Dublin, 1891-92. 590.6.

Meads Marvel–the ass (q.v.) as Meath. 479.9.

*****Meagher,** Wally–appears to have inherited a pair of trousers, to have been involved in some kind of "troth". I do not think he is Thomas Meagher. 61.13,19,22; 211.11; 214.4; 508.15.

Mealterum–see Matharan.

Meath–see Ass.

Mebbuck at Messar–see Nebuchadnezzar. 344.16.

Medard, St–6th century French bishop, patron of rain. 185.21; 433.35.

Medea – Greek enchantress — see Jason. 348.7.

Medici–great family of the Italian Renaissance. 517.6.

Meehan, Mr R. E.–see Ahriman. 466.33.

*****Meelisha's** deelishas–Lisa? Melissa? Isha? Elisha? Dilys? Delia? (q.q.v.). 351.23.

Meg–see Maggies.

Meg, Mons–big gun on Castle Rock, Edinburgh—see Scott's "Bonnie Dundee". 537.34.

*****Megan,** St, 243.27; 378.19.

*****Megrievy,** widow, 227.6.

*****Meiklejohn,** Dan, 60.31.

*****Meinfelde,** Mistress B. de B. Minefields and BeeBee guns? 184.27-28.

Meithne–see Eithne.

*****Melamanessy,** Dr, 505.24.

Melampus–legendary seer, introduced the worship of Dionysus (q.v.) into Greece. 380.7.

Melanchthon, Philipp (1497-1560) German theologian. 416.19-20.

Melba, Nellie (1861-1931)–Australian soprano. She sang Juliet to Jean de Reszke's Romeo (q.q.v.) in Gounod's opera. 200.9; 494.29.

*****Meldon,** Dan, 94.2.

Melecky–Arabic for "angel" or "king". See Festy King. 86.8.

*****Melekmans,** Milcho–Milcho or Milchu (q.v.) was the man for whom St Patrick tended cows when a slave in Ireland. See Melecky. 366.17.

Melkarth–god of Tyre, associated with Baal (q.v.). †91.13—with Mark of Cornwall, King Arthur (q.q.v.); 538.8.

Melmoth, Sebastian – see Oscar Wilde and C. R. Maturin (q.q.v.). 228.33; 587.21.

*****Melooney,** Tommy – see Tom Malone? 331.12.

Melpomene–muse of tragedy. 569.29 (Moll Pamelas).

*****Melton,** Andraws–possibly Andrew Mellon. 328.5-6.

Melville, Herman (1819-91)–American novelist. I am not sure the following references are to Melville. See Ahab, Billy Budd. 40.11; †283.28—with Herman (q.v.); †342.20—see Entwhistle.

Mencius–Latinized form of Mangtaze or Mr Mang, Chinese philosopher, d. 289 B.C. 159.34; 486.13.

?Mencken, H. L. (b. 1880)–American writer. 110.13.

Mendelssohn-Bartholdy, Jacob Ludwig Felix (1809-47)–German composer. 377.15; 528.8.

Mendoza–the devil in Shaw's (q.v.) *Man and Superman.* See John Tanner, Anne Whitefield. †312.8 —with Thor (q.v.).

Meno–title character of a Platonic (q.v.) dialogue in which a slave boy is given a geometry lesson. 294.12 (me now); 297.6; 341.4 (menody); 415,34,35; ?615.8-9.

Menshikov, Alexander Sergeivich, Prince (1787-1869)–Commander-in-Chief of the Russian forces in the Crimean war. He was responsible for the field operations around Sebastopol. 339.12 (manchokuffs).

Mephistopheles–first appeared in the German *Faust* (q.v.) of 1587 as the evil spirit to whom Faust sells his soul. See Countess Cathleen. 441.11-12 (Mavis Toffeelips).

Mercadante, Saverio (1789-1870)–Italian composer. 327.18; 360.8 (Smirky Dainty).

Mercius or Mercy is Shem (q.v.). See Justius. 193.31.

Mercury–Roman god of merchants, etc., identified with Hermes (q.v.), also a planet, an alchemical substance, a medicine, perhaps even Shakespeare's Mercutio (q.q.v.). 163 and 484 play on a remark of Pythagoras (q.v.), who, meaning we can't all read FW, said: *Non ex quovis ligno Mercurius fit*. 163.15; 183.35; 184.9; 251.15; 454.20-21; 484.36; 494.12; 548. 31.

Mercutio–see Mercury?

Mereshame, Mistress – a meerschaum (sea-foam) pipe—see Cad. Perhaps also, as the *Skeleton Key* suggests, Venus (q.v.). 241.14.

Merlin–powerful enchanter in the Arthurian (q.v.) stories. *The Birth of Merlin or The Child Hath Found His Father* is a pseudo-Shakespearean (q.v.) play. 5.35; 28.20; 151.31; 285.2; 358.15; †387.28—with Martin Cunningham (q.v.).

Merodach or Marduk–Babylonian sun-god. 254.28; †325.32—with St Mark (q.v.).

Merope–there are a good many Meropes in Classical myth. I fancy Joyce is thinking of the mother of Daedalus (q.v.). 273.10.

?Merriwell, Frank–hero of a series of American boys' stories. †440.36 —with Mary (q.v.).

Merry Monarch–see Charles II. 525.16-17.

Merrytricks, Honorbright – see Honor Bright. 60.6; 211.33.

Merry Wives of Windsor–Shakespeare's (q.v.) Mrs Ford and Mrs

Page. See Anne Page. 183.26; 227. 1-2.

*Meschiameschianah – probably Hebrew for "horrible death". 358.19.

Mesmer, Franz (1733-1815)–Austrian doctor who gave us the word "mesmerism". 360.24; 476. 7.

*Mesopotomac, old mother–the reference is to Anna Livia (q.v.) who, I guess, combines Mesopotamia and the Potomac (old world and new) because Eve, mother of the old world and the new, was born in Eden which was in Mesopotamia. 559.35.

Messop, Mr–see Mossop.

Metellus–a number of distinguished Romans. 252.15.

Methodius–and Cyril—the two great saints of the Eastern church. 159.31; 528.23.

Methusalah–lived 187 years and begot Lamech (q.v.). 378.15.

Metternich - Winneburg, Prince (1773-1859)–Austrian statesman. 339.5.

Mettresson, Master–the mattress of the Earwicker's (q.v.) bed. See Glimglow. 585.6.

Meurice, François Paul (1818-1905) –French dramatist who, with Vacquerie and Gautier, produced an imitation *Falstaff* (q.v.) and with Dumas a sort of a *Hamlet* (q.v.). †123.4—with St Maurice (q.v.).

Meyerbeer, Giacomo (1791-1863)– German composer. 360.7 (mere Bare).

*Mezienius, 483.32.

*Mezosius, 483.32.

Mezzofanti, Giuseppe Caspar (1774-1849)–Italian cardinal and linguist. He spoke fluently some fifty or sixty languages of the most widely separated families, and was less perfectly acquainted with many more. 260.21.

Micah–an Old Testament book and a man whose history enters into that of the foundation of the Israelite sanctuary at Dan (Judges 17 ff.). 153.32.

Micawber, Wilkins–character in Dickens's *David Copperfield* (q.q.v.), modelled on Dickens's own father, John. John Shakespeare (q.v.) has been called "an Elizabethan Micawber" and John Joyce (q.v.) was the same fine kind. 131.16.

Miccheruni–Micky Rooney's band, *Ulysses*, 284/373. 407.33.

*Micgranes, Malachus – Magrath (q.v.)? 4.4.

Michael–the archangel. His day is 29 September. See Father Michael, Mick.

Michael Cerularius–broke from the supremacy of the Popes and es-tablished the Greek Church in 1054. In the context of FW he is Father Michael (q.v.)—I don't know why. 573.4.

*Michael, Father–the man Anna Livia (q.v.) loved and seduced when she was young, before she married HCE (q.v.). He appears but once in FW, in the "Anna Livia Plurabelle" section where beyond question he assumes the role of Adam, tempted to his fall. Otherwise he is a character always off-stage, always absent, always hoped for in Anna Livia's letter from Boston, Mass. Mrs von Phul thinks Father Michael is composed of Michael Bodkin (q.v.) and the young James Joyce. This seems to me the best solution yet, but not exactly right. At any rate, he is the lost lover, "the boy in his innocence" who the woman has destroyed and wishes she hadn't. I do not think he is exactly "Mick" (q.v.), a Shaun role, though the two are surely connected. Father Michael is a real live lover, a man of flesh and blood, while Mick-Shaun is, I think, that lover recollected by the frustrated female and sent walking like a zombie around the world. Father Michael *is* the archangel (see above); Mick only plays at being. 11.23; 94.36; 111. 15; 115.26.29; 116.7; 203.18 (see Arklow); 215.21; 279.note 1; 280. 13; 365.1; 369.32; 382.12; 432.7; 447.12; 458.3; 459.2; 461.21; 533. 29,32; †573.4—with Michael Cerularius (q.v.), 15,18,23; 617.25; 618.3.

Michael, Grand Duke–various prominent Russian nobles. 329.29.

Michael, Hetman–character in *Jurgen* (q.v.). †243.14—with Finn (q.v.).

Michan, Bishop and Mrs–not people but St Michan's church in Dublin, a Church of Ireland church, whose vault is full of well-preserved corpses. St Michan was Danish. 36.29; †443.35—with Michael (see Mick); 455.18; †541.5—with Michael (q.v.).

Michelangelo (1475-1564)–Florentine painter. †81.23—with Michael (see Mick); 161.1; †230.3—with Michael (see Mick) and Angelo (q.q.v.); †407.15-16—with Michael Kelly (q.v.).

Michele, Chelli–see Michael Kelly. 199.28.

Michelet, Jules (1798-1874)–French historian, friend and collaborator of Quinet's (q.v.), translator of Vico (q.v.). 117.11.

*Michelides Apaleogos–possibly Michael Palaeologus (1234-84)— Byzantine emperor. See Mick. 349.23.

Mick and Nick–archangel and devil, Shaun and Shem (q.v.)—also called Chuff and Glugg (q.v.). These are the parts played by the Earwicker (q.v.) twins in "The Mime of Mick, Nick and the Maggies" (q.v.). I do not understand "The Mime", I don't even know what happens in it. I assume that its subject is Milton's (q.v.) dubious battle on the plains of heaven, presented by a company of child actors, "little eyases" of *Hamlet*, who rival the adult players, parody their parts. See Father Michael, Lucifer, Maggies.

505.32-33,34-35 looseaffair . . .
            knickknaver, knacked
            . . . knechtschaft
506.1   nickelname
508.33   knickt
515.7,8   Nock . . . Mock
520.1   feelmick's
538.4   mick
540.30   hairtrigger nicks (Nick
            Carter?)
†541.4-5   Nicholas Within . . .
            Michan (q.v.)
†546.4   neckamesh—with Shem
            (q.v.)
549.4   nickenbookers
559.11-12 Michael . . . Satan
567.16   Michalsmas
570.22-23 mic . . . mac . . . mick's
596.32   mickwhite
602.17   "Mike" Portlund—see
            Mackpartland?
621.2-3   santomichael . . . lausa-
            fire

Micky and Minny Mouse–characters in Disney cartoons. 12.24-25.

Micmacrobius – see   Macrobius. 255.20.

Midas–legendary king of Phrygia. Dionysus (q.v.) gave him power to turn all he touched into gold; he nearly starved before the god revoked the gift. In a musical contest, he voted against Apollo (q.v.), who gave him ass's ears. Midas's ears were known to his barber who whispered the secret to river reeds, and they told it to the world. 158.7; 481.33; †482.4 —with de Sade (q.v.)?; 496.20-21.

*Midweeks–perhaps Luke Tarpey (q.v.)—see 399.stanza 3. Perhaps Odin (q.v.). 63.8.

*Migo, 146.36.

Milchu or Milcho–owner of St Patrick (q.v.) when he was a slave in Ireland. When Patrick returned, a missionary, to Ireland, he sought out Milchu to convert him. Milchu burned himself and his house up when he saw the saint coming. 241.22; 366.17.

Mildew Lisa—see Lisa.

*Milikens, 176.16; 318.15; 334.35.

*Miliodorus and Galathee — see Galatea. 32.12.

Mill, John Stuart (1806-73)–English philosopher and economist. Among his works are: *England and Ireland* (1868) and *Subjugation of Women* (1869). The joke about "Ditto on the Floss" can be found in the 11th *Britannica*, "Index". 213.2; ?414.34; 416.33.

*Miller, 84.1.

Miller, Joe (1684-1738)–English actor who gave his name to any time-worn joke. †71.7-8—with Josephine Brewster and Milton (q.q.v.).

*Millicent, 123.15.

Milligan, Alice–author of *The Last Feast of the Fianna* which was played at the Abbey (q.v.). 133.26.

Milltown–see Milton.

Milner, Alfred, Viscount (b. 1854)– British colonial administrator, annexed the Transvaal. See Whang. 341.5.

Militiades Strategos–led the Greeks at Marathon. 307.left margin.

Milton, John (1608-74)–English poet. I can't help feeling that there must be a great great deal more Milton in FW than I have found. Milltown is an environ of Dublin and an end to care. †71.7 —with Joe Miller (q.v.); 96.10.

*Mimi, 194.4.

Mina—not a person but a place in Arabia. The pilgrim to Mecca must stop at Mina and throw stones at pillars. 318.18.

*Minace, old–menace? See Minos. 95.1.

Mindelsinn–see Mendelssohn.

Minerva–the Roman Athena (q.v.). 61.1.

*Ming, Ching, and Shunny, 57.5.

Minnehaha–Hiawatha's (q.v.) girl. Her name means "Laughing Water". 206.15-16; 450.5; 600.7.

Minos – semi-legendary king of Crete, son of Zeus (q.v.), husband of Pasiphaë, father of Ariadne and Phaedra, patron of Daedalus (q.v.) who built a labyrinth for him. After death he became a judge in the underworld with Aeacus and Rhadamanthus (q.v.). 95.1.

Minthe–one of those pursued maidens who ended up a plant. 417.16.

*Mippa, 280.18.

Miranda–heroine of Shakespeare's (q.v.) *The Tempest.* Her name has to do with Latin *mirandus* and Ferdinand (q.v.) addresses her as "O you wonder!". (See *Ulysses,* 193/250.) As "Wonder" she appears in FW. See Prospero, Caliban, Perdita, Marina, Elizabeth Hall. 147.28; ?248.34; 265.15-16; 270.20; 281.2; 295.15,16; 300.19; 318.17 (*bis*); 327.7; 331.1; †363.23 —with Perdita (q.v.); 336.16; 374.3,9; 375.35; 388.2-3; 395.31; ?443.36; 454.23; 508.6; †576.21— with Perdita (q.v.); 597.29.

Mireille–heroine of a Mistral (q.v.) epic and a Gounod opera. 527.28.

Miriam–Moses's sister (Exodus 15). See Mary. 265.22; 366.35; 427.25; 561.21.

Mirilovis–see Marie Louise.

*Miserius, 128.13.

*Mishe Mishe to Tauftauf–Joyce says "Mishe" means "I am (Irish) i.e. Christian", and he says "Tauf" is "baptise (German)". (Joyce to Miss Weaver, 15 November 1926). I do not understand the theme, but it is obviously an important one in FW and refers, at least some of the time, to persons. See Meath, Issy, Taff? 3.21; 12.22; 65.31; 80.7; 87.24; 92.31; 96.11, 12; 102.28; 104.23; 117.17,18; 125.1; 145.7,8,24; 148.2; 167.19; 191.36; 202.30; 203.29,30; 225. 20,21; 228.3; 240.24,25; 249.29; 277.11; 290.21; 291.24; 320.23; 338.12; ?341.16; 342.3; 349.24; 352.12; ?354.28; 366.13; 434.24;

446.18; 457.25; 459.3-4; 460.24; 466.12; 468.8; 481.26; 483.8; 486.14; 505.20,23; ?537.5; ?549.4; ?561.13; 605.2; 606-607.

Mistinguette–French dancer (d. 1956). 32.12.

Mistral, Frederic (1840-1913) Provençal poet. 241.18.

*Mitchel, Miry, 13.9.

Mitchells–see Mick. 281.note 4.

Mithra or Mithras–Persian god of light, whose worship rivalled Christianity in the Roman empire. Also an avatar of Vishnu's (q.v.). 80.24; 578.10.

Mix, Tom–American star of silent western pictures. See Tom. 50.34; 58.24.

*Mmarriage, Llewelyn, 210.12.

Mnepos–see Nepos. 392.18.

Mobbely, Eva–fickle Eve. "mobled queen"? 210.30.

Mock-Comic, Joan–see John McCormack. 222.7.

Mockmacmahonitch – see MacMahon. 529.16.

Mock Turtle and Gryffin–characters in *Alice in Wonderland* (q.v.). †358.21-22—with Mookse and Gripes (q.v.); †393.11 — with Mookse (q.v.).

Modred or Mordred–son and nephew of King Arthur (q.v.) who brought down the Round Table. Joyce also plays on Irish *madradh,* dog. 8.24; 132.5; 250.17; †517.11 —with Mardrus (q.v.).

*Moedl's, Suzy's – in Austrian dialect *süsse Mädls* are "sweet girls". See Susanna? 405.15.

*Moels–Welsh for mountains. 390. 9.

*Moffat–see Ham, Shem, Japhet. 87.10.

*Mofsovitz, 514.30.

Mohammed or Mahomet (570-632)–founded the Moslem religion. 156.22; 244.36; 312.20 (maomette); 353.6; †418.18 — with

Hamlet (q.v.); 623.12 (me homage me hamage).

*Mohorat, 33.16.

Moke–see Ass.

Molly–see Bloom.

Moloch–Jewish god to whom children were sacrificed (Lev. 28; 2 Kings, 23). In *Paradise Lost*, one of the chief fallen angels. †473.7 —with Malachy II (q.v.).

Molroe, Mrs–"Moll Rowe", the air to which Moore's (q.v.) "One Bumper at Parting" is sung. 87.2.

Moltke, Helmuth, Count von (1800-91)–Prussian field-marshal. 333. 13.

Mommsen, Theodor (1817-1903)– German historian, wrote of Rome. 155.33.

*Momonian, 387.18.

*Momuluius, Saint – Mamalujo? See Four. 484.11.

*Mona–moon (q.v.)? 61.1; 464.32.

Moncrieff, Algernon–character in Wilde's (q.v.) *The Importance of Being Earnest* (q.v.). 536.12.

*Mongan, Roche–Mongan was a 7th century Irish hero, a reincarnation of Finn MacCool (q.v.). The whole name doubtless refers to Stone Mountain, Georgia, traditional meeting-place of the Ku Klux Klan. Roche Mongan is first known as Peter Cloran (q.v.) and the Kloran is the sacred book of the KKK. St Roche is patron of the plague-stricken. 41.4.

Monks, Dolly–Dollymount (q.v.), an environ of Dublin. 294.21.

Montague – a noble family in *Romeo and Juliet* (q.v.). 516.21.

Montaigne, Michel de (1533-92)– French essayist. 225.15.

*Montan–perhaps the Phrygian heretic, Montanus. 260.29.

Montez, Lola (1818-64)–stage name of Marie Dolores Eliza Rossana Gilbert, an Irish girl who became a dancer and mistress of Ludwig I of Bavaria. She devoted her last years to visiting outcasts of her own sex in New York and lecturing on "gallantry". ?434.23; 525.14.

Montezuma–emperor of the Aztecs, conquered by Cortez. See Atahualpa. 339.33.

*Montgomery – perhaps James Montgomery, Dublin wit. 426.11; 525.7; 543.28.

*Montmalency, 318.2.

Moody, Dwight Lyman (1837-99) and Ira David Sankey (1840-99), American evangelists who had a great success in England and were famous for their *Gospel Hymns*. They visited Dublin in 1875. †60.19 — with Gautama (q.v.); 533.20.

Mookse and Gripes (Fox and Grapes??)–Shaun and Shem (q.v.). Joyce said their little fable has to do with the "Old Catholics" who in 1870 broke with the Vatican over papal infallibility and the *sacrificio del intelletto*. The Mookse is the Pope, specifically Adrian IV (q.v.), born Nicholas Breakspear, an Englishman, whose bull, *Laudabiliter*, was later used to sanction Henry II's (q.v.) conquest of Ireland. (This bull is held by some to be a forgery.) The Gripes is whoever does not submit to the Pope, particularly Adrian's enemy Barbarossa (q.v.) — the Barbarossa is a kind of grape. Beyond this I am all at sea and by no means steadied by Joyce's cryptic post-card to Miss Weaver (16 April 1927): ". . . you must not think it a silly story about the mouse [sic] and the grapes." In the 17th century a "gripes" was a crooked gambler. See Fox.

70.32	Mooxed
72.10,20,27-28	Sower rapes . . . gripes . . . mocks . . . grapes
78.24	druiven . . . muskating
87.22	creepfoxes
†105.27	Smocks . . . Graces — with Gracehoper (q.v.)

†140.2 Antwarp . . . Musca—Ondt (q.v.)

141.21 must begripe

152-159 Mookse and Gripes (*passim*)

†155.31 Niklaus Alopsius—with Nicholas Breakspear (q.v.) (I am told *alopex* is Greek "fox" and *alopecis* is Latin for a grape vine whose grapes look like a fox's tail.)

192.3-4 monkax . . . ape

231.35-36 Mookery mooks . . . grippe . . . gripes

†234.2,10 griposly . . . mookst kevinly—with Kevin (q.v.)

268.11 mugs . . . grooser's

271.left margin hyperape . . . mink

299.13 mooxed and gaping

301.26 griper

306.9 mugs and the grubs

†331.16-17 mokes . . . gribes (see Moke)

339.35 monkst

343.24 smooking

†358.21-22 amock . . . gryffygryffygryffs—with Mock Turtle and Griffin (q.v.) and see also Vogel Gryff

364.25 Mucias and Gracias

365.14-15 meekst . . . graced

†20 Marx . . . Groups—with Marx (q.v.)

†393.11-12 muckstails turtles . . . griesouper — with Mock Turtle (q.v.)

412.17 verjuice

418.33 mocks . . . gropes

432.34-35 mokst . . . grapce

465.35 gripes

489.4 Fullgrapce . . . muxy

568.11 Muchsias grapcias

579.13 Monks . . . Grasps

†614.1 Mopsus . . . Gracchus (q.q.v.)

*Moon—the following references are a most inadequate sampling of moons. Only lately, I have seen the great importance of the moon in FW, and my remarks about it are crude and hasty. It is clear that Anna Livia (q.v.) is Artemis (q.v.). See also Delia, Diana, Selene, Phoebe, Hecate, Lamp, Elizabeth I, Biddy Doran, Amazia, Gallagher. The moon is also the lamp carried by Shaun the Post (q.v.)—see Moonshine; now and then the moon is the Ark (see 244.26), for the story of Noah (q.v.) has been interpreted as a lunar myth. The twenty-eight or twenty-nine (q.v.) girls are "lunar sisters". I am sure there is something which pulls all these diversities together, but I have not seen it. Perhaps the nature of the moon is governed by its phase. In Irish "moon" is *ré* and *gealach*. 27.15; 61.1; 64.6; 65.9; 90.10; 92.12,24; 94.14-15; 104.13; 144. 25; 157.15; 167.34-35; 190.32; 192.30; 201.10; 202.22,28; 212.16; 215.4; ?219.31; 244.4,5,26; 245.7; 256.36 (*bis*); 264.4; 267.3,22; 271.note 1 (*bis*); 276.note 3; 285. note 5; 329.19-20; 340.20-21,32; 341.16; 360.25; 364.13; 375.12; †377.15-16 — with Horniman (q.v.); 385.29; 389.5; 395.13; 408.34; 413.13; 428.8; 436.28; 439.8; 449.35; 464.7,32; 477.27, 30; 478.15; 502.14; 504.36; 507. 17; 519.21; 528.5; 538.23; 549.13; 566.5; 623.26; 627.28,30 (Amazia . . . Niluna, q.q.v.), 34.

Mooney, Mrs–landlady in Joyce's story "The Boarding House", whose daughter waits upstairs while an argument rages. See Moon. 17.1-2; 157.15.

Moonlight, Captain–during the 19th century land agitation, groups of Irish shot people and maimed cattle and said it had been done by Captain Moonlight, as the Luddites smashed machines in the name of Captain Lud. 495.14.

Moonshine–whisky, nonsense, the role played by Starveling (q.v.) in "Pyramus and Thisbe" (q.v.) in Shakespeare's (q.v.) *A Midsummer Night's Dream.* I believe that in III,i,ii Shaun (q.v.) plays, among other things, Moonshine, while Shem plays Bottom (q.v.), translated into an ass (q.v.). 73. 21; 138.31; 440.31; 489.27.

Moonshine, Miss Cecilia and Edgar –characters in *Boots About the Swan*—see Jacob Earwig. See also above. 64.6.

Moor–see Othello, Maurice, Thomas Moore, Thomas More, George Moore, Sycamore.

Moore and Burgess–black-faced minstrels whose troop came to London in 1862 and was not dissolved till 1904. One of their catch-lines was, "Take off that White Hat"—see Finn MacCool. See also Thomas and George Moore and Charles Burgess, who may be comprehended here. 62. 30-31; 160.25; 516.31-32.

Moore, George (1852-1933)–born at Moore Hall in Galway, novelist, author of *The Lake, Esther Waters* (q.v.), *Hail and Farewell*, all of which are mentioned in FW. See Dean, Dayne, Four, George, Gogarty. Moore very often turns up near references to his good friend AE (q.v.); I have not succeeded in separating him from references to Thomas Moore (q.v.).

George Moore had, like Swift, a Stella (q.q.v.) whom he somewhat chilled. Thus, he is included in all the Moore Park references. Incidentally, Moore Park is not just Sir William Temple's (q.v.) estate, but also an apricot (mentioned in *Mansfield Park*). This ties Moore Park to fruit and temptation. 28.9; 140.30,34 (see Four); 160. 25; ?†229.3—with St George (q.v.); †281.20-21—with Othello, Sycamore (q.q.v.); 305.8; †316.7; 359.35-36; ?399. stanza 4; 410. 29; 449.31-32; 599.18-19 — (see George).

Moore, Mot–1) *Old Moore's Almanack*, still published in England and 2) Thomas Moore (q.v.). 206.12.

Moore, Thomas (1779-1852)–Irish poet, song writer. Mr M. J. C. Hodgart discovered that the opening phrase of most of Moore's *Irish Melodies* appears in FW and near at hand are the airs to which they are sung. Mr T. Wilder discovered that "Moore" or "more" or "Tom", etc. occurs near every one of the quoted *Melodies*, but I have not attempted to list all these. There is a statue of Moore in Dublin.

It is hard to separate all Thomas and George Moore (q.v.) references. Many Tom (q.v.) references may be to Moore. Some of the references below may be to St Thomas More (q.v.).

15.14; 20.2-3; 106.8; 184.15; †206.12—see Mot Moore; 316.7; †331.12—see Tom Malone; 439.9; 468.27; 477.29; 492.34.

*****Moore,** Unity, 101.8.

*****Moorehead,** 426.8.

*****Moors** or lett's, 78.28.

Mopsus–1) soothsayer of the Argonauts or 2) son of Apollo and Manto, also a soothsayer. †614.1 —with Mookse (q.v.).

Mora and Lora–two hills which abound in "Fingal" and "Temora" (q.q.v.). 131.23-24.

Moran–Counsellor of Feredach the Just. Moran devised a collar which strangled the wearer if he deviated from the strict rules of equity. ?102.18; 133.2.

?More, St Thomas (1478-1535)– English humanist.—May be comprehended in some Tom Moore references (q.v.). 534.8,14.

*****Morehampton,** S.E.–a Dublin road. 354.16.

Morell, Lady Otoline–English patroness of artists. 229.35.

*****Morfydd,** 529.25.

*****Morgan,** 127.31; 518.26; 530.13; 584.25.

Morgan, Appleton–anti-Stratfordite, author of *The Shakespeare Myth*, 1881. 36.5.

Morgan, Lady Sidney (1783-1859) –Irish novelist, author of such works as *O'Donnell, The Wild Irish Girl.* 60.33-34.

Morgana–as Morgana le Fay, a sorceress in the Arthurian stories. She dispenses treasure in *Orlando Furioso.* In *Ogier the Dane* she rejuvenates Ogier when he is over 100 and marries him. The *Fata Morgana* in Sicily is a mirage at sea. 20.33; †224.29—with Anna Livia (q.v.); 570.12.

*Morgen–maybe just morning. See Morgan. 221.30; 547.35; 584.25.

Morialtay–see Rowley the Barrel. 376.30; 602.9.

Moriarty, Biddy–one of the guests at Finnegan's (q.v.) Wake. Perhaps also Biddy Doran (q.v.) in her fatal phase. 453.4.

*Morion, Lap ap–from context, Luke Tarpey (q.v.). 398.1.

Morkan–the ladies who give the musical party in Joyce's "The Dead". 90.8.

*Morland-West, 514.24-25.

Morley, John (later Viscount) (1838-1923)–English statesman and author, Home-ruler, Irish secretary in 1886 under Gladstone (q.v.). I think his interest for Joyce lay in his entrancing *Life of Gladstone* which contains a heroic portrait of Parnell (q.v.), who at one point he calls Ireland's "erring chief"—cf. FW, 198.12. 541. 12.

*Morna, Missmisstress, 189.25.

Morpheus–Greek god of sleep who becomes Murphy (q.v.) in *Ulysses.* †88.9—with Pan and Socrates (q.q.v.); 142.29; 599.16.

Morris the Man–Sir William Morris was the first to apply mass-production methods to the manufacture of British motor cars, named for himself. 205.28-29.

Morris, William (1834-96)–English poet, writer, author of *News from Nowhere,* 1891. 333.36.

*Morrisons, 192.4.

*Morrissey, 410.14.

Morse, Samuel (1791-1872)–American inventor of the telegraph. 87.3; 99.6; 123.35; 530.19.

*Mortimer, Sister Anne – three guesses: 1) the sister Anne of the Bluebeard (q.v.) story; 2) Parnell's (q.v.) sister Anne, who drowned herself; 3) Richard III's (q.v.) grandmother, Anne Mortimer. 210.24.

Mortimor, Morya–common Irish expression of mild distress. 316. 21.

*Moscas – character in *Volpone?* Moscow? 84.1.

Moses–Jewish lawgiver, prophet, leader. *The Book of Moses* is an esoteric, theosophical work. 4.23; 47; †123.35—with Morse; 167.36; 307.left margin; 313.5; 354.12; 463.30; †518.2—with Mars (q.v.).

Mosse, Bartholomew–18th century Dublin doctor and philanthropist, built the Rotunda Hospital. 43.3; 428.10; 545.32; 552.30.

*Mosses, Diggin, 69.9.

Mossop, Henry (1729-74)–Dublin-born actor who long played with Barry (q.v.). 569.30.

Moth–character in Shakespeare's (q.v.) *Love's Labour's Lost.* See Costard, Biron. 360.25.

Motley, John Lothrop–19th century American historian, author of *The Rise of the Dutch Republic.* 338.11.

Mountain–usually HCE (q.v.).

Mountjoy–English prison in Dublin where Ireland's martyrs did time. I cannot decide whether the name has further meaning in FW. Mountjoy was the name of the Huguenot (q.v.) family with whom Shakespeare lived on Silver Street in London. He is known to have been involved in one of their lawsuits; it has been suggested that the daughter of the family,

Mary, taught him French for *Henry V* (q.v.). Christopher Mountjoy was a tyre-maker. 45 (*bis*); 76.4-5; 460.9; 587.6.

*Mountsackvilles, Misses, 375.12.

Mowy, St–Saint Mo-bhi of Glasnevin, Columba's (q.v.) tutor. Pleasant grin comes from a false etymology which assumes Glasnevin to mean *glas* (green) *aoibhinn* (pleasant). Glasnevin and Mount Saint Jerome (252.11) are Dublin cemeteries. The twins wish each other in the grave. 252.7.

Moyhamlet–Mohammed and Hamlet (q.q.v.). 418.18.

*Moynihan, 307.9.

Mozart, Wolfgang Amadeus (1756-91)–German composer. 360.12.

*Mozos, Santos, 455.36.

Mozzaccio–see Masaccio. 435.9.

*Mtu or Mti–In Kiswahili (see 204.3) *mtu* means "man", *mti* "tree". 204.21.

Mud Island, King of–hereditary robber chieftain who ruled a gang of smugglers and highwaymen. 87.26.

*Mudson, Mr, 133.22.

Muggleton, Lodowick (1609-98)–English sectarian. He was a tailor who in 1651 began to have revelations; he proclaimed himself and his cousin the two witnesses of Rev. 10:3; they wrote *The Divine Looking Glass* (1656) in which they said God had a human body. See Lodowick. †123.21—with the Maggies (q.v.); 312.26; †538.3—with Ludwig and Lewis Carroll (q.q.v.).

Mulachy–see Malachy II. 32.1.

*Muldoons, 94.3.

Mullans, Mad–see Mullinx. 279. note 1.

*Mullarty, Mahmullagh–Mad Mullah? 390.9-10.

*Mullen, Pat, 94.1.

Mulligan, Malachi "Buck"–character in *Ulysses*—see Gogarty. Many "bucks", perhaps even Buckley (q.v.) may refer to him. In *Ulysses* he is Antinous, Claudius and Aegisthus (q.q.v.). †64.9, 10—with Canaan (q.v.); 193.6,18; 303.20.

Mullinx, Mad–18th century Dublin street beggar. Swift (q.v.) put him in a poem, "Mad Mullinx and Timothy". 279.note 1.

Mullocky–see Malachy II, 151.24.

Mulo–Celtic mule god. 499.5.

Mumblesome – see Mendelssohn. 377.15.

Mumfsen–see Mommsen. 155.33.

Mumm–champagne. 451.23.

Mumsell–see Maunsel. 185.1-2.

?Munday, Anthony (1553-1602)–minor playwright, ridiculed by Ben Jonson (q.v.). 149.5; 350.13.

*Murdoch, 274.left margin.

Murdrus–see Mardrus. 374.12.

*Murnane, 613.30.

*Murphy–often potatoes. See Morpheus. 161.29; 190.4; 333.32; 446.30; 529.25.

*Murphy, Andrew Paul–anthropomorphic. 31.35.

*Murphy, Martin – may include Martin Chuzzlewit. 434.32.

*Murphy, Mary Anne, 293.10-11.

Murray, Lindley (1745-1826)–Anglo - American grammarian whose *Grammar of the English Language* (1795) was a standard text for fifty years in England and America. 269.29.

Murray, Mary Jane–maiden name of Joyce's mother. See Mary, Mary Shakespeare. †63.27—with Mary; ?208.35.

*Murrey, Wat, 227.29.

*Murrough, Mick na–MacNamara? See Mick. 330.16.

*Murry–see Mary? 433.19.

Murtagh of Tirconnell–in 941 conducted the first midwinter campaign ever seen in Ireland and won the name "Murtagh of the Leather Cloaks". The campaign was called "The hosting of the frost"—see FW 501.33. 289.20; ?314.30.

Musketeers–see Three Musketeers. 379-380.

Mustardseed – fairy in Shakespeare's (q.v.) *A Midsummer Night's Dream*. See Bottom. Mustard perhaps carries the further significance of Ben Jonson's (q.v.) gibe at Shakespeare's coat of arms—"Not without mustard". 279.note 1 ; 409.16; 455.32.

Mut–Egyptian goddess, consort of Amon (q.v.), whose name means "mother". 53.3; 230.14; 287.5.

*__Muta__ and Juva see Mutt and Jute.

*__Mutantini__, Bianca, 238.23.

Mutt and Jute–take their names from Mutt and Jeff, American comic-strip characters. Americans were chosen because, as Sir Sidney Lee (q.v.) pointed out at length, Caliban (q.v.) is an American Indian. Mutt is a mutt or mutton-head. The Mutt and Jute episode (15-18) is partly based on Caliban and Stephano-Trinculo in *The Tempest*. It also owes something to the meeting of Polyphemus and Ulysses (q.q.v.). Mutt or the native seems to be identical with the Man Servant (q.v.). 16-18 (*passim*); 110.26; 143.23; †168.5-6 —with Japhet (see Ham); ?249.30 (Mettencough); 266.23,24; 273.18; 327.1; 359.18; 467.16-17; 488.29; 517.13; 609-610 (Muta and Juva, *passim*).

*__Mycock__, Lizzy and Lissy–see Elizabeth? 538.22.

Myles–see Myles na Copaleen. 246.19.

*__Myles__, 433.10; 516.12; 567.1.

Myles the Slasher – see Myles O'Reilly. 99.24-25.

Mynn, Alfred (1807-61)–English cricketer. 584.14-15.

Myrrdin–see Merlin. 151.31.

*__Myrtle__, 291.note 4.

*__Mysterion__, Mr–until the Reformation, *Mysterium* was engraved on the Papal tiara. 301.18-19.

N

*__Naama__, Nautic–*naam* is Hebrew "pleasantness", so I take it Anna Livia's (q.v.) new name is something like *felix culpa*. 204.5.

Naaman–(2 Kings, 5) cured of leprosy when he washed in the Jordan. 103.8.

*__Nabuch__, 103.8.

Nagle, Irish informer. 516.12.

Namar–see Raman. 374.22.

Nan, Nancy–see Anna Livia.

Nansen, Fridtjof (1861-1930)–Norwegian statesman, arctic explorer. See Fram. 326.21; 477.20; ?535.19.

Naomi–Ruth's (q.v.) mother-in-law. 491.29.

Napier, John (1550-1617)–Scottish mathematician. 300.32; 345.21.

Napoleon I (1769-1821)–Emperor of France, born Napoleon Bonaparte or Buonaparte in Corsica. In FW he is usually Wellington's (q.v.) opponent and in the Museyroom episode is the Three Soldiers (q.v.). Napoleon is the hero of Shaw's *Man of Destiny*, to which reference is made on 162. Napoleon was also known as the Corsican, and as The Little Corporal. See Corsican Brothers, Joséphine and Marie Louise, Marengo. 8-10 (Lipoleum, *passim*); 9.6,29; 10.35; 33.2; 81.33-34; 83.26; †84.33—with Billy Bones (q.v.); 94.35; 133.21; 162.

3; 175.11; 238.26; †246.16—with Paul Léon (q.v.); †273.26-27—with Apollyon (q.v.), left margin; †321.8—with Nolan (q.v.); 327. 33-34; †334.14—with Nolan; 336. 24-25; 337.16; 340.3; 368.10; 388.8,16,21; 412.29.

Narcissus–beautiful youth of classical legend who loved his own image and drowned in pursuit of it. †212.31-32—with Narcissus Marsh (q.v.); 234.14; 526.34.

Narsty–see Tristram. 395.2.

***Nash**–*nahash* is the Hebrew for "serpent". See Pierce Pennilesse. Elizabeth Hall, Shakespeare's (q.q.v.) granddaughter, married Thomas Nashe. 75.32; ?222.27; 290.28.

Nasoes–among the graffiti on the walls of Pompeii, there is a rude caricature of Perigrinus with an enormous nose and one of Naso with almost no nose. 403.19.

***Nast**–maybe Thomas Nast (1840-1902) — American caricaturist. 369.3.

***Naster,** Bouncer–Pater Noster? 455.14.

Nathan ("gift")–prophet who rebuked David (q.v.) for causing Uriah's (q.v.) death (2 Sam., XII, 1-9). There is a remote possibility that it takes in Nathaniel Hawthorne (q.v.). †3.24—with Jonathan, Swift (q.q.v.); 184.18 (an athanor); 588.16.

***Natigal,** 40.25.

Nausicaa–princess in the *Odyssey*, episode and Gertie MacDowell in *Ulysses*. 229.15.

***Nautsen,** 479.36.

Navellicky Kamen–Russian, Mr Prescott says, for "on the great stone". 392.25.

***Naville,** 61.21.

***Naylar-Traynor,** 370.22.

Neanderthal Man–a man of the Old Stone Age. 18.22; 19.25.

Neandser, Allbroggt and Viggynette Neeinsee–see Nyanza. 600. 12-13.

***Neaves,** 577.21.

***Neblonovi's** Nivonovio, 230.15-16.

Nebo–Babylonian god whose name means "proclaimer", son of Merodach (q.v.), god who introduced writing and general wisdom to the people. 11.5,16; 235.16.

Nebuchadnezzar–became king of Babylon in 606 B.C. and made it a world's wonder. Twice he marched on Jerusalem. 24.35; 177.14; 319.29-30; 344.16.

***Ned**–I imagine all refer to the ass (q.v.), but they may take in any Edward you find knocking about. 82.17; 273.11; 288.5; 325.33; 330.4; 368.36.

Ned of the Hill–poem by Samuel Lover (q.v.). See ass. Edmond O'Ryan, 18th century outlaw of Tipperary, hero of a Gaelic song. 477.6.

Neeblow's–Niblo's Garden, 19th century New York music-hall. 552.19.

***Neelson,** Mr Heer Assassor, †242.1 —with ass (q.v.).

***Nefersen,** 415.33.

Nell, Little–died in Dickens's (q.v.) *The Old Curiosity Shop*. Oscar Wilde said that one must have a heart of stone to read the death of Little Nell without laughing. 324.28.

Nelly, Fresh–see *Ulysses*, 214/278. 34.32.

Nelly–probably always Helen (q.v.), at least in part. In Shakespeare's *Troilus and Cressida*, Paris (q.v.) calls Helen "Nell". †224.30—with Cinderella (q.v.); 227.14; †243.9 —with Parnell (q.v.); †291.14— with Elizabeth, Anna Livia (q.q.v.); †326.13-14—with O'Connell (q.v.); 332.29; 361.14; 423. 12; 431.17; ?445.11; 450.10; †512. 16—with Anna Livia (q.v.); †561.

25—with Virgin (q.v.); 584.17; 604.36.

Nelson, Horatia–daughter of Nelson and Lady Hamilton (q.q.v.). 329.4.

Nelson, Horatio, Viscount (1758-1805)–English naval hero. There is a Nelson Pillar in Dublin. 322.32; 422.30; 466.24; 553.13.

Nema Knatut–see Tut-ankh-amen. 395.23.

*****Nemon**, Niscemus–maybe Noman or Ulysses (q.q.v.), maybe Nemon the Venomous, a Celtic war goddess. 175.33; ?274.25; 318.6.

*****Nenni**–perhaps composed of 1) Nennius (fl. 796)—Welsh author of *Historia Britonium* which contains the earliest legends of King Arthur (q.v.) and an account of Ireland; 2) Ninus, in Greek myth, the eponymous founder of Nineveh, husband of Semiramis (q.v.). It was at Ninny's tomb that Pyramus (see Bottom) was to meet Thisbe (q.v.—see Flute) and did, in fact, meet death. 452. 27.

Nephew–usually refers to Tristram (q.v.).

Nepos, Cornelius (99-24 B.C.)– Roman historian, letter writer, collector of anecdotes. 134.28; 389.28; 392.18.

Neptune–Italian god of the sea, Dublin rowing club. 203.12; 391. 18; 585.2.

Nereids–in Greek myth, nymphs of the Mediterranean. 267.24.

Nero (37 68) Roman emperor, popularly believed to have burned Rome. 177.14; 306.left margin.

Nerses the Gracious (d. 1165)– Armenian poet. 242.9.

*****Nessans**, St–church on Ireland's Eye, which Weston St John Joyce describes as "an antiquarian forgery". 26.34.

Nessie–the Loch Ness sea-serpent.

†365.28—with Stella and Vanessa (q.v.); †379.16—with Stella and Vanessa (q.v.).

Nessus – centaur whose blood-soaked shirt killed Hercules (q.v.). 508.14.

Nestor–wise old warrior in the *Iliad*, Mr Deasy (q.v.) in *Ulysses*. 307.left margin.

Net or **Neith**–Egyptian virgin goddess. 148.4.

*****Netta** and **Linda**, 527.27.

*****Nettle**, Nelly, 604.36.

Neuclidius–see Euclid. 155.32.

*****Neville**, 61.21; 552.12.

Newcomen's–Bank that once stood in Castle Street, Dublin. †130.21 —with Comyn (q.v.).

Newman, John Henry (1801-90)– English cardinal, whom Joyce considered the greatest writer of English prose. He helped found the Catholic University in Dublin. The Irish nationalists held him their enemy and Manning (q.v.) their friend. 282.20-21; †487.33— with Numa (q.v.); 493.31; 596.36; 614.17.

Newnes, Sir George (1851-1910) publisher of *Tit-Bits, The Strand Magazine*, etc. 363.6.

Newton, Sir Isaac (1642-1727)– English natural philosopher. 126. 29; 293.27; ?†611.20 (Entis-On-ton)—with Einstein (q.v.); 625. 25-26.

Ney, Marshal–one of Napoleon's (q.v.) marshals, fought at Waterloo. 10.15 (hncy); 337.16.

Nial or **Niall** of the Nine Hostages– ruled Ireland in the 4th century. He raided Scotland and Britain, but was finally deserted by his own men and conquered by the Romans. A later Nial was perhaps slain by Hamlet (q.v.)—see also Olaf, Sitric. I think FW doesn't distinguish between Nials. ?282.32; 346.33; 580.24.

Niall, Mrs–see Hamlet, Olaf. 96.4-5.

Nichiabelli–Nick and Machiavelli (q.q.v.). 182.20.

Nicholas–see Nick.

Nicholas of Cusa (Nicholaus Cusanus) (1401-64)–Cardinal, theologian, scholar. His principal work was *De docta ignorantia.* He is said to have influenced Joyce. †49.34 — with Michael Cusack (q.v.); 163.17.

Nichtian–see Nietzsche. 83.10.

Nick–see Mick.

*****Nickies,** Nancy–see Two. 422.32-33.

Niece–in FW the word is used as Shakespeare (q.v.) uses it in his will and in his plays, meaning "granddaughter". I believe Joyce means it to refer to that very niece of Shakespeare's, Elizabeth Hall (q.v.) or "Lizzie, grampa's little lump (q.v.) of love"; by extension a niece becomes any young woman loved by an older man—Issy, Isolde of Ireland, Grania, Guinevere, etc. (q.q.v.).

Nielsen–see Horatio Nelson. 553.13

*****Nieman** from Nirgends–German *niemand,* "nobody", *nirgends,* "nowhere". 202.19.

Nietzsche, Friedrich Wilhelm (1844-1900)–German philosopher. 83.10; 344.14.

Nightingale, Florence (1820-1910) –founded the nursing profession during the Crimean War. †360.2 —with Jenny Lind and Philomela (q.q.v.); 514.33-34.

Nijinsky (1890 - 1950) – Russian dancer. 513.11.

Nike or Nice–Greek goddess of victory. †270.24 — with Nick (q.v.); †296.28—with Nick (q.v.).

Niklaus Alopysius–see Mookse and Gripes. 155.31.

Nile–see Cleopatra, see Amazon.

*****Nilfit**–*nihil fit*? 194.17.

Nilsens–see Nelson. 322.32.

Niluna–Cleopatra (q.v.) as moon (q.v.) and river. 627.30.

Nimb or Niav of the Golden Hair– took Oisin (q.v.) to the Land of Ever Young. 143.20; 199.34; 375.31.

Nimrod – Biblical hero, mighty hunter (Gen. 10). 435.13.

Ninon–see Lenclos. 153.4-5.

Nippoluono–see Napoleon. 81.33-34.

Nippy–see Napoleon. A Nippy is a waitress in a Lyons (q.v.) tea-shop. 388.8.

*****Nivynubies,** 66.36.

Noah – 10th patriarch in direct descent from Adam, father of Ham, Shem, Japhet (q.v.), builder of the Ark in which he and his family escaped the flood. After the flood subsided, God made a covenant of peace with Noah and its sign was the rainbow (q.v.). Noah was first to cultivate the vine and get drunk. This is why he occurs so importantly on p. 3 of FW where everyone is concerned with water and/or drink. Joyce does a good deal with various mythological interpretations of the Noah story, e.g. the Ark as moon, the whole tale as a second creation, Noah as a Jewish Dionysus (q.v.). Joyce links Noah with the Guinness (q.v.) family. 5.9; 7.1,15; 16.15; ?20.29; 47.6; 80.25; 89.27; 102.3; †105.14 — with Nyanza (q.v.); 125.18; ?168.5; 175.16; 178.12; 244.26; 275.note 5; 307.left margin; 317.22; 335.29; 383.21; 387.21; 388.18-19; 393.11; 420.23; 463.30; 490.23; 514.14; 521.17; 531.11; †549.34—with Guinness, Ass (q.q.v.); 561.5; 581.15.

Noal–see Noah. 393.11.

Noasies–see Noah. 463.30.

*****Nobbio** and Nuby, 230.16.

Nobel, Alfred (1833-96)–Swedish inventor of dynamite who founded prizes for eminence in science, idealism in literature, and peace. 211.3;306.4—with Noblet's (q.v.); 356.11; 536.12.

Noble, King–lion in the Reynard (q.v.) cycle. See Mark Lyons. 184.34; †488.14—with Nolan.

Noblet's–sweet shop at 34 Abbey Street, Dublin; see Nobel. 306.4.

*Nobnut, Norris, 376.9.

Nobody–see Ulysses.

Noel–see Noah. 490.23.

*Noel–see Knowell? 337.15; 594.35.

*Noggens–seems to be the Man Servant (q.v.). 370.26.

Noh–Japanese plays. See Noah? 244.26.

Nolan–see Browne and Nolan.

Nolan, Jibbo–hero of Liam O'Flaherty's *The Informer.* †587.36— with Nolan (q.v.).

Nolan, Philip–hero *A Man Without a Country* by Edward Everett Hale. †187.28—with Nolan (q.v.).

Noll–see Oliver, Oliver Cromwell, Knowall.

Nomad–see Ulysses, Damon.

Noman–see Ulysses.

Nomario–see Mario. 450.24.

*Noodynaady's, 253.16.

Nora Creina–title and air of a melody of Thomas Moore's (q.v.). 348.26-27.

*Norgel's – *nörgeln* is German "grumble", "grouse". 15.14.

*Norreys, Soothbys, Yates and Welks–the Four (q.v.) as compass points. Yates may be Yeats (q.v.) since Joyce seems to have, at first, meant him for one of the Four. Norris, Wilkes and Yates were actors. 557.2.

Norreys, Sir John–English general who fought Tyrone in 1594. His sister, Lady Mabel Bagnal eloped with Tyrone. 311.35.

*Norris, Southby, Yates and Weston–see Norreys, etc. See Jessie Weston. 534.15-16.

North, J. H. and Co.–Dublin auctioneers. 529.13.

Northcliffe, Alfred Charles William Harmsworth, Viscount (1865-1922)–newspaper magnate, born in Chapelizod (q.v.). 10.36; 137. 35; 246.31-32; 363.6; †458.23— with O. W. Holmes (q.v.); 618.2.

*Northeasts, 30.19.

Norval–old shepherd in Home's *Douglas.* (Where's your Willy Shakespeare now?) He has a son, young Norval, who turns out to be somebody else. 569.36; 570.1.

Norwegian Captain–Philip McCann told John Joyce a story of a hunchbacked Norwegian Captain who could not get a suit properly fitted by the Dublin tailor, J. H. Kerse (see Kersse), and they had a slanging-match over it (Ellmann, 22). The captain is on p. 60/72 of *Ulysses.* He is a character in *Hamlet* (q.v.). I must say that I really do not know what happens in the Norwegian Captain episode. The Captain is a hunchbacked pagan of a Norse invader who wins (or is won by) an Irish bride and is converted to Christianity. I think he is HCE (q.v.) courting Anna Livia (q.v.) or being courted. On the other hand, his fight with Kersse seems to be one of the brother battles in which FW so abounds. They are Set and Horus (q.v.), and peace at last is made between them by an old codger, the Ship's Husband, who is father of the girl. See Pukkelsen, Gobbo. 23.11; 49.28; †67.13-14—with Kersse (q.v.); †241.18-19—with Dick Whittington (q.v.); 311.9; 312.2; 316.34; 319.18; 320.25; 322.25; †325.27 — with HCE (q.v.); 327.30; 330.18; 343.10; 511.2.

Nothing, Mary–"airy nothings" from *A Midsummer Night's Dream.* 52.20.

*Novus Elector, 365.19.

Nowhare–see Noah. 335.29.

Nox–Roman goddess of night. 35. 23; 143.17; 555.22; 594.29; 602. 35; 614.13.

Nu–Egyptian sky god. 240.8; †493. 31—with Newman (q.v.).

Nuad or Nuadu–god of the Tuatha De Danaan, who had a silver arm. 138.20; 344.36.

Nuancee, Victrolia and Allbart Noahnsy—see Nyanza. 105.14.

*****Nuathan,** 244.31.

Nugent, Monsignor James (1822-1905)–helped the Irish during the famine and the cholera years when they landed in Liverpool. Later he took up the problem of emigration. 24.26; ?537.19.

Numa Pompilius–second legendary king of Rome (715-672 B.C.). †467.33—with Newman (q.v.).

Nunn–father of Joshua (q.v.). In the Egyptian religion he is the personification of the germ of all things which slept in the flood till creation. 231.18; 291.1; 523. 17.

Nupiter Privius–see Jupiter. 390. 22-23.

*****Nur**–Arabic for "light". 310.24.

?Nurse–Juliet's (q.v.). †242.9— with Nerses (q.v.); 257.16; 522.33.

Nut–in the Egyptian religion the sky goddess who laid the cosmic egg, the Great Cackler. I fancy she ties up with Artemis-Delia-Biddy Doran (q.q.v.), a nut-tree goddess and a hen. 113.3; 360. 15-16; 370.15; 623.32.

Nutter–character in LeFanu's (q.v.) *The House by the Churchyard.* Nutter is steward to Lord Castle-mallard (q.v.); he fights a comic duel with Fireworker O'Flaherty (q.v.) in Phoenix Park. 16.15; 80.9.

Nuvoletta–Issy as cloud and little girl. See Letty? Mr Wilder has pointed out the resemblance between FW, 159 and Pound's (q.v.) *Canto* XXIX. 73.35; 87.23; †157. 8,17,24—with Lucia Joyce (q.v.); 159.5,6; †256.33—with Issy and Elizabeth (q.q.v.); 304.19; 329. 35; 561.11.

Nyanza, Victoria and Albert–two great African lakes, the two western reservoirs of the Nile (q.v.). Their waters mingle and flow north to the Mediterranean. The word *nyanza* comes from an ancient Bantu word, *anza*, meaning river or lake. See Cleopatra. Albert and Victoria Quays, opposite each other on the Liffey, were the last quays, as you come in from the sea. †23.20-21—with HCE and Anna Livia (q.q.v.); 105.14; 126.27; 202.20-21; 558. 27-28; 598.6; 600.12-13.

O

Oakley, Annie – female sharp-shooter, also a term for a seat given free at a theatre. 52.1.

Oates, Titus (1649-1705)–English conspirator. †70.14—with Titus Andronicus (q.v.), 18.

Obadiah (servant of Yahweh, q.v.) –4th of the Old Testament minor prophets. 531.11.

O'Bawlar, Faugh MacHugh–see O'Byrne. The battle-cry of the Irish Brigade was *fág à bealach,* "Clear the way". 382.22.

O'Bejorumsen–see Bjornson. 529. 16.

Oberon–king of the fairies, husband of Titania (q.v.) in Shakespeare's (q.v.) *A Midsummer Night's Dream.* According to Celtic tradition, he was son of Julius Caesar and Morgana le Fay (q.q.v.). See Indian Boy.

†339.14–with Brian Boru (q.v.); †357.2—with Aubrey Beardsley (q.v.).

*O'Breen's–Joyce is playing on Moore's "O breathe not his name" which is sung to the air of "The Brown Maid". 56.32.

*O'Brien, 291.10; 370.21.

O'Brien, Boris–see Brian Boru. 385.15.

O'Brien, Lynn–see Brian O'Linn. 70.7.

O'Brien, The–see Four, see Five Bloods. 270.36.

?O'Brien, William–editor of Parnell's (q.v.) paper, *United Ireland*. In 1883 he exposed homosexuals in the police and the post-office— see Cornwall. †41.16—with H. J. Byron (q.v.).

O'Brien, William Smith–leader of the Irish insurrection of 1848. 588.31 (the o'briartree).

*O'Briny rossies – Rosse? Rose? (q.q.v.). See Brie on Arossa. 95.4; 207.15.

O'Bryony, Bryony–plant of the cucumber family. 450.32.

O'Byrne, Fiach MacHugh–Irish chief who helped Owen Roe O'Neill escape from the Anglo-Normans. They finally slew him in Dublin in 1598. See O'Bawlar. 382.22.

*O'Cannochar, Conno–maybe Conchobar (q.v.). 348.18.

Occidentaccia, Cardinal –Johnny MacDougal (q.v.) as west. 180.15.

*Ochtroyd, 538.7.

O'Clery, Michael, Peregrine and Conary–see Four Masters.

O'Connell, Daniel (1775-1847)– Irish statesman, known as the Liberator. He gave his life to freeing Irish Catholics from their disabilities. By formation of the Catholic Association and by his powerful (if scurrilous) oratory in Parliament, O'Connell won much for Ireland and the Irish

worshipped him as they were later to worship Parnell (q.v.). Nevertheless, in old age, he was passed by and vilified as conservative by the more radical Young Irelanders, was defeated at a mass-meeting at Clontarf, and died in Italy a disappointed man. There is a statue of him in Dublin, wearing a great cloak. Yeats (q.v.) once made a speech in the Dail, saying you could not throw a stone in Dublin without hitting one of O'Connell's bastards. The O'Connells opened a brewery in Dublin in the 19th century. See Dan, D'Esterre.†7.12—with Danu (q.v.); 56.14; 70.29; 81.9; 133.3; 141.25; 198.34; ?†211.1—with Mangan (q.v.); 277.2; 303.8,10, 12; 310.28; 311.18; †317.31—with The O'Connor Don (q.v.); 319.4; 321.1; 322.3; 323.26; 326.13-14; ?330.6; 336.24; 365.9; †379.9-10 —with Michael Gunn (q.v.); 382. 5; †386.22—with Danu (q.v.); †392.30—with Danu (q.v.); 466. 36; †525.18—with Conal (q.v.); †553.14—with Conal (q.v.); 588. 35-36; 590.14; †625.12—with Conal (q.v.).

*O'Connor–some of these may refer to William O'Connor, author of *Harrington* (q.v.). All references double with O'Connell (q.v.). 141. 25; 319.4; 321.1.

O'Connor, Eily–see Colleen Bawn.

O'Connor, Roderick (c. 1116-98)– last high king of Ireland, defeated by the Anglo-Normans. (See McCarthy). Rory O'Connor, an IRA general who was in charge of the Four Courts when they were burned in the Easter Rebellion, may also be comprehended here. The part of FW which deals with Roderick O'Connor was the first part of FW Joyce wrote. 3.25 (rory); 129.11; 130.13-14; †369.18—with Ruric (q.v.); 378. 13; 380.11-12,33; †381.11—with Roderick Random (q.v.), 24-25; 498.23-24 (Dodderick Ogonoch Wrack); 510.26; 539.1.

O'Connor, The–see Five Bloods, Four. 271.1.

O'Connor, Thomas Power, "Tay Pay" (b. 1848)–Irish M.P., Parnellite (q.v.), journalist, founder of a weekly paper, *Mainly About People,* known as MAP—see 261. left margin. 262.left margin (*put thounce otay ithpot*).

O'Conor, Don, The–19th century Irish nationalist politician, M.P. under Parnell (q.v.). †317.31— with Daniel O'Connell (q.v.).

*****O'Crian,** Roaring, Jr–O'Brien? 87.18.

*****O'Cronione**–perhaps Cronus (q.v.) or his son Zeus (q.v.). 415.21.

Octavius Caesar–see Augustus.

Octoroon–I do not know her name, but she is heroine of Boucicault's play. 468.36.

O'Daffy–see O'Duffy.

?O'Daly – composer of "Eileen Aroon" (q.v.) in 1385. 48.25.

*****O'Darnel,** a duna, 94.31.

O'Dea, Kevineen–I assume, Kevin (q.v.) of God. 59.23; 210.14.

*****O'Deavis,** Lisa–clearly O'Mara (q.v.). See Lisa. 41.3-4.

?Odet–female in Proust (q.v.). 200.33.

Odin–one-eyed chief of the Norse gods. Other forms of his name are, Auden, Ase, Asa, Woden, Wotan. 69.10; 82.16; 88.21; 130.5 (asama); 246.7; 279.note 1 (Asa and Auden); †319.27—with Olaf (q.v.); 325.31; 535.5 (this takes in the "Wooden Man", a statue which used to stand on Essex Street, Dublin); 565.5; 577.17.

O'Doherty, Kevin Isod – patriot Irish poet of the 19th century. He was sentenced to transportation but would have been pardoned if he pleaded guilty. Such a plea would have implied acceptance of English rule in Ireland, so he refused and was confirmed in his refusal by his sweetheart, Mary Anne Kelly (also a poet, Eva of the *Nation*) who said, "I'll wait for you, O darling". She did wait. 231.14 (coffin acid odarkery); 232.13 (O doherlynt).

O'Domnally–see Domnall. 420.27-28.

*****O'Donnell,** Hyacinth–may have something to do with the O'Donnell who killed Patrick Carey (he had informed on the Invincibles). See John MacDonald, Hyacinth. 86.15; 87.12,32.

*****O'Donner**–see O'Donnell.

O'Donough–Moore's song "Of All the Fair Months" is sung to the air "Song of O'Donohue's Mistress". O'Donohue's white horses are the white waves on a windy day. 106.2.

O'Donough, The–chieftain of Killarney, hero of many legends. 439.19-20 (Theo Dunnohoo).

*****O'Dowd**–possibly a reference to Daddy O'Dowd (q.v.). Cornelius O'Dowd was a pseudonym of Lever's (q.v.). Joyce is playing on the fact that Moore's (q.v.) "O! Doubt Me Not" is sung to the tune "Yellow Wat and the Fox". 89.13.

O'Dowd, Daddy–title character of a play by Boucicault (q.v.). 439.20.

*****O'Doyles**–see Doyles. 48.25.

*****O'Duane,** Mr–Dane? Dane's son or Hamlet (q.v.)? 365.25.

O'Duffy, General–leader of a daffy Irish fascist movement (Blueshirt) in the 1930s. Yeats (q.v.) wrote songs for the Blueshirts. 84.14.

*****O'Dungaschiff,** Pumpey – see O'Dunnochoo. Pompey (q.v.)? 350.7.

*****O'Dunnochoo,** Danno–or some such name seems to be the name of the Russian General — see Buckley. 348.19; 349.20; 350.7.

*****O'Dwyer,** 116.16; 446.31; 529.25.

*O'Dwyer of Greyglens–see Dwyer Gray. 602.14-15.

*O'Dyar–see O'Dwyer.

Oedipus ("swollen footed")–in classical legend, killed his father and married his mother. See Jocasta. 128.36; 306.left margin; 434.19; ?445.23; 499.16; 513.21.

Oetzmann and Nephew–cabinet makers, house furnishers of Dublin (Grafton St.), London, Constantinople.

*O'Farrell, Philomena, 212.12-13.

Offa–hero of the early Angli, king of Angel. According to *Widsith* he had to fight in single combat for his throne against the Saxons. He won. 82.13.

O'Flagonan–see Demetrius O'Flanagan McCarthy. 27.25.

O'Flaherty, fireworker–comic Irish officer in LeFanu's (q.v.) *The House by the Churchyard.* He fights a comic duel in Phoenix Park with Nutter (q.v.). 80.8-9.

*O'Flanagan, Teague, 210.20.

*O'Fluctuary, Posidonius – see Poseidon. 80.28-29.

*O'Ford, Flatter, 512.31.

*Oga, 203.32.

Oglethorpe, James Edward (1696-1785)–English general, philanthropist, founder of Georgia (see Peter Sawyer). Much of his philanthropy was directed toward helping criminals. 81.21.

Ogma Sun-face–Irish god who invented ogam (or ogham) letters. Joyce's use of cryptographic ogham may be learned from Macalister's *The Secret Languages of Ireland.* 89.30,32; †90.1,2— with Sun-yat-Sen (q.v.); 223.4; ?602.11.

O'Gorman–see Gorman.

O'Grady, Rosy – "Sweet Rosy O'Grady", a song. See Rose. 133.7.

O'Growney, Father Eugene (1865-99)–authority on Gaelic, helped found the Gaelic League. He died in America, was dug up and brought to Ireland for reburial. 102.19.

O'Hagan, Thomas O'Hagan, 1st Baron (1812-85)–lord chancellor of Ireland. A great orator, he began as a nationalist but sold out to the English. 299.23.

O'Hara–see Burke and Hare. 580. 32.

O'Heffernan, Blind–Irish bard. 519.6.

Ohm, George Simon (1787-1854)– German electrician. 310.1.

*O'Hollerins of Staneybatter, †291.11–with Holly (q.v.).

*O'Huggins, Dora, 519.5.

*O'Hurry, Hairy–as in Tom, Dick, Harry. See Harry. 8.27.

*O'Hyens of Locklaunstown – Ohioians? 291.10.

Oil, Olive–girl friend of Popeye (q.v.) in an American comic-strip, "The Thimble Theatre" (cf. 268. 15-16). 279.note 1.

Oincuish–Oengus or Aengus (q.v.). 90.34.

*Okaroff, 49.3.

O'Keef-Rosses and Rhosso-Keevers –reference is to the town of Kiev and its early Scandinavian rulers, sometimes called *Rhossisti.* See Ross. The Swiss-German word *russenkäfer* means a beetle, nearly related to the earwig (q.v.). 310. 16-17.

*O'Kehley, Rhian, 90.28-29.

*O'Kneels–see O'Neill. 291.10.

Olaf the White–came to Ireland and became the first Norse king of Dublin about 852. According to Giraldus Cambrensis (q.v.), three (q.v.) brothers, Olaf, Ivor and Sitric (q.q.v.), built respectively the cities of Dublin, Limerick, and Waterford, and ruled them. The story is apparently a fairy-tale, but Joyce uses it at 12.31. On 201.30, however, Joyce begins and hardly ever stops associating Olaf with Alpha (since he was the first Norse King?), Hamlet, and Lamb (q.q.v.) who wrote up *Hamlet* for *Tales from Shakespeare* (q.v.). Olaf becomes, in fact, indistinguishable from Hamlet. The Olaf—son of Sitric —who fought at Dublin in 919 and may have been Hamlet, is not of course, Olaf the White, but throughout FW Joyce identifies people because they have the same name—e.g. Tristram of Lyonesse and Sir Amory Tristram (q.q.v.). Norse and Irish history crawls with Olafs and Sitrics and I doubt if Joyce greatly bothered to sift them out. In Irish Olaf is *Amhlaoibh*, anglicized as Humphrey (q.v.). The Irish word means "curled". 7.10; 12.31; 13.18,19; †44.music—with Cromwell (q.v.); †45.3 — with Cromwell (q.v.); 100.26; 132.17-18; 134.27; 159.27; 201.30; 287.15 (olfa); 294.8,9; †319.27 — with Odin (q.v.); 378.23; 443.30; 492.4; 498.7; †532.8 — with MacAuscullpth; 567.18-19.

Olaf Trijggvesson or King Olaf I of Norway (969-1000)–converted his country to Christianity. 335.13.

Olcott, Chauncey (1860-1932) – American actor, wrote "Mother Machree". 451.2.

?Oldcastle, Sir John–the original of Falstaff (q.v.). 45.stanza 2.

Old Grog–nickname of Admiral Edward Vernon (1684-1757). 428.19.

O'Leary, Caoch–subject of a poem, "Caoch the Piper" by John Keegan (1809-49). Caoch is an aged, blind piper who outlives his friends. 43.20-21.

*Olecasandrum – Johnny MacDougal (q.v.) as Alexandria? Cassandra (q.v.)? 124.36.

Ole Clo–an itinerant seller of old clothes as described by Mayhew

in *London Labour and the London Poor*. 453.15.

Oleg–successor to Ruric (q.v.) in Kiev. 310.16.

Olga the Slav–an Eastern saint. 528.23.

Olim, Priam–see Priam, Brian O'Linn. 6.23.

O'Linn, Brian–hero of an Irish ballad, first to wear clothes, make them out of simple materials like sheepskins, shells, etc. I think he usually doubles with Brian Boru (q.v.). †6.23—with Priam (q.v.); †17.12—with Briand (q.v.); 60.11; 70.7; 148.36; 275.1; 328.2.

Oliphant, Laurence (1829-88)–British author, foreign correspondent, eccentric, associated with countries of the east. 427.22.

Oliver–see Cromwell, Roland and Oliver, Gogarty, Goldsmith.

Olivia – in Shakespeare's (q.v.) *Twelfth Night*. See Viola. 227.14; 525.29.

*Oliviero–see Oliver? 456.10.

Olona Lena Magdalena–Olona is the Italian form of Magdalene (q.v.), Lena the Russian, Magdalena, the South American. See also Maggies. 211.7-8.

*O'Looniys, 464.7.

*O'Loughlin, 49.33; 106.7.

O'Malley, Charles–title hero of a novel by Lever (q.v.). †93.34-35 —with Molly Bloom (q.v.).

O'Malley, Grace–female pirate of Elizabeth I's (q.v.) time. Her Irish name was Granu Wail or Grania (q.v.) Ui Mhàille, a name which came to stand for Ireland like Dark Rosaleen (q.v.) or Cathleen Ni Houlihan. See also Grace, and William Grace, Gracehoper.
  According to report, she sailed up to Howth, went to the Castle and demanded admission. The Earl of Howth refused her because he was at dinner. In revenge,

she kidnapped his young heir and did not return him until the Earl promised that his doors would always stand open at mealtime. As so often happens, I can see Joyce's source standing behind what he does with the source and still not understand it all. Joyce calls Grace O'Malley "the prankquean" (q.v.), and joins her on to his temptress theme. Since Anna means "grace" she is probably some aspect of Anna Livia (q.v.). She is also, in some measure, Grania stealing Dermot from Finn (q.v.).

A possible level of meaning in the prankquean episode (pp. 21-23) is that Jarl van Hoother (q.v.) is Shakespeare (q.v.); and his twin boys, Tristopher and Hilary (q.q.v.), are Tragedy and Comedy. The prankquean is the Muse who mixes up comedy and tragedy, as they are mixed up in Shakespeare's later plays. There are certainly other levels, e.g. the Biblical, the Viconian, that of the Masterbuilder. It is also likely that the episode is an "Endgame" at chess.

?7.6; 21.20-21; 22.12; 71.19; 83.23; 89.11; 95.3-4; 105.27; 106.34; 115.20; 119.20; 146.30; 201.32; 227.25; 312.27; 318.1; †335.31—with Maggy (q.v.); 356. 7; 361.12-13; 364.25; 365.15; 377.30; 395.24; 419.6; 428.16; 460.6; 509.30; 512.28; 550.35; 561.14; 570.6; 577.15; 597.9; 623.11.

Omar–see Khayyam. 319.34.

O'Mara, Joseph–Irish tenor who sang in *Tristan und Isolde* (q.q.v.). See also Mildew Lisa, A'Hara. 40.16.

O'Mara, K. M.–primarily Omar Khayyam (q.v.), but I wonder if it cannot also be a reference to Kipling's Kim or Kimball O'Hara who really ought to be in FW, since he was Irish and went in quest of a wonderful river. 122. 19.

O'Mario–see Mario. 407.16.

*Ombrellone–umbrella? shadow? 361.19.

*O'Morum, Mrs, 460.18.

O'Mulcnory, Ferfessa – see Four Masters.

Onan–spilled his seed upon the ground—see Genesis 38:8-10. 24. 34; 40.25 (nano); 361.21; 435.31; 481.7.

Ondt and Gracehoper–Joyce's version of La Fontaine's (q.v.) fable, a praise of prudence. Joyce's version is easy enough to read: the Gracehoper—Shem (q.v.) or Time —has all the fun in this world, but is a social failure in the afterlife; the Ondt—Shaun (q.v.) or Space —gets all the goodies and houris in heaven. I have read that "Ondt" is the Danish word for "evil": it is also an anagram of Don't. The episode may owe something to Robert Greene's (q.v.) recension of the fable in *A Groatsworth of Wit.* I am sure it has a philosophical meaning that I have not made out. See Grace.

63.1,4	crassopper . . . aunt (see Aunt)
87.23	andt grousuppers
93.5	an't
105.28	Aunt . . . Clodshoppers
147.16-17	groupsuppers . . . Anty Pravidance
158.16,17	undths . . . grice
197.27-28	grasshoop . . . antsgrain
253.7-8	ants . . . sauterelles
257.5	gracehoppers, auntskippers
268.11-12	andt's . . . grossopper
278.note 1	Gosem pher, gezumpher, greeze
307.16	Grasshopper . . . Ant
331.15-16	aandt . . . grosskropper
335.10-11	hundt . . . ground sloper
338.17-18	unt . . . groundsapper
339.36	emt . . . greaseshaper
340.33	ant's
†343.23	antiants . . . grandoper —with Iago and (implied) Othello (q.q.v.)

†360.34,36 anthill . . . groatsupper —with Antheil (q.v.)

361.12-13 Hopping Gracius, onthy

364.23 merryaunt . . . gravesobbers

414.20-21 Ondt . . . Gracehoper (these forms continue, *passim* to 419.6.)

440.2 An Traitey

515-516 end . . . grass . . . hopping

531.22 La Sauzerelly

563.28 Formio and Cigalette (Romeo and Juliet?)

568.12 sautril . . . a meise

579.12 Endth

613-614 Owned . . . grazeheifer

*O'Neill, 291.10; 495.27.

?*O'Neill, Michael, 212.20 (My colonial).

O'Niell, Outlawrie–Hugh O'Neill (1540-1616)—outlawed by the Irish parliament in 1613. 550.31.

Onions–FW has jokes based on *unio* being Latin for pearl (q.v.) and for onion. Rabelais called Cleopatra (q.v.) a "crier of onions" in hell because she drank a pearl. Thus onions tie on to the Margaret-Maggie (q.v.) theme.

O'Nonhanno–see Hanno. 123.32.

*Oodles of Anems, Miss–"anems" could be an anagram of "names". 226.35.

Oonagh–the air to which Moore's (q.v.) "While Gazing on the Moon's Light" is sung. 64.8.

*Oozle, Dinny–*dhuine uasail* is Gaelic for "fine fellow". The Ouzel was a Dublin ship which was thought lost and all her insurance was paid; in 1700 she sailed into Dublin, causing a nice how-do-you-do in Poolblack. 35. 16; 332.33.

Ophelia–heroine of *Hamlet* (q.v.). Like St Kevin's (q.v.) Cathleen, she drowned herself because of masculine coldness — see also Biddy Doran. ?72.4; 105.18; 110. 11; 465.32.

*O'Phelim–see Ophelia. Plays on *felix culpa*. 72.4.

Oppel, Carl Albert (1831-65)–German palaeontologist who devoted special attention to fossils of the Jurassic system. 315.32-33.

*O'Prayins–O'Briens (q.v.)? 291. 10.

Ops–Roman goddess of fertility and agriculture, wife of Saturn (q.v.). 425.30.

O'Purcell–see Purcell. 187.18.

O'Rafferty, Paddy–the air to which Moore's (q.v.) "Drink of this Cup" is sung. 345.25.

*O'Rahilly–one of the leaders of the IRA in the Easter Rebellion so spelled his name. 174.29.

Oram, Elsie–Eilis Oram is a false-tongued character in Tipperary folk-lore. 211.12.

*O'Rangans, Lili–see Lily, Orange. 30.13-14.

Orange is William III (q.v.). 3.35; 19.5; 23.1-2; 30.13-14; 43.8; 59.8; 63.23; 69.35; 96.22-23; 102.25; 110.27,29; 111.34; ?132.29; 135. 12; 140.19; 143.25; 203.27; 208. 15; 226.31; 246.26; 343.1; 361. 24; 374.31; 396.16; 405.33; 450.9; 477.36; 478.1; 479.31; 488.5; 495.9; 498.8; 504.24; ?522.16; 528.5; 541.34; ?555.31; ?556.11; 596.1; 611.6,30.

*Orani–see Cloran. 49.19.

*O'Rann, O'Ryne – the above? Orion (q.v.)? 372.32.

O'Rarelys, Parks – see Persse O'Reilly.

*Orbiter, 257.35.

Orcus–Roman name for Pluto (q.v.), considered as the angel of death. 393.32.

O'Reilly, John Boyle (1844-90)–Irish-American, Fenian, journalist, versifier. 231.13 (gumboil owrithy).

O'Reilly, Miles the Slasher–hero of

the Confederate Wars of 1798. 99.24-25.

*O'Reilly, Molloyd – see Persse O'Reilly. 616.1.

O'Reilly, Persse – the name by which HCE (q.v.) is execrated in Hosty's "The Ballad of Persse O'Reilly". It has to do with French *perce-oreille* or earwig (see Earwicker) and maybe something to do with the expression, *avoir la puce à l'oreille*. In the ballad HCE is identified at length with an insect as in the (supposed) Shakespearean (q.v.) ballad, Sir Thomas Lucy is identified with another insect, the louse.

You would expect the name to tie on to Patrick Pearse of the Easter Rebellion, or to Lady Gregory (née Persse), but I cannot see that it does. Persse O'Reilly does tie on to St Peter, Raleigh, and Percival (q.q.v.). He is firmly tied to Shakespeare, or at any rate to Shakespeare pretenders by the fact that FW 44.10-14 echoes the dedication of a book by Brig. Gen. S. A. E. Hickson, *The Prince of Poets*, 1926: "In Memory of One of the Greatest of Men Who Had No Name of His Own But Who May Be Called by a Whole Library of Names: Gascoigne—Laneham— Immerito — Lyly — Broke — Gosson —Webbe—Puttenham—Watson — Lodge — Daniel—Greene— Nash—Peele—Marlowe—Spenser —Cervantes—Montaigne—Bacon —and Shakesepare.

26.32	Reilly Parsons
†37.32	rawly—with Raleigh (q.v.)
38.34-35	pierce . . . aurellum . . . parse . . .
44.9,14	piersified . . . Persse O'Reilly
†49.14	perished . . . rawl— with Raleigh (q.v.)
71.25	O'Reilly's
84.34	pierced
90.30	pearced our really's
105.10-11	Prszss Orel Orel

†133.11	piercers, ally . . . raw- lies—with Raleigh
162.12	Persic-Uraliens
175.28	Perce-Oreille
240.10	Experrsly
243.34	Saint Pursy Orelli
262.8,10	pearse. . . O really
270.3-4	orations parsed
†289.3-4	perished . . . rock o'ralereality — with St Peter (q.v.)
332.9	Peace, O wiley
340-341	peer's aureolies
342.16-17	Pitsy Riley
†343.21	rawlawdy — with Ral- eigh (q.v.)
347.8,31	Reilly Oirish . . . orus- saheying and patron- ning
352.10	Percy rally
353.18,24	erseroyal . . . Parsuralia
354.14	Parkes O'Rarelys
357.9,18	perssian . . . owe, real- isimus . . . oreillental
358.20	Perseoroyal
?†359.35	our allies—with Alice (q.v.)
362.2	rally
373.33	parssed our alley
378.9	P.R.C.R.L.L. Royloy
390.5	pierce of railing
†419.25	shunt Persse—with St Persse (q.v.)
†447.24	Fino Ralli—with Finn MacCool (q.v.)
467.29	parses orileys
482.4,5	oreils. Piercey, piercey, piercey . . . Pig Pursriley
491.25	Pirce! Perce
493.3	Erill Pearcey O
?495.17	Riley
496.15	Piers Aurell
497.27	Persee and Rahli
498.18-19	beers o'ryely
512.20,24	reely, O reely . . . ap- pierce
525.16	Parasol Irelly
556.35	peirce the yare
580.30	Purses Relle
581.7	Big Reilly
†593.15-16	O rally, O rally, O rally, Phlenxty O rally—with Planxty O'Reilly (q.v.)

616.1,32   Molloyd O'Reilly . . .
            unperceable
620.24   pearse orations

O'Reilly, Planxty–the air to which Moore's (q.v.) "What Life Like That of the Bard Can Be" is sung. †593.16—with Persse O'Reilly (q.v.).

Orestes–Greek tragic hero. 305.left margin.

Orexes–see Orestes.

Oriana–heroine of *Amadis of Gaul.* Name applied by the poets to Elizabeth I (q.v.) and by Ben Jonson (q.v.) to Anne (q.v.), queen of James I (q.v.). †504.24—with Urania (q.v.).

Origen (185-254)–theologian. 161.8.

*Orimis, 418.5.

Oriolopos–see Orion. 107.14.

Orion–in Greek myth a mighty hunter who, after death, became a constellation. 107.14; 185.24-25; 254.3.

Ormazd and Ahriman–principles of good and evil, supreme gods of the Zoroastrian religion. Ormazd or Ormuzd was the god and creator of light, good, intelligence: Ahriman was lord of evil, dark, ignorance. Their conflict lasts forever. †14.36—with Esau, Heremon (q.ç.v.); 73.36; 163.1-2; 239.34; 390.31; 425.28,34; 426.3; 466.33 (Mr R. E. Meehan).

Ormonde–see Butler.

Ornery, Lord–see Orrery

*O'Roarke, Colonel John Bawle—see John Bull. 99.32-33.

*Oropos Roxy and Pantharhea–see Oedipus, Rhea, Panthar? Greek *panta rhei* means "everything flows". 513.21-22.

Orr, William–United Irishman, alluded to in the street ballad "By Memory Inspired" which is quoted here. 69.8 (ter), 9 (ter).

Orrery, Roger Boyle, earl of (1621--79) – Irish-born British soldier, statesman, author of *An Answer*

to a *Scandalous Letter, Irish Colours,* and several plays. Possibly also the 4th Earl who translated Plutarch and had a controversy with Bentley (q.v.). 144.9; 533.34.

*Orwell–George? 41.9.

*Orwin–partly "Planxty Irwin" the air to which Moore's (q.v.) "Oh Banquet Not There" is sung. 397.6.

O'Ryan–see Orion. 185.25.

*Osborne, 122.8; 429.34.

Oscar–son of Ossian (q.v.), grandson of Finn MacCool (q.v.). Joyce may connect him with Oscar Wilde (q.v.). ?46.stanza 4—see Wilde; 66.35; 68.11; 326.7,16; 384.22; 476.22.

O'Shea, Katherine (popularly, Kitty), born Wood (q.v.) – a clergyman's daughter who brought Parnell (q.v.) low. I think she is the Helen (q.v.) of *Ulysses,* but Cleopatra (q.v.) is her natural role. Parnell called her "Queenie" (q.v.). For many years she was his mistress, mother of two of his children. The various accounts of their love are contradictory (her own account is of surpassing interest) and colored by partisan feeling, but it appears that while Parnell held the world well lost for Mrs O'Shea, he really didn't think he was going to lose it. When Captain William O'Shea divorced his wife, naming Parnell as co-respondent, the scandal gave Parnell's friends and enemies a chance to blast his career, which seemed (but perhaps was not) the same as blasting the chance of Home Rule. A few months before he died, Parnell married Mrs O'Shea. The many references to her in FW are too elaborate to explain here—see a biography of Parnell (O'Brien's is best). Generally, she is a temptress, and there is sometimes a suggestion (which was a part of Irish folklore at the time) that she destroyed

Parnell at the behest of the British government, sold him. Her name often doubles with *shee*, the Irish word for "fairy". 6.13; 9.7; 29.12; 49.28; 62.9-10 (papishee . . . qvinne); †68.21-22 —with Prankqucan (q.v.); †92. 31,32—with Shaun (q.v.); †123. 25—with Ossian (q.v.); 143.30; 182.30; 192.8,30; 243.17; 248.2; ?269.11; 290.1,5; 389.27-28; 395. 14,15,25; 409.2 (Captain O'Shea?); 486.33; 508.27; 536.36; 570.24, 25; 603.12.

Oshean–see Ossian and O'Shea. 123.25.

*O'Sheen–Ossian? 223.18.

Osiris–see Isis.

*Osler–perhaps Sir William (1849-1919), Canadian doctor. 317.16.

Osman–towel manufacturers who advertise "white as Osman towels". 235.6.

*Osmund, 88.23.

*O'Somebody, Morbus, 88.14.

Ossian or Oisin–legendary Irish warrior and bard, son of Finn MacCool (q.v.). After the Fianna were defeated by Carbery (q.v.), Ossian was carried off to the Land of the young by Nimb'(q.v.) and returned centuries later, like Rip van Winkle, to find his companions dead, himself ancient, and St Patrick (q.v.) in Ireland. He was baptised by St Patrick. Ossian was the supposed author of Macpherson's (q.v.) poems. †123.25 — with O'Shea (q.v.); ?139.22 (the reference is primarily to Lear, q.v., as the sea); 294.13; 326.6,18; 385.36.

Ostia or Osti–see Hosty.

*Ostman Effendi, 131.7-8.

*O'Strap, Patsy, 70.11-12.

?Oswald–of Ibsen's (q.v.) *Ghosts*. 264.27 (ashwold).

Ota–wife of Turgesius (q.v.). She and her husband were pagan, and when they ruled Armagh, Ota

held court on the high altar and prophcsied in the cathedral. 493. 19.

Othello–title hero of a play by Shakespeare (q.v.) and of operas by Rossini and Verdi (q.q.v.), *Otello*. In FW he typifies the sick sorrows of the polluted imagination of the impotent voyeur. Many "Moor" references include him. See Sycamore, Desdemona, Iago, Cassio. 196.13-14; 200.10; 281.20-21; 452.11; 460.23; 586.18; 607.27.

*Other Fellow–because he is associated with the Four (q.v.), I guess him to be the ass (q.v.) and Christ, present but uncounted as in "The Waste Land". (See Joyce to Miss Weaver, 7 June 1926.) There is, however, a letter of Stevenson's (q.v.) which reads: "I fell asleep and woke, and for the rest of the night repeated to myself a nonsense word . . . all night long one part of my mind (*the other fellow*) kept informing me that I was not repeating the word myself, but was only reading in a book that Swift had repeated it in his last sickness. . . . It was probably the same part that bid me compare it with the nonsense words of Lewis Carroll." 162.24; ?205.33; 384.13; 385.13; 386.28; 419.26; 598.11,19-20.

Otho, Marcus Salvius (32.69)–Roman emperor for three months. 132.6.

O'Toole, King–subject of a legend related (or invented) by Samuel Lover (q.v.). King O'Toole, a great hunter in the mountains, had an old goose which he dearly loved. St Kevin (q.v.) made the goose young again and won from the king a gift of land. 557.7.

O'Toole, St Lawrence – see St Lawrence O'Toole.

Ottavio, Don–in *Don Giovanni* (q.v.), Octavius in *Man and Superman*. †467.8—with Octavius Caesar (q.v.).

*Otto, Sands and Eastman, Limericked–the Four (q.v.)? Eastmans Ltd., Victuallers, are listed in *Thom's* (q.v.) *Directory* for 1906. 67.17,18.

Otus and Ephialtes–sons of Poseidon (q.v.), renowned for strength and daring. At nine years they threatened Olympus and would have destroyed it, had not Apollo (q.v.) destroyed them first. Ephialtes became a nightmare-causing demon. 493.23-24.

?O'Twomey or O'Tuama, Sean– 18th century Irish bard. †252.20 —with Tom and Tim (q.v.).

*Ouida Nooikke–yes no. Maybe novelist Ouida, M. L. de la Ramée (1839-1908). 221.28.

Outis–see Otus. Perhaps also see Noman or Ulysses (q.v.). 493. 24.

Ovid (43 B.C.—A.D. 17)–Roman poet. 166.11; 306.left margin.

*Owen, 202.6; 300.25; 397.2; 421. 8; 601.3.

Owen K–probably Owen Kerrigan, Dublin undertaker. 66.24.

Owen Mor–King of Munster—see Conn. 475.7.

Owens–brand of American glass. 101.29.

*Owens, D'Oyly–see Doyle and D'Oyly Carte. 574.1.

Owens, Mary–Merrion, an environ of Dublin. 294.20-21.

Oxford, Edward de Vere, 17th earl (1550-1604)–a Shakespeare pretender. †182.26—with Hog (q.v.); ?†266.10—with Bedevere (q.v.); 463.7; 467.31; 492.16.

Oxmantown–see Rosse. Oxmanstown is an environ of Dublin.

Oxthievious–see Augustus. Possibly includes Hermes (q.v.) who stole oxen or Ulysses's men who did likewise. 271.5-6.

P

*Paas and Pingster's, 550.13.

*Paddishaw, Serge–Shaw (q.v.)? 131.8.

Paddrock–see St Patrick. 611.2.

Paddy–either St Patrick (q.v.) or a generic name for an Irishman.

*Paddybarke's, 378-379.

Paderewsky, Ignace (1860-1941)– Polish statesman and pianist. 335.24.

Paganini, Nicolo (1782-1840) – Italian violinist. 50.15.

Page, Anne–heroine of Shakespeare's (q.v.) *The Merry Wives of Windsor* (q.v.)—see the play, I, i, 46-47. †513.27—with Virgin (q.v.); 553.1,2.

*Pagets, Lady of Tallyhaugh–perhaps the "honourable Mrs Paget" of *Ulysses*, 248/324. Dorothy Paget (d. 1960) was a famous horse-breeder. 622.27.

Palamon–with Arcite, subjects of Chaucer's (q.v.) "Knight's Tale" and of the Shakespearean (q.v.) or not-Shakespearean, *Two Noble Kinsmen*. 462.18.

Pales–Italian goddess of flocks. Also William Paley, author of *Evidences of Christianity*, who pointed out that for a watch there must be a watch-maker. 289.9.

Palestrina, Giovanni Pierluigi da (1526-94) – Italian composer of church music. 407.14.

?Palisse, Marchal de la–French soldier, killed at Pavia, 1525, subject of a humorous poem by Monnaye to which Stephen (q.v.) refers in "Scylla and Charybdis", *Ulysses*, 182/235. †380.25—with Ass (q.v.); †495.15 with Ass (q.v.).

Palladino, Eusapia – spiritualist medium, fl. 1905-7. 528.14.

Palliser, Lady Glencora (later Duchess of Omnium) – leading character in such novels of Trollope's (q.v.) as *Phineas Finn, Phineas Redux,* and *The Prime Minister.* 242.13.

*Palmer, ?384.18; 539.8.

Palmer, Paddy–see St Patrick. 254.10.

?Palmer, Mrs Bandman–played Hamlet and Leah (q.q.v.) in Dublin in the spring of 1904. 221.13.

Palmerston, Henry John Temple, 3rd viscount (1784-1865)–Irish peer and absentee landlord, British secretary for war. Palmerston Park is an environ of Dublin. 383.18-19.

Palumbus, Prestopher–Columbus (q.v.) affected by P-Celtic. 484.32.

Pamelas, Moll–Melpomene (q.v.). Perhaps also Moll Flanders (q.v.) and Pamela Andrews. Or Molly Bloom (q.v.) and Pamela, Lord Edward Fitzgerald's (q.v.) wife. 498.17; 508.19; 569.29.

Pamphilius, Cneius Babius–died while asking a boy the time. 596. 18.

Pan–Greek god of shepherds, flocks, forests. †14.20—with Pandora (q.v.); †88.9—with Morpheus, Socrates (q.q.v.); 158.35; 237.15; 340.31; 598.18.

Pancras, St–patron of children. 550.13.

Pandora ("all giving")–according to Hesiod, the first woman, the Greek Eve (q.v.). Anna Livia (q.v.) is Pandora when she distributes her gifts "for evil and ever", pp. 209-212, to her children. (See Joyce to Miss Weaver, 7 March 1924.) Pandora's box is—I don't know why—the letter from Boston, a combination of whine and hope springing eternal.

Pandora is connected with Biddy Doran (q.v.) whose last name comes from Greek *doron* or "gift".

Pandora is connected with Delia Bacon (q.v.) whom Hawthorne (q.v.) wrote of as "a gifted woman". I fancy—but have not much looked into it—that Pandora is connected with Dora, Dorothy, Dot, Doll (q.q.v.). †14. 20—with Biddy Doran (q.v.); 211.10 (see Hopeandwater); †369. 25-26—with Biddy Doran (q.v.).

Pango–see Pepigi.

Pankhurst, Sylvia–English advocate of women's rights. 388.26,28.

Panniquanne–see Prankquean and Anna Livia. 606.30.

Pantagruel–son of Rabelais's Gargantua (q.v.), "the all-thirsty one". 513.17 — with Taglione (q.v.).

Pantaloons, Dirty Daddy–HCE (q.v.) intended. In the modern pantomime or harlequinade, Pantaloon is a foolish, vicious old man. In Italian comedy he was a Venetian. 94.35; 513.21.

Panther or Pantherus–by one tradition, a Roman centurion, father of Jesus. 480.25; †513.22—with Rhea (q.v.); 565.19.

Paoli, Pasquale (1725-1807)–Corsican general, friend of Boswell (q.v.). Pauli's is a waterfront district of Hamburg. †117.24— with Peter and Paul (q.v.).

Paolo–loved his brother's wife, Francesca, and when their love was discovered, they died together. Dante (q.v.) meets them in hell at the end of the 5th canto of *The Inferno.* See Galeotto. 182.22.

Pappagallus and **Pumpusmugnus** —see St Gallus. *Pappagallo* is Italian "parrot". Pope Pius IX was known as "Papa Gallo". 484.35.

Paracelsus, Phillipus Aureolus, born Theophrastus Bombastes Ab Hohenheim, (1493-1541)–Alchemist, charlatan. 306.1.

Paragraph, - Peter – name under

which Samuel Foote, in *The Orators* (1762), satirized George Faulkner, a Dublin bookseller. See also Peter and Paul. 438. 19.

Pardonnell of Maynooth–I assume the reference to be to Parnell's (q.v.) statue in Dublin. (It was made by St Gaudens.) "The Pardon of Maynooth" was the ironic title of a massacre of an Irish garrison by the English in 1535. 553.12-13.

*Parimiknie, 194.28.

Paris–son of Priam (q.v.), abductor of Helen (q.v.), character of Homer's and Shakespeare's (q.q.v.). Would he be Parnell (q.v.) in *Ulysses*? 131.9; 230.13.

Parish–see Parrish. 199.8.

Park, Mungo (1771-1806)–Scottish explorer of the Niger. 51.20.

Parker, Charley–one of Wilde's (q.v.) boys, a soldier, who was prepared to testify against him in court. 138.13; 587.27,28.

Parnell, Charles Stewart, "the Chief" (1846-91)–in many ways Parnell is the pattern fallen-hero-expected-to-rise-again; and although his name does not perpetually occur in FW, references to his career abound. Parnell was a strange, Shakespearean, kingly man, who managed to frighten the English, and for this reason if no other, deserved the title that Tim Healy (q.v.), his Judas (q.v.), gave him, "The Uncrowned King of Ireland". (In FW Stephen Dedalus, q.v., is tied to him by plays on "crown").

The English made strong attempts to destroy Parnell. One of these began with *The Times* publishing articles, "Parnellism and Crime". They contained damning "Parnell" letters, especially one letter in which Parnell, an advocate of peaceful resistance to England, condoned the Phoenix Park assassinations.

A most dramatic trial—for it was, in effect, a trial of Parnell and Ireland—was the sitting of a commission, empowered to sift this, and other charges. The letter's forger, Richard Pigott (q.v.), was trapped on the witness stand because he misspelled "hesitancy". (When the word is "hesitency" in FW, someone is lying.) Pigott fled to Spain and when Scotland Yard closed in, he shot himself.

Parnell was now on a peak of power and popularity, but the peak was dizzy and he fell. He fell by his own faults, by English hypocrisy, by Gladstone's (q.v.) political shiftiness, by the late-roused fury of the Irish priesthood, and by the traditional faithlessness of the Irish people. Parnell was cited in a divorce action brought by Captain William O'Shea, husband of Parnell's long-time mistress, "Kitty" O'Shea (q.v.). The record of this liaison was neither more nor less sordid than any other, but it showed Parnell an adulterer, a user of false names—see Steward, Fox. Perjured testimony described him sneaking down a fire-escape to avoid Captain O'Shea.

If Parnell had laid low for a while he might have surmounted the scandal, but he insisted on fighting it out in an Ireland bitterly divided for and against him. (See the Christmas dinner scene in *Portrait of the Artist*.) On 6 October 1891 (Ivy Day) Parnell died because he did not change wet socks or because he was murdered by the priests—the Irish—Tim Healy—Gladstone—Mrs O'Shea—you pays your rancor and takes your pet enemy.

For FW the best Parnell books are by Barry O'Brien and Mrs O'Shea; the best account of the Parnell Commission is by John MacDonald (q.v.). Joyce often quotes the words on Parnell's statue "No man has a right to fix the boundary to the march of a nation". Other Parnell quotations in FW are his words to his followers when they were ratting: "When you sell, get my price" and "Do not throw me to the wolves". 41.36; 43.32; 169.25; 173.11; 243.9; 289.30; †291.note 8—with Charles the Simple (q.v.); 307.14; 334.14; 384.23; 455.34-35; 498.10-11; †553.12-13 — see Pardonell; †564.28—with the Scarlet Pimpernel (q.v.).

Parolles–knave in Shakespeare's (q.v.) *All's Well That Ends Well*. 565.28.

Parr, Thomas or Old Parr (1483-1635)–English centenarian, who when over a hundred was accused of incontinence and of getting a girl with child. Joyce often plays on the fact that, like Tristram Shandy or "cold Ham", his name is self-contradictory, for a "parr" is a young salmon. On the first page of FW (in the company of Miss Weston, q.v.) Old Parr begins the Fisher King (q.v.) theme. 3.29; 36.6; 81.22; ?170.28; 205.2-3; 332.5,7; ?458.4; ?533.28; 584.9; 597.17.

Parrio, Porvus–*corvus cario*. 484.32.

Parrish–strengthening food. 199.8; 432.1.

*Parrylewis – maybe Wyndham Lewis (q.v.). 352.14.

Parsifal–see Percival.

Parsuralia–see Persse O'Reilly. 353.24.

Parthenope – ancient name of Naples, a siren so chagrined by Ulysses (q.v.) that she drowned herself. 542.21.

Partholan–early Scythian invader of Ireland who landed at Innish Saimer in 1500 B.C. Keating says he was a giant, who invented Hebrew, Latin, Greek and Irish letters. 15.30.

*Partick Thistle, 378.18.

Partlet, Dame–heroine of Chaucer's (q.v.) "Nun's Priest's Tale". Toward Biddy Doran (q.v.) in the section called "The Hen" (I,v) Joyce adopts precisely Chaucer's tone. 124.24.

Partridge, John–see Bickerstaff, Perdix. †301.30—with St Patrick (q.v.); 344.7.

Pascal, Blaise (1623-62)–French religious philosopher and mathematician, worked in conic sections, infinitesimal calculus, probability and hydromics. See Jacqueline Pascal. 128.34; 302.3; 432.30; 446-447.

Pascal, Jacqueline (1625-61)–sister of Blaise Pascal (q.v.), infant prodigy who became a nun and converted her brother. Euphemia (q.v.) was her name in religion. She is quoted, 446.36. 432.30; 447.1; 528.24.

*Passivucant, 553.15.

Paster de Grace–see Peter the Great. 329.30.

Pasteur, Louis (1822-95)–French chemist. 356.24.

*Patathicus, 602.27.

*Patchbox, Merry Anna, 562.14.

Pater, Walter (1839-94)–English essayist and critic. 507.31.

*Patersen's, 421.1.

*Paterson and Hellicott, 529.30-31.

Patholic–see St Patrick.

Patkins, Paddy–an Irish Tommy Atkins (q.v.). 8.6.

Patomkin–see Potemkin. 290.note 7.

Patriack, Madre–Mother Patrick, a Dominican nun at the Eccles Street convent, pioneer in the Gaelic Revival. 408.32.

Patrick, St (b. 389)–male patron saint of Ireland as Bridget (q.v.) is the female. He was probably born in Britain. According to the *Vita Tripartita*, his baptismal name was Succat and FW is full of plays with "suck" and "suck it" (the Suck is an Irish river); his name in slavery was Cothraige, meaning *mog cethrair* or "the servant of four masters" (q.v.), which helps account for the strong connection between St Patrick and the ass (q.v.), also a servant of Four Masters—see also Man Servant; his name while studying for the priesthood with St Germanus in Gaul was Magonis because he was *magis agens* or more powerful than the other monks; the name given him at ordination was Patricius (which the Irish turned to Patrick), derived from *pater civium*. Mr Kelleher points out that these derivations are absurd, but they are all over FW. Patrick had yet another name: the Irish called him "Adzhead" from, it is thought, the shape of his tonsure, but it is also a maker's name and it is applied to Shem on 169.23. His father's name was Calpurnius, his mother's, Concessa (q.v.). See also Lorette.

As a boy, Patrick was kidnapped and sold into slavery in Ireland, where, according to one tradition, he tended herds for a chief, Milchu (q.v.), and his three brothers near Mount Slemish in Antrim; but Bury (q.v.), Patrick's most scholarly biographer, thinks he lived in Connaught near Croagh Patrick. Joyce adopts both views. After six years in slavery, Patrick escaped from Ireland on a ship that was exporting Irish wolfhounds. He entered the Church and returned to Ireland in 432 in response to a dream in which "The Voice of the Irish" prayed his return. There he labored for the rest of his life, having great success at converting pagans (see Laoghaire, Druid), but something less than success at getting on with fellow churchmen(see Ciaran) who attacked him for his bad Latin and for some sin committed in youth and confided to a friend who betrayed it. His so-called

"Confession"—a · most moving document—is a defense of himself and his works against their slanders. It is used in FW. A song of St Patrick's is mentioned—the *Lorica* or Breast-plate, known also as *Cry of the Deer*.

Many legends concerning St Patrick are used in FW. The one about his father's lighthouse in Boulogne is not known to me. The famous lighthouse at Boulogne was built by Caligula (q.v.) when he meant to invade Britain. (See Joyce to Miss Beach. 24 August 1926.) Others are: Patrick's driving the snakes from Ireland; Patrick's illustrating the Trinity by a shamrock plucked from the old sod; Patrick's lighting the paschal fire and vanquishing the Druids at Slane; and his discovery of a cave in an island in Lough Derg, Patrick's Purgatory (see Magrath), believed to be a real door, opening into Purgatory; his bringing into being a holy well in Dublin; his introducing Roman letters to Ireland.

St Patrick is a role of Shem's (q.v.)–see Joyce to Miss Weaver, 16 August 1924—opposed, as it were, to St Kevin (q.v.), a role of Shaun's (q.v.). In III,i,ii, Shaun assumes almost all Shem's roles and plays St Patrick as a picture-postcard saint. The real Patrick was a most attractive saint and Joyce must have found him so, for, on p. 3.line 22 he is peatreek or whisky, the water of life which raises Tim Finnegan (q.v.) from his bier. Patrick is supposed to have taught the Irish to make whisky. See also Cleopatra.

†3.22   thuartpeatrick—with St Peter (q.v.)

7.10-11 Singpantry's

12.22   somepotreek

?13.28   Succoth (a Jewish festival)

17.14-15 patwhat

†19.15-16 Paddy Wippingham— with Whittington and Wippingham (q.q.v.)

24.22	Cotterick's donkey (see ass)
27.2	pathoricks
35.24	Sempatrick's
51.8	Slypatrick
53.30	Puddyrick
54.15	A'Cothraige
58.23	Tap and pat and tapat-again (see Three)
69.25	triplepatlock
76.12	patly
78.23	patrizen
80.7	Pat's Purge
†81.18	cropatkin—with Kropatkin (q.v.)
28	patrecknocksters
84.13	Paddybanners
85.32	appatently
87.11	patrified
†91.6	Cliopatrick—with Clio, Cleopatra (q.q.v.)
96.24	it suck (the Suck is an Irish river)
120.2	Kat Kresbyterians
129.18	patricus
169.23	adze of a skull
177.4	pawdry's purgatory
179.23	patricianly
210.27	Patsy Presbys
228.6	Trichepatte
230.32	patriss
249.18	pat
254.10	Paddy Palmer
288.22	flop hattrick
292.9	pastripreaching
301.13	patpun
†30	croakpartridge — with Partridge (q.v.)
307.22-23	Saint Patrick
316.5	Prepatrickularly
-317.2	Patriki
326.3,4,25	Paddeus . . . Pat . . . Saint Petricksburg
347.16-17	San Patrisky
352-353	pungatories of sin practice
361.3-4,7	sen peatrick's . . . Pat
369.10	Mr Q. P. Dieudonney (see Jonathan and Nathaniel)
387.15	patrician
393.10	oldpoetryck
394.12	Oldpatrick
404.35	Haggispatrick
411.20	Glorious Patrick

425.28	Paatryk
†30	pucktricker's—with Puck (q.v.)
442.36	Saint Patrice
†447.29	pet ridge—with W. P. Ridge (q.v.)
463.1,4	Pat's . . . Paddyouare
464.16	sympatrico
475.35	patsy watsy
†478.26	Trinathan partnick dieudonnay—with Tristram, Nick, Nathan, Nathaniel, Jonathan (q.q.v.)
34	padredges
479.12	Pat
485.1,7,8	patrician . . . Suck at . . . Suck it
486.2	cawthrick (see Crow?)
487.23	Mr Trickpat
490.8,10,14	Mr Gottgab . . . pat . . . gabgut
491.11	Patrick's
†508.23	P. and Q. Clopatrick's—with Cleopatra (q.v.)
530.10-11	Saint Patrick's
531.33	primapatriock
550.7	S. S. Paudriac's
563.7	pat
565.18	pawdrag
582.29	patrick's purge
†611.2	Paddrock — with St Peter (q.v.)
7,10	Patholic . . . Same Patholic
24,27-28	Rumnant Patholic . . . patfella
612.15,18,19	Sukkot . . . blackinwhitepaddynger . . . apatstropied
618.15	sympowdhericks purge

Patti, Adelina (1843-1919)–Italian soprano. 184.23.

*Pattorn, Lorencz, 537.10.

Paudheen, Gus–*gospodin*, Russian "Mr" or "gentleman". 332.32.

*Paudheen Steel the Poghue–see Arra-na-Pogue. 600.32.

Paul, St–see St Peter.

*Pauline–refers in part to the "Pauline privilege": if at the time of marriage both partners are unbaptised, and later one is baptised, he may dissolve the marriage if the other refuses to dwell peacefully and sinlessly with him. 34.33.

*Paullabucca, Pandoria – plainly Biddy Doran (q.v.). See also Pandora. 369.25-26.

*Paullock, 39.5.

*Pautheen–whisky? 82.9.

Pavier, Thomas–printer who in 1619 attempted to put out a collection of Shakespearean (q.v.) and pseudo-Shakespearean (q.v.) plays. See Jaggard, Butter. 534. 23.

*Pavl the Curate–possibly the Man Servant (q.v.) since the Irish call a bar-assistant a "curate". 210.36.

Pavlova, Anna (1882-1931)–Russian dancer. †207.8-9—with Anna Livia (q.v.).

Paycock – protagonist of Sean O'Casey's, *Juno and the Paycock*, 1924. 551.4-5.

Payne, Howard (1791-1852)–American actor, playwright, author of "Home Sweet Home". 533.20.

Peabody, George (1795-1869) – American philanthropist. 101.13.

*Peace, Pieman–wasn't there an English murderer named Charles Peace? 202.14.

Peacer the grave–see Peter the Great. 503.27.

Peaches–born Frances Heenan, a young girl who in the 1920s figured in a scandalous case with an elderly man named Daddy Browning. The Isabel (see Issy) is an old variety of peach. 57.4; 65.26; 113.17; 251.24; 365.7; 485.20.

Peachum, Polly–heroine of Gay's (q.v.) *The Beggar's Opera*. Note *The Threepenny Opera* at 485.17. 147.13; 235.21; 485.20.

Peacock, George (1791-1858)–English mathematician who engaged in the famous (to whom?) struggle of "d-ism" over "dot-age" which

ended in the introduction into Cambridge of the continental notation in the infinitesimal calculus to the exclusion of the fluxional notation of Newton (q.v.). Peacock also dealt with Imaginaries. 303.note 2.

Pearcey, Erill – Persse O'Reilly (q.v.). It is also possible that Mrs Pearcey is included here. She was a London murderess, whose career is outlined in F. Tennyson Jesse's *Murder and Its Motives*. A not very innocent bystander in the case was referred to by the trial judge as "the man Hogg"—cf. FW 199.20. See also Hogg, hog. 493.3.

Pearl, Cora (1846-71)–born Emma Elizabeth Crouch, daughter of the man who wrote the music for "Kathleen Mavourneen". She became a noted Parisian courtesan. See Pearl. 225.26; 363.3.

Pearl, Little–see Maggies for listing. She is the symbolic little daughter of Hester Prynne (q.v.) in Hawthorne's (q.v.) *The Scarlet Letter*. Her changeable nature, her association with a brook are echoed on 153, 159. A child named Pearl and a stream are also principals in "The Pearl". See Onion, Tears.

Pears–English soap. A *Punch* cartoon has someone say, "I used Pear's soap three years ago, and since then I have used no other". 593.21.

?Pearse, Patrick – see Persse O'Reilly.

*Pearson, 60.25.

?Peaseblossom–fairy in Shakespeare's (q.v.) *A Midsummer Night's Dream*, waits on Bottom (q.v.). 412.31; 578.8.

Pedersen–see Kapp, Kappa, 221. 29.

*Pedersill–German *petersilie* is parsley. 161.28.

*Peebles–a place in Scotland. See

T. P. O'Connor. 260.left margin; 390.26; 537.13.

Peel, John–subject of an English hunting song. His "View Halloo would waken the dead". 31.28.

Peel, Sir Robert (1788-1850)–English statesman who divided his name between the English and the Irish police. 42.34; 332.11.

Peele, George (1558-97)–English playwright, author of *David and Bethsabe*, 1599—see David and Bathsheba. ?167.35; †468.36—with Shakespeare (q.v.).

Peeler and Pole–see Peter and Paul. 86.12.

Peena and Queena, 377.18-19; 508.23.

Peer, Gynt–Norwegian folk hero, subject of a play of Ibsen's (q.v.), a suite of Grieg's. 199.8; 365.6; 540.22-23.

Peer Pol–see Peter and Paul. 330.5.

Peg–see Maggies. A number of "Pegs" refer to J. H. Manner's play, *Peg o'My Heart*. Peg often melts into Pig (q.v.).

Pegasus–horse of the muses on which Bellerophon tried to fly to heaven. He fell, but Pegasus dwells among the stars. 231.21.

Pegger–see Festy, Beggar.

Peggylees, 508.19.

Pelagius (360-420)–heretic about free will and grace. He opposed the Augustinian (q.v.) idea of total depravity and said, "If I ought, I can". He was probably Irish and his ideas were for a time popular in Ireland. 182.3; 358.10; 387.6; 525.7; 538.36.

Pelican–brand of European ink. 359.1.

Pembroke, William Herbert, 3rd earl (1580-1630)–a leading contender for the part of Shakespeare's Mr W. H. (q.q.v.) and his mistress, Mary Fitton (q.v.) for the part of the Dark Lady (q.v.). He and his brother Philip are the "incomparable pair of brethren" to whom the First Folio is dedicated. He was described as "the Hamlet of the English court". Pembroke is an environ of Dublin. See also Strongbow? The Herbert is or was a bridge across the Dodder, near Dublin. I have little faith in the following references referring to Pembroke. †6.7—with Mr W. H. and Butt; †31.25—with St Hubert (q.v.); 74.15; 277.20; †376.5-6—with St Hubert (q.v.); †525.35—with Butt (q.v.).

Pen or Penman–see Shem.

Pender, 210.8-9.

Penelope–wife of Ulysses (q.v.); in *Ulysses*, Molly Bloom (q.v.). See also Penelope Rich, Ann Hathaway. 123.4-5; 212.10 (Penelope Inglesant); 359.14 (Danelope—with Dunlop).

Penn, William (1644-1717)–English Quaker, founder of Pennsylvania. Early in his career he was imprisoned for attending a Quaker meeting in Cork. 13.28; 19.32.

Penniless, Pierce–*His Supplication to the Devil* (1592), a prose satire against Gabriel Harvey, Martin Marprelate and other vices of the day by Thomas Nash (q.v.). See Ellmann, 300. I wonder if Stanislaus got the joke. See Persse O'Reilly? †210.22—with St Peter (q.v.).

Peny-Knox-Gore–see Knox? 606. 19.

Penzance, Lord–a Baconian. 501. 21.

Pepette–may come from French *pipet* and "Ppt", a name Swift (q.v.) gave to Stella (q.v.) in *Journal to Stella*. Issy often addresses people by this name and —somewhat less frequently—is so addressed. See Pip and Estella, Sir Philip Sidney. 14.8; 79.23; 96.14; 143.31,32; 144.17; 147.29, 33; †178.27—with Pip (q.v.); †232.9-10—with Pip (q.v.), 25;

248.19; 272.note 4; †276.20-21—with Pip (q.v.), note 6; 301.7; †314.25-26—with Pip (q.v.); 327. 29; 366.1; 374.11; 413.22,24; 449.31; 459.25; 470.21; 478.3,27; 500.23,25,32; 502.9; 540.14; †563. 5,7—with Pip (q.v.); 571.17; 588.6; 590.4; 601.28; †624.9—with Pip (q.v.).

*Pepigi–perfect tense of Latin *pango* (q.v.) which means to make fast or, figuratively, to compose or write. 575.29; 576.6,8.

Pepin the Short (d. 768)–King of the Franks. 568.34.

Pepper–19th century exhibitor of "ghosts" which were illusions made with mirrors and a magic lantern. Samuel Lover (q.v.) wrote a play, *The White Horse of the Peppers.* 120.14-15; 173.26; 214.16.

Pepys, Samuel (1633-1703)–English diarist. 614.15.

Percival, Parsifal–Grail Knight in early Arthurian (q.v.) legend, subject of a Wagnerian (q.v.) opera. He is certainly a part of the Grail Quest theme in FW, which begins on the first page of the book and is consummated when Michael Arklow (q.v.) drinks of Anna Liffey (p. 203). I am not sure whether the quest is repeated in the later sections of FW, but I think so. I do not understand Percival's relation to Persse O'Reilly (q.v.). See Miss Weston, Fisher King.

To understand the use of Percival on p. 43 it is helpful to know that the "Percival" was the hunting-horn, a term I have not found in dictionaries, but which is used by Surtees (q.v.) in *Handley Cross.* (FW 43 may imitate Surtees.)

43.31,35; 44.9; 72.35; 92.1-2; 106.5; 124.1; 125.16; 168.3; 222. 32; ?235.29; 240.10; 242.14; 251. 14; 332.7; 333.22,28; †339.18—with St Peter and Perseus (q.q.v.); 363.6; 426.21; 474.24-25; 491.25.

*Percy the pup–Percival? Percy Wyndham Lewis? 235.29.

Percy, Bishop Thomas (1729-1811) –in 1765 published *Reliques of Ancient English Poetry* which contains many old ballads. 493.3; 616.32.

Perdita–heroine of Shakespeare's (q.v.) *The Winter's Tale*, "that which was lost". It is impossible to understand her place in FW unless one compares FW 80.14-19 with *Ulysses*, 192-193/249-251, where Joyce, like Shakespeare, identifies her with the word "lost". See also Marina, Miranda, Elizabeth Hall, Florizel, Fawnia. 80.15 (*bis*); 95.29; 147.2; 213.33; 214.1; ?225.28; ?257.36; 270.20; 282.3; 293.33; 318.18; †363.23—with Miranda (q.v.); 376.17; 388. 4; 443.35; 454.23; 480.20; 527.4; 547.7; 556.19; †576.21 — with Miranda (q.v.).

Perdix–nephew of Daedalus (q.v.), killed by Daedalus who feared he might become a great artificer. Perdix became a partridge (q.v.). †447.28—with St Peter (q.v.).

Peregrine–see Four Masters.

Pergolesi, Giovanni Battista (1710-36)–Italian composer. 360.7 (pere Golazy).

Pericles (490-429 B.C.)–Athenian statesman. That he doubles with Shakespeare's (q.v.) Pericles, Prince of Tyre, may be seen from 306.note 3 which refers to the Prince's daughter, Marina (q.v.), and her unpaid, virtuous servitude in Mytilene. 306.left margin.

Perkin–see Warbeck. 39.4.

Perkun–Lithuanian thunder god. Perun, the Slavic thunder god, is also here. 23.5-6.

*Perousse–maybe the French dictionary *Larousse*, plus "peruse". *La Perousse* is a ballet of Balfe's (q.v.). 439.35.

*Perperp, 298.25-26.

*Perrichon, 254.14.

Perry, Matthew Galbraith (1794-1858)–American naval officer who negotiated the treaty that opened Japan to the west. He doubles with Pyrrha (see Deucalion). 288.22; 367.20.

Perse, St John–pen name of Alexis Leger, contemporary French poet. 419.25.

Persee and Rahli – see Persse O'Reilly. 497.27.

Persephone–see Proserpine.

Perseus–son of Zeus (q.v.) and Danae who slew Medusa (see Gorgon) and saved Andromeda. †339.18—with Percival (q.v.).

*****Pervenche**–periwinkle—see Selskar Gunn.

Petault–King Pétaud, at whose court everyone is master. From *le roi Pétaud* (Latin *peto*, I beg), title of the chief of the fraternity of beggars. Also Charles Perrault (1628-1703), French author who wrote fairy tales, *Contes de fées*. 118.28.

Peter, Jack and Martin–represent the Catholic, the Anglican, and the Lutheran creeds in Swift's (q.v.) *Tale of a Tub*. 7.4; 26.5; 86.2; †549.23-24—with Mathurin (q.v.).

Peter and Paul, Saints–usually occur as a pair and seem to be almost entirely a verbal theme. I do not know their precise significance to Joyce, but I assume they are respectively Shem and Shaun (q.v.). Their day is June 29. They were held opposed in early centuries of Christianity. A great many "rocks" or "stones" refer to St Peter—see Tree and Stone. †3.19 (rocks)—with Peter Sawyer (q.v.), 22—with St Patrick (q.v.); 13.23; 34.33; 38.28; †39.4-5—with Perkin (q.v.); 86. 12; 111.17-18; †117.24 — with Paoli (q.v.); 131.11,12; 142.27; 157.13; 159.4,5; 192.13; 199.19; 202.11,30; †203.31—with Petrarch and Petrock (q.q.v.); 205.34

(St Petersburg and New York—see Stuyvesant); †210.22—see Penniless; †269.8—with Peter Wright (q.v.); 274.7; 277.10; 288.note 6; 291.25; 326.26; 330. 5; 377.18,22,24; 339.18,22; 340. 19; 349.24; 350.18-19; 351.14; 355.2; †372.6—with Peter Sawyer (q.v.); 405.35; 407.15; †438.19—see Paragraph and Puff; †447.28 —see Perdix; 449.16; 451.17,22-23; 497.8; 520.14; 527.26; 535.19; †580.4-5—with Paoli (q.v.); 622.2.

Peter the Great (1672-1725)–Tsar of Russia. ?134.6-7; ?289.21; ?329.30; 344.27; 464.31; 497.28; 503.27.

Peter Paragraph and Paulus Puff–see Sts Peter and Paul and see Paragraph and Puff. 438.19.

Peter the Painter–Russian anarchist of the early 20th century. 85.5; 616.9.

Peter Parley–pseudonym of Samuel Griswold Goodrich (1793-1860)—author of children's books. 288. note 6.

*****Peter,** Roaring, 212.2.

Peters, Joe–see Jupiter.

*****Peters,** Pickedmeup – see Pickwick. 106.20.

Petersen–a coil which has to do with lightning protection. †310.3 —with Thor (q.v.).

*****Petitbois,** Bishop – French for peas? 440.12.

*****Petite** Bretagne, la princesse de la, 157.32-33.

Petrarch and Laura – Petrarch (1304-74) was an Italian poet, Laura a married woman with whom he fell in love and to whom he wrote sonnets. 203.30,31; 264. 12,14, †26—with St Lawrence O'Toole (q.v.); 397.15; 561.19.

*****Petries** – maybe George Petrie (1789-1866), a Celtic scholar, and/or Flinders Petrie (b. 1853), Egyptologist. 77.1; 481.35.

Petrock, St–6th century Cornish

saint. †203.31—with St Peter and Petrarch (q.q.v.).

*Pettit, Sequin, 372.11.

Petty, Sir William (1623-87)–English statistician and political economist, made a survey of Ireland called *The Down Survey*, because its results were set *down* in maps. †609.2—with Vaughan (q.v.).

Petulengro–head of the English gipsies, died in the '50s. 472.22.

Peurlachasse–see La Chaise. 76.36.

*Pferdinamd Allibuster – maybe Wellington's (q.v.) big "white" horse, Copenhagen (q.v.). Ferdinand (q.v.)? 535.9.

Phaethon–son of Helios (q.v.) who drove his father's chariot too near earth and fell to his death, struck by a bolt by Zeus (q.v.). 110.10.

Pharaoh–title of the rulers of ancient Egypt. Used in the Bible as a proper name for the ruler under whom Joseph (q.v.) served and also for the king who drowned in the Red Sea (Exodus, 14). 62.20-21; 129.36; 326.18; 387.26; 452.20; 580.12; 625.3.

*Phelan, 370.21.

*Phenitia – Phoenicia? Perhaps Fenicia, the original of Shakespeare's Hero (q.q.v.), heroine of Bandello's Twentieth Story. 85.20; †576.28-29—with Phoenix (q.v.).

*Phibbs, John, 187.20.

Phil the Fluter–song by Percy French (q.v.). See Flute? 6.8; 58.11-12; 63.27; 230.21; 297.18-19; 363.15; 444.8.

*Phil Phishlin–seems to be Philly Thurnstone (q.v.), whoever he is. Perhaps Percy French's (q.v.) "Whistlin' Phil McHugh". 50.33.

*Philadolphus – loving brother? 167.9.

Philip–see Pip, Sidney.

Philip of Macedon (reigned 359-336 B.C.)–Father of Alexander the Great (q.v.). A woman was once unjustly condemned by the king when he was drunk and she said she would appeal from Philip Drunk to Philip Sober. This may include Philippe Soupault who helped translate "ALP" into French. 542.9.

Philip the Good (1396-1467)–Duke of Burgundy about whom many medieval stories were told. †463.36—with Puck (q.v.).

*Phillyps, Captain–see Philip? 67.22,26; ?537.20.

Philomela and Procne–ravished sisters, turned into a nightingale and a swallow. In FW they are identical with Stella and Vanessa (q.v.). See also Tereus. 237.36; 248.2; 307.left margin.

Philpot, Saara–see Sarah Curran. 210.30.

Phiz–pen-name of Hablot Knight Brown, who illustrated Dickens (q.v.). 67.27; 231.17; 580.8.

Phoebe–the Moon (q.v.) personified. Phebe is shepherdess in Shakespeare's (q.v.) *As You Like It*. In the list of opera girls on 147 she may be Phoebe from *The Yeomen of the Guard*. "Phoebe Dearest" is a song. 147.14; 200.10; 415.10; 583.19.

Phoenician Sailor, Drowned–character in Eliot's (q.v.) "The Waste Land". The one-eyed merchant "melts" into him, he into Ferdinand (q.v.). I think this explains Joyce's phrase "Phenician blends". See Phoenix with whom the following double. 197.31; 221.32; 608.32.

Phoenix–fabulous sacred bird of the Egyptians (by them called *bennu*) who lived on air for 500 years, then flew to the temple at Heliopolis and burned to ashes, from which was generated a young bird to repeat the process. It is usually taken to symbolize the rising sun and resurrection. The word "phoenix" comes from the Greek word for "date palm" —see Artemis.

In FW Phoenix is a resurrection symbol, as it is in the poem in "Ivy Day in the Committee Room"—cf. FW, 27.13; but it takes on further meanings. The Eden of FW is sometimes Phoenix Park, which lies across the Liffey from Dublin and Chapelizod (q.v.). Joyce wrote Miss Weaver, 14 August 1927: "As to 'Phoenix'. A viceroy [Chesterfield, q.v.] who knew no Irish thought this was the word the Dublin people used and put up the mount of a phoenix in the park. The Irish was *fiunishgue* = clear water from a well of bright water there." Chesterfields' mistake was useful to Joyce, for in FW water, not fire, is the element of resurrection. In 1882 the Phoenix Park was the site of the assassinations of Lord Frederick Cavendish and T. H. Burke (q.v.) by the Invincibles, thus making it criminal ground, even as Eden. (See Parnell.) There is or was a Phoenix Tavern in Chapelizod and I have always thought it ought to be HCE's (q.v.) tavern, but there is no evidence of this. There was, in one of the environs of Elizabethan London, a Phoenix Theatre. I think the "Feenichts Playhouse", where the childrens' company presents "The Mime of Mick, Nick and the Maggies" (q.q.v.) combines park and theatre.

4.17; 17.23; 24.11; †27.13—with Phoenix and Turtle (q.v.); 55.28; 80.6; †85.17,20—with Phenitia, Phoenix and Turtle (q.q.v.); 88. 24; 128.35; 130.11-12; †136.35— with Phoenix and Turtle (q.v.); 196.23; †197.31—with Phoenix and Turtle and Phoenician Sailor (q.q.v.); 205.25; 219.14; †221.32 —with Phoenician Sailor (q.v.); 265.8; 311.26; 321.16; 322.20; †324.7—with Sphinx (q.v.); 331. 2; 332.31; 346.36; 382.4; 406.10; 454.34; 461.10; †473.16,17,18—

with Sphinx (q.v.); 520.1; 534.12; 553.25; †564.8—with Finn (q.v.); †576.28-29—with Phenitia (q.v.); 587.25; †608.32—with Phoenician Sailor (q.v.); 621.1.

Phoenix and Turtle–the identification is unsure, but I think these may refer to Shakespeare's poem. See Phoenix. 27.13,18; †85.17,20 —with Phenitia (q.v.); †197.31-32 —with the Phoenician Sailor (q.v.).

Phogg, Phineas–hero of Verne's (q.v.) *Around the World in Eighty Days*. See Ffogg? 5.33.

***Phyllis,** 60.4; 435.10-11; 491.30.

***Piaras** UaRhuamhaighaudhlug –Persse O'Reilly? *Thom's* (q.v.) *Directory*, 1906, lists O'Reilly & Co., 16 Eustace St., mantle manufacturers. 310.11.

Pickett, George Edward (1825-75) –Confederate general, led a charge at Gettysburg. 10.7; 291.19.

Pickle, Peregrine–title hero of Smollett's (q.v.) novel. 29.7.

Pickwick, Samuel–head of the club that jaunts about England in *The Pickwick Papers* by Dickens (q.v.). See Sam Weller. 106.20.

***Pieder,** Poder and Turtey—see 12.36. 220.20.

Pierrot–leading character in French pantomime. 594.34.

***Piersse,** Jetty – perhaps Black Peter, Santa's (q.v.) helper in Holland and, I suppose, elsewhere. 420.24.

Piers–see Pears. 593.21.

***Pig**–the ass and the hen (q.q.v.) of FW turn out to be persons. I dare not, therefore, ignore the pig in or out of the parlor, paying or not paying the rates. I do refuse to try to explain the relation of pigpork-hog-swine-boar, etc. to Francis Bacon, Richard III, Ham, Hamlet, Bach, Pigott, Cleopatra (q.q.v.). 9.36; 15.30-31; 25.12,33; 39.17; 41.17; 57.15; 60.15; 64.8; 69.7,19,22-23; 70.20-21; 71.12,23,

24; 72.14,15 (*bis*), 36; 83.7; 86.14,27; 87.9,21; 88.20; 89.15, 34; 91.8; 92.15; 99.19; 100.6; 101.9-10; 106.11; 119.7; 122.19; 128.14; 130.2,5; 132.5; 133.15; 136.8,14; 137.12; 141.8; 143.35; 149.7; 152.22; 163.6,17,27; 167.3; 170.20; 173.19; 176.29; 180.35; 186.14; 199.21 (*bis*), 23,26; 200. 13; 202.9; 205.30; 210.13; 212.5, 23; 227.32; 230.28; 232.36; 241.9; 243.7; 245.2; 253.11; 254.3; 260. left margin; 261.left margin; 262. 19; 269.12; 278.27; 282.3.note 4; 285.8; 296.21,31; 304.18; 313.16, 22; 314.23; 323.32; 326.33,36; 327.32; 331.12; 349.3; 359.26; 362.1; 366.26; 368.10,11; 369.23; 373.18; 374.35; 381.35; 407.19; 409.15; 410.16; 411.36; 415.34; 420.9,10-11; 422.17; 424.27; 430. 7; 432.15; 433.2,11,12; 435.7,24-25; 438.7,26; 442.35; 447.2,11; 455.9-10; 460.10; 462.35; 463.1,6; 482.5; 483.25; 485.31,32; 487.7; 496.18,19,20; 511.18; 517.5,15; 521.11; ?522.36; 533.35; 535.20; 538.32; 550.11; 566.26; 568.22; 576.26; 581.12; 584.4; 595.11; 603.19; 609.4; 613,27-28; 615.12; 619.11.

Pigeon–lived at the end of Dublin's South Wall and gave his name to the Pigeonhouse. See Raven and Dove. 197.32.

Pigott, Richard – obscure Irish journalist who forged the letters which *The Times* printed in "Parnellism and Crime". See Parnell for a fuller account. References to Pigott often double with Pigott's, a Dublin music store. Does his name tie him to Pig (q.v.)? 16.6; 43.32; 99.19; 133.15; 282.note 4; 349.3; 350.18; 1.537.

Pilate, Pontius–Roman governor of Judea under whom Jesus was crucified. 92.36 (see Four); 156.5.

Pilkington–see Polkington.

*Pill, Jom–from context John Peel (q.v.). 31.28.

Piltdown Man–a human skull and an ape's jaw (or the other way around) found near Lewes in Sussex and hailed as a missing link until unhailed. 10.30.

*Pim–maybe always Pim Brothers, Dublin drapers (q.v.). AE (see Russell) worked there a while. Champagne? 10.16; 232.15; 307. note 3; 333.9; 533.33-34.

Pim's and Slyne and Sparrow's. For Pim see above. Slyne and Co. is a ladies' tailor, Sparrow another. See also Kerse. 548.26-27.

*Pim, Peter, 43.9.

*Pinchapoppapoff, 461.15.

Pinker–Joyce had a literary agent so named. 43.28.

Pinkerton, Lieutenant – hero of Puccini's *Madame Butterfly* in which Patti (q.v.) sang. 184.23.

Pinkham, Lydia–purveyor of female tonic. 128.12.

*Pinpernelly, Miss, 445.11.

Piowtor the Grape–see Peter the Great. 497.28.

Pip and Estella–hero and heroine of Dickens's (q.v.) *Great Expectations*. Pip often ties to Pepette (q.v.) and Estella to Stella (q.v.). Since Pip is short for Philip, I am inclined to think the references include Sir Philip Sidney (q.v.) who wrote the sonnet sequence; "Astrophel and Stella" to Lady Penelope Rich (q.v.). 178.27; 232.9,11; †276.20-21—with Pepette (q.v.); 314.26 (four times); 563.7; 624.9.

*Piper, Peadher, of Colliguchuna–Peter Piper? 346.15-16.

Pipette–see Pepette.

*Pipkin, Josiah, 372.9.

Pippa–Browning's (q.v.) passing girl optimist. See Pip? Pepette? 55.16; 272.5; 301.7; 337.1.

?Pistol–in Shakespeare's *2 Henry IV* (q.q.v.). 63.4.

Pitre, Sinner and Poule–see Sts Peter and Paul. 192.13.

Pitt, William (1759-1806)–English

prime minister during the Napoleonic wars. His father, William Pitt the Elder, was also prime minister. 32.11.

Pitymount, Madame of–*Mont-de-Piété* is French for pawnshop. 541.13.

Pius, Pope–twelve popes. 67.22; 156.20.

Pius XI (1857-1939)–born Achille Ratti. 458.6.

Pivorandbowl, S.–see Sts Peter and Paul. 351.14.

Planck, Max (1858-1947)–German physicist. 505.28.

Plantagenets – surname conveniently but unhistorically applied to the royal line descended from Geoffrey, Count of Anjou, and the Emperess Maud. 504.2; 516.24.

Plato (b. 427 B.C.)–Greek philosopher. See Meno, Gorgias, Socrates. 164.11; ?192.17; 241.15; 257.11; 262.2 (*A*pproach *to* lead *o*ur *p*assage); ?286.3,18 (*p*lates *to* lick one), right margin (*a*potheosis of *t*he lustral *p*rincipium); 292.30; 307.left margin; 348.8; 417.15; 622.36.

Plautius, Aulus–Roman general, helped conquer Britain in A.D. 43. 581.22.

Plautus, Titus Maccius (254-184 B.C.)–Roman comic poet. Shakespeare's (q.v.) *Comedy of Errors* is based on Plautus's *Menaechmi.* See Dromio. †269.27—with Pluto (q.v.).

Playboy–Christie Mahon, hero of Synge's (q.v.) *Playboy of the Western World,* a play which was an insult to Irish womanhood. I think it unlikely he is included in Mahon (q.v.) references. 27.9; 183.4; 584.17.

Playfair, Tom–book by Father Finn (q.v.). 439.35.

Plimsoll, Samuel (1824-97)–British politician, reformer. The "Plimsoll line", a load line on ships, bears his name. 397.17.

Pliny the Elder (23-79)–author of the *Naturalia historia.* Pliny the Younger, his nephew, (61-113) was an orator and letter writer. 255.18-19; 281.4; 319.7; 354.26; 615.2.

Plooney–see Pliny.

Plotinus (203-62)–founder of Neo-Platonism. 470.20 (*bis*).

*****Plundehowse**, Herrin, 525.21-22.

Plunkett, Luke–a Dubliner who played Richard III's (q.v.) death-scene so comically that the audience demanded an encore. The corpse rose, bowed, and died again. 127.19.

Plurabelle–see Anna Livia.

Plussiboots, Auld Letty–I suppose Anna Livia, Letty, Puss-in-Boots (q.q.v.). 415.3.

Pluto–Greek god of the underworld. 78.12; 267.9; †269.27 — with Plautus (q.v.); 292.30; 387.13.

Plyfire–see Playfair.

Pobble that has no toes–protagonist of a poem by Edward Lear (q.v.). In German *pöbel* means rabble. 334.24; 454.35.

Pocahontas (1595-1617) – Indian princess, character in Brougham's burlesque, *La Belle Sauvage.* See John Smith. 106.16.

Pocahontas, the Mare – greatest dam of English race-horses. 559. 32.

Podex – see Johnny MacDougal. 398.2.

Podomkin–see Potemkin. 333.4.

*****Podushka**, 333.28.

Poe, Edgar Allan (1809-49)–American poet and prose writer, author of *The Purloined Letter.* 315.35; 534.21.

Poincaré, Jules Henri (1854-1912) –French mathematician. 304.5.

*****Poindejenk**, Dr, 179.28.

Poins–friend of Prince Hal (q.v.) in Shakespeare's *Henry IV* (q.q.v.). †143.19—with Poyning (q.v.).

*Pointefox–maybe just *pontifex*, maybe the Pontifex family of Butler's (q.v.) *The Way of All Flesh*. 242.35; 293.note 2.

Pointer the Grace–see Peter the Great. 289.21.

*Poirette–didn't there used to be a Paris designer with a name like this? 235.34.

Polkingtone, the rubberend Mr– title of a song. Swift (q.v.) also had a friend, the Reverend Mr Pilkington who wrote memoirs of Swift and his circle, including Sheridan (q.v.). His wife's name was Laetitia. 144.30.

Pollard and Crockard–the Dublin Annals for 1300 says base coins were so called. I always feel that these references ought to include Carter and Pollard who unmasked the Wise (q.v.) forgeries. †350.11 —with Oscar Wilde; 537.29.

*Pollockses–partly Pollux—see Castor. 28.6.

Pollux–see Castor.

Polo, Marco (1254-1324)–Venetian traveller. 567.35.

?Polonius–Ophelia's (q.v.) father in Shakespeare's *Hamlet* (q.q.v.). 616.24.

Polycarp, St (69-155)–Bishop of Smyrna, martyred at Rome. 254.9-10; 600.5.

Polygonus–son of Proteus. 231.30; ?339.35.

Polyphemus – cyclops, outwitted by Ulysses (q.v.) who told him his name was Noman (q.v.) and got him drunk. See Michael Cusack. 55.22; †73.9—with Ham (q.v.); 222.12; 229.15.

*Pomeranzia–from context Bare-niece Maxwelton (q.v.). Pomerania is a German province. 38.11-12; 249.16.

Pomfret, John (1667-1702)–author of a rather fun poem, "Choice". 19.15.

Pompadour (1721-64)–mistress of Louis XV. 351.34; 545.25.

Pompeius Magnus or Pompey (106-48 B.C.)–Roman triumvir. Pompey is a bawd and tapster in Shakespeare's (q.v.) *Measure for Measure*. 64.15; 153.17; 155.8; 307.left margin; 329.25; 484.35; 568.24,25,26.

Pompey–see Pompeius.

Ponce de Leon, Juan (1460-1521)– Spanish discoverer of Florida. 321.34.

Ponds–brand of cosmetics. 461.2; 526.29.

*Pondups, 616.35.

Pooley–19th century cricketer. 584. 12.

Poor Old Woman or Shan Van Vocht–poetically Ireland. 13.25-26; 48.15; 54.4.

Pope, Alexander (1688-1744)–English poet. See Belinda, Curll. 133. 20; 448.17; 466.11.

Pope, John (1822-95)–Union general at 2nd Bull Run. Lost. See Grant. 78.28 (*bis*); 84.6.

Popeye–character in "The Thimble Theatre" an American comic-strip. See Olive Oil. Also a character in Faulkner's *Sanctuary*. 13.30; 189.10.

Poppaea–wife of Nero (q.v.). 572. 36.

Poppagenua–Papageno and Papagena are low comedy in Mozart's (q.v.) *Magic Flute*. 513.20.

Poppakork, Rinseky–see Rimsky-Korsakov. 497.28.

Popper, Amalie–one of Joyce's pupils in Trieste for whom he had a tenderness—see Ellmann, 353 ff. 370.3.

Population Peg – see Margaret Sanger. 436.10.

Pork–see Pig.

Porphyry (233-304)–Greek scholar, historian, Neo-Platonist. ?100.17; 264.note 3.

?**Porpora,** Niccolo (1686-1767)–great singing teacher, composer of such operas as *Berenice* and *Camille.* 185.10.

Porsena, Lars–king of Clusium who was kept from Rome by Horatius at the bridge. This incident is the subject of one of Macaulay's (q.v.) *Lays of Ancient Rome.* 83.7-8.

Porson, Richard (1759-1808)–English classical scholar. 18.22.

Porteleau–Sir John Gray, head of Dublin's waterworks from 1863-75. His statue is in O'Connell Street. 553.13-14.

*__Porter__–Earwicker's name is sometimes Porter. HCE (q.v.) is a publican and sells porter, no doubt; he is also said to be a janitor or door-keeper, but I think there is more to it than that. Perhaps the drunken porter of *Macbeth* (q.v.) comes into it, for his soliloquy is indicated, 63.20 ff. See Janus. 16.4; 21.18-19; 22.6, 29-30; 23.10; 69.26; 72.3; 78.21; ?288.33; 89.16; 91.15; ?94.32; 104.30,35; 106.32; 114.25; 135.7; 136.4; 142.17; 186.35-36; 187.16, 17; 204.9; 219.18; 257.27; 260.18; 276.left margin; 327.33-34; 371.1; 372.4,9; 405.23; 406.2,10; 510.24; 511.19; 530.12; 531.25; 548.12; 560.8,22,24,26,31-32; 561.3; 563. 23; 570.15,19,20; 609.33; 624.15.

*__Porterscout__ and Dona–possibly Danu (q.v.). 388.15.

Portia–heroine of Shakespeare's (q.v.) *Merchant of Venice.* Note that an argument of Justice and Mercy follows. 186.36.

*__Portlund,__ "Mike"–see MacPartland. 602.17.

Poseidon–Greek god of the sea. †80.28-29—with Posidonius(q.v.).

Posidonius (b. 135 B.C.)–Stoic philosopher. †80.28-29—with Poseidon (q.v.).

Possum—see T. S. Eliot.

Post or **Postman**–see Shaun.

Posthumus Leonates–husband of Imogen (q.v.) in Shakespeare's *Cymbeline* (q.q.v.). 316.34; 377.9; 422.14; 563.4-5; †607.9—with Esau (q.v.).

Potemkin, Prince (1739-91)–Russian statesman, lover of Catherine the Great (q.v.). 290.note 7; 333.4.

Potiphar's wife–tempted Joseph (q.v.) and falsely accused him (Gen. 39). 193.20.

Potollomuck Sotyr–see Ptolemy Soter. 254.22-23.

*__Pott,__ Miss Butys–Miss Beauty Spot, stage name of Issy (q.v.) in "The Mime". 220.7.

Pott, Mrs Constance (fl. 1880)–author of *Did Francis Bacon Write "Shakespeare"? Thirty-Two Reasons for Believing That He Did.* (Cf. 64.35?) 111.23; 543.7.

*__Potter,__ 50.4.

Potter the Grave–see Peter the Great. 134.6-7.

Potter, Mr, of Texas–title hero of a novel by Archibald Clavering Gunters. 274.note 3.

Pott's Fracture–a bone fracture named for an 18th century Dr Potts. 73.8.

Pouilly-Fuissee–French wine. 547. 24.

Poulard, Mère–a restaurant at Mont Saint-Michel, noted for egg dishes. Joyce adds on Madame Puard who nursed him in Paris —letter to Miss Weaver, 28 May 1929. 184.31.

Poulichinello–see Punch. 43.23.

*__Pouncefoot,__ 367.5.

Pound, Ezra (1885-   )–American poet. 56.6; 89.25; 116.2; 167.29; 190.6; 322.14; 378.24; 566.1.

*__Powell,__ 376.22.

Power, Frank, "Ghazi" (1858-84)–Irish journalist, famous for practical jokes. He claimed to have been at Plevna and gained the title of "Ghazi" or "Brave" when he led a Turkish cavalry charge, crying, "Hooroo for Dublin!". He nearly hoaxed Parnell (q.v.) into believing Dublin had risen in rebellion and showed him a bullet wound in his leg, which turned out to be an "illconditioned ulcer", a blind boil. Power later became foreign correspondent for *The Times* and was killed trying to escape Khartoum. 56.11; 58.18; ?98.26; ?345.19; 346.21; †369.10—with Peer Gynt (q.v.); ?393.35; 521.22-23,24.

Power, O'Conor–19th century Irish politician. 317.30-31.

Power, William Grattan Tyrone (1797-1841)–best stage-Irishman of his generation. 569.35.

Power's – Dublin whisky-makers whose trademark is three swallows. 321.1; 495.4.

Powther and Pall–see Sts Peter and Paul. 349.24.

Poyning, Sir Edward–after cowing Perkin Warbeck (q.v.) in 1459, he induced the Irish parliament to pass "Poyning's Law" which said that all acts of the English parliament were in force in Ireland and that the Irish parliament could pass no laws without the king's approval. †143.19—with Poins (q.v.).

*Poynter, Reverend, 622.26-27.

Pranjapansie – son of Gautama (q.v.). 59.14.

*Prankquean–see Grace O'Malley, Queen. Irish *práiscín*, "apron", may apply. 20.32 (frasques); 21-23 (*passim*); 68.22; 95.5; 128. 17; 139.26; 223.33; 224.13; 250. 29; 269.21; 312.22; 337.22; 340. 11; 394.28; 398.36; 508.28; †606. 30.

?*Pratt, 124.25; 265.9-10.

Precious Stream, Lady – title heroine of a Chinese play by S. I. Hsiung. †332.22-23—with Anna Livia (q.v.).

*Prehistoric, 59.15; 385.18.

Prendergast, Cecil–hero of Swinburne's (q.v.) *Sadopaidia.* 144.6.

Prendergast, Reverend Patrick (d. 1824)–last Lord Abbot of Cong. He kept the Cross of Cong in an unlocked cupboard. A valuable collection of Irish manuscripts was left by him on his table one day and when he returned, his tailor had cut them up for measures. 124.15.

Presbutt, S. and other Dublin churches, are identified by Mr Kelleher in *The Analyst* No. X. 569.

Presbys, Patsy–see St Patrick. 210.27.

*Prestissima, 256.4.

Preston, Ethelred–book by Father Finn (q.v.). 439-440.

*Prettyplume, Ethna–Ethna Carberry? Eithne? 318.12.

Prévost, Abbé (1697-1763)–French author of *Manon Lescaut* (q.v.) and *Le Doyen de Killérine.* The reference is also to the ever-suspended coffin of Mohammed (q.v.). 5.22.

Prezioso, Robert–an Italian journalist who was attracted to Nora Joyce (q.v.)—see Ellman 327-328. Joyce dreamt of seeing him in tears (Ellmann 451) and, in his dream, associated him with the word "precious"—see FW 148.27. Mr Ellmann quotes a list of words which Joyce associated with Nora: garter, precious, Prezioso, Bodkin (q.v.), music, palegreen, bracelet, cream sweets, lily of the valley, convent garden (Galway), sea. Almost all of them occur FW 143-148. 143.31; 144.12; 146.31; 460.19; 500.25,28; 571.21.

Priam–last king of Troy, character of Homer's and Shakespeare's (q.q.v.). †6.23—with Brian O'Linn (q.v.); 131.8; 240.36; 513.20.

Priapus – son of Dionysus and

Aphrodite (q.q.v.), god of fruit-fulness, often represented as a phallus. 115.32.

*Priars, 438.17.

Pride, Colonel–Puritan responsible for Pride's Purge of the House of Commons in Cromwell's (q.v.) time. 355.13.

Priestley, J. B. (1894-)–British author of *The Good Companions*, etc. 237.8.

*Primrose, Galopping–from the context a tavern, but I wonder if it may not take in the Vicar of Wakefield? 39.35-36.

Prince, Morton–Boston neurologist who studied the personalities of Miss Christine Beauchamp (q.v.). ?239.29; 242.26; ?278.26; 280.22 (prints); 346.30; ?365.28; 460.12, 22 (prince . . . mort).

Princes of the Tower–little princes murdered in Shakespeare's *Richard III* (q.q.v.). 566.20.

*Prior–see Priars. 196.33; 358.9; 422.36; 438.17.

Priscian or Priscianus Caesariensis (fl. 500)–Latin grammarian. 467. 32.

*Pritchards – partly Vicar Pritchard (1579-1644), author of moral rhymes, *Canwyll y Cymry* (464.6) or *Welshman's Candle*. 44.8; 176.2 (in Joyce's correction).

Procne–see Philomela.

*Proctor, 366.23.

Prometheus (whose name means "forethought")–taught the arts of life to the Greeks, stole fire from heaven for mankind. 22.7; 297. left margin; 307.left margin; 560.1; 585.11.

*Promptboxer–possibly a reference to Shakespeare (q.v.), rumored to have been for a while a prompter in the theatre. 49.30.

Proserpine or Persephone – daughter of Zeus and Demeter (q.v.), raped by Pluto (q.v.), became Queen of the Underworld.

See Kore, Two Goddesses. 267.11; 583.13.

*Proud, Nicholas–the devil? 12.25.

Proudie, Bishop–character in Trollope's (q.v.) Barchester novels. 484.19-20.

Proust, Marcel (1871-1922)–French novelist—see Swann. 303.14.

Prout, Father (1804-66)–pen-name of F. S. Mahoney, an Irish Jesuit who was dismissed from his order in 1830. He wrote light verse and is best known for "The Bells of Shandon". 482.31.

*Prue, 337.27.

*Prunella, 206.35.

Pruny-Quetch, Mrs–Prunikos or Sophia (q.v.). According to certain Gnostics, she was a female Holy Ghost, sister of Jesus. She sent the serpent to tempt Eve (q.v.) or maybe was the serpent. See "Ophites" in the 11th *Britannica*. She is one of a string of fruit ladies—prune and German *Zwetsche* or "plum". 550.32-33.

Prynne, Hester–heroine of Hawthorne's (q.v.) *The Scarlet Letter*. In FW, I think Joyce takes Lawrence's opinion of her as avenging herself on Dimmesdale. Thus she ties to the various Hesters listed under those other avengers, Stella and Vanessa (q.v.). See also Little Pearl.

Pshaw–see G. B. Shaw. 303.7.

Psyche–in the *Golden Ass* and Freud (q.v.), the personification of the soul. 416.6.

Ptah–Egyptian god, artist, master-builder. 411.11; 415.26; 590.19.

Ptolemy–2nd century Alexandrian mathematician, astronomer and geographer. In *Geographike syntaxis* he gives an early, inaccurate description of Ireland which he places farther north than any part of Wales. He called Dublin "Eblana" and thought Howth (q.v.) an island. 13.11; 529.34; 540.7.

Ptolemy Soter–founder of the Ptolemaic dynasty in Egypt. Cleopatra (q.v.) was the last of the line. 198.2; 254.22-23.

Puard–see Poulard. 184.31.

Puck–mischievous sprite in medieval folklore—see Lob. In Shakespeare's (q.v.) *A Midsummer Night's Dream* he plucks a flower (a pansy) whose juice mixes up the heart's natural impulses. In *The God of the Witches*, Miss Murray derives his name from *bog*, the slavic word for "god". 37.30; 90.33; 210.35 (see Ellen Terry); 227.29; 231.21; 236.31; 278.13, †note 1—with Jerry (q.v.); 304.right margin; 326.3; 338.32; 369.29; 371.12; †425.30—with St Patrick (q.v.); †463.36 — with Philip the Good (q.v.); 496.20; 524.35; 569.25; 604.3.

Puff, Mr–character in Sheridan's (q.v.) play *The Critic*. 438.19.

Pugases–see Pegasus. 231.21.

Pugh – family of Dublin glass-workers. I am not sure any but the first reference belongs to them. 76.11; 349.3; 350.18.

Pukkelsen–from Norwegian *pukkel* or hunchback. It is applied to the Norwegian Captain (q.v.) and links him to HCE (q.v.) who is also hunchbacked. 316.1; 319.23; 323.16; †325.29—with Buckley (q.v.); 326.11-12; 339.2.

Pulcinella–female of Punchinello —see Punch. Joyce puns on *pulcino* or "chick". 220.21.

***Pules,** Master, 166.20.

Pumpusmugnus – see Pompey. 484.35.

Punch and Judy–best known puppets. I think there is a very remote possibility that they may be Judith Shakespeare and her vintner husband, Thomas Quiney (q.q.v.). 4.25; 29.35; 40.12; 43.23; 116.23; 133.23; 255.26; 257.23; 261.1; 334.20-21; 368.26; 455.2; 468.16; 514.13,33; 594.35; 620.23-26.

Punchus and Pylax—two of the Four (q.v.) as Justices. See also Pilate. 92.36.

Purcell, Patch–in the 19th century, the principal mail-coach owner in Ireland. ?187.18; 412.22; 516.23-24.

Purefoy, Mrs–birth-giving Mrs Pure Faith (plus Betty Foy?) in *Ulysses*. 296.2.

***Puropeus** Pius–Pope Pius? 14.9.

***Purple** top, 82.3.

Pusey, Edward (1800-82) – English divine, leader of the Oxford movement. 510.33.

Puss-in-Boots–clever cat in fairy-tale and pantomime. †415.3—see Plussiboots: 531.22; 622.11.

***Pykemhyme** – Packenham? See Kehoe. 379.36.

Pylax or Pilax–see Pilate.

Pyncheon–family which owns the House of the Seven Gables—see Hawthorne, Maule. ?69.33; 435.33.

Pyramus–see Bottom.

Pyrrha–see Deucalion.

Pythagoras–Greek philosopher of the 6th century B.C. 116.30; ?310.32.

Q

***Quarta** Quaedam, 101.9.

Quasimodo–Hugo's (q.v.) hunchback of Notre Dame. 248.1.

Queen or Quean–in FW a few of the meanings of this word are: prank-quean, Elizabeth I, Kitty O'Shea (q.q.v.).

Queen of Night–character in Mozart's (q.v.) *The Magic Flute*. 147.13; 241.22; 497.32.

Queenie–what Parnell (q.v.) called Mrs O'Shea (q.v.). There is a chance that it may also refer to Judith Quiney (q.v.), whose name was so pronounced. †147.13—with Queen of Night (q.v.); †234.13—with Maya (q.v.); 577.2.

Queen's Men–Elizabethan theatrical company, rivals of Shakespeare's (q.v.) company. See King's Men, Strange. 219.28.

Queequeg–African in Melville's (q.v.) *Moby Dick*. 270.14.

Quemby, P. P.–see Quimby.

*Questa and Puella–see Two. 61.16.

*Quickdoctor, Mrs Wildhare–maybe Mistress Quickly (q.v.). 227. 4-5.

Quickenough, Mrs – the washwoman who turned into a tree. 620.19.

*Quicklow, 175.3.

?Quickly, Mistress – character in Shakespeare's *1 Henry IV*, *2 Henry IV*, Henry V (q.q.v.) and *The Merry Wives of Windsor*. 227.4-5.

Quilbhe–provided the ale which kept the Irish gods immortal. †406.33—with Gilbey (q.v.).

*Quilty, Peggy, 212.7.

Quimby, Phineas P. (1808-86)– mental healer of Portland, Maine, who cured Mrs Eddy (q.v.). Some say she borrowed most of Christian Science from him. 536.6.

*Quin–some Quin or Quinn reference ought to include John Quinn, a New York lawyer, and patron of James Joyce. Joyce would have liked the late ado over Quinn's letters. 58.10; 305.20.

Quinet, Edgar (1803-75)–French historian, translator of Vico (q.v.), associate of Michelet (q.v.). 117. 11.

Quiney, Judith Shakespeare (1585-1661) – Shakespeare's (q.v.) younger daughter, twin of Hamnet Shakespeare (q.v.). In 1616 she married Thomas Quiney (pronounced Queenie, q.v.), a vintner, later keeper of the Cage Inn. They married in such haste and informality that they were excommunicated. Tradition has it that Shakespeare, Jonson (q.q.v.) and Drayton drank too much from a silver bowl (which Shakespeare left Judith in his will) at this wedding and Shakespeare took ill from drink and died some weeks later. This wedding party may lie behind FW 510 ff.
In *Ulysses* Stephen Dedalus (q.v.) never mentions Judith. She does not fit his theory, for she gave Shakespeare three grandsons and Stephen denies him even one —see *Ulysses*, 205/267. Shakespeare also seems to have felt she did not fit in, for the author of *King Lear* made an unequal will, leaving most of his money to Susanna and Elizabeth Hall (q.q.v.).
All the same, I keep feeling that Judith lurks in FW, disguised as something or other. Maybe she and her husband are Punch and Judy (q.v.), maybe with Susanna she makes up the double girl or Sosie (q.v.), maybe, like Viola (q.v.), she dresses up as a boy and is mistaken for her twin, Hamnet or Hamlet. See also Judith.
57.19; 127.24; ?171,24,25; †207. 36—with Judith (q.v.); 254.31; 256.19; 297.16; 327.1; 358.33; 379.16; 444.22; 600.25.

Quinn, Father–air to which Moore's (q.v.) "When E'er I see" is sung. See Father Flynn? 562.27.

Quixote, Don–title hero of a novel by Cervantes (q.v.). 198.35; †234. 4—with Ass (q.v.); ?286.note 3; †482.14—with Ass (q.v.).

R

Ra–Egyptian sun-god. See Aten. 415.11-12.

Rabworc–Crowbar, probably in reference to the Crowbar Brigade. See Festy King and Meleky. 86.13.

Rachel and Leah (Ewe and Languid)–the wives for whom Jacob (q.v.) served (Gen. 29-30). Their use as mirror girls takes off from Dante's (q.v.) *Purgatorio* xxvii, 100 ff. The editor explains that they were Old Testament types of the Contemplative and Active lives, as Mary and Martha (q.v.) are in the New Testament. ?57.5 (lea); 145.5 (ewe); †221.12—see Kate, Varian; 271.6,7 (you . . . lie); 279.note 1; †371.33-34—see Rose; 396.14; 466.6,25-26; 580.5.

Radouga, Rab–Russian "rainbow", "slave". 248.35.

Raffles–gentleman cracksman, hero of novels by Hornung. 50.26.

Raglan, Fitzroy James Henry Somerset, 1st Baron (1788-1855)–commander of British troops in the Crimea. 132.21; 339.10.

Ragnar Lodbrok–Viking chief, subject of a saga. He fought mainly in Northumbria, but tradition says he died in Ireland and some attempt has been made to identify him with Turgesius (q.v.). 19.4; 22.36; 64.3; 89.17; ?169.16; 313. 15,23-24; 360.17; 373.29; 444.5.

Ragonar Blaubarb – see Ragnar Lodbrok? 169.16.

Rahoulas or Rahula–son of Gautama (q.v.). 62.5.

Rainbow–see Seven.

Raleigh, Sir Walter (1552-1618)–favorite of Elizabeth I (q.v.), soldier, poet, author of a *History of the World.* Delia Bacon (q.v.) believed he joined with Francis Bacon (q.v.) to produce Shakespeare's (q.v.) plays. Raleigh explored the new world, founded the first Virginia colony. Suppressed Irish rebels, planted protestants in Munster, and was an absentee Irish landlord. He brought tobacco to England and the potato in 1610, perhaps to Ireland (see Hawkins). In FW there are times (e.g. 271.25-28) when the apple of Eden seems to be the earth-apple or potato. A potato may have been *moly* in *Ulysses,* but it was at first considered an aphrodisiac. The 11th *Britannica* calls it Raleigh's "fatal gift" and a "demoralizing esculent". In the 19th century famine years, the potato brought a glut of death and exile to the Irish. Because of pride and atheism and a tax on drink, he became the most unpopular man in England, the devil incarnate, and under James I (q.v.) he had a great fall. His name was often spelled "Rawley" and so pronounced, for James greeted him with "I have heard but rawly of thee". In FW he doubles with Persse O'Reilly (q.v.). 37.32; 49.14; 133.11; 301. 27; 343.21; 362.2; 626.25.

Ralli, Baron–Greek to whom Joyce owned his "liberation" from Austria in 1915. 174.29.

Ralli, Fino–see Finn MacCool and Persse O'Reilly. See Ralli? 447.24.

***Ralph** the Retriever, 613.21.

Rama or Raman–the 6th, 7th, and 18th avatars of Vishnu (q.v.). Rama and Krishna (q.v.) are the avatars most worshipped by Hindus. 18.29; 374.22 (Namar).

***Ramasbatham**–can be broken into Rama and Bottom (q.q.v.), but must take in someone named Ramsbottom. 18.29.

Rameses–several Egyptian pharaohs. 452.21.

Ramrod–see Nimrod. 435.13.

Ran–Norse sea god. 316.20.

Random, Roderick–title hero of Smollett's (q.v.) novel. 28.36; †381.11 - 12 — with Roderick O'Connor (q.v.); 405.9; 583.6.

Ranji or Ranjitsinhji – Rajput cricketer, played for England, made over 3,000 runs. 10.9.

*Rantipoll, 193.20.

Raoul–hero of Meyerbeer's (q.v.) opera, *Les Huguenots*; character in *Sweets of Sin*. 133.20; 456.25.

Rask, Christian Rasmus (1787-1832)–Danish philologist, master of 25 languages. 233.34.

Raskolnikov–hero of Dostoievsky's *Crime and Punishment*. In Russian *raskol* means a heretic or dissenter of a particular sort. 156.10.

Ravel, Maurice (b. 1875)–French composer whose works include "Ma Mère l'oye"—see 428.7. 366.20.

*Raven and Dove–one of the large verbal themes of FW. The reference is sometimes to Noah's (q.v.) raven and dove, sometimes to the southern constellations Corvus and Columba. See Stars. 7.6,8; 8. 33,34; 10-11; 49.9,10,11; ?61.2; 62.4; ?67.36; 68.26; 72.13; 105.27, 32; †129.30,31—Poe's (q.v.) raven and Columbus (q.v.); 136.13,29, 30; 178.35,36; 197.20,30,32; 238. 25; ?247.35; 248.35; 266.note 3; 327.35,36 (see Huggin); 329.13; 333.17; 338.31; 354.28; 357.16,17, 20; 358.1,4,5,12-13; 360.28; †361.1 —with Columbine (q.v.); 363.7; 364.25; †365.23—with Rosaline (q.v.); 371.0,7; 377.22; †409.15,17 —with Columbus (q.v.); 480.1,3; 491.14; 495.18,19; †496.30,32— with Columbus, Le Caron (q.q.v.); 521.17; 523.29,30; 579.14,15; 622.1,2.

*Rayburn, Gladeys, 387.35.

Reacher the Thaurd–see Richard III. 319.20.

*Readbreast, Reuben–the robin redbreast formerly symbolized Jesus. 211.27; 537.9.

Reade, Charles (1814-84)–English novelist and dramatist, author of *The Cloister and the Hearth* and *Love Me Little, Love Me Long*. ?63.2; 364.21.

Reade, Lector–probably not a person. A lector is one who reads lessons in the church service. 197.6.

*Real, Kirschie–*kirsch(e)* is German "cherry" and a brandy. 207.12.

Rebecca – wife of Isaac (q.v.), mother of Jacob and Esau (q.v.). 203.4; †483.19—with Anna Livia (q.v.).

*Recknar Jarl or Roguenor–possibly Ragnar (q.v.). 313.15.

Redfern–late 19th century Paris couturier. 548.25.

*Redmond–Parnell (q.v.) had two loyal followers of this name. 552. 11.

Red Riding Hood–heroine of a nursery tale. 33.1; 307.note 1; 411.24; 551.8.

*Reed–Shem (q.v.)? Charles Reade? 94.6.

Reeves, John Sims (1818-1900)– English vocalist, first a baritone, then a tenor, sang in some of Balfe's (q.v.) operas. †408.21-22 —with Shem (q.v.).

*Reginald, Loudin, 342.34.

Reich, Roamer – Roman empire. 553.35.

Reid's Family Stout–widely guzzled in the British Isles. 52.4.

*Reilly, Big – perhaps Persse O'Reilly (q.v.). 581.7.

*Reilly-Parsons – probably Persse O'Reilly (q.v.). 26.32.

Rejane, Gabrielle – 19th century French actress. 64.19.

Relle, Purses–see Persse O'Reilly. 580.30.

Rembrandt (1606 - 69) – Dutch

painter. 54.2; †176.18—Riangbra (q.v.); 403.22.

Remus, Uncle – Joel Chandler Harris's old negro story-teller. See Brer Fox. †442.8—with Remus (see Romulus).

Renée–see Descartes. 269.note 2.

Renshaw–see Grimshaw. 132.10.

*Reparatrices, Marie, 618.14-15.

*Repippingham, 298.26.

Reszke, Jean de (1850-1925)–Polish tenor. He and Nellie Melba (q.v.) sang in *Romeo and Juliet* (q.v.). 81.34; †200.9—with Romeo (q.v.); 408.4.

Reuters–British news agency. 364. 19; 421.32; 495.2; 593.18.

*Reynaldo, 192.14.

Reynard the Fox–title character of a medieval beast epic. See Fox, Noble, Baldwin, Fyrapel. 97.28; 480.23 (wrynecky fix).

*Reynolds, Leatherbags–possibly Thomas Reynolds who informed on the United Irishmen. He got a £5,000 pension. 26.1.

*Reyson-Figgis, Mrs, 550.32.

Rhea–wife of Cronos (q.v.), mother of Zeus (q.v.) and other Olympic gods. †283.28-29—with Herman and Dorothea (q.v.); 327.11; 513.22—with Panther (q.v.); †583.17—with hen (q.v.).

Rhea Silva–by Mars (q.v.) became mother of Romulus and Remus (q.v.). †467.35—with Romulus (q.v.).

*Rhoda–Mr Wilder knows a song about Rhoda who lived in a pagoda and sold tea and soda— it sounds like a lovely song. He also says Roda Roda is a humorous German novelist. 78.17; 81.9; 266.21-22; 434.7; 466.19; 469.34; 478.13.

*Rhodagrey, 583.18.

*Rhoss's, 443.29.

Rhosso - Keevers – see   O'Keef - Rosses. 310.17.

Riangbra, Loeg mac–in Cuchulain's (q.v.) fight at the ford of Glas Cruind his steam makes a rainbow round his charioteer, Riangbra. †176.18—with Rembrandt (q.v.).

Rib–see Eve.

*Ribboncake, Bishop, 340.27.

Rich, Lady Penelope (née Devereux) (1562-1607)–the Stella (q.v.) of Sir Philip Sidney's (q.v.) "Astrophel and Stella"—see Pip and Estella. She has been a candidate for Shakespeare's Dark Lady (q.q.v.). See *Ulysses,* 199/258. See Penelope. 252.23; 357.17; 406.15; †563.20—with Gipsy Devereux; †571.32—with Mr W. H. (q.v.); 622.33.

Richard III (1452-85) – English king of the House of York (q.v.), crook-backed, known as the Boar or the Hog (q.v.), from his crest. In Shakespeare's (q.v.) play he is a brother-battler—see Princes in the Tower, George, Duke of Clarence. In *Ulysses,* 199, 206-209/258, 268-272, he is associated with Burbage (q.v.) and with Shakespeare's brother Richard (q.v.). See also Tom, Dick, Harry? Luke Plunkett, Richard Rowan. 48.17; †71.12 (York's porker)— with Bacon (q.v.); 126.30; 127.17; †134.11—with Burbage (q.v.); 138.33; 230.22; 241.9; 319.20; †604.29 — with Dicky Tierney (q.v.).

*Richman, 515.4.

*Richmond Rover, 375.21.

Rick–see Richard III, Burbage.

*Rickets–possibly Charles Ricketts, 19th century illustrator. 212.27; 293.5.

Ridge, William Pett (b. 1864)– English author of such works as *Mord Em'ly* and *Erb.* †447.29— with St Patrick (q.v.).

Ridley, Nicholas (1500-55)–English bishop, burned as a heretic under Bloody Mary. 49.18.

*Rigagnolina, 225.15.

Rigoletto–title character of Verdi's (q.v.) opera, a hunch-backed jester. 234.26.

Riley, Paddy–subject of Percy French's (q.v.) song "Come Back, Paddy Riley, to Ballyjamesduff". 485.15-16.

Riley, Pitsy–see Persse O'Reilly. 342.16-17.

Rimbaud, Arthur (1854 - 91) – French poet. 319.5.

Rimsky-Korsakov, Nicholas (1844-1908)–Russian composer. 497. 28.

Ringling Bros.–American circus. 367.31.

Riviere, Anne–singer who married a composer, Sir Henry Rowley Bishop. †289.25-26—with Anna Livia (q.v.).

*Riviers, 586.23.

*Rizzies–Izzies? 454.21.

Roastin the Bowl–see Rosin the Beau. 231.33.

Robber and Mumsell–see Maunsel. 185.1-2.

Robert of Retina–Englishman who made the first Latin translation of the Koran. 443.2.

Robert the Devil–hero of French romance and Meyerbeer (q.v.) opera. 540.29-30.

*Robidson, Jo–see Man Servant? 199.29.

*Robinson, 480.32.

Robinson, Paschal, Monsignor–papal nuncio to Ireland in the 1030s. †243.21 with Robinson Crusoe (q.v.).

Robinson, Peter–London department store. †65.15—with Robinson Crusoe (q.v.).

Robinson, Swiss Family – title characters of a novel by J. S. Wyss, 1813. 129.34-35.

*Robort, P. C.–Robert and Robot? 86.7.

*Roby – English music-hall performer? 156.27.

Roche, Sir Boyle (1743-1807)–Irish M.P. noted for his bulls. Once in the House, he said, "Mr Speaker, it is impossible I could have been in two places at once, unless I was a bird". †449.16—with St Peter (q.v.).

*Roche, Pomeroy, of Portobello, 290.note 5.

*Rochelle–see Rachel who married Jacob (q.v.) who was associated with pottage. 466.25-26.

Rochester, John Wilmot, earl of (1647-80)–English author who wrote erotic books. 439.26.

Rock or Stone–see Tree and Stone.

Rockefeller–American family, symbolizing money. 129.21.

Roderick–see Roderick O'Conor.

Rodin, Auguste (1840 - 1917) – French sculptor. 435.36.

Rody the Rover or The Ribbonman –novel by William Carlton, 1845. Rody is a provoking agent for the English government. 228.24; 551.14.

Roe–large Dublin distillers. 122.12; 543.33.

*Roe of the fair cheats, 394.18; 397.36.

*Roe, Williams, Bewey, Greene, Gorham, McEndicoth, Vyler–are doubtless so many well-known Dubliners but, as Mr Higginson points out, they are also the spectrum—see Seven. Roe is a reddish color; Williams is William of Orange (q.v.); buidhe is Irish for yellow; Greene is green; gorm is Irish for blue; McEndicoth sounds kind of like indigo; Vyler really does sound like violet. 277.note 4.

*Roebucks, 70.12.

*Roga, 602.12,13; 604.2; †604.18— with Shem (q.v.).

*Roger (famous with the spear)–it was a bawdy word in the 18th century. It ought to refer sometimes to Casement (q.v.). See also Rogers, Rogger, Rutland. 66.21; 177.36; 290.note 3; †363.8—with Almayne Rogers (q.v.); 373.15; 439.26; 554.3 (*bis*); 559.36.

*Rogers, Almayne–possibly Roger Casement (q.v.). 363.8.

Rogers, Romeo–one of Joyce's friends in Trieste. †481.16—with Romeo.

Rogerson – Sir John Rogerson's Quay is on the Liffey. †211.16—with Crusoe (q.v.).

Roggers–see Roger. The reference here is to an incident in Swift's (q.v.) life. When he first went to Ireland, he had few parishioners. On Wednesdays and Fridays he would read prayers to himself and his clerk, named Roger, beginning, "Dearly Beloved Roger, the Scripture moveth you and me in sundry places". 413.25.

*Rogue, Allan, 588.28.

Roguenaar–see Ragnar Lodbrok. 360.17.

Rohan, Benjamine, Duc de Soubise (1589 - 1642) – Huguenot leader, soldier. 251.33-34.

*Rohan, Roxana–the Rohans were a famous French feudal family; superficial investigation reveals no Roxana. Roxana was the wife of Alexander (q.v.), also a racehorse and a Defoe heroine. 212. 11.

Rolaf–see Rolf Ganger and Olaf. 301.30.

Roland and Oliver–beloved friends in the *Chanson de Roland* and in Ariosto's *Orlando Furioso*. They were killed in battle by the Saracens because Roland would not blow his great horn and summon help from Charlemagne (q.v.). When he did blow it was too late. Orlando and Oliver are brothers in Shakespeare's (q.v.) *As You Like It*. 56.15; 73.33; 74.4,5; 117.20; 323.26; 352.9;

353.15-16; †385.35—with Childe Roland (q.v.); 548.8-9; 610.6-7.

Roland, Childe–Byronic (q.v.) hero. †385.35—with Roland (q.v.).

Rolf Ganger or Rollo (d. 927)–chief of the Normans who invaded France, first duke of Normandy —see Gisela. I do not know what on earth links him to Rafe Smith (q.v.), or to Cinderella. I wish I did. 221.9; 230.5; †263.15—with Rafe Smith (q.v.); †301.30—with Olaf (q.v.); 330.20; 378.9; 389.8 (ter); †444.32—with Rafe Smith (q.v.); †619.17—with Cinderella (q.v.).

Rollo–see Rolf Ganger.

*Romain–French novelist? 302.25.

Romano, Julio (1492-1546)–Italian painter, architect, engineer, sculptor. See *The Winter's Tale*, V, ii, 105. †144.14—with Romeo and Juliet (q.v.).

Romanov–Russian royal family. 361.32-33.

Romany Rye–see George Borrow. 600.30.

Romas and Reims–cities and Romulus and Remus (q.v.). 209. 25.

Romeo and Juliet–hero and heroine of Shakespeare's (q.v.) play and Gounod's opera — see Reszke. Joyce plays, as Shakespeare does, with "Romeo" as a medieval term for a pilgrim. Dante (Paradiso VI) has an account of a Romeo who came from the shrine of St Iago (q.v.)—hence he would bear a scallop shell—and got all the daughters of Raymond Berengar IV of Provence married. See Julia. 81.10; †144.14—with Julio Romano (q.v.); 148.13; †152.21—with Antony, Rowley (q.q.v.); †200.9—with Reszke (q.v.); 236. 2; ?260.note 1; 291.12; 303.2; 313.25; 326.13; †350.23—with Anna Livia (q.v.); †391.21—with Giliette (q.v.); ?430.36 (see Julia); 463.8; †553.16-17—with Gregory I and Julius Caesar (q.q.v.).

Romeo, Antony–see Romeo, Anthony Rowley, and Mark Antony. 152.21.

Romulus and Remus – twins, suckled by a she-wolf, who prepared to found Rome together. Romulus killed Remus and founded Rome by himself. See Rhea Silva. 12.34; 98.31-32; 122.9; 209.25; 236.19; 286.note 1; 358. 13; †467.35—with Rhea Silva (q.v.); 525.33-34.

*Ronayne, Rina Roner Reinette, 373.22.

Roneo and Giliette–see Romeo. 391.21.

Rooney, Annie–song. The name is applied to Anna Livia (q.v.). 7.25,26; 327.12; 426.3-4.

Rooney, Handy Andy–title hero, a bumbling servant, of Lover's (q.v.) novel. He turns out to be an Irish peer. 129.17; 229.2; 279.note 1; 409.31.

Rooters and Havers–Reuters and Havas (q.q.v.). 421.32.

Rorke relly–see Persse O'Reilly. 373.30.

Rory–see Roderick O'Connor.

Rosa, St, of Lima–patroness of the impossible. See Rose. 264.24.

*Rosairette's–see Rose? 376.7.

Rosaleen, Dark–poetic name for Ireland. Mangan's (q.v.) poem begins "My dark Rosaleen, do not sigh, do not weep . . .". In FW I think she doubles with the dark Rosalines (q.v.) of Shakespeare's (q.v.) Love's Labour's Lost and Romeo and Juliet (q.v.). The Rosalines have frequently been identified with Shakespeare's own Dark Lady (q.v.). See Rose. Mangan wrote also a poem "The Little Black Rose". 15.1; 93.27; 277.16; 351.9; 365.23-24; 583.21-22.

Rosaline and Rosalind–Rosaline is an off-stage dark charmer in Romeo and Juliet (q.v.); Rosaline is heroine of Love's Labour's Lost, also a dark girl—see Biron; Rosalind is heroine of As You Like It—see Hero, Benedict, Jacques. See also Rosaleen, Rose.

Roscranna–daughter of Cormac (q.v.) in Macpherson's "Temora" (q.v.). She married Fingal (q.v.). 329.17.

*Rose–In FW Rose is a theme or element which I do not see steadily or whole. Sometimes it is a masculine rose, connected—goodness knows why—with Ross, Rosse and with The Russian General (q.q.v.). Perhaps the masculine rose looks to Shakespeare's (q.v.) identification of flower and Mr W. H. (q.v.), who, Wilde (q.v.) says, inspired Shakespeare's heroines and played them on the stage—see Rosaline, Rosalind, Rosaleen—see also Seven. The Rose of FW is, however, more often female, for, Havelock Ellis says, in the poetry of many countries, the imagery of the rose as the feminine labia "may be traced in a more or less veiled manner". The rose was also sacred to Aphrodite (q.v.). Sometimes the feminine roses of FW are two (q.v.) girls, Rose and Lily (q.v.), or the red and white roses of Lancaster and York (q.v.), but often there is only one rose—as in the reference (290.1) to Yeats's (q.v.) Mystic Rose or Rose of the World. Joyce also puns now and again on rose and ros (Lat. "dew"). See Budd. 3.25-26; 21.15; 28.24; †32.11—see Lily, Mistinguette (q.q.v.); 34.29; †40.13—with Eros (q.v.); †42.11—with Russian General (q.v.); 43.27; †64.27—with Snow White and Rose Red (q.v.); 92.18; †93.7—with Jenny (q.v.), 14, †27—with Dark Rosaleen (q.v.); †94.30—with Elizabeth (q.v.), 36 (see York and Lancaster); 95.4; 96.1, 2—see Dark Rosaleen; 101.7; †122.16—with Rosse (q.v.), 25; 127.8-9; †133.7,8—with O'Grady (q.v.); 140.26; 142.36; †143.25—

see Rosered; 144.1; †146.24 (anagram)—with Hero (q.v.); 147.19; 182.11; ?210.10; 223.6 (see Viola, Spectrum); †229.11—see La Gilligan; 231.20; 235.13; 236.8; 239. 36; †245.18—see Rosimund; 264. note 3; 267.28.note 1; 277.16 (see Rosaleen); 290.1; 302.27; 314.34; 317.32; 321.32; †327.16—with Rosse; 336.27; 337.16; 339.8 (dew here); †340.27 — with Russian General (q.v.); †346.21 — with Russian General (q.v.); †351.9 (see Dark Rosaleen), 13—with Rosse (q.v.); †359.33—see Rosini; 363.10; †365.23-24—see Rosaline, John Lane; †371.33-34 — with Rosaline, Rachel (q.q.v.); ?376.7; †391.30—with Rosse (q.v.); 395. 16; 430.22-23; 441.16; 444.29; ?450.18; 463.9, †24—with Rosse (q.v.); 470.18; 485.12 (see York and Lancaster); 495.24; 502.7; 526.28; 528.6; 548.24; ?553.6; 561.19; †563.30—with George (q.v.); 569.33; 583.21-22; 594.18; †609.11—see Rosina; †620.4— with Russian General (q.v.).

*Rosemary—see Rose.

*Rosimund–Yeats's (q.v.) Rose of the World? Shakespeare's (q.v.) Rosaline or Rosalind (q.v.)? Possibly an allusion to the 18th century "Rosamond's Pond" in St James's Park—a meeting place for lovers, a suicide place for lorn maidens. See Rose. 245.18.

Rosin the Beau–song sung to the tune "Men of the West", about a man, fond of drink, who begs his friends to drink at his funeral and sprinkle his corpse with whisky— see Tim Finnegan. 231.33.

Rosina–heroine of Rossini's (q.v.) *The Barber of Seville*. See Rose. 609.11.

Rosmer, Johannes–male protagonist of Ibsen's (q.v.) *Rosmersholm*. 540.25.

*Ross–I can't account for Joyce's steady punning on Ross or Rosse (q.v.) and Rose (q.v.). Some

"Ross" must surely refer to Robbie Ross, Wilde's (q.v.) faithful friend. 122.16; 250.3; 327.16; 351.13; 391.30; 463.24; 465.30; 535.8.

*Ross, Bart—Rosse? 246.27; 247. 10,20.

Rossa, O'Donovan–19th century Irish nationalist. A bridge in Dublin bears his name. 212.4.

Rosse, William Parsons, 3rd earl of (1800-67)–Irish astronomer and telescope-maker, known until his father's death as Lord Oxmantown. In 1845 he finished his celebrated 6-foot reflector and it was used constantly from 1848 on, particularly to observe the nebulae. In FW he belongs to the peeping-tom theme, peeps at the stars or Stellas (q.v.). He also has a mysterious connection with Rose (q.v.). 8.36; ?47; ?73.28; 248.21; ?250.3; 340.35; 355.24; †391.30—with Rose (q.v.).

*Rossies, ruderic, 285.note 3.

Rossini, Gioachino Antonio (1792-1868)–Italian composer. †359.33 (rose-scenery)—with Rose (q.v.).

Roth, Samuel – American who pirated *Ulysses*. 176.23.

Rothschild–Jewish family which has acquired an unexampled position from the magnitude of its financial transactions. 10.35; 129. 20; 328.35-36.

Rotshield–see Rothschild. 129.20.

Rourke, Felix (1765-1803)–United Irishman, hung for his part in Emmet's (q.v.) rebellion. 373.30.

Rousseau, Jean Jacques (1712-78) –French philosopher. In all cases he doubles with James and John (q.v.). 463.9; 469.11-12; 471.14.

Rovy the Roder–see Rody.

Rowan, Archibald Hamilton – United Irishman. His wealth and importance and the transparent naïveté of his character saved him from the severities which befell his fellows. 588.31.

Rowan, Richard–hero of Joyce's terribly boring play, *Exiles*. I assign two "Richards" to Rowan only because I am sure Joyce put him into FW. See Richard III, see also Archibald Hamilton Rowan, for Richard Rowan has a little son, Archie. Mr Senn points out that 215.7 echoes Bertha's (q.v.) last speech in *Exiles*— "Forgive me, Dick." 230.22; ?†544.35—with Rowntree (q.v.); 565.10.

Rowe, Nicholas (1674-1718)–English dramatist, poet laureate, author of *The Fair Penitent,* and of the first (and by no means the worst) biography of Shakespeare (q.v.). 72.24-25; 202.23.

Rowena–heroine of Scott's and Ireland's (q.q.v.). See Ivanhoe, Vortigern. 39.9.

Rowlandson, Thomas (1756-1827) –English caricaturist, best known for his tours of Dr Syntax. †602. 11—with Rowley the Barrel (q.v.).

*Rowley – may include William Rowley (1585 - 1642) – actor, dramatist, friend of Shakespeare's (q.v.), with whom his name is associated on the title-page of *The Birth of Merlin: or the Child Hath Found His Father*—see Merlin. Since Rowley's play is false Shakespeare, it may tie onto Chatterton's (q.v.) "Rowley Poems". 330.14; 376.31.

Rowley, Anthony–appears in some versions of "The Frog He Would A-wooing Go": "Gammon and spinach, says Anthony Rowley". †152.21—with Antony and Romeo (q.q.v.).

Rowley the Barrel–see Rowley. Song, "Roll Out the Barrel". The principal reference is, however, to Dermot (q.v.), to an adventure of his which may be found in "The Green Champions" in Lady Gregory's *Gods and Fighting Men*. Dermot performed tricks for his enemies—kept upright on a barrel rolling downhill, walked the edge

'of a sword, *Mór-alltach*—see Kniferope Walker and Morialtay. *Mór-alltach* (great jointed) is also at 602.10. 376.31; †602.11—with Rowlandson (q.v.).

*Rowleys, Red, 330.14.

Rowntree, B. Seebohm (d. 1954)– English sociologist, author of *Poverty: A Study of Town Life* which, as Mr Atherton has shown, is the basis of FW 543-545. 544. 35.

Roy, Rob–Scottish outlaw, title character of Scott's (q.v.) novel. 546.18.

Royce–cf. *Ulysses,* 11/10: ". . . old Royce sing in the pantomime of Turko (q.v.) the terrible . . .". †205.29—with Rolls Royce.

*Royde, 282.20; 284.1.

Royloy, P.R.C.R.L.L. see Persse O'Reilly. 378.9.

Roze–see Maas. 204.2.

Rubens–1) Peter Paul (1577-1640) —Flemish painter; and 2) Paul Rubens (1875-1917)—composer of "Under the Deodar". †160.8— with Vernet (q.v.).

Rubeus, Verney–see Rubens and Vernet.

*Rubiconstein, Cadacus Angelus, 211.16-17.

*Ruby, 156.26; 379.16; 440.28.

Rudge, Barnaby–title character of Dickens's (q.v.) novel, which is about the Gordon No-Popery riots of 1780. †292.note 1—with the Russian General—see Buckley.

*Rue, 227.14,17.

Ruffian–not a person but a pandar —see *Inferno,* xviii, 66, and the notes thereto in the Oxford edition of Dante (q.v.), especially as they refer to *ruffian* and *sipa*. 366.23.

Ruffo, Fabrizio (1744-1827)–Neapolitan cardinal and politician who worked with a gang of brigands, including Fra Diavolo (q.v.). 247.10.

Ruff's *Guide to the Turf*, 1854, as Mr Thompson points out. 623.20.

Rufus, Villain–see William Rufus. 122.17.

*****Rumoury,** Sir–see Amory. 96.7.

Rupert, Prince (1619-82)–nephew of Charles I, for whom he fought gallantly in England's Great Rebellion. 88.22; ?241.31.

Rupprecht–see Rupert. 88.22.

Ruric or Rurik – semi-legendary prince of Rus (part of Sweden) who took over vast territories in what is now Russia, in 862. He had to become a Christian in order to marry a sister of the Byzantine emperor. †309.22—with Roderick O'Connor (q.v.); †369.18—with the same.

Rurie, Thoath and Cleever – in Scribbledehobble, 6: "3 waves of I = Thoth, Ruri, Cleeva." According to AE (q.v.) the three great waves are "the wave of Toth, the wave of Rury, and the long, slow, white-foaming wave of Cluna". In Bardic stories, AE says, these waves shout round the Irish coast in recognition of great kings and heroes. The three waves become, I think, Four (q.v.) in FW. 254.2.

Ruskin, John (1819-1900)–English writer. †220.15—with Russian General (q.v.).

Russell, George William, AE (1867-1935), born in Ulster (see Four), poet, journalist, character in *Ulysses*. His pseudonym was a printer's error for Aeon. See Draper. In FW he often turns up in the vicinity of his good friend, George Moore (q.v.). †77.7—with Ariel (q.v.), 15; 95.31; †99.10—

with Ariel (q.v.); 141.4,7; 174.29-30; 231.30; 281.21; 300.4; 303. note 1; 316.4; 325.22; 338.36; 375.13; 379.11; †445.36—with HCE (q.v.); †449.30—with Ariel; 462.34; 540.35; 552.8 (*bis*); ?594. 34; 601.30 (ter); †608.5—with Draper (q.v.).

Russian General–see Buckley.

Ruth–title heroine of a book of the Old Testament. 3.24; 58.31; 192. 28; 257.21; 596.21.

*****Ruth**–since these are opera girls, maybe the female heavy in *The Pirates of Penzance*, but I think they are all sopranos. 147.13.

Rutland, Roger Manners, 5th earl (1576-1612)–married a daughter of Sidney's (q.v.), is a Shakespeare (q.v.) pretender—see *Ulysses*, 205/267. The 4th duke of Rutland was lord-lieutenant of Ireland in 1784. Rutland Square (the Rotunda was on it) was named for him, but is now Parnell (q.v.) Square. See Roger. 42.36; 57.3; 97.12; 148.8-9; †349.16—with Shakespeare (q.v.); ?363.8; 369.20; 373.15, ?36; 378.6; 386.2; 437.5; 457.14; 559.36; 582.32.

*****Rutter,** 88.21.

*****Ruttledges,** 72.4.

Rutty, Dr–eccentric 18th century Dubliner, Quaker, naturalist, physician. 525.4,13; 537.9-10.

*****Ryall,** Stewart – maybe Royal Stuart? Charles I? Parnell? 227.29.

*****Ryan,** 288.note 6.

Ryan, John–last bailiff of Dublin for the title was afterwards (1548) changed to sheriff—see 540.19-20. 77.14.

S

Saar–wife of Finn (q.v.), mother of Ossian (q.v.), changed into a sad doe. †210.30—with Sarah and Sarah Curran; †571.24 — with Sarah (q.v.).

*Sabina, S., 512.11.

*Saccharissa–name Edmund Waller gave Lady Dorothy Sidney (b. 1617); *sécheresse* is French for dryness or barrenness. 204.1.

Sackerson or Sacksoon–see Man Servant. Sackerson was a famous Elizabethan (q.v.) bear. See *Ulysses*, 186/240. See Hunks.

Sackville, Lionel Cranfield, first duke of Dorset–lord-lieutenant of Ireland (1750-54). Sackville (now O'Connell) Street bore his name. 14.3, etc.

*Sackville-Lawry–Lower Sackville (now O'Connell) Street, Dublin? 514.24.

Sade, Marquis de, Seigneur de La Coste (1740-1814)–French writer, author of *Justine* (q.v.). 184.29, ?36; 445.8; †482.4—with Midas (q.v.).

Sailor King–see William IV.

St Austell, Ivan and Hilton St Just–mentioned *Ulysses*, 648/774, as Dublin tenors. 48.23-24.

St Lawrence, Armoricus Tristram –Anglo-Norman invader of Ireland who founded the St Lawrence family of Howth (q.v.). His name was originally Armoricus or Amory Tristram, but he came to Ireland, fought a battle on 10 August (feast of St Lawrence the Spaniard) and took the saint's for his family name. (See Evora.) For FW he represents a Viconian father or founder of a city. He is almost always coupled with Tristram, lover of Isolde (q.v.) and I have listed him under Tristram (q.v.).

St Leger, Sir Anthony–16th cen-

tury Irish viceroy, also a horse-race. 498.3.

Salaman–see Solomon. 116.1.

*Salamoss, Pfarrer, 161.27.

Sally–subconscious self of Christine Beauchamp (q.v.). She often doubles with Sarah (q.v.) because Sarah with her laugh became a new personality. Sally wrote her hopes and buried the page near Boston, Mass. See Issy, the Maggies, Two. 11.17,35; 13.22,23; 19.29; 75.15; 76.27,29; 129.14;144. 34; 198.11; 200.19; 204.15 (Sally Gap is on the Liffey); 272.10; †280.23—with Issy (q.v.); 281.21; 293.note 2; 334.3; 358.20; 359.18; 360.23; †364.30 — with Sarah (q.v.); 446.6; 491.23; †526.32— with Alice (q.v.); 609.12 (*bis*).

Salmon and Gluckstein–proprietors of the Lyons Corner Houses, English restaurants. 170.27, †32— with Gladstone.

Salmonson–see Solomon. 297.3.

Salmosalar–*Salmo salar*, genus of salmon. See Fisher King. Finn MacCool (q.v.) burnt his thumb when cooking the Salmon of Wisdom and had only to suck his thumb to know All. Salmon's wisdom ties to Solomon (q.v.). 7.16.

Salome–daughter of Herodias who got the head of John the Baptist (q.v.) on a platter as a dancing prize. Play of Wilde's (q.v.), opera of Strauss's. 497.33.

*Saltarella–Issy (q.v.). The saltarella is a dance, the galliard. †627.5—with Cinderella?

*Salvator–Latin "savior". Salvator was Roman god of bodily health. 409.31.

Salvatorious Ledwidge–see Muggleton. 538.3.

Salvini, Tommaso (b. 1829)–Italian actor, played Lear and Shylock (q.q.v.), but was best known for his Othello (q.v.). See Silvayne. 495.36.

*Sam, Sammy, Samuel–Beckett (q.v.)? 49.21; †87.10—with Ham, Shem, Japhet (q.v.); 222.36; 341. 36; †342.5—with Sammael; 466. 10; 467.18.

Saman–the first native dynasty of Persia. Here, however, I think the reference mainly to Sanscrit *saman*, a solemn tune to which verse is chanted. 387.31.

Sammael–in Jewish folklore, the enemy of God against whom Michael (q.v.) wars eternally. ?49.21; 185.8 (Sam Hill); ?466.10; ?467.18; 586.22.

*Sampson, 431.12.

Samson–antagonist of the Philistines, unmaned and unmanned by the wiles of Delilah (q.v.). Blind and captive, he pulled down the temple of the Philistines. (Judges 16). 307.left margin; 340. 23;523. 16—with John Jameson (q.v.).

Sancho Panza–servant of Don Quixote (q.v.). 234.6; 360.36; 464.11.

Sand, George (1804-76)–pen-name of the Baronne Dudevant, French novelist. See Lelia, Consuela. 189.14.

Sandeman, Robert–18th century leader of the Glasites or Sandemans, a sect now extinct, who believed that "the bare death of Jesus Christ without a thought or deed on the part of man, is sufficient to present the chief of sinners spotless before God". ?491.1; 492.1.

*Sanders–all the Sanders, Anders, Saunders (q.q.v.) refer to the sender of the letter from Boston, but may very well be real people too. 363.36; 412.23; 413.5.

*Sangannon's, 297.note 3.

Sanger, Mrs Margaret (1883-)– American advocate of birth-control. 436.10.

Sankey–see Moody.

Santa Claus–comes down the chimney at Christmas. 200.14-15; 209.23; 295.7; 307.16; 434.23.

*Santalto, Holy, 247.20.

*Santoys, 58.32.

Santry, Lord–first nobleman tried for murder (of a porter) in the Irish House of Lords, 1739. He was convicted but escaped punishment. As Mr Kelleher reminds us, HCE is often Mr Porter (q.v.). Santry is an Irish river and a town near Dublin. 14.13.

*Saom Plaom, 179.9.

Sapphira–wife of Ananias (q.v.). 479.8 (zephyros).

Sappho (fl. 610 B.C.)–Greek poetess. 307.left margin; †542.19—with Sapphrageta (q.v.).

Sapphrageta and Consciencia–suffragettes and conscientious objectors. See Sappho. 542.19-20.

Sarah–see Abraham.

Sardanapalus–according to Greek myth, last king of Assyria, who, in the face of rebellious subjects, burned up himself, his wives and his palace. 146.13; 182.18; 254.23.

*Sarmon, Master–salmon (q.v.)? 615.18.

Sassoon, Siegfried (1886-)–English poet, author of *Memoirs of an Infantry Officer*, etc. 344.1.

Satan–see Mick and Nick, Lucifer, Sammael.

*Sators of the Sowsceptre, 230.28.

Saturn–ancient Italian god, planet. †90.17—with Slattery (q.v.); 137. 9; 366.15-16; 415.9; 449.2-3; 494. 10; 534.20; 583.19.

*Saucy–maybe Susanna (q.v.) in Mozart's (q.v.) *Marriage of Figaro*. 147.14.

Saul–king of Israel—see the 2 Samuels. 306.left margin.

Saunders *News Letter* – Dublin newspaper, founded in the 18th century. See Sanders. 389-390; 534.20.

*Saunderson–seems usually to be the Man Servant (q.v.). It was a

Unionist Colonel Saunderson who brought up the forged Parnell (q.v.) letters in the House of Commons. 221.6; 413.14.

Savage, Richard (d. 1743)–inferior poet and playwright, subject of a superior life by Samuel Johnson (q.v.). He claimed to be the illegitimate son of the 4th earl Rivers by the wife of the 2nd earl of Macclesfield. 63.34; ?191.11; ?350.36.

?Savile, Lord Arthur–his crime is a story of Wilde's (q.v.). 353.9.

Savonarola, Girolamo (1452-92)– Italian monk, reformer, hell-fire preacher, burner of books. Himself burned by order of the Pope. 439.35.

*Sawabs, Lightnints Gundhur, 351. 32.

*Sawy, Fundally, Daery, or Maery, Milucre, Awny, or Graw – see Seven. 200.19-20.

Sawyer, Peter–Founder of Dublin, Georgia, USA, a town in Laurens (q.v.) County, on the Oconee River. Its motto "Doubling all the time". Joyce's source on Dublin, Ga., has not yet been found, and there may be a great deal about Peter Sawyer in FW. He is, like Tristram Amory or St Peter (q.q.v.), a founder. He seems to be Shaun (q.v.), Georgia ties him to George (q.v.). His personal name begins the Tree and Stone (q.v.) theme since a "sawyer" is a tree fast in the bed of a stream with its branches projecting to the surface and bobbing up and down with the current. 3.19; 104.22; 211.28; 372.0; 549. 25; 580.4.

Sawyer, Sid–Tom Sawyer's (q.v.) brother. 410.36.

Sawyer, Tom–title hero of Mark Twain's (q.v.) book. He ties always perhaps to Peter Sawyer. Tom Sawyer may become "Tom-saw-you" and so tie on to the voyeurist theme. Tom Sawyer is

really inconsequential in FW. See Huck Finn. 132.36; ?173.29; 299.28; 338.26; 374.34-35; 410.35.

Saxo, Grammaticus (1150-1206)– Danish historian, poet, author of *Gesta Danorum* or *Historia Danica* which is one of the old sources of the Hamlet (q.v.) story. 16.7; 304.18; 388.31.

Saxon Chromaticus–see Saxo.

Scaliger–1) Julius Caesar Scaliger (1484-1558) scholar, philosopher, botanist; 2) his son, Joseph Justus Scaliger (1540-1609), classical scholar. 491.28; 524.31.

*Scapolopolos, Machinsky, 64.31- 32.

Scarlet Pimpernel–*nom de guerre* of Sir Percy Blakely in Baroness Orczy's novels. †564.28—with Parnell (q.v.).

Scarlett, Sir James Yorke (1799- 1871)–British general who commanded a brigade in the Crimean war. 339.12; 352.6.

Sceptre–horse in *Ulysses*. 32.3; 290.1.

Schaff, Fritzi–dancer, singer, played in *Frou-Frou* (q.v.). 510.35.

Schaurek, Frantisek – Joyce's brother-in-law. 423.36.

Scheekspair–see Shakespeare. 191. 2.

Scheherazade – narrator in the *Arabian Nights*. 32.8; 51.4.

Schelling, Wilhelm (1775-1854)– German philosopher. 234.4; 305. note 1; 416.4.

Schoolmaster–refers, I think to Joyce (Stephen Dedalus in *Ulysses*) and to Shakespeare (q.q.v.) who was, Aubrey (q.v.) says, a schoolmaster.

Schopenhauer, Arthur (1788-1860) –German philosopher. 414.33.

*Schott–German "wall". 149.19; 161.23; 514.9,27.

*"Schottenboum", 116.6-7.

Schratt, Kathe–dancer, mistress of

Kaiser Franz Joseph (q.v.) in Vienna. 556.35.

Schubert, Franz Peter (1797-1828)– German composer who set many of Shakespeare's (q.v.) songs to music. See Antheil. 133.27.

Schultz, Dutch or Arthur Flegenheimer–American gangster, shot in 1935. 602.24.

*Schwalb, 542.21.

Schweep's – Schweppe's Tonic Water is drunk in England. †146. 11-12—with Swift (q.v.); 556.36.

Schwitzer's – Dublin department store, Switzer's. Mr Hart suggests that because of Bach (q.v.) the reference may include Albert Schweitzer. 176.35.

Scipio – patrician Roman family which produced many famous men. 293.8.

Scolastica, St (d. 543)–St Benedict's (q.v.) sister. One day she wanted him to linger at her convent and prayed for a thunderstorm, which came out of a clear sky. She is patroness of the Benedictine nuns. 431.23.

*Scott, great tropical–perhaps the Antarctic explorer. 211.29.

Scott, Sir Walter (1771-1832)–Scottish poet and novelist. 177.35.

Scrooge–protagonist of Dickens's A Christmas Carol. See Marley. 227.20.

Scrope–English family of Norman origin which produced many prominent men. 302.21.

Scylla and Charybdis–a rock and a whirlpool in the sea between Italy and Sicily, a section of Ulysses in which Stephen Dedalus (q.v.) sets forth a Shakespearean (q.v.) theory which I believe to be the basis of FW. Joyce told Stuart Gilbert that Stephen's Scylla and Charybdis are Plato and Aristotle (q.q.v.), but I can think of other pairs. 229.14; †231.18—with Silla (q.v.).

Sea or Ocean–see Lear, Lir.

Seagull, Mother–"Mother Seigel's Syrup", a digestive tonic, sold in the British Isles. 26.31-32.

*Sealy, 370.21.

Sean the Post–low-born hero of Boucicault's Arrah - na - Pogue (q.q.v.). He marries Arrah. See Atherton, The Books at the Wake, 159-161. See Shaun.

*Searingsand, 137.17.

Sebastian–Viola's (q.v.) twin, believed drowned but come to life and courted by Olivia (q.v.), in Shakespeare's (q.v.) Twelfth Night. He is listed under Wilde (q.v.).

Seddon–English murderer. †60.6— with Siddons (q.v.).

Seeboy–see Wellington.

Seekersenn–Man Servant (q.v.). Seker was the Egyptian god of the night sun. 586.28.

Sejanus–minister and favorite of Tiberius (q.v.). Title character of a play by Ben Jonson (q.v.) in which Shakespeare (q.v.) acted. 361.3 (comes againus).

Selene–in Greek myth, the moon (q.v.). See also Artemis. 192.30; 244.26; 513.1.

Selfridges – London department store. 137.34; 497.36.

Selkirk, Alexander (1676-1721)– Scottish shipwrecked sailor, model for Robinson Crusoe (q.v.). 243.1.

Selskar–see Selskar Gunn.

Sem–Shem (q.v.) whose name is so spelled in the Townley Noah (q.v.) play.

Semiramis (b. 800 B.C.)–Assyrian princess to whom sexual excess and every stupendous work of antiquity in Iran have been ascribed. 553.11-12.

Semperkelly, Mr Wallensten. Washington – see Wallenstein, Washington and W. W. Kelly, 32.29.

Sempronius–see Gracchi. 128.15.

*Sencapetulo, 54.34.

Sender–see Anders, Sanders.

Seneca, Lucius Annaeus–1) the elder or the rhetorician (54 B.C.—A.D. 39), author of *Controversiae* in which he discusses *colores* or devices for making black appear white and extenuate injustice; 2) the younger (3 B.C.—A.D. 65), Stoic, statesman, playwright, tutor of Nero (q.v.). 612.15.

Sennacherib–Assyrian who came down like a wolf on the fold. 150.16.

Senta–heroine of Wagner's (q.v.) *The Flying Dutchman.* See Vanderdecken, Eric. 268.3.

*Sepulchre, Saint – maybe the Church of the Holy Sepulchre in Jerusalem, one of the remote causes of the Crimean war. 343.5.

Sereth Maritza–the Sereth is a Rumanian river, the Maritza a Turkish. The whole refers to Anna Livia (q.v.) who is all rivers —see Artemis. 469.14.

*Sergo, 186.33.

Set or Sett–see Horus.

Seter–see Soter. 153.24.

Seth–born to Adam and Eve (q.v.) after Cain (q.v.) murdered Abel. Eve called him "Seth", "For God", saith she, "hath appointed (*shath*) me another seed instead of Abel." †29.28—with Set (q.v.); 287.12.

Seton–Satan (q.v.). 441.4.

Seumas, thought little – see St James the Little. 211.4.

Seven Rainbow and/or Gamut "Girls"–an important strand in FW's theme of unity and diversity, a theme I am not within a hundred miles of understanding. It seems plain that white light (which contains all colors) is unity and the seven spectrum colors, opposing diversity (see 215.15-22, 611-613). The opposition of white

light and spectrum is resolved (only for the moment perhaps), declared an illusion (613.13-14) in the dialogue of the Christian St Patrick and the pagan Archdruid Berkeley (q.q.v.). St Patrick, who triumphs, states that fallen man can see only the spectrum, but must firmly believe in the white light. It seems, therefore that this diversity and unity are our battered old friends, the many-colored glass and the white radiance of eternity. Bacon's (q.v.) "Colours (pretenses) of Good and Evil" come into it too, somehow.

If seven are resolved into one in the dialogue, FW opens with a burst of diversity, the human race. The second paragraph of the book is composed of seven clauses, which move backward through the spectrum from violet to red. It is, in short, a reversed or secondary rainbow, secondary because it has all happened before. Joyce plays on Arc and Ark, signifying, I guess, that there is no great peace between God and man. These seven clauses are, I think, the seven strings of the *viole d'amour* or what Kepler called, "the seven-stringed harp of the Creator's wisdom". Thus spectrum and gamut are identified and continue off and on identified throughout FW—an "iridescent huecry" (see 68.20-21; 260.25, left margin).

As Mr Kelleher points out, seven is the number of garments HCE (q.v.) wears, and at least once (23.1-2) he wears the seven colors. Most often however, the colors are personified in seven spectrum or rainbow "girls" who are Anna Livia's (q.v.) rivals. They are associated with, but are not precisely Issy (q.v.). It seems blankly impossible that seven should belong to one man and to seven girls, but the contradiction goes (at least it partly goes) if the one man is Shakespeare's Mr

W. H. (q.q.v.), "A man in hue all hues in his controlling". In "The Portrait of Mr W. H." Wilde (q.v.) took this and other lines from Shakespeare's sonnets and deduced from them a young actor, Willie Hughes who played Shakespeare's heroines. Wilde names seven heroines. I think FW alters and adapts Wilde's theory, I think all "hues" refer to Willie Hughes and that the seven girls are Shakespeare's illusory heroines from Violet to Rosaline (q.q.v.). I do not think that this completely explains the Seven "girls". The Rainbow Girls are young female Masons. See also Noah, Iris.

3.16,25,26 violer . . . rory . . . regginbrow
?4.13 skysign
10.35 seven
†11.12 huemeramybows—with Mr W. H., Mary Fitton (q.q.v.)
23.1-2 rudd yellan gruebleen orangeman . . . violet indigonation
†63.12-13 Myramy Huey—with Mr W. H., Mary Fitton (q.q.v.), Colores Archer
66.14 seven
68.20-21 iridescent huecry of down right mean false sop lap sick dope
102.25-26 Poppy Narancy, Giallia, Chlora, Marinka, Anileen, Parme
27 rainbow huemoures
104.25 Arcs
106.31 Seven wives
107.12 rainbowl
126.31 sevenal successivecoloured serebanmaids
?129.22 seven dovecotes (the reference is primarily to Homer)
133.31 rain bowed
143.25-26 roserude . . . oragious . . . gelb . . . greem . . . blue . . . ind . . . Violet (see Rose, Rosered)

158.22 sevens
171.16-17 rhubarbarous maundarin yellagreen funkleblue windigut
175.16 Arcobaleine
178.24 sevenspan ponte *dei colori*
182.8-10 cries . . . gember! inkware! chonchambre! cinsero! zinnabar! tincture and gin
186.28 arch girl, Arcoiris
†202.17-18 maids were in Arc—with St Joan (q.v.)
203.26-29 red . . . reignbeau's heavenarches arronged orranged . . . violetian
207.10-11 strawberry reds to extra violates
215.17-21 seven hues . . . cry . . . pinky limony creamy birnies . . . turkiss indienne mauves
223.6-7 Rose, Sevilla . . . Citronelle . . . Esmeralde, Pervinca . . . Indra . . . Viola (see Rose, Pervinca, Viola)
226-227 (*passim*)
228.9 bow of the shower
231.20 roseaced . . . violast
238.10-11 Brick, fauve, jonquil, sprig, fleet, nocturne, smiling bruise
248.35 Seven Sisters
260.left margin Don't retch meat fat salt lard sinks down
260-261 rougey . . . pulshandjupeyjade . . . petsybluse indecked o'voylets (see Punch and Judy)
267.13-16 grene . . . red, blue . . . yellow . . . blewy blow . . . windigo
273.4-5 heptarched span of peace
277.note 4 Roe, Williams, Bewey, Greene, Gorham, McEndicoth . . . Vyler (see Roe)

284.28-285.5 turquo-indaco . . .
    viridorefulvid . . .
    redor . . . enviolated
    . . . seven
285.15   rainborne
  note 6 Tomatoes . . . Blues . . .
    violens
304.9   rayingbogeys
316.2-3   ulstravoliance . . . in-
    froraids
318.33   spectrum (seven deadly
    sins)
319.5   rinbus
339.28-29 Rent, outraged, yew-
    leaved, grained, bal-
    looned, hindergored
    and voluant
379.14-17 seven hores . . . Two
    Idas, two Evas, two
    Nessies and Ruby-
    juby . . . rheinbok
432.29-31 sung . . . rubrics, man-
    darimus, pasqualines,
    or verdidads . . .
    bruiselivid indecores
    of estreme voyoulence
    (see Jacqueline Pas-
    cal, Verdi)
?433.1   Purpalume . . . Ultra-
    mare
474.36   sevenply
475.13   rainbowpeel
494.2-5,29 arch of chrome . . . iri-
    decencies! Ruby and
    beryl and chrysolite,
    jade, sapphire, jasper
    and lazul . . . seventh
495.8   siven
498.31   spectrem
?525.17   seven parish churches
    (in Glendalough)
†527.29-30 Mon ishebeau! Ma re-
    inebelle!—with Issy
    (q.v.)
?551.32   sevendialled
552.16   seven wynds
558.19   seven honeymeads
562.9-10   seventip . . . blue to
    scarlad
568.2-4   A ruber, a rancher, a
    fullvide, a veridust . . .
    crerdulous . . . a dam-
    son . . . sloe

572-573   Gillia . . . Poppea,
    Arancita, Clara, Mari-
    nuzza, Indra . . .
    Iodina (see Gillia)
579.33   seven sisters
589.20   seven
590.8-10   true falseheaven colours
    from ultraviolent to
    subred . . . reignbolt's
605.30   sevenfold
611.6   heptachromatic seven-
    hued septicoloured
    roranyellgreenlindi-
    gan
  14   spectacurum . . . iridals
612.27,28 Great Balenoarch . . .
    Greatest Great Bale-
    noarch (q.v.)
613.24   rainbow

Seven Wonders of the Ancient World—not people, but associated with certain deities. They were: 1) the pyramids of Egypt; 2) the pharos of Alexandria; 3) the walls and hanging gardens of Babylon; 4) the temple of Artemis (q.v.) at Ephesus; 5) the statue of Zeus (q.v.) at Ephesus; 6) the mausoleum built by Artemisia at Halicarnassus; 7) the colossus of Rhodes. 81; ?192; 241; 261; 347; 553; 625.

*Sexton—William Sexton was a lieutenant of Parnell's. See Fox-Goodman? 230.11; 281.left margin; 416.13; 552.23.

*Shackleton—see Shekleton. 317. 15; 392.33; 393.1; 397.17.

*Shackleton, Roy, 541.21-22.

Shahryar—king who listened for 1001 nights. See Scheherazade. 357.19.

Shakefork—see Shakespeare. 274. left margin.

Shakespeare, Ann—see Hathaway.

Shakespeare, Edmund—see Edmund.

Shakespeare, Gilbert—if I am right in thinking FW is about Shakespeare (q.v.), all the Shakespeare family is in FW, and his brother

Gilbert (himself an actor) is the mysterious Gill (q.v.) or Gilly. If not, not.

Shakespeare, Hamnet (1584-96)– Shakespeare's son, Judith's twin. It is said that Hamnet and Hamlet (q.v.) were used without distinction in Elizabethan times. *Ulysses*, 186/241, identifies Hamnet-Hamlet and calls them "twins".

Shakespeare, Joan – William's sister—see Hart.

Shakespeare, John and Mary– William Shakespeare's parents. Given Joyce's simple - minded pleasure in "correspondences", I don't think he missed the fact that his own parents were also John and Mary (see Joyce). John Shakespeare and John Joyce were also fathers who enjoyed some modest prosperity in the years of their oldest sons' childhoods, and declined sharply in their sons' adolescence. Both sons, by the bye, after wild youth exiled themselves from their native place.

John Shakespeare was, at various times, a dealer in corn, wool, malt, skins, leather. He was a glover, a butcher (q.q.v.), an ale-taster, a constable, a J.P., an alderman, High Bailiff or Mayor of Stratford, and a recusant. FW is full of references to these occupations, but John Shakespeare's great importance to FW is less savory. He was twice fined for keeping a dunghill (see Biddy Doran, Humpty-Dumpty) or dump in Henley Street, outside his front door. It probably also matters that Voltaire said Shakespeare's plays were a dung-hill in which some pearls (q.v.) could be found. See John.

Shakespeare, Judith–see Quiney.

Shakespeare, Richard—see Richard III.

Shakespeare, Susanna–see Susanna, see Hall.

Shakespeare, William (1564-1616) English playwright. It is my belief that FW is about him. See Will, Bill, Bard, Swan, William, Mr W. H., Ann Hathaway, Elizabeth, Hall, Francis Bacon, Delia Bacon, Orange, and all Shakespeare's major characters. Below I list only references to the poet's surname. It may seem extravagant to take all "shakes" and "spears" (or "lances") in FW as referring to Shakespeare, but there has been complaint that Shakespearean scholars do just that when combing through Elizabethan literature and Joyce steadily mocks the scholars' search. Shakespeare himself punned on his name in his writings and in his coat of arms. So did his contemporaries, e.g. Ben Jonson's (q.v.) "shake a Lance", Greene's (q.v.) "shake-scene". Thomas Fuller derived Shakespeare from *Hasti-vibrans* and Charles Mackey from Celtic *seac speir* or "dry shanks". I think that the lance puns in FW refer also to the lance as one of the Grail symbols.

6.9	shake
15.26	shake
21.36	shaking
22.31	lance
28.2,4	Shirksends, Shakeshands . . . hayfork's
36.20	Shshshake
40.25-26	shakedown
47	Shikespower
?59.7	lallance
73.36	lancer
?75.29	peer
78.14	spearway
96.23,24	shakeahand . . . schenkusmore
107.31	heartshaker
128.16	shopkeeper
131.14	speared
139.3	taken with a lance
140.18	sheverin wi'all . . . we'll . . . orange (see Will, Orange)
143.21,22	shakeagain . . . shakealose

145.24   Chickspeers (see Biddy Doran)

†152.31,33 lancia spezzata . . . Bragspear — with Adrian I (q.v.)

159.19   nattleshaker

161.31   shakespill

172.22   shaking

174.9,12,28 shakers . . . seer . . . spiers

177.32   shaggspick . . . Shakhisbeard

184.7   shaking

191.2   Scheekspair

194.27,31 dry yanks . . . shaking

209.14   bearb . . . Shake

222.35   shimmershake

225.29   Shape your reres

229.9   sheepcopers

242.15   shake

244.4   spearing

248.23   Shake

251.14,21 pierce . . . shake

254.32   ashaker

†257.20   Missy Chickspeer—with Issy (q.v.) (The reference is to a Shakespeare daughter, see Susanna, Judith, Elizabeth)

267.4   speer

273.9.note 1 shake . . . Shake

274.left margin Shakefork

275.note 5 shaik . . . sheeks

280.10,27,35 Schlicksher . . . Schlicksheruthr . . . shake

282.note 4 Lancydancy

285.note 4 boneshaker

288.27   shuck

295.3   Shapesphere (the sphere is the globe in all senses)

336.28   shimmeryshaking

342.29   shaking

343.21   Schtschuptar

344.6   sheepskeer

346.6   devilances

347.24   shake

†349.16   rutilanced—with Rutland (q.v.)

†350.14   melovelance—with Lovelace (q.v.)

352.26   shorpshoopers

354.15   shaken

†32   lancifer—with Lucifer (q.v.)

360.34   alancey

†365.6   peer . . . shakes—with Peer Gynt (q.v.)

395.25   shaking

415.6   shake

435.28   shake

441.34   chigs peel

447.31   boneshaker

450.14   spearlight

451.24-25 shake a pale

?466.16   shuck

468.33,36 shacks . . . peeling—see George Peele

?471.21   Shanks

485.19   *Spira* . . . spear

505.11   shaking

506.8   bellance

508.1   shaken

513.34   lancers

514.19   shakeup

535.11   handshakey

539.6   Shopkeeper

541.6,18   spearing . . . shraking

546.9   lanciers, shaking

549.3,8   spearhead . . . trembling . . . quaked

559.11   lance

566.11   shakenin

578.1   shivering shanks

595.5   shake

597.24   shivery anilancinant

*Shallwesigh, Mr or Mr Shallwelaugh, 37.27-28.

Shalmanesir – Assyrian king (2 Kings 17-18). 150.16-17.

Shalott, Lady of–poem by Tennyson (q.v.). 550.15-16.

Shandy, Tristram–title hero of Sterne's (q.v.) novel. "Shandy" means boisterous mirth, and the name, therefore, exemplifies the antithetical sorrow and hilarity which Joyce personifies in the two little jiminies of Jarl von Hoother (q.v.). See also Tristram. 21.21-22; 141.6-7 (does this include John Shand of *What Every Woman Knows*?); 323.2; ?324.33 (Streamstress Mandig—see Dignam); 588.12; 621.36.

Shanks–see Shakespeare.

*Shannon, Nancy–probably just the Irish river. 211.9; 213.34.

Sharadan–see Thomas Sheridan. 184.24.

Sharkey, Jack–American boxer. †307.20—with John (q.v.).

Sharman, John – 19th century author of a textbook of astronomy. 427.14.

Sharp–when Shakespeare's (q.v.) mulberry tree was cut down in 1758, its wood suffered the fate of the True Cross and appeared in an almost infinite number of cups, ink-stands, etc. Most of these were the work of a Mr Sharp of Stratford. 6.23; 566.9.

Shasser, Bill–see Belshazzar, Bill. 494.20.

Shaun–see Shem.

*Shaw, Major A., 263.7.

Shaw, George Bernard (1856-1951) –Irish playwright. Many, perhaps all, his principal characters appear in FW and "Burrus and Caseous" (q.v.) imitates his prefaces. See Four, George. 41.8 (bis); 98.13; 112.34,36; 116.6; ?131.8; †132.10 —see Grimshaw; ?144.4; 162.18 (wash); 211.2 (Barney-the-Bark), 36 (swash); 221.33; †256.13—with Wilde (q.v.); 303.7; 304.20 (whas); ?331.21; ?366.34; ?369.7-8; 378. 24; ?497.30; ?527.8; ?553.36.

*Shawe, Lamppost, 193.18.

*Shaws, Skowood, 257.12.

*Shea–O'Shea? 378.25.

Sheba, Queen of–see Balkis.

Shee–see O'Shea.

Sheehy–friend of Joyce's youth, professor of law at the University of Galway. Joyce associated him with the Four (q.v.)—see letter to Miss Weaver, 23 October 1923. 385.28.

Sheepskeer–see Shakespeare. 344. 6.

*Sheila, 451.23.

*Sheilmartin, E. N.–Sheelmartin is a place near Dublin. See St Martin. 354.16-17.

Shelley, Percy Bysshe (1792-1822) –English poet. 231.12; 450.10.

Shem and Shaun–Irish forms of James and John (q.v.). They are the Earwickers' twin sons. Shem is called Shem the Penman (q.v.). Shaun is Sean the Post from Boucicault's Arrah - na - Pogue (q.q.v.). The twins are also known as Jerry and Kevin, Mick and Nick, Mookse and Gripes, Ondt and Gracehoper, Burrus and Caseous, Glugg and Chuff, Butt and Taff, Horus and Set, etc. (q.q.v.). Most of the time it is possible to tell which twin plays which part in these and other episodes, but ever so often Joyce deliberately muddies the waters by having the twins coalesce into a single character, or divide into the mysterious Three (q.v.) who are usually soldiers; more often yet, the twins swap parts like quick-change artists. In FW there is never the smallest difficulty in recognizing the older generation, HCE and Anna Livia (q.q.v.); confusion is confined to the younger generation, male and female.

It is a commonplace that the twins illustrate Bruno's (q.v.) theory of the identity of opposites. Shem is the artist (as a young man) and Shaun is the philistine. They represent man at war with other men and with himself, and it is the same war, whether fought over a girl or a philosophic principle. It is my opinion that Shem and Shaun are as yet imperfectly understood.

As characters, Shem and Shaun are vivid enough examples of two kinds of unpleasant young men. Shem is a sort of burlesque of Joyce, or rather, of Stephen Dedalus (q.v.), the impotent artist, Hamlet (q.v.), awash in self-pity. Shaun, on the other hand, is full of self-satisfaction, a philistine saint, forged from the basest metal of religious imagination. With Shaun, Joyce scourges the intellectual and esthetic abuses of Irish Catholicism with a ferocity positively medieval. See John McCormack. It is a mistake to suppose that Joyce means Shem to stand for good and Shaun for bad, Shem for a desirable freedom and Shaun for a contemptible authoritarianism. Joyce's readers are likely to be bookish people and suppose that an artist in revolt must be heroic, but HCE (q.v.) is the only hero of FW.

13.28	penn . . . polepost
†19.32	Penn — with William Penn (q.v.)
29.4	showm
†35.24	Sempatrick's—with St Patrick (q.v.)—see Sem
57.18	semmingly
75.23	shamed and shone
†92.13,32	Show'm the Posed . . . shayshaun — with O'Shea (q.v.)
93.13,21	Shun the Punman . . . Skam! Schams! Shames!
94.11-12	Shem . . . Shaun
125.25	Shem the Penman
126.16	Shaun Mac Irewick
152.36	Shinshone
162.27-28	sin . . . semagen
168.14	Semus
169.13,23,32	Shem . . . Shemus . . . Shem's . . . Master Shemmy
170.15,19,22,24,29	Sem . . . semi-sized . . . Shem . . . Shem sham . . . sham (see Ham Shem and Japhet)
173.32	sematics
177.5,23	shemozzle . . . Shem
†30	Sheames de la Plume —see Jeames
179.6	Shem
180.6	Shemlockup
182.1,17	shamians . . . Shem
185.35	alshemist

†187.34-35	Shem Macadamson — with Adam, MacAdam (q.q.v.)
188.5,18-19	Sheem . . . Shehohem
190.33	shemming
192.23	Pain the Shamman
193.28	Shem
206.11	Shaun the Post
211.31	Shemus O'Shaun the Post
212.18	Shem, her penmight
215.35	Shaun or Shem
216.1,2,3-4	Shaun . . . Shem and Shaun . . . stem . . . stone
219.34	Mr Seumas McQuillad
220.11	Mr Sean O'Mailey
225.14	Shem . . . shome
228.15	Shimach
237.5	mesh
249.18,28	Sem . . . shem
258.11	Semmi
286.30	Sem
†305.5	Sunny Sim—with Sunny Jim (q.v.)
317.28	himshemp
324.5	spume and spawn
†364.8	Shaum Baum's—with John Brown (q.v.)
369.27-28	Schelm the Pelman
?376.6	chemins
384.27,28	vicemversem . . . huntsem
385.5,6	Nush . . . Mesh
393.15-16	shems and shawls
404.7	Shaun! Shaun! Post the post
405.7,9	Shaun . . . Shaun
407.13,28	Shaun . . . Shaun
†408.21	Sim—with John Sims Reeves (q.v.)
33-34	Shaunti . . . shaunti . . . shaunti
409-414	Shaun (passim)
415.23	sham (see Ham Shem Japhet)
419.18,20,21,25	Lettrechaun . . . shemletters . . . Shaun . . . sem
420.17,18,19	Shaun . . . Shem . . . Shaun . . . Shem . . . Shaun
421.15-21	Shaun . . . Shaun
†25	Mr O'Shem the Draper —see Draper

422.19,24   Shaun . . . Shaun
423.1,15   Shemish . . . Shem
            Shrivenitch
424.8,14,17,24,26 Shim . . . Shaun
            Shaun . . . Shaun . . .
            Shaun
425.3,6,7,9 Shemese . . . Shamous
            Shamonous . . . Shaun
            . . . Shaun
426.1   Shaun
427.19,27   Shaun . . . Sean Moy
437.33   Mistro Melosiosus Mac-
            Shine MacShane
'442.22   Shaun
453.22   Sh the Po
†454.6-7   Ann Posht the Shorn—
            with Anna Livia (q.v.)
461.25   Shane
†462.8   Shaunathaun—with
            Swift, Jonathan,
            Swift (q.q.v.)
464.10   mesh
   †13   Shemuel Tulliver—with
            Gulliver (q.v.)
477.24   meshing
483.3,4   Shaum . . . Sameas.
            Shan-Shim-Schung
†489.28   shemblable—with Abel
            (q.v.)
   †30   S. H. Davitt — with
            David, Michael Davitt
            (q.q.v.)
?515.7   scheme of scorn
517.17,18   shine his puss . . . shin
            the punman
526.14   Shem and Shaun
†528.21-22 shone yet shimers—with
            Sun-yat-Sen (q.v.)
530.3-4   shamshemshowman
533.34   Shaun Shemsen
534.32-33   Shame . . . Shames . . .
            Shamus
†546.4   neckamesh—with Nick
            (q.v.)
556.30   Shuhorn the posth
558.23   toppingshaun
565.36   Shoom
580.18   Sheem . . . Shaam
593.34   Nuahs . . . Mehs
603.4-5   Shoen! Shoan! Shoon
            the Puzt
604.18   Shamus Rogua
613.10   Shamwork
620.15,16   Som . . . Sim . . . sehm
            asnuh

Shem–son of Noah—see Ham, Shem
Japhet.

Shemans, Mrs–see Hemans.

Shen–what certain Chinese Christ-
ians call God. 3.25.

*****Shenstone**–English poet? 332.13.

Sheppard, Jack (1702-24)–English
robber, rival of Jonathan Wild
(q.v.), hung at Tyburn. †540.27—
with John (q.v.).

*****Shepperd**, 552.11-12.

Sheridan, Richard Brinsley (1751-
1816)–Irish playwright, member
of the British parliament. See
Languish, Surface. †256.12-13—
with Goldsmith (q.v.); 545.35.

Sheridan, Thomas (1687-1738)–
grandfather of the above, "a
punster, a quibbler, a fiddler and
a wit", author of The Art of Punning. 184.24.

Sherlock, Lorcan–called a "coun-
cillor" in *Ulysses*, 470/602, became sheriff. †534.31—with Sherlock Holmes (q.v.).

*****Sherratt**, Katey – Kate (q.v.).
380.1-2 (*bis*).

Sherry, Marienne–dear Marianne,
the personification of France, also
Mariana of the Moated Grange
(q.v.). 625.1.

Shiel, Richard Lalor – became
Master of the Irish Mint in 1850.
280.left margin; 520.14.

Shikespower–see Shakespeare. 47.

*****Shimar** Shin–Shem and Shaun?
10.6,18.

Shimmyrag, Terry–Terence Shamrock or Ireland. 366.21.

*****Shing**-Yung-Thing in Shina, 231.9.

Shitric Shilkanbeard—see Sitric.
532.8.

Shoolbred's–London department
store. 127.11-12.

Shopkeeper–see Shakespeare. Here
and elsewhere "shopkeeper" also
refers to Napoleon's calling the
English "a nation of shopkeepers".
See Draper. 539.6.

*Shop-Sowry, 221.34.

*Shortbred, Lady Marmela–just eatables? 235.32-33; 236.6.

*Shorty, Frisky, 39,18-19; 50.7; 172.28; 212.2; 419.16; 523.23,30; 524.7,10.

*Shouldrups and Kneesknobs– Mookse and Gripes (q.v.) obviously intended. 157.10-11,12.

Shousapinas, Mary Louisan–see Joséphine. 223.2.

*Shovellyvans–see Sullivan. 495.2.

Showpanza, Sin–see Sancho Panza. 234.6.

*Shunders–see Sanders, Anders. 413.6.

*Shuter, P.–Paul Suter was a Zurich friend of Joyce's. 265. note 5.

?Shylock – in Shakespeare's *The Merchant of Venice*. See Antonio. 180.6.

Sickerson–see Man Servant.

Sid Arthar–see Gautama, Sidney. 59.7.

Siddons, Sarah (1755-1831)–English actress. Her tragic question, "Will it wash?" is at 290.19-20. 58.35; †60.6—with Seddon (q.v.).

Sidney, Sir Philip (1554-1586)– English poet, statesman, soldier, son of Sir Henry Sidney who was three times lord-deputy of Ireland. In FW I have found only two references which I consider certainly to him—88, 500. The second reference is to his alleged incest with his sister Mary, Countess of Pembroke. It is, however, tempting to identify him and his "Stella" (q.v.)— Penelope Rich (q.v.)—with Pip and Estella (q.v.). †59.7—with Gautama (q.v.); 60.27; 88.31-32; 177.6; †463.36—with Philip the Good (q.v.); 489.31; 500.21; 553. 31; 595.33.

Siegfield–see Ziegfeld. 106.12.

*Siegwin, Martiell, 539.27.

Siemens – two brothers, Ernest (1816-92) and Sir William (1823-83), electrical engineers who fitted out the lighthouse at Arklow. 245.8; 549.18.

*Sigerson, Sigurd–see Man Servant, Sigurd. There was a Dr George Sigerson (1838-1925), Dubliner, translator. His daughter, Dora, was a poetess. 608.10.

Silanse, Unkel–villain in LeFanu's (q.v.) novel *Uncle Silas*. 228.17.

Silas (fl. 50)–Christian missionary, companion of St Paul (q.v.) on his second journey. 470.7.

Silence, Sylvia–detective heroine in an English schoolgirl's magazine in the 1920s. She suggests that HCE (q.v.) be prosecuted under the act which was used against Oscar Wilde (q.v.). See Sylvia? 61.1; 337.17,25.

Silent, Solomon Reading–as Mr Hodgart has shown, the games on 176 come almost entirely from Norman Douglas's *London Street Games*. One of these games is Solomon Silent Reading. It is probably significant that both Douglas and Frazer trace these games back to primitive fertility rites. 176.8.

*Silkebjorg–Sitric (q.v.)? 163.30.

*Sillayass – Scylla? Perhaps the heroine of Barnabe Rich's *Apolonius and Silla*. Silla is the original of Shakespeare's Viola (q.q.v.) —see 231.20. †231.18—with Ass (q.v.).

Silvayne, Alexander–his *Histoires Tragiques* (trans. 1506) is the source of *The Merchant of Venice*. See Salvini. 495.36.

Silver, Captain John–in Stevenson's (q.v.) *Treasure Island*. See Billy Bones, Flint. The reference is also to *Navire d'Argent*, where some of FW was published. 291.2.

Sim, Sunny–see Shem, Sunny Jim. 305.5.

Simba the Slayer–see Siva. Simba is the word for "lion" in Bantu. 203.32.

Simon, Simple – nursery - rhyme character. 408.20.

Sinbad the Sailor–subject of an *Arabian Night's* story and of an English pantomime. 94.33; 256. 26,33; ?263.note 4; 314.18; 327. 25; 548.14; 620.7.

Sindat–see Sinbad.

*Sindy and Sandy, 491.1.

Singabob–see Sinbad.

Singer–American sewing machine. 626.14.

Singpantry's–see St Patrick. 7.10-11.

Sinnett, Alfred Percy – aide to Madame Blavatsky (q.v.), author of *Esoteric Buddhism.* 352.13.

Sinobiled–see Sinbad. 263.note 4.

Siranouche–see Cyrano de Bergerac. It may also have to do with Scaramouche, a stock character in Italian farce. 338.24.

Sirdarthar–see Gautama, Wellington, Arthur. 347.9.

Sirius – constellation named for Orion's (q.v.) dog. 426.24; 513.1.

Sirr, Major–British officer who, with Major Swann (q.v.), captured Lord Edward Fitzgerald (q.v.). He was noted for his brutality to the Irish: half-hanging was one of his happiest thoughts. 355.28; 516.15.

*Sistersen–see Man Servant. 186. 19.

Sitric or Sictric or Sygstrygg or Cedric–there are a good many Norse King Sitrics in Irish history. One of them may have been Hamlet's (q.v.) father—see Olaf the White. Another, Sitric Silkbeard, was defeated at Clontarf by Brian Boru (q.v.) in 1014. 12.32; 16.34; 77.13; 80.1; †221.34 —with Silken Thomas (q.v.); 313. 24; 348.18 (see Gormleyson); 353. 14; 376.31; 393.8; 532.8.

Sittons–see Siddons.

Siva the Slayer–with Brahma and Vishnu (q.q.v.) he forms the supreme trinity of the Hindus. Siva destroys and recreates. In one aspect he is an ascetic, in another the *linga.* 80.24; 203.32; 338.14.

Sixtus, Pope–five popes. 153.33; 234.13.

Skavar, Ivan Skavinsky–Russian who fought Abdul (q.v.) in Percy French's (q.v.) song. 355.11.

*Skelly, 390.7.

*Skerretts, 44.8.

*Skerry–possibly Skerry's Academy, *Ulysses,* 751/910—see Badbols. 376.26.

Skertsiraizde–see Scheherazade. 32.8.

Skilly–see Scylla. 229.14.

Skin-the-Goat–one of the Invincibles, keeper of the cabman's shelter in *Ulysses.* 507.6.

Skinner–stocking manufacturers. 414.32-33.

Slater, Oscar–convicted of murdering an old woman with a hammer. Conan Doyle (q.v.) got him released from prison. 511.4.

Slattery's Mounted Foot–song of Percy French's (q.v.). †90.17 and 137.9—with Saturn (q.v.); 181. 18-19.

*Slavocrates, 328.12.

Sleeping Beauty–fairy tale and English pantomime. 477.23; †541. 30-31—with Beauty and the Beast (q.v.); 620-621.

Slobabogue–Russian for "thank God". 350.30.

*Sloomysides, Sig, 399.stanza 2.

Slow, Mr Melancholy–Goldsmith's (q.v.) *The Traveller* opens: "Remote, unfriended, melancholy, slow. . . ." 56.30.

Sludge, Mr, the Medium–poem by Browning (q.v.). Mr Sludge is D. D. Home (q.v.). 439.23.

Sluttery–see Slattery. 181.18.

Slyne and Co.–Dublin ladies' tailor —see Sparrow. 548.27.

Smacchiavelluti–see Machiavelli. 251.26-27.

*Smell, The–probably Luke Tarpey (q.v.). 305.note 3.

Smeth–see Captain John Smith. 106.15-16.

Smirky Dainty–see Mercadante. 360.8.

Smith, Erasmus–patron of Trinity College, Dublin. 504.26.

Smith, Mr Frank–Shaun (q.v.). See Frank. 48.23-24.

*Smith, Hardy, 372.10-11.

Smith, Captain John (1579-1631)– president of the English colony in Virginia. His life was saved by Pocahontas (q.v.). 106.15-16.

*Smith, Miss–perhaps Madeline Smith, the Scottish poisoner. 468.10.

*Smith, Neoliffic, 576.36.

Smith, Rafe – see John Lane, Susanna for his identity. All these Smiths may not refer to him. See also Gow. ?75.33; 79.33; 148.32; ?197.11; 238.25,27,29; ?248.35; †263.15 and left margin—with Rolf Ganger; 434.36; †444.32— with Rolf Ganger (q.v.); ?481.21; 589.30; 594.11; 595.17.

Smollett, Tobias (1721-77)–English novelist, author of *Roderick Random, Humphrey Clinker, Peregrine Pickle* (q.q.v.). The pun on p. 28 depends on a smolt being a young salmon (q.v.). 28.35; 170.28; 580.8.

Smyly Boys Home–in Dublin. The reference may include Samuel Smiles. 209.33-34.

Smyth, Edward–Dublin sculptor who did the sculptures at the Custom House. 552.12.

*Smythe, Lady–battle of Ladysmith? 178.22.

*Snider–maybe Jacob Snider who converted the muzzle-loading Enfield to a breech-loader. 320.4.

Snooks, Robert–English highwayman, hanged in 1802. 493.14-15; 507.19.

Snorryson–see Sturlason. 551.4.

Snout, Tom–tinker who plays Wall (q.v.) in Shakespeare's (q.v.) *A Midsummer Night's Dream.* ?179. 6; 342.3.

Snow White and Rose Red–sisters in a fairy tale. See Rose. 64.27; 143.25; 380.3.

*Snuffler, 260.note 1.

*Soakersoon–see Man Servant. 566.10.

Soboostius–see Augustus Caesar. 468.3-4.

*Sobrinos, Alby, 488.29.

*Sockerson–see Man Servant. 370. 30.

Socrates–Greek philosopher. †88.9 —with Pan and Morpheus (q.q.v.); 306.left margin.

Soddy, Frederick–British mathematician, author of *Chemistry of the Radioactive Elements.* 264.note 1; 299.note 1.

*Sogermon, Master, 222.9-10.

*Sohan, Simpatica, 212.11-12.

*Solasistras, 90.2.

Soldiers Three–heroes of Kipling's stories. See Three Soldiers.

*Soldru, 124.30.

*Solidan–Isolde and Anne? Solid Dan? Saladin? 355.21.

*Soll–probably Sol or Solomon (q.v.). 44.13.

Sollis, Clive–Matt Gregory (q.v.) as the sword of Nuad (q.v.), one of the four (q.v.) magic objects brought to the battle of MagTured. 219.23-24.

*Solman Annadromus – salmon? 451.11.

Solness, Halvard–see Masterbuilder. 624.11.

Solomon–wise, magnificent king of Israel, reputed author of "The Song of Solomon". Joyce often relates him to the salmon (q.v.) because it was the giver of wisdom in Irish folk-lore. See Finn MacCool. 116.1; 126.28; 167.16; 188. 25; 198.4; 297.3; 307.left margin; †330.8—with Solveig; 337.10; 344.5; 416.5; †546.2—with Cromwell (q.v.); 625.16.

Solomon, Dr Bethel–former president of Dublin's Rotunda Maternity hospital. 542.28.

Solon (638-558 B.C.) – Athenian legislator, celebrated for wisdom and for repealing the severe laws of Draco (q.v.). 94.27; 167.27; 239.5; 307.left margin; 384.1; 476.14.

*Solsking the First–Louis XIV? Amenhotep? Heliogabalus? (q.q.v.). 607.28.

Solveig–heroine of Ibsen's *Peer Gynt* (q.v.) whose song ends the play. The Russian for nightingale is *solovei*. †330.8—with Solomon (q.v.).

Solyman–see Dr Bethel Solomon. 542.28.

Somers, Sir George–admiral of an English fleet, whose ship, *Sea Adventure*, was wrecked on Bermuda's reefs. Two crew members, Sylvester Jourdan and William Strachey, wrote accounts of the wreck. These Shakespeare (q.v.) used in *The Tempest*. ?16.13; ?319.10; 331.26; 453.16; 502.29.

Somers, Will–Henry VIII's (q.v.) fool. *Sommervogel* is Swiss-German for "butterfly". See Will. 415.27; 602.7.

Sonia – heroine of Dostoievsky's *Crime and Punishment*. See Raskolnikov. 348.34; 528.25.

*Soothbys–see Norreys. Perhaps the London auctioneers. 557.2.

Soothsayer–character in *Julius Caesar* (q.v.). 366.25.

Sophocles–Greek tragic poet. 47.

Sophy or Sophia (wisdom)–see Pruny-Quetch, see also *Ulysses*, 183/287. 9.34; 31.16; 450.18; 534.28.

Sorge–according to some medieval romances, the son of Tristram and Isolde of Ireland (q.q.v.). 189.18; 578.11.

Sorley Boy–see Sorley Boy MacDonnell. 499.22.

Sosie–see Susanna. It is French for double, counterpart, second self —see Two, Rachel and Leah, Christine Beauchamp, etc.

*Sostituda, 271.note 4.

Soter, Pope–pope from 167 to 174. 153.24.

Soteric Sulkinbored–see Sitric. 393. 8.

Sothis–Egyptian goddess, both Isis and Sirius (q.q.v.). 14.2; 452.6.

*Soulard, 292.23.

Soult, Nicolas Jean de Dieu, Duke of Dalmatia (1769-1851)–French marshal who fought Wellington (q.v.) in the peninsula and at Waterloo. 10.14 (insoult).

Souslevin, Jean–see John Sullivan. 222.8.

Sousymoust–see Zosimus. 232.7.

Southampton, Henry Wriothesley, 3rd earl–Shakespeare's (q.v.) patron to whom "Venus and Adonis" and "Lucrece" (q.q.v.) are dedicated. He is a leading candidate for the role of Mr W. H. (q.v.), but (and this makes me quite nervous) I cannot find a certain reference to him in FW. I list two instances of Harry (q.v.) which may be him. All Harrys could be, of course. 454.19; 511.24.

Sow–see Pig, Francie, Cleopatra.

Sowyer–see Peter Sawyer. 372.6.

*Spadebeard, Magnus, 480.12.

Sparkes, Isaac–according to Fitzpatrick (q.v.), "the greatest favourite that ever trod the Irish boards". Foote was an 18th century actor. 199.35; 376.23.

*Sparrem–see Warren. 575.30.

Sparrow's–Dublin store. See Slyne. 548.27.

Spartacus–leader of the Slave or Gladiatorial War against Rome, 73-71 B.C.; also a German revolutionary socialist party, c. 1918. 116.11.

Spectrum girls–see Seven.

?Speed – clown in Shakespeare's (q.v.) *Two Gentlemen of Verona.* 448.17.

Speke, John Haning – explorer, author of *Journal of the Discovery of the Sources of the Nile.* I think his name is in the "O Answer" which accompanies the Nile (q.v.) theme, for to "O Answer" is to speak. 202.20.

*Spence, Father Petrie – Peter's Pence. See Petrie? 350.28.

Spendlove, Mrs–Dublin prostitute who went into prolonged and public mourning weeds for Edward VII (q.v.). Gogarty (q.v.) has an amusing account of her. 625.8.

Spengler, Oswald (1880-1936)–German historian. 151.9; 521.1.

Speranza–see Lady Wilde.

Sphinx–a monster in Greek myth whose riddle Oedipus (q.v.) guessed. †473.18—with Phoenix (q.v.).

*Spillitshops, Misto Teewiley – Spirit shops? HCE (q.v.)? 355.30-31.

*Spilltears, Rue, 60.1.

Spinoza, Baruch (1632 77) Dutch philosopher. 150.8; 414.16, 32-33; 611.36.

Spofforth, F. R.–English cricketer. 583.32.

*Squalchman, Mrs Dowager Justice, 390.35-36.

Squeers, Mr–educator in Dickens's (q.v.) *Nicholas Nickleby.* 151.15; 384.10; 420.22; 556.24.

*Squintina, 567.29.

Staffetta–in Italian *staffa* is "stirrup", *staffetta* is "courier", or Shaun (q.v.). 462.5.

Stainusless–St Stanislaus Kosta, Confessor–a young Polish nobleman, model of religious perfection. As a joke, Joyce may join on his atheist brother Stanislaus (q.v.). 237.11.

*Stakelum, Selina Susquehanna, 212.6.

Stalin, Joseph (1879-1953)–Russian dictator. 272.27.

Standfast Dick–reef of rock across the Liffey at Dublin. 210.28.

Stand-Fast, Mr–character in the second part of *The Pilgrim's Progress*, who is tempted by Madame Bubble (q.v.). 275.8.

Starlin–see Stalin.

Starn–see Sterne. 303.6.

*Starr, Lord Joe, 549.35.

Stars – see Stella and Vanessa, Esther, Swift, Sterne, Pip and Estella, Raven and Dove, etc. According to Joyce (to Miss Weaver, 23 October 1928) the Germans call glaucoma the Green Star; cataract the Gray Star; dissolution of the retina, the Black Star. These are the "sesthers" wroth with Swift on the first page of FW and throughout the book they represent female vengeance. In the 18th century "star over garter" meant the vagina and "star gazer" meant the penis. See Sterne.

Starveling, Robin–a tailor who plays Moonshine (q.v.) in Shakespeare's *A Midsummer Night's Dream.* In FW III,i,ii, Moonshine is Shaun (q.v.) who eats like a starved man (see John McCormack) and converses with Shem (q.v.) who plays Bottom-as-ass (q.q.v.). See also Moon. 466.17.

Stator and Victor–epithets of Jupiter (q.v.). 179.11.

Steal–see Steele.

Steele, Sir Richard (1672-1729)– English man of letters, born in Dublin. 303.5.

Steevens, Grisel – founder of Steeven's Hospital, Dublin, in the 18th century. She was believed to have a snout like a pig. 40.34.

Stein, Gertrude – 20th century American expatriate writer who was in Paris in Joyce's time. 287.19.

Stella and Vanessa–Esther Johnson and Esther Vanhomrigh (called by Swift Vanessa—see Cadenus) —the two young spinsters with whom Jonathan Swift (q.v.) so obscurely involved himself. Joyce's opinion of that involvement may be guessed from his identifying the Esthers (q.v.) with Philomela and Procne (q.v.). Swift is Tereus (q.v.) who ravishes the girls with cold: they are the vengeful stars (q.v.) who blind him. The "Venice" prince, as Mr Litz suggests, may bring in Desdemona (q.v.). In FW they are women, furies, stars, flowers, disease, and dangerous as hell. Vanessa is also a butterfly—see 107.18, 232.11. See also Issy, Ishtar, Venus, Hester Prynne, Sterne, Pip and Estella, George Moore.

†3.22   venissoon—with Venus (Hebrew name for that planet is Esther)

†24   vanessy — with Venus (q.v.), sesthers

†7.4   issavan essavans—with Issy (q.v.)

†21.13   homerigh—with Homer (the reference may be to Bartholomew Vanhomrigh, q.v.)

27.11   Hetty Jane

†14-15   Essie Shanahan . . . Essie—with Jonathan (see Swift)

28.9,23   nesters . . . Stilla Star

29.13   Artsa

?†52.29-30   d'Esterre (q.v.)

61.20   fastra sastra

65.11,13   stars . . . stars (q.v.)

†69.14   Isther Estarr . . . Yesther Asterr — with Issy, Ishtar, Astarte(q.q.v.)

101.4,8,29   ussies . . . Estella Swift (see Swift) . . . izarres

104.24   Hesterdays

†107.18   persequestellates his vanessas—with Percival (q.v.)

135.11   hestens

143.22   disaster . . . starring

155.25   starabouts

177.10-11,17   stellas vespertine . . . vanessance

†178.27   peepestrella — see Pip and Estella

184.22   Asther's . . . Huster's

212.31-32   estheryear's . . . vanitty

†214.1   histereve — with Eve (q.v.)

†232.11   venicey . . . a stell—with Venus, Pip and Estella (q.q.v.)

234.30   essies

?236.17   jessies (q.v.)

246.13-14   stars astir and stirabout

248.7,13   asters . . . stars

†257.2   Fain Essie . . . stella's vispirine—with Issy (q.v.)

261.note 1   happnessied

†276.20-21,23   peepeestrilling . . . still here—with Pip and Estella (q.v.)

†278.note 3   Enastella . . . Essatessa —with Ena, Tessa (q.q.v.)

280.7   yesters

†281.14-15   pervinciveness—with Pervenche (see Solskar Gunn), Venus

295.1-2   hesterdie . . . istherdie . . . Vanissas Vanistatums . . . nesse—(see Ishtar)

25-26   very nesse

319.6-7   hesteries

327.13   ester

364.17   starvision

†365.28-29   estelles, van Nessies von Nixies voon der pool —with Nessie (q.v.)

†379.16   Nessies (q.v.)

382.17   stargaze
406.30   Mesthress Vanhungrig
407-408   hesternmost
413.6,7,8,25, †29 shester . . . mudi-
             cal dauctors . . . Eas-
             ther's . . . M.D.D.O.D.
             . . . venusstas — with
             Venus (q.v.) (M.D.
             was what Swift called
             Stella in *Journal to*
             Stella)
426.32   asterisks
427.1,7,10 Killesther's . . . vanes-
             shed . . . stellas
439.10   stardaft
†449.3-4   stellar . . . vanity of
             Vanissy — with Issy
             (q.v.)
454.23   still and
457.28   fluster
†458.10   sester   Maggy — with
             Maggy (q.v.)
†461.2-3   star . . . Pouts Vanisha
             Creme—see Issy, Ish,
             Pond's
462.7   Esterelles
†471.8-9,11-12 estellos and venous-
             sas . . . star . . . hes
             sthers — with Venus
             (q.v.)
486.26-27 still a vain essaying
500.21   ersther
503.4-5   steller . . . starey
511.28   star stellar
†526.23   Stilla Underwood—see
             Underwood
528.11-12 hister . . . esster
539.21   starrymisty
?562.32   veen nonsolance
†605.12   Yssia and Essia—with
             Issy, Esther Waters
             (q.q.v.)
608.4   essenesse
609.30   aster
624.25   Yesthers . . . Yhesters

*Stena, 608.16.

Stentor–loud-voiced Greek herald
in the *Iliad*. 454.9-10.

Stephen, St – first martyr. See
Stephen Dedalus. 326.2.

Stephens, Davy – a professional
Irishman with long ringlets and
wild eyes who sold newspapers
on Kingston Pier. Every year he
dressed up like a gentleman in
frock-coat and tall-hat and went
to the Derby. 300.note 2.

Sterne, Laurence (1713-68)–English novelist, born in Ireland. See
Tristram Shandy. In FW he is
usually coupled with Swift (q.v.)
and I remember reading somewhere that Joyce said Sterne and
Swift should have exchanged
names in order to describe their
writing properly. They are further
connected in that *sterne* is German
for "stars" (q.v.) and the stars
always accompany Swift. 4.21;
36.35; 66.21; 77.6; 123.9; 199.7;
256.14; 282.7; 291.note 4; 292.30;
303.6; 454.21-22; 486.28.

Stetson–hat. 54.32.

Stevenson, Robert Louis (1850-94)
–Scottish novelist—see Silver,
Billy Bones, Jekyll, Other Fellow.
106.9 (Polynesia*l* Entertaine*r* Ex-
hibit*s*).

Stoddard–English cricketer. 584.1.

Stoker, Bram (1847-1912)–Irish
journalist and novelist, author of
Dracula. FW, 145.24-32 becomes
somewhat more comprehensible
if you know Stoker wrote a jesting
piece, claiming that Elizabeth I
(q.v.) was really a man. This was
taken seriously by a Mr Titterton
who claimed in *New Witness*,
1913, that Elizabeth - the - man
wrote Shakespeare's (q.v.) plays.
145.32.

Stokes, Whitley (1830-1909)–Celtic
scholar. 619.32.

*Stolterforth, Sigismond, 537.8-9.

*Stoney–from context, an architect
or sculptor. 552.12.

Stopes, Marie–British advocate of
birth-control. 444.8.

?Stow, John (1525-1606)–English
chronicler and antiquary. 503.21.

Strabo (b. 63 B.C.)–Greek geographer and historian. 295.17.

?Strachey, Lytton (1880-1932)–

English biographer. See also Somers. 595.4.

Strange, Baron Ferdinand – see Derby, 5th earl. 39.32, 351.2-3.

*****Stranaslang,** 338.22.

Strindberg, Johann August (b. 1849)–Swedish author who wrote, among other things, *Sömngångarnätter.* 221.30.

Strong, Kate–Chart (q.v.) says, "The most odious of Dublin tax collectors . . . a woman, Kate Strong. The people erected an effigy of her, armed with a tolldish of utterly unfair proportions." According to Fitzpatrick (q.v.), "Katherine Strong, a widow, inherited from her deceased husband the post of city scavenger, and a grant of tolls for performing the duties of that office. The lady in question seems to have been much more active in collecting her dues than in removing the abundant filth of the city, notwithstanding the oath which the city scavengers (79.34, 80.5) were bound to take." See Kate the Cleaner. 79.27.

Strongbow, Earl of Pembroke– leader of the Anglo-Normans who invaded Ireland in 1170. He married Eve Macmurrough (q.v.) and, not without difficulty, ruled Leinster till his death in 1176. He was buried in Christ Church Cathedral; his tomb was long a Dublin landmark and a recognized place for the payment of debt, transaction of business, etc. See Pembroke. 23.3; 68.19; 82.24; 87.28; 129.32; 288.15; 311.15; 343.4; ?376.31; 547.31; 626.2.

Struldbrugs – miserable, epicene immortals in the third part of *Gulliver's* (q.v.) *Travels.* I think the Four (q.v.) are Struldbrugs in II,iv. 623.23-24.

Stuarts – Scottish royalty, uncrowned, and by Joyce not infrequently associated with Charles

Stewart Parnell (q.v.). 41.36; 227.29; 498.1.

Studds – 19th century cricketer. 583.36.

*****Stumblestone,** Davy–see David? 210.29.

Sturk–character in LeFanu's (q.v.) *House by the Churchyard.* In Phoenix Park he is stunned and given up for dead by Archer (q.v.); Black Dillon (q.v.) performs an operation which "resurrects" him. 17.14; ?34.1; 80.10.

Sturlason, Snorri (1178-1241) – author of the *Prose Edda.* 257.36; 551.4; 578.2.

Stuyvesant, Peter (1592-1672)– Dutch governor of New Amsterdam. 117.24; ?205.34 (Pete-over-Meer may be Peter Sawyer and Dublin, Ga., rather than Stuyvesant and New York); 550.31.

Suck at–see St Patrick. 485.7,8.

Sudley, Planty–air to which Moore's (q.v.) song "Oh the Sight Entrancing" is sung. 566.28.

Sudlow, Bessy–Dublin actress, Mrs Michael Gunn (q.v.). 32.10; 434.8.

Sue, Eugène (1804-57)–French novelist who wrote *Le Juif errant.* 437.31.

Suetonius–Roman historian of the 1st and 2nd centuries B.C., wrote the lives of the twelve Caesars from Julius (q.v.) to Domitian, great letter-writer. 6.7; 271.7.

Suffoclose–see Sophocles. 47.

Sukkot–see St Patrick. 612.15.

Sulla, Lucius Cornelius (138-78 B.C.)–Roman general and dictator. He mixes with Sully the Thug (q.v.). 573.6,13,31.

*****Sulleyman**–see Sullivan? Sully the Thug?

*****Sullivan** and Doyle (q.v.)–apparently the composite names of the Twelve (q.v.). Their leader is Sully the Thug (q.v.). 58.10; 142.26; 435.29; 495.2,7; †573.7,

13—with Sir Arthur Sullivan (q.v.); 581.4; 602.26; 622.23.

Sullivan, Sir Arthur–see Gilbert and Sullivan. †573.7—with Sullivan above.

Sullivan, John–Irish tenor, enthusiasm of Joyce's. 222.8.

Sullivan, T. D.–author of "God Save Ireland" which is sung to the tune of "Tramp, Tramp, Tramp". I think Joyce confuses him with his brother A. M. Sullivan, himself a versifier. 93.30.

*Sully the Thug–leader of the Twelve (q.v.). See also Sullivan. He is said to be a henchman of Magrath's (q.v.) and a bootmaker. 212.3; 435.29; 495.1,7; 525.3; 558.12,14; †573.6,13,31 — with Sulla (q.v.); 618.8,29.

Sulpicius (121-88 B.C.)–Roman orator, led a democratic revolt and was put to death by Sulla's (q.v.) forces. 254.8.

Summanus–Saline or Etruscan god of the nocturnal heavens and thunder by night. 7.18; 241.2.

Sunday, Billy (1862-1925)–American evangelist. 436.27.

*Sunfella's, 96.2.

Sun-Yat-sen (1866-1925)–father of a Chinese revolution. 90.1; †528. 21-22—with Shem and Shaun (q.v.).

Sunny Jim–advertising figure for a breakfast food, "Force". Joyce was so called as a child. See Bodkin, James. 211.6; 305.5.

Surface, Joseph and Charles – brothers of opposing character in Sheridan's (q.v.) *School for Scandal.* 208-209.

Surtees–1) Robert (1803-64), author of sporting novels. FW 43 is rather in his style—compare the welcome of Mr Jorrocks to Handley Hall. See Percival. 2) Reverend Scott of Dinesdale-on-Tee, author of *William Shakespeare of Stratford-on-Avon. His Epitaph*

Unearthed and the Author of the Plays Run to Ground. 57.30.

Susan, Susy, Sue, Sosie–see Susanna.

Susanna (Hebrew "Lily", q.v.)– title heroine of an Apocryphal book. Because she rejected the advances of two Elders (q.v.), they accused her falsely of being unchaste with a young man. Daniel (q.v.) proved her innocent. In FW she is identified with Susanna Shakespeare Hall (q.v.) who was accused by John Lane (q.v.) of being "naught" with Rafe Smith (q.v.). See also Sosie, Elizabeth, Ann Hathaway. See also *Ulysses,* 209/272. 3.24; 11.16; 19.29; 96.13; 116.1; 123.27; †127. 19—with Anne (Hathaway? Anna Livia? q.v.); 130.18; 135.8; 143. 5; 146.11; 147.14; 148.9; 154.8; 173.1; 184.2; 192.2; 209.35; ?210. 25; ?†212.6—with Hen and Anna Livia (q.q.v.); ?212.8; 213.26; 232.28,29; 246.14; 301.note 1; 308.28; 311.22,23,34; 313.34; 317. 22; 324.12,29,30; 326.24; 327.30; 329.2; 330.1; 363.18; ?376.14; 384.27; 413.18; 418.14; ?435.15 (see Moedl's); 437.29,31; 446.6; 454.19; 459.10-11; 508.31; 513.6; 531.22; 534.33; 538.30; 552.20; ?561.16; ?562.13-14; ?564.36; 567. 30; †594.30—with Hen, Anna Livia, Hathaway (q.q.v.); 595.8; 601.12.

Suso, Heinrich (1300-66)–German mystic, the *minnesinger of Gottesminne.* 11.16.

Suzy–Paris hat-maker. See Moedl's, Susanna. 435.15.

Svea–personification of Sweden. 607.20.

Swan–William Shakespeare (q.v.) the Swan of Avon. Swan references also surround his Cordelia (q.v.), Lir's (q.v.) lonely daughter and, not unnaturally, spread out to take in Zeus (q.v.) as Leda's (q.v.) swan, Leda is connected with another poet named William. The Swan was an Elizabethan

theatre. Swan Water is a sub-
terranean river which once merged
with the Liffey (q.v.). See also
Swann, Jacob Earwig. 7.1; †21.18
(Mark the Wans)—with Mark of
Cornwall (q.v.); 63.35; †127.15—
with Joseph Swann (q.v.); †139.
12-13 (his wan); 171.4; 202.9 (see
Bacon); 204.11; 208.19; 226.
5; 248.23; †289.2—with Anna
Livia (q.v.); †326.36 — with
Sweyne (q.v.); †372.4—with Mark
of Cornwall and Moke (q.q.v.),
16; 383.27; †410.3—with Charles
Swann (q.v.); 423.21-22; †450.5—
with Charles Swann (q.v.); †465.
35—with C. Swann (q.v.); 511.13;
†516.18 — with Major William
Swann (q.v.); 548.33; 557.9;
577.3; 581.6; 600.31.

Swann, Charles – protagonist of
Proust's (q.v.) *Swann's Way*. He
doubles with Swan above. 410.3;
450.5; 465.35.

Swann, Sir Joseph (1828-1914)–
British physicist, inventor of an
incandescent lamp. See Swan.
127.15.

Swann, Major William – with
Major Sirr (q.v.), captured Lord
Edward Fitzgerald (q.v.). See
Swan. 516.18.

Swaran–in Macpherson's "Fingal"
(q.q.v.), leader of the Norsemen
against whom Fingal fights. The
Norsemen are defeated and a
general reconciliation of the foes
takes place. 131.22; 348.14; ?521.
1; ?524.17.

*****Sweainey,** Sister Evangelist, 391.
33.

*****Sweatagore**–Tagore (q.v.)? 37.2.

Swedenborg, Emanuel (1688-1772)
–Swedish philosopher, scientist,
mystic. 552.16.

Sweeney–as among Nightingales—
see T. S. Eliot. See also swine,
swan. Sweeney was an Irish
king who went mad at the battle
of Mog Rath. 92.15; 424.27;
504.23.

*****Swenson,** 372.16.

Sweyne–son of Harold Bluetooth
(q.v.), baptised in infancy, re-
verted to paganism and warred
against the Christian faith. 254.3;
†326.36—with Swan (q.v.).

Swift, Jonathan (1667-1745)–born
in Hoy's Court, Dublin, secretary
to Sir William Temple (q.v.) at
Moore Park (see George Moore);
Dean of St Patrick's—see Dean,
St Patrick; author of *Gulliver's
Travels* (q.v.), *A Tale of a Tub*
(see Peter, Jack, Martin), *Journal
to Stella*, "Cadenus and Vanessa"
(q.q.v.), the *Drapier Letters* (see
Draper). See also Bickerstaff,
Yahoo, Philomela, Godolphin,
Partridge, Struldbrugs.
  Swift is of immense importance
in FW, and Mrs Mackie Jarrell
has written a comprehensive
piece about it (ELH, June 1959).
She does, however, miss two
points I think important. 1) The
Irish pronounce "Dean" as
"Dane", which ties Swift to
Hamlet (q.v.), both men having
unsweetened imaginations and
behaving with notable coldness
to their women. 2) Stella and
Vanessa are the stars (q.v.) of
blindness who blind Swift in
revenge for his having ravished
them with cold. Sterne (q.v.) is
German *sterne* or "stars". (See
Joyce to Miss Weaver, 28 October
1928.) See Philomela, Tereus.
  In FW Swift, like Bacon, is split
between Shem and Shaun (q.v.).
As a writer, he is, I think, Shem
or Draper, as a man he is Shaun
or Jonathan. The remarks in this
paragraph are tentative.

†3.24	nathanjoe — with Nathan, Jonathan (q.q.v.)
4.23	swiftly
36.35	swift
†146.11-12	Tame Schwipps — with Schwepps (q.v.)
165.2	swift
192.22	Jonathan (q.v.)
252.35	jomtom sick
256.13	swiftly

282.8	swift
289.17	priesto
292.24	swiftshut
294.16	swiftshut
303.6	Swhipt
†307.5	Brother Jonathan (q.v.)
347.29-30	swiping a jonny dann sweept
449.3	swift
450.6	swift
†454.9	Jaunathaun–see Jonathan, Shaun
20	swifter
†462.8	Shaunathaun—with Shaun (q.v.)
467.27	swift
486.26	swift
?555.32	Jerry Godolphing—with Jerry (q.v.), see also Godolphin
?563.25-26	godolphing lad in the Hoy's Court—see Godolphin
568.30	swift
596.33	swift

Swinburne, Algernon Charles (1837-1909)–English poet. See Wippingham. 41.7; 434.35 (Algy).

Swine–see Pig.

***Swingy,** MacSmashall – *Ulysses*, 315/416: "smashall sweeney's moustaches". 516.5.

Swithin or Swithun, St (d. 862)– "St Swithin's day if thou dost rain,/For forty days it will remain;/St Swithin's day if thou be fair,/For forty days 'twill rain na mair." 34.28; 178.8; 433.35; 520.16.

***Swordsmeat,** 490.20-21.

Sycamores–the Scriptural sycamore was the fig-tree. In FW the Four (q.v.) as impotent old men —Struldbrugs, Tiresias from "The Waste Land"—are the sycamores, avidly watching love-making and dirtying it because they cannot participate. The sycamore is also firmly associated with the sickamour of Othello (q.v.). See also Elders. 24.31; †95.21—with John Lane (q.v.); 115.21; 203.21-22; †281.20-21—with Othello and perhaps George Moore (q.q.v.); 384. 1; 388.24; 397.23-24; †460.23— with Othello (q.v.); 533.17; 555. 20.

Sygstryggs–see Sitric. 77.13.

***Sylvanus** Sanctus, 570.32.

***Sylvester,** 388.26.

Sylvester, St (d. 335)–the Pope who baptised Constantine (q.v.). His day is December 31. 473.3.

Sylvia–girl in Shakespeare's (q.v.) *Two Gentlemen of Verona.* Sylvia references may now and then include Sylvia Beach (q.v.) who ran Shakespeare and Co. See Julia, Valentine, Sylvia Silence. ?133.15; 148.8; 211.36; †360.13— with Carmen Sylva (q.v.); ?495. 36; ?564.25; 619.30.

***Symmonds**–maybe J. A. Symonds (1840-92)–English writer. 310.14.

Synge, John Millington (1871-1909) –Irish poet, playwright—see Playboy. The references may include a most zealous Dublin preacher of the 18th century. 244.7; 251. 10; †256.13—with Yeats (q.v.); ?267.8; 466.21; 549.3.

***Synodius,** Saint, 487.36.

T

Taafe–family that was prominent in the North of Ireland from the 13th century. One went with Charles II (q.v.) into exile, another fought at the Boyne, others —still in exile—rose to prominence in Austria. See Taff. 320.23; 582.8.

Tabarins–name assumed by Jean Soloman (1584-1633) – Parisian street charlatan who sold quack medicine with farcical patter. 360.26; 415.9.

***Tabitha** or Tib (see Tibbs)–the

Earwicker family cat who sometimes seems to be Issy (q.v.) for "Tib" is short for Isabel. 28.5; 235.30; 603.5; 624.18.

*Taboutot, Blaize, 372.10.

Tacitus, Cornelius (55-120)–Roman historian. 17.3.

*Tad, 273.note 8.

Taff–see Butt.

*Taft, toft–see Taff. I suppose this could be President Taft, for I have an idea Joyce puts in all the U.S. presidents. 277.11.

Taglioni, Maria (1804-84)–Italian dancer. 513.17.

Tagore, Sir Rabindranath (1861-1941)–Indian poet. His play *The Post Office*, produced in Ireland in 1913, probably helped suggest Shaun (q.v.) as the king's royal post, carrying the divine word. 37.2.

Tailor–see Kersse, Starveling.

Tailte–queen of the Firbolg, foster-mother of Lug (q.v.). He established the Tailtean games in Meath in her honor; the games were revived by the Free State. 83.23; 344.17; 386.27; 550.25.

*Taiocebo, 43.23.

Talbot, Lord – valiant English leader against Joan of Arc (q.v.) in Shakespeare's *1 Henry VI* (q.q.v.). He was several times a bad Irish viceroy. There is a Talbot Street in Dublin. 229.25; 447.13.

Talbot, Matt–Dublin laborer who put himself under the obligation of perpetual prayer, covered himself with ropes and cart chains which were hung with religious medals. He always entered churches by crawling on his tummy. 262.note 6.

Taliessin–late 6th century British bard of whom nothing is known except the attribution to him of the poems known as the *Book of Taliessin*. 151.22.

?Tallis, Thomas (1515-85)–father of English cathedral music. 150.1.

*Tallulah–maybe Tallulah Bankhead, American actress; maybe the American river for which (I suppose) she was named. 358.22.

Talop, Aasdocketor–see Plato. 241.15.

Talos–1) nephew of Daedalus (q.v.); 2) bronze giant made by Daedalus which guarded Crete. 539.26.

Tam–see Tom.

Tam O'Shanter–subject of a poem by Burns (q.v.). Joyce associates him with the peeping-Tom theme. See Kate. 227.22; 229.21; 315.25.

Tamagno, Francisco (1851-1905)–Italian tenor. 404.26.

Tamar–see Genesis, 38. †200.31—with Tamora (q.v.).

Tamerlane or Timur (1336-1405)–Oriental conqueror, subject of two plays by Marlowe. 71.16; †136.21 — with Thomas Moore (q.v.); †550.30-31—with Michael Cusack (q.v.).

Tamlane – see Tamerlane. "The Young Tamlane" is a Scottish ballad. 550.30-31.

Tammany–wire Delaware chief of the 17th and 18th centuries, facetiously canonized as patron saint of the USA. His name was adopted by a New York City fraternal organization whose building Tammany Hall is a symbol of corrupt Democratic politics, long an Irish-American prerogative. †379.34—with Tem, Tim (q.q.v.).

Tammuz–Babylonian slain god, called Adonis (q.v.) by the Phoenicians. Tammuz is the 6th month in the Babylonian calendar. The annals, 13-14, are zodiacal. 13.26; 598.15.

?Tamora–queen of the Goths, Roman empress in Shakespeare's *Titus Andronicus* (q.q.v.). †200.31 —with Tamar (q.v.); 255.4.

Tancred (d. 1194)–King of Sicily who fought against the Romans to maintain his Norman kingdom. He lost. 337.35-36.

Tandy, James Napper (1740-1803) –United Irishman, immortalized in "The Wearing of the Green": "I met with Napper Tandy . . .". He was neither intelligent nor reliable. 345.24; 408.30; 464.24; 516.31.

Tanner, John–hero of Shaw's Don Giovanni (q.q.v.) play, *Man and Superman*. His girl's name is Anne Whitefield (q.v.) and the name "Anne" is included in his own. See Mendoza, Ottavio. 71. 28; 182.23; 294.30; †312.9—with Anne Whitefield, Anna Livia (q.q.v.).

*Tan-Taylour, Mrs – Anna Livia (q.v.) as tailor's (q.v.) daughter? 511.29.

Tappertit, Simon–anarchical apprentice in Dickens's *Barnaby Rudge* (q.q.v.). 505.1; 594.35.

Tark or Tarik–sky and lightning god of the Hittites. 356.17.

Tarpey, Luke–the third of the Four (q.v.). He is the number 3; the third letter of the Hebrew alphabet; the province and Leinster and places in that province (excepting Dublin which belongs to HCE); he is east, east wind; the element earth; the copper age, the third age of man or death. He lives with Lilly Tekkles (q.v.) at the Eats; his road is Waddlings (q.v.) Raide; his beast is the ox or calf. See Four Evangelists. 142.6; †184.34-35—with Charles Lucas (q.v.); 214.34; 368.33; 384.11; 386.6; 389.10; 390.13,23, 34; 398.22,26; 405.5; 475.27-28; 476.26; 482.7; 485.30,32; 519.31; 520.8; 526.30; 573.8,28.

Tarquin–various prominent Romans (of Etruscan background) were so named. I think Joyce means the Tarquin who raped Lucrece (q.v.), both of them

Shakespearean (q.v.) characters. 278.note 7.

Tarquinius, Priscus Lucius and Tarquinius Superbus – respectively the 5th and 7th (or last) legendary kings of Rome. 467.32, 35.

Tarrant, G. (1838 - 70) – British cricketer. 583.29.

*Tarriestinus, 157.2.

*Tarry the Tailor–see tailor. 43.17.

Tartarin de Tarascon–title hero of a novel (1874) by Daudet. 227.35.

Tass–Russian news agency. 338.22; 593.18.

*Tate and Comyng–see Tut-ankhamen. 295.8.

Tattu, Lord of–see Osiris. 486.14.

*Taubiestimm, Mrs–In German *taubstumm* means "deaf and dumb"; *Taube*, "dove", *Tau*, "dew", *Biest*, "beast", *Stimme*, "voice". 546.29.

*Taverner, Mass–HCE (q.v.) the tavern keeper? 54.21-22.

Tawfulsdreck–see Teufelsdröckh. 68.21.

*Taylor–tailor (q.v.)? Jeremy? 61. 28; 365.33-34.

*Teague–a name, like Paddy, for an Irishman. 281.note 2.

Tears–see Pearl.

Tearsheet, Doll–whore in Shakespeare's *2 Henry IV* (q.q.v.). See Doll? 22.1; 266.18; 268.note 7; 298.9,11.

*Teddy–Edward? 191.23.

Tefnut–goddess in Egyptian myth. 570-571; 624.17-18.

*Tekkles, Lilly–see Lily, Luke Tarpey. 373.3.

Telemachus–son of Ulysses and Penelope (q.q.v.), Stephen Dedalus (q.v.). 176.36.

Telesphorus–pope from 126-127. He may have been martyred. 154.6.

†**Televox,** Mr–Valentine Vox (q.v.)? 546.29.

Telford, Thomas (1757-1834)–British civil engineer, builder of bridges and harbors. 552.26.

Tell, William – legendary Swiss champion of freedom. 154.35.

Tellus–ancient Italian earth goddess. 101.2; 275.left margin; 499. 34; 527.1.

Tem or Atem–according to *The Book of the Dead,* Ra (q.v.) as the night sun. He was self-created, created gods and men. He seems to merge with Tom (q.v.). I don't know why. 56.34; 88.35; 223.36; 224.1,3,7; ?258.21; 353. 29; †379.34 — with Tammany (q.v.); 608.31.

*Temple–maybe Swift's (q.v.) patron, Sir William Temple (1628-99) of Moor Park—see George Moore. 192.35; 288.21.

Tenducci–18th century tenor who made his reputation singing "Water Parted from the Sea". 541.32.

Tennyson, Alfred, Lord (1809-92)– English poet. 48.35; 214.27.

Teobaldo, Fra–see Father Mathew. See also Fra Diavolo. 553.13.

Teresa or Therese, St–I cannot be sure whether Joyce intends St Teresa of Avila (1515-82) or The Little Flower, St Teresa of Lisieux (1873-97). 432.29 is certainly the latter. 155.26 ought to be a Dublin convent. 155.26; 432.29; ?491.16.

Tereus–ravisher of Philomela (q.v.) and Procne, turned into a hawk. See Swift. 360.4.

*Terriss, 105.35-36; 111.6.

Terry and Kelly–Terry Kelly, a Dublin pawnbroker. 206.19.

Terry, Ellen (1848-1928)–English actress. She played Puck (q.v.) in Shakespeare's (q.v.) *A Midsummer Night's Dream.* 210.34-35.

*Tessa–perhaps the heroine of *The Gondoliers.* †278.note 3 — with Stella (q.v.).

Tethra–legendary leader of the Fomorians. †457.13—with Hera (q.v.).

Teufelsdröckh, Professor–hero of Carlyle's (q.v.) *Sartor Resartus.* In German *teufelsdreck* means "asafetida", literally "devil's dirt". 68.21.

Thackeray, William Makepeace (1811-63)–English novelist, whose *Vanity Fair* is mentioned on the first page of FW. See Jeames. 177.35; 434.26.

*Thacolicus, pro-Brother, 193.21- 22.

Thaddeus–hero of *The Bohemian Girl,* rival of Florestein (q.v.). 246.18.

Thaddeus–according to apocryphal tradition, the brother of Jesus, sometimes called Judas Thaddeus. 281.note 2; ?456.30.

Thalia–muse of comedy and merry, idyllic poetry. See Melpomene, Clio. 569.29.

*Tham the Thatcher, †318.16–with Ham (q.v.)?

Themis–titaness, some say mother of Prometheus (q.v.), divine justice as opposed to Dike or human justice. Jane Harrison wrote a book, *Themis.* 101.4; 138.10; 167.10,25.

*Theobald–see Tibbs, Tybalt? 117. 19; 236.8; 423.2-3; 424.29.

Theobald, St–church father, anchorite. 159.31; †263.5-6—with Balder (q.v.).

Theobalder – see St Theobald, Balder. 263.5-6.

Theocritus (fl. 3rd century B.C.)– creator of pastoral poetry. 307. left margin.

*Theophil–maybe Theophilus, East Roman emperor (829-842), or Théophile de Viau, French poet (1591-1626), author of a *Pyramus and Thisbe* (q.q.v.); maybe

Gautier, French poet (1811-72). 163.25.

*Theophrastius Spheropneumaticus–possibly Paracelsus (q.v.). 484.30-31.

Thersites – Homeric, Shakespearean (q.q.v.), Joycean character, a railer. †137.24—with Thor (q.v.); 228.31 (othersites).

Theseus – Greek hero, duke in Shakespeare's (q.v.) *A Midsummer Night's Dream*. See Amazon. 266.left margin.

Thisby–see Flute, Pyramus. 75.27; 116.36; 140.23; 472.15-16; 518.10.

Thom's–Dublin's city directory. See Tom. 90.26; 534.27.

Thomar – Danish invader from whom Malachy (q.v.) won the circle of gold. 90.26.

Thomas, St (Doubting)–see St John, 20:4/24. He had to touch the risen Christ in order to believe. In the middle ages, the ass (q.v.) became his symbol. The last boy to enter school on St Thomas's day was called "Ass Thomas". See Tom, Toucher Tom. 8.26-27; †93.9—with Ass and Aquinas (q.q.v.); †101.9—with Ass (q.v.); 210.15; 347.10; 506.28; 507.1-2.

Thomas, Silken or Lord Thomas Fitzgerald, 10th earl of Kildare (1513-37)–Irish rebel, hanged at Tyburn. †221.34 (silktric twomesh)—with Sitric (q.v.).

Thompson, Dr William–Australian who wrote a pamphlet unfavorably contrasting Shakespeare's (q.v.) views on vivisection with those of Bacon (q.v.). It was called *A Minute Among the Amenities*. I cannot help hoping that Joyce refers to it on 502.25-26 and that he indicates Dr Thompson in some of the Toms (q.v.).

Thon–see Thonar.

Thonar or Thon–god worshipped in England and on the Continent who may be a form of Thor (q.v.),

for his name is that of the Teutonic word for "thunder". 11.3,4, 5; †18.16—with Thor (q.v.); 31. 10; 106.15; 176.1; 294.6 (noth); 334.32; 354.34; 365.22; 415.31; 582.32.

Thor–Scandinavian god who wields the thunderbolts. Tomar is the Irish form of his name. See also Thon. All thunder-gods are of great importance in FW because, according to Vico (q.v.), a crash of thunder started civilization. 36.35; 53.26; 77.7; 80.14; 86.11; 90.26; 130.4; †137.24—with Thersites (q.v.); 154.23; 198.29; 246. 6-7; 279.note 1; †310.3—with Petersen (q.v.), 20; 311.6; †312.8 —with Mendoza (q.v.); †353.25— with Ivan the Terrible (q.v.); 360.16; 378.12; 424.22; 532.9— with MacAuscullpth (q.v.); 537. 4-5; 543.16; 568.17; 609.26; †626. 28—with Thorir (q.v.).

Thorir or Domrair–Viking conqueror who came to Ireland with Turgesius (q.v.). †626.28—with Thor (q.v.).

Thorkill–see Turgesius.

*Thorne's, 192.11.

Thorneycroft, William Hamo (1850-1925) – English sculptor. 552.13.

Thornton, Ned–see Matthew Kane. 63.6.

*Thorp, 77.7; 310.3; 331.21.

?Thorpe, Thomas–printed Shakespeare's (q.v.) sonnets in 1609. See Butter. 4.27.

Thorror–see Thor, Thorir. 626.28.

*Thortig, Enoch, 283.1.

*Thortin, 378.12.

Thoth–Egyptian god of letters, invention, and wisdom. See Hermes Trismegistus. 224.33; 238.8; 410. 36; 415.28; 452.10,13; 457.31; 485.36.

*Three Soldiers – "characters" about whom I do not think we have even begun to ask the right questions. The three of them and the two (q.v.) girls are always about when HCE did whatever he did do in Phoenix Park.

For some reason, the three are often Welsh Fusiliers. Two of the soldiers are Shem and Shaun (q.v.), or, at any rate, it says so on 526. It is also possible that the three soldiers are something to do with the two soldiers of *Ulysses*, Privates Carr and Compton. As will be seen below, the three soldiers manifest themselves under a great many different names, none of which go very deep. (If, as I think, FW is about Shakespeare (q.v.), it probably matters that he has been thought to have been—as Ben Jonson (q.v.) was —a soldier in the low country.) See Tom, Dick, Harry, and Tommy Atkins.

†7.4   patterjackmartins — see Peter, Jack, Martin
†8-10 (*passim*) the three lipoleum boyne—see Napoleon
†11.1   three of crows—see Crow
†12.31-32 Olaf . . . Ivor . . . Sitric (q.q.v.)
20.24   three's
†26.5   Pete, Jake or Martin (q.v.)
†31.14-20 William the Conk . . . Michael . . . Elcock (q.q.v.)
34.17   Ted . . . Tam . . . Taffyd (Edward, Thomas, David?)
36.7   triplehydrad snake
†40-42   Peter Cloran . . . O'Mara . . . Hosty (q.q.v.)
†51.12-15 Will, Conn, Otto . . . Vol . . . Pov . . . Dev . . . three Enkelchums — see Will, Conn, DeValera
52.13-14 triad of precoxious scaremakers
57.5   Ming, Ching and Shunny
†58.24-32 three Tommix . . . soldiers free . . . private Pat Marchison — see Tom Mix, Soldiers Three

61.27   three drummers
†64.22-23 musketeers!   Alphos, Burkos and Caramis —see Three Musketeers (q.v.)
†65.16   Arty, Bert . . . Charley Chance (q.v.)
†86.2   padderjagmartin tripiezite — see Peter, Jack, Martin
88.27   three wicked Vuncouvers Forests
94.17   three meddlars
105.33   Trion of Battlewatschers
†106.33   Tripple of Caines–see Cain
107.7   Raincoats
113.14   three men
128.17   three caskles
129.3   three desertions
†134.11   Rick, Dave and Barry —see Burbage, Garrick, Barry
137.26-27 tripplescreen
161.30   three
166.17   THREE male ones
†167.4   Antonius - Burrus - Caseous — see Antony, Brutus, Cassius
176.5   Threes
†193.24   Kelly, Kenny and Keogh (q.q.v.)—KKK?
196.22   thried
202.18   three
†203.13   leandros three — see Leander
238.26,31 three chancers . . . triel
241.29-30 three Dromedaries
†245.19-20 hunt - by - threes . . . musketeering — see Three Musketeers
253.19-20 tiercely . . . three
†254.2-4   Rurie, Thoath and Cleaver (q.v.) . . . three stout sweynhearts (see Sweyne), Orion of the Orgiasts, Meereschal Mac Muhun (q.q.v.), the Ipse dadden
257.12   fellows of Trinity
†264.5   three saturnine settings —see Saturn
267.17   trebly
268.18   third person

†271.5-6 tryonforit of Oxthe-vious, Lapidous and Malthouse Anthemy — with Octavius, Lepidus, Mark Antony (q.q.v.)

279.note 1 peeper coster . . . salt sailor . . . mustied poet (the last is Shakespeare—see Mustardseed)

†281.left margin Threes Totty Askins — see Tommy Atkins

284.23-24 three comseekwenchers

†285.13-14 threehandled dorkeys— see Ass

288.10 thirds

294.22-23 Blake-Roche, Kingston . . . Dockrell (Dublin environs)

?299.1 trist (see Tristram?)

†302.23-24 Smith - Jones - Orbison —see Smith, Jones

†312.28-30 three blend cupstoomerries . . . the Gill gob, the Burklley bump, the Wallisey wander-look — with Gill, Berkeley, Burke, and —probably Wellington or Wellesley (q.q.v.)

317.23,24,27,29 first breaches-maker . . . second-snipped cutter . . . thricetold . . . three's

?319.11 three swallows (see Power's whisky)

322.26-28 three newcomers . . . three

†330.4-5 Ned . . . Fred . . . Peer Pol—see Peter and Paul?

331.8 threelegged

337.4-5,20-21 three oldher patrons' . . . three longly lurking lobstarts (a "lobster" is a redcoat)

†343.3 Boyle, Burke and Campbell (q.q.v.)

†348.18,19,21 Cedric said Gormleysonson . . . Danno O'Dunnochoo and Conno O'Cannochar

(q.q.v.) . . . thurkmen three

†351.7,26 praddies three . . . three tankers hoots ('sham! hem! or chaffit!)—see Ham, Shem and Japhet

358.12 threespawn bottery parts

†360.4 jemcrow, jackdaw, prime and secund with their terce—with James and John, Crow, Tereus (q.q.v.)

366.27 Houtes, Blymey and Torrenation

374.31-32 Basil and the two other men

†376.25-27 three blows . . . three Skerry Badbols . . . Grey One (q.q.v.)

377.11-12 Three . . . threequicken-threes

†379-380 Keyhoe, Dannelly and Pykemhyme, the three muskrateers—see proper names and Three Musketeers

386.3-4 three jolly topers

389.24 troad of thirstuns

†398.5-6 Gowan, Gawin and Gonne (q.q.v.)

410.34 three masses

420.8 treefellers

†434.12 Hayes, Conyngham and Erobinson (q.q.v.)

446.30-31 Murphy, Henson and O'Dwyer, the War-chester Warders (q.q.v.)

†449.14-16 Saint Jamas Hanway . . . Jacobus . . . Peter Roche (q.q.v.)

465.18 tertius quiddus

478.20 Three persons

480.3 pigeons three

506.4 three barrels

†526.11-22 Grenadiers . . . tertium quid . . . Three . . . three . . . Shem and Shaun (q.v.) and the shame . . . three slots . . . trefoil

†529.15,25-6 three tailors on Tooley Street . . . doughboys

three . . . Hansen,
Morfydd and O'Dyar
(q.q.v.)

537.30   three pipples

538.14   three pock pocks

†546.8-9,15-16 terce of lanciers (see
Shakespeare) . . .
three surtouts

584.10   Three

587.6   three jolly postboys

589.8   three golden balls

594.11   Smud, Brunt and Rub-
binsen

595.25   triple conjunction

†606.14   three Benns—with Ben
Jonson and Franklin
(q.q.v.)

†608.6,8,9 three droopers assessors
. . . Billyhealy, Bally-
hooley and Bullyhow-
ley—see Draper, Billy

616.10-11 three Sulvans of Dukley
—see King of Dalkey

623.2   three poach dogs

Three Musketeers–title characters
of Dumas's novel. They are
always identified with the Three
Soldiers (q.v.). See also Soldiers
Three. 64.22-23; 245.19-20; 379-
380.

*****Thumpsen**–see Kelvin? 155.33.

Thunder—The 1001 letters the
thunder says form themselves
into 200 odd names of gods and
heroes and the men and women
to whom gods spoke. Most names
occur elsewhere in FW.

Thurn und Taxis–noble Austrian
family which secured a monopoly
on the national postal service.
5.32; 554.1.

*****Thurnston**, Philly, 38.35; 50.33.

Thursitt, R.–Arthur's Seat. 541.4.

Thursmen–see Thor. 80.14.

Thurston (d. 1140)–Archbishop of
York (q.v.), involved in a state-
church controversy and exiled
from England. ?53.14; 319.34.

?Thwackum and Square–characters in *Tom Jones*. 561.4 and
560.10.

Tib–see Tabitha.

Tibble, Dr–*Ulysses*, 619/734: "Dr
Tibble's Vi-Cocoa." 26.30.

Tibble, St–see Theobald.

Tibb's Eve–means never for there
is no St Tibbs. See Tib, Theobald,
Tybalt. 117.19; 236.8; 424.29.

Tiberius–Roman Emperor under
whom Christ was crucified, 14-37.
Character in Ben Jonson's (q.v.)
Sejanus (q.v.). Shakespeare (q.v.)
is known to have acted some
part in *Sejanus* and doubtless
somebody has suggested that he
acted Tiberius. 115.11; 119.16;
123.30; 424.9.

Tich, Little – English music-hall
comedian, early 20th century.
465.29.

*****Tichiami**, Comes, 289.29.

*****Tickell**, James H., 386.26.

Tieck, Johann Ludwig (1773-1853)
–German poet, novelist, Shakespearean (q.v.) critic of no great
powers. 18.20.

*****Tierney** of Dundalgan, 91.8,9.

Tierney, Tricky Dicky–candidate
in Joyce's "Ivy Day in the Committee Room". †604.29—with
Richard III (q.v.)?

Tiger – see Shakespeare, Robert
Greene.

Tiger Tim–character in an English
comic paper, nickname of Tim
Healy (q.v.). 210.15.

*****Tigh**, Madges–majesty—see Mag-
gies. 369.30.

*****Tighe**, 408.23.

Tilley, Vesta (b. 1864)–stage name
of Matilda Alice, Lady de Frece,
who won great popularity as a
male impersonator in the music
halls. She retired in 1919. †526.30
with Vesta (q.v.).

Tilly the Tailor–Anna Livia (q.v.)
as tailor's (q.v.) daughter? "Tilly
the Toiler" used to be an American comic-strip. 385.33.

Tim–see Tom.

Tim, Uncle–see Uncle Tom, Tim Healy, Tom. 622.7.

*Timmy the Tosser–Tim Healy (q.v.)? 27.1.

Timon of Athens–title hero of Shakespeare's (q.v.) play. 143.5; ?197.33; 241.10.

*Timoth–see Tom and Tim? 342.5.

Timothy–companion of St Paul (q.v.) on many journeys (Acts 14, etc.). Two of Paul's epistles are addressed to him. 274.11; 599.3.

Timour–see Tamerlane. 136.21.

*Tina-bat-Talur–Anna Livia (q.v.) as a tailor's (q.v.) daughter? 327.4.

*Tinbullet, Mrs, 193.20-21.

Tinkerbell–fairy in Peter Pan. 346. 27.

Tintoretto, Jacopo Rubusti (1518- 94)–Venetian painter. 435.8.

*Tipperuhry Swede, 82.3.

Tipple, Dr–see Tibble. 26.30.

Tippoo Sahib (1753-99)–Sultan of Mysore who was defeated by Wellington (q.v.). 302.2.

Tiptoft, John, earl of Worcester– 15th century Irish viceroy. See Taff. 5.2.

Tiresias–blind Theban soothsayer who had been both a man and a woman. His role in "The Waste Land" inspired, in part, the Four (q.v.). 307.left margin; ?538.2.

*Tisdall, 468.28.

Titania–Queen of the Fairies in Shakespeare's (q.v.) A Midsummer Night's Dream. See Oberon, Indian Boy, Bottom, etc. 583.17; ?627.1.

Titius–see Gracchi, Titus Andronicus. 128.15.

Titteretto–see Tintoretto. 435.8.

Titus Andronicus–title hero of Shakespeare's (q.v.) play in which Caius and Sempronius are also characters. ?5.18; ?†70.14—with

Titus Oates (q.v.); †128.15—with the Gracchi (q.v.); 527.2.

Toadlebens–see Todleben. 339.21.

*Toaro–Bull? 136.14.

*Tob – Hebrew "good" (Judges 11:3). 90.3.

Tobias–son of Tobit (q.v.). 580.8.

?Tobit–an Apocryphal book. 40.31 (two bits).

*Tobkids, Long Lally–see Lally, Man Servant. 67.11.

*Toby–perhaps Uncle Toby in Tristram Shandy (q.v.) — see Trim; perhaps Sir Toby Belch in Twelfth Night, perhaps Punch's (q.v.) dog or anybody's jug. 172. 6; 211.12; 406.25.

Todd, Sweeney–in London myth, a barber who converted customers into pork pies. The main piece of English Grand Guignol is Sweeney Tod, the Demon Barber. 261.left margin.

Todhunter, Isaac (1820-84)–English mathematician whose texts were widely used in English schools. 283.25-26; 293.note 2.

Todleben, Franz Eduart Ivanovich, Count (1818-84)–Russian officer in charge of the fortifications of Sevastopol in the Crimean war. 339.21.

Toffeelips, Mavis–see Mephistopheles. 441.11-12.

*Toffler, Old–see Taff? 606.29.

Tolan–see Toland. 601.34.

Toland, John (1670-1722)–deistical writer who was hounded out of Dublin and fled to England. 601. 34.

*Tolearis, Bearara–perhaps the pole star. See Bear. 255.15.

*Toler–partly Toller (see Gill), partly perhaps John Toler, the unpopular judge who tried Robert Emmet (q.v.). †16.5; 82.4; 127.7; †326.1—with Horus and Horrocks (q.q.v.); 320.9; 372.3.

*Tollertone, Titentung – a bell? 512.11.

?Tolloller, earl–character in Gilbert and Sullivan's (q.v.) *Iolanthe.* †65.17—with Lot (q.v.).

Tom, Uncle–saintly old negro in Mrs Stowe's *Uncle Tom's Cabin.* See Tim Healy. 622.7.

Tom, Dick and Harry–see Three Soldiers. 8.26-27; 19.27-28; 55.15; 90.3-4; 291.7; 323.28; 325.34; 329.3; 337.30; 351.1-2; 354.32; 376.25-26; †410.35-36—with Tom and Sid Sawyer and Huck Finn (q.q.v.); 425.25; 485.11; 503.26; 506.1-2; 575.26; 597.6.

*Tom and Tim–names that run strongly and—to me—mysteriously through FW. It has been suggested that Tom is the name of the Man Servant (q.v.). Tim must sometimes refer to Tim Finnegan and Tim Healy (q.q.v.), and Tom to Tom the Piper's son, Peeping Tom, Doubting Tom, a Becket, Aquinas, Eliot, Quiney, O'Shanter, Moore, etc. (q.q.v.). See also Tem, Atem. Tammuz. It is probably significant that Thomas means "twin".
I think that Tom is also, at times, A-Tom or atom, as in the Annals passage, 13-14, where the initial letters of the entries spell MO AT and represent, I think, a split and scattered Atom.
6.10-11; 7.5; 12.5; 15.14, †26—with Tim Finnegan (q.v.); 19.4, 27; 27.1,20; 28.24; 34.17; 39.14, 16,28 (see Treacle Tom); 52.23; 55.15; 56.34;†88.35-36—withTem (q.v.); †90.26—see Thomar and Thom; 93.3; †101.9—with Ass (q.v.); 108.11; 130.17; 139.10; 149.35; †176.1—with Thom and Thon (q.q.v.), †21—with Wellington (q.v.); †178.27—with Pip (q.v.); 180.26; †187.22 — with Ham (q.v.); †191.21—see T. S. Eliot (q.v.); 196.34; 204.21 (Mtu or Mti, q.v.); †210.15—with Tiger Tim (see Healy) and the Tombigby river; 215.33; 227.20; 234.

32-33; †238.19,25—with Wellington (q.v.); 244.30; 252.10-20,35; 258.20-21,30,31,35,36; †260.14—with Tom-Tit-Tot (q.v.); ?265. note 5; †276.21-22—with Tim Finnegan (q.v.); 279.note 1; 284. 9,15; †291.7,8—with Tim Healy (q.v.); 311.12,13; 318.16-17,26; 326.30; †331.11-12 — see Tom Malone?; †333.34-35—with Mrs Beeton (q.v.); 334.3; 336.9; 340. 5; †341.32—with Whittington (q.v.); 342.3,5; 344.17,30,35; †347.10—with Ass (q.v.), 26; 352. 14,15; 353.22,29; 361.1; 362.4; 363.12; 367.30; †379.34—see Tem (I suppose Tammany Hall is around); †385.10—see Tom the Piper's son; †390.13—with Luke Tarpey (q.v.); 406.17; 413.2; †419.16—see Treacle Tom; 426. 21; 442.3; 459.27; 463.1; 481.31, 32,36 (Tom Tower is at Oxford); 489.17; 496.20; †504.19—with Zeus (q.v.); 505.1; †506.28—see Doubting Thomas; 507.1-2,34 (see Thoms); 509.5; †510.10,18—see Thorneycroft, Aquinas; 519. 10; 525.24 (Long Tom is a tobacco); 526.8; 534.17-18,27; 543.17; 561.4; 570.4; 579.17; 582.1; 584. 7; ?586.12; 588.23; 597.30; 598. 21,27; 599.23; 603.6; 608.31-32; †617.12-13—with Becket (q.v.); †622.7—with Uncle Tom and Tim Healy (q.q.v.).

Tom Quad, old–Old Tom is a strong gin. Tom Quad is the great quadrangle at Oxford. See Tom and Tim. 57.24.

Tom Thumb–minute hero of a nursery tale. "General Tom Thumb" was the name adopted by Charles Sherwood Stratton (1838-83), American dwarf, exhibited by Barnum (q.v.). 253.28; 412.6.

Tom Tit Tot–title of a book, studying primitive religions by E. Clodd (q.v.). 260.14.

*Tom Toucher–certainly in part St (Doubting) Thomas. Beggar? †8. 26-27—with St Thomas (q.v.);

210.15 (Tombigby River); 242.18; 506.28.

*Tom, Treacle—at least partly Tom-Tom the piper's son (Cad's son?) who stole a pig (q.v.)—or a *Hamlet*. 39.16,28; 172.28; 212.2; 379.4; 385.10; 419.16.

Tomar–see Thor.

*Tombigby, Techertim–"Toucher Tom" (q.v.) in *transition*. The Tombigby is an American river. See Tom, Tiger Tim. 210.15.

*Tombs, 329.22.

Tombuys, Judy–probably Judith Shakespeare or Mrs Thomas Quiney. 358.33.

*Tomkins, Madam–67.23-24; ?326. 30; 328.5.

*Tomley–see Tom. 265.note 5.

Tompion, Thomas (1639-1713)– English watchmaker, inventor of the first dead-beat escapement. 151.18.

*Tompkins, †290.note 7—with Potemkin (q.v.).

Tone, Theobald Wolf (1763-98)– leader of the Irish rebellion of 1798, founder of the United Irishmen. It may be that all, or many, wolves in FW refer to him. †80.13—with James Wolf (q.v.); 99.14; 318.33 (ulver); 323.34; 516.21; 565.5; 572.15-16.

*Tony–Lumpkin? Mark Antony? (q.q.v.); †6.7—with Suetonius (q.v.).

*Toole, 468.28.

Tooley Street, Three Tailors of– began a petition, "We, the people of England". 529.15-16.

Top–see Tom Sawyer. 410.35.

Toragh or Torah–Hebrew "law". The Pentateuch of the Laws of Moses is called The Torah. 29.17.

*Torba, 125.9.

Torquells–see Turgesius. 493.20.

Tosti, Francesco (1847-1916) – Italian composer; another was a

radio pioneer. †309.31 — with Bellini (q.v.); 408.19.

Toto–Baron Corvo (see Raven?) wrote *Stories Toto Told Me*. 537. 17.

Tottenham, Charles (1685-1758)– M.P. for New Ross in the Irish parliament. He rode sixty miles by night to parliament in 1731 to cast (in his boots) a vote against handing over an Irish financial surplus to England. 284.note 2.

*Totty, 327.7.

Totty, Sir John–Lord Mayor of Dublin in 1671. †281.left margin —with Don John (q.v.).

Totumcalmum – see Tut-ankh-amen. 26.18.

Touchstone–jester in Shakespeare's (q.v.) *As You Like It*. See Jacques, Rosalind. 332.12-13.

Toughertrees–see Tristopher.

Toulouse-Lautrec–French painter whose works include a picture of a dancer called "La Goulue". See also Avril, Desossé. 531.15,18 (lautterick's . . . touloosies).

*Toun, Mr Tupling–Dublin town? 481.14.

Toussaint L'Ouverture, Pierre-Dominique (1746-1803)–one of the liberators of Haiti. †455.5— with Madame Tussaud (q.v.).

Tower, Geesyhus–see Turgesius. 464.32.

Tower, Tam–Tom Tower on Christ Church, Oxford. See Tom Quad, Tom. 481.36.

*Townsends, 283.15.

*Trabezond, Lady–maybe a reference to Offenbach's opera *Princess de Trebizonde*. 165.22.

*Treble Stauter–Trouble's Daughter? 490.20.

Tree, Iris–English actress, taking in, I think, Iris (q.v.) and the tree of Eden. 30.13.

*Tree and Stone–this theme which runs through FW may have some overriding symbolism, but I see parts, not whole. Tree is the tree of Eden, the Cross (associated with Tristram, q.v., because he is a man of sorrow). It is Yggdrasill, it is the tree at Howth Castle on which the luck of the St Lawrence (q.v.) family depends; it may be the crab apple tree under which Shakespeare (q.v.) slept off a drunk or the mulberry tree he planted in Stratford. The stone is St Peter, the stone on which Jacob (q.v.) dreamed, the stone of Destiny (see Pierre Dusort) or Scone, the *lia fail*, or the Dublin stone, or the long stone. It may matter that in all Celtic languages the word for "letters" is the word for "tree". At the end of "Anna Livia Plurabelle" the washwomen turn into a tree and a stone. 3.19 (sawyer, q.v.); 25.30,31; 44.9; 53.14-16; 80.29-30; 83.10; 88.26-27; 94.4,5; 100.13; 103.8,9; 106.36; 112.19; 128.2-3; 133.4-5; 136.31-32; 146.34; 159.4-5; 176.8; 202.30; 215.35; 216.1,3-4; 221.31-32,33-34,35; 230.26,35-36; 247.4; 259.1,2; 264.12,13-14; 267.26,27; 279.2,3; 293.24; 314.15-16; 331.4-5; 332.12,13; 350.2,4; 371.30; 420.11-12; 430.4,6; 474.7; 503.26,30; 504.32-33; 505.16,17; 539.3,11 (*cram* is Irish "tree"); 563.20; 564.30; 579.4-5.

Treestam, Armoury–see Tristram and St Lawrence. 104.22.

Treestone–see Tristram, Tree and Stone. 113.19.

Trelawney, Sir Jonathan, Bart (1650-1721)–Cornish bishop whose imprisonment inspired twenty thousand Cornish men to want to know why. 91.18.

Trestrine von Terrefin–see Tristram. 279.note 1.

***Trevi**–people throw pennies in the Trevi fountain in Rome. 192.12.

Trichepatte–see St Patrick. 228.6.

***Tricks** and Doelsy–seems to be Issy (q.v.). Is Tricks Beatrice (q.v.)? Doelsy Dulcy (q.v.)? 398.18.

Trilby–title heroine of Du Maurier's (q.v.) novel. 285.note 1; 548.29.

?Trim, Sergeant – of *Tristram Shandy* (q.v.). See Uncle Toby. 408.9.

Trinculo – character in Shakespeare's (q.v.) *The Tempest.* See Mutt and Jute, Caliban. 16.30.

***Tripier,** Abraham, 167.25-26.

Tristopher–see Hilary. The name may include a 16th century, Christopher, 20th Lord of Howth (q.v.).

Tristram has three possible meanings in FW: 1) sorrow as opposed to joy–see Hilary, Tree and Stone; 2) it can refer to Sir Armory Tristram, founder of the St Lawrence (q.v.) family of Howth (q.v.); 3) it can refer to Tristram (Tristan) of Lyonesse, nephew of King Mark of Cornwall (q.v.), lover of Isolde of Ireland (q.v.), husband of Isolde of the White Hands, father perhaps of Sorge (q.v.). Tristram was a great hunter and harper. His story is well-known, especially in the versions of Malory and Wagner (q.q.v.). (Joyce told Miss Weaver to read Bédier's *Tristan et Iseult.*) Tristram woos the Irish princess Isolde (Chapelizod, q.v., is said to be named for her) for his uncle. Crossing from Ireland to Cornwall (as in FW II,iv) the young people accidentally drink a love potion and love forever, though Isolde marries Mark and Tristram marries Isolde of the White Hands. Because they fell through drink the lovers appear on p. 3 of FW where all is connected with water, plain or strong. Tristram and Isolde run away from Mark and die together in circumstances variously reported. See Mildew Lisa. I think Tristram is Shem but I am not always sure. Isolde is Issy (q.v.). Too little

attention has been paid Sir Amory
Tristram.

3.16,17,19	Sir Tristram . . . Armorica . . . the stream
†20	Laurens (q.v.)
5.31	tramtrees (in Ireland Tristram reversed his name)
21.12,21	Tristopher . . . Tristopher (q.v.)
22.17,24,29	tristian . . . Toughertrees . . . Tris
†66.21	twist stern—with Sterne (q.v.)
28-29	tristinguish
92.7	tristone
96.7	Sir armoury
100.28	tristurned
104.22	Armoury Treestam
†106.36	Tree . . . Stone (q.v.)
†113.19	Treestone (q.v.)
119.30	tryst
†136.34	trees down (q.v.)
146.7	trysting
148.31	Amory
158.1	Tristis Tristior Tristissimus
159.32	Tristan da Cunha (an island)?
169.32	tristended
189.5	trysting
202.30	tough . . . oaktrees
211.26	Armoricus Tristram Amoor Saint Lawrence
226.14	tryst
230.13	trist in
234.3	tristiest
279.note 1	Trestrine von Terrefin
288.22	tristar (see Star?)
299.1	trist
301.16	trieste . . . trieste (city)
302.6-7	bistrispissing
317.36	trystfully
363.26,28	trisspass . . . theactriss calls
383.23,30	Tristy's . . . Trustan
384.32	Trisolanisans
388.3,6	natsirt . . . thrysting
389.24	thirstuns
394.24	trustin
395.2,35	Narsty . . . Armoricas Champius
398.29	Tristan
424.28	treestem

?442.1	ministriss
449.7	tristys
467.7	Triss
480.3	trustyman
?481.10	tristich
486.4,7,20	tryst . . . tantris . . . tryst . . . tistress
491.12	tryst
499.30	Tris tris
513.26	Trists
†521.22	tristy minstrel—with Christy Minstrels (q.v.)
550.1	trissed
571.7,10,14,18	tantrist . . . trysting . . . triste . . . tryst
588.29	Triss

Triton–in Greek myth, the personification of roaring waters. See Lir. There is a Tritonville Road near Dublin. 203.13; 531.30; 547.24; 585.2.

*Trivett, 377.17.

Trollope, Anthony (1818-82)–English novelist who worked for the Post Office department in Ireland, author of *Phineas Finn, Phineas Redux*. See Palliser, Proudie, Twentyman. †409.6-7—with St Anthony (q.v.); 520.25; 582.34-35; 603.28.

Tromp, Martin and Cornelius–Dutch admirals who harried the English in the 17th century. 23.26-27.

Trot, Mrs–a pony or a whore—see *The Taming of the Shrew*, I,ii, 77-80. 440.17.

Trotsky, Leon (1879-1942)–pseudonym of Lev Davidovitch Bronstein, Russian revolutionary leader, murdered in Mexico. 59.36.

Troutbeck, Rev John (1832-99)–minor canon of Westminster, translated Bach's (q.v.) *St John Passion* and many foreign libretti. 76.26.

*Trouvas, Jeremy – Jerry - Shem (q.q.v.), the finder of the letter, as Kevin-Shaun (q.q.v.) is the keeper. At times, however (e.g.

110, 482), Kevin both finds and keeps. 370.8.

Trumper–English cricketer. 584.1.

Tubal–see Jubal Cain.

Tuck, Friar–one of Robin Hood's merry men. 441.32; 530.36.

Tudor–English royal family—see Elizabeth I, Henry VIII. 93.8; †307.14—with Sir Henry Tudor (q.v.); 498.2; 504.21.

Tudor, Major General Sir Henry– headed the Black and Tans.†307. 14—with Henry VIII (q.v.).

Tuhal–character in Macpherson's "Fingal" (q.q.v.). 329.16.

Tullbutt, beautified–see Matt Talbot. 262.note 6.

Tullius, Servius–6th legendary king of Rome. 467.36.

*****Tulloch**–Turnbull girl, 171.31-32.

Tullus Hostilius (672-640 B.C.)– third legendary king of Rome. 467-468.

Tully, Vesta–see Tilly. 526.30.

Tummer the Lame–see Tamerlane. 71.16.

*****Tung**-Toyd–tongue tied? 123.20.

*****Tunnelly,** Mr, 435.34-35.

Tunnicliffe–English cricketer. 583. 35-36.

*****Tuomush,** Touchole Fitz – see Tom, Dick, Harry, Toucher Tom. 8.26-27.

Tuonisonian–see Tennyson. 48.35.

Turgesius or Thorgil–Viking who invaded Ireland in 832. He and his death were likewise violent. See Ota. 51.16; 91.9; 464.32; 493.20.

Turko the Terrible–title character of a pantomime by Edwin Hamilton (q.v.). See *Ulysses,* 11/10. See also Royce. 132.18; 205.29; 520.2.

?Turner, Joseph Mallord William (1775-1851)–English painter. 390. 6.

Turpin, Dick (1706-39)–English highwayman, famous for a sup-

posed ride from London to York. 457.12.

Turridu–hero of Mascagni's opera *Cavalleria Rusticana.* 60.31; ?580. 17.

Tuskar–light ship at the S.E. corner of Ireland. 25.26; 245.1.

Tussaud, Madame (1760-1850)– founder of "Madame Tussaud's Exhibition" of wax figures, which is specially famous for its "Chamber of Horrors". 57.20; †455.5— with Toussaint L'Ouverture (q.v.).

Tut-ankh-amen – Egyptian king whose resplendent tomb was opened in the 1920s and the king "resurrected". A curse was popularly supposed to have been laid on those who moved his bones. 26.18; 29.28; 102.22; 242.18; 291.4; 295.8 (Tate and Comyng); 335.29; 367.10; 385.4-5; 395.23 (Nema Knatut); 512.34.

*****Tutu**–see *Ulysses* 43/52? 113.8,9; 145.1; 238.17; 337.19; 397.33; †449.10—see Mona Vera; 461.30; 486.14 (see Tattu); 491.13,14.

Twain, Mark or Samuel Langhorne Clemens (1835-1910) – American writer, author of *Tom Sawyer* and *Huckleberry Finn* (q.q.v.). Mark Lyons (q.v.) stands for the number 2. †425.29-30—with Mark of Cornwall (q.v.); 431.35; 455.29.

Twath–boar (see Pig) in the *Mabinogion.* 132.5.

Tweedledum and **Tweedledee**– twins in a nursery-rhyme and in *Alice in Wonderland* (q.v.). 258.23.

*****Twelve**–a mysterious and recurring group in FW whose collective name seems to be Sullivan or Doyle (q.q.v.). They are various Twelves—apostles, jurymen, customers at the inn, environs of Dublin, exagminators of *Work in Progress.* They stand for all that is pompous and obtuse. 48.25; 76.2-3; 142.8-28 (*passim*); 147.5; 194.29; 283.note 1; 284.18-19; 312-313; 325.5; 327.35; 335.6-7; 364.3; 369.7-12; 370.20-22; 375.

11; 408.34; 435.9; 443.12; 479.14;
497.17-22; 511.6,13; 557.13-558.
20; 566.12; 573.6-7,13; 574.30-32;
†575.35-36—with Judas (q.v.).

Twentyman, Larry–hero of Trollope's (q.v.) *The American Sena-
tor,* a young hunting squire,
coming up in the world but
not quite a gentleman. I cannot
for the life of me explain his connection with King Lear (q.v.).
†582.19,35—with King Lear (q.v.).

*****Twenty**-nine – the leap-year or
February daughters of whom Issy
(q.v.) is the 29th. See Moon. They
are also hens or Biddies—see
Biddy Doran, St Bridget. 10.29;
64.35; 92.12-15 (*passim*); 93.12;
147.11-15 (*passim*); 157.16; 159.
16; 212.6-15; 220.3-5; 242.17-18;
247-248; 249.36; 279.note 1; 283.
note 1; 289.12; 327.7,35; 375.14;
430.1,3; 450.18; 469.30; 470.4;
470-471 (see Frida); 558.22.

Two goddesses–a title of Demeter
and Persephone (q.q.v.). 508.31.

Two temptresses–the two girls who,
with the three soldiers (q.v.), are
involved in HCE's (q.v.) crime
in Phoenix (q.v.) Park. They were
probably suggested to Joyce by
the two young women (coyly
pulling up their skirts to display
their ankles) on Dublin's coat of
arms. I am by no means secure in
my understanding of the two,
but they are evidently worked
out in terms of a double or split
personality. They have many
names in FW. See especially
Rachel and Leah, Isolde, Issy,
Sosie, Christine Beauchamp, Jinnies, Stella and Vanessa.

10.36   pigeon pair
11.4   Nixy girls
20.24   two's
†30.13-14 Iris Trees and Lili
         O'Rangans (q.q.v.)
†32.8,11 Skertsiraizde . . . Dony-
         ahzade . . . Rosa and
         Lily Miskinguette—
         see Scheherazade,
         Mistinguette

34.19   pair of dainty maid-
         servants
51.14-15 two Curchies
†52.3   Lili and Tutu (q.v.)
†57.4   two peaches (q.v.)
60.15   two bitches
61.16   Questa and Puella
†64.27   Snowwhite and Rosered
         (q.v.)
65.23-30 (*passim*)
†67.33,36 Lupita Lorette, Luperca
         Latouche (q.q.v.)
†75.17   liliths (q.v.)
88.25   two childspies
90.16   two disappainted solici-
         tresses
†94.12,16,36 Una and Ita (q.q.v.)
         . . . pair of sycopanties
         . . . two roses (q.v.)
†95.4-5 O'Moyly gracies . . . O
         Briny rossies — see
         Grace O'Malley,
         O'Brien, Ross, Rose
†96.13   saucicissters—see Sosie,
         Susanna
†102.3   adazillahs—see Adah
†105.20,34 Dual of Ayessha (q.v.)
         . . . Totties a Doeit of
         Deers
†106.21,32,34 Two Lice . . . Abbrace
         of Umbellas . . . Misses
         O'Mollies—see O'Mal-
         ley
107.6   Pair of Sloppy Sluts
†113.16,17 mollvogels . . . peaches
         —see Molly Bloom,
         Peaches
†115.22 'alices (q.v.)
†126.30 twomaries—see Mary
†128.17 two queans (q.v.)
†129.3,30 two psychic espousals
         . . . Giroflee Giroflaa
         (q.v.)
132.10   rival queens (play by
         Nicholas Lee)
†134.9-10 brace of girdles — see
         Bracegirdle
137.26   pair of pectorals
†156.26-27 Ruby and Roby (q.q.v.)
160.1   Picea and Tillia (a genus
         of pines and a genus
         of lindens)
166.16-17 TWO domestics
176.4   Twos
192.2   two scissymaidies

194.26   two belles (see Bell)
196.22   two
201.1   two
†203.13-14 heroines two—see Hero and Leander
†207.11-12 two boudeloire maids . . . Ciliegia Grande and Kirschie Real— see Baudelaire, Grande
†230.14-15,16 Mondamoiseau of Casanuova (q.v.) and Mademoiselle from Armentières (q.v.) . . . Nobbio and Nuby
†238.23   Kicky Lacy . . . Bianca Mutantini (q.q.v.)
†241.4   lilithe maidinettes—see Lilith
†245.19-20 tempt-in-twos . . . Brace of girdles—see Brace-girdle
246.35   Two
†257.11,20-21 a plattonem blondes named Hips and Haws . . . Missy Cheekspeer (q.v.) . . . Ruth Wheatacre—see also Plato, Ruth
264.4-5   two lunar eclipses (see Moon)
267.17-18 To brace cogeners . . . twainly
268.19-20 a person . . . her second
269.3-4   dual in duel
271.14   duo of druidesses
†279.note 1 Olive d'Oyly and Winnie Carr (q.q.v.)
284.22-23 two antesedents
289.27   two trueveres
290.23-24 duel mavourneens
†291.14   a nelliza the second— see Nell, Elizabeth, Anna Livia
†294.20-21 Mary Owens and Dolly Monks (q.q.v.)
295.27,30,31 pair of accomplasses . . . tew . . . twain
307.6-7   Two Young Spinsters (see Stella, Philomela)
314.28   tuone tuone
331.7   two
†337.16   twee cweamy wosen— see Rose

342.24   Furstin II and The Other Girl
348.22-23 twum plumymnietcies
†351.29-30 Misses Celana Dalems (q.v.)
†358.32-33 two Gemuas . . . Jane Agrah . . . Judy Tombuys (q.q.v.)
†359.32   dewfolded . . . naughtingels — see Jenny Lind, Philomela
360.2-3   twittwin twosingwoolow
377.18-19 Peena and Queena
†380.3   blashwite and Bushred —see Snowwhite
†389.23   peer of quinnyfears— see Guinevere
398.5   braceolanders
407.22   sisterwands
410.34   two chaplets
†415.2   Dehlia and Peonia—see Delia and Poena
†422.32-33 liliens of the veldt, Nancy Nickies and Folletta Lajambe (q.q.v.)—see also Lily
†423.12   Kates and Nells—see Kate the Shrew, Nell
432.11,13 two viragoes . . . coppall of geldings (see Capel?)
†433.19-20 Minxy . . . Murry—see Mary
†434.7   Rhidarhoda and Daradora—see Rhoda
435.34   braces of couples
446.10   two pure chicks
†461.9   duess of yore–see Duessa
?480.1   two lay payees
483.8   two turkies
†485.12   Rose Lankester and Blanche Yorke—see York, Rose
†491.13   two a tutu—see Tutu
492.6   Pairaskivvymenassed
†502.13-14,24,29 pair of pritty geallachers (see Gallagher) . . . Julie and Lulie (q.v.) . . . Miss Somer's . . . Mad Winthrop's (q.q.v.)
503.15   two
†508.6,22-23,24,29 Pax and Quantum . . . subligate sisters, P. and Q., Clopatrick's . . . two

goddesses—see Cleo-
patra, St Patrick, Two
Goddesses
511.23   too woman
522.9   two serious charges
†526.23-24 two stripping baremaids,
            Moth MacGarry (q.v.)
527.3-528.25 (passim)
†529.11-12 Misses Mirtha and
            Merry, the two dree-
            per's assistants—see
            Martha and Mary,
            Draper
537.29   two punt scotch
†538.14,21-22 two claps . . . tew
            cherripickers . . . Lizzy
            and Lissy Mycock
            (q.v.)
546.5,16   two young frish . . . two
            twin pritticoaxes
561.2   two
584.10   two
†587.26-27 Elsies from Chelsies, the
            two legglegels (see
            Elsie)
588.35   Two pretty mistletots
589.28,33   two . . . two hussites
595.24-25   double preposition
608.5-6,7-8 the two drawpers as-
            sisters (see Draper)
            . . . two cozes from
            Niece (q.v.)

616.11-12 two Peris of Monacheena

Tybalt–character in Shakespeare's
    Romeo and Juliet (q.q.v.). See
    Theobald, Tib, Tibbs. 28.5; 75.29
    (toe bout . . . saft eyballds).

Tykingfest–see Festy King. 86.
    13.

Tyldesley–English cricketer. 583.
    35.

Typette–see Pipette. Typtology is
    the science of the taps of the
    table-turning spirit. 478.3,27.

*Typus, Mister, Mistress Tope and
    all the little typtopies–typo-
    graphical errors—it has been
    suggested that during his "lost
    years" Shakespeare (q.v.) was a
    typesetter. 20.13.

Tyrone–Irish county and earldom.
    The most famous Tyrone was the
    2nd earl, Hugh the rebel, who
    fled Ireland in 1607. 49.7; 163.9,
    30.

Tyrrel, Kitty–air to which Moore's
    (q.v.) "Oh Blame Not the Bard"
    (q.v.) is sung. 60.9.

*Tytonyhands and Vlossyhair,
    265.21.

U

Uachet (Green Water)–in The Book
    of the Dead, a serpent goddess and
    lady of flame. 494.15.

*Ubeleeft, Dr's Het, 150.9.

Uggugg–nasty boy in Lewis Car-
    roll's (q.v.) Sylvie and Bruno. Ugh
    is Irish for "egg". 249.27; 276.9-10.

Ugolino see the Inferno, xxxiii.
    513.8.

†Ulerin's–Lord Ullins daughter?
    194.14.

*Ulikah's–partly Uriah (q.v.) Heep
    and Hittite. 434.29.

Ulysses–character in the works of
    Homer, Shakespeare, Joyce
    (q.q.v.). To Polyphemus (q.v.),
    he gave his name as "Noman".

See Bloom, Penelope, Telema-
    chus, Pericles. 41.12; 59.16; 75.
    32; 79.8,9; 123.16; 162.13; 175.
    33; 179.26; 196.33,35; 229.13;
    321.14; 324.9; 546.4; 611.11.

*Una–I cannot make the girl in
    The Faerie Queene (q.v.) fit it.
    94.12; ?147.14; ?212.12; 267.25;
    ?576.6.

Uncle–usually a dirty word in FW,
    referring to Mark of Cornwall or
    Claudius (q.q.v.).

Undershaft, St Andrew–London
    church, Shaw (q.v.) hero. See St
    Barbara. 147.26-27.

*Underwood, Stilla–maybe Under-
    wood typewriters, maybe Ben

Jonson's (q.v.) *Underwoods*, a collection of religious and amatory poems, epigrams, including both tributes to Shakespeare (q.v.). See Stella. 248.28; 360.15; 526.23.

Undine–Greek water sprite, title heroine of a novel (1811) by de la Motte-Fouqué; in it, Undine, a personification of water, marries a human being, and when set aside for another woman, kills her husband with a kiss. 139.21; 547.8.

Undset, Sigurd (b. 1882)–Norwegian novelist, Nobel (q.v.) Prize winner. 248.6.

Urania–muse of Astronomy, planet. 171.28; †504.24 — with Oriana (q.v.); 583.16.

Urban–name of eight popes. Urban I was Pope, 222-230. 154.20; 539.32.

Uriah the Hittite–husband of Bathsheba (q.v.), sent by David (q.v.) into the forefront of the battle and killed. (2 Samuel 11.) 102.7; †434.29—with Heep (q.v.); 468. 36 (hourihaard).

*Urloughmoor, 577.14.

Ursula, St–leader of a band of 11,000 virgins, all martyred by the Huns near Cologne. 471.31.

Usher, Arthur–son of Sir William Usher, Elizabethan clerk of the Dublin council; Sir William was drowned in the river Dodder. Usher Quay lies along the Liffey. 52.16,17.

*Ursussen, Ussur–partly the USSR —see Bear. 353.12.

*Usquadmala, 184.28.

V

Vaast, St–introduced Christianity into Arras, c. 500. 338.14.

*Val from Skibereen, 210.18-19.

Valdemar–a number of noted Danish kings. 255.16; 317.17.

Valentine–saint whose festival is February 14; character in Shakespeare's (q.v.) *Two Gentlemen of Verona*. See Sylvia, Julia. The following references include Valentino (q.v.). 249.4; 289.28; 458.2.

Valentino, Rudolph–cinematic sex-symbol of the 1920s. He doubles with Valentine (q.v.).

*Valkir–Walker? Valkyrie? 99.16.

Valkyries–Teuton battle-maidens. 68.15; 210.5-6; 565.3.

Valsinggiddyrex – see Vercingetorix 281.note 1.

*Valtivar and Viv, 331.26.

*Vance, 539.19.

Vance, Joseph–title hero of a novel (1906) by William De Morgan. †211.32 — with Don Giovanni (q.v.).

Vanderbilt – monied American family. 543.11.

Van der Decken–hero of Wagner's *The Flying Dutchman* (q.q.v.). See Senta, Eric. 323.1; †530.20— see Man Servant; †620.7—with Dekker (q.v.).

?Vanderpool, Lew – a forger — I know no more. 365.28-29.

Vanessa–see Stella.

*Vanhaty, 178.3.

Van Homryk, Homereek – see Homer, Vanhomrigh. 314.23-24.

Vanhomrigh, Bartholomew–father of Swift's Vanessa (q.q.v.). He was lord-mayor of Dublin in 1697 and, according to the Dublin Annals, "obtained from William III (q.v.) a royal donative of a collar of SS. in lieu of that lost in 1688". The collar of SS is the lord-mayor's chain of office. I think he is connected somehow with Jarl von Hoother (q.v.). †21.13—with Homer (q.v.); 44. 13; 174.26; 314.23-24; 352.5; 393.8; 535.2; 623.16-17.

Vanhomrigh, Esther–see Vanessa.

*Van or von Hoother, Jarl–protagonist of the Prankquean (q.v.) episode, 21-23. At the base of the episode is the encounter of the Earl of Howth and Grace O'Malley (q.q.v.), but I do not perfectly understand what Joyce builds on his base. See Tristopher and Hilary, Dermot and Grania, Mark of Cornwall, Bartholomew Vanhomrigh, St Lawrence. 21.10,22, 32,34-35; 22.9,19,22,31-32; 23.14; 44.13; 100.4; 106.33; ?†111.12— with Van Houtens (q.v.); 130.33; 140.1; 312.19-20; 314.22; 394. 28-29; 414.4; 491.16; 541.15; 560.24-25.

Van Houtens–a brand of Dutch cocoa. ?†111.12 — with Van Hoother (q.v.); 414.4.

Vania–short for Ivan—see John. 239.14-15.

Van Nost, John–sculptor who made the equestrian statue of George II which stood on Stephen's (q.v.) Green in Dublin. It was destroyed by political hooligans. 552.12 (Vnost).

Vardon, Dolly–character in Dickens's *Barnaby Rudge* (q.q.v.), also a picture hat. 451.1; †600.33— with Molly Bloom (q.v.).

Varian, J. S.–a brush factory, Talbot Street, Dublin. The name is given to Kate the Cleaner (q.v.). 211.19; 221.12; 380.1,2; 451.17.

*Varina – perhaps Swift's (q.v.) name for Jane Waring, an early interest of his. 101.8.

*Vartry–perhaps "Vartry water", *Ulysses*, 268/351. 290.19.

Varuna–Hindu creator and storm god. 3.28.

Vasa, Gustavus (1496-1560)–became King Gustavus I of Sweden, freed his country from the Danes. 255.16.

*Vasilleff's, 49.13.

Vaughan, Father Bernard, S.J.– author of *The Worker's Right to Live*. 609.2—with Petty (q.v.).

Vaughan, Thomas (1622-66)–English alchemist, probably Eireneaus Philalethes who claimed to have found the philosopher's stone in America. †482.18—with Kevin (q.v.).

Vayu, Vata–spirit of wind in Vedic myth. 597.25; 599.5.

*Vedette, screendoll–a *vedette* is a French military term for a mounted sentry. 577.16.

Vega, Carpio, Lope Felix de (1562-1635)–Spanish playwright and poet. 440.17.

Vega, Garcilasso de la (1535-1616)– author of a history of the Incas. 423.2.

Vellentam, Herzog van–see Wellington. 238.24-25.

Venus–Roman goddess of beauty and fertility, Shakespearean (q.v.) character. The discussion of "Venus and Adonis" (q.v.) in *Ulysses* is germane to FW, especially to "Anna Livia Plurabelle" (q.v.). See also Aphrodite. †3.22—with Issy (q.v.); 6.17 (Cythera); †24—with Vanessa (q.v.); 79.18; 93.17; 105.1; 113. 21; 203.20; †232.11 — with Vanessa, Issy (q.q.v.); 267.22; †281.14-15 — with Pervenche (q.v.), left margin; 299.left margin; 103.26 27 (most beautiful of women—the Italians call Venus *donna bellissima*—see Bellezza); 435.3; 551.34.

*Vera, 532.18.

Vercingetorix (d. 46)–Gallic chieftain who revolted against Rome in the time of Julius Caesar (q.v.). 54.3-4; 66.12; 88.22; 281.note 1; 346.20; 518.25; 617.12.

Verdi, Guiseppe (1813-1901) – Italian operatic composer. 7.30; 231.7; ?412.33.

*Verdons–the Verduns came to Ireland with King John in 1185. 4.4.

Vere, Captain Edward Fairfax, "Starry"–character in Melville's *Billy Budd* (q.q.v.). 312.11; 334.2; 343.35; 344.23 (with Very lights); 346.24.

Vereker, Hugh–novelist in Henry James's (q.v.) "The Figure in the Carpet". Some "James" (q.v.) reference doubtless takes in Henry. 536.17.

Verges – headborough in Shakespeare's (q.v.) *Much Ado About Nothing.* 395.22.

Vergobretas–not a person but a magistrate of ancient Gaul. 48.19.

Vergognese–see Veronese. 435.8.

*Vericus, Ericus, 373.24.

?Verlaine, Paul (1844-96)–French poet. 250.23 (verveine).

Verne, Jules (1828-1905)–French author of such works as *Around the World in Eighty Days, Twenty Thousand Leagues Under the Sea.* 469.18.

Vernet–three French painters. 160.8.

Verney–see Vernet.

Vernon, Kathleen May–the song "Kathleen Mavourneen" contains the words: "It may be for years and it may be forever. . . ." 93.31.

Vernons–an Irish family which owned—or owns—Clontarf Castle, near the battlefield of Clontarf. In their possession is an ancient sword, traditionally believed to be that of Brian Boru (q.v.). 498.25.

Veronese, Paul (1528-99)–Italian painter. 435.8.

Veronica, St–the pious woman who gave Jesus her handkerchief to wipe His brow when He was carrying His Cross. When He returned it to her, His image was impressed on the handkerchief. 204.30; 458.14.

Vespasian–Roman emperor, 70-79. 132.18.

Vespatilla–from Latin *vespa* or wasp. 414.25; 417.30; 418.16; 458.33.

*Vespian, 484.17-18.

Vesta–Roman goddess of fire. 12.9; 183.16; 242.34; †526.30—with Vesta Tilley (q.v.); 536.18.

*Vestray, Papa – probably *vester pater* or the Pope. 26.7.

Vianney, St Jean-Marie (1786-1859) –Curé d'Ars, patron of parish priests. 440.10 (Curer of Wars).

Vicker–see Vico.

*Vicky–Victoria (q.v.)? 527.16-17.

Vico, Giovanni Battista (1668-1744) –Italian jurist and philosopher. From his great work, *Scienza Nuova,* Joyce took an immense lot for FW. Joyce's debt to Vico has not, thus far, been fully or accurately explained. There is a Vico Road in Dalkey, one of Dublin's environs. See John the Baptist, Hosty. 3.14,22,25; ?26.31; 98.19; 117.12 (jambebatiste); 134.16; 215.23; 246.25; 255.27; 260.27; 287.24; ?330.13; 417.6; 473.6; 497.13; 551.34; 596.29 (Jambudvispa Vipra); 614.9; 614.27.

Victoria (1819-1901)–queen of the United Kingdom of Great Britain and Ireland, Empress of India. Victoria and Albert are two quays along the Liffey. 6 Victoria 15 is, Mr Graham tells me: an act to impose an additional duty on spirits, and to repeal the allowance on spirits made from malt only, in Ireland. See Nyanza, Nile. 57.28; 82.12-13,27 (law); 146.34 (bigtree); 351.1; 495.31.

*Victory, Michael–the Archangel, I assume — see Mick, Father Michael. 94.36.

*Vike–Viking? Vico (q.v.)? 44.10.

Vikramaaditka, King–legendary

Hindu king of Uzjaiv at whose court the "nine gems" of Sanscrit literature flourished. 493.12.

Vilikins and his Dinah–subjects of an old cockney ballad. 250.31.

Vincentio–Duke in Shakespeare's (q.v.) *Measure for Measure.* See Lodewijk, Isabella, Angelo. 38.26.

Vining, E. P.–author of *The Mystery of Hamlet*, 1881. The solution is that Hamlet (q.v.) is a woman and in love with Horatio (q.v.). See *Ulysses*, 196/254. 93.8.

Viola – heroine of Shakespeare's (q.v.) *Twelfth Night.* She was shipwrecked, masqueraded as a boy, was loved by Olivia (q.v.). See Seven Rainbow Girls, Rose. 3.16; 143.26; 223.7; 231.20 (see Sillyass); 261.2; 275.18; 403.27, 34; 612.11.

Vipra–see Vico. 596.29.

Virag–the original family name of Bloom (q.v.). 432.11.

Virchow, Rudolph (1821-1902)– German pathologist, politician. 537.5.

Virgil (70-19 B.C.)–Roman poet. *Sortes Virgilianae* is fortune-telling by opening a volume of Virgil and reading the first passage hit upon. 270.25; 281.right margin; 569.16; 618.2.

Virgin–see Mary, Elizabeth I, Jinnies. 115.19,26; 171.3 (see Swan); 250.23; 304.25; 342.27; 365.9-10; 408.8; 433.3; †513.27—with Anne Page (q.v.); †553.1—with Anne Page (q.v.); †561.25—with Helen (q.v.); 602.12.

Vishnu–in Hinduism, the second god of the triad which includes Brahma and Siva (q.q.v.). One of his incarnations was Matsya, a fish who saved Manu (q.v.). See also Krishna, Rama. 525.20,27.

Vitellius, Aulus–Roman emperor from 2 January to 22 December 69. He was murdered by Vespasian's (q.v.) soldiers. Vitellius means veal or calf in old Latin, and the name is applied to Luke

Tarpey who as St Luke (q.q.v.) is symbolized by an ox or calf— see Four Evangelists. 307.left margin; 406.14,18.

Vitruvius–Roman architect, engineer, author of *De Architectura Libri Decem.* 255.20.

Vitus, St–patron of nervous disorders who has given his name to the disease chorea, St Vitus's dance. 141.9.

*Vjenaskayas, Vjeras, 348.23.

Vnost–see Van Nost. 552.12.

Vogelweide, Walter von der–German minnesinger. 486.7.

Vogt, Alfred–Swiss oculist who helped restore Joyce's sight. 54.5.

*Vol, Pov and Dev–See Three. Vol is will (q.v.), Dev is DeValera (q.v.). 51.13.

Volta, Alessandro (1745-1827)– Italian physicist after whom the volt is named. 549.16.

?Voltaire, François Marie Arouet de (1694-1778)–French philosopher, author of *Candide*, which is quoted FW, 193.19-23, etc. 509. 33.

Volumina–mother of Shakespeare's Coriolanus (q.q.v.). 155.20.

Vortigern–king of Britain when the Saxons arrived, led by Hengist and Horsa (q.v.). *Vortigern and Rowena* (q.v.) is one of Ireland's (q.v.) Shakespeare (q.v.) forgeries. 565.12.

Vousden, Val–Dublin music-hall entertainer at the turn of the century. 50.15; 439.17-18.

Vox, Valentine, the Ventriloquist– title hero of a novel (1840) by Henry Cockton. On one occasion, Vox makes a voice come from an Egyptian sarcophagus and bystanders think the dead has come to life. 142.19; 439.17.

*Vuggy, 106.26.

Vulcan–Roman god of fire. 79.18; 89.28;334.9;481.14;494.7;514.12.

*Vyler–see Roe. 277.note 4.

W

*Waarft, Jetty de–probably the wharves and jetties of the Liffey (q.v.). 332.18-19.

Wadding, Luke (1588-1657)–Irish Franciscan, historian. His chief work was the *Annales Minorum*. 377.15; 573.26.

Wagner, Richard (1813-83)–German dramatic composer, significant in FW for having written *Tristan und Isolde* (q.v.—see also Mildew Lisa, Wesendonk) and perhaps also for *Parsifal* (q.v.) and *Lohengrin*. 230.12; 540.24; 577.13 (voguener).

Waldemar–see Valdemar. 317.17.

?Waldmann, Hans–Zurich burgomaster. 345.4.

*Walker, 170.18; 361.32; 603.15.

*Walker – Matt Gregory, Mark Lyons, Luke Tarpey, and Johnny MacDougal (q.q.v.) all are called Walker—I don't know why. It probably matters that Johnny Walker is a brand of whisky; I don't think it does matter that Matthew Gregory is a knot. Walker was the name of some Stratford friends of Shakespeare's (q.v.), for whose son, William, the poet stood godfather. Tim Finnegan (q.v.) lived in Walker Street.

*Walker, doctor, 394.12.

*Walker, Gus–seems to be the ass (q.v.). See Walker above. 555.24.

Walker, Kniferope–see Rowley the Barrel. 376.30.

Walker, "Whimsical"–professional name of a clown, Thomas Walker (1850-1934). 473.3-4.

*Wall–in FW "wall" refers to the wall Tim Finnegan (q.v.) was building when he fell. This becomes the magazine wall in Phoenix (q.v.) Park. No one has ever explained the particular significance of the magazine wall, nor can I; but anyone who will take the trouble to trace "wall" through FW, will see that it slides constantly in and out of identification with "will" and "well" (q.v.).

A minor significance of wall is, I think, occasionally Wall as played by Tom Stout (q.v.) in Shakespeare's (q.v.) *A Midsummer Night's Dream* (e.g. 90-91), a wall with a hole in it as in FW (5.30; 6.9,12; 69.5-6,7-8; 78.3; 90.21-22; 365.16; 587.15,16) a wall where Pyramus and Thisby (q.v.) met.

Wallaby–see Whalley. 601.34.

*Wallat–maybe London's Wallace Collection. 153.30.

Wallenstein, Albrecht Eusebius von (1583-1634)–German statesman and general who aimed to unify Germany but was murdered. Hero of Schiller's (q.v.) drama. †8.1—with Wellington (q.v.); †32.29—with Washington and W. W. Kelly (q.q.v.).

Waller, Lewis (1860-1915)–English actor. 151.23; 181.3.

Walleslee – see Wellington, Lee. 133.21.

Wallinstone–see Wellington, perhaps also Wallenstein. 8.1.

Wallor, Loose–see Waller. 181.3.

Walpole, Horace (1717-97)–English letter-writer whose account of the great Gunning (q.v.) battle is used in FW. †307.left margin—with Horace (q.v.).

Walsh, William John (1841-1921)–Roman Catholic archbishop of Dublin. He helped bring Parnell (q.v.) down, but was an enthusiastic Sinn Feiner. The word "walsh" may well have some further significance for FW. 282.22; 318.19; 338.9; 340.3; 495.27.

Walsingham, Lilias – heroine of LeFanu's (q.v.) *The House by the Churchyard.* She dies for love of Gipsy Devereux (q.v.). See Lily. 563.20 (Lylian).

*Walter – Meagher?   Raleigh? (q.q.v.). 64.20 *(bis)*; †76.27—with Walton (q.v.); 320.10; 373.6 *(bis)*; 473.4.

Walton, Isaac (1593-1683)–author of *The Compleat Angler.* 61.19,24; †76.27-28—with Walter, Isaac (q.q.v.).

*Wanda–possibly the title heroine of Doppler's opera, possibly the water-spirit in "Babil and Bijou" (1872), a *Féerie* by Boucicault (q.v.), Planché and Brough. 147. 14; 199.12.

*Wandervogel, 419.15.

Wangel–Dr Wangel of Ibsen's (q.v.) *The Lady from the Sea* (q.v.), his wife, or his daughter Hilda, heroine of *The Master Builder* (q.v.). 300.5; 390.14.

Warbeck, Perkin (1474-99)–pretender to the English throne who was strongly supported by the Irish. †39.4—with St Peter (q.v.).

*Ward, Pruda, 212.6-7,20.

Ware, Sir James (1594-1666) – author of *The Antiquities and History of Ireland.* 542.13; 572.32.

*Warner, 245.8.

*Warre, Abbot, 539.27.

*Warren–seemingly Brer Rabbit (q.v.), turns into Barren and Sparrem (q.q.v.). 574.4.

?Warren, Viv–heroine of Shaw's (q.v.) *Mrs Warren's Profession.* Viv's mother was no virgin. 28.27.

Wars, Curer of–see Vianney. 440.10.

Washington, George (1732-99)– first president of the United States. †32.29—with Wallenstein, W. W. Kelly (q.q.v.); 107.1; 434. 22-23.

Waterhouse, Alfred (1830-1905)– English architect, designer of the clock which is, or was, the Big Ben of Dublin. 88.1; 213.16.

Waterlow, Sir Ernest Albert (1850-1919)–English painter, famous for "Galway Gossips". I have a feeling there is another Waterlow. 105.30; 202.17.

Waterman–American fountain pen. 447.11.

Waters, Mrs 'Boss'–Anna Livia (q.v.). 342.24-25.

Waters, Esther–title heroine of a novel (1894) by George Moore (q.v.). Only the name has any significance for FW. See Esthers. 305.29; 605.12.

*Watkins, Fred–probably Fred Atkins (q.v.). 587.20; 588.2,6,12.

*Watsy Lyke–seems to be the Man Servant (q.v.)—what's he like? 245.33.

Watt, James (1736-1819)–Scottish inventor of the steam engine. 321.9.

Waves–see Rurie, Four.

Weary Willy–tramp character in an English comic-strip. See Willy. 56.22.

*Weaver – Bottom?   Penelope? (q.q.v.) Miss Harriet Weaver? In a letter to this last (9 November 1927) Joyce tells of dreaming he was a "carpetweaver". 43.18; 211.18; 313.1.

Webley–brand of pistol. 82.16.

*Webster, 479.30.

Webster, Noah (1758-1843)–American lexicographer. I agree with Mr Wilder that for FW, Joyce's English-language dictionary was Webster's. 36.11.

Wedgwood–family famous for the manufacture of china. 72.18.

Wei-Ling-Taou–see Wellington. 81. 34.

*Weisingchetaoli, 609.10.

Welikins–William as in William and Mary (see William III) and Wilkins (q.v.) 106.17.

*Welkins–sky. Wilkins (q.v.)? 178. 11.

*Welks–Johnny MacDougal (q.v.) as west. 557.2.

Weller, Sam–of Dickens's *Pickwick* (q.q.v.) *Papers*. †93.34 — with Lover and Lever (q.q.v.).

Wellesley, Richard Colley Wesley, Marquis (1760 - 1842) – older brother of Wellington (q.v.). He had a distinguished diplomatic career and in 1821 became lord-lieutenant of Ireland. An advocate of Catholic Emancipation, he so annoyed the Orange (q.v.) faction that in 1822, at a performance of Goldsmith's (q.v.) *She Stoops to Conquer* the audience rioted and threw bottles at him. Some of the Wellesleys, listed under Wellington, may refer to him. †273.25-26—with Wellington (q.v.); 510.22.

Wellington, Arthur Wellesley, 1st Duke of (1759-1852)–called by Shaw (q.v.) "the most typical Irishman that ever lived". He was probably born in Dublin, his memorial stands in Phoenix Park and the iron bridge across the Liffey is named for him. In FW there are many references to Wellington, Wellesley (q.v.), Iron Duke, the Sepoy, Arthur (q.v.). A charming episode is the tour of the Wellington "museyroom" (8-10), a tour conducted by Kate (q.v.) where Waterloo mixes in with HCE's (q.v.) misadventures with two girls and three soldiers (q.q.v.)—see also Napoleon, Jinnies, Willingdon, Will, Wall, Well, Wolsey, Wesley. For an account of Joyce at Waterloo, see a letter from Thomas Wolfe to Aline Bernstein, 22 September 1926.

†8.1   Wallinstone—with Wallenstein, Wall (q.q.v.)

†8-10 (*passim*) Willingdone — with Willingdon (q.v.)

†10.2   Stonewall Willingdone—with Stonewall Jackson (q.v.)

10.14,15,19 seeboy (ter) (Wellington fought the Sepoys and was called "The Sepoy" by Napoleon)

17.11   woolseley
36.18   *duc de Fer's*
41.1   welleslays... wallasdays
47   Wellington's monument
†49.8   Wolsey (q.v.)
52.27   woolselywellesly
71.23   Arthur
81.34   Wei-Ling-Taou
85.10   Wellington Park road
93.7   Arthrc
97.34   willingsons
126.24   Wellingtonia sequoia
128.16   the duke
†133.21   Walleslee—with Robert E. Lee (q.v.)
†137.11   artful Juke of Wilysly—with Jukes (q.v.)
†162.4   the juke—with Jukes (q.v.)
175.11   Arth out of Engleterre
203.7   wellingtonorseher
209.33   artesaned wellings
238.24-25   Herzog van Vellentam
252.20   artthoudux
†273.25-26 muckwits of willesly—with Wells and Wellesley (q.q.v.)
286.11   Wellington's Iron Bridge
312.29-30   Wallisey wanderlook
333.18   Bullingdong ("the Bullingdon" is mentioned in *Brideshead Revisited*, sounds like a stodgy sort of club or eating place)
334.13   willingtoned
335.17,18,30 Wullingthund . . . Wellingthund . . . Arthurduke
†337.21   Will Woolsley Wellaslayers — with Will (q.v.)
339.26   jupes of Wymmingtown
†347.9   Sirdarthar Woolwichleagues—with Gautama (q.v.)
358.29   arthouducks
†371.36   Dook Weltington—with Dick Whittington (q.v.)
377.13   Welsey Wandrer
†420.36   Well, Sir Arthur—with Cromwell (q.v.)

460.1   wellingtons
†492.10   Wolossays—with Wol-
             sey (q.v.)
510.30   Orther
529.33   wellingtons
531.6   ironing duck
541.21   Duke Wellinghof
567.2-3   Wellington memorial
568.19   Woolington bottes
†578.7   wollsey — with Wolsey
             (q.v.)
595.22   vellumtomes muniment,
             Arans Duhkha
30   Conk a dook (Welling-
             ton was called "Old
             Conky")
620.9   Iren duke's

Wells–the man who broke the bank
at Monte Carlo—see 11th *Britannica*, "Wells, Charles Jeremiah".
†273.26—with Wellington (q.v.).

Wells, H. G. (b. 1866)–British
novelist and historian. 58.29; 79.
23.

Wenceslaus (1361-1419)–German
and Bohemian king. St Wenceslaus was a 10th century duke of
Bohemia, slain by his brother.
539.29-30.

*Wendell, 581.11.

Wesendonk, Mathilde–mistress of
Wagner's (q.v.) who inspired
Tristan und Isolde (q.q.v.). 230.12.

Wesley, John (1730-91)–founder of
Methodism. See Wellesley, Wellington. 86.33.

West, Mae–American actress of the
1930s. 330.26,28; 457.20.

West, Rebecca–heroine of Ibsen's
(q.v.) *Rosmersholm*—see Rosmer.
203.4-5.

Westinghouse–American electrical
firm. 372.17.

Weston, Jessie–author of *From
Ritual to Romance*. There is a large
Grail theme in FW and many
"wastes" and "wests" take in
Miss Weston. 3.33 (west in quest);
77.3.

*Wet, Pinter, 92.7.

Wetherby, Fred – prolific song-
writer. He did not write "I'm
sitting on the stile, Mary . . .".
445.32.

Wettingstone, Dirk–see Dick Whittington. 550.31.

W. H., Mr–the fair young man to
whom (presumably) Shakespeare's
(q.v.) sonnets are dedicated and
mostly addressed—see Dark
Lady. It has been suggested that
he was Pembroke, Southampton
(q.q.v.), William Hall, William
Hathaway, even Mr William Himself. Joyce glances at these
theories in *Ulysses* and FW; but,
as far as I can see, he uses mostly
in FW a theory (or his own
variations of it) advanced by
Wilde (q.v.) in "The Portrait of
Mr W. H.". Wilde fancies that
Mr W. H. was Willie Hughes, a
beautiful youth who inspired and
acted Shakespeare's heroines at
the Globe—see Seven Rainbow
Girls.
    Mr. W. H. has other uses (Wilde
felt Shakespeare punned on that
word) in FW: he is the object of
an older man's homosexual love
—an Alfred Douglas (q.v.) figure.
He is the young man—a Tristram
figure—who is taken by the Dark
Lady (q.v.) from the older man—
see Mark of Cornwall, Finn,
Arthur. I think there are uses and
interpretations of Mr W. H. which
I have not listed or seen. See
Will, Fitton, Rich, Arrah-na-
Pogue. Margaret Hughes was the
first woman to act a Shakespeare
heroine, Desdemona (q.v.).
†6.7   hugh butt—with Pem-
             broke (q.v.)
†30,32,36   Well, Hlm . . . Hom
             well . . . wail him—
             with Hamlet (q.v.)—
             see also Will
†11.12   huemeramybows — see
             Mary Fitton, Seven
?†31.25   Saint Hubert (q.v.)—
             see also Pembroke
34.2   hue
†63.12-13   Myramy Huey — see
             Mary Fitton, Seven

?66.13   huge
68.20   huecry
?70.1   the U.S.E.
84.15   hugely
91.27   t'yous
102.27   huemoures
103.5   hues
106.2   Hue
†118.20   wall will hue—see Wall
182.8   outhue
†197.7-8   Billyclub . . . Hughes
            Caput Earlyfouler—
            with HCE and Hugh
            Capet (q.q.v.)
215.17   hues . . . hue
†220.12-13 fine frank fairhaired fel-
            low of the fairytales
            —with Frank (q.v.)
223.13-14   hugh . . . will
227.25   whose hue
233.5,8   hues . . . will
234.26-27   finehued, the fairhailed,
            the farahead
240.3,6   honaryhuest . . . whooze-
            become
256.10   hued
?257.11   Hips and Haws
34-35   When the h, who the
            hu, how the hue,
            where the huer
259.9   hu
273.13   hugh
316.33   you's
333.14,16   willowy . . . uses
336.12-13   dapplehued
?342.22-23 Mr Whaytehayte's . . .
            Homo
†350.11   Mr Lhugewhite Cadder-
            pollard—with Wilde
            (q.v.)
30   huguenottes
371.36   hugon
†376.5-6   wollan . . . Hubert—see
            Pembroke, St Hubert
23   Huggins
†385.32   poghuing and poghuing
            —see Arrah-na-Pogue
411.24   greenridinghued
414.8   ghuest
417.28   hugely
423.2   huw
453.3   yous
454.4,11,15-16 Haugh! Haugh!
            woollys . . . huges
            huges huges hughy

hughy   hughy — see
Will
?456.14   Huguenot
462.1   yous
474.23,24,27 hooh . . . phew . . .
            Hwoah
†480.18,36 Bill . . . Whu's . . . Whu's
            Whoah — with   Bill
            Bailey (q.v.)
?499.35-36 Whoishe (7 times)
520.24,25,28,30 use . . . bil . . . will
            . . . Will . . . Will
521.4   well . . . yous Essexelcy
            —with Essex (q.v.)
535.3,24   yous . . . will yous
541.14   yous . . . hugheknots
549.25   hew
557.20   whose
†571.32   Huesofrichunfolding-
            morn. Wakenuprise-
            andprove — with
            Penelope Rich (q.v.)
†574.15   Wieldhelm, Hurls—with
            Shakespeare   (q.v.),
            Wilde?
576.7,9   Will . . . whew whew
            whew whew
588.18,20   whoer . . . hue (a lot of
            W. H.s in here)
589.9   hugest
598.34   hugibus hugibum
602.4   highhued
604.20   who is who will
609.20   hue
†611.6,13,18,19 sevenhued . . . hue-
            ful . . . heupanepi . . .
            huepanwor — see
            Seven
622.26,33   Honourable Whilp . . .
            hue

Whalley, Dr John (b. 1653)–Dublin
quack, astrologer, writer of alma-
nacks.   In trouble, he fled to
England, later returned to Dublin. †536.32-33—with Jonah (q.v.)
and Jonah Barrington (q.v.);
601.34 (Wallaby).

*Whambers, Carry, 562.13.

Whang the Miller–character in
Goldsmith's (q.v.) *Citizen of the
World.* Whang has a prosperous
mill which collapses when he digs
under it for non-existent treasure.
122.13,15,16,17,18; 297.note 5;

†341.5—with Milner (q.v.); 520. 25.

*Wharrem–see Warren. 576.7.

?Wharton, Edith (1862-1937) – American novelist. 34.10-11 (what's edith ar home).

Wharton, Thomas, Marquis of (1648-1715) – Whig politician, author of "Lilliburlero". While lord-lieutenant of Ireland, he had built the magazine in Phoenix Park which inspired Swift (q.v.) to his last joke: "Behold a proof of Irish sense!/Here Irish wit is seen!/Where nothing's left that's worth defense,/They build a magazine." 12.23; 269.12.

*Whatarwelter, Herrschuft–Seems to play around the German *Der Herr schuf die Welt*, "The Lord created the world", with *Schuft*, "rogue, rascal", thrown in. *Weltherrschaft* is the "domination of the world". 12.9.

Whately, Richard (1787-1863) – Anglican archbishop of Dublin. His celebrated tract, *Historical Doubts Relative to Napoleon Bonaparte* (q.v.) may have to do with the Museyroom episode of FW. 342.22-23; 387.25.

*Whaytehayte – partly Whately, Mr W. H. (q.q.v.). White hat? 342.22-23.

*Wheatacre, Ruth–Whittaker? See Ruth. 257.21.

Wheatley's Dublin hop bitters, *Ulysses* 80/100, 443.29.

Wheatstone, Sir Charles (1802-75)– English physicist, practical founder of telegraphy, inventor of the "acoucryptophone", which was a light box, shaped like an ancient lyre and suspended by a metallic wire from a piano in the room above. When the piano was played, its vibrations were transmitted silently and became audible in the lyre, which appeared to play itself. 13.16.

Whenchehislaws–see Wenceslaus. 539.29-30.

*Whilp, the Honourable, 622.26.

*Whisperer, Father, 96.10.

Whistler, James (1834-1903) – American painter. 626.13.

*Whiston, John–possibly the translator of Josephus. 359.23.

White, White Head, White Hat— see Finn.

White, Blanco (d. 1841)–Irish-Spanish priest who became an Anglican clergyman and then a Unitarian minister. His autobiography may be used in FW. 43.24; 49.7,8.

White   Knight–character in *Through the Looking-Glass*. 501. 30, 31.

White, Luke–18th century Dublin bookseller and auctioneer who became a civil power and great property owner. 529.20.

*White, Oliver–maybe just "white livered", maybe Olaf (q.v.) the White. 334.15.

*White, Patch–seems to be Shem (q.v.). 63.5; 83.26; 93.4; ?149.18; 223.17; ?251.26; ?253.24; ?350. 12; 379.9; 419.1; 468.17; 488.30; 559.25.

White, Pearl–movie actress, noted for her performance in *The Perils of Pauline*. †394.35-36—with the Maggies (q.v.).

*Whitebeaver, Alderman, 160.15-16.

Whitefield, Ann–the heroine or Donna Anna of Shaw's (q.v.) *Man and Superman*—see Don Giovanni, Tanner. Shaw says, "every woman is not Ann, but Ann is Everywoman". She doubles in every case with Anna Livia (q.v.). 294.29; †312.9—with John Tanner (q.v.).

Whitehead–see Finn MacCool. 535. 22.

*Whiteknees–Whitneys? 302.14.

Whiteleys – London department store. 127.12.

Whiteside, James (1804-76)–Dublin legal light, defended O'Connell and William Smith O'Brien (q.q.v.). †95.15 — with Kaffir Whiteside (q.v.); 352.4.

Whiteside Kaffir – White-eyed Kaffit was, I am told by Miss Worthington, an entertainer of the 1920s who wore a white, diamond-shaped patch over one eye. See Patch White? †95.15— with James Whiteside (q.v.).

Whitestone–at the Irish bar, Counsellor Shannon, whose witnesses had been accused of perjury by Counsellor Whitestone, responded: ". . . all the water in the Shannon, with the Liffey to back it, could not wash a Whitestone into a Blackstone." 5.17; 106-107.

*Whitlock, Mr, 98.25.

Whitman, Walt (1819-92)–American poet whose influence is certainly to be seen in FW, 532-554. 263.9.

Whittington, Dick (d. 1423)–three times Lord Mayor of London. The real Richard Whittington has been confused with the folk-figure Dick Whittington who was recalled to London by the prophetic peal of Bow bells: "Turn again, Whittington." The story of Dick's cat, who rid a ship of rats, is told in many languages. Also an English pantomime. Perhaps also Thomas Whittington, a shepherd from whom Ann Hathaway (q.v.) Shakespeare borrowed 40 shillings. †19.15-16 (Paddy Wippingham)—with St Patrick and Wippingham (q.q.v.); †52.10 —with Wilde (q.v.); 140.1; †241. 18—with the Norwegian Captain (q.v.); 248.7; 341.32 (Wittyngtom); 346.29; †371.36—with Wellington (q.v.); 372.17; 550.31; 625.35-36.

*Whitwell, 536.25.

*Whitworth, 84.27.

Wholyphamous–see Polyphemus. 73.9.

Whooley the Whooper–see Willy the Weeper. 368.29.

*Whoyteboyce of Hoodie Head– the Whiteboys were 18th century anti-landlord agitators. 4.5.

*Whyforyou, 76.31.

?Whymper, Edward (b. 1840)– Englishman, first to climb the Matterhorn. 410.30.

*Widger, Winny Willy–seems to be Anna Livia (q.v.). See W. W. 20.35; 21.1; 39.2,11; 40.3 (W. W.); ?227.14; 327.8; 610.22,36.

*Wieldhelm–William (q.v.)? 574. 15.

Wigham, J. R.–Dublin inventor who, in 1865, made a 108-jet gas burner for the Bailey (q.v.) Light on Howth (q.v.). The jewels of Wigan, however, are pieces of coal. 551.3.

Wikingson, Meistral–see Whittington, Norwegian Captain, Mistral. 241.18-19.

Wilberforce, William (1759-1833)– English philanthropist, chiefly associated with the abolition of the slave trade. He was an M.P. 126.32.

Wild, Jonathan (1682-1725)–English criminal, hanged, subject of Fielding's *Jonathan Wild, the Great.* †540.28—with John (q.v.).

Wild Man from Borneo–subject of a song: "The Wild Man from Borneo has just come to town". *Il Bornio* is Italian for "the one-eyed". †130.23-24—with Hulme (q.v.); 331.35-36; 345.4-5; 382.25-26; 415.8.

Wildair, Sir Harry–character in Farquhar's play *The Constant Couple.* It was one of Peg Woffington's (q.v.) breeches parts. 210.25.

Wilde, Jimmy–English boxer. †307. 20—with James (q.v.).

Wilde, Lady–mother of Oscar Wilde (q.v.), herself a writer of books on

Irish legend and a quantity of verse which appeared in *The Nation*, signed Speranza (q.v.). 211.24; 297.note 1.

Wilde, Oscar Fingal O'Flahertie Wills (1856-1900)–Irish writer. There are many Wilde characters in FW—see Ernest, Moncrieff, Lady Windermere, Dorian Gray and—most important—Mr W. H.; many, maybe all Wilde's works are mentioned; *De Profundis* is echoed, so is *Psychic Messages from Oscar Wilde*, (1924) by Hester Travers Smith, in which Wilde savages *Ulysses.* But, as always, more is made of Wilde's life and character—mostly as reported by Frank Harris (q.v.). Wilde's love for Lord Alfred Douglas (q.v.) is identified with Shakespeare's (q.v.) love for Mr W. H.; much is also made of Wilde's love of soldiers (see Atkins), his trial (see Sylvia Silence), his fall; there are also references to Sebastian Melmoth (q.v.)—the name Wilde adopted, but did not much use, after his trial—and to Great White Caterpillar, which was what Wilde reminded Lady Colin Campbell of. See also Constance Lloyd, Beggar, Oscar, Fingal?

All Wilde references are not homosexual. Wilde was, like Shakespeare, bi-sexual and the father of two sons. Moreover, some Wilde references must take in his father, Sir William Wilde (q.v.), a notorious heterosexual.

33.23	great white caterpillar
34.25	wildest
39.29	wild
†40.13	whilde roarses — with Eros (q.v.)
?†46	Fingal Mac Oscar Onesine Bargearse Boniface—see Fingal
49.5	wild
69.3	wilde
81.17	wilde
98.2	wildewide
149.9	wiles

157.2	wildest
†160.19	wildsbillow—with Billy (q.v.)—Sir William?
223.3	wiles
226.32	O while
228.33	subustioned mullmud—see Melmoth
241.9,31,32	greyed vike cuddlepuller . . . askors . . . osghirs
246.22	wilds
250.33	wild
†256.13	wildeshaweshowe—with G. B. Shaw (q.v.)
269.11	wild's
303.7	Wiles
319.4	ersewild
†350.11	Mr Lhugewhite Cadderpollard—with Mr W. H. (q.v.)
22	askormiles'
†358.23	the Wildemanns—with Wild Man from Borneo
363.22	wild
†371.22	Fingool MacKishgmard Obesume Burgearse Benefice — see Finn, Boniface
374.29	Ascare winde
403.25,27	wild . . . veilde
408.19	os so ker
419.25	Oscan wild
488.25	Erse clare
503.34	Wilds
510.11	wilde
511.20	oska
525.32	wild
526.21	wild
535.26,28,29	Old Whitehowth . . . woyld . . . O.W.
536.1,13,21,34	Sebastion . . . whiles . . . Oscarshals . . . wild
549.26	wildth
571.28	Notwildebeestsch
587.21	Melmoth
588.3	woyld
589.23	wild
?602.23	Oscur Camerad
615.33	wiles
622.24	moskors

Wilde, Sir William (1815-76)–some of the above references take in, I feel sure, Oscar Wilde's (q.v.) father, an eminent Dublin eye-doctor, who, like his son, was involved in a notorious sexual scandal and trial. Mary Josephine Travers accused him of having assaulted her when she was his patient. The jury found for Miss Travers with one farthing's damages.

Wilde references may also include Oscar's brother, Willy (223. 3?), a journalist who after Oscar's trial said to Frank Harris, "Oscar was not a man of bad character. A woman was perfectly safe with him."

Wildemanns–see Oscar Wilde and Wild Man from Borneo. 358.23.

*Wilfrid's–St Wilfrid (634-709)? 449.8.

Wilhelmina's,   S. – the   Dublin churches on p. 601 have been almost completely identified by Mr Kelleher in *The Analyst*, No. X.

Wilkes,   John   (1727-97)–English politician. 269.12.

Wilkins, George (fl. 1607)–minor playwright who wrote for Shakespeare's (q.v.) company. He also wrote a novel about Pericles (q.v.)—see also Marina. Sidney Lee (q.v.) thinks he helped Shakespeare with *Pericles*. Wilkin is a diminutive of William (q.v.). 90. 11; †106.17—with William III (q.v.); †131.16—with Micawber (q.v.); ?178.11; 464.19.

Will, Willy–when he can, Joyce associates important characters with common words, sometimes in direct references, sometimes to remind us that language is at once alive with people and a repository of the vaster race. Examples: HCE-he; Anne-an; Issy-is; Stella-still; O'Shea-she; Ham-him; Hamlet-let him; Cain-can; Abel-able; Butt-but; Noah-no (q.q.v.), etc. In the same way, I think Joyce links "will" to William Shakespeare (q.v.), and, by extension, to other Wills,

notably Mr W. H. and W. B. Yeats (q.q.v.). As a *leitmotiv* of FW, "will" is inseparable from "well" and "where theirs is Will there's his Wall . . ." (q.v.). Not infrequently   or   unnaturally, "will" turns up in the neighborhood of "free", which I take to refer to Frank or Francis Bacon (q.q.v.).

It is well known (see Knowell) that Shakespeare punned on "Will" in his sonnets. Sidney Lee (q.v.) disdained the pun: "To what depth of vapidity Shakespeare   and   his   contemporary punsters sink is nowhere better illustrated than the favour they bestow   on   efforts   to   extract amusement   from   parities   and disparities of form and meaning between the words 'will' and 'wish'."

Joyce certainly knew that to Elizabethans "will" meant not only volition and obstinacy, but also lust. Obsessed as a primitive with the meaning and potency of names, a lover to end all lovers of "the fatal Cleopatra", Joyce has Stephen Dedalus (q.v.) say (*Ulysses*, 207/269): "He has hidden his own name, a fair name, William, in the plays, a super here, a clown there, as a painter of old Italy set his face in a dark corner of his canvas. He has revealed it in the sonnets where there is Will in overplus."

I think that in FW all occurrences of "will", "well", "wall" are either direct references to Shakespeare or reminders that "He is all in all" (*Ulysses*, 210/ 272). I have gathered the wills-wells-walls of FW (even an occasional we'll), but I list below only such wills and willys as occur in passages very obviously Shakespearean. See William, Bill, Bard, Swan, Butcher, Maltster.

6.4,30,32,36; †8-10—with Wellington (q.v.); 13.17,18; 28.6; 36.24; 39.29; 44.13; 51.12,13; 56.22; 66.10; †70.7—with Lamb (q.v.); ?75.27 (see William III); 79.24; 80.5,13; †90.11—with Wilkins (q.v.); 92.14,20; †93.34—with Lever, Lover (q.q.v.); 102.27 (see Mr W. H.); 111.26; 112.19, 20,21,22,34; 116.36; 118.16,19,20, 26; 119.5,7,9; †130.23 — with Wilde (q.v.); 139.6; 140.18 (*bis*); 146.11; 150.30,31; 151.16,30; 152. 12; 154.3,26; 159.19; 163.27 (*bis*); 164.21; 167.34; 170.21; 172.6,27; 175.19; 180.32; 181.31; 184.5; 190.21; 191.1; 196.35; 207.4 (willow); 211.2 (see Will-of-the Wisp), 36 (swilly); 213.27; †223.3—with Wilde (q.v.), 14; 225.20; †227.2—with Wilde (q.v.); 232.24; 233.8, 12,13; 238.6,11,15,16,34; 239.29; 245.1; 246.22,30; 248.22,35; 250. 3,36; 253.12,16; 264.30; 272.4; †273.26—with Wellesley (q.v.); 277.6,13,note 3; ?278.8; 281.17, note 4; 287.8; 292.24; 297.7; 300. note 3; 302.note 2; 308.3; 318.14, 35; 321.12; 326.4; 328.36; 329.2; 331.22; ?334.26; †337.21—with Wolsey, Wellesley (q.q.v.), 22,24; ?347.26—with Longaville (q.v.); 350.36; 357.3; 360.23; 366.28; 368.29 (see Willy the Weeper); 370.12; 373.16; 377.9; 378.20; 381.26; 404.15,22; 408.22; 410.22; 411.11,28; 412.21,30; 413.17; 423. 24; 425.30; 440.19; 442.17,21,22, 28,29; 449.31; †454.11—with Mr W. H. (q.v.); 457.2,14; †464.19—with Wilkins (q.v.); 468.26; 473. 15; 482.31; 483.2; 487.29,30; 511.32; 516.22; 518.10; 521.29, 33; 525.10; 526.3,4,21; 528.3; 532.11; 535.24 (see Mr W. H.); 540.8; 556.21; 562.28,29,35; 563. 7,11,20; 566.6 (see Keeper); 567. 19,26,35; 568.7,19,36; 569.24,30; 573.24; 575.29-30 (see Breakfast), 576.7; †578.7 — with Wolsey (q.v.); 582.28; 593.24; 598.31 (see Mr W. H.); †602.7—with Will Somers (q.v.); 604.20; 606.25; 607.29; 609.9,10; 620.27; 625.5,7; 627.30.

*Will, Conn and Otto–will, can, ought to. See Vol, Pov, Dev. See Will. 51.12.

*Will-of-the Wisp—either Shakespeare or Yeats (q.q.v.) fits the context. Perhaps both are intended. See Will. 211.2; 404.15.

William–I believe that all Williams in FW—see also Will—refer primarily to Shakespeare (q.v.), who is manifest as many Williams (see below), manifest, for that matter, as every character in the book—see *Ulysses*, 210/272. He is particularly likely to turn up as one of the four King Williams of England (q.v.) since it is said that Shakespeare acted "kingly parts". It will be noticed that almost all Williams are English.

†6.30-36	Well, Him . . . let . . . Hom, well . . . wail him—with Hamlet, Mr W. H. (q.q.v.)
25.31	Liam Failed
†27.17-18	Williamswoodmenufactors — with William Wood (q.v.)
†31.11	sailor king—see William IV
†14	William the Conk—see William I, William III
†25	our red brother—see William Rufus (note that William Gladstone also occurs on this page)
?88.21	Helmingham—with Ham?
†33	Wirrgeling—with William III (q.v.)
†90.11	wilkinses (q.v.)
100.13	Limestone
†106.17	Welikin's Douchka Marianne—with Wilkins, William III and Mary, Marina (q.q.v.)
120.32	uus
†122.17	Villain Rufus — with William Rufus (q.v.)
124.32	the sailor—with William IV (q.v.)
†131.10	one Liam Fail — with William I (q.v.)

†16 welkins—with Wilkins, Micawber (q.q.v.)

†135.12 prince of Orange and Nassau—with William III (q.v.), see also Orange

†138.32 woollem the farsed— with William I (q.v.)

†160.2-3 Cricketbutt Willown— with William Grace (q.v.)

179.31 vellum

186.14 killim our king (the reference is to Parnell, q.v.)

†211.34 Billy Dunboyne—with William III (q.v.)

226.32 W

242.1 Villumses

277.note 4 Williams—see Roe

281.left margin shillum

302.note 2 sweet willings

310.29 whilom

†322.33 Kongbullies — William III's (q.v.) statue

331.4 liamstone

†336.34 whilom eweheart — with Gladstone (q.v.)

345.16 meanwhilome

†347.32 Crummwiliam — with Cromwell (q.v.)

?376.5 wollan

380.21 whilom

387.19 Swede Villem

†388.1 old conk—see William I

?†440.3-4 William Archer (q.v.)

460.5 villain

461.18 welluminated

†464.19 Wilkins (q.v.)

?478.12 vallums

507.35 Shivering William

543.17-18 William Inglis . . . that man de Loundres

†553.14 Guglielmus Caulis—see William III (statue)

†567.16 mellems the third and fourth—see Williams III and IV

?568.32 vellum

573.24 Guglielmus

574.15,36 Wieldhelm . . . whilom

575.15 pinkwilliams

578.3 villen

581.20,21 illian . . . willyum

†583.28 King Willow — with William Grace (q.v.)

†595.22 vellumtomes — with Wellington (q.v.)

607.22 Whyle om

613.4 Fullyhum towhoom

†615.20 Williamstown and the Marrion Ailesbury— with William III (q.v.)

William I or William the Conqueror (1028-87)–Norman noble who, by defeating Harold (q.v.) at Hastings in 1066, became king of England. I think that all the King Williams of England come to see HCE (q.v.) on FW, 31. William I is at line 14, William II or Rufus at line 25 ("our red brother"), William III, who did conquer Ireland at line 14, William IV ("the sailor king") at line 11. And for good measure William Gladstone (q.v.) often called "William the Conqueror", is at lines 30,32. See William above, see all these kings below.

In *Ulysses*, p. 199/258, Shakespeare (q.v.) is identified with William the Conqueror.

Incidentally, the first personal name in the Domesday Book is William—see FW, 485.5-6.

26.28; 31.14; 128.8; 131.10; 138.32; 388.1.

William II or William Rufus (1056-1100)–king of England, and a villain, sure enough. It has been suggested that in *Satiromastix*, William Rufus is William Shakespeare (q.v.), reference being made to Shakespeare's complexion. (Brandes, q.v., p. 299). See William, William I. 31.25; 122.8, 9,11,14,15,16,17,19,25.

William III (1650-1720)–Prince of Orange (q.v.), later, with his wife Mary (q.v.), ruled as King of England. After the revolution of 1688, William beat James II (see James) at the Battle of the Boyne in 1690. (This victory was celebrated July 12). William conquered Ireland, remained a popular symbol to the Orange or Ulster faction and a symbol of foreign, protestant domination to the Green. His equestrian statue on College Green, Dublin, was a target of vandals whenever political feeling ran high. It was finally blown up, but little statues of his white horse are still displayed as tokens of Orange feeling. I am inclined to think that it is William's white horse on which Wellington (q.v.) rides — see Copenhagen. I also think he is Shakespeare (q.v.) in some manner. See William, William I. †31.14 —with William I (q.v.); 53.36; 75. 27; 88.33-34; †106.17—with Wilkins and Marina (q.q.v.); 135.12; ?†160.27-28—with Faust (q.v.); 186.14; †211.34—see Dunboyne; ?242.1; 248.21; 322.33; 337.16; †347.32—with Cromwell (q.v.); 553.14; †567.16—with William IV (q.v.); ?573.24; 615.20.

William IV ("The Sailor King") (1765-1837)–King of England. See William, William I. 31.11; 124.32; †567.16—with William III (q.v.).

Willingdon, Marquess of — appointed Indian viceroy in 1931. India was in a period of revolutionary turmoil which sounds very much like Ireland's. Willingdon suppressed a "no rent" movement, arrested Gandhi (q.v.) and generally treated disaffection as a crime. With Wellington (q.v.) he makes up the name Willingdone in the Museyroom episode, FW 8-10. Willingdon is also "Whose will be done".

Wills, William Gorman (1828-91)– Irish dramatist and song writer, author of *A Royal Divorce* (see Henry VIII) and of "I'll Sing Thee Songs of Araby". See Will. 4.1; 577.21.

Willy–see Will.

Willy the Weeper–subject of an American song about a dope fiend who dreams he is a king. He is brought before a judge and jailed. The name is applied to the ass (q.v.) and is also a reference to Shakespeare (q.v.) since Joyce calls Willy a "whooper" and a "whooper" is a wild swan (q.v.), see also 255.9. See Will. 368.29.

Wilysly, Juke of–see Wellington. 137.11.

Windermere–probably a reference to Wilde's (q.v.) play, *Lady Windermere's Fan.* 212.36.

Winestain–see Einstein. 149.28.

*****Wingh** and Wangh, 351.21.

*****Winnie**–see Widger.

*****Winthrop,** Mad–the reference is partly to *The Winter's Tale.* 502. 29.

Wippingham, Paddy–made up of: 1) St Patrick; 2) Dick Whittington; 3) *The Wippingham Papers* by A. C. Swinburne (q.q.v.). 19.15-16.

Wisden, J. (1836-84) – English cricketer, founder of *The Cricketer's Almanack,* still published annually. 584.16.

Wise, T. J.–one who muddied the nature and origin of certain 19th century pamphlets. 16.24; 281. note 3.

Wiseman, Nicholas Patrick (1802-65) – English cardinal. 282.22 (weisswash).

*****Withers**–maybe George Withers, English poet (1588-1667). 4.29; 386.33.

*****Wit-upon-Crutches,** 209.7-8.

Woden–see Odin.

Woeful Dane Bottom–see Hamlet and Bottom. Shakespeare's (q.v.) greatest tragic and greatest comic characters are opposites, here united. Both are roles belonging to Shem (q.v.). Is it also a place? 340.9; 369.12; 503.21; 594.12.

Woffington, Peg (1714-60)–Irish actress, toast of Dublin. See Wildair. 210.25.

Woldomar–see Valdemar. 255.16.

Wolf the Ganger–see Rolf Ganger. 444.32.

Wolfe, James (1727-59) – British general, won the battle but died on the Heights of Abraham (q.v.). †80.13—with Wolfe Tone (q.v.).

Wolff–news agency. 593.18.

Wolfgang–see Goethe. 480.36.

Wolossay–see Wellington, Wolseley. 492.10.

Wolseley, Garnet Joseph, Viscount (1833-1913)–British field marshal, b. Co. Dublin, fought in the Crimea, the Indian Mutiny, China, Canada, Egypt, etc. 49.8; 292. note 3; 492.10; 578.7.

*Wombwell, Ida–perhaps in some way Wombwell's Wild Animal Show. 60.22-23; 529.1.

Wommany Wyes–see Borrow. 600. 30.

Wonder–see Miranda.

Wood–maiden name of Mrs O'Shea (q.v.).

Wood, Anthony à (1632-95)–antiquary and historian. 80.3.

Wood, Hickory–writer of pantomime scripts. 98.35-36.

Wood, Mrs John–her company played *She Stoops to Conquer* and *La Belle Sauvage* at the opening of the Gaiety Theatre in Dublin. †223.20—with Joan of Arc (q.v.).

Wood, William–see Draper for an account of Wood's halfpence; see also William. 11.21; 16.33; 27. 17-18; 77.16; 82.31; 98.26,35; 112.4,5 (Swift, punning with his name, called Wood "Son of a Beech"); 413.36; 574.1; 586.23; 602.9.

Woodbine, Willie – see Stoddart Kennedy. 351.12.

Woodenbeard – see Beardwood. 467.15.

Woodward, Henry–founder of the Crow Street Theatre in Dublin. It was also the name of a panto-mime company. Woodwards and Regarders were forest officers who saw no hurt was done to vert or venison. 34.15; 189.24; 280.4.

Woolley–English cricketer. 454.11.

Woolley–these references usually combine Willy and Lamb (q.q.v.).

Woolworth–chain of five and ten cent stores. The Woolworth Building in New York was one of the first skyscrapers. In FW it equals the Tower of Babel. 4.35; 72.14; 127.35; 541.6.

Woppington–see Woffington. 210. 25.

Worde, Wynkinde–succeeded to Caxton's press. 249.4.

Wordsworth, William (1770-1850) –English poet. 539.5.

Worth, Charles (1825-95)–famous dressmaker, born in Lincolnshire. 28.31; 548.23,25.

*W. P., 86.34.

*Wramawitch, 27.28.

*Wright–possibly Frances, a 19th century feminist, possibly Sir Almroth Wright, author of *The Unexpurgated Case Against Woman's Suffrage*, 1913. 466.15.

Wright, Mr Fortunatus–18th century Englishman who captured a French ship under conditions that the French considered piracy. 327.26.

Wright, Peter–published in the 1920s a scandalous book about political figures, including Parnell and Gladstone (q.q.v.). He accused the latter of saving fallen girls for fallen purposes. Gladstone's sons, believing that "no property in law can exist in a corpse" (FW, 576.5) forced Wright to sue for libel. He lost. †269.8— with St Peter (q.v.); 301.7; 422. 34.

*Wucherer–German for "usurer". 422.34.

W. W.–his translation of the *Menaechmi* of Plautus (q.v.) is the source of Shakespeare's (q.v.) *Comedy of Errors*. See Widger.

*Wwalshe – possibly John W. Walshe (d. 1915), colleague of Parnell's (q.v.), prominent in the Land War. 495.27.

Wyer, Daddy de–see ass, Dwyer Gray. 398.2.

Wymmingtown, Jupes of–see Wellington. 339.26.

Wyndham, Sir Charles (b. 1837)– English actor, attended medical school in Dublin. 181.2.

*Wynn's Hotel, 609.15-16.

*Wynns, Percy–book by Father Finn (q.v.). Percy Wyndham Lewis (q.v.)? 440.9.

X

Xenia–heroine of *Boris Godunov*. 147.14.

Xenophon (b. 430 B.C.)–Greek historian. 308.left margin.

Xerxes–Persian king who fought the Greeks at Thermopylae and was finally defeated at Salamis. 286.8.

Y

Yahoos–ill-bred humans in the land of the Houyhnhnms (q.v.) in the 4th part of *Gulliver's* (q.v.) *Travels*. 205.30; 310.17; 348.1; 387.10; 490.13; 553.33.

*Yakov Yea–Jacob (q.v.)? 201.34.

*Yaman, Judgity, 386.36.

Yardley's–brand of soap and toilet articles. 156.28.

*Yasha Yash, 240.1,2.

*Yateman–maybe Yeats, maybe J. P. Yeatman (q.q.v.), author of *The Gentle Shakespeare* (q.v.), 1896. 225.18-19.

Yates–Yeats and Luke Tarpey (q.q.v.) as east. See Four. 557.2.

*Yates, Pam–Yeats (q.v.)? 27.27.

Yawn–Shaun (q.v.) in III,iii. 97.29; 200.15; 474.13,23; 476.19; 477.3 (yun), 27,31 (Y); 511.17; 588.1.

*Ydwalla, 88.23.

Yeats, William Butler (1865-1939)– Irish poet and playwright, whose use in FW is pretty extensive and needs study. A number of his works are quoted or mentioned— e.g. *Reveries Over Childhood and Youth* (482.5-6), *Countess Cathleen* (q.v.), *The Twisting of the*

Rope (427.19)—and Joyce pretty well agrees with Yeats's view of Swift and Stella (q.q.v.) as expressed in *The Words Upon the Window Pane*. Yeats's love for Maud Gonne (q.v.) is implicit in Joyce's references to her and to Leda (q.v.). Because of Yeats's Leda-Helen poems, Joyce joins him with the Swan (q.v.) of Avon, whenever a "will" (q.v.) is near a Leda passage. This is especially true in FW II,ii, the most Yeatsian section of FW; here *A Vision* (297.left margin) is quoted, parodied, perhaps (though I do not think so) its phases absolutely worked out, a Yeatsian within a Viconian (q.v.) cycle. This section is full of technical terms from *A Vision*—Other (q.v.), Will, Creative Mind, Primary Tincture, Body of Fate, Mask, Husk, Spirit, Shift, Byzantium, Gyres, Sphere, Phase, Concrete Man (q.v.). The most extensive quotation from *A Vision* deals with a dream Yeats had about his father (295.10-14). See Four, George, Abbey, Rose, Will, Yates. ?27.27; 41.9; 112.30 (teasy); ?135.10; 167.18 (mister Abby); 170.16; ?211.2 (Will-of-the-Wisp, q.v.); 237.33; †256.13

—with Synge (q.v.); 260.16 (will); ?262.19 (Sow byg eat — anagram?); 272.4; 285.1 (habby); 303.7-8; 306.4; ?404.15; 483.8-9; ?527.9 (Strip Teasy); †557.2—with Luke Tarpey (q.v.), see also Four.

Yellowman – Elleman's yellow brand of embrocation. 184.22.

Yellowtooth–Queen Victoria (q.v.) —see *Ulysses*, 44/53. 303.3.

*Yem or Yan, 246.31.

*Yennessy–perhaps the river Yemassee and Hennessy's brandy. 212.1.

*Yggely ogs Weib, 267.19-20.

Yo–Japanese female principle. 424.22.

*Yokan, 531.35.

*Yokeoff, 531.35.

*Yopp, Jeremy, 372.10.

Yorick – 1) Hamlet's (q.v.) old friend, the jester; 2) his descendant the parson in *Tristram Shandy* (q.v.). All references double with York (q.v.). 190.19; 230.1; 283.15; 465.32-33.

*York, Archbishop? †190.19—with Yorick (q.v.); 491.19-20.

*York, Duchess of, †461.9–with Duessa and Duse (q.q.v.).

York and Lancaster–noble houses, which, in the Wars of the Roses (q.v.), fought for the English crown. "To pluck a rose" is a medieval euphemism for "to make water" (see 21.15-16; 22.3). This accounts for the association of the two (q.v.) girls with The War of the Roses. Shakespeare's *2* and *3 Henry VI* (q.q.v.) were first published as *The Whole Contention between the two Famous Houses, Lancaster and York*. There are, of course many Yorks and Lancasters in other plays of Shakespeare. See Yorick, York's Porker. See also *Portrait of the Artist*, pp. 7-8. 95.2,18; †190.19—with Yorick (q.v.); †283.15 — with Yorick (q.v.); 348.28; 442.9; †465.32-33—with Yorick and Cassius (q.q.v.); 485.12-13 (see Rose); 500.11; 534.2; 567.36; ?583.36.

York's Porker–combines Francis Bacon (q.v.) whose town residence was York House and Richard III (q.v.) whose crest was a boar. See Pig, York and Lancaster. 71.12.

Young, Brigham (1801-77)–Mormon leader. 542.27.

*Younger, Lilien–see Lily? 548.20.

Yssia and Essia–are Issy plus Stella and Vanessa plus Esther Waters (q.q.v.). 605.12.

Yul–see Yule.

Yule, Sir Henry (1820-98)–British orientalist. 245.6.

*Yussive, 262.note 1.

Z

*Zachary, 580.8.

*Zara, 340.34.

Zarathustra–form of Zoroaster. Nietzsche (q.v.) wrote *Also Sprach Zarathustra*. 281.left margin.

*Zaza, 248.2.

Zerubabbel–prince of Judah in *Ezra*. †536.32—with Barrington (q.v.).

*Zessid, 34.31.

*Zetland, marquess of, 544.1.

Zeus–greatest of Greek gods. See Hera, Leda, Jupiter. 269.18; 414.36; †504.19—with Tom (q.v.); 524.30.

Ziegfeld, Flo–American showman of the 1920s and 30s who put on the Ziegfeld Follies every year for a while. 106.12.

Zilla–see Adah. 102.3.

Zimmermann – as in Lortzing's opera *Czar and Zimmermann.* 349.4.

Zingari I–known as I.Z., meaning The Wanderers, an English cricket club which had a festival during the Dublin horse-show. 112.7.

Zita, St–patron of servants and the city of Lucca. 285.3.

Zoans–Blake's (q.v.) "Four Zoas". See Four. 57.7; 611.14.

*Zoe–literally "life"—see Eve. 479. 8.

Zolfanerole–see Savonarola. 439. 35.

*Zovotrimaserovmeravmerouvian, 113.4-5.

Zozimus–1) 5th century Pope; 2) 5th century Greek historian who lived in Constantinople; 3) 6th century hermit who came on every Good Friday eve to give the Sacrament to St Mary the Egyptian in a cave on the banks of the Jordan; 4) a strolling bard of Dublin, a beggar, sometimes called the last of the minstrels; 5) an illustrated Dublin paper (1870-71). 63.32; 154.8; 186.16; 232.7; 567.30.

Zwilling–Augustinian eremite who sided with Luther (q.v.). German *zwilling* means "twin". 187.33.

Zwingli, Huldrych (1484-1531)– Zurich reformer. 371.3.

Author . . .

Adaline Glasheen has taught at Wheaton
College and has contributed articles on
Finnegans Wake to various periodicals.
Mrs. Glasheen claims her only qualifica-
tions for this work are a deep and con-
tinuing interest in *Finnegans Wake*. To
this might be added that she is an
inspired researcher whose work simplifies
the Joyce novel for her readers.